RUTGERS BYZANTINE SERIES

PETER CHARANIS
General Editor

St. John Chrysostom; icon of miniature mosaic, set in wax (Constantinople, first half of the 14th century; approximately $7 \times 5''$). Dumbarton Oaks Collections, Washington, D.C. Photo courtesy of the Dumbarton Oaks Collections.

DEMETRIOS J. CONSTANTELOS

BYZANTINE
PHILANTHROPY
and
SOCIAL WELFARE

RUTGERS UNIVERSITY PRESS
New Brunswick   *New Jersey*

Dedication

To my parents Joannes and Christina
ἀνθ' ὧν ὑπὲρ ἐμοῦ ἐμόχθησαν

To my teacher Peter Charanis
τιμῆς καὶ εὐγνωμοσύνης ἕνεκεν

To my wife Stella
διὰ τὴν ἄφατον αὐτῆς φιλανθρωπίαν

Epigraph

" Ἡμῖν δέ παρ' ὅλην τὴν ἱστορίαν τὰ μὲν γραφέντα καλῶς μὴ μετε-
χέτω φθόνου, τὰ δὲ ἀγνοηθέντα τυγχανέτω διορθώσεως ὑπὸ τῶν δυνα-
τωτέρων."

Throughout our entire history it is to be hoped that what we
have written well may not cause jealousy, and that what we have
omitted because of ignorance may be corrected by more compe-
tent historians.

—Diodoros Siculus, «Βιβλιοθήκη Ἱστορική», Bk. I. v. 3

Acknowledgments

Because the present work is based primarily on sources, many of which depend upon or quote each other, a certain repetition has been unavoidable. In the spelling of Greek names and terms in English I preferred to preserve their original Greek form, although the most common of them appear Anglicized.

It is my duty to record here my gratitude to my friends Professors David Evans of Princeton Theological Seminary and Walter Kaegi of the University of Chicago for editorial assistance. Dr. Evans read the third and the fourth parts and Dr. Kaegi read the second section. My gratitude goes also to Mrs. Betty Mezines of Washington, D.C., who read the first part for the same purpose. Professor Donald Nicol of the University of Edinburgh read the final form of the whole work and made additional corrections. To all four I convey my hearty thanks.

Furthermore, I am grateful to a number of other scholars who also read the manuscript and offered me the benefit of their criticism: Professors Richard Brown, John Lenaghan, and Ernest McDonnell of Rutgers University; Francis Dvornik, Romilly Jenkins, and John Meyendorff of the Dumbarton Oaks Research Library of Harvard University. However, in no way are they responsible for any mistakes and inaccuracies.

It is a pleasure to acknowledge the generosity of the history department of Rutgers University. Its assistance in the form of a teaching assistantship and two fellowships were decisive for the completion of my doctoral studies. Later, when difficulties attending the completion of my dissertation seemed insurmountable, a junior fellowship from the Dumbarton Oaks Research Library of Harvard University came as a unique blessing. I am grateful to its director of studies Professor Ernst Kitzinger, its faculty, and its staff for their most helpful cooperation. My gratitude goes also to the staffs of the Rutgers University Library and the Library of New Brunswick Theological Seminary.

I am grateful, too, to His Eminence Archbishop Iakovos, Primate of the Greek Orthodox Archdiocese of North and South America, who relieved me of pastoral duties and assisted me for two years through the Taylor Scholarship Foundation of the Greek Archdiocese, to enable me to complete my graduate studies.

Above all I express my profound gratitude to my esteemed teacher Professor Peter Charanis for his great philanthropia toward me. It was Professor Charanis who both encouraged me to undertake the study of Byzantine civilization and guided me in my graduate work at Rutgers. His careful reading of this work and his criticism has contributed greatly to its improvement. May the *Philanthropos Theos* reward him with good health and many more years of wisdom and happiness. My gratitude goes also to my colleague Dr. Costas Proussis, who undertook the burdensome job of reading proofs of the footnotes.

I wish also to thank my wife Stella and my children Christine, John, Helen, and Maria for their "unfathomable philanthropia" in accepting me once again in their midst. For several years they enjoyed only my corporeal presence and that only at times, while my mind and thoughts were wandering in the vast territories of the Byzantine Empire.

D. J. C.

Preface

Theophylactos of Simocatta, who held the office of imperial secretary under Heraclios (610–41), has preserved an interesting address which reflects in some measure the ethos of Byzantine civilization. He describes the later Roman or Byzantine Empire as a state which excelled in *philanthropia* over all other nations.

Theophylactos relates that during the reign of Maurice (582–602) the Avars were besieging Anchialos, a city in Eastern Thrace. The Emperor dispatched two ambassadors to the Khagan in order to deter further raids and to negotiate peace. Comentiolos, one of the two ambassadors, addressed the chief of the Avars, saying that the leaders of nations must be more prudent and wise than their subjects. They must excel in virtue as much as they are pre-eminent in authority. "The Romans [Byzantines] on behalf of peace are throwing into oblivion previous calamities and they have already forgotten the injustices which you have brought upon them. And because they are superior in philanthropia to all other nations, they are not eager to resort to arms." [1] The entire address is indicative of Byzantine diplomacy, revealing at the same time the ethical and social notions of Byzantine society.

The same author has preserved elsewhere advice which the Emperor Tiberios II (578–82) addressed to his son-in-law, the

1. Theophylactos of Simocatta, *Historia*, I. 5, ed. Charles De Boor (Leipzig, 1887), 48. "Τοιγαροῦν διὰ τὴν ἐκ τῆς εἰρήνης εὔνοιαν ἀμνημονοῦσι Ῥωμαῖοι τῶν ὑπὸ σοῦ προϋπηργμένων δεινῶν, καὶ πολλῶν ἀδικημάτων γεγόνασιν ἐπιλήσμονες, καὶ φιλανθρωπίᾳ πάντων τῶν ἐθνῶν διαφέροντες οὐ πρὸς ὄρεξιν ἀντιλυπήσεως κεκινήκασιν ὅπλα."

Emperor Maurice. "Let philanthropia precede wrath"[2] is the testament of Tiberios to his successor. This passage also constitutes an element of Byzantine social and political philosophy. Theophylactos claims elsewhere that the Byzantines were a state wealthy in material possessions and very humane; in fact, he adds, Byzantium was a glorious nation because of its philanthropy.[3]

Three centuries later, the celebrated scholar and patriarch of Constantinople, Photios (858–67, 877–86), employed similar language to describe the Byzantine Empire. In his appeal to the Emperor Basil I (867–86), Photios writes that the king should treat him humanely, as is fitting for the head "of the most philanthropic nation of the Romans."[4]

Nicholas Mysticos of the tenth century emphasized Byzantine philanthropia also. During the early part of the tenth century the Saracens, influenced by the rumor that their mosque in Constantinople had been destroyed, were preparing an attack against the Byzantines. Nicholas Mysticos, patriarch of Constantinople at that time (901–07, 912–25), appealed to the "leader" of the Arabs, counseling him not to believe such unfounded reports. Among other arguments Nicholas wrote: "There are many objects for which the nation of the Romans is distinguished; however, what stands above all others is their philanthropia and leniency. Nor is this my own opinion," Nicholas wrote, but "men everywhere and the whole of history verify this testimony. . . ."[5]

Similar claims are made as late as the fourteenth century. The Emperor Joannes VI Cantacuzenos (1347–54) describes the Byzantines as a nation which was characterized by its many works of practical philanthropy. He relates a case in which philanthropia is pictured as a virtue not only of the rich and prominent,

2. *Ibid.*, p. 42. "ἡγείσθω τῆς ὀργῆς τὸ φιλάνθρωπον."
3. *Ibid.*, VI. 2: "αὐτούς τε τῶν Ῥωμαίων ἔθνος ἀκηκοότας ἐπί τε πλού- τῳ καὶ φιλανθρωπίᾳ λίαν, ὡς ἔστιν εἰπεῖν εὐκλεέστατον." Cf. V. 16, where the "Romans" of Constantinople and vicinity are described as Byzantines (Βυζαντίοις).
4. Photios, *Epistle No. 218*, ed. Joannes N. Valetas «Φωτίου Ἐπιστολαί», (London, 1864), p. 533. "τοῦ φιλανθρωποτάτου γένους τῶν Ῥωμαίων."
5. Nicholas Mysticos, *Epistle No. 82*, ed. J. P. Migne, *Patrologia Graeca*, CXI, col. 312A. "Καὶ γὰρ πολλῶν ὑπαρχόντων οἷς τὸ Ῥωμαϊκὸν σεμνύ- νεται γένος, ἓν τοῦτο ὑπάρχει ἐξαίρετον τὸ τῆς φιλανθρωπίας αὐτῶν καὶ ἐπιεικείας. Καὶ τούτου μάρτυς οὐχ ὁ ἐμὸς λόγος . . . πάντες ἄνθρωποι κατὰ πᾶσαν γῆν, καὶ πᾶσα ἱστορία ταύτην παρέχονται τὴν μαρτυ- ρίαν. . . ." Migne's *Patrologia Graeca* is cited hereafter as MPG.

but of all organizations and classes of people. He describes the empire as a state devoted to philanthropy.[6] Alexios Makrembolites, in about 1348, emphasized that the Byzantines were forgiving and generous, even to enemies who abused their kindness, because philanthropia was one of their innate qualities.[7]

But are the claims of these Byzantine authors supported by other evidence? Was philanthropia an element of Byzantine religious, moral and social philosophy, and if so, to what extent was it applied? Admittedly even critics who have seen only barbarism and superstition in Byzantium have words of praise for Byzantine philanthropic philosophy and its practical application.[8] Nonetheless, this aspect of Byzantine civilization has been hitherto almost unknown and insufficiently studied.[9]

The aim of this book is to investigate philanthropia as a philosophy and as a way of life among the Byzantines, and to determine if the claims of the five Byzantine sources quoted above are substantiated by concrete examples from Byzantine daily life. Their claims are supported by certain modern authors.[10] The present work, therefore, is hermeneutic and a synthesis.

My research has covered a number of important and representative sources from the whole of Byzantine history. I have made, however, as complete a study as was possible of all the outstanding sources of the tenth, eleventh, and twelfth centuries, i.e. histories, chronicles, *typika* and *practika* of monasteries, episto-

6. Joannes Cantacuzenos, *Historia*, ed. by L. Schopenus, Corpus Scriptorum Historiae Byzantinae, III (Bonn, 1832), 223. "Τὸ θαυμαστὸν τοῦτο παρὰ Ρωμαίοις ἔργον καὶ πολλῆς φιλανθρωπίας γέμον. . . ." Corpus Scriptorum Historiae Byzantinae is cited hereafter as CSHB.

7. Alexios Makrembolites, "Λόγος Ἱστορικός," ed. by A. Papadopoulos-Kerameus, «Ἀνάλεκτα Ἱεροσολυμιτικῆς Σταχυολογίας», I (Petropolis, 1891) 146.31:" . . . τὴν ἔμφυτον Ρωμαίων φιλανθρωπίαν καὶ ἡμερότητα."

8. Edward Gibbon, *The History of the Decline and Fall of the Roman Empire*, III (London, 1887), 252, n. 73. Cf. A. N. Diomedes, «Βυζαντιναὶ Μελέται», I (Athens, 1951), 263.

9. Peter Charanis, "Some Aspects of Daily Life in Byzantium," *The Greek Orthodox Theological Review*, VIII, Nos. 1–2 (Summer 1962–1963), 67; cf. also n. 39.

10. Constantine Amantos, " Ἡ Ἑλληνικὴ Φιλανθρωπία κατὰ τοὺς Μεσαιωνικοὺς Χρόνους," *Athena*, XXXV (Athens, 1923), 164; «Ἱστορία τοῦ Βυζαντινοῦ Κράτους», 2nd Edition (Athens, 1953), p. 26; Phaedon Koukoules, «Βυζαντινῶν Βίος καί Πολιτισμός», II, part 1 (Athens, 1948), 64. The Koukoules is cited hereafter as BBΙΙ; R. Janin, *La Géographie Ecclésiastique de l'Empire Byzantin* (Paris, 1953), pp. 564–65.

lography, state laws and church canons, hagiographical texts, and related writings. Any reference to Byzantine philanthropy beyond the twelfth century may be considered incidental.

Nevertheless, the resultant study does not claim to be exhaustive or definitive. Such an ambitious project would require several years of careful investigation if it were to include all the historians, chronicles, laws and canons, sermons, epistles and orations, *practika* and *typika* of monastic and church institutions, wills and numerous hagiographical texts, *synaxaria,* and other related texts, many of which remain unedited. The author entertains the hope of continuing his investigation of Byzantine philanthropy and the social consciousness of the medieval Greek world.

Demetrios J. Constantelos
Holy Cross Greek Orthodox Theological School
Brookline, Massachusetts

Contents

Acknowledgments   vii

Preface   ix

List of Illustrations   xv

List of Abbreviations   xviii

Foreword by Peter Charanis   xxviii

Part I: Philanthropia in the Thought-World of Byzantium
  1. The Hellenic and Christian Background   3
  2. The Motives behind Byzantine Philanthropic
     Thought   18
  3. Philanthropia in Byzantine Religious Thought   29
  4. Philanthropia as an Imperial Virtue   43

Part II: Application and Agencies of Philanthropy
  5. Byzantine Philanthropy   65
  6. Philanthropy and the Church   67
  7. Philanthropy and Monastic Establishments   88
  8. Philanthropy and the Byzantine State   111
  9. Private Benefactors   137

Part III: Philanthropic Institutions
  10. Administration   149
  11. Hospitals   152
     Hospitals in the Early Empire · The Sixth Century ·

Four Centuries of Incomplete Evidence · The Hospital of Pantocrator and Other Comneni Establishments · Additional Testimony

12. Xenones (Hospices)   185
    Xenones during the First Three Centuries · The Hospice of Sampson · The Macedonian Era and Its Hostels · Xenones during the Comneni Dynasty · The Unknown Institutions · Administration
13. Gerocomeia (Homes for the Aged)   222
    Gerocomeia in the Early Byzantine Empire · The Gap in Evidence · Gerocomeia under the Macedonians and the Comneni · The Director
14. Orphanages   241
    The Orphanage of St. Zoticos · The Orphanage of St. Paul · Other Homes for Children · The Office of Orphanotropos
15. Ptocheia (Houses for the Poor)   257
16. Other Institutions   270
    Reformatory Houses · Xenotapheia · Homes for the Blind

Part IV: Conclusion
17. Conclusion   279

Bibliography   290

Index   316

List of Illustrations

FIGURES

Frontispiece: St. John Chrysostom; icon of miniature mosaic, set in wax (Constantinople, first half of the 14th century; approximately 7 × 5″). Dumbarton Oaks Collections, Washington, D.C.

1. Christ the Merciful; icon of miniature mosaic, set in wax (Constantinople, 11th–12th century). Formerly in the Berlin State Museum; present location unknown.   40

2. John VI Cantacuzenos as Emperor and as Monk; miniature from MS *grec* 1242, fol. 123 (second half of the 14th century). Bibliothèque Nationale, Paris.   44

3. An Emperor (Basil I or Leo VI) kneeling before Christ enthroned; mosaic panel over the Imperial Door, narthex of Hagia Sophia, Istanbul (9th–10th century).   47

4. St. John Chrysostom; mosaic panel, north tympanum of Hagia Sophia, Istanbul (9th century).   72

5. St. Gregory, St. Basil the Great, and St. John Chrysostom; mosaic panel, Cappella Palatina, Palermo, Sicily (12th century).   73

6. St. Ignatios the Younger; mosaic panel, north tympanum, Hagia Sophia, Istanbul (9th century).   77

7. Penteles Monastery, Greece, showing its *Gerocomeion* outside the monastery walls; after a drawing by Barskij.   82

8. *Gerocomeion* of Penteles Monastery, Greece; exterior.   82
9. *Gerocomeion* of Penteles Monastery, Greece; section
and ground plan.   83
10. Hospital of Barlaam Monastery, Meteora, Greece; section and ground plan.   103
11. Hospital of the Great Meteoron, Greece; exterior before its collapse.   104
12. Hospital of the Great Meteoron, Greece; the *tetrakionion* which supported the central dome.   104
13. Hospital of a Meteora monastery; section and ground
plan.   105
14. Christ crowning Emperor Constantine VII Porphyrogenitos; ivory plaque (c. 945; approximately
7⁵⁄₁₆ × 3¹¹⁄₁₆″). Pushkin Museum of Fine Arts, Moscow.   117
15. Christ crowning Emperor Romanos IV Diogenes and
Empress Eudocia; ivory plaque (c. 1068). Cabinet
des Médailles, Bibliothèque Nationale, Paris.   120
16. Christ enthroned between Emperor Constantine IX
Monomachos and Empress Zoë; mosaic panel, south
gallery of Hagia Sophia, Istanbul (11th century).   124
17. Emperor Constantine IX Monomachos; detail from
mosaic panel (see Figure 16), south gallery of Hagia
Sophia, Istanbul.   125
18. Alexios, son of John II Comnenos, proclaimed co-
Emperor in 1122; mosaic panel, south gallery of
Hagia Sophia, Istanbul (first half of the 12th century).   127
19. Ring of Michael Attaleiates (d. 1081); gold and cloisonné enamel (Constantinople, 10th century; diameter approximately 1″ [2.3 cm.]). Dumbarton Oaks
Collections, Washington, D.C.   143
20. Foundations of a building in Jerusalem excavated by
Roland De Vaux and identified by him as the ruins
of the Hospital of Justinian.   161
21. Inscriptions which indicate the existence of hospitals
(*nosocomeia*) as institutions distinct from *gerocomeia*
(homes for the aged).   163

22. Emperor John II Comnenos; mosaic panel, south gallery of Hagia Sophia, Istanbul (first half of the 12th century). 173
23. Empress Irene, wife of John II Comnenos; mosaic panel, south gallery of Hagia Sophia, Istanbul (first half of the 12th century). 173
24. Church of the Pantocrator, south flank and apse; Istanbul. From a 19th century engraving. 176
25. Church of the Pantocrator, southeast view of the entire complex; Istanbul. 176
26. Church of the Pantocrator, west façade; Istanbul. 177
27. Church of the Pantocrator, exterior of the apse; Istanbul. 177
28. Hospital of Pantocrator in Constantinople; ground plans. 178
29. Three Seals of the Xenon of Sampson in Constantinople. 194
30. Three Seals of Xenon Directors. 201
31. Church of St. John Studion, interior looking toward the apse; Istanbul. 211
32. St. Theodore Studites, mosaic panel, Monastery of Nea Mone, Chios, Greece. 217
33. The *Gerocomeion* in the Quarter of Armatiou in Constantinople, derived from a miniature in a Byzantine manuscript. 228
34. Seal of Kyritsios, Gerocomos of Eugeniou, a *Gerocomeion* in Constantinople. 234
35. Seals of Directors of Two *Gerocomeia*. 238
36. Five Seals Relating to Orphanages and their Officers. 253

MAPS

The Byzantine Empire Endpapers
Locations of Known Philanthropic Institutions 17
Constantinople 42
Important Monastic Communities in the Holy Land 62

List of Abbreviations

Periodicals

AB	*Analecta Bollandiana*
B	*Byzantion*
BIAB	*Bulletin de l'institut archéologique bulgare*
BIARC	*Bulletin de l'institut archéologique russe à Constantinople*
BNJ	*Byzantinisch-Neugriechische Jahrbucher*
BS	*Byzantinoslavica*
BZ	*Byzantinische Zeitschrift*
CH	*Church History*
DIEEE	*«Δελτίον τῆς Ἱστορικῆς καὶ Ἐθνολογικῆς Ἑταιρείας τῆς Ἑλλάδος»*
DOP	*Dumbarton Oaks Papers*
EA	*«Ἐκκλησιαστικὴ Ἀλήθεια»*
EEBS	*«Ἐπετηρὶς Ἑταιρείας Βυζαντινῶν Σπουδῶν»*
EHR	*English Historical Review*
EO	*Echos d'orient*
GOTh. R	*Greek Orthodox Theological Review*

GP	«Γρηγόριος ὁ Παλαμᾶς»
GRBS	*Greek-Roman and Byzantine Studies*
HE	«Ἑλληνικά»
HTh. R	*Harvard Theological Review*
JHS	*Journal of Hellenic Studies*
M	«Μακεδονικά»
MX	«Μικρασιατικὰ Χρονικά»
NE	«Νέος Ἑλληνομνήμων»
NS	«Νέα Σιών»
O	«Ὀρθοδοξία»
OCP	*Orientalia Christiana Periodica*
P	«Παρνασσός»
REB	*Revue des études byzantine*
ROC	*Revue de l'orient chrétien*
Th	«Θεολογία»
Thr	«Θρακικά»
VV	*Vizantiiskii Vremennik*

General Works

Altaner, *Patrology*	B. Altaner, *Patrology*
Beck, *Kirche und Theologische Literatur*	Hans Georg Beck, *Kirche und Theologische Literatur in Byzantinischen Reich*
Dolger, *Regesten*	Franz Dolger, *Regesten der Kaiserurkunden des ostromischen Reiches*
Grumel, *Chronologie*	V. Grumel, *La Chronologie*
Grumel, *Régestes*	V. Grumel, *Les Régestes des actes du patriarcat de Constantinople*
Halkin, *Hag. Graeca*	F. Halkin, *Bibliotheca Hagiographica Graeca*
Krumbacher, *Geschichte*	K. Krumbacher, *Geschichte der Byzantinischen Litteratur*
Monnier, *Hist. Asst. Publ.*	Alexandre Monnier, *Histoire de l'assistance publique dans les temps anciens et modernes*

Moravcsik, *Byzantinoturcica*	G. Moravcsik, Vol. I, *Die byzantinischen Quellen der Geschichte der Turkvolker;* Vol. II, *Sprachreste der Turkvolker in den byzantinischen Quellen*
Quasten, *Patrology*	J. Quasten, *Patrology*
Ramsay, *Historical Geography*	William M. Ramsay, *The Historical Geography of Asia Minor*

Sources

AASS	*Acta Sanctorum*
"Actes de Chilandar"	"Actes de Chilandar," *Vizantiiski Vremennik*
Actes de Lavra	*Actes de Lavra*
Anna Comnena, *Alexias*	Anna Comnena, *Alexias,* Anne Comnène Alexiade
Basil, *Epistles*	*Saint Basil—the Letters,* Loeb Classical Library
Cecaumenos, *Strategicon de Off. Reg.*	*Cecaumeni Strategicon et . . . de officiis Regiis Libellus*
Chronicon Paschale	*Chronicon Paschale*
Codinos, *De Officialibus*	G. Codinos, *De Officialibus Palatii Constantinopolitani*
Continuatus, *Chronographia*	*The Chronographia of Theophanes Continuatus*
Delehaye, *Deux Typica*	Hippolyte Delehaye, *Deux Typica byzantins de l'époque des Paleologues*
Delehaye, "Monumenta Latrensia"	Hippolyte Delehaye, "Monumenta Latrensia Hagiographica," *Milet*
Delehaye, "Une Vie"	Hippolyte Delehaye, "Une Vie inédite de saint Jean l'aumonier," *Analecta Bollandiana*
Dmitrievsky, *Euchologion*	A. Dmitrievsky, *Euchologion*

Dmitrievsky, *Typika*	A. Dmitrievsky, *Typika, Opisanie Liturgicheskikh Rukopisei*
Doukakis, «Συναξαριστής»	Constantine Chr. Doukakis, «Μέγας Συναξαριστὴς Πάντων τῶν Ἁγίων»
Ephraemios, *Patriarcharum*	Ephraemios, *Imperatorum et Patriarcharum*
Eusebios, *Eccl. History*	Eusebios of Caesarea, *Historia Ecclesiastica*
Evagrios, *Eccl. History*	*The Ecclesiastical History of Evagrius with the Scholia*
Fourmy-Leroy, "S. Philarète	M. H. Fourmy and M. Leroy, "La Vie de S. Philarète," *Byzantion*
Gedeon, Ἑορτολόγιον	Manuel Gedeon, «Βυζαντινὸν Ἑορτολόγιον»
Gelzer, *Leontios*	*Leontios' von Neapolis, Lebendes heiligen Iohannes des barinherzigen erzbischofs von Alexandrien,* ed. H. Gelzer
Goar, *Euchologion*	Jacobus Goar, *Euchologion Sive Rituale Graecorum*
Ioannou, «Μνημεῖα»	Theophilos Ioannou, «Μνημεῖα Ἁγιολογικά»
Julian, *Epistles*	*L'Empereur Julien, oeuvres complètes*
Justinian, *Novels*	*Corpus Juris Civilis*
Kataskepenos, *Cyril Phileotes*	*La Vie de Saint Cyrille le philéote, moine byzantin*
Khitrowo, *Itinéraires*	B. de Khitrowo, *Itinéraires russes en orient*
Latysev, *Menologii*	*Menologii Anonymi Byzantini*
Malalas, *Chronographia*	J. Malalas, *Chronographia*
Manasses, *Synopsis*	Constantine Manasses, *Synopsis Chronike*
Mansi	J. D. Mansi, *Sacrorum Conciliorum nova et amplissima collectio*

Menologium	*Patrologia Graeca,* ed. J. P. Migne
Meyer, *Athoskloster*	Ph. Meyer, *Haupturkenden für die Geschichte der Athoskloster*
Miklosich-Muller, *Acta et Diplomata*	Fr. Miklosich and J. Muller, ed., *Acta et Diplomata Graeca Medii Aevi Sacra et Profana*
Monachos, *Chronicon*	George Monachos, *Chronicon*
MPG	*Patrologia Graeca,* ed. J. P. Migne
Nazianzenos, *Epistolae*	Gregory Nazianzenos, *Epistolae, Patrologia Graeca,* ed. J. P. Migne
Nic. Callistos, *Eccl. History*	Nicephoros Callistos Xanthopoulos, *Ecclesiastical History, Patrologia Graeca,* ed. J. P. Migne
Nich. Mysticos, *Epistles*	Nicholas Mysticos, *Epistles, Patrologia Graeca,* ed. J. P. Migne
Palladios, *Hist. Lausiaca*	*The Lausiac History of Palladius*
Palladios, *Vita S. Jo. Chr.*	*Palladii Dialogus de Vita S. Joannes Chrysostomi*
Papadopoulos, «Εὐχολόγιον»	«Εὐχολόγιον τὸ Μέγα», ed. N. P. Papadopoulos
Papadopoulos-Kerameus, «'Ανάλεκτα»	A. Papadopoulos-Kerameus, «'Ανάλεκτα Ἱεροσολυμιτικῆς Σταχυολογίας»
Papadopoulos-Kerameus, *Varia*	A. Papadopoulos-Kerameus, *Varia Graeca Sacra*
Petit, "Typikon de . . . Pacourianos"	L. Petit, "Typikon de Gregoire Pacourianos pour le monastère de Petritzos," *Vizantiiskii Vremennik*
Philotheos, *Kletorologion*	J. B. Bury, *The Administrative System in the Ninth Century,* with a revised text of the *Kletorologion of Philotheos*

Photios, *Epistles*	«Φωτίου Ἐπιστολαί», ed. J. N. Valetas
Porphyrogenitos, *De Cerimoniis*	Constantine Porphyrogenitos, *De Cerimoniis, Constantine VII Porphyrogenete le livre de ceremonies*
Psellos, *Chronographia*	*Michel Psellos chronographie*
Regel, *Analecta*	W. Regel, *Analecta Byzantino-Russica*
Regel, *Fontes*	W. Regel, *Fontes Rerum Byzantinarum*
Rhallis-Potlis, «Σύνταγμα»	G. A. Rhallis and M. Potlis, «Σύνταγμα τῶν θείων καὶ ἱερῶν Κανόνων»
Sathas, «Μεσ. Βιβλιοθ.»	Constantine N. Sathas, «Μεσαιωνικὴ Βιβλιοθήκη»
Schwartz, *Kyrillos*	Edward Schwartz, *Kyrillos von Skythopolis*
Sozomenos, *Eccl. History*	*Sozomenus Kirchengeschichte*
Studites, *Epistles*	Theodore Studites, *Epistles, Patrologia Graeca,* ed. J. P. Migne
Symeon Magister, *Chronographia*	Symeon Magister, *Chronographia, Corpus Scriptorum Historiae Byzantinae*
Symeon Metaphrastes	Symeon Metaphrastes, *Patrologia Graeca,* ed. J. P. Migne
Synaxarium	*Synaxarium Ecclesiae Constantinopolitanae,* Propylaeum ad Acta Sanctorum Novembris
Pseudo-Codinos, *Patria,* Th. Preger	Pseudo-Codinos *Scriptores Originum Constantinopolitanarum,* ed. Th. Preger
Theodoretos of Cyrus, *Eccl. History*	*Theodoret Kirchengeschichte*
Theophanes, *Chronographia*	*The Chronographia of Theophanes Continuatus*

Theophylactos, *Epistles* Theophylactos, *Epistles,*
Patrologia Graeca,
ed. J. P. Migne

Timothy, *Historia* *Subsidia Hagiographica No.* 34
Monachorum (Brussels, 1961)

Wagner, *Carmina* G. Wagner, *Carmina Graeca*
Medii Aevi

Zepos-Zepos, *Jus* J. Zepos and P. Zepos, *Jus*
Graecoromanum

Modern Works

Amantos, «Ἰστορία» Constantine Amantos, «Ἰστορία
τοῦ Βυζαντινοῦ Κράτους»

Barker, *Soc. Pol. Thought* Ernest Barker, *Social and*
Political Thought in
Byzantium

Baynes, *Byzantine Studies* Norman H. Baynes, *Byzantine*
Studies and Other Essays

Baynes-Moss, *Byzantium* *Byzantium,* ed. Norman H.
Baynes and H. St. L. B. Moss

Bréhier, *Civilisation* L. Bréhier, *La Civilisation*
byzantine. Le Monde
byzantin III

Bréhier, *Institutions* L. Bréhier, *Les Institutions de*
l'empire byzantine. Le
Monde byzantin II

Bréhier, *Vie et mort* L. Bréhier, *Vie et mort de*
Byzance. Le Monde
byzantin I

Byzantios, «Κωνσταντινούπολις» Scarlatos D. Byzantios,
«Ἡ Κωνσταντινούπολις»

Champagny, *Char. Chret.* Franz de Champagny, *La*
Charité chrétienne dans les
premiers siècles de l'église

Charanis, "Coronation" Peter Charanis, "Coronation
and its Constitutional
Significance in the Later
Roman Empire," *Byzantion*

Charanis, "Monastic Properties"	Peter Charanis, "The Monastic Properties and the State in the Byzantine Empire," *Dumbarton Oaks Papers*
Charanis, "Social Structure"	Peter Charanis, "On the Social Structure of the Later Roman Empire," *Byzantion*
Chastel, *Influence de la charité*	Etienne Chastel, *Etudes historiques sur l'influence de la charité*
Diehl, *Société byzantine*	Charles Diehl, *La Société byzantine à l'époque des Comnenes*
Dittenberger, *Sylloge*	W. Dittenberger, *Sylloge Inscriptionum Graecorum*
Dolger, *Beitrage*	Franz Dolger, *Beitrage zur Geschichte der byzantin-ischen finanzverwaltung, besonders des 10 und 11 Jahrhunderts*
Downey, "Philanthropia"	Glanville Downey, "Philan-thropia in Religion and Statecraft in the Fourth Century After Christ," *Historia*
Du Cange, *Constantinopolis Christiana*	Charles de Fresne Du Cange, *Historia Byzantin*
Festugière, *Les Moines*	A. J. Festugière, *Les Moines d'orient* 111/2 *Les Moines de Palestine*
Hunger, *Prooimion*	Herbert Hunger, *Prooimion-Elementeder Byzantinischen Kaiseridee in den Aregnen der urkunden*
Janin, *Constantinople*	R. Janin, *Constantinpole byzantine*
Janin, *Geogr. Eccles.*	R. Janin, *La Géographie ecclésiastique de l'empire byzantine*

Koukoules, ΒΒΠ — Phaedon Koukoules, «Βυζαντινῶν Βίος καί Πολιτισμός»

Lecky, *Eur. Morals* — William Lecky, *History of European Morals from Augustus to Charlemagne*

Lallemand, *Hist. Char.* — Leon Lallemand, *Histoire de la charité*

Laurent, *Corpus de sceaux* — V. Laurent, *Le Corpus de sceaux de l'empire byzantine*

Louillet, "Saints de Constantinople" — G. DaCosta Louillet, "Saints de Constantinople aux VIIe, IXe, et Xe siècles," *Byzantion*

Marin, *Moines* — Abbé Marin, *Les Moines de Constantinople*

Millingen, *Byzantine Churches* — Alexander Van Millingen, *Byzantine Churches in Constantinople*

Oeconomos, *La vie religieuse* — L. Oeconomos, *La Vie religieuse dans l'empire byzantin au temps des Comnènes et des anges*

Orlandos, «Ἀναπαράστασις» — A. Orlandos, «Ἡ Ἀναπαράστασις τοῦ Ξενῶνος τῆς ἐν Κωνσταντινουπόλει Μονῆς τοῦ Παντοκράτορος», *Epeteris Etaerias Byzantinon Spoudon*

Ostrogorsky, *History* — G. Ostrogorsky, *History of the Byzantine State*

Paspates, «Ἀνάκτορα» — A. G. Paspates, «Τὰ Βυζαντινὰ Ἀνάκτορα»

Paspates, «Βυζ. Μελέται» — A. G. Paspates, «Βυζαντιναὶ Μελέται—Τοπογραφικαὶ καὶ Ἱστορικαὶ»

Richter, *Quellen* — J. P. Richter, *Quellen der Byzantinischen Kunstgeschichte*

Schlumberger, *Sigillographie* — G. Schlumberger, *Sigillographie de l'empire byzantin*

Uhlhorn, *Christian Charity* — G. Uhlhorn, *Christian Charity in the Ancient Church*

Vasiliev, *History*	A. A. Vasiliev, *History of the Byzantine Empire 324–1453*
Zakythinos, «Βυζάντιον»	D. A. Zakythinos, «Βυζάντιον— Κράτος καὶ Κοινωνία Ἱστορικὴ Ἐπισκόπησις»

Foreword

There is no need for the General Editor of this series to discourse at length on the book by Dr. Constantelos. The book, which is the first serious and comprehensive attempt to elucidate one of the most important features of Byzantine society, speaks for itself. Philanthropy, whatever its original meaning may have been, eventually came to mean charity to man by man, and it is primarily in that sense that Dr. Constantelos has sought to examine it as a feature of Byzantine society. And an important feature it was, as an idea, as a practice of private persons, of the State, of the Church and monastic establishments, as the basis in the development of certain institutions: hospitals for the sick; houses for the poor, the old, the orphans; and hospices for the traveler and the stranger. The thoroughness with which Dr. Constantelos has treated this three-fold aspect of philanthropy as it obtained in the Byzantine Empire is what gives distinction to his book. The first original work to be included in this series, we are happy indeed that we are able to offer it to the public.

Peter Charanis
General Editor
Rutgers Byzantine Series

Part I

Philanthropia in the Thought-World of Byzantium

1. The Hellenic and Christian Background

Philanthropia as an element of Byzantine civilization was an inheritance from Greek and Christian antiquity. Although it is "a word which defies translation,"[1] philanthropia, which is a pure Greek compound word, describes man's love for his near ones, his affection and active concern not only for his kin and friend but for his fellow man in general. Philanthropia as a Byzantine concept is identified with *agape* and implies an active feeling of benevolence toward any person, independent of that person's identity or actions. Byzantine philanthropia designates a deliberate, religious, and purposeful expression of love and compassion for humanity, a definition similar to but more advanced in depth and catholicity than that of ancient Greece,[2] as the present study

1. Norman H. Baynes, *The Byzantine Empire* (London, 1946), p. 70.
2. For the concept of philanthropia in Greek literature and culture see S. Lorenz, *De Progressu Notionis* φιλανθρωπίας (Leipzig, 1914). This unique dissertation traces the development of philanthropia from its earliest appearance down to the time of Cicero; S. Tromp de Ruiter, "De Vocis quae est φιλανθρωπία significatione atque usu," *Mnemosyne*, LIX (1932), 271–306; Marie-Therese Lenger, "La Notion de 'bienfait' (philanthropon) royal et les ordonnances des rois Lagides," *Studi in onore di Vincenzo Arangio-Ruiz*, I (1935), 483–99; H. I. Bell, "Philanthropia in the Papyri of the Roman Period," *Hommages à Joseph Bidez et à Franz Cumont*, Collection Latomus, II (Brussels, 1949), 31–37; John Ferguson, *Moral Values in the Ancient World* (London, 1958), pp. 102–17; Herbert Hunger, «Φιλανθρωπία» –*Eine griechische Wortpragung auf ihrem wege von Aischylos bis Theodoros Metochites* (Vienna, 1963); Roger Le Deaut, "Φιλανθρωπία dans

3

will indicate. The Greeks who conceived and coined the term attributed much significance and ethical value to it.

In ancient Greece philanthropia meant the love of the deity for man. Plato defines it as the love of God for humanity, explaining that daemons took charge of men in order to establish peace and justice among them and to free men from feuds and wars.[3] Although God made the universe and all the creatures dwelling in it, he does not love animals as he loves man.[4] This concept of philanthropia was not merely an abstraction. Prometheus undertook to bring fire to men and to teach them arts and handicrafts out of love for them.[5] Aeschylos has Prometheus exclaim: "Behold me a doomed god, enchained . . . because of my very great philanthropy for men." [6]

The gods further reveal their love for men by granting them various goods and provisions for their livelihood, as well as the seasons of the year, the moon and the stars, water, fire, and other benefactions or philanthropies.[7]

Nonetheless, in Greek antiquity philanthropia implied man's love for man or mankind in general.[8] But it also meant politeness or courtesy, kindness and generosity, or any kind of act which befits a civilized and cultured being.[9] Further, a citizen's love toward his equals and a king's benevolence to his subjects, so-

littérature grecque jusqu'au Nouveau Testament," *Mélanges Eugene Tisserant,* I (Rome, 1964), 255–94.

3. Plato *Leges* iv. 713 d, ed. Joannes Burnet, *Platonis Opera,* V (Oxford, 1959), "ὁ θεὸς ἄρα καὶ φιλάνθρωπος ὤν, τὸ γένος ἄμεινον ἡμῶν ἐφίστη τὸ τῶν δαιμόνων. . . ."

4. Plutarch *Numa* iv, ed. Carolus Sintenis, *Plutarchi Vitae Parallelae,* I (Leipzig, 1895), 121: "τὸν θεὸν οὐ φίλιππον οὐδὲ φίλορνιν, ἀλλὰ φιλάνθρωπον ὄντα τοῖς διαφερόντως ἀγαθοῖς ἐθέλειν συνεῖναι. . . ."

5. Aeschylos *Prometheus Bound* 28–30: "τοιαῦτ' ἐπηύρου τοῦ φιλανθρώπου τρόπου. θεὸς θεῶν γὰρ οὐχ ὑποπτήσσων χόλον βροτοῖσι τιμὰς ὤπασας πέρα δίκης." Cf. Grace H. Macurdy, *The Quality of Mercy—The Gentler Virtues in Greek Literature* (New Haven, Conn., 1940), pp. 98 ff.

6. Aeschylos *Prometheus Bound* 118–23.

7. Xenophon *Memorabilia* IV. iii. 3–7: "ὡς ἐπιμελῶς οἱ θεοὶ ὧν οἱ ἄνθρωποι δέονται κατεσκευάκασι . . . ἐπεὶ τροφῆς δεόμεθα, ταύτην ἡμῖν ἐκ τῆς γῆς ἀναδιδόναι καὶ ὥρας ἁρμοττούσας πρὸς τοῦτο παρέχειν . . . πάνυ . . . καὶ ταῦτα φιλάνθρωπα."

8. Plato *Definitiones* 412C, ed. Burnet, *ibid.:* "Φιλανθρωπία ἕξις εὐάγωγος ἤθους πρὸς ἀνθρώπου φιλίαν· ἕξις εὐεργετικὴ ἀνθρώπων, χάριτος σχέσις, μνήμη μετ' εὐεργεσίας."

9. Hubert Martin, Jr. "The Concept of Philanthropia in Plutarch's Lives," *American Journal of Philology,* LXXXII (April 1961), 164–75.

ciety's concern for the orphans and the aged, the sick and the strangers, were succinctly described as philanthropia. In addition, a man's pity for and aid to those in any kind of tribulation, and his anguished concern for those in captivity, were expressions of philanthropia.

It is obvious that in the ancient Greek world philanthropia was not only a literary or philosophical ideal but was also a practical virtue applied by both the individual citizen and the city state.[10] In the Homeric age philanthropy was associated with assistance to beggars as well as to the poor and to strangers. Hesiod counseled his brother to work hard if he were to avoid asking for charity from others. One's neighbors can be expected to contribute once or twice but not forever.[11] The people were expected to be hospitable, especially to strangers and the needy. When Odysseus reached Ithaca, without knowing that the land was his beloved island, his first concern was the nature of the inhabitants. As he awoke and observed the land, he wondered whether the natives were just, hospitable, and God-fearing, or barbaric and insolent.[12] The stranger in ancient Hellas was considered as dear as a brother.[13] A modern scholar describes Greek hospitality as follows: "The virtue of hospitality so sacred to the Greeks is emphasized even in the *Iliad* by Achilles' reception of old Priam and by the fact that even Helen found hospitable reception in Troy. Paris' abuse of hospitality was his great crime and the cause of woe to himself and others. In the *Odyssey* regard for hospitality is evident in the treatment that Odysseus received at the hands of Alcinous and his court . . . the terrible fate meted out to the suitors is a striking instance of the retribution that follows its abuse." [14]

Orphans also deserved philanthropic providence, and their

10. See Monnier, *Hist. Asst. Publ.;* Leon Lallemand, *Hist. Char.* I, 55–100.

11. Hesiod *Works and Days* ll. 390–402.

12. Homer *Odyssey* xiii. 200–03: " "Ω μοι ἐγώ, τέων αὖτε βροτῶν ἐς γαῖαν ἱκάνω; Ἦ ῥ' οἵ γ' ὑβρισταί τε καὶ ἄγριοι οὐδὲ δίκαιοι, ἦε φιλόξεινοι καὶ σφιν νόος ἐστὶ θεουδής. . . ." Cf. Hesiod *Homer's Epigrams, ibid.,* p. 466.

13. Homer *Odyssey* viii. 546–47: "ἀντὶ κασιγνήτου ξεῖνος θ' ἱκέτης τε τέτυκται ἀνέρι. . . ."

14. Frederick A. G. Beck, *Greek Education* (New York, 1964), p. 59; cf. H. J. Marrou, *Histoire de l'éducation dans l'antiquité* (Paris, 1948), pp. 29–38, 297–309.

condition was viewed with compassion.[15] Plato proposed that orphans be placed under the care of public guardians and urged love and compassion for them: "Men should have a fear of the loneliness of orphans. . . . A man should love the unfortunate orphan (boy or girl) of whom he is the guardian as if he were his own child; he should be as careful and diligent in the management of the orphan's property as of his own or even more careful still." [16] Hippodamos, in his plan for the benevolent state, provided that the orphans of citizens who died in battle should be maintained at public expense.[17] Aristotle adds that this condition already existed in Athens and in other Greek cities.[18] This is also confirmed by Thucydides; the funeral oration of Pericles reveals the concern of Athenians for the orphan.[19]

The ancient Greeks were also very philanthropic and affectionate toward the aged.[20] Not only was reverence for aged parents advocated, but also respect and consideration for all persons of advanced age. Demosthenes, for example, praised the young who had reverence for their parents and respect for their elders.[21] In Homer's works we encounter over and over again the Greek veneration and esteem of old age. But this was not merely a sentimental attitude; the Greeks had legislated and taken measures to protect the aged and to make the last years of life less miserable. An authority on the subject observes: "In their attitude toward the aged and orphans we see a most redeeming feature in the character of the Greeks." [22]

The poor in general were assisted in ancient Hellas in diverse ways. Legal enactments were introduced for release of debts; poor-relief was distributed to the sick, and loans of different

15. Homer *Iliad* xxii. 490–500.
16. Plato *Leges* xi. 927A; tr. R. G. Bury, Loeb Classical Library, II (London, 1932), 434.
17. Aristotle *Politica* xi. 8, ed. Immanuel Bekker, *Aristotelis De Republica Libri VIII* (Oxon., 1837), p. 42.
18. Aristotle, *ibid.*: "ἔστι δὲ καὶ ἐν ᾿Αθήναις οὗτος ὁ νόμος νῦν καὶ ἐν ἑτέραις τῶν πόλεων."
19. Thucydides *History of the Peloponnesian War* ii. 46.
20. For the Greek attitude toward old age see the exhaustive monograph by Bessie Ellen Richardson, *Old Age Among the Ancient Greeks* (Baltimore, 1933), especially pp. 48–58.
21. Demosthenes *Aristogiton* i. 24–25.
22. Richardson, *Old Age*, p. 58; cf. C. B. Gulick, "Notions of Humanity Among the Greeks," *Harvard Essays on Classical Subjects,* ed. Herbert W. Smyth (Boston and New York, 1912), pp. 38, 41.

nature were extended to those in want. Peisistratos, for example, who is described as philanthropic, lent money to the poor so that they might earn a living.[23]

The sense of philanthropy developed by the Greeks manifested itself also in philanthropic institutions. Strangers and needy foreigners received shelter and food in public guest-chambers or *xenones* maintained for them. To look after the needs of strangers there were brotherhoods of hospitality known as *xenoi* or guest-friends. For example, in the city of Hierapolis the brotherhood of hospitality had a common fund chest and Apollo was their patron.[24]

In addition to the xenones, the Greeks had hospices or *katagogia* attached to various temples or near them to serve as resting places or even as clinics. The sanctuary of Hera, north of Argos, included such an institution, two hundred feet square, with rooms on two floors.[25] A similar two-storied establishment (katagogion) has been discovered at the temple of Asclepios in Epidauros.[26] It included a section of four colonnaded courts with one hundred and sixty rooms for the sick and for visitors to the temple.[27] Such institutions existed adjacent to the temples because of belief in the healing power of the gods resident in them.[28] Priests of Asclepios attended the poor and sick gratuitously.

Another Asclepieion at Gortyn in Dorian Crete could shelter at least two hundred patients. A large proportion of the temple funds was used for charities. The "sacred treasuries," as they were called, were destined for philanthropic uses, although the state could borrow from the temples in time of need.[29] In addition to the temple xenones and hospitals there was an organiza-

23. Aristotle *Athenian Constitution* xvi: "Πεισίστρατος, . . . ἔν τε γὰρ τοῖς ἄλλοις φιλάνθρωπος ἦν καὶ πρᾶος καὶ τοῖς ἁμαρτάνουσι συγγνωμονικός, καὶ δὴ καὶ τοῖς ἀπόροις προεδάνειζε χρήματα πρὸς τὰς ἐργασίας. . . ." Cf. Gulick, "Notions of Humanity . . ." p. 45.

24. William M. Ramsay, *The Cities and Bishoprics of Phrygia*, I (Oxford, 1895), 97.

25. Thucydides iii. 68; Plato, *Leges*, xii. 952D–953B.

26. Pausanias *Corinthiaca* ii. 30.

27. R. C. Rosanquet, "Archaeology in Greece, 1899–1900," *JHS*, XX (1900), 177; cf. C. S. Loch, *Charity and Social Life* (London, 1910), pp. 49 ff.

28. Walter A. Jayne, M.D., *The Healing Gods of Ancient Civilizations* (New York, 1962), pp. 257–59 *et passim*.

29. J. Papadopoulos, "Τὰ Ἱερὰ χρήματα εἰς τὴν Ἀρχαίαν Ἑλληνικὴν καὶ Βυζαντινὴν Περίοδον," ΕΕΒΣ, XIX (1949), 188–93.

tion which furnished medical aid and relief for strangers and the poor.

Hippocrates' rules provided that a physician should give his services with no compensation when the need arose.[30] When visiting a town the physician was urged to attend the sick. The state or the city physician would visit without fee any poor man who sought his services. Hippocrates emphasized that the motive of the doctor in offering his services should be the love of man. True philanthropia causes a physician to love the art of healing as well.[31] The benevolent physicians included those who visited country people specifically for the care of children and the poor.

In Athens there was also a system of public relief for those who were unable to earn a livelihood by reason of illness, bodily defects, and infirmities. The qualification was a property test. The value of an applicant's property must be no more than three minae. Socrates may serve as an illustration, since he adopted this method in estimating his modest circumstances.[32]

The spirit of brotherhood and friendship which is the basis of philanthropia is well expressed by Sophocles in his *Antigone*.[33] And Xenophon projects Heracles as the embodiment of this spirit of humanism. He adds that "if one desires the protection of the gods, one must practice piety toward them; if a man would be loved by his friends he must help them; if he would be honoured by a city he must serve it; if he would be admired by all Greece, he must be her benefactor." [34]

Xenophon relates that philanthropia was a regular policy of Agesilaos, King of Sparta (398–360 B.C.). He had followed a humane and compassionate policy toward prisoners of war, destitute children, and elderly men.[35] Agesilaos, by virtue of his philanthropia, was described as a fortress impregnable to assault.[36]

30. Hippocrates *Precepts* vi.

31. *Ibid.*: "ἢν γὰρ παρῇ φιλανθρωπίη πάρεστι καὶ φιλοτεχνίη."

32. Xenophon *Oeconomicos* ii. 5–10; cf., Aristotle *Atheniensium Respublica*, Ch. 49.

33. Sophocles *Antigone* 50–70, 150–75, *et passim*.

34. Xenophon *Memorabilia* II. i. 28.

35. Xenophon *Agesilaos* i. 21–23.

36. *Ibid.*: "τῶν κατὰ κράτος ἀναλώτων τειχέων τῇ φιλανθρωπίᾳ ὑπὸ χεῖρα ἐποιεῖτο."

In addition to political dignitaries, other civil servants and private citizens advocated the practice of philanthropia in ancient Greece. Demosthenes counseled that philanthropia alone must govern the relations between citizens, while their enemies deserved their wrath and hatred.[37] His rival Athenian orator Isocrates urged King Philip of Macedonia to a policy of philanthropy toward all the Greeks, together with meekness and good works.[38] He exhorted Philip to imitate the example of Heracles, who spent his life in the establishment of moral order, virtue, and justice.[39] Men of philanthropic feelings are described as demigods or Olympians.

Among individual Greeks who were given much credit for actual philanthropy we may mention a few. We are told that Epaminondas, the great general of Thebes, ransomed captive fellow citizens with his own money and collected dowries for impoverished girls.[40] Cimon, the son of Miltiades, used his private wealth for philanthropic purposes. He fed the hungry and clothed the naked. Plutarch avers that Cimon, in his generosity, "surpassed even the hospitality and philanthropy of the Athenians of olden times." [41] And Bias, one of the seven wise men of ancient Greece (c. 570 B.C.) used his personal funds to emancipate captive girls of Messenia, restoring them to their families and giving them dowries.[42]

In general we may observe that the philosophers played an important role in reminding the government and the citizenry of their duties toward the disinherited classes. Philanthropia was an ideal as well as a practical virtue of the ancient Hellenes. In their welfare institutions the Greeks displayed the agility of

37. Demosthenes *On the Chersonese* ll. 70–71.

38. Isocrates *To Philip*, par. 49: ". . . διὰ παντός σε τοῦ λόγου πειρῶμαι προτρέπειν ἐπί τε τὰς εὐεργεσίας τὰς τῶν Ἑλλήνων καὶ πραότητα καὶ φιλανθρωπίαν."

39. *Ibid.*, par. 48: "λέγω δ᾿ οὐχ ὡς δυνησόμενον ἁπάσας σε μιμήσασθαι τὰς Ἡρακλέους πράξεις . . . ἀλλὰ κατά γε τὸ τῆς ψυχῆς ἦθος καὶ τὴν φιλανθρωπίαν καὶ τὴν εὔνοιαν, ἣν εἶχεν εἰς τοὺς Ἕλληνας, δύναι᾿ ἂν ὁμοιωθῆναι τοῖς ἐκείνου βουλήμασιν."

40. Cornelius Nepos, *Epaminondas* III, 5–6; for philanthropy in the ancient Greek world see also Hendrik Bolkestein, *Wohltatigkeit und Armenpflege im Vorchristlichen Altertum* (Utrecht, 1939), pp. 67–286.

41. Plutarch *Cimon* x. 1–6; B. Perrin, Loeb Classical Library, II (London, 1928), 434: "ἡ δὲ Κίμωνος ἀφθονία καὶ τὴν παλαιὰν τῶν Ἀθηναίων φιλοξενίαν καὶ φιλανθρωπίαν ὑπερέβαλεν."

42. Diogenes Laertios *Bias*, Loeb Classical Library, I, 84.

their varied genius: a noteworthy solicitude, a restrained ego-
tism, and a more compassionate spirit.[43]

The classical Greek conception of philanthropia was inherited
by the Hellenistic world.[44] The theoretical aspect of it was expressed by St. Paul. Writing to his disciple Titus, Paul asserts
that the love and philanthropia of God has manifested itself
toward men.[45] This notion, of the philanthropia of God expressed
in the incarnation of Jesus Christ, is found frequently in medieval Greek texts.

The practical application of the term is well expressed by St.
Luke in the book of Acts. He describes the compassion shown
after the wreck of the ship transporting St. Paul as a prisoner
to Rome. Luke alleges that the natives of the island of Melita
(Malta) "showed them no little philanthropia." They "kindled
a fire and received every one because of the rain and the cold" [46]
thereby rendering deeds of hospitality and benevolence.

As in classical Greek antiquity so in the Hellenistic world
humanistic feeling and activity was not lacking.[47] In particular
the physicians exercised philanthropia extensively on a voluntary
basis and made no distinction between rich and poor, free and
slave, in their services.[48] At the same time there were provisions
for the poor. Food liturgies were organized in Rhodes and
Athens, special concern was shown for the crippled, and there
were other works of assistance and philanthropy.[49] Aristotle had
advocated that in a true democracy the Athenians should imitate
the people of Tarentum, who shared the use of their property
with the poor.[50]

Nevertheless, in the Greek world before Christ, despite the
many acts of private and state assistance to the aged, orphans,

43. Monnier, *Hist. Asst. Publ.*, p. 79.
44. Bell, "Philanthropia in the Papyri," *Hommages Bidez et Cumont* II, 33.
45. Titus 3:4: "ὅτε δὲ ἡ χρηστότης καὶ ἡ φιλανθρωπία ἐπεφάνη τοῦ
σωτῆρος ἡμῶν θεοῦ. . . ." Cf. Le Deaut, "Φιλανθρωπία dans Litterature
Grecque," *Mélanges Tisserant* I, 291–94.
46. Acts 28:2.
47. Cf. William Tarn and G. T. Griffith, *Hellenistic Civilization*, 3rd ed.
(London, 1959), pp. 79–125; Le Deaut, *Tisserant*, pp. 278–90; M. Spanneut,
"L'Amour de l'hellénisme au christianisme," *Mélanges de science religieuse*,
XX (1963), 12–19.
48. Dittenberger, *Sylloge*, 2, 163, 400; cf. Tarn and Griffith, *ibid.*, pp.
108–10.
49. Aristotle *Republica*, Ch. 49.
50. Aristotle *Politica* vi. 5.

impoverished, handicapped, strangers, and destitute; despite the great benevolence of Epaminondas, Agesilaos, Pericles, Cimon, and others; although philosophers such as the Stoics had created an atmosphere of humanism and philanthropic attitudes, and the city-states had organized public assistance, philanthropia in Greek antiquity depended mostly upon the policies of those in charge of the government. When their treasuries were exhausted, all forms of public assistance generally collapsed. As a rule no underlying and widespread spirit of philanthropia prevailed.[51] What was current could not be compared to what we encounter in the Graeco-Christian civilization of the Byzantine world— well-organized philanthropy, spontaneous expression of selfless love and compassion, church- or privately- or state-organized institutions.[52]

The limitations of ancient Greek philanthropia were defined by their ideas of responsibility for one's fellow man.[53] Their philanthropy was practiced in a limited field and was directed mostly toward the civilized Hellenes. "The 'love of man for man' found its actual outlet in application to relatives, friends, fellow citizens, or allies." [54] With several exceptions allowed, Greek philanthropia was a type of kindness and liberality.[55]

While philanthropia in the ancient Greek world was mostly anthropocentric, in Christianity it became eminently theocentric. The principle of philanthropy was the love of God rather than the love of man.[56]

The teaching of the Christian religion which made philanthropia theocentric was the sermon of Jesus Christ: "The son of man came not to be served but to serve, and to give his life as a ransom for many." [57] Thus the philanthropist becomes a servant as God became a servant. God did not manifest his love for man out of selfish interest, but that man might be saved. Here, then, is the basis of altruism, selfless love, Christian philanthropia.

51. Monnier, *Hist. Asst. Publ.*, p. 134.
52. Tarn and Griffith, p. 110.
53. Cf. Glanville Downey, "Who Is My Neighbor? The Greek and Roman Answer," A Th. R, reprint (January 1965), pp. 3 ff.
54. Ferguson, *Moral Values in the Ancient World*, pp. 107–08; Martin, "Philanthropia in Plutarch," *AJP*, LXXXII, 166.
55. Cf. A. H. M. Jones, *The Later Roman Empire* 284–602 II (Norman, Okla., 1964), 970–71.
56. Cf. Lecky, *European Morals*, II, 79.
57. Mark 10:45; Matt. 20:28.

Jesus advised his disciples to love one another as he had loved them.[58] God is the prototype and His creature should imitate the Creator. In the words of Jesus: "A new commandment I give to you, that you love one another; even as I have loved you, that you also love one another. By this all men will know that you are my disciples, if you have love for one another." [59]

Christianity is revolutionary, so far as social relations are concerned, in another way. In Christianity all are presumed to be equal; there is no distinction between patrician and barbarian, citizen and slave, elect and proselyte; thus Christian philanthropy, at least in theory, becomes universal and embraces all men. The difference between the Christian notion and the Greek, Roman, or Judaic is found in the following: "You have heard that it was said, 'You shall love your neighbor and hate your enemy.' But I say to you, love your enemies and pray for those who persecute you. . . . For if you love those who love you, what reward have you? Do not even the tax collectors do the same? And if you salute only your brethren, what more are you doing than others? Do not even the Gentiles do the same?" [60]

The preaching of universal *agape* becomes the slogan of the disciples of Christ [61] and the cornerstone of the early Church. It was not just a theoretical abstraction but an applied virtue as well. The followers were admonished to practice charity to the needy, the stranger, and the orphan, and to develop a sense of social and ethnic equality and justice.[62] And this practice of philanthropy was not to be the result of coercion, expediency, or selfish motives, but the fruit of free will.[63]

This revolutionary concept inspired an enthusiasm for charity which displayed itself in the erection of numerous philanthropic institutions.[64] Most probably it was the "new commandment" [65]

58. John 15:12.
59. John 13:34–35. For the concept of agape in the New Testament see Ceslaus Spicq, *Agape in the New Testament*, tr. Marie A. McNamara and Mary H. Richter, Vols. I–III (B. Herder: St. Louis, 1963–1966); Anders Nygren, *Agape and Eros*, tr. Philip S. Watson (Philadelphia, 1953); see especially pp. 61–145.
60. Matt. 5:43–48.
61. Rom. 13:8; Eph. 5:2; I Pet. 1:22; I John 2:10, 3:11, and especially I Cor. 13.
62. Cf. Rom. 12:13; James 1:27, 2:14, I Pet. 4:9 *et passim*.
63. II Cor. 9:7; Rom. 12:8; Acts 5:1 ff. *et al*.
64. Lecky, *European Morals*, II, 80.
65. John 13:34.

of agape which helped to introduce Christianity to the ancient world.[66]

The apostolic Church organized philanthropies and looked after the poor, the widows, and the orphans;[67] it held common meals; and Christians extended their assistance to the local congregation and also to others.[68] They believed that they were living members of the same organism. Thus if one were sick all shared in his affliction by extending a helping hand. They cared also for those in prison, and for them the application of philanthropia became the essence of the Christian community.[69] This attitude of the early Christians adhered to the teaching of Christ: "Insofar as you did it to one of the humblest of these brothers of mine [i.e. the needy], you have done it to me."[70] God caused philanthropia to be practiced. As God had reached out to save man, so the man of God was expected to reach out and help his fellow man. Thus, to receive strangers and extend hospitality to transient visitors was considered a sacred duty. Nevertheless, the philanthropia of the host was not to be abused. If the guest could earn his living he should be put to work.[71]

After the first century the Church continued the philanthropic policy of the Apostles. The concept of agape had taken hold of the hearts of the believers to the extent that active philanthropy became the concern of all. Charitable offerings were taken every Sunday for the poor of the local congregation and for believers in other cities. The poor were accepted as the "temple of God,"[72] and tithes were established in order that the Church might have sufficient funds for its philanthropic mission.[73] We

66. Cf. Ignatios, *Epistle to the Smyrneans*, VI; Polycarp, *Epistle to the Philippians*, X; all references and citations from the fathers of the Church or early ecclesiastical writers are from the editions of «Βιβλιοθήκη Ἑλλήνων Πατέρων καὶ Ἐκκλησιαστικῶν Συγγραφέων», ed. Apostolic Diaconate of the Church of Greece (Athens, 1955–), unless otherwise stated.

67. Cf. Rom. 15:31; I Cor. 16:1 ff.; II Cor. 8:9 ff.; Gal. 2:10, I Cor. 7:8; Acts 6:1–6; Acts 2:42; Heb. 13:16; Jas. 1:27 *et al.*

68. Acts 11:29; Rom. 15:21; II Cor. 8:4, 7–14; 9:1–2, *et passim.*

69. S. Agourides, «Ἡ Κοινοκτημοσύνη ἐν τῇ πρώτῃ Ἐκκλησίᾳ» (Thessalonike, 1963), p. 14; M. Siotes, «Ἡ Φροντὶς τῆς πρώτης Ἐκκλησίας ὑπὲρ τῶν Ὀρφανῶν Κορασίδων» (Athens, 1964), pp. 67–85.

70. Matt. 25:40; cf. Matt. 25:42–43; Matt. 19:21, Mark 10:21; Luke 18:22.

71. *Didache of the Twelve Apostles*, XII, 1–5.

72. *Apostolic Constitutions*, III. 6; IV. 3 *et passim.*

73. Justin, *First Apologia*, 67. 6; Tertullian *Apologeticus* 39, ed. tr. T. R. Glover, Loeb Classical Library (London, 1931).

encounter often the view that it was the sermon of agape which prompted Christians to exercise philanthropies.[74]

Philanthropia had become the badge of distinction between Christian and pagan. Ignatios, Bishop of Antioch, writes to the Christians of Smyrna: "Take notice of those who have contrary opinions concerning the grace of Jesus Christ . . . how different they are. . . . They do not care for acts of love, they don't care about the widow, the orphan, the distressed, the afflicted, the prisoner, or for him released from prison, neither do they worry about the hungry or the thirsty." [75]

The members of the Church were admonished to offer the first fruits of their products—wine, oil, clothes, wheat, sheep, and other goods—to the "prophets" of the congregation, but if there were no prophets they should give their sacrifices to the poor.[76]

Charity was not always limited to fellow Christians. The time came when the faithful were advised to give "to all who need, not doubting to whom you shall give and to whom not: give to all, for to all God wishes gifts to be made of his own bounties." [77] The believers were even urged to fast and to save the money for charity to be contributed to a widow, an orphan, or someone destitute.[78]

Christian philanthropy was institutionalized very early and the bishop entrusted with the administrative responsibility for the charities of the Church. He was expected to exhibit "to the orphans the care of parents; to the widows the care and the protection of husbands; . . . to the invalid commiseration; to the strangers a shelter, to the hungry food; to the thirsty drink; to the naked clothing, to the sick visitation, to the prisoners assistance. . . . " [79] The orphans, the elderly, the sick, and those

74. *Epistle of Barnabas*, 20. 2; Ignatios, *Epistle to Smyrnaeans*, 6:2; *Didache of the Twelve Apostles*, 4:5, 13:3, 15:4.

75. Ignatios, *Epistle to Smyrnaeans:* ''καταμάθετε δὲ τοὺς ἑτεροδοξοῦντας . . . περὶ ἀγάπης οὐ μέλει αὐτοῖς, οὐ περὶ χήρας, οὐ περὶ ὀρφανοῦ, οὐ περὶ θλιβομένου, οὐ περὶ δεδεμένου ἢ λελυμένου, οὐ περὶ πεινῶντος ἢ διψῶντος.'' Cf. *Epistle of Barnabas*, 20. 2.

76. *Didache of the Twelve Apostles*, XIII. 3–7; cf. also Chaps. IV. 5–8; XV. 4; also *Epistle of Barnabas*, XIX. 9–11.

77. The Shepherd of Hermas, *Mandate*, 2. 2; cf. also *Parable*, 1. 8; Aristides *Apologia* XV. 7.

78. The Shepherd of Hermas, *Parable*, 5. 3; Aristides *Apologia* XV. 8.

79. *Apostolic Constitutions*, IV, sect. 1, 2; cf. Tertullian *Apologeticus* 39.

families with many children were recommended for special support.[80]

Those recommendations were not empty words. Aristides describes the Christians as people who actually did many charitable works.[81] The philosopher Justin provides us with similar information. He defends the followers of Christ as people peaceful and mindful of the needy, and testifies that they are benevolent who plead for the widow, provide for the orphan, do justice to all, do not exploit the humble, and deliver the poor and the weak out of the hands of the wicked.[82]

The third-century manuscript sources continue to indicate that philanthropia was a great concern of the Christian Church, both in the East and the West. Cyprian (d. 258) asserts that the Church diligently looked after the welfare of the sick, the poor, the widows, and others in need.[83] Tertullian (d. c. 220), the champion of the Christian cause, relates that "every man once a month brings some modest coin—or whenever he wishes, and only if he does wish, and if he can; for nobody is compelled; it is a voluntary offering. You might call them the trust funds of piety. For they are not spent upon banquets nor drinking-parties nor thankless eating-houses; but to feed the poor and to bury them, for boys and girls who lack property and parents, and then slaves grown old and shipwrecked mariners; and any who may be in mines, islands, or prisons, provided that it is for the sake of God's school, become the pensioners of their confession." [84]

A few years after Tertullian's eloquent testimony about the work of the church, we learn that the Church of Rome under Bishop Cornelius (c. 250) was feeding more than fifteen hundred widows and afflicted persons.[85]

In the fourth century Christian philanthropy must have taken

80. *Apostolic Constitutions*, IV. 9, II. 25; III. 3 *et passim*.
81. Aristides, *Apologia*, XV. 6–7: "χήραν οὐχ ὑπερορῶσιν, ὀρφανὸν οὐ λυποῦσιν, ὁ ἔχων τὸν μὴ ἔχοντα ἀνεπιφθόνως ἐπιχορηγεῖ· ξένον ἐὰν ἴδωσιν, ὑπὸ στέγην εἰσάγουσι καὶ χαίρουσιν ἐπ' αὐτῷ ὡς ἐπὶ ἀδελφῷ ἀληθινῷ.''
82. Justin, *First Apology*, chaps. 44, 61; Justin, *Dialogue with Trypho*, chaps. 27, 127 *et passim*.
83. Cyprian, *Epistles*, Nos. 35 and 36; *Treatise 8; The Ante-Nicene Fathers*, Alexander Roberts and James Donaldson, eds., V (Buffalo, 1886), 314–15, 476–84.
84. Tertullian *Apologeticus* 39, 5–6.
85. Eusebios, *Eccl. History*, VI. 43, 11–12.

on new dimensions. It was extended to believers and unbelievers alike. The Emperor Julian (361–63) complained that the Christians were extending their philanthropies not only to people of their own faith but to followers of the Olympian gods as well. In a letter to Arsacios, the high priest of Galatia, Julian writes: "It is disgraceful that . . . the impious Galilaeans support not only their own poor but ours as well." [86] In another letter to an unknown pagan priest, Julian prescribes: "You must above all exercise philanthropia, because from it result many other blessings." [87] Perhaps the example of the Christians exerted a telling influence upon Julian.

As the evidence indicates, one can clearly discern that in the early Christian societies of both the East and the West philanthropia had assumed an integrated and far-reaching meaning. The term was used to describe man's love for the totality of humanity. Its application was directed to even the humblest among men. Philanthropia appropriated the meaning of selfless love and willing sacrifice.[88] It was extended to the underprivileged, as it proclaimed freedom, equality, and brotherhood, transcending sex, race, and national boundaries. Thus, conclusively, philanthropia was not limited to equals, allies, and relatives, nor to citizens and civilized men, as was most often the case in ancient Greece. Christianity adopted the Greek concept of philanthropia but it went much further in its application.[89]

86. Julian, *Letters,* ed. tr. W. C. Wright, Loeb Classical Library, III (London, 1913), 71.

87. *Ibid.,* II, 299; cf. Sozomenos, *Eccl. History,* V. 16; Gibbon, *The Decline and Fall of the Roman Empire,* ed. J. B. Bury, II (London, 1897), 50.

88. Cf. Edwin Hatch, *The Influence of Greek Ideals on Christianity,* reprint (New York, 1957), p. 350.

89. For charity in the early church see: Uhlhorn, *Christian Charity;* A. Harnack, *Die Mission und Ausbreitung des Christentums,* IV (Leipzig, 1924), 186 ff.; Filaretos Vafides, " Ἡ Ἀγάπη καὶ τὰ ἔργα αὐτῆς ἐν τῇ Ἀρχαίᾳ Ἐκκλησίᾳ," ΓΠ, II (1927), 215 ff.; P. Demetropoulos, «Ἡ Πίστις τῆς Ἀρχαίας Ἐκκλησίας ὡς κανὼν ζωῆς καὶ ὁ Κόσμος» (Athens, 1959), pp. 142 ff.; H. Leclercq, "Charité," *Dictionnaire d'archéologie chrétienne et de liturgie,* ed. F. Cabriol and H. Leclercq, III, part 1 (Paris, 1913), 598–653; Leon Lallemand, *Hist. Char.,* II, 1–38; Chastel, *Influence de la charité,* pp. 23–70; Champagny, *Char. chret.;* Lecky, *European Morals,* II, 79–136. Frances J. Niederer, "Early Medieval Charity," CH, XXI (1952), 285–95; Augustus Neander, *General History of the Christian Religion and Church,* tr. Joseph Torrey, I (Boston, 1847), 255 ff.; E. F. Bruck, *Kirchenväter und Sozialen Erbrecht* (Berlin, 1957).

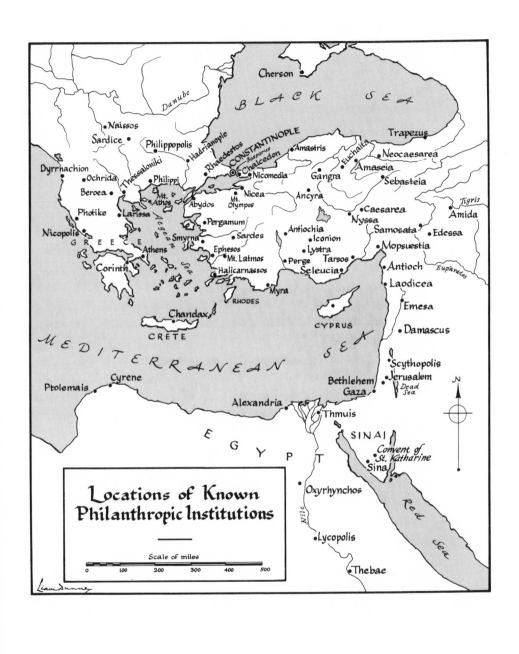

Locations of Known Philanthropic Institutions

Scale of miles

0   100   200   300   400   500

2. The Motives behind Byzantine Philanthropic Thought

The Greek notion of philanthropia, broadened and deepened both in theory and in practice under the impact of the Christian teaching of *agape,* was adopted by the Byzantine Empire. As a Graeco-Christian Commonwealth,[1] the medieval Greek world was a new creation and synthesis, and philanthropia was developed into a special concept.

Philanthropia in Byzantium was not what we understand today as philanthropy and charity. In practical application this it was, but in the Byzantine thought-world philanthropia assumed a theological meaning which is not easy to translate in any single modern English term. Today philanthropy implies prophylactic and therapeutic welfare, concern for the general public, and charity properly so called, directed toward alleviation of individual suffering.[2] But in the thought and life of the Byzantines philanthropia was: first, a philosophical and theological abstraction; second, a political attribute; third, charity directed to the individual in want; and fourth, philanthropy properly so called and expressed in organized institutions. We may note here that it was markedly similar to the ancient Greek understanding of

1. Cf. Ostrogorsky, *History,* p. 193; Peter Charanis, "The Transfer of Population as a Policy in the Byzantine Empire," *Comparative Studies in Society and History,* III, no. 2 (January, 1961), 154.

2. Cf. *Webster's New International Dictionary of the English Language,* ed. William Allan Neilson, *et al.* (Springfield, Mass., 1961), p. 1840.

18

philanthropia. As we already have seen, all these meanings of the term were current in ancient Greece, from the view of philanthropia as love of the deity for men and love of man for man, to hospitality, help to the orphans and the aged, and organized philanthropy. However, in Byzantium philanthropia assumed new dimensions.

If we were to ask a Byzantine what prompted him to believe in and apply philanthropia, he would have answered in the following terms, which formed the philanthropic philosophy of a monastery.[3] Become not only merciful, as your Heavenly Father is merciful,[4] but also just; for, as it is written, the just man gives liberally every day and lends,[5] he distributes freely to the poor, his righteousness endures to the ages of ages.[6] Blessed are the merciful for they shall obtain mercy;[7] blessed is he who considers the poor and the beggar;[8] he who sows in *eleemosyne* shall reap the fruit of life;[9] he who is charitable to the poor lends to the Lord;[10] he who oppresses a poor man insults his Maker;[11] through eleemosynary works and faithfulness sins are forgiven.[12]

These rules were the foundation of Byzantine philanthropic philosophy because God demanded man's mercy for his fellow man rather than sacrifices.[13] The practitioner of charities was admonished that his deeds of mercy would lead him to the eternal habitations of the Almighty.[14] This philosophy of philanthropy is expressed in many medieval Greek writings, in seals of monasteries, of churches, of other establishments, and of in-

3. Delehaye, *Deux Typica*, p. 69.
4. Cf. Luke 6:26.
5. Cf. Ps. 37:25–26.
6. Cf. Ps. 112:9.
7. Matt. 5:7; cf. St. Basil the Great, *Homilia in Divites*. 4, MPG, XXXI, col. 292AB.
8. Cf. Ps. 41:1.
9. Cf. Hosea 10:12; cf. S. Murray, *A Study of the Life of Andreas, The Fool for the Sake of Christ* (Leipzig, 1910), pp. 95–97.
10. Cf. Prov. 19:17; cf. Gregory of Nyssa, *De Pauperibus Amandis*, MPG, XLVI, col. 484B: ''οὐκοῦν ὅλον τὸ πλήρωμα τῶν ἐντολῶν ἐν τούτοις ἔχεις πληρούμενον, καὶ αὐτὸν τὸν τῶν ὅλων Κύριον ὑπόχρεών σοι διὰ τῆς εἰς τοῦτον φιλανθρωπίας γινόμενον.''
11. Prov. 14:31; cf. Murray, *Life of Andreas*, p. 102.
12. Cf. Prov. 16:6; "Life of St. Theodore Sykeon," ed. Ioannou, «Μνημεῖα», p. 384.
13. Delehaye, *Deux Typica*, p. 69; cf. Hosea 6:6.
14. Delehaye, *Deux Typica*, p. 69; cf., Lk. 16:9.

dividuals, of which several have survived to the present day.[15]

The metaphysical anxieties of the Byzantines were concentrated on the question of salvation and the inheritance of the eternal Kingdom of God. To achieve that goal perfection on the earth was viewed as a prerequisite. Thus some of them became monks to live a life of prayer and mortification of material needs, while others distributed their possessions to the poor to free themselves and achieve their theosis as hermits, that is, in constant communion with God. There is much that is admirable in this philosophical quest, much that cannot be dismissed as excessive religious zeal. A third category had dedicated themselves to the practice of philanthropia or selfless love, within society. To keep love alive one was to practice works of philanthropy which repel wickedness afar, while lack of them makes man's love grow cold.[16] Thus many of them, though poor, found means and ways to practice the salutary commandment. We are told that certain monks solicited money from the rich in order to distribute it to the poor.[17] They considered philanthropy as one of the five most important virtues.[18]

These views were well expressed by Dionysios of Alexandria (d. 264–65) and were re-emphasized by John of Damascos (660–750) and other writers: "Nothing is more honorable or philanthropic to us than to be merciful and to do good, because nothing is more desirable to God."[19]

It is obvious that the background of philanthropia is theological, that is, intended to please or to imitate God. Gregory Nazianzenos counseled his people: "Prove yourself a god to the unfortunate, imitating the mercy of God. There is nothing more godly in man than to do good works."[20] Other motives were

15. Gustave Schlumberger, "Monuments numismatiques et sphragistiques du moyen âge byzantin," RA, XL, new series (1880), pp. 193–212.

16. Cf., Matt. 24:12.

17. Macarios, *Homily 17.* 8, ed. Hermann Dorries, *Die 50 Geistlichen Homilien Des Makarios* (Berlin, 1964), p. 171.

18. *Ibid.*, p. 269; cf. p. 183.

19. Joannes Damascenos, *Sacra Parallela*, MPG, XCV, col. 1473C: "τοῦ ἐλεεῖν καὶ εὐεργετεῖν, οὔτε προτιμότερον, οὔτε φιλανθρωπότερον ἐστὶν ἡμῖν τι ἕτερον, ἐπεὶ μηδὲ τῷ Θεῷ." Cf. *Actes de Lavra*, p. 31: "οὐδὲν οὕτω θεραπαύει Θεόν, ὡς ἐκ πολλῶν μαθεῖν ἐστίν, ὡς ἐλεημοσύνη καὶ ἡ πρὸς τοὺς δεομένους."

20. Gregory Nazianzenos, *Oratio No. 15*, quoted by J. Damascenos, *ibid.*, col. 1465D: "γενοῦ τῷ ἀτυχοῦντι θεός, τὸν ἔλεον Θεοῦ μιμούμενος. Οὐ-

either religious or ethical in nature. It was believed that possession of philanthropia was an expression of repentance and re-
dedication to God. To illustrate this view Palladios of Eleonopolis (d. c. 431) relates that a virgin nun was once seduced by
a church reader (anagnostes), an act which imprinted a great
guilt upon her soul. To alleviate her moral stigma she devoted
her life to the service of the sick and the lepers.[21] Philanthropia
was viewed as the great antidote to injustice and to sin because
it was considered also the point of balance in God's attributes.[22]

In application, too, philanthropia was built on moral and religious foundations. Basil the Great was very emphatic about it.
If you have not been merciful, he wrote, you will not receive
mercy; if you have not opened your house to the poor, you will
be locked out of the Kingdom of Heaven; if you have refused
bread to the hungry, you will be deprived of life eternal.[23]

Next to God, the Byzantines were advised to imitate the great
patriarchs of the Old Testament in works of hospitality, because
one patriarch was host to God the Savior; another entertained
the angels; a third was rewarded by a son in his advanced age,
while yet another was delivered with his daughters from the
fires of Sodom.[24] Furthermore, hospitality had been urged by the
Apostle.[25] Charity was viewed as the wings of prayer. St. John
Climacos wrote that the soul needs wings to fly to heights which
are provided by eleemosyne. But as fire is extinguished without
oil, he wrote, likewise prayer fails in its goal when it is not
accompanied by charity.[26]

δὲν γὰρ οὕτως ὡς τὸ εὐποιεῖν ἄνθρωπος ἔχει Θεοῦ." I have not been able
to find this passage in Gregory's fifteenth oration.

21. Palladios, *Hist. Lausiaca*, p. 165; cf. Joannes Climacos, *Scala Paradisi*,
MPG, LXXXVIII, col. 845AB.

22. Gregory Nazianzenos, *Oration*, no. 15, quoted by John of Damascus,
Sacra Parallela, MPG, XCV, col. 1465C: "Οὐδὲν γὰρ ἄλλῳ τινὶ ὡς φιλανθρωπία τὸ φιλάνθρωπον ἀντιδίδοται παρὰ τοῦ δικαίως ἀντιμετροῦντος
ἐν ζυγῷ καὶ σταθμῷ τὸν ἔλεον."

23. Basil the Great, *Homilia in Divites*, 4, MPG, XXXI, col. 292B; cf.
Joannes Climacos, *Scala Paradisi*, MPG, LXXXVIII, col. 1144C.

24. Palladios, *Vita S. Jo Chr*, pp. 71 ff.

25. Hebr. 13:2.

26. Joannes of Climacos, *Scala Paradisi*, MPG, LXXXVIII, col. 1144D:
"πτερόν ἐστι τῆς εὐχῆς ἡ ἐλεημοσύνη· ἐὰν μὴ ποιήσῃς πτερὸν τῇ εὐχῇ
σου, οὐκ ἀνέρχεται εἰς ὕψος.... Ὥσπερ γὰρ πῦρ ἐὰν μὴ ἔχῃ ἔλαιον ἀπο-
στάζον, σβέννυται, οὕτως καὶ ἡ εὐχή, ἐὰν μὴ ἔχῃ ἐλεημοσύνην ἀφανί-
ζεται." Cf. Kataskepenos, *Cyril Phileotes*, p. 69.

This view of philanthropy must be universal in character and all-embracing. The trans-ethnic nature of Byzantine society was well expressed by Maximos the Confessor who proposed agape as the supreme attribute. The perfect in love sees no difference between his own people and the stranger; between the Christian and the infidel, the free and the slave, male and female. He is liberated from the tyranny of the passions and sees men everywhere as equals. For him there is no Greek or Jew, male or female, slave or free, but all and in all they are one in Christ.[27]

Philanthropy was not to be practiced, however, on the basis of selfish motives. It is possible that a man might offer charity to a poor and young girl but with evil intentions, to exploit her loneliness and her youth. One may offer charity to the sick, to individuals of advanced age, to poor people, but the offering might be grudgingly made. Such philanthropy is of no merit. The Byzantine should offer generously, joyfully, and selflessly.[28] A man should practice charity while alive and not wait for his relatives to distribute philanthropies after his death on his behalf.[29] The contribution of material goods was not considered sufficient, but one was supposed to show one's feelings by actual and altruistic service to the needy,[30] for a man's expression of love was of greater importance than the material goods given to the poor. This view is frequently found in writings throughout the Byzantine era.[31]

Not all the eleemosynary philosophy was expressed in moral and religious hortatory writings. One may say that economic terminology properly so called was employed for the use of riches. Wealth which remains static is useless, St. Basil wrote. He advised the rich people of his diocese to imitate the earth and be fruitful like her lest they prove her inferior. The earth does not produce fruits for herself but for the benefit of man. When a man uses his wealth in good works, the benefit comes

27. Maximos the Confessor, *De Caritate*, Century II. 30, MPG, XC, col. 993B; cf. Gal. 3:28; Col. 3:11.

28. Palladios, *Hist. Lausiaca*, p. 138.

29. Joannes Chrysostomos, *Ecloga*, 33, MPG, LXIII, col. 730.

30. Maximos the Confessor, *De Caritate*, Century I. 26, MPG, XC, col. 965C.

31. Kataskepenos, *Cyril Phileotes*, p. 69: "Οὐ γὰρ τοσοῦτον διὰ τὸ τραφῆναι τὸν πένητα ἡ ἐλεημοσύνη ὥρισται, ὅσον διὰ τὴν ἀγάπην."

back to him.[32] Basil adds that the wealth which is used becomes beneficial to all society.[33]

However, despite the great results that philanthropia was expected to effect upon the human soul after death, it was accepted that no charity was great enough to lead a habitual sinner to the presence of God after death. Eleemosyne was able to deliver a malefactor from eternal hell but was not powerful enough to take him to paradise, where he could enjoy the light of God.

This philosophy was expressed in a conversation between Archbishop Arcadios of Cyprus and his bishops in the seventh century. All were admirers of a certain magnate named Philentolos who had performed many philanthropies, including the erection of institutions. Philentolos, however, was a slave to the passion of fornication. Until his death he continued his charities as well as his obsession for women.[34] Despite his many philanthropies, Philentolos was deprived of the joy of paradise, although he escaped the eternal punishments of hell. He found himself in a neutral category.[35]

Forgiveness of sins after death as a philosophic motive for philanthropic action was maintained throughout the Byzantine period. A few illustrations will suffice to support this view. This Byzantine notion was based upon the teachings of Jesus himself. When a rich ruler asked Christ, "What shall I do to inherit eternal life?" Jesus answered, "You know the Commandments, do not commit adultery, do not kill, do not steal, do not bear false witness, honor your father and mother." But the young ruler answered, "All these I have observed from my youth." It was after his answer that Christ uttered the now-famous words: "One thing you still lack. Sell all that you have and distribute

32. Basil the Great, *In Illud Dictum Evangelii*, 3, MPG, XXXI, col. 265C.
33. *Ibid.*, col. 272B: "Τὰ φρέατα ἐξαντλούμενα εὐροώτερα γίνεται· ἐναφιέμενα δέ, κατασήπεται. καὶ πλούτου τὸ μὲν στάσιμον ἄχρηστον, τὸ δὲ κινούμενον καὶ μεταβαῖνον κοινωφελές τε καὶ ἔγκαρπον." Cf. Eustathios of Thessalonica, *De emendanda vita monachica*, Ch. 36, ed. Tafel, *Eustathii Opuscula* (Frankfurt am Main, 1832), pp. 222–63 ff.
34. "Περὶ τοῦ Φιλεντόλου 'Ολυμπίου," ed. Halkin, AB, LXIII (1945), p. 62: "Εἰς γῆρας οὖν ἐλθὼν ἐτελεύτησεν μήτε τῆς ἐλεημοσύνης παυσάμενος μήτε τῆς ἁμαρτίας [πορνείας] ἀποκόψας."
35. *Ibid.*, p. 63. Philentolos was told in Hades:"Διὰ μὲν τῆς ἐλεημοσύνης ἐλυτρώθης τῆς γεέννης· διὰ δὲ τὸ μὴ ἀποστῆναί σε τῆς πορνείας ἐστερήθης τῆς χαρᾶς τοῦ παραδείσου."

to the poor and you will have treasure in heaven. . . ."[36] The philosophy of this passage contributed greatly to the development of Byzantine monasticism and charitable works. Even the great donations of laymen to monasteries and churches, hospitals and additional philanthropic establishments were given for the salvation of the soul and the accumulation of treasures in heaven.[37]

Through philanthropia one not only receives benefits on earth and treasures in heaven, but one's sins are forgiven. This notion persists from the Apostolic Age to the very end of the Byzantine Empire. The writings known as Constitutions of the Holy Apostles state: "If you have by the work of your hands, give, that you may labour for the redemption of your sins; for 'by alms and acts of faith sins are purged away.' You shall not grudge to give to the poor, nor when you have given shall you murmur; for you shall know who will repay you your reward."[38]

The same theory exists in other writings. St. John Chrysostom in a sermon on charity pleads: "I am begging you constantly, spare your souls, and redeem them from the last judgment by means of money . . . relieve yourselves from the burden of sins through philanthropia . . . be charitable that you may receive charity . . . as holy baptism cleanses man from his sins likewise philanthropia cleanses the soul of the benevolist from its sins."[39] Even if we accept the opinion which considers this sermon spurious, the fact remains that it presents a concept which is found frequently in religious writing of the Byzantine era. Theodore the Studite (759–826) also brings philanthropia into relationship with Christ, with the result that the donor would gain the bosom of Abraham.[40] Eustathios of Thessalonica (b. c. 1125) also emphasized that the philanthropist would not be left without satisfaction from God.[41]

36. Luke 18:18–22; cf. Mat. 19:16–21; Mark 10:17–21.

37. Cf. Miklosich-Müller, *Acta et Diplomata*, 6, 277 *et passim;* cf. Joannes Chrysostomos, *Homilia 52—Commentarius in S. Matthaeum Evangelistam,* MPG, LVIII, cols. 522–26.

38. *Apostolic Constitutions,* Bk. VII. 1; cf. Murray, *Life of Andreas* (Leipzig, 1910), p. 93.

39. Joannes Chrysostomos, *De Eleemosynis,* MPG, LX, col. 750; see Otto Plassman, *Das Almosen bei Joannes Chrysostomus* (Münster, 1961).

40. Joannes Damascenos, *Sacra Parallela,* MPG, XCV, cols. 1456–1524; Theodore Studites, *Iamboi,* MPG, XCIX, col. 1792.

41. Eustathios of Thessalonica, *Oratio in Psalmum XLVIII,* MPG, CXXXV,

Symeon of Thessalonica (d. 1429) perpetuated the same precept, namely that philanthropia is a good means for the forgiveness of sins and the improvement of the state of the soul after death. He writes: "Through memorial services and prayers and the Holy Eucharist and by means of philanthropia to the poor, forgiveness of sins is granted to those who while they sinned on earth, yet died in repentance. . . . Let every believer know that if he loves his relative who has died, he does him a great deal of good when he gives on his behalf. The philanthropist becomes the source of much happiness for his dead relative when he gives to the poor and ransoms prisoners of war. . . ."[42]

Frequently we encounter the view that to be *philotheos* and *philoptochos*, that is, *God-loving* and *poor-loving*, was to achieve the supreme state of perfection possible.[43] Once a monk from a coenobitic monastery approached and asked Cyril Phileotes how he could become worthy of God. Cyril admonished him that *eleemosyne* was one of the essential virtues that he ought to pursue, dear even to the pagans (Hellenes).[44] But charity should not be extended indiscriminately, that is, to people who could earn their living. The orphan, the widow, and the stranger deserved every assistance, but not the hypocritical and the lazy.[45] To give to those who do not deserve it is to deprive those who merit it.[46] If an individual were in need, the philanthropist should not consider his character, origin, faith, or appearance. In imitation of God he, too, should not discriminate.[47]

This philosophy was especially held by the monastic establishments, whose social service cannot be overemphasized. The monks were counseled to be especially lovers of God and the poor.[48] The influence of the Christian teaching of agape is very

cols. 524–525; cf. François Halkin, *Inédits byzantins d'Ochrida, Candie et Moscou*, Subsidia Hagiographica, No. 38 (Brussels, 1963), p. 134.

42. Symeon of Thessalonica, *De Fine et Exitu nostro e vita*, MPG, CLV, col. 693AB; cf. *ibid.*, *De Eleemosynis*, MPG, CXX, col. 219.

43. Dmitrievsky, *Typika*, p. 702.

44. Kataskepenos, *Cyril Phileotes*, p. 164.

45. *Ibid.*, p. 95.

46. *Ibid.*, p. 80: "Τὸ δὲ διδόναι οἷς μὴ δεῖ ὅμοιόν ἐστι τῷ μὴ διδόναι οἷς δεῖ."

47. Maximos the Confessor, *De Caritate*, Century I. 24, MPG, XC, col. 965AB.

48. Delehaye, *Deux Typica*, p. 21; "Vita S. Lazari," AASS November, III (Brussels, 1910), Ch. 192, p. 566; Miklosich-Muller, *Acta et Diplomata*, V, 407.

obvious. The Typikon of Neilos Damilas, for example, centers its rules on the concept of agape, and quotes several passages from the New Testament.[49]

These views of the Byzantine religious writers were shared by the state and the imperial court as well.

This principle is exemplified by Romanos Lecapenos (920–44), who is credited with many philanthropies for the benefit of his soul after death.[50] Other emperors or members of the imperial family were motivated by the same notions to practice charity, that is, to improve the state of their souls after death.[51]

These views reflect also the political philosophy that the emperor was required to imitate God in works of altruism not simply for the sake of imitation but in order to please the Almighty. A poem addressed to an emperor reflects: "Clothe a naked beggar and give bread to the hungry, comfort those who are in mourning and sorrow, and visit the sick. For when you give something to the poor and when you perform some good, consider it as if you are doing it to God himself who will compensate you in Paradise in a hundred-fold."[52]

The humanitarian emperor knew that he pleased God when he attended to and cared for the poor. The same "poem of exhortation" adds that "he who is hospitable to the poor is hospitable to the angels of God."[53] God would favor and reward an emperor who believed in and practiced philanthropia. Another text composed during the Comnenian era[54] praises the character of Alexios Comnenos and attributes his successes to his philanthropic and God-fearing personality. "You go against your enemies crowned with virtues which you have as your best allies. . . . Christ remunerates you because you make others rich by superb contributions."[55]

Alexios Comnenos, the author of a hortatory poem known as

49. S. Petrides, "Le typikon de Nil Damilas pour le monastère de femmes de Daeonia en Crete," BIARC, XV (1911), 95–97.

50. Theophanes Continuatus, *Chronographia,* pp. 429 ff.; cf. Leo VI, *Tactica,* MPG, CVII, col. 860.

51. Dmitrievsky, *Typika,* pp. 664 ff.; Miklosich-Muller, *Acta et Diplomata,* V, 358; *Actes de Lavra,* pp. 128, 139.

52. Wagner, *Carmina,* p. 4.

53. *Ibid.,* p. 20.

54. Pseudo-Codinos, *Patria,* Th. Preger, II, xv.

55. *Ibid.,* II, 290–91.

"Spaneas," sums up the motives for imperial philanthropia in these comprehensive words: "When you see a poor man or a beggar, don't turn your back against him . . . my son, love the poor . . . for God wills it." [56] Thus it is the will of God which prompts an emperor to believe in and practice philanthropia.

It is interesting to note here that there were individual officers in the royal court who practiced philanthropia as an expression of gratitude to God, to whom their success in life was attributed. Michael Attaliates, who served in various capacities in the Byzantine government from the 1060s down to the 1080s [57] is a good example. In 1077 he established a *ptochocomeion* (house for the poor) and a monastery and proved himself exceedingly philanthropic as a token of gratitude to God. He writes: "I, a sinner and unworthy of all, who came from a humble and poor environment, became the recipient of innumerable blessings from the Almighty, philanthropic and merciful God, to the extent that I became one of the leading members of the Senate, and one of the most prominent political magistrates and upon whom many public honors were bestowed, I ought to be mindful and express my due gratitude to the donor God." [58]

To invoke the mercy of God upon the ailing Emperor Alexios, his wife Irene made numerous donations to the poor and sick. "When the Empress saw that the disease [of Alexios] was gaining ground and she quite despaired of any human help, she made still more fervent intercessions to God on his behalf . . . and all those who were sick or confined in prison and worn out with suffering she made very rich by contributions and invited them to offer prayers for the Emperor." [59] Isaac Comnenos, son of Alexios Comnenos, established the monastery of Kosmosotera with its philanthropic functions, granting to it all his real estate "for the salvation of his soul." [60] And John II Comnenos established the famous Monastery of Pantocrator with its many

56. Wagner, *Carmina*, pp. 23, 22.
57. Sathas, «Μεσ. Βιβλιοθ.», I, introduction, pp. 7–16; cf. J. M. Hussey, *Church and Learning in the Byzantine Empire*, 2nd issue (New York, 1963), pp. 183–84.
58. Sathas, «Μεσ. Βιβλιοθ.», I, 4–5, 7–11.
59. Anna Comnena, *Alexias*, XV. 11; tr. E. A. S. Dawes, *The Alexiad* (London, 1928).
60. Petit, "Typikon du monastère de la Kosmosotira," BIARC, XIII (1908), 22.

charitable institutions as a token of gratitude to the Almighty for His many blessings upon the emperor.[61]

Attaliates, mentioned above, claims that he established his *ptochotropheion* (poor house) of Raedestos "for the redemption and forgiveness for his many and great and innumerable sins." [62]

In addition to religious motivations for the practice of philanthropia [63] on the part of the State as well as the Church, one cannot exclude other considerations, such as vanity, self-interest, self-projection, political expediency, and other egotistical drives. Nonetheless, very little evidence is found in the sources which would indicate any motives other than religious and moral ones for the practice of philanthropia, a mention of which will be made in another chapter.

The Byzantine concept that philanthropy prepares the way and opens the gates of eternal bliss exerted perhaps a great deal of influence upon their conquerors, the Ottoman Turks. They, too, felt that compassion and charity toward fellow believers were indispensable for the inheritance of heaven.[64]

61. Dmitrievsky, *Typika*, p. 558.
62. Sathas, «Μεσ. Βιβλιοθ.», I, 8: ". . . εἰς ἐξιλέωσιν καὶ ἄφεσιν τῶν ἐμῶν πολλῶν καὶ μεγάλων καὶ ἀναριθμήτων ἁμαρτιῶν."
63. Cf. Diomedes, «Βυζαντιναὶ Μελέται», I, 291 *et passim*.
64. G. G. Arnakis, «Οἱ πρῶτοι 'Οθωμανοί. Συμβολὴ εἰς τὸ πρόβλημα τῆς πτώσεως τοῦ Ἑλληνισμοῦ τῆς Μικρᾶς 'Ασίας» (Athens, 1947), pp. 110 ff.

3. Philanthropia in Byzantine Religious Thought

W hile the term *agape* is predominant in the early Christian literature and life, beginning with the third century there is a tendency to substitute it in favor of the word philanthropia. In the writings of the New Testament agape is used frequently [1] but philanthropia is rarely employed [2] and never by the Apostolic Fathers.[3] Even among the Greek Apologists (second century) the term philanthropia is infrequently used. Justin the Philosopher (d. c. 165) uses it once, and once more he utilizes the adjective philanthropos.[4] Theophilos of Antioch uses philanthropia as an attribute of God. In his discussion of the nature of man, Theophilos writes that God created man free, and what man lost through the abuse of his freedom and his disobedience, God restores through His own philanthropia and mercy toward man.[5]

1. John 13:35, 15:9, 17:26; Rom. 5:5; 8; 8:35; 12:9; 13:10; I Cor. 13:1–13, 14:1, *et passim*.

2. Acts 27:3, 28:2; Titus 3:4.

3. We do not include here the Pseudo-Clementines, which is considered the work of two authors of the fourth century; cf. Quasten, *Patrology*, I, 59–62. It is interesting that in this literature the noun "philanthropia" is used several times; see: *Letter to James*, IX. 12; *Homily*, XIII. 25; *Epitome*, XCVII. 9, *et al.*

4. Justin, *First Apology*, X. 1; *ibid.*, *Dialogue with Trypho*, XXIII. 2.

5. Theophilos, *To Autolycos*, II. 27: " Ἐλεύθερον γὰρ καὶ αὐτεξούσιον ἐποίησεν ὁ Θεὸς τὸν ἄνθρωπον. Ὃ οὖν ἑαυτῷ περιεποιήσατο δι' ἀμελείας καὶ παρακοῆς, τοῦτο ὁ Θεὸς αὐτῷ νυνὶ δωρεῖται διὰ ἰδίας φιλανθρωπίας καὶ ἐλεημοσύνης."

29

In the last quarter of the second century and the first of the third, Clement of Alexandria (d. c. 215) used the word philanthropia to indicate God's love for mankind, manifested through the incarnation of the Logos. Both God the Father, the originator of His Son's incarnation, and God the Logos, who assumed human flesh, are described as lovers of man.[6] It seems that in Clement's writings philanthropia has replaced agape as an attribute of God. In the New Testament God is designated as agape, and those who abide in agape abide in God.[7] Clement, on the other hand, characterizes philanthropia as the greatest of God's properties.[8] Clement's *Paedagogos* is Christ who is philanthropos both as God and man. His human philanthropia derives from His personal experience of becoming flesh and feeling its weaknesses, while as the Logos of God he is the true associate of God's philanthropia.[9] Throughout his *Paedagogos* Clement utilizes the term philanthropia several times, a practice which is carried further by Origen. Perhaps it was Origen who was most responsible for the growing use of the term philanthropia in Byzantine Christendom. Many views that Clement expressed are repeated by his successor to the catechetical school of Alexandria. Origen writes in contradiction to the Platonist philosopher Celsos that it was because of philanthropia for man that the Logos divested himself of His heavenly glory, in order that He might be capable of being received by men.[10] Not only is Jesus Logos Philanthropos but his influence produces a complete transformation in ·the character of men who themselves become humanitarians and philanthropists.[11] The incarnation of the Logos was not achieved according to the Platonic theory of metempsychosis but was the result of a nobler theory, the concept and the property of God's philanthropia.[12]

6. Clement of Alexandria, *Paedagogos*, Bk. I, VIII. 20: ''Φιλάνθρωπος ἄρα ὁ Θεός, φιλάνθρωπος ἄρα ὁ λόγος.''

7. I John 4:16.

8. Clement, *Paedagogos*, Bk. I, VIII. 5: '' Ἐνταῦθα ἐπιφύονταί τινες οὐκ ἀγαθὸν εἶναι φάμενοι τὸν κύριον διὰ τὴν ῥάβδον καὶ τὴν ἀπειλήν . . . , ἐκλαθόμενοι δὲ τὸ μέγιστον αὐτοῦ τῆς φιλανθρωπίας, ὅτι δι᾽ ἡμᾶς ἄνθρωπος ἐγένετο.'' Cf. VIII. 10. 43 *et passim*.

9. Clement, *ibid.*: ''ὅς ἐστὶ τῆς τοῦ Θεοῦ φιλανθρωπίας συναγωνιστὴς γνήσιος.''

10. Origen, *Against Celsos*, Bk. IV. 15; for an English translation see Henry Chadwick, *Origen: Contra Celsum* (Cambridge, 1953), p. 193.

11. *Ibid.*, Bk. I. 67.

12. *Ibid.*, Bk. I. 18; cf., Bk. VII. 41 *et passim*.

One can easily discern that both Clement and Origen [13] much preferred philanthropia to agape. The reason might have been that philanthropia as love of God or the gods for man, and love of man for man, was known to the Graeco-Roman world and could commend Christianity to the pagans much more easily than agape.[14] Whatever the case may be, philanthropia becomes very popular in the following centuries and finds its place in many patristic, liturgical, hagiographical, and even historical writings in the Byzantine Empire.

The historian Eusebios declares in his address to Marcellus that through God's unfathomable philanthropia man can direct himself to Him and ask for forgiveness.[15] Another historian, Sozomenos, in the introduction to his Ecclesiastical History, praises the Emperor Theodosios II as humanitarian and adds that the Emperor acquired the virtue of philanthropia by imitating the prototype, the Heavenly King who is the source of this virtue.[16] For Sozomenos, as well as for Eusebios, Origen, and Clement, philanthropia is considered the chief or one of the supreme properties of God [17] and becomes common in his writings.

According to another historian, however, the philanthropia of God has limits. God is also righteous, and His justice manifests itself when man abuses God's philanthropia for man. Theodoretos of Cyrus, who expounds this view, says that as God is merciful to the penitent so is He just to those who do not appropriate His long-suffering philanthropia. He uses both philanthropia and punishment because of His *dikaeosyne* or justice. Nevertheless, in general God is philanthropos and humanitarian in His relationship with men.[18]

Among the outstanding Greek Fathers who exerted a permanent influence upon Byzantine religious thought, Athanasios,

13. Cf. Nygren, *Agape and Eros*, p. 374, n. 1.
14. Cf. Ferguson, *Moral Values in the Ancient World*, pp. 110–12.
15. Eusebios of Caesarea, *Fragments to Marcellos*, No. 99, ed. Erich Klostermann, *Eusebius Werke* (Leipzig, 1906); cf. *ibid.*, No. 107.
16. Sozomenos, *Eccl. History*, Introduction, 9.
17. *Ibid.*, Bk. I. 4, 18–19.
18. Theodoretos, *Eccl. History*, Bk. V. 1, 7: "οἶον γὰρ τισι σταθμοῖς καὶ ζυγοῖς οἴκτῳ καὶ δικαιοσύνη χρώμενος ὁ φιλάνθρωπος, ὅταν ἴδῃ τινὰ τῷ μεγέθει τῶν πλημμελημάτων ὑπερβάλλοντα τῆς φιλανθρωπίας τὰ μέτρα." Cf. Methodios, *On the Resurrection*, Bk. I. 43, 4, ed. D. G. N. Bonwetsch, *Methodius* (Leipzig, 1917).

Basil the Great, Gregory Nazianzenos, Gregory of Nyssa, Maximos the Confessor, Theodore Studites, John of Damascos, and later the Archbishops Nicholas Mysticos, Theophylactos of Ochrida, and others added new dimensions to the perception and application of philanthropia. Fundamentally all of them expressed the view that philanthropia is one of the paramount attributes of God expressing itself toward His relationship with man, and that as a result man ought to possess the same attributes and to apply it toward his fellow man.

In particular we read that in St. Athanasios' writings philanthropia is described as the leading motive of God for the incarnation of the Logos. The disobedience of the first man summoned the philanthropia of man's Creator, who reached out to save him.[19] God became man that man might be made god. The corruption of man caused his alienation from God, with whom relations were severed. Man's restoration could not be achieved except by the fatherly love of God the Creator, who becomes an actual adopting father.[20] This fatherly philanthropia is expressed by the fact that God did not spare His First-Born Son the Logos, who assumed humanity that His brothers might partake of divinity.[21] The philanthropic attribute of God demands that man should imitate it and manifest it in his relations with his fellow men.[22] Humanitarian concern and philanthropy for the poor, widows, strangers, orphans, and the needy in general

19. Athanasios, *De Incarnatione*, IV, 2–3, ed. Frank L. Cross, *Athanasius De Incarnatione* (London, 1939), p. 6: "ἡ ἡμῶν αἰτία ἐκείνῳ γέγονε πρόφασις τῆς καθόδου, καὶ ἡ ἡμῶν παράβασις τοῦ Λόγου τὴν φιλανθρωπίαν ἐξεκαλέσατο, ὥστε καὶ εἰς ἡμᾶς . . . φανῆναι τὸν Κύριον." Cf. *ibid.*, pp. 7, 19, *et passim;* cf. Athanasios, *Oratio Contra Arianos*, XXXI, XXXIII, ed. Anton Stegmann, *Die pseudo-athanasianische "IVte Rede gegen die Arianer"* (Rottenburg A. N., 1917), pp. 80, 82.

20. Athanasios, *Oratio II Contra Arianos*, LIX, MPG, XXVI, col. 273A: "Αὕτη δὲ τοῦ Θεοῦ φιλανθρωπία ἐστὶν ὅτι ὧν ἐστι ποιητής, τούτων καὶ πατὴρ κατὰ χάριν ὕστερον γίνεται." Cf. *ibid.*, Ch. LXXV, col. 305C.

21. Athanasios, *Vita S. Antoni*, Ch. XIV, MPG, XXVI, col. 865B: "τῆς εἰς ἡμᾶς γινομένης τοῦ Θεοῦ φιλανθρωπίας, ὃς οὐκ ἐφείσατο τοῦ ἰδίου Υἱοῦ, ἀλλ' ὑπὲρ ἡμῶν πάντων παρέδωκεν αὐτόν." Cf. *ibid.*, *De Incarnatione*, I, 2; *ibid.*, *Oratio Contra Gentes*, XXXV, MPG, XXV, col. 69A, 81D *et passim.* Gregory Nazianzenos, *Theological Oration IV. 6*, ed. A. J. Mason, *The Five Theological Orations of Gregory of Nazianzus* (Cambridge, 1899), pp. 116, 130.

22. Athanasios, *Epistola Episcoporum Aegypti et Libyae Nonaginta*, Ch. VII, MPG, XXVI, col. 1041B *et passim.*

should be practiced by virtue of the commandment of the Lord.[23]

In the writings of the Cappadocian Fathers we find the same meanings of the term philanthropia but with much emphasis on its practical application. Philanthropia indicates charity, altruism, kindness, selfless love, and good works. The connotation of philanthropia as an attribute of God is used frequently. In the Liturgy of St. Basil, from the office of the prothesis to the eucharistic thanksgiving, the concept of the philanthropia of God is invoked fifteen times. The love of God for man is described as ineffable. God is described frequently as "good and philanthropos," He is "merciful and lover of man," His love for man is "untold and immeasurable." God is a loving Lord who is called upon to protect the widows, to support the orphans, to free the prisoners of war, to heal the sick, to accompany voyagers and travelers, to assist all who need some form of help and protection.[24]

There are many properties attributed to God. Basil writes that God is called Bridegroom when He presents to Himself the blameless soul. On other occasions He is described as physician. These properties of God should strike man with consternation, and at once man should rejoice at God's mighty power and His philanthropia for man. There is no doubt that Basil here identifies philanthropia with agape.[25] What Athanasios expressed about the incarnation of the Logos, Basil repeats in these words: "Every time we kneel down and rise up we show by deed that because of our sin we fell down upon the earth, and that we were invited back to heaven through the philanthropia of our Creator."[26]

Basil applied philanthropia as an attribute of God in his

23. Athanasios, *Historia Arianorum*, Ch. LX, MPG, XXV, col. 765C.

24. Basil the Great, *The Divine Liturgy*, ed. Papadopoulos, «Εὐχολόγιον», p. 74 *et passim*.

25. Basil the Great, *De Spiritu Sancto*, VIII. 18, ed. Benoit Bruche, *Basil de Césarée traité du Saint-Esprit*, Sources Chrétiennes (Paris, 1946), p. 137: "ἢ τὸ ἐναντίον ἔκπληξιν τῆς μεγάλης δυνάμεως ὁμοῦ καὶ φιλανθρωπίας τοῦ σώζοντος ἐμποιοῦσιν, ὅτι καὶ ἠνέσχετο συμπαθῆσαι ταῖς ἀσθενείαις ἡμῶν. . . ."

26. *Ibid.*, XXVII. 66, p. 238: "Καθ' ἑκάστην δὲ γονυκλισίαν καὶ διάνάστασιν, ἔργῳ δείκνυμεν, ὅτι διὰ τῆς ἁμαρτίας εἰς γῆν κατερρύημεν, καὶ διὰ τῆς φιλανθρωπίας τοῦ κτίσαντος ἡμᾶς εἰς οὐρανὸν ἀνεκλήθημεν." Cf. Hypatios of Ephesos: "καὶ ἡμεῖς δὲ γόνυ κλίνοντες ἔργῳ δείκνυμεν, ὅτι διὰ τῆς ἁμαρτίας εἰς γῆν κατερρύημεν, καὶ ἀνιστάμενοι πάλιν, ὅτι διὰ τῆς θείας φιλανθρωπίας εἰς οὐρανὸν ἀνεκλήθημεν." Franz Diekamp, *Analecta Patristica*, Orientalia Christiana Analecta 117 (Rome, 1938), p. 151.

liturgy proper, in which he employed the term ten times. It is repeated twelve times in the Liturgy of John Chrysostom and ten more times in the Liturgy of the Presanctified Gifts.

In the writings of John Chrysostom the terms agape and philanthropia are used interchangeably. Both words are employed by the great Church father to convey the concept of love,[27] the love of God for man and also as love manifested in personal relations between man and man. However, Chrysostom emphasized the philanthropy of God compounded with His justice and judgment.[28] Philanthropia isolated from *dikaeosyne* is dangerous because it degenerates into harmful sentimentality. On the other hand, overemphasis on the justice of God tends to obscure the fatherhood and mercy of God. Not only in Chrysostom but in other Greek Church fathers these two attributes (philanthropia and dikaeosyne) are blended in perfect union.[29] One may safely aver that philanthropia as a divine attribute is used as a refrain in the many liturgical and ceremonial books of the Byzantine Church. The services of vespers and orthros, the hymns and prayers of everyday services reveal that sinful man is redeemed through the philanthropia of God, which is described as "unfathomable," "indescribable," "immeasurable," [30] and so on.

In many instances God is described as *philanthropos* and *philoptochos, philanthropos evergetes, Lord philanthropos* and *philopsychos*.[31] This early Christian tradition is incorporated in the prayer life and the theological beliefs of the Byzantines of later centuries. In hymns and prayers attributed to Romanos Melodos, Andreas of Crete, John of Damascos, Leo VI Wise, Theophanes, and Theodore Doukas Lascares one frequently finds *philanthropia* as an attribute of God.[32] It is the philanthropia of

27. Joannes Chrysostomos, *Commentarius in Sanctum Joannem Apostolum et Evangelistam*, Homily XXVI. 3, MPG, LIX, col. 160: ''ἐντραπῶμεν τοίνυν αὐτοῦ τὴν ἀγάπην· αἰσχυνθῶμεν τῆς φιλανθρωπίας τὴν ὑπερβολήν.'' Cf. *ibid.*, Homily XXVIII. 1, col. 161.

28. Chrysostomos, *ibid.*, Homily XXVIII. 1, MPG, LIX, col. 161–65.

29. Cf. *ibid.*, cols. 161–62.

30. Cf. Goar, *Euchologion*, prayers 5, 6, 7, p. 29, pp. 31–32 *et passim*.

31. Cf. Prayer of Serapion of Thmuis, ed. Dmitrievsky, *Euchologion*, p. 14: ''Αἰνοῦμέν σε πάτερ ἀόρατε . . . φιλάνθρωπε καὶ φιλόπτωχε. . . .'' Cf. pp. 17–20, 22, 30 *et passim;* «Παρακλητική», ed. Fos (Athens, 1959), pp. 4, 5, 8, 17, 24, 25; cf. Dmitrievsky, *Typika*, p. 770.

32. Papadopoulos, «Εὐχολόγιον», pp. 17–22, 25, 156–58, 174, 183, 188, 480, 482, 484 *et passim*.

God which teaches man true knowledge and which can forgive the greatest sinners following a genuine repentance.[33] God is never disappointed with man's lack of cooperation in His divine plans, but He manifests His philanthropia toward man ceaselessly.[34]

The Byzantines attributed many beneficent events in their lives to the philanthropia or love of God. Cyril of Scythopolis asserts that it was God's philanthropia which terminated a disastrous drought in Palestine.[35] In days of natural catastrophes or in commemoration of such past experiences they conducted litanies to satisfy or invoke the philanthropia of God upon themselves.[36] So great was believed to be God's supreme attribute that God is always eager to manifest it toward his children. Maximos the Confessor wrote that just as the pregnant woman is eager to give birth, so God is eager to bestow his mercy upon men.[37] He added that just as it is natural for the sun to send out its light, so by His innate nature God shows His philanthropia throughout creation.[38]

It is due to God's philanthropia that He does not seek the impossible from man.[39] Independently of what man might be able to achieve he is saved through the grace and the philanthropia of God.[40] These and similar views are repeatedly found in diverse Byzantine authors from the fourth down to the fifteenth century.[41] Philanthropia as an attribute of God appears like a re-

33. Basil the Great, *Prooimium in Regulas Brevius tractatas,* MPG, XXXI, col. 1080A; 1089C.

34. Timothy, *Historia Monachorum,* cf. Cyril of Scythopolis, "Vita S. Joanni Hesychasti," ed. Schwartz, *Kyrillos,* p. 220.

35. Cyril of Scythopolis, *Life of St. Sabas,* ed. Schwartz, *Kyrillos,* pp. 167–68.

36. *Chronicon Paschale,* I, 586; cf. Symeon Magister, *Chronographia,* p. 710.

37. Maximos the Confessor, *Capita Theologica,* Ser. 26, MPG, XCI, col. 869A; cf. Kataskepenos, *Cyril Phileotes,* p. 226.

38. Maximos the Confessor, *Capita Theologica,* Ser. 7, MPG, XCI, col. 769B.

39. Joannes Climacos, *Scala Paradisi,* MPG, LXXXVIII, col. 1169D.

40. Kataskepenos, *Cyril Phileotes,* p. 73.

41. Theodore Studites, *Small Catechism,* ed. Emmanuel Auvray, **Sancti Patris nostri et Confessoris Theodori Studitis Praepositi Parva Catechesis** (Paris, 1891), pp. 14, 74, 110, 121, 166, 317 *et passim;* cf. Joannis Damascenos, *Sacra Parallela,* MPG, XCVI, cols. 392C–397B; Photios, *Epistle No. 23,* cf. Jean Darrouzès, *Epistoliers byzantins du Xe siècle* (Paris, 1960), pp. 118, 133, 380–81; Papadopoulos-Kerameus, *Varia,* pp. 221, 238–39, 253;

frain. The view persists in other centuries that the Son of God assumed the form of a servant in order to redeem man the servant from his captivity to the devil.

In the sixth century Hypatios of Ephesos (d. between 537–38 and 552) reiterates that Christ our God humbled and allowed Himself to be crucified and buried because of His "inexpressible philanthropia" for man. Hypatios no doubt identifies philanthropia with agape.[42] In answers to questions of his suffragan bishop Julian of Adramyttion, Hypatios adds that though we cannot depict the essence of God we can describe His "inexpressible" and "incomprehensible" philanthropia [43] which is manifested also in diverse other ways.[44]

Philanthropia replaces agape almost completely in the teaching of Pseudo-Dionysios the Areopagite, whose writings belong to the sixth century.[45]

Pseudo-Dionysios writes that the philanthropia or agape of Jesus for man is a mystery revealed only to angels.[46] When God punished the Israelites of old, it was because of His "fatherly philanthropia." [47] Just as a father punishes an undisciplined child because he loves him, so God manifests his love even when He punishes his children.[48] This philanthropia is an innate quality of

Miklosich-Muller, *Acta et Diplomata*, VI, 62, 70; "Vita et Acta S. Macarii Hegumeni Monasterii Pelecetes," ed. I. Van Den Gheyn, AB, XVI (1897), 163; Gregorios Monachos, "Vita S. Lazari," AASS, November, III, 515, 516, 520, 521, 526 *et passim;* "Vie et récits de l'abbé Daniel de Scété," ed. M. Leon Clugnet, ROC, V (1900), 61–62, 72; Delehaye, *Deux Typica . . . ,* pp. 25–26, 90, 136; Basilike Papoulia, ed., "Die Vita des Heiligen Philotheos vom Athos," *Sudost-Forschungen*, XXII (Munchen, 1963), 274.

42. Franz Diekamp, *Analecta Patristica*, Orientalia Christiana Analecta 117 (Rome, 1938), p. 126: "Πᾶσαν ὑπὲρ ἡμῶν ἑκουσίως ὑπομείνας . . . ὑπὲρ ἀφάτου φιλανθρωπίας γυμνὸς καὶ ἄταφος ἀπορριπτεῖται καὶ πρὸς τοῦ Ἰωσὴφ κηδεύεται. . . ."

43. *Ibid.*, pp. 127–28: "Τὴν ἄρρητον δὲ καὶ ἀπερίληπτον εἰς ἡμᾶς τοῦ θεοῦ φιλανθρωπίαν . . . ἐν γράμμασι μὲν ἡμεῖς ἱεροῖς ἀνευφημεῖσθαι διατυποῦμεν."

44. *Ibid.*, p. 128; cf. *ibid.*, pp. 151–53.

45. Cf. Jean-Michel Hornus, "Les recherches récentes sur le pseudo-Denys l'Areopagite," *Revue d'Histoire et de Philosophie Religieuses*, XXXV, no. 4 (Paris, 1955), pp. 404–48.

46. St. Dionysios the Areopagite, *De Coelesti Hierarchia* IV. 4, MPG, III, col. 181B; see also the edition of Gunter Heil, *Denys l'Aréopagite sources chrétiennes* (Paris, 1958), p. 99.

47. St. Dionysios, MPG, III, col. 240D.

48. Cf. *ibid.*, col. 241B.

God and because of it God reaches out to bring man to *theosis*.[49] Other passages in Pseudo-Dionysios confirm the use of philanthropia for agape.[50] When Pseudo-Dionysios uses the term agape as an independent concept he identifies it with eros,[51] using philanthropia for Christian agape.[52]

Later in the tenth century Symeon Metaphrastes repeats that "because of unfathomable philanthropia [Christ] appropriated human flesh." [53]

Because of the philanthropia of the Creator, man owes philanthropia to his fellow man. Thus in imitation of this philosophy Michael Attaleiates applied himself to charitable work,[54] because God is served by our philanthropia to our fellow man.[55] Inequity and lack of philanthropia might cause the manifestation of God's

49. St. Dionysios the Areopagite, *De Ecclesiastica Hierarchia* II. 1, MPG, III, col. 393A.

50. Cf. *ibid.*, col. 437A, 441A, 444AC, 561D; cf. also *De Divinis Nominibus*, col. 592B, 640C *et passim*. *Epistles*, col. 1069B, 1072B *et passim*.

51. St. Dionysios the Areopagite, *De Divinis Nominibus*, MPG, III, col. 709B: " Ἐμοὶ γὰρ δοκοῦσιν οἱ θεολόγοι κοινὸν μὲν ἡγεῖσθαι τὸ τῆς ἀγάπης, καὶ τὸ τοῦ ἔρωτος ὄνομα. . . ." Cf. col. 709C: " Ἐπὶ τοῖς ὀρθῶς τῶν θείων ἀκροωμένοις ἐπὶ τῆς αὐτῆς δυνάμεως τάττεται πρὸς τῶν ἱερῶν θεολόγων τὸ τῆς ἀγάπης καὶ τὸ τοῦ ἔρωτος ὄνομα. . . ." Cf. col. 712C and Maximos the Confessor, *Scholia in Librum de Divinis Nominibus*, MPG, II, col. 264B and col. 265B.

52. Cf. St. Dionysios the Areopagite, *De Divinis Nominibus*, MPG, III, col. 648D, 856C; cf. George Pachymeres, *Paraphrasis*, MPG, III, col. 861C, 993D *et passim*. Professor Jean-Michel Hornus, an acknowledged authority on Pseudo-Dionysios, in a letter to this writer, dated November 17, 1963, agrees that philanthropia "replaces altogether ἀγάπη in pseudo-Dionysius."

53. Symeon Metaphrastes, *Precationes*, MPG, CXIV, col. 220A: "ὁ δι' οἶκτον φιλανθρωπίας ἀνεκδιήγητον, τὸ ἡμέτερον ὅλον προσλαβόμενος φύραμα." Cf. also Theodore Studites, *Small Catechism*, ed. Duvray, pp. 158, 346: "βαβαὶ τῆς ἀφάτου φιλανθρωπίας! Ἐλήλυθεν ὁ δεσπότης πρὸς τὸν δραπετεύσαντα δοῦλον ἐν δουλικῷ σχήματι ἵνα αὐτὸν τῆς τοῦ διαβόλου δουλείας ἐλευθερώσειεν. . . ." Photios, Epistle No. 4, par. 36, ed. Valetas, p. 178; Nicholas Mysticos, *Epistle No. 12*, MPG, CXI, col. 91C; *Epistle No. 15*, *ibid.*, col. 108B *et passim*; "Διαθήκη Παύλου τοῦ Λατρηνοῦ," ed. Spyridon Lampros, NE, XII (Athens, 1915), 200; Sathas, «Μεσ. Βιβλιοθ.», I, pp. 5, 6–7; "Actes de Chilandar," Suppl. No. 5, VV, XVII (1911), p. 32.

54. Sathas, «Μεσ. Βιβλιοθ.», I, pp. 7, 46, *et passim*; cf. Theophylactos of Ochrida, *Epistle No. 11*, MPG, CXXVI, col. 325B: "Φιλανθρώπου τοίνυν καὶ δεσπότου καὶ φιλαδέλφου ὑπηρέτης ὤν, φιλανθρωπίαν [another reading: φιλαδελφίαν], καὶ φιλαδελφίαν ἐπίδειξαι."

55. Papadopoulos-Kerameus, *Varia*, pp. 238–39: "οὐδὲν γὰρ οὕτως, ὡς τῇ φιλανθρωπίᾳ καὶ ἐλεημοσύνῃ ὁ φιλάνθρωπος καὶ ἐλεήμων θεὸς θεραπεύεται."

justice and wrath, as was the case of Thessalonica's siege by the Saracens in 904.[56]

This theological concept appears quite stereotyped to the very end of the Byzantine era. The philanthropia of God was able to absolve even a dead man though he had died in great sin, provided that prayers and charities were offered in his behalf. The Empress Theodora, wife of Theophilos (829–42) had asked a group of bishops and monks to absolve her husband of the sins he had committed through his iconoclastic policy. After the initial refusal, the influential abbot Symeon of Studios[57] assured Theodora that relying on the philanthropia of God, they had received the dead king among the orthodox and that they had him forgiven for his sins. It was made clear, however, that God's love was the only source of absolution, which Theodora entreated with tears, prayers, and charities.[58]

The concept of philanthropia as an attribute of God, proclaimed by Athanasios and Basil as well as Maximos the Confessor and Theodore Studites, was revived by the fourteenth-century mystical theologian Nicholas Kabasilas (d. c. 1370). He identifies philanthropia with agape and describes it as the ultimate definition of God's relationship to man. Because of God's noble attribute His plan for man's salvation was executed through the incarnation of Christ.[59]

As one reads various histories and chronicles, epistles and wills, typika of establishments and hagiographical texts, it becomes evident that the philanthropia of God is overemphasized. It is either love in the Christian sense, providence, kindness or for-

56. Nicholas Mysticos, " Ὁμιλία εἰς τὴν ἅλωσιν τῆς Θεσσαλονίκης," ed. John Tsaras, *Makedonica*, I (Thessalonike, 1940), 243, 244, 245; Joannes Cameniates, *De Excidio Thessalonicensi*, ed. Immanuel Bekker (Bonn, 1838), p. 516.

57. "Acta Graeca SS. Davidis, Symeonis et Georgii, Mitylenae in insula Lesbo," AB, XVIII (1899), 247–48.

58. "De Theophili imperatoris absolutione," ed. Regel, *Analecta*, pp. 30–31: " Ποιήσομεν οὖν ἅπαντες νηστείαν καὶ δέησιν καὶ προσευχὴν πρὸς τὸν φιλάνθρωπον . . . σὺν δάκρυσιν καὶ ἐλεημοσύνῃ· καὶ πάντως ποιήσῃ . . . τὸ ἔλεος αὐτοῦ καὶ τὴν φιλανθρωπίαν. . . ." Cf. p. 33.

59. Nicholas Kabasilas, *Life in Christ*, IV. 25, ed. W. Gass and M. Heinze, *Die Mystik des Nikolaus Cabasilas* (Leipzig, 1899), pp. 87–88: " Πρόδηλον ὅτι τὸν ἔσχατον τῆς φιλανθρωπίας ὅρον ἐπὶ τοῦ σωτῆρος ἔγνωμεν, καὶ δι' ὧν εἰργάσατο μόνος ἐδίδαξεν ἀνθρώπους, ὅπως ἠγάπησεν ὁ θεὸς τὸν κόσμον καὶ ὅση τις ἐστίν αὐτῷ περὶ τὸ γένος κηδεμονία. . . ." Cf. pp. 88, 128, 143.

giveness. One gets the impression that the Byzantines believed much more in the love of God than in His judgment or justice. The influence of St. John the Evangelist is evident. Very seldom do we encounter admonition to the sinner not to abuse the philanthropia of God, which might yield to His justice.[60] In contrast to the Latin West, which since the times of St. Jerome had held a rather puritanical concept of God, the God of the Byzantines was the personification and the manifestation of love. Because of such beliefs the founder of the Monastery of Theotokos Eleousa at Stroumnitza in Thrace counseled the monks of his institution to raise themselves above weaknesses and imitate the philanthropia of Christ.[61] The greeting "may the philanthropia and the grace of God be with you" was common among Byzantine ecclesiastics.[62]

We are told that during the great theological controversies of the fourteenth century philanthropia was considered one of the supreme energies of God of which man can partake, even if imperfectly.[63] One wonders whether Origen had not exerted a permanent influence upon Byzantine theology. His theory of the final restitution of the cosmos to its pristine immateriality and primitive harmony, which was disrupted by man's rebellion against God, essentially relies on the concept of the philanthropia of God.

In any case, our investigation reveals that the God of the Byzantines was especially philanthropic and merciful; that is, the Byzantine theologians and religious thinkers emphasized love and mercy as chief attributes of the Almighty. Their God was a *philanthropos* and *eleemon Theos*. This view was expressed not

60. Theodoretos, *Eccl. History*, Bk. 5, 1, p. 278: "Οἷον γάρ τισι σταθμοῖς καὶ ζυγοῖς οἴκτῳ καὶ δικαιοσύνῃ χρώμενος ὁ φιλάνθρωπος [Θεός] . . . ὅταν ἴδῃ τινὰ τῷ μεγέθει τῶν πλημμελημάτων ὑπερβάλλοντα τῆς φιλανθρωπίας τὰ μέτρα, τῇ δικαίᾳ τιμωρίᾳ κωλύει τὴν ἐπὶ τὰ πρόσω φοράν." Cf. Delehaye, "Monumenta Latrensia," pp. 143, 153.
61. Petit, "Le Monastère de Notre-Dame de Pitié," BIARC, VI (1900), 80; cf. Nicholas, Patriarch of Constantinople, "De Vita Monastica," ed. Angelo Mai, *Scriptorum Veterum Nova Collectio*, IX (Rome, 1837), 618.
62. "Τυπικόν . . . Μάμαντος," ed. S. Efstratiades, E, I, no. 2 (1928), p. 307.
63. Alexios Makrembolites, "Διάλογος Πλουσίων καὶ Πενήτων," ed. Ihor Ševčenko, "Alexios Makrembolites and his 'Dialogue between the Rich and the Poor,'" *Zbornik Radova*, LXV (Belgrade, 1960), 191; but cf. Gregorios Palamas, *Theophanes*, MPG, CL, col. 925C.

Figure 1. Christ the Merciful; icon of miniature mosaic, set in wax (Constantinople, 11th–12th century). Formerly in the Berlin State Museum; present location unknown.

only in the several texts already cited, but also in their art. The ideal Christ is the *Pantocrator Philanthropos* [64] or the *Eleemon,* depicted as the prototype whose philanthropy men are expected to imitate.

The adjective *philanthropos* becomes a permanent attribute of Christ to the extent that it appears often as a proper name substituted for His more familiar names, such as Jesus, Son of God, Logos, and so on. When the Byzantines spoke of *The Phi-- lanthropos* they meant either God or His Son. Christ, in particular, is often described in many liturgical and hagiographical texts as the only philanthropos.[65] Their concept of Christ as philanthropos is confirmed by the fact that the Byzantines even had a men's monastery named after the *Philanthropos Soter.*[66] Thus, even as Asklepios, the god of mercy and healing, was called in Greek classical antiquity "Soter" and "Philanthropos," [67] so the God of the Byzantine Greeks was known as "Philanthropos Soter."

It is interesting to note that a philanthropic God has under His command an army of philanthropic angels to look after the welfare of men [68] and to protect the Byzantines in wars against their enemies.

64. Cf. Heinrich Brockhaus, *Die Kunst in den Athos-Klostern* (Leipzig, 1924), p. 93; Walter Felicetti-Liebenfels, *Geschichte der Byzantinischen Ikonenmalerei* (Lausanne, 1956), p. 78.

65. See Goar, *Euchologion,* pp. 334–35; *Menaeon,* September, ed. Fos (Athens, 1961), pp. 177, 191, 193 *et passim;* "De SS. Hierone et Sociis Martyribus," AASS, November, III (1910), 332B. Cf. Papadopoulos-Kerameus, «'Ανάλεκτα», I, 390–92.

66. Miklosich-Muller, *Acta et Diplomata,* V, 380, 383; V. Laurent, "Une Princesse byzantine au cloître," EO, XXIV (1930), 29–60; R. Janin, "Les Monastères du Christ Philanthrope à Constantinople," REB, IV (1946), 135–62.

67. G. I. Karvelas, «'Ασκληπιός», *Megale Hellenike Encyclopaedia,* V (Pyrsos, Athens, 1928), 834; cf. E. R. Dodds, *The Greeks and the Irrational* (Berkeley and Los Angeles, 1959), pp. 110–16 *et passim.* P. Kabbadias, «Τὸ 'Ιερὸν τοῦ 'Ασκληπιοῦ ἐν 'Επιδαύρῳ καὶ ἡ Θεραπεία τῶν 'Ασθενῶν» (Athens, 1900), p. 6. Cf. A. P. Aravantinos, «'Ασκληπιὸς καὶ 'Ασκληπιεῖα» (Leipzig, 1907), pp. 72, 192.

68. François Halkin, *Inédits byzantins d'Orchrida, Candie et Moscou,* Subsidia Hagiographica, No. 38 (Brussels, 1963), p. 134.

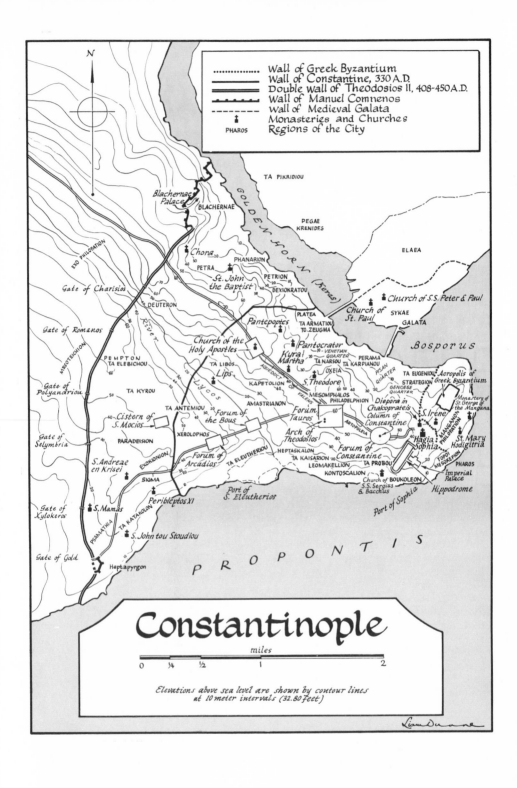

Wall of Greek Byzantium
Wall of Constantine, 330 A.D.
Double wall of Theodosios II, 408-450 A.D.
Wall of Manuel Comnenos
Wall of Medieval Galata
Monasteries and Churches
PHAROS **Regions of the City**

N

TA PIKRIDIOU

Blachernae
Palace
BLACHERNAE

PEGAE
KRENIDES

ELAEA

EXO PHILOPATION

Chora
PETRA   PHANARION

Church of S.S. Peter & Paul

Gate of Charisios

St. John
the Baptist   PETRION
DEXIOKRATOU

Church of
St. Paul   SYKAE
GALATA

DEUTERON

PLATEA

Gate of Romanos

Pantepoptes   TA ARMATIOU
TO ZEUGMA

PERAMA   B O S P O R U S

PEMPTON
TA ELEBICHOU

Church of the
Holy Apostles   Pantocrator   VENETIAN
QUARTER

Kyra
Martha   TA NARSOU   TA KARPIANOU   PISAN
QUARTER

GENOESE
QUARTER

TA EUGENIOU Acropolis of
STRATEGION Greek Byzantium

Gate of
Polyandriou

TA KYROU   TA LIBOS
Lips   OXEIA

S. Theodore

KAPETOLION   MESOMPHALOS
PHILADELPHION

Diepona in
Chalcoprateis

Monastery of
St. George of
the Mangana

Gate of
Selymbria

Cistern of
S. Mocios   TA ANTEMIOU   Forum of
the Bous   AMASTRIANON

Forum
Tauros   Column of
Constantine   S. Irene

MANGANOY
PHILOPATION

St. Mary
Hodigitria

PARADEISION   XEROLOPHOS   Arch of
Theodosios

Forum of
Constantine   Hagia
Sophia   PHAROS
TOPOI
MESOKEPION

S. Andreae
en Krisei   EXOKIONION   Forum of
Arcadios   TA ELEUTHERIOU

HEPTASKALON
TA KAISARION
LEOMAKELLION
KONTOSCALION   TA PROBOU

Imperial
Palace

Gate of
Xylokeros   SIGMA   Peribleptos XI

Port of
S. Eleutherios   Church of BOUKOLEON
S.S. Sergius
& Bacchus

Hippodrome

S. Mamas
TA KATAKOLON

S. John tou Stoudiou   Port of Sophia

Gate of Gold   Heptapyrgon

P R O P O N T I S

Constantinople

miles

0   ¼   ½   1   2

*Elevations above sea level are shown by contour lines
at 10 meter intervals (32.80 feet)*

4. Philanthropia as an Imperial Virtue

Philanthropia was one of the most important of the many virtues expected of a Byzantine emperor.[1] However, the Byzantine concept of philanthropia as a political attribute was inherited from the Hellenistic thought-world. One of the several elements inherited from antiquity by Graeco-Christian Byzantine civilization was the Hellenistic theory of kingship.[2] This legacy can be traced in some measure to classical Greece, especially to Plato, Aristotle, and Isocrates. The ancient Greek, the Hellenistic, and the Christian views of kingship were amalgamated by such Christian thinkers as Clement of Alexandria, Eusebios of Caesarea, Synesios of Cyrene, and Deacon Agapetos, to mention only a few, and by such pagan authors as Libanios, Themistios, and Julian, to give us the Byzantine doctrine of the single universal ruler who was an earthly god, the representative of the heavenly prototype.[3]

Eusebios of Ceasarea is considered the first thinker to lay the foundation of the Byzantine concept of kingship.[4] He Christianized the theory that the emperor is the image and the projection

1. Cf. Baynes, *Byzantine Studies*, p. 55.
2. A. H. M. Jones, "The Greeks under the Roman Empire," *Dumbarton Oaks Papers*, XVII (Washington, 1963), 11.
3. Cf. *ibid.*, p. 17.
4. Cf. Baynes, "Eusebius and the Christian Empire," *Byzantine Studies*, pp. 168–69.

Figure 2. John VI Cantacuzenos as Emperor and as Monk; miniature from MS *grec* 1242, fol. 123 (second half of the 14th century). Bibliothèque Nationale, Paris. Photo courtesy of the Bibliothèque Nationale.

of the archetype. Because God possesses philanthropia, Eusebios writes, the emperor also must acquire the same attribute.[5] "Philanthropia is the only attribute that makes a king an imitator of God," adds Themistios,[6] Eusebios' contemporary, who placed philanthropia above *praotes, dikaeosyne,* and *eusebia.* The pagan author and rhetorician advised the Emperor Constantius (337–61) not only to believe in philanthropia as an abstraction but to practice it. If it is a virtue necessary for every man, it is much more important as the primary characteristic of an emperor.[7]

The Emperor Julian (361–63), a pagan thinker in his own right, shared Themistios' views and urged the application of philanthropia, in the sense of mercy and clemency.[8] Libanios, too, "looked upon philanthropia as one of the greatest qualities which both the Emperor and his subjects might possess."[9]

During the same important century Synesios the Bishop of Cyrene (b. 370–75, d. 413–14) counseled the young Emperor Arcadios (395–408) on the ideal image of an emperor. He, too, emphasized that the king is the projection of the archetype, God the Universal King. God provides and maintains the cosmos and makes clear what He expects from the king. People, cities, and nations must be the beneficiaries of the emperor's policy in imitation of the Heavenly King.[10] The emperor must be a com-

5. Eusebios, *De Laudibus Constantini,* ed. I. A. Heikel, *Eusebius Werke,* I (Leipzig, 1902), 200: "Πράξεσί τε βασιλικαῖς τὴν τοῦ κρείττονος ζηλῶν φιλανθρωπίαν. . . ." Cf. pp. 202–06.

6. Themistios, *Oration 19,* ed. by Wilhelm Dindorf, *Themistii Orationes* (Hildesheim, 1961), p. 276: "ἡ πραότης καὶ ἡ δικαιοσύνη καὶ ἡ εὐσέβεια καὶ ἡ τούτων ἔξαρχος φιλανθρωπία, καθ' ἣν μόνον δύναται βασιλεὺς θεῷ ὁμοιοῦσθαι." Cf. *Oration 1, Ibid.,* p. 8: ". . . βασιλικωτέρα φιλανθρωπία τοῦ λοιποῦ χοροῦ τῶν ἀρετῶν. . . ." *et passim.*

7. Themistios, *Oration 11,* ed. by Dindorf, p. 174: "φιλανθρωπία δὲ καλὸν μέν που κτῆμα καὶ ἰδιώτη, βασιλέως δὲ ἴδιος κόσμος καὶ ἐμπρέπων ὑπὲρ τὰς ἀρετὰς τὰς λοιπάς. . . ." Cf. Themistios, *First Oration,* 8, tr. Glanville Downey, *Greek and Byzantine Studies,* I, no. 1, p. 58; *ibid.,* "Philanthropia," *Historia,* IV (1955), 201; *ibid.,* "Themistius and the Defense of Hellenism in the Fourth Century," H Th. R, I, 4 (October, 1957), pp. 268–73.

8. Julian, *Epistle No. 89,* tr. Wright, p. 71: ". . . ἀσκητέα τοίνυν πρὸ πάντων ἡ φιλανθρωπία." For Julian's concept of philanthropia see J. Kabiersch, *Untersuchungen zum Begriff der Philanthropia bie dem Kaiser Julian* (Wiesbaden, 1960); cf. Walter E. Kaegi, Jr. "Research on Julian the Apostate; 1945–1964," *The Classical World,* 58. 8 (April, 1965), p. 235.

9. Downey, "Philanthropia," p. 204.

10. Synesios, *De Regno,* MPG, LXVI, col. 1065BC.

mon good to all, a lover of man.[11] To practice good deeds is the one common characteristic shared by God and man,[12] while the stamp of kingship must be to do good, to be merciful, to possess the attributes of God.[13] As the sun holds brightness in its very being so the emperor ought to be a fountain of light and beneficent works. Thus early Byzantine political philosophy adopted the Greek, Hellenistic, and Roman teaching that philanthropia is one of the basic virtues of an emperor.[14] While eusebia or piety was emphasized by certain Christian authors of the fourth century as the prime imperial virtue, other writers added Greek philanthropia to Christian piety. Thus for later Byzantine authors both eusebia and philanthropia came to be viewed as primary imperial virtues.[15]

Writers of the sixth century on political philosophy or administration express views strikingly similar to those of the fourth or early fifth century. Deacon Agapetos, for example, urged Justinian to apply philanthropia. He advised the emperor that, since he had received the rule by the consent of God, he should imitate Him through good works. As the work of the sun is to shed light on nature with its rays, the king's duty is to practice philanthropia. The recipient of authority should imitate the donor of it.[16]

Justinian himself, however, emphasized that his legislation was philanthropic and that he was himself a lover of humanity. That he was forced to impose certain heavy penalties was not an indication that he lacked humanitarian beliefs. To have delighted in punishment would have been foreign to his philanthropic

11. *Ibid.*, col. 1104A: "Κἀντεῦθεν οὖν παρὰ τὸ θεοφιλὴς εἶναι, φιλάνθρωπός ἐστι παντὸς μᾶλλον, οἵου τυγχάνει τοῦ βασιλέως, τοιοῦτος τοῖς βασιλευομένοις φαινόμενος." Cf. cols. 1085D.

12. *Ibid.*, col. 1209 ff. "τὸ γὰρ εὖ ποιεῖν ἓν τοῦτο μόνον ἔχουσι κοινὸν ἔργον ἄνθρωποι καὶ Θεός."

13. *Ibid.*, col. 1104AB: "Χαρακτῆρα βασιλείας εὐεργεσίαν ἐτίθεμεν, τὸν δωρητικὸν πάλιν τῶν ἀγαθῶν, τὸν ἵλεων, τὰς ὁμωνυμίας ἀναπεμπαζόμενοι τοῦ Θεοῦ." For an English translation see Augustine Fitzgerald, *The Essays and Hymns of Synesius of Cyrene,* I (London, 1930), 108–47.

14. Cf. Glanville Downey, "The Perspective of the Early Church Historians," *Greek-Roman and Byzantine Studies,* V. 1 (Spring, 1965), 62–63.

15. Sozomenos, *Eccl. History,* Praefatio, "Σὺ δέ . . . ἔνδοθεν ἀεὶ τὸν ἀληθῆ κόσμον τῆς βασιλείας ἠμφίεσαι, τὴν εὐσέβειαν καὶ τὴν φιλανθρωπίαν."

16. Deacon Agapetos, *Expositio Capitum Admonitoriorum,* MPG, LXXXVI. 1, Chs. 1, 20, 37, cols. 1164 ff.

Figure 3. An Emperor (Basil I or Leo VI), kneeling before Christ enthroned; mosaic panel over the Imperial Door, narthex of Hagia Sophia, Istanbul (9th–10th century). Photo courtesy of the Byzantine Institute, Washington, D.C.

views. His legislation was intended to introduce more philanthropic laws [17] because in former times Roman law lacked any
philanthropia toward certain classes of people,[18] such as the children, although humane legislation was first introduced by Constantine the Great. Justinian claimed further that his philanthropic legislation was all-embracing and inclusive,[19] extended
to the capital as well as the provinces and the villages. Not only
his legislation but even his personal attitude manifested his views
on philanthropy. There is no offense which is not judged according to the standards of philanthropy. Justinian adds that justice
is applied against the malefactors, but the remedy of admonition
is applied and then anger is transformed into leniency, and philanthropia prevails over wrath.[20]

On another occasion Justinian asserted that he viewed philanthropia as one of the most important attributes of the emperor
and the State. Justice and philanthropia are described as the
supreme virtues which must characterize the State and govern
the lives of its subjects.[21]

Such views thoroughly impregnated the Byzantine thought-
world. An anonymous diatribe which has been attributed to the

17. Justinian, *Novel 81*, Prooimion, p. 397: "νῦν δὲ φιλανθρωπότερόν
τι καὶ σεμνότερον τῇ πολιτείᾳ διανοούμενοι."

18. Justinian, *Novel 89*, Prooimion, pp. 428–29: "Τὸ τῶν νόθων ὄνομα
τῇ Ῥωμαίων νομοθεσίᾳ πρώην οὐ διεσπούδαστο οὐδέ τις ἦν περὶ αὐτὸ
φιλανθρωπία. . . ."

19. Justinian, *Novel 147*, Prooimion, p. 718: "Πᾶσαν ὅμως ἐπινοοῦμεν
ὁδόν, ὡς ἂν καὶ τὰ τῆς χορηγίας ἀκώλυτα γένοιτο καὶ μηδὲν φιλανθρωπίας εἶδος περὶ τοὺς ὑποτελεῖς τοὺς ἡμετέρους παραλιμπάνοιτο . . . οὐδεὶς
φιλανθρωπίας δεηθεὶς ἄπρακτος ἐκ τῆς ἡμετέρας ἀνεχώρησεν ὄψεως . . .
ἀλλ' ἐπειδὴ μικρὸν καὶ βασιλείας ἀνάξιον εἶναι νομίζομεν . . . ἢ καὶ μέχρι
χωρίων ἢ πόλεων μόνων ἢ καὶ ὅλων ἐπαρχιῶν τὴν ἡμετέραν ἐκτείνειν φιλανθρωπίαν."

20. Justinian, *Novel 129*, Prooimion, p. 718: "Οὐδὲν οὕτω μέγα τῶν ὑ-
πηκόων τινὸς τῶν ἡμετέρων ἐστὶν ἁμάρτημα, ὡς μὴ τῆς ἐξ ἡμῶν ἀξιω-
θῆναι φιλανθρωπίας . . . τὸν καιρὸν θεραπεύοντες καὶ τοῖς προσήκουσι
τοὺς ἁμαρτάνοντας νουθετήσαντες τρόποις πάλιν πρὸς τὴν ἡμῶν αὐτῶν
φιλανθρωπίαν ἐπάνιμεν, τὸ δίκαιον τῆς ὀργῆς ἀγαθότητος καταλεαίνον-
τες λογισμοῖς."

21. Justinian, *Novel 163*, Prooimion, p. 749: "Μέγιστα τῶν ἐν ἀνθρώποις ἐστὶν ἀγαθὰ δικαιοσύνη τε καὶ φιλανθρωπία, ἡ μὲν τὸ ἴσον ἑκάστῳ
νέμουσα καὶ τῶν ἀλλοτρίων οὐκ ἐφιεμένη, ἡ δὲ πρὸς ἔλεον τρέχουσα καὶ
χρεὼν τοὺς δεομένους ἐλευθεροῦσα δυσκόλων. Ταῦτα τὴν βασιλείαν ἔδει
κοσμεῖν καὶ ἀσφαλῶς καὶ τὸ πολίτευμα διασῴζειν καὶ τὸν ἀνθρώπινον καλῶς διακυβερνᾶν βίον." Cf. Hunger, *Prooimion*, pp. 143–53.

sixth century [22] describes the imperial office as divinely ordained and states that the emperor is an earthly god. The essence of the emperor's mission is to imitate the heavenly God in the administration of his people. The king bears the image of the Universal and Heavenly King.[23] Although he is human, because he derives his authority from God the king is *isotheos* in authority upon the earth.[24]

The philanthropia of the emperor manifested itself in his personal life as well as in his legislation and policies toward his subjects. Philanthropia, which was viewed as a divine virtue characteristic of a ruler by such earlier pagan and Christian authors as Dio Chrysostomos, Themistios, Julian, Synesios, Deacon Agapetos, and others, assumed an even more accentuated Christian meaning in the seventh-century writings of George of Pisidia.[25] Thus the Emperor Heraclios (610–41) asserted that power must shine more in love than in fear.[26] The concept of philanthropia and social justice was the foundation of an Emperor's legislative activity.[27] Such a philosophy was enunciated by Leo III, the Isaurian (717–41), who issued the *Ecloga* with a view to greater humanity—*eis to philanthropoteron*. In the Preface of this selection of laws Leo writes: "Since God has put in our hands the imperial authority, according to His good pleasure, and thereby has given us an acknowledgement of the love which we reverently cherish toward Him . . . we believe that there is nothing higher or greater that we can do in judgement and justice

22. Barker, *Soc. Pol. Thought*, p. 65.
23. Anonymous, *De Scientia Politica*, ed. Angelo Mai, *Scriptorum Veterum Nova Collectio*, II (Rome, 1827), 602: "ἡ τοιάδε ἀρχὴ ἡ μόνη βασιλεία τε καὶ βασιλεὺς τῷ οὐρανίῳ ὅμοιός τε κατὰ τὸ δυνατὸν καὶ ὁμώνυμον, εἰ καὶ φθαρτὸν ἀφθάρτῳ χρῆμα· φέρων ὅμως ἐν ἑαυτῷ τὴν θείαν ὁμοιότητα." Cf. Cyril of Scythopolis, "Life of St. Sabas," Schwartz, *Kyrillos*, p. 152.
24. Maximos Confessor, *Capita Theologica*, Sermon 9, MPG, XCI, cols. 781AC: "τὸν βασιλέα δεῖ μνημονεύειν, ὅτι ἄνθρωπος ὢν ἐξουσίαν εἴληφεν ἰσόθεον, ἵνα προαιρῆται μὲν τὰ καλὰ καὶ θεῖα. . . ."
25. Cf. Marcello Cigante, "Sulla Concezione Bizantina dell' Imperatore nel VII Secolo," *Synteleia*, Vincenzo Arangio-Ruiz (Naples, 1964), pp. 546–51; see especially pp. 549–50.
26. George of Pisidia, *Expeditio Persica*, 11. 92–94, ed. by Agostino Pertusi, *Giorgio di Pisidia Poemi*, Studia Patristica et Byzantina (Buch-Kunstverlag Ettal, 1960), p. 101.
27. Walter Ashburner, "The Farmer's Law," JHS, XXX (1910), 97; cf. Wilhelm Ensslin, "The Emperor and the Imperial Administration," Baynes and Moss, *Byzantium*, p. 278.

for those who are committed by Him to our care, to the end that the bonds of all manner of injustice may be loosened, that the oppressing of covenants imposed by force may be negated, and so that the assaults of wrongdoers may be repelled. . . . " [28]

A controversial oration whose anonymous authorship has been placed in the age of Photios or even later [29] repeats the above views more profusely. The unknown royal counselor urged the king to occupy himself with works of piety, justice, education, and philanthropia. The king to whom it is addressed is described as "divine and philanthropos basileus" [30] and all his subjects are aware of the king's justice and philanthropy. [31] He was lenient in matters of taxation and proved himself "most righteous" and "most philanthropic." [32]

There is nothing more praiseworthy than the king's philanthropia which makes him resemble the Universal King. [33] The Byzantines urged their emperors to imitate the philanthropia of God. [34] It is not so much bravery in war that glorifies and saves an emperor as his kindness and his philanthropia toward his fellow citizens. [35] Photios had attempted to transmit Byzantine political and moral views to the Bulgarian King Boris, whom he instructed to set an example of justice and philanthropy because the king's behaviour becomes a law for the subjects. [36]

28. Zepos-Zepos, *Jus,* II, 12–13; Barker, *Soc. Pol. Thought,* pp. 84–85; cf. Zacharia von Lingenthal, *Geschichte des Griechish-Romischen Rechts* (Berlin, 1892), pp. 122–23.

29. Barker, *Soc. Pol. Thought,* pp. 220–21. Other views on authorship have placed this oration in the third century after Christ. While Barker attributes it to a latter Byzantine scholar, the oration gave me the impression that it might have been written by a pagan in a much earlier century. Cf. also the criticism of Romilly Jenkins in *The Journal of Theological Studies,* New Series, X. 2 (October, 1959), 420–21.

30. Anonymous, "Εἰς Βασιλέα," ed. Bruno Keil, *Aelii Aristidis,* II (Berlin, 1898), 253.

31. *Ibid.,* p. 257.

32. *Ibid.,* p. 257: "οὐ μόνον δικαιότατος ἀλλὰ καὶ φιλανθρωπότατος βασιλέων περὶ ταῦτα γενόμενος."

33. *Ibid.,* pp. 258–59.

34. Porphyrogenitos, *De Cerimoniis,* II, 123, 173: "Μιμήσασθε Θεοῦ φιλανθρωπίαν."

35. Photios, *Epistle No. 6,* ed. Valetas, p. 235: "οὐχ οὕτως ἡ ἐν πολέμῳ ἀνδρία τὸν ἄρχοντα κοσμεῖ καὶ σώζει, ὡς ἡ πρὸς τοὺς ὁμοφύλους εὐμένεια καὶ φιλανθρωπία."

36. Photios, *Epistle No. 6,* ed. Valetas, p. 233: " Ὁ τῶν ἀρχόντων τρόπος νόμος γίνεται τοῖς ὑπὸ χεῖρα." Cf. also pp. 228, 231, 233, 248.

The kings themselves considered philanthropia as an important basis of their education. Basil I (867–86), advising his son Leo about the content of true education, counseled the study of the Holy Scriptures as the first method of education. The second, of equal importance, is the practice of benevolent works. He urged his successor to be merciful and philanthropic.[37] In his first exhortation to his son, Basil writes: "Give mercy to those who need mercy in order that you may receive mercy from the King of all. . . . Don't count among the days of your life that one in which you failed to be benevolent to those whom God appointed you to rule. Make philanthropy your possession so that you may receive the same from God. Give . . . to those who ask of you . . . be merciful to the tears of a widow and don't reject the orphans."[38] Elsewhere Basil repeats, "don't postpone to do good until tomorrow . . . love philanthropia and practice it."[39]

The same moral political philosophy is found in Leo VI's collection of laws whose preface is the same as that of Leo III the Isaurian, emphasizing the need for a collection of laws more philanthropic.[40] But that philanthropia and social justice continued in their prominence as imperial virtues can be seen from the following definition of kingship: "The King is an upright overseer of the laws [*ennomos epistasia*], a common good to all the subjects. . . . His purpose is to be beneficent to all, and therefore he is called benefactor. Once the King loses his virtue of benevolence [*philanthropia*], he adulterates his royal character [*kivdilevi ton basilikon charactera*]. . . . The king must interpret the laws humanely and when dealing with dubious questions the manner of interpretation must be philanthropic . . . ."[41]

It is obvious that philanthropia and *evergesia* as political attri-

37. Basil I, *Paraenesis to Leo*, MPG, CVII, col. XXI.
38. *Ibid.*, col. XL; cf. cols. XLVII and XLIX.
39. *Ibid., Second Paraenesis*, MPG, CVII, cols. LVII–LX.
40. Constantine Porphyrogenitos, *Selectus Legum*, MPG, CXIII, col. 453A; cf., Zepos-Zepos, *Jus*, II, 11.
41. "Epanagoge," Title 2. 1–8, Zepos-Zepos, *Jus*, II, pp. 240–41: "Βασιγεύς ἐστιν ἔννομος ἐπιστασία, κοινὸν ἀγαθὸν πᾶσι τοῖς ὑπηκόοις. . . . Τέλος τῷ βασιλεῖ τὸ εὐεργετεῖν, διὸ καὶ εὐεργέτης λέγεται, καὶ ἡνίκα τῆς εὐεργεσίας ἐξατονήσῃ, δοκεῖ κιβδηλεύειν κατὰ τοὺς παλαιοὺς τὸν βασιλικὸν χαρακτῆρα. . . . Φιλαγάθως δεῖ τοὺς νόμους ἑρμηνεύειν τὸν βασιλέα· ἐν γὰρ τοῖς ἀμφιβόλοις τὴν φιλόκαλον [φιλάνθρωπον] ἑρμηνείαν προσιέμεθα." Cf. "Procheiros Nomos," pp. 114–15.

butes are interchangeable terms.⁴² At the acclamation of a patrician, thanks were expressed to the *evergetis basileus* who had bestowed the honor.⁴³ At a reception the emperor and his wife were greeted and acclaimed as benefactors of the world.⁴⁴ On many occasions those acclamations and views might have been empty words, but the evidence indicates that many Byzantine emperors had a strong sense of social justice and made many attempts to maintain a social equilibrium. Such were the motives of Nicephoros Phocas (963–69) ⁴⁵ and Basil II (976–1025) ⁴⁶ who had issued special laws to effect social justice. Moreover, the titles "philanthropos" or "evergetis basileus" were justified on account of the many charitable works which the Byzantine Emperors initiated, as we shall see. Suffice it to note here that Basil I is credited with the erection of one hundred houses for the poor, hospitals, homes for the aged, establishments for strangers and travelers, churches, and monasteries.⁴⁷

Nicholas Mysticos, the celebrated Patriarch of Constantinople, expressed the above philosophy in very concrete terms. The basileus must be philanthropos because of his religious nature. Nicholas propounded his views in a letter to Symeon,⁴⁸ the Bulgarian king, in which he counseled the king to imitate the philanthropia and the forbearance of God, from whom Symeon had received the royal authority.⁴⁹ Nicholas perhaps abused the use

42. Cf. Porphyrogenitos, *De Cerimoniis*, II, pp. 127, 129, 130, 155.

43. *Ibid.*, pp. 58, 59, 72, 89, 121.

44. *Ibid.*, p. 89: "χαίρετε, δεσπόται τῶν Ρωμαίων· χαίρετε . . . ἄνακτες . . . οὓς ἡ Τριὰς [the Holy Trinity] ἀνηγόρευσεν νικητὰς καὶ κόσμου εὐεργέτας."

45. Zepos-Zepos, *Jus*, I, 253–54.

46. *Ibid.*, p. 264; cf. D. A. Zakythinos, «Ἱστορία τοῦ Βυζαντινοῦ Κράτους», I (Athens, 1953), 149–55.

47. Theophanes Continuatos, *Chronographia*, pp. 258, 339; cf. Zakythinos, Ἱστορία, p. 150.

48. Cf. Ostrogorsky, "Die Kronung Symeons von Bulgarien durch den Patriarchen Nikolaos Mystikos," *Actes du IVᵉ Congrès International des Etudes Byzantines*, I (Sofia, 1935), 276–86.

49. Nicholas Mysticos, *Epistle No. 3*, col. 40C: " Ἐπεὶ καὶ παρὰ τοῦ πάντων ἄρχοντος Θεοῦ παρεσχέθη τοῖς ἄρχουσιν ἡ ἀρχή, οὐδενὸς ἄλλου χάριν, ἢ ἵνα πρὸς μίμησιν τοῦ τιμήσαντος . . . ἐπίστασαι τὴν τοῦ Θεοῦ φιλανθρωπίαν καὶ τὴν χρηστότητα καὶ τὸ συμπαθές . . . οἵ γε ὡς ἀληθῶς ἄξιοι τῆς παρὰ Θεοῦ δεδομένης αὐτοῖς ἀρχῆς, πλείστων ὑπαρχόντων δι' ὧν ἔστιν αὐτοῖς θεραπεύειν Θεόν, ταύτην μάλιστα τὴν ἐξαίρετον θεραπείαν προσφέρουσι, τὸ φιλάνθρωπον . . . καὶ τὸ ἀνεξίκακον. . . ." Note that the epistle throughout deals with the importance of philanthropia as a

of the popular term. While he described the Bulgarian ruler as a very philanthropic king,[50] on the other hand he urged him to adhere to humane attitudes and to leave behind him the reputation of a *philanthropos* lord. The diplomatic technique of the eminent patriarch is evident. He used a persuasive language to avert any Bulgarian hostilities and to establish peace.[51]

There must be a common understanding between the Byzantine emperor and a non-Christian ruler because both receive their authority from God. In a letter to the leader of the Saracens, perhaps to Al-Muktadir, Calif of Bagdad,[52] Nicholas Mysticos appealed for peace on that basis.[53]

Because of the above moral political views, the Byzantine emperor was expected not only to be philanthropic in his feelings and attitudes but in his practical application of the virtue. Michael Psellos described it "as the most characteristic"[54] of all royal virtues. Thus Constantine IX Monomachos (1042–55) considered himself not to be emperor during that day on which he undertook nothing philanthropic for his subjects.[55]

If one were to point out a single source which incorporates the Byzantine concept of social justice and philanthropia as an imperial virtue, one would undoubtedly point to two works attrib-

royal attribute. Nicholas emphasized that God will manifest his philanthropia only toward a *philanthropos basileus*, col. 41C; cf. *Epistle No. 4*, col. 44C; *Epistle No. 8*, col. 68B *et passim*.

50. Cf. *ibid. Epistle No. 14*, cols. 101AB, 104C; *Epistle No. 22*, col. 148C *et passim*.

51. *Ibid., Epistle No. 8*, col. 68B; cf. *Epistle No. 11*, col. 89A; cf. J. Gay, "Le Patriarche Nicolas et son rôle politique," *Mélanges Charles Diehl*, 1 (Paris, 1930), 91–101.

52. Cf. Romilly J. H. Jenkins, "A Note on the 'Letter to the Emir' of Nicholas Mysticos," DOP, XVII (Washington, 1963), 399; Grumel, *Les Régestes*, I, Fasc. 2, p. 163.

53. Nicholas Mysticos, *Epistle No. 102*, col. 309B: " "Όσῳ πάντων τῶν σῶν ὁμοφύλων, ὦ εὐγενεστάτη τῶν Σαρακηνῶν κορυφή, παρὰ Θεοῦ ἔλαβες τὸ ὑπερέχειν, καὶ ὑπεράνω καθῆσθαι, τοσοῦτον καὶ τῇ ἄλλῃ ἀρετῇ πάντων ὀφείλεις τὸ ἐξαίρετον ἔχεις. . . ." Thus "μᾶλλον κατάλιπε ὁπόταν ἐκ τοῦ βίου παρέλθῃς, μνημόσυνον φιλανθρωπίας, μνημόσυνον ἐπιεικείας καὶ δικαιοσύνης, καὶ ὅτι ἐν ταῖς ἡμέραις τῆς σῆς ἀρχῆς φιλανθρωπία καὶ δικαιοσύνη τοῖς ὑπηκόοις ἐμπολιτεύεται." Cols. 317D–319.

54. Psellos, *Chronographia*, Bk. 6. 5, I, 119: "χαρακτηριστικωτάτη μὲν γὰρ τὸ εὐεργετεῖν τοῖς βασιλεύουσιν ἀρετή."

55. *Ibid.*, Bk. 6. 169, II, 54: "ἐκεῖνος γὰρ ὥσπερ ἐπὶ τούτοις τὸ βασιλεύειν λαχὼν οὐδ' εἶναι τὴν ἡμέραν ἐκείνην βασιλεὺς ἐδόκει ἐν ᾗ μήτε τι φιλάνθρωπον ἐνεδείξατο. . . ."

uted to an eleventh-century author known as Cecaumenos. The first is addressed as *Logos noutheticos pros basilea* (de officiis regiis libellus) and the second as Strategicon (military manual).[56]

The first treatise, whose authorship is still disputed, though it has been attributed to Cecaumenos by scholars,[57] incorporates much of the mentality and the Graeco-Christian tradition before the eleventh century.[58] It is clear that God places a king on the imperial throne to rule and makes him a terrestrial god,[59] nevertheless the king is subject to the laws [60] and he must set an example for his subjects to imitate.[61] His example must be one of prudence, truth, justice, and impartiality toward all,[62] as befits the earthly representative of the heavenly prototype.[63]

In the Strategicon,[64] which is written in the form of instructive literature,[65] the king is urged to restore social justice and to be impartial in his benefactions to all.[66] Cecaumenos further counseled the king to make justice a pursuit of his life, to look after the philanthropic institutions such as the hospitals, and to care for the needs of the poor, the orphans, and the widows.[67]

It has been suggested that the emphasis of the Strategicon on

56. B. Wassiliewsky and V. Jernstedt, ed., *Cecaumeni Strategicon et . . . de officiis Regiis Libellus* (Petropoli, 1896).

57. Georgina Buckler, "Writings Familiar to Cecaumenos," B, XV (1940–1941), 133; but cf. Barker, *Soc. Pol. Thought*, pp. 121, 125; Vladimir Valdenberg, "Nikoulitza et les historiens byzantins contemporains," B, 3.1 (1926), 95–121; Paul Lemerle, *Prolegomenes à une édition critique et commentée des "Conseils et Récits" de Kekaumenos* (Brussels, 1960), pp. 20 ff.

58. Cf. Valdenberg, B, 3.1, 97–99.

59. Cecaumenos, *De Off. Reg.*, p. 93: "ἀνεβίβασέ σε ὁ Θεὸς εἰς τὴν βασίλειον ἀρχὴν καὶ ἐποίησέ σε τῇ αὐτοῦ χάριτι, τὸ δὴ λεγόμενον θεὸν ἐπίγειον ποιεῖν καὶ πράττειν ἃ βούλει."

60. *Ibid.*, "ὁ βασιλεὺς ἄνθρωπος ὢν νόμοις εὐσεβέσιν ὑπόκειται."

61. *Ibid.*, p. 99.

62. *Ibid.*, p. 93.

63. On the divine nature of the byzantine king cf. Peter Charanis, "Coronation," B, XV, 48–66; Rodolphe Guilland, "Le Droit divin à Byzance," REB, XVII (1959), 207–32.

64. For discussion on authorship and literature in addition to works cited in footnote no. 57 see also Hans-Georg Beck, *Vademecum der Byzantinischen Aristokrate. Das Sogenannte Strategikon des Kekaumenos* (Graz, et al., 1956), pp. 5–19; G. Buckler, "Authorship of the Strategikon of Cecaumenos," BZ, XXXVI (1936), 7–26; *ibid.*, "Can Cecaumenos be the Author of the Strategikon?" B, XIII (1938), 139–41.

65. Cf. Cecaumenos, *Strategikon*, p. 75 *et passim*.

66. *Ibid.*, pp. 4, 7, 57, *et passim*.

67. *Ibid.*, p. 52:"ἔστω ἡ ἐπιμέλειά σου εἰς τὸ ὀρφανοτροφεῖν καὶ χήρας τρέφειν καὶ εἰς νοσοκομεῖα καὶ ἀνάρρυσιν αἰχμαλώτων καὶ εἰς τὸ εἰρηνεύειν καὶ ἀδυνάτων προΐστασθαι. . . ."

help for the poor and its appeal for restoration of social justice reveal the internal conditions of the Empire [68] during the reign of Michael VII (1071–78), when the treatise was written.[69] The ethical essence of this treatise is its declaration that the emperor should believe in and practice philanthropia, which is translated in terms of justice, courtesy, morality, tolerance, and prudence.

Such views are expressed in other documents as well. When Alexios Comnenos decided to avail himself of the wisdom of St. Cyril Phileotes, the saint advised the emperor to pursue a policy of justice, peace, and philanthropia.[70] While Archbishop of Ochrida (ca. 1090–1118), Theophylactos, in a letter addressed to an imperial dignitary who was the brother-in-law of Alexios Comnenos, counseled him to exercise his office with generosity, honor, and philanthropic feelings.[71]

Despite the hortatory nature of our sources there is no reason to doubt their validity as writings for the mentality and the ethos of the Byzantines. They reveal the religious nature of Byzantine society. And philanthropia, whether as theological concept or political philosophy, whether as an ideal or as an applied virtue, derived its value from the religious attitudes of the Byzantines. It is understandable, therefore, why the Byzantine emperor competed with the bishop, the saint, or the wealthy magnate in the erection and endowment of philanthropic institutions, such as *nosokomeia, xenones, ptochotropheia,* and *gerocomeia.*[72] These institutions, as well as charity toward the aged, travelers, lepers, orphans, and others in need of assistance, came as a result of Byzantine moral philosophy and of the notion concerning the nature of the emperor and of man in general.[73]

The spirit of philanthropia as political attribute in the later Byzantine Empire is expressed in a poem of exhortation attributed to Alexios Comnenos, the son of John II Comnenos, and directed to Nicephoros Bryennios the Younger, son of Anna Comnena.[74] The author advised the royal recipient of the poem to be

68. G. Buckler, "Writings Familiar to Cecaumenos," B, XIII (1938), 135, 143.

69. Ostrogorsky, *History*, p. 281; see also n. 2; cf. Beck, *Vademecum*, etc., pp. 5–19.

70. Kataskepenos, *Cyril Phileotes*, p. 229.

71. Theophylactos of Ochrida, *Epistle No. 12*, MPG, CXXVI, col. 521D.

72. Cf. A. M. Adreades, "Public Finances," Baynes-Moss, *Byzantium*, p. 76.

73. Cf. Diehl, *La Société byzantine*, pp. 50–51.

74. Wagner, *Carmina*, p. 1.

a philanthropist and imitator of God because "the king is a projection of God" and "the emperor too is called a god." [75] As such
the emperor was believed to receive his inspiration and to determine his decisions not as an ordinary human being. As the vice-
regent of the *theanthropos* or God-man Christ on earth, the emperor was expected to think and to act like a demigod in matters
of philanthropia, justice, and other moral and religious virtues.[76]

This notion is expressed once again in an epigram in honor of
Constantine IX Monomachos. The emperor is described as a
person who grants forgiveness to sinning men, "imitating the
philanthropic nature of his co-regent Lord," i.e. Christ.[77] This
concept was held by Byzantine emperors themselves. The
twelfth-century historian Nicetas Choniates concludes that the
Emperor Isaac Angelos "believed that kings are allowed to do
anything, and that the difference between god and king in the
rule of earthly affairs is not at all incompatible and antithetical,
like affirmation and denial." [78] If we are to accept another text
of the same passage, we see that Nicetas becomes even more
daring in his comparison of the king to God: "there is no difference in authority between God and the King upon the affairs of
the earth, for the Kings are permitted to do anything, and they
possess in common all that belong to God and to the Kings,
because they have received the reign from God, and there is no
disagreement between them [God and kings]." [79]

A similar concept was expressed by Eustathios, the celebrated
archbishop of Thessalonica who wrote in the twelfth century.
In an address to Manuel Comnenos, Eustathios says that an emperor must be "a guide in every virtue, a teacher in righteousness,
a prototype of the good life." [80] Eustathios adds that an emperor
must constitute the eyes of the universe "looking toward men in
order to offer himself as an example for their instruction." [81]

75. *Ibid.*, p. 4.
76. Cf. Cecaumenos, *De Off. Reg.*, pp. 93–94.
77. Spyridon P. Lampros, " Ὁ Μαρκιανὸς Κῶδιξ 524," NE, VIII (1911) 6.
78. Nicetas Choniates, *Historia*, III. 7, ed. J. Bekker, CSHB (Bonn, 1835),
p. 583; n. 2: "πάντα γὰρ ἐξεῖναι τοῖς βασιλεύουσιν ποιεῖν διετείνετο, καὶ
θεοῦ καὶ ἄνακτος κατὰ τὸ ἄρχειν τῶν ἐπιγείων μὴ ὡς ἐπίπαν εἶναι τὸ
διεστὸς ἀσύμβατον καὶ ἀντίθετον, ὡς τῇ καταφάσει ἀπόφασις."
79. *Ibid.*, n. 16; cf. Vasiliev, *History*, p. 469.
80. Regel, *Fontes*, p. 6.
81. *Ibid.*, p. 8.

But an emperor should not believe in philanthropia as only an abstract ethical ideal, for he ought to apply philanthropia at the same time for the practical benefit of his subjects. Eustathios further avers that as the sun moves everywhere contributing to life and to progress, so a good emperor must be characterized by his constant activity of good deeds, using his wealth for the help of the needy, and by being philanthropic to the utmost of his ability and means.[82]

Another author of the twelfth century, Michael the Rhetorician, describes philanthropia (efpiia) as one of the two most important attributes of an emperor. In an oration in honor of Manuel Comnenos, Michael proposes, "May you, o victorious one, be adorned by two virtues. . . . Bravery is the first one . . . and philanthropia [efpiia] is the other."[83] The same author indicates that it was an old custom for the Byzantines to entrust their poor to the emperors, not in order that the poor should give anything, but rather that they may receive aid from the king, especially on such days as Christmas, Easter, and Pentecost. "By doing so an emperor would be granted to reign until advanced old age."[84]

An unknown author of the twelfth century claims, in a letter directed to the Emperor John Comnenos, that it matters not whether one directs one's prayers to the heavenly God or to the earthly god.[85] The earthly god is none other than the emperor, who is reminded to distribute his wealth to the needy, to poor maidens, and to old women. Let the emperor imitate the rain which is dispersed everywhere upon the earth, even upon the stones and the seas.[86] As the good tree is identified by its good fruits, likewise a good king is known by his philanthropies and the application of justice.[87]

One may, however, question the validity of this literature, in view of its poetical and rhetorical nature. Should we take seri-

82. *Ibid.*, p. 14.
83. *Ibid.*, p. 138.
84. *Ibid.*, pp. 164–65.
85. G. Mercati, "Gli aneddoti d'un Codice Bolognese," BZ, VI (1897), 140: '' ᾿Άκουσον τοῦ λόγου μου βασιλεῦ—διὰ γὰρ τοῦτο σὺ βασιλεύς—ἵνα μὴ ἀδίκως ἀλλὰ δικαίως προσαγορεύῃ καὶ βασιλεύς, ἴσον δὲ εἰπεῖν καὶ θεὸς ἐπίγειος καὶ οὐράνιος.''
86. *Ibid.*, p. 142.
87. *Ibid.*: "ὡς γὰρ τὸ δένδρον ἐκ τοῦ καρποῦ, οὕτω βασιλεὺς ἐκ τοῦ εὐεργετεῖν καὶ μᾶλλον τὸ κοινόν, οὐκ ἐκ τοῦ ἀδικεῖν γνωρίζεται."

ously the philosophy expressed in such hortatory and sermonic speeches? Certainly we cannot exclude them, for some of the noblest ideals and philosophies of man are expressed through poetry and rhetoric. Thus, though we must be cautious about drawing conclusions from such literary sources, we cannot underestimate them. If this philosophy were expressed in one or two poems only, or even in certain rhetorical speeches, our reservation could be wholly justified. But a considerable number of sources by both churchmen and laymen prove their intrinsic value.

One of the most prominent writers of the twelfth century or late eleventh, Theophylactos, Archbishop of Ochrida, maintains the same philosophy about the nature of the emperor and his attitude toward philanthropia. In his *paedeia vasilike*, or royal education, addressed to his pupil the Crown Prince Constantine, son of the Emperor Michael VII, Theophylactos asks: "How great should the philanthropia of the emperor be?" He answers, "as great as is the philanthropia of God toward men." [88] Theophylactos is using the term *philanthropia* in the sense of clemency. He further proposes that the emperor "should imitate the heavenly King," and that "the king who resorts to his sword with easiness is not a king but an executioner; such a king does not have God as his archetype, neither is the king made after Him." [89] Elsewhere Theophylactos reminds Constantine of his mother's philanthropic character as a model for him.[90]

We may assume that other authors of the Age of the Comneni might have expressed similar views about the nature of the emperor and the concept of philanthropia as an imperial virtue. There is no doubt that philanthropia in theory and in practice was developed under the influence of Christianity. Philanthropia as a royal attribute derived of necessity from the Byzantine concept of the nature and function of the emperor. Christianity was a necessary qualification for holding the imperial office [91] and philanthropia was a part of it. Thus the emperor must imi-

88. Theophylactos, *Institutio Regia*, Ch. 26, MPG, CXXVI, col. 284D: " Ἡ φιλανθρωπία δὲ πόση τις ἔσται τοῦ αὐτοκράτορος; Ὅση Θεῷ πρὸς ἀνθρώπους. . . . Τὸν γὰρ ἄνω βασιλέα μιμήσεται."
89. *Ibid.*, col. 284D.
90. *Ibid.*, col. 261B.
91. Cf. Charanis, "Coronation," p. 50.

tate Christ, and to his subjects the emperor must be "the rule and the example in every good thing," [92] for "the imperial office is after the image and the likeness of God." [93]

The emperor must hold devoutly to Christian practices, because "all look upon him as the example and archetype and he must be adorned with these elements both in word and in deed." [94] Nicephoros Blemmydes, active in the last quarter of the twelfth century and the first half of the thirteenth, wrote in his political eulogy in honor of the Emperor John III Vatatzes: "I write an apophthegm that it may survive as a teaching to those rulers who will follow. They must follow the example of Emperor John III and rule peacefully, gently, mildly, sympathetically, philanthropically." [95] These virtues constitute the ethos and the characteristics of the imperial office. And on another occasion Blemmydes advises that the king must be not only free from passions but should be able to free others from their passions, and must display a knowledge and experience in these things, in word and in example as well as in holy songs (paeans).[96]

Since there was a law "prohibiting the coronation of a new emperor unless he took an oath of fidelity to the established tradition," [97] we may infer that the emperor was expected to be philanthropic. The religious coronation ceremony performed for each new emperor indicates that the source of imperial power was God [98] and that the emperor should thus act as a representative of God.

This philosophy was in perfect agreement with the oath that the emperor had to take before assuming his imperial office. The oath written by the emperor was handed to the patriarch by the emperor himself shortly before the coronation. It includes a provision by which the emperor promised to be "kind" and "philan-

92. Nicephoros Blemmydes, *Oratio de Regis Officiis*, MPG, CXLII, col. 633B.
93. *Ibid.*, col. 659A.
94. *Ibid.*, col. 657BC.
95. Nicephoros Blemmydes, «Στίχοι Πολιτικοί», ed. A. Heisenberg (Leipzig, 1896), p. 104.
96. Nicephoros Blemmydes, *De Regis Officiis*, MPG, CXLII, col. 659D.
97. Charanis, "Coronation," p. 57.
98. *Ibid.*, p. 61.

thropos." "The Confession of Faith" reads: "Also I promise . . . to be kind and philanthropic to my subjects as is reasonable and fitting, to refrain from infliction of death and mutilation and anything resembling these insofar as it is possible, and to submit to all truth and justice." [99]

Thus the concept of philanthropia as an imperial virtue in the Byzantine Empire followed of necessity the Christian idea of the nature and the destiny of the emperor. But were there any other motives which prompted an emperor to be philanthropic? Undoubtedly there must have been others, such as vanity, selfish interests, political expediency, and other human weaknesses.

Despite any secular motives which might have contributed to the formation of Byzantine political theories, there is abundant evidence which underlies the religious foundations of philanthropia as an imperial virtue. This philosophy was maintained to the very end of the Empire. [100]

If this were the theoretical aspect of the nature of an Emperor, not all people believed in it. *Timarion,* an anonymous fourteenth-century satire, ridicules the idea of the divine nature of the emperor. [101] On the other hand Patriarch Antonios IV of Constantinople (1391–97) in a letter to Basil, the prince of Moscow, emphasized that the Byzantine emperor was not like any ordinary man. Why, then, is so much honor paid the emperor? Because, Antonios answered, the emperor plays a major role in the life of the Church. Not only is the Byzantine emperor a *Christomimetos basileus* [102] (an imitator of Christ), but he also invokes the ecumenical councils, he supports the faith, fights heresy, and in general embodies piety. [103] Royalty and the Church have much in common and thus cannot be divided. [104] This has

99. Codinos, *De Officialibus,* p. 87; cf. Charanis, "Coronation," p. 58.
100. Cf. Paul J. Alexander, "A Chrysobull of the Emperor Andronicus II," B, XV (1940–1941), 177; Miklosich-Muller, *Acta et Diplomata,* II, 190; Demetrios Cydones, *Epistles,* No. 11, ed. Raymond J. Loenertz, *Demetrius Cydones Correspondance,* I (Vatican City, 1956), 38: ''καὶ βασιλεῖ προσήκοντα ταῦτα νομίζων βασιλικώτερον ἡγῇ τὴν φιλανθρωπίαν.'' Cf. Theodulos Monachos, *Oratio de Regis Officiis,* MPG, CXLV, cols. 452–56.
101. Timarion, ch. 33, ed. Adolf Ellissen, *Analekten der mittel- und neugriechischen Literatur,* IV (Leipzig, 1860), 76.
102. Kataskepenos, *Cyril Phileotes,* p. 231.
103. Antonios Patriarch of Constantinople, "Adhortatio Patriarchae ad Basilium, regem Moscovii," Miklosich-Muller, *Acta et Diplomata,* II, 190.
104. *Ibid.,* p. 191: ''ἡ γὰρ βασιλεία καὶ ἡ ἐκκλησία πολλὴν ἕνωσιν καὶ κοινωνίαν ἔχει καὶ οὐκ ἔνι δυνατὸν ἀπ' ἀλλήλων διαιρεθῆναι.''

been, Antonios adds, the verdict of the fathers, the synods, and the canons. That is, there are two natural kings, one in heaven and the other on earth. Thus the laws and rules affect the whole *oecumene*.[105]

The theoretical aspect of philanthropia which we have investigated in the preceding pages, whether as a theologico-philosophical concept or as a political attribute, reveals the extent to which Byzantine authors depended on each other, and demonstrates the continuity in their rationale and outlook. Repetition is evident and originality in the social order or in secular thinking is negligible. This is easily understood if we consider that Byzantium was a medieval state concerned primarily with soteriological, anthropological, and theological questions. Though the Byzantines did not speculate in secular disciplines,[106] there is much originality in their fields of speculation and interests. Their concern with the origin and the destiny of man is a field in itself. Their views on philanthropia as a theological or religious abstraction deserve serious consideration.

Nevertheless, we are safe in stating that the Byzantines were much concerned with rather practical virtues: justice, social action, practical philanthropy, and humanitarian works in general.[107] It will be shown in the following two chapters that these virtues were widely applied.

105. *Ibid.*, p. 192.
106. Cf. D. C. Hesseling, *Essai sur la civilisation Byzantine* (Paris, 1907), pp. 281–82.
107. Cf. Koukoules, BB II, II. 1, pp. 64 ff.; Zakythinos, «Βυζάντιον», pp. 59–62.

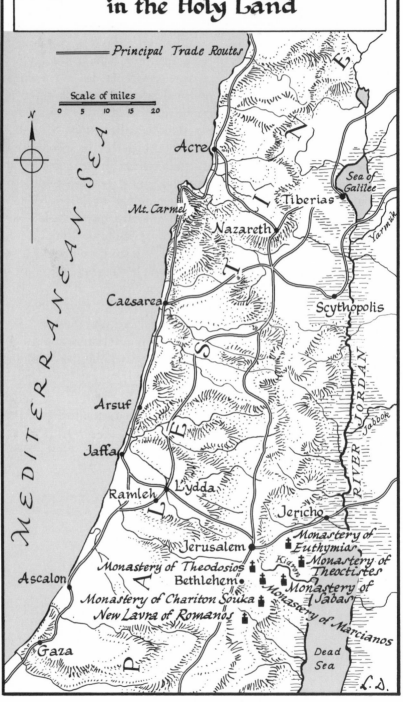

Important Monastic Communities in the Holy Land

Principal Trade Routes

Scale of miles
0 5 10 15 20

N

MEDITERRANEAN SEA

PALESTINE

Acre

Sea of Galilee

Tiberias

Mt. Carmel

Nazareth

Caesarea

Scythopolis

RIVER JORDAN

Yarmuk

Jabbok

Arsuf

Jaffa

Ramleh

Lydda

Jericho

Jerusalem

Monastery of Euthymias

Kidron

Monastery of Theoctistes

Monastery of Theodosios

Bethlehem

Monastery of Sabas

Ascalon

Monastery of Chariton Souka

New Lavra of Romanos

Monastery of Marcianos

Gaza

Dead Sea

L.D.

Part II

Application and Agencies of Philanthropy

5. Byzantine Philanthropy

Philanthropy in the Byzantine Empire as elsewhere was the work both of institutions solely dedicated to charity and of organizations primarily directed toward more temporal purposes as well as, of course, the work of individual persons. The great accomplishments of the former, the purely philanthropic institutions, are discussed in Part III. In the present chapter, the charities of the latter, the institutions not philanthropic by definition, and the philanthropic individual, will be considered.

A sharp line of differentiation between the Church and the State, the monastery, or the individual, as we know this differentiation today, could not be clearly made in Byzantium. The Byzantines, whether they were state dignitaries or humble citizens, church officials or unknown hermits, were primarily members of one organism and organization, the visible body of Christ on earth, His Ecclesia.[1] The emperor was the embodiment of the State, yet also the chief servant of God and the defender of His holy people. The emperor's concern for the Church was as great as his interest in the welfare and administration of the Empire.[2]

The same is true of the Byzantine monasteries. Though they were independent religious institutions, they met certain needs and aspirations of the Church as a whole, both laity and clergy, and nurtured the holiest part of the Church's function and life. The Byzantine Church was an all-embracing organism. When

1. Cf. Baynes, *The Byzantine Empire*, p. 98.
2. Cf. Baynes, *Byzantine Studies*, pp. 74 ff.

we speak, therefore, of the Byzantine Empire we ought to think of it as an organic entity rather than as a collection of autonomous units.

The aforementioned observations may be difficult for modern man to understand, in view of the present-day structure of many twentieth-century states, in which religious organizations are markedly divided from the state or other secular organizations. In the middle ages, however, the concepts of church and state did not differ much from each other. This blending of authorities and functions had its shortcomings as well as its merits.

Much in Byzantine culture that deserves our admiration to-day—and indeed our emulation—centers on the value of man. It is an error to identify humanism solely with the fine arts and with literary culture and to deprive it of its semantic foundation: man himself. The Byzantines loved man and expressed this love or philanthropia in active efforts to alleviate his miseries, to prolong his life, to guide him into the certainties of faith, and to orient him to a purposeful life.

The Church may well have been the most significant institution in the Byzantine Empire. In philanthropy, she played a protagonist's role. The British historian Robert Byron may have been over-romantic in some of his observations on Byzantine civilization, but the following remark is not without truth: "Had Christianity remained as the Byzantines perfected it, and not been distorted by the common sense of the Latin peoples and the romanticism of the Northern peoples, it might have merged harmoniously with the present mode of thought." [3]

In any case, there is no doubt that Byzantine Christianity was a positive and constructive force in the lives of its followers. The Byzantines gave serious thought to their "brethren, the poor," including the sick and the deformed. They extended protection to orphans and widows and provided relief to the needy, to those advanced in age, the captives, strangers, and foreigners in want. And they did this not out of mere liberality or lukewarm kindness but out of *agape*—love.

3. Robert Byron, *The Byzantine Achievement* (New York, 1929), p. 31.

6. Philanthropy and the Church

From the very beginning, the philosophy of the Christian Church induced a revolution in the realm of philanthropy "by regarding the poor as the special representatives of the Christian Founder, and thus making the love of Christ rather than the love of man the principle of charity."[1] This statement by William Lecky concerning the early Christian Church is applicable also to the Byzantine Church, for the achievements of the Byzantine Church were great in the sphere of charity.[2]

The theological and philosophical speculation of the Byzantine Church was no mean achievement; but her true greatness lay perhaps more in her civilizing and humanitarian work, both among her own people and among the new tribes and nations.

The Church had established a sound tradition of philanthropic works, as is revealed by several canons. The fifty-ninth Canon of the collection of Church laws, which has survived under the name of Apostolic Canons, states that both bishops and presbyters must practice philanthropy. As supervisor of the properties and the money of the Church, the bishop was expected to distribute all the surpluses to the poor.[3] The twenty-first Canon of the Synod of Gangra (343?) extols and encourages the tradition

1. Lecky, *Eur. Morals,* II, p. 79.
2. Cf. *ibid.,* p. 85; cf. Neander, *General History of the Christian Religion and Church,* tr. Torrey, II (Boston, 1848), p. 137.
3. Rhallis-Potlis, «Σύνταγμα», II, 76–77.

of Church charity: "We praise the exceeding charities done by the brethren to the poor, according to the traditions of the Church. . . ." [4]

Priests not only preached sermons influential in strengthening the philanthropic and humanitarian work of the Church,[5] but also set an example of generosity themselves. It is well known that many of the fathers of the Church distributed their personal wealth in the welfare work of the Church. They urged their people to make personal sacrifices in order to maintain distributions to the poor.[6] John Chrysostom, the celebrated Patriarch of Constantinople, not only distributed his personal wealth to the poor in Antioch, but manifested his concern for the "brethren, the poor," wherever he served the Church.[7] So powerful was his work to effect an equilibrium in the social order, speaking on behalf of the poor, the slaves, and other underprivileged, that J. B. Bury characterized him as "almost a socialist." [8]

St. Basil, Bishop of Caesarea, is given credit for much charitable work in his diocese. When a famine befell his diocese, Basil was the only hope for many unfortunate beings.[9] He is described as the wealth for poverty, the steward for the wealth, the pro-

4. Rhallis-Potlis, «Σύνταγμα», III, 118; cf. also the commentaries of Zonaras, Balsamon, and Aristenos, *ibid.*, pp. 118–21.

5. Basil the Great, *Homilia in Divites; Homilia dicta tempore famis et siccitatis,* MPG, XXXI, cols. 278D–328C; cf. *ibid., De Jejunio Homilia 1, ibid.,* cols. 164 ff.; Gregory Nazianzenos, *Oratio XIV—De Pauperum Amore,* MPG, XXXV, cols. 857A–909C; Gregory of Nyssa, *De Pauperibus Amandis et Benignitate Complectendis,* MPG, XLVI, cols. 453A–490B; Joannes Chrysostomos, *De Eleemosyna Sermo,* MPG, LI, cols. 261–72; cf. also cols. 271–302; Anastasios Sinaites, *Quaestiones, XII–XIV,* MPG, LXXXIX, cols. 445B–468B; Joannes Damascenos, *Sacra Parallela,* MPG, XCV, cols. 1456C–1524C; Cyrillos of Alexandria, *Homiliae Paschales,* IV, MPG, LXXVII, cols. 452A–472B *et passim;* Neilos of Ancyra, *Peristeria,* sect. IV, Chs. 13–17, sect. V, chs. 1–3, MPG, LXXIX, cols. 840B ff.

6. Cf. Athanasios the Great, *Epistles,* nos. I. 11, IV. 3, XLV. 1, XLVII, ed. tr. Archibald Robertson, *Nicene and Post-Nicene Fathers,* ed. Philip Schaff and Henry Wace, IV (Grand Rapids, Mich., 1953), 510, 516 *et passim.*

7. Cf. J. Milton Vance, *Beitrage zur Byzantinischen Kulturgeschichte* (Jena, 1907), pp. 66–69.

8. J. B. Bury, *History of the Later Roman Empire* (New York, 1958), reprint, I, 139; cf., Chrysostomus Baur, *Der heilige Johannes Chrysostomus und seine zeit,* I (Munich, 1929), 319.

9. Gregory Nazianzenos, *Oratio XLIII—In Laudem Basilii Magni,* ed. Fernard Boulenger, *Gregoire de Nazianze discours funèbres* (Paris, 1908), p. 132 *et passim.*

tector of the widows, and the father of the orphans, the generous friend of the poor, and the friend of the strangers.[10]

Less famous bishops, such as the humble Spyridon of Trimithous in Cyprus, surpassed many of their fellow clergymen in works of philanthropy.[11]

Churchmen, whether of the fourth, the ninth, or the fifteenth century, were conscious of social injustice and inequality. Many, such as Chrysostom in the fourth century or Ignatios in the ninth or others of the fourteenth, made appeals to the rich for contributions and saw that the philanthropic work of the Church was carried out.[12] When the city of Agathoupolis, a city between ancient Apollonia and Salmydessos, fell to the Turks in 1389, its bishop complained that his diocese, which had been rich and able to feed the hungry and provide generous philanthropies, could no longer continue its charitable functions. The Turks had deprived the bishopric not only of its wealth but even of the bishop's residence.[13]

In the "golden age" of the Eastern Church, Church legislation provided for the erection of the first philanthropic institutions, such as hospitals, houses for the poor and the elderly, orphanages, and similar establishments.[14]

The seventieth Canon of a corpus of eighty attributed to the first Council of Nicaea (325) advised that hospitals should be erected in every city of the Empire.[15] The eighth and the tenth rules of the Council of Chalcedon (451) were issued in order to maintain good administration of the existing institutions, namely xenones, ptochotropheia, and others.[16]

In addition to ecumenical canons, local bishops issued encyclicals concerning the establishment or the maintenance of existing philanthropic institutions. They ruled that the local congregation should spare neither labor nor money in philanthropic en-

10. *Ibid.*, p. 228: "ἡ πενία, τὸν ποριστήν· ἡ εὐπορία τὸν οἰκονόμον. Δοκοῦσί μοι καὶ χῆραι τὸν προστάτην ἐπαινέσεσθαι· καὶ ὀρφανοὶ τὸν πατέρα· καὶ πτωχοί, τὸν φιλόπτωχον· καὶ τὸν φιλόξενον οἱ ξένοι."
11. Theodore of Paphos, *Life of St. Spyridon*, ed. Paul Van Den Ven, *La Legende de S. Spyridon évêque de Trimithonte* (Louvain, 1953), pp. 48 ff.
12. Cf. Mansi, XVI, 273D.
13. Miklosich-Muller, *Acta et Diplomata*, II, 130.
14. Cf. Champagny, *Char. Chret.*, pp. 310–29.
15. *Decrees and Canons of the Seven Ecumenical Councils*, The Nicene and Post-Nicene Fathers, Series 2, XIV (Grand Rapids, Mich., 1956), 50.
16. Rhallis-Potlis, «Σύνταγμα», II, 234–42; cf. commentary of Balsamon to the first canon of the Seventh Ecumenical Council (787), VI, 650–53.

deavors. The bishops placed the orphans, the widows, the strangers in want, and others in need of help under the philanthropic care of the priests and deacons. Athanasios the Great and Theophilos, Patriarchs of Alexandria during the fourth and early fifth centuries, may serve as good illustrations.[17]

The bishops themselves were bound by universal Church law to do charitable works, such as visiting prisoners, and protecting the weak, the orphans, the widows, and others. They were instructed to set aside all surpluses of their dioceses for charities, called *ptochica.*[18]

These early Church canons, whether issued by an ecumenical or local council or by a bishop of distinction, were incorporated into the canon law of the Byzantine Church and were valid throughout the Byzantine era. Many canons of a local synod or of a bishop were ratified by the Council in Trullo (692).[19]

The philanthropic work of the Church, however, was not a matter of cold legalism, which in theory might say much but have little application. The Byzantines did not need laws forcing them to express their love of mankind. From the bishop to the most humble believer, philanthropy was a daily preoccupation. On many occasions the bishop led his flock in expressing the concern of the whole Church for philanthropy.

Epiphanios (d. 403), Bishop of Constantia in Cyprus, was such a leader. The historian Sozomenos relates that Epiphanios applied both the treasures of his church and his own patrimony to the relief of the needy, especially of those who were the victims of shipwreck or any other calamity. Epiphanios' humanitarian policy was so impressive that it induced many pious men of the island to bequeath their properties to him for charitable purposes.[20]

17. See *The Canons of Athanasius of Alexandria*, W. Riedel and W. E. Crum, eds. (Oxford, 1904), pp. 38, 40, 42, 127 *et passim;* Rhallis-Potlis, «Σύνταγμα», IV, 350; VI, 272, 495; cf. "Διήγησις μερικὴ τῶν ἐπιστολῶν Ἀλεξίου βασιλέως καὶ Νικολάου Πατριάρχου," Meyer, *Athoskloster*, pp. 178–79.

18. Rhallis-Potlis, «Σύνταγμα», II, 77.

19. "Second Canon," Rhallis-Potlis, «Σύνταγμα», II, 308–12.

20. Sozomenos, Bk. VII, 27: "πολλὰ θαυμάσια αὐτῷ ἀνατιθέασι . . . μεταδοτικὸς ὢν περὶ δεομένους ἢ ναυαγίοις ἢ ἄλλως δυστυχήσαντας, ἐπειδὴ πάλαι τὴν οὐσίαν ἀνάλωσε, εἰς δέον ἐσπάθα τοῖς τῆς ἐκκλησίας χρήμασιν. πλεῖστα δὲ ἦν. πάντοθεν γὰρ πολλοὶ τὸν πλοῦτον εὐσεβῶς ἀναλίσκειν προθέμενοι. . . ." Cf. "S. Epiphani Vita," MPG, XLI, cols. 61D–75B.

Zeno, Bishop of Maiuma in the fourth century, pursued his previous profession of weaving linen even though he was a bishop, in part to supply his personal wants and also to obtain means of helping others in poverty.[21]

St. John Chrysostom will always stand as a brilliant example of a bishop consumed by his sense of duty, justice, and love toward his fellow man.[22] In Antioch as well as in Constantinople his ecclesiastical program included a great concern for the destitute. The famous patriarch was fully conscious of the social responsibilities of the church, finding time not only for religious services and private study but for personal ministration to the needs of the less fortunate. He tended the sick, the orphans, the widows, the prisoners, and those in distress.[23] Chrysostom built charitable institutions, such as hospitals and old-age homes,[24] and redeemed many prisoners held by Isaurian robbers.[25] All had a friend in his person.[26]

Chrysostom applied stern discipline in his private life and in diocesan expenditures for charity. He avoided dinners and expenses that might reduce his capability to assist the poor. He restricted the expenditure of his diocesan stewards in order to provide food for the orphans and the poor.[27]

Charitable works were initiated not only by such prominent churchmen as Basil, Gregory Nazianzenos, and Chrysostom, but by many humble clergymen and unknown individuals as well. Cyril of Scythopolis relates that a certain bishop named Aetherios, from the diocese of Asiana,[28] visited Jerusalem where he distributed on his arrival a large amount of money to the poor.[29]

21. *Ibid.*, Bk. VII, 28: "λινῆν ἐσθῆτα ὕφαινεν ἐπὶ μονήρους ἱστοῦ, ἐντεῦθεν τε τὰ ἐπιτήδεια εἶχε καὶ ἄλλοις ἐχορήγει, καὶ οὐ διέλιπεν ἄχρι τελευτῆς τὸ αὐτὸ διέπων ἔργον. . . ."
22. Cf. Otto Plassmann, *Das Almosen bei Johannes Chrysostomus* (Münster, 1961), pp. 9 ff.
23. Symeon Metaphrastes, MPG, CXIV, col. 1097C.
24. *Ibid.*, col. 1096B.
25. Sozomenos, *Eccl. History*, VIII, 27. 8, ed. Bidez-Hansen, p. 388; cf. Symeon Metaphrastes, MPG, CXIV, col. 1096C.
26. Palladios, *Vita S. Joannes Chrysostomi*, ed. Coleman-Norton, p. 80: "ἡ τῶν χηρῶν κηδεμονία, ἡ τῶν παρθένων παραμυθία, ἡ τῶν ἀρρωστούντων νοσοκομία, ἡ τῶν καταπονουμένων ἐπικουρία, ἡ τῶν πλανωμένων ἐπιστροφή, ἡ τῶν συντετριμμένων φροντίς, ἡ τῶν ἐν φυλακαῖς ἐπίσκεψις."
27. *Ibid.*, p. 70.
28. Cf. Ostrogorsky, *History*, p. 32.
29. Schwartz, *Kyrillos*, p. 213.

Figure 4. St. John Chrysostom; mosaic panel, north tympanum of Hagia Sophia, Istanbul (9th century). Photo courtesy of the Byzantine Institute, Washington, D.C.

Figure 5. St. Gregory, St. Basil the Great, and St. John Chrysostom; mosaic panel, Cappella Palatina, Palermo, Sicily (12th century). Photo courtesy of Fratelli Alinari, Florence (Alinari no. 3314).

Abraamios, Bishop of Krateia in Bithynia [30] or perhaps of Craeteia of Paphlagonia [31] during the fifth century, proved himself a worthy follower of his Master. His biographer avers that Abraamios carried out numerous philanthropic works benefiting the orphans, the sick, the poor, and the strangers of his diocese. [32]

As previously stated, the brilliant tradition of charity of the early Christian centuries continued in later years. No other bishop is better known in the seventh century or any other epoch, perhaps with the exceptions of Basil and Chrysostom, than John the Eleemosynary, Patriarch of Alexandria (d. 620). It was because of the numerous charities he performed that he was surnamed John the Alms-Giver (Eleemosynary). Leontios of Neapolis writes that when John was elected Pope of the See of St. Mark, he sent out emissaries to compile a list of all the poor living in Alexandria. These unfortunates numbered more than seventy-five hundred, and all were placed under the welfare program of the great patriarch. [33] Furthermore, he established justice in the administration of the patriarchate and eliminated abuses against the poor and the weak. His philanthropic work reached its apex when in 613 [34] the Persians invaded Syria and throngs of refugees swarmed to his diocese. The patriarchate became a peaceful and secure haven for many of them. John extended hospitality to the refugees, not as strangers and foreigners but as true brethren. In Alexandria he caused to be built several philanthropic institutions (to be discussed below) for the aid of these refugees. All of the sick and injured received free treatment; [35] the healthy received monetary help. The motive of his philanthropic policy was, of course, to emulate the philanthropia of Christ toward men. [36]

Leontios asserts that the Patriarch's charities were too numerous to count. He considered the poor as his "brethren," [37] and

30. Cf. Ramsay, *Historical Geography*, p. 191.

31. A. H. M. Jones, *The Cities of the Eastern Roman Provinces* (Oxford, 1937), pp. 142–53 *et passim*.

32. Schwartz, *Kyrillos*, p. 247: "τῆς συντομίας φροντίδα ποιούμενος παρασιωπῶ τὰς ὑπ' αὐτοῦ ἐν τῇ ἐπισκοπῇ κατὰ μέρος γεγενημένας θεαρέστους πράξεις τάς τε ὀρφανοτροφίας καὶ ξενοδοχίας καὶ νοσοκομίας . . . καὶ τὰς τῶν δεομένων ἐπικουρίας."

33. Gelzer, *Leontios*, pp. 8–9.

34. Cf. Ostrogorsky, *History*, pp. 85–86.

35. Gelzer, *Leontios*, p. 13.

36. *Ibid.*, p. 16.

37. *Ibid.*, pp. 18–20, 27, 42, 43 *et passim*.

set before himself the example of other fathers and saints of the Church who had distinguished themselves in deeds of love (such as St. Serapion, who sold himself as a servant and gave the money to help a widow and her orphans [38]). The Patriarch's selfless love influenced many residents of his episcopate, and they responded with generous contributions to help him in his work.[39] Furthermore, his philanthropic program was not limited to relief for the refugees of the Persian invasions nor for the poor of his diocese, but was extended to include people in general need, such as those who had been shipwrecked. He worked also for restitution of social justice.[40]

Andrew, Archbishop of Crete (d. 740), is another illustrious person who followed in the steps of his Master and made charity one of his primary concerns. Even as a layman and monk he was very compassionate to the poor, a father to the orphans, the champion for the cause of justice, and a refuge for the persecuted.[41]

The Church maintained an institution called *diaconia* (diaconate). The members of it were in charge of distributions of charities and of other welfare and religious duties. We may assume that the members of a *diaconia* were from both religious strata, lay and clergy. It seems that many dioceses, local churches, and monasteries supported such organizations. For example, either the Church of the Virgin or the Church of St. Michael located in the *Eugeniou* section of Constantinople, had such a ministry. St. Andrew served as its director before his election as Archbishop of Crete. V. Laurent, who has studied numerous seals belonging to sundry diaconates of various churches and individuals, concludes that such philanthropic organizations served the social and charitable programs of the Byzantine Church for more than seven centuries. When St. Andrew became Archbishop of Crete his philanthropies multiplied and were extended to include the erection of institutions, as will be seen in the next chapter.[42]

The Byzantine Empire never lacked great churchmen either

38. *Ibid.*, pp. 48–49.
39. *Ibid.*, p. 54; cf. p. 76 *et passim.*
40. *Ibid.*, pp. 60, 62, 64, 66–67.
41. Papadopoulos-Kerameus, «'Ανάλεκτα», V, 172.
42. *Ibid.*, pp. 174, 176, 178 *et passim.* Laurent, *Corpus de sceaux*, V, pt. 2, 125–27.

as theologians or as social workers. Tarasios, Patriarch of Constantinople (784–806), whose personality is associated with the
iconoclastic controversies, belonged to the second category. His
biographer writes that it is not easy to enumerate all of Tarasios'
philanthropic works, including his efforts to shelter the strangers,
to help the lepers and the deformed, to feed the hungry, and to
protect orphans and widows.[43] As Patriarch, Tarasios reserved
several church houses in Constantinople for hospitality to strangers and needy foreigners. Every day he made distributions of
food to the poor who knocked at the door of his residence. The
deformed, crippled, blind, and sick who visited Constantinople
during Holy Lent and Easter received help from the patriarch.
During the winter months Tarasios distributed clothes and
blankets to the needy. On Easter Sunday the patriarch himself
visited an institution named "old royal house" to companion with
and serve the poor.[44]

In order to illustrate the compassion and the sense of justice
which governed the patriarch's life, Ignatios the Deacon relates
an interesting episode. An imperial dignitary was accused of
abusing a great sum of money and was imprisoned. While the
guards were sleeping the prisoner escaped and found refuge at
the Altar of Hagia Sophia. The guards discovered their prisoner
but they could not force the inviolability of the Holy of Holies.
They then guarded the Church continuously, hoping that hunger
and other physical needs would induce the prisoner to give himself up. No one was allowed to visit the Holy Altar except the
patriarch. Tarasios, through compassion for the prisoner and
conviction of his innocence, not only brought him food but had
the prisoner found innocent and set free.[45] Ignatios adds that
Tarasios was a man of justice and impartiality (favoring neither
the poor nor the rich) and a father to all. It is no wonder that
when Tarasios died he was mourned as a great benefactor.[46]

43. Ignatios the Deacon, *Vita Tarasii Archiepiscopi Constantinopolitani,*
ed. I. A. Heikel, Acta Societatis Scientiarum Fennicae, XVII (Helsingforsiae,
1891), 402; cf. p. 419; cf. A. Vogt, "S. Theophylacte de Nicomedie," AB, I
(1932), p. 69.
44. Ignatios the Deacon, *Vita Tarasii*, pp. 402–03.
45. *Ibid.*, pp. 380–82.
46. *Ibid.*, pp. 386–87: "Οἱ πτωχοὶ ἔκλαιον τὸν δοτῆρα, οἱ τυφλοὶ τὸν
ὀφθαλμόν, οἱ χωλοὶ τὴν βακτηρίαν, οἱ ξένοι τὸν ξενοδόχον, αἱ χῆραι τὸν
προστάτην, οἱ ὀρφανοὶ τὸν βοηθόν. . . ."

Figure 6. St. Ignatios the Younger; mosaic panel, north tympanum, Hagia Sophia, Istanbul (9th century). Photo courtesy of the Byzantine Institute, Washington, D.C.

Tarasios had consecrated a certain Theophylactos (d. c. 840) as Archbishop of Nicomedeia. The anonymous biographer of Theophylactos writes that, upon his election, Theophylactos initiated a wide program of philanthropic work in his diocese. Not only did he erect institutions for the sick and the poor but he supported the orphans, the widows, and others in need in his diocese. He visited patients in the hospital, distributing gifts and expressing his love and humility by personally washing the victims of leprosy.[47] When he died all people felt the loss, especially the great numbers who had benefited from his philanthropies.[48]

Yet another representative of the Church who followed in the steps of his Master was the Archbishop of Amastris [49] in Paphlagonia, named George (d. c. 807). Like Theophylactos of Nicomedeia, George, whose see was elevated to an archbishopric in about 800,[50] was ordained by the Patriarch Tarasios. Upon his election to the bishop's office, George distributed all his money to the poor, a practice not uncommon for Byzantine clergymen and monks.[51] When he assumed his duties his attention turned not only to purely ecclesiastical matters but to the social conditions of his people. In days of foreign invasions or natural catastrophes the bishop was the personification of hope for his people. Thus, when the Arabs invaded his diocese, his people suffered many losses, and George became their champion. He spared neither money nor labor to save them.[52] These catastrophes occurred most probably when the Muslims under Harun-al-Raschid invaded the region of Ancyra in 806.[53]

In his ministry Archbishop George worked to bring justice to the relationships of his people, "to exorcise *misanthropy* and to substitute it with philanthropia." [54] Even after his death the

47. Anonymous, *Life of St. Theophylactos Archbishop of Nicomedeia,* ed. A. Vogt, "S. Théophylacte de Nicomédie," AB, L (1932), 74–75.

48. *Ibid.,* p. 81.

49. Ramsay, *Historical Geography,* p. 91.

50. *Ibid.,* p. 91.

51. "Life of St. George, Archbishop of Amastris," ed. V. G. Vasilievskii, *Trudy,* III (Petrograd, 1915), 25; cf. "Synaxare of Stephanus Confessor, Archbishop of Sougdaia," ed. V. G. Vasilievskii, *Trudy,* III (Petrograd, 1915), 73.

52. *Ibid.,* pp. 36–37.

53. Ostrogorsky, *History,* p. 173. Because the Archbishop was alive during the Muslim invasion we may be safer in placing his death on or after 806. F. Halkin suggests the years 802–807; see his *Hag. Graeca,* I, 211.

54. "Life of St. George Archbishop of Amastris," ed. Vasilievskii, *Trudy,* III, p. 60.

saintly bishop remained the philanthropic patron of his people. When the Russians, "who lacked every sense of philanthropia," attacked Amastris during a raid on Constantinople in 860,[55] it was the beloved patron who saved the city through his intercessions in Heaven.[56]

Another bishop who distinguished himself in philanthropic work and social action in his diocese was a certain Michael, Bishop of Synnadon in Phrygia. Michael (d. c. 826) was a social force in his diocese and expressed his social consciousness with the erection of several institutions. In addition to churches and monasteries, he built resorts for strangers and homes for orphans, while his social program included special provisions for widows, for the poor, and for others in distress, as well as visitation of needy people of all walks of life.[57]

In days of famine, natural calamity, and barbaric invasion, the bishops and priests played a great role in the actual survival of their people. They conducted relief drives and did everything in their power to assist the victims. Nicholas Mysticos, Patriarch of Constantinople, may serve as an illustration.

The Bulgarian raids under Symeon during the first quarter of the tenth century laid waste several cities and villages in Eastern Macedonia and Thrace, such as Adrianople, Dyrrachium, and others. The victims must have been many and the need to feed and clothe them not less paramount. Nicholas Mysticos initiated drives for charities. He appealed to fellow bishops for collections and provisions for the unfortunate victims. In a dramatic letter to an unknown dignitary, perhaps a metropolitan who had several suffragan bishops under his jurisdiction, Nicholas indicates that his appeal is to meet a great emergency. He advised his correspondent to do his utmost, together with the other bishops, in order to relieve the pressure of the times. If it is the clergyman's duty to look after the everyday needs of the unfortunates, it is of greater importance to initiate philanthropic enterprises in times of general catastrophe.[58] Eustathios of Thessalonica

55. A. Vasiliev, *The Russian Attack on Constantinople* (Cambridge, Mass., 1946), pp. 75 ff.

56. "Life of St. George Archbishop of Amastris," *Trudy*, III, pp. 64 ff.

57. "Βίος τοῦ ἁγίου Μιχαὴλ Συννάδων τῆς Φρυγίας," ed. Doukakis, «Συναξαριστής», May, IX, second edition (Athens, 1963), 224; cf. Theodore Studites, *Epistolarum*, Bk. II, No. 94, MPG, XCIX, col. 1613D.

58. Nicholas Mysticos, *Epistle No. 92*, Col. 297BD: "εἰ γὰρ καὶ ἰδίᾳ στενοχωρουμένοις τισὶν ὀφείλομεν χορηγεῖν κατὰ δύναμιν πρὸς τὸ λῦσαι

(b. 1125) relates that a certain priest named Philotheos believed that he who imitates God in philanthropia becomes God himself. Thus in days of need he opened the storage of his Church to feed the poor.[59]

Of course, the pastorage and the episcopal residence were centers of much philanthropic activity. Those in want turned to the local clergy for help. It was common to find xenones and institutions for orphans and elderly people located next to the bishopric. On many occasions the clergy were expected to champion justice and the cause of the underprivileged or the unjustly persecuted. Even academicians turned to the clergy for help.

A certain Alexander [60] a teacher at the University of Constantinople, was exiled by the authorities to the region of Chimmerious in Armenia. He suffered there from malnutrition and other calamities to the extent that he considered himself "alive among the dead." Alexander solicited the intervention of Philaretos, Metropolitan of Euchaita,[61] a city in the Armeniacon theme, telling him that his last hope rested with the philanthropia of the bishop,[62] whose virtue would be reminiscent of the philanthropia of God. Alexander made it clear that the intervention of a bishop for the restoration of justice was viewed as a worthy manifestation of philanthropia. He expressed these views in another letter addressed to Ignatios, Metropolitan of Nicomedeia.[63]

Nicephoros, the tenth-century Bishop of Miletos, believed and taught that the passionate part of man's soul is pacified and subjugated through love and active manifestation of philanthropy toward his fellow man.[64] Thus he felt very close to all people

τὴν στενοχωρίαν τῶν ἀπορουμένων, πόσῳ μᾶλλον ἐν τῇ παγκοίνῳ ταύτῃ στενοχωρίᾳ τοῦτο πράττειν ὀφείλομεν. . . ."

59. Eustathios of Thessalonica, *Laudatio S. Philothei Opsiciani*, MPG, CXLVIII, col. 149; cf. col. 148.

60. Jean Darrouzés, *Epistoliers Byzantins du Xᵉ Siècle* (Paris, 1960), pp. 27–32.

61. See Ramsay, *Historical Geography*, pp. 20–21.

62. Jean Darrouzés, *Epistoliers*, p. 74.

63. *Ibid.*, pp. 74–75.

64. "Vita S. Nicephori," ed. H. Delehaye, "Monumenta Latrensia Hagiographica," *Milet*, III. 1 (Berlin, 1913), 161: "θατέρῳ δὲ τὸ θυμοειδὲς τῆς ψυχῆς τιθασσεύεται καὶ μαλάττεται φιλοπτωχίας καὶ συμπαθείας θεσμοῖς, καὶ τοῖς πένησιν ἐμβραβεύεται τὸ φιλάνθρωπον καὶ τῷ ταπεινῷ μέρει τοῦ γένους. Ἐξ ὧν τῷ μακαρίτῃ συνέβαινε πάντας μὲν οἰκείους εἶναι καὶ προσφιλεῖς διὰ τὴν μετάδοσιν."

and especially to the lonely and needy, who looked upon him as their father and guardian. Nicephoros, a contemporary of Nicephoros Phocas (d. 969),[65] not only used the finances of his diocese for charity but visited the rich, soliciting donations which he added to his philanthropies.[66]

Zealous clergy who endeavored to breathe new life into their jurisdiction applied philanthropy as one of the most effective means. Theophylactos of Ochrida relates that when Clement became Bishop of Ochrida (+916) he found distressing conditions among the people of his diocese. Clement began a program of restoration. Through preaching, teaching, and social work Bishop Clement extended hope and protection to the orphans, the widows, and the lonely stranger, whose well-being is always provided for in Byzantine hagiographical texts.[67]

Contrary to the allegations of certain scholars that Byzantine bishops were subservient to imperial whims, many clergymen maintained a high morale and stature. They counseled as well as reprimanded members of the imperial court. Patriarch Euthymios of Constantinople (907–12) instructed Emperor Leo VI (886–912) to govern the people with piety as well as with justice, charity, and compassion.[68] Stylianos Zaoutsis, the chief magistrate under Leo, appears to have been an unprincipled man. The Patriarch castigated him for his injustices, abuses, and lack of compassion, and advised him to repent.[69] In addition, Euthymios performed many charitable acts and distributed his own possessions among the poor.[70] He was a great philanthropos because he believed in a philanthropic God.[71]

Frequently, the clergy acted as spokesmen for the poor. The fate of the poor was deplorable during certain centuries; the rich exploited them and actually made them their servants.[72]

---

65. *Ibid.*, p. 162.
66. *Ibid.*, p. 199.
67. *Monumenta ad SS. Cyrilli et Methodii successorum vitas resque gestas pertinentia*, ed. N. L. Tunitskij, I (Sergiev Posad, 1918), 124: "διὸ καὶ πατὴρ μὲν ὀρφανῶν καὶ χηρῶν βοηθός, πάντα τρόπον αὐτῶν κηδόμενος, ἡ δὲ θύρα παντὶ ἁπλῶς ἀνέωκτο πένητι, καὶ ξένος ἐκτὸς οὐκ ηὐλίζετο."
68. "Vita Euthymii," ed. C. De Boor, *Vita Euthymii—Ein Anecdoton zur Geschichte Leo's des Weisen A. 886–912* (Berlin, 1888), p. 3.7.
69. *Ibid.*, p. 7.12.
70. *Ibid.*, p. 63.12.
71. Cf. *ibid.*, p. 78.8–9; cf. p. 16.16 *et passim*.
72. Theophylactos of Ochrida, *Epistolae*, No. 7, MPG, CXXVI, col. 513D;

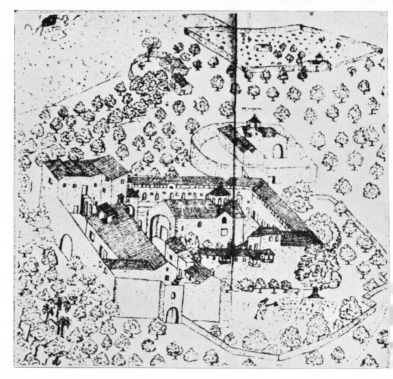

Figure 7. Penteles Monastery, Greece, showing its *Gerocomeion* outside the monastery walls; after a drawing by Barskij. Reproduced with permission from A. K. Orlandos, *Monastic Architecture*, p. 56.

Figure 8. *Gerocomeion* of Penteles Monastery, Greece; exterior. Photo reproduced with permission from A. K. Orlandos, *Monastic Architecture*, p. 56.

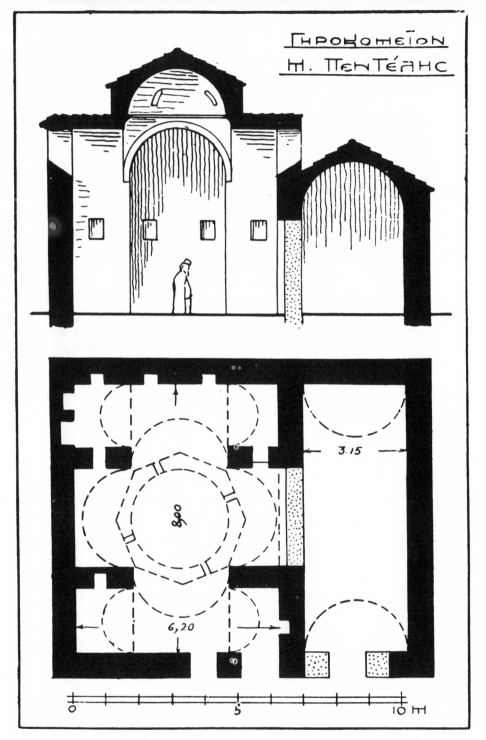

Figure 9. *Gerocomeion* of Penteles Monastery, Greece; section and ground plan. Reproduced with permission from A. K. Orlandos, *Monastic Architecture*, p. 55.

Theophylactos, the celebrated Archbishop of Ochrida (1091–1108),[73] wrote a letter to John, the son of the Sebastocrator Isaac, the brother of Alexios Comnenos, in which he pleaded for the poor of his diocese, who suffered under the land-hungry magnates. John, who apparently held a responsible position in the administrative machinery, was advised not to reject the bishop's plea. A rejection of the poor would have been rejection of God, while benevolence to the poor was considered imitation of the Lord.[74]

In the realm of practical philanthropy there must have been many unknown or obscure Chrysostoms in the Byzantine Empire. One such was Gregorios, Bishop of Assos in Asia Minor during the twelfth century. He was distinguished as a religious teacher, church administrator, and social paragon, in his great concern for the welfare of the poor.[75] A little-known Bishop of Adramyttion, Athanasios,[76] was highly praised for his philanthropic work.[77] Constantine Acropolites, a great Logothetes, in an oration of 1296 [78] described him as a churchman whose daily preoccupation concerned measures to help his flock.

In her philanthropic work the Byzantine Church must have utilized the services of the order of deaconesses. It is well known that this class of women played an important role in the religious and social work of the early Church.[79] Outside of their

cf. Diogenes A. Xanalatos, "Θεοφύλακτος ὁ Βουλγαρίας καὶ ἡ δρᾶσις του ἐν ᾽Αχρίδι," *Th.*, XVI, no. 63 (Athens, 1938), 230.

73. Diogenes A. Xanalatos, *Beitrage zur wirtschafts unde Sozialgeschichte Makedoniens im Mittelalter, hauptsachlich auf Grund der Briefe des Erzbischofs Theophylaktos von Achrida* (Munich, 1937), pp. 15–17.

74. Theophylactos, *ibid.*, *Epistle No. 6*: "τὸ μὲν ἀγαθοποιεῖν Θεοῦ, τὸ δὲ κακοποιεῖν ἐρινννώδες, ὑπὲρ τῆς ταλαιπωρίας τῶν πτωχῶν, καὶ τοῦ στεναγμοῦ τῶν πενήτων, . . . μηδὲ ἄλλο τι προτιμότερον ἡγοῖο τῆς θεομιμησίας, καί σε Θεοῦ οἱ πένητες. . . ."

75. "Life of Saint Gregory, Bishop of Assos," Doukakis, «Συναξαριστής», March, pp. 46–47.

76. Philemon Photopoulos, "Anecdota," NS, XII (Jerusalem, 1912), p. 665.

77. Constantine Acropolites, "Λόγος εἰς τὸν ἅγιον ᾽Αθανάσιον τὸν ᾽Ατραμυττίου," Papadopoulos-Kerameus, *Varia*, pp. 142–43.

78. Beck, *Kirche und Theologische Literatur*, p. 698.

79. See Cecilia Robinson, *The Ministry of Deaconesses* (London, 1898), pp. 1–99; C. H. Turner, "Ministries of Women in the Primitive Church," reprinted in *Catholic and Apostolic*, ed. H. N. Bate (London and Oxford, 1931), pp. 328–43; see also "On the Early History and Modern Revival of Deaconesses," *The Church Quarterly Review*, XLVII. 94 (January, 1899), 302–17; Leopold Zscharnack, *Der Dienst der Frau in den ersten Jahrhunder-*

religious duties, such as assisting in the baptism of women, the deaconesses attended the sick and the afflicted and ministered to the needs of the poor and the orphans.

In the early Byzantine Empire, from the fourth century until the age of Justinian, deaconesses were a well-established institution,[80] very active in the social work of the Church.[81] The nineteenth Canon of the first Ecumenical Council indicates that the deaconesses constituted an ordained ministry. The same is implied by the fifteenth rule of the Council of Chalcedon (451). This practice of ordination was later discontinued,[82] perhaps because the order had lost its religious significance. The prevalence of infant baptism, for example, eliminated the assistance of the deaconesses in the baptism of adult women. Thus their order appropriated more social significance in later centuries.[83] Because the welfare work of the Church was administered by local churches and congregations, deaconesses were assigned to serve and were attached to such churches as Hagia Sophia. Thus Justinian prescribed that forty deaconesses should be included among the clerical staff of the Great Church,[84] and we can be sure that deaconesses were in the service of other churches as well.[85]

This class of dedicated women was active also during the seventh century. Heraclios preserved Justinian's law and kept forty deaconesses attached to Hagia Sophia [86] while he ordered that nine deaconesses should be assigned to the Church of Theotocos in Blachernae.[87] The Council in Trullo prescribed that a deaconess should not be received by the Church before her

ten der christlichen Kirche (Göttingen, 1902), see especially pp. 99–156; E. Theodorou, «Ἡρωΐδες τῆς χριστιανικῆς ἀγάπης—αἱ διακόνισσαι διὰ τῶν αἰώνων» (Athens, 1949); F. Stephana, " Ἡ Διακόνισσα στὸ Βυζάντιο," *Aktines* (1946), pp. 270 ff.

80. Cf. *Codex Theodosianus*, XVI. 2, 27; Sozomenos, *Ecclesiastical History*, VII. 16.

81. Cf. Basil the Great, *Epistle No. 105*, ed. Deferrari, II, 198; Theodoret, *Ecclesiastical History*, III. 14 and 19; cf. Turner, p. 341; Robinson, pp. 64–67; Zscharnack, pp. 123–39.

82. Rhallis-Potlis, «Σύνταγμα», II, p. 255; cf. IV, p. 477.

83. Cf. Theodoret, *Ecclesiastical History;* cf. Rhallis-Potlis, «Σύνταγμα», IV, 477, Question 38.

84. Justinian, *Novel III. 1*, Schoell and Kroll, *Corpus Juris Civilis*, p. 21.

85. *Ibid.*, Prooimion; *Heraclios, Novel XXII*, Zepos-Zepos, *Jus*, I, 29.

86. *Ibid.*, p. 28; cf. Photios, *Nomocanon*, I. 30, Rhallis-Potlis, I, 69.

87. Heraclios, p. 29; cf. Joannes Moschos, *Pratum Spirituale*, 3.

fortieth birthday.[88] After a long silence about this order in the following two centuries, we learn that women were joining the deaconesses during the reign of Leo the Wise and were still in the service of various churches.[89] Later, in the twelfth century, deaconesses served in the philanthropic work of the Church. These women were not ordained, although certain nuns had appropriated the term uncanonically. This is confirmed by the canonist Theodore Balsamon.[90]

In the fourth century the social responsibilities of the deaconesses had been defined: they visited poor families and reported cases of illnesses, poverty, and distress to the bishop who supervised the philanthropic work of the Church.[91] Though we lack evidence as specific as that which we possess in the *Apostolic Constitutions* (c. 380), there is no reason to doubt that the work of the deaconesses remained substantially the same in later centuries. We may assume that with the appearance of hospitals and organized institutions, deaconesses played an even greater role in the charitable work of the Byzantine Church. Anna Comnena corroborates the existence of this class of women in the twelfth century, relating that her father Emperor Alexios made the work of the deaconesses his personal concern.[92] Anna adds that her father introduced female choristers to the Church of St. Paul. It is probable that deaconesses served in that capacity also. But their primary duty must have been nursing and attending the female patients, aged people, and orphans who were confined in Alexios' "new city" of charity.[93] We may also assume that deaconesses served as nurses and attendants in other hospitals, homes for the aged, leprosaria, and orphanages. In addition to

88. Rhallis-Potlis, «Σύνταγμα», II, 337.

89. *Basilica*, Bk. IV. I, 7, ed. H. J. Scheltema and N. Van der Wal, *Basilicorum Libri LX*, I (Gravenhage, 1955), 114.

90. Rhallis-Potlis, «Σύνταγμα», II, 255: "διακόνισσα γὰρ σήμερον οὐ χειροτονεῖται, κἂν καταχρηστικῶς τινὲς τῶν ἀσκητριῶν διακόνισσαι λέγονται."

91. *Apostolic Constitutions*, Bk. III, Ch. 19: "χρὴ οὖν ὑμᾶς τοὺς διακόνους [male and female, deacons and deaconesses, see the opening of Chap. 19] ἐπισκέπτεσθαι πάντας τοὺς δεομένους ἐπισκέψεως καὶ περὶ τῶν θλιβομένων ἀναγγέλλετε τῷ ἐπισκόπῳ ὑμῶν."

92. Anna Comnena, *Alexias*, XV. 7: "ἐπιμελὲς γὰρ καὶ τὸ τῶν διακονισσῶν πεποίηκεν ἔργον."

93. Cf. *ibid.* and Georgina Buckler, *Anna Comnena* (London, 1929), p. 121; Oeconomos, *Vie Religieuse*, pp. 195–96.

the deeds of deaconesses and other persons in the service of the Church, much philanthropic work of the Patriarchate of Constantinople as well as of other Eastern Patriarchates and dioceses was carried out under the supervision of the Syncellos, the chief confidant of the Patriarch.[94]

Thus there is much evidence to indicate that the Byzantine Church took under her aegis the lower classes, and her contribution toward the improvement of their lives must not be underestimated.[95] Even if the Church had achieved nothing else in the life of the Empire, her philanthropies proved her very great worth.

94. Athenagoras, Metropolitan of Paramythia and Parga, " Ὁ Θεσμὸς τῶν Συγκέλλων ἐν τῷ Οἰκουμενικῷ Πατριαρχείῳ," ΕΕΒΣ, IV (1927), 4–9; *ibid.*, VI (1929), 140–41.

95. Cf. Chastel, *Influence de la Charité*, pp. 303–44; Champagny, *Char. Chrét.*, pp. 290–329 *et passim*.

7. Philanthropy and Monastic Establishments

The monks and monastic establishments were great factors in the application of philanthropia, the noble virtue. It was not without reason that Theodore the Studite (d. 826) described the monks as "the nerves and the foundations of the Church." [1]

It was virtually an established tradition among the poor, the orphans, the sick, and the needy to turn to the Church and her monastic communities for help and consideration. Many of these less fortunate Byzantines would visit the monasteries (especially on days such as Christmas, Epiphany, Holy Thursday, Good Friday, Easter, Pentecost, and the Dormition of Theotocos) in order to receive gifts of wheat, wine, meat, honey, beans, and other foodstuffs.[2] On most days during the year, the monks and their institutions were instruments of philanthropy and charity.

It is true that early Christian monasticism was not concerned with the affairs and the social problems of this world. The ideal of early hermits, anchorites, and monks in general was to achieve the perfect life in Christ, to attain a mystical experience of God and to strive for the *theosis* of human nature apart from the

1. Theodore Studites, *Parva Catechesis*, MPG, XCIX, col. 393: "καὶ μο-ναχοὶ τὰ νεῦρα καὶ ἑδραιώματα τῆς Ἐκκλησίας." Cf. Marin, *Les Moines*, p. 520.
2. Cf. Joannes Moschos, *Monachus et Eremita*, MPG, LXXXVII, col. 2911; cf. *Pratum Spirituale*, col. 2941BC.

pandemonium of secular life. Because of his constant endeavor to approach his goal and his escape from worldly concerns, the perfect monk was considered to be "the man of God." [3]

Beginning, however, with the fourth century under the influence of Basil the Great, religious isolation and mystical *theoria* were not deemed sufficient for the monk to achieve the *summum bonum* of his vocation. Basil decreed that monasticism should not be divorced from the needs of human society, and that the practice of philanthropia ought to become an element of the monk's life. The love of the monk should be turned not just to his own spiritual salvation but toward charity for his fellow man, and to productive work.[4] Basil encouraged the monks to perform deeds of philanthropy not only for fellow monks but for all people, and to compete with each other in works of charity.[5]

As a result of the new monastic philosophy of love and service to mankind, the monasteries became centers of hospitality, almsgiving, and care for the sick, the pilgrims, and the wayfarers. The philanthropic program of a monastic establishment depended upon the fruits of its inhabitants' labor. Basil counseled the members of his monastic city to work not only to keep the body under subjection, but to provide their institutions with

3. A. J. Fytrakis, «Οἱ Μοναχοὶ ὡς Κοινωνικοὶ Διδάσκαλοι καὶ Ἐργάται ἐν τῇ Ἀρχαίᾳ Ἀνατολικῇ Ἐκκλησίᾳ» (Athens, 1950), pp. 5–12 *et passim;* J. M. Hussey, "Byzantine Monasticism," *Historia,* XXIV, no. 93 (June, 1939), 92; A. Theodorou, "Das Mönchtum der Orthodoxen Ostkirche," *Die Orthodoxe Kirche in Griechischer sicht,* ed. P. Bratsiotis, I, part 1 (Stuttgart, 1960), 83–88; Baynes, *Byzantine Studies,* pp. 27 ff.; C. G. Bonis, "Τὰ Ἰδεώδη τοῦ μοναχικοῦ βίου ἐν Βυζαντίῳ κατὰ τὴν ια΄ ἑκατονταετηρίδα," *Th.,* XVI, No. 64, 356–57; George Soteriou, «Αἱ Μοναὶ τῆς Ἑλλάδος καὶ ἡ Ἐθνική των δρᾶσις κατὰ τοὺς Βυζαντινοὺς Χρόνους» (Athens, 1936), pp. 14 ff. Demosthenes Savramis, *Zur Soziologie des Byzantinischen Mönchtums* (Leiden/Koln, 1962); R. Janin, "Le Monachisme byzantin au moyen âge. Commende et typica (Xᵉ–XIVᵉ siècle)," REB, XXII (1964), 5–44. [For monasticism as a social force in late Roman Egypt see: Farag Fofail Farag, *Sociological and Moral Studies in the Field of Coptic Monasticism* (Leyden, 1964), pp. 35–43; for the role of monasticism in the civilization of Western Europe see: Jean Decarreaux, *Monks and Civilization,* tr. Charlotte Haldane (London, 1964).]

4. Basil the Great, *Sermo Asceticus,* 10, MPG, XXI, col. 648B: "Γίνου μιμητὴς Χριστοῦ . . . ἐλεήμονος, καὶ μὴ ἀνηλεοῦς· φιλανθρώπου, καὶ μὴ μισανθρώπου . . . ἑκάστης ἡμέρας ἐργασίαν ἐπισκεπτόμενος, σύμβαλε τῇ πρὸ αὐτῆς, καὶ σπεῦδε πρὸς τὴν βελτίωσιν." Cf. *Regulae Fusius Tractatae,* XXXVII. 2–4, cols. 1012A–1016A.

5. Basil the Great, *Regulae Fusius Tractatae,* 35, MPG, XXXI, col. 1004C.

sufficient goods to feed those in want.[6] Thus very early in the Byzantine Empire a monastery became a constructive force in the social life of the state. A monastery was both a worshiping community and a working society as well. A monk was often advised to work not only to escape the grievous sin of idleness but also to produce and be able to help the needy.[7] Monasteries were usually havens for travelers, strangers, and the poor. The charters or *typika* of monastic establishments often prescribed that the monks should have the monastery's doors open to all the needy, a tradition which we find in all centuries of the Byzantine State.[8] Philanthropy became a daily practice of many monastic establishments, as diverse hagiographical texts indicate and the *typika* of the monasteries reveal. On the basis of the positive contributions of Byzantine monasticism, one of its former but converted critics writes: "What a new and rich life was to be found in Greek monasticism, and how great its significance was in relation to the theory and practice of penance and the formation of the inner life and of spiritual devotion."[9]

One of the rules of a monastery provided that distribution of food be made each day at the gate of the establishment. The Typikon of the Monastery of *Vevaias Elpidos* for women rules that all the surpluses of the daily meals should not be preserved for the following day but be distributed to the "brethren in Christ, the poor," and to those who for one reason or another knocked at the monastery door.[10] Charities were to be performed with compassion and love as if being offered to Christ.

6. Basil the Great, *Regulae Fusius Tractatae*, 37.1, MPG, XXXI, col. 1009C: "οὐ μόνον διὰ τὸν ὑπωπιασμὸν τοῦ σώματος χρησίμου οὔσης ἡμῖν τῆς τοιαύτης ἀγωγῆς, ἀλλὰ καὶ διὰ τὴν εἰς τὸν πλησίον ἀγάπην, ἵνα καὶ τοῖς ἀσθενοῦσι τῶν ἀδελφῶν, δι' ἡμῶν ὁ Θεὸς τὴν αὐτάρκειαν παρέχῃ. . . ." Cf. Eph. 4:28.

7. Cf. Georges Florovsky, "Empire and Desert: Antinomies of Christian History," GOTh.R, III, no. 2 (Winter, 1957), 148–50. Cf. "The Social Problem in the Eastern Orthodox Church," *The Journal of Religious Thought*, VIII, no. 1 (Autumn–Winter 1950–1951), 42–43.

8. Cf. M. I. Gedeon, "Διαθήκη Μαξίμου μοναχοῦ κτίτορος τῆς ἐν Λυδίᾳ μονῆς Κοτινῆς," MX, II (1939), 278: " Ἔστω δὲ ἡ τῆς μονῆς πύλη ἀείποτε ἀνεωγμένη· καὶ τοὺς ἐρχομένους οἱ μοναχοὶ ὑποδεχέσθωσαν, εἰς τὸ μηδένα τῶν ξένων ἢ τῶν ἐνδεῶν παρορᾶσθαι, ἀλλ' ἅπαντας φιλοτίμως δέχεσθαι, καὶ φιλοξενεῖσθαι ἐν οἷς ἂν εὐπορεῖν ἔχῃ ἡ μονὴ ποτοῦ καὶ σίτου."

9. A. von Harnack, *Aus der Werkstatt des Vollendeten* (Giessen, 1933), p. 282, quoted by J. Hussey, "Byzantine Monasticism," p. 56.

10. Delehaye, *Deux Typica*, pp. 68–69.

In addition to the everyday charities, practically every monastic establishment was more generous on certain holidays, such as the observance of the Dormition of Theotocos, the day of commemoration of the founder's death,[11] or St. John the Forerunner's day (Monastery of Lips).[12] In addition to bread, wine, wheat, and other goods, some monasteries also distributed money when it was necessary,[13] and extended hospitality in the xenon of their monastery to all strangers, pilgrims, and wayfarers in need. Hospitality was viewed as the "most royal virtue," and was denied by male monasteries to women only because they might be a source of temptation to the monks.[14]

It was a stereotype rule of many monasteries to distribute charities regularly and extend hospitality to all in need. Their typika suggest that either they copied each other or that they all had a common practice. We learn further that the poor who solicited help from a monastic establishment were many. Thus one monk was assigned each day the sole duty of making distributions to the poor.[15] Some monasteries gave more generously than others, and the less wealthy were instructed by their typikon to be discreet in their charities.[16] Limitations on the humanitarian activities of a monastery were due sometimes to outside factors. The monastery of Neophytos in the eparchy of Paphos may serve as an illustration.

The Typikon of Neophytos indicates that Cyprus suffered from heavy taxation under Richard the Lionhearted when he conquered the island in 1191 or 1192.[17] The Latin oppression had caused such poverty that the inhabitants were deprived of even their daily necessities.[18] While the poor multiplied, the monastery

11. *Ibid.*, pp. 79, 81, 99.
12. *Ibid.*, p. 127; cf. "Typicon of Theotocos Eleousa," Petit, BIARC, VI (1900), 86.
13. Delehaye, *Deux Typica*.
14. "Typicon Neilou," Miklosich-Muller, *Acta et Diplomata*, V, 422, 431 *et passim;* Neophytos, "Τυπικὴ Διαθήκη," ed. Frederick E. Warren, *Archaeologia*, XLVII (London, 1882), 31; J. P. Tsiknopoulos, «Νεοφύτου Πρεσβυτέρου Μοναχοῦ καὶ Ἐγκλείστου Τυπικὴ σὺν Θεῷ Διαθήκη» (Larnaca, 1952), pp. 32–33.
15. "Typicon of the Monastery of Theotocos of Elegmon," Dmitrievski, *Typika*, pp. 730–31.
16. "Typicon Neilou," Miklosich-Muller, *Acta et Diplomata*, V, p. 398.
17. Ostrogorsky, *History*, pp. 361–62.
18. Neophytos, "Τυπικὴ Διαθήκη," ed. Warren, *Archaeologia*, p. 14: "ἀλλ' ὠθεῖσα ἡ χώρα ἡμῶν παρὰ τῶν Λατήνων [Λατίνων] καὶ στενωθέντες πάντες ἄνθρωποι ἐκ παντὸς ἀναγκαίου."

could not cope with its daily obligations toward them because of the "grievous slavery."[19] Nevertheless, the monks were instructed to continue their humanitarian contributions even on a moderate scale.

The typika are very emphatic in instructing the monastic establishments to practice charities and the monks to look upon the poor, orphans, widows, wayfarers, and others in want with compassion and love. Agape, philanthropia, eleemosyne, and humility are virtues to be practiced because God is pleased and because of which God became man and man becomes like God.[20]

That a monastery or an isolated Lavra had been a salutary refuge for those in want is demonstrated by rules and regulations of early monastic communities. The rules of St. Sabas (d. 532), while excluding a number of people from entering the monastic establishment, provide that foreigners, wayfarers, and others in need be received and hospitality be extended to them for as long as seven days.[21] The poor who received help at St. Sabas were many.

Other isolated monasteries, such as those of the tenth century on Mount Athos, maintained the traditional policy of hospitality, charity, and help to the needy. Athanasios the Athonite writes in the typikon of his monastery that hospitality should be extended especially to seamen forced by the weather to spend days or months at the port of Athos, to shipwrecked seamen, and to all who need help, whether they come from the land or the sea.[22]

The emphatic recommendations for charity in the monastic typikon often resulted in competition between monasteries to surpass each other in hospitable services, thus imitating the hospitality of Abraham.[23]

19. *Ibid.*, p. 27.
20. Timothy, "Typicon of the Monastery of Theotocos Evergetis," Dmitrievsky, *Typika*, pp. 645–46: "ἡ δὲ ἀγάπη κεφαλὴ καὶ ἀπαρτισμός· καὶ γὰρ καὶ τὴν ὑψοποιὸν ταπείνωσιν συνεζευγμένην ἑαυτῇ δείκνυσι, καὶ τὴν ἐλεημοσύνην καὶ τὴν φιλανθρωπίαν, δι' ἃ καὶ μᾶλλον ὁ Θεὸς γέγονεν ἄνθρωπος, καὶ ἃ καλεῖται Θεός, καὶ δι' ὧν ὁ ἄνθρωπος θεὸς ἀποδείκνυται καὶ τῷ οὐρανίῳ πατρὶ ὅμοιος. . . ." For the monastery which was established in the eleventh century see Janin, *Geog. Eccles.*, pp. 186–92.
21. "Τύπος καὶ παράδοσις . . . τῆς λαύρας τοῦ [ἁγίου] Σάββα," Kurtz, BZ, III (1894), p. 170; Dmitrievsky, *Typika*, p. 224.
22. "Τυπικὸν ἤτοι Κανονικὸν τοῦ . . . Ἀθανασίου τοῦ ἐν τῷ Ἄθῳ," Meyer, *Athoskloster*, pp. 114, 130; Manuel J. Gedeon, «Ὁ Ἄθως» (Constantinople, 1885), p. 262; Dmitrievsky, *Typika*, p. 245.
23. Cf. "Laudatio S. Paul Junionis," ed. H. Delehaye, *Milet*, III. 1 (Berlin,

One can easily discern that the rules of the monastic community recommended *necrosis* of the passions and carnal desires not only through prayer and *theoria* but by means of *exascesis* or *ascesis* in the application of love toward man. It was an ideal of Byzantine monasticism for the monk to be *philotheos* and *philoptochos.*[24]

But the important question is whether Byzantine monks fulfilled the duties and demands expected of them. Theories and rules can be mere empty words or rhetorical recommendations without much practical value, and it is naive to believe that every word of a typikon was followed faithfully by all. However, it is equally unjust to reject or seriously doubt the practice of philanthropy by Byzantine monasteries. Examples from the lives of individual saints indicate that many of them were actively engaged in practical charity. But the information we possess is general. The first point which a saint's biographer emphasizes is that the monk or priest or bishop was a lover of both God and man—*philotheos* and *philoptochos.* The latter was manifested in his concern for the poor. Usually such "a man of God" is described as "the eye of the blind, the feet of the lame, the clothes of the naked, the roof of the homeless, the physician of the sick, etc." [25]

The first demonstration of a saint's compassion for the needy was the distribution of his private possessions to the poor before taking up the life of a monastic, or to use part of it for churches and charitable institutions. This action was carried out also by men of the higher clergy. In addition to St. Anthony, St. Basil the Great, and Chrysostom, we may cite here Hypatios, Archbishop of Gangra, who distributed his wealth to help the poor, and

1913), 150–51; "Διάταξις . . . Μανουὴλ Μοναχοῦ," Petit, BIARC, VI (1900), 87; Daniel the Abbot, "Περὶ τῆς Πατρικίας," ed. M. Leon Clugnet, "Vie et récits de l'Abbé Daniel," ROC, V (1900), 54; Callinicos, *De Vita S Hypatii Liber,* Seminarii Philologorum Bonnensis Sodales (Leipzig, 1895), p. 19 *et al.*

24. "Typicon of the Monastery of St. Mamas," Efstratiades, HE, I, no. 2 (1928), 256: "Μέγα τι καὶ θεῖον χρῆμα καὶ τίμιον ψυχὴ φιλόθεος καὶ φιλόπτωχος." Cf. "Typicon of the Monastery of Evergetis," Dmitrievsky, *Typika,* p. 615.

25. Symeon Metaphrastes, MPG, CXIV, col. 496B-D; cf. Theodoros of Petra, *Life of St. Theodosios,* ed. Hermann Usener, *Der Heilige Theodosios* (Leipzig, 1890), p. 98; cf. "Life of St. Eudocimos," ed. Ch. M. Loparev, BIARC, XIII (1908), 206; "Vita S. Martha," AASS, May, V (1866), col. 400E ff.

built churches and houses for orphan girls.[26] Others pursued manual professions not only to maintain themselves but in order to supply charities to the poor.[27] The vision of God through a clean heart and mind was to be supplanted by applied love for man.[28]

We learn from the history of the monastic communities in Egypt that the monks were supporting many of the poor in Alexandria. A priest named Serapion was in charge of all the products of the monasteries in the region of Arsenoita. He saw that no one in his jurisdiction went hungry and that wheat was shipped to the poor of Alexandria.[29] Since they had set an example of charity, some influential fathers often led rich people to follow this example.[30]

Palladios, the historian of early Eastern monasticism, relates that the sons of a very rich businessman named Spanodromos distributed their inheritance to charities. One of them offered his wealth to monastic establishments, churches, and prisons while the second founded a monastic center which became an asylum for the stranger, the sick, the poor, and the elderly.[31] A priest named Philoromos from Galatia, Asia Minor, who had earned two hundred and fifty nomismata by his own manual labor, donated all his savings to the lepers.[32]

In the monastic community of Oxyrhynchos in Egypt foreigners and wayfarers were received well, and a cordial hospitality was extended to all. The officials of the city placed guards at the gates in order to lead in all strangers in need of food and shelter.[33]

The motive governing the charitable work of the monks and the church fathers was always emulation of the example of the

26. "Life of Hypatios, Archbishop of Gangra," Ioannou, «Μνημεῖα», p. 256; cf. Palladios, *Hist. Lausiaca*, pp. 38, 109–10.

27. Schwartz, *Kyrillos*, p. 14.

28. Timothy of Alexandria, *Historia Monachorum*, pp. 34, 58–59 *et passim*.

29. *Ibid.*, pp. 114–15.

30. *Ibid.*, p. 131.

31. Palladios, *Hist. Lausiaca*, p. 38: "ὁ μὲν γὰρ πάντα διασκορπίσας ἀ- σκητηρίοις καὶ ἐκκλησίαις καὶ φυλακαῖς, . . . ὁ δ' ἄλλος . . . ποιήσας ἑαυ- τῷ μοναστήριον . . . πάντα ξένον ἐδεξιοῦτο, πάντα ἄρρωστον, πάντα γέ- ροντα, πάντα πένητα, κατὰ κυριακὴν καὶ σάββατον τρεῖς τραπέζας ἱστῶν· οὕτως αὐτοῦ κατηνάλωσε τὰ χρήματα."

32. *Ibid.*, p. 133.

33. Timothy, *Historia Monachorum*, p. 42; cf. p. 106.

Lord.[34] Some monks went so far in their zeal to serve their needy fellow man that they were forced to steal in order to give to the poor! Innocent, a priest from the Monastery of Elaeon in Jerusalem, was such a man.[35]

We often read in hagiographical texts that the words of Christ, "Come, o blessed of my Father, inherit the kingdom . . . for I was hungry and you gave me food . . . I was a stranger and you welcomed me, . . . "[36] exerted a telling influence upon many Byzantines, clergymen and laymen alike, who proved themselves humanitarian.[37]

The influence of Byzantine monks upon the life of their state is well known. In the social realm we learn that some outstanding figures of the monastic world were the spokesmen for the poor, and for the lower masses in general. The biographer of St. Hypatios relates that the poor in Thrace suffered greatly during the first half of the fifth century. The hegoumenos of the monastery in Halmyrissos,[38] Thrace, made a special trip to Constantinople to plead with the authorities on behalf of the poor. His appeals did not fall upon deaf ears. Not only the official government but rich individuals as well sent him sufficient "wheat and beans" for distribution to the poor.[39] This monastery was apparently celebrated for its humanitarian work among those in want.[40]

In addition to the poor, the persecuted individual, the orphan, the naked, and especially the sick found a good shelter in this monastery. The monk Hypatios, familiar with the art of Hippocrates, became a symbol for many people. He treated various patients suffering from sores of some sort (perhaps leprosy) who, because they were poor, had been refused treatment by other physicians. No poor person left the monastery with empty

34. Schwartz, *Kyrillos*, p. 139.
35. Palladios, *Hist. Lausiaca*, p. 131.
36. Matt. 25:34–37.
37. Cf. Callinicos, *De Vita S Hypatii Liber*, pp. 13–14.
38. *Ibid.*, p. 17.
39. *Ibid.*, p. 16: "ὃ δὲ κύρις Ἰωνᾶς εἰσερχόμενος ἐν τῇ μεγαλοπόλει ἔλεγεν τοῖς ἰλλουστρίοις μετὰ παρρησίας· πεινῶσιν οἱ πτωχοὶ παιδευθέντες ἐν τῇ Θρᾴκῃ καὶ ὀχλοῦσί μοι. Ἀποστείλατε αὐτοῖς ἀναλώματα. Ἐκεῖνοι δὲ ἀκούοντες . . . καὶ οἱ λοιποὶ τῶν μεγάλων . . . πλοῖα γεμίζοντες σίτου καὶ ὀσπρίων ἔπεμπον αὐτῷ, ἵνα διαδώσῃ αὐτοῖς."
40. Cf. *ibid.*, pp. 23, 24–25, 30–32, 34, 65, 72.

hands.[41] Hypatios' slogan was the biblical passage: "A man's almsgiving is like a signet with him." [42] Hypatios continued his humanitarian work when he moved to Bithynia, where he organized his own monastic community.[43] His major preoccupations were the needs of the sick, the stranger, and the poor.[44] This *vita* demonstrates once again that the monasteries were the refuge of the persecuted, the sick, and the underprivileged.[45]

Another illustration from a hagiographical text indicates the spontaneous and altruistic hospitality among the Byzantines, men of the cloth as well as laymen. An unknown author relates that during the reign of Justin I (518–27) the Abbot Daniel of the great Scete in Constantinople visited Thebais in Egypt with one of his disciples. They had no lodging for the evening; suddenly, Eulogios, a layman of advanced age and a woodcutter by trade, approached them holding a lantern. He was searching the streets of the town for strangers, to extend hospitality to them. Eulogios led Daniel and his companion to his house, where he washed their feet and offered them food and shelter for the evening.[46] He practiced this kind of hospitality for several years.[47]

We read often in hagiographical narratives that parents of pious monks, laymen, or clergymen who distinguished themselves in works of charity, were themselves humanitarian. St. Martha (+551), the mother of St. Symeon Stylites the Younger (+592) may serve as a typical example. Martha carried on extensive charitable work in her native town of Edessa in Syria.[48] She distributed clothes and bedding to peasant families [49] who apparently were visiting Edessa. She attended the sick, fed the hungry, and helped all those in need of assistance.[50] She imitated

41. Callinicos, *Vita S Hypatii*, p. 36: "πολλοὺς γάρ, οὕσπερ οἱ ἰατροὶ ἀπηγόρευσαν ὡς μὴ δυναμένους θεραπείας τυχεῖν διὰ τὸ εἶναι πένητας, καὶ οἷς ἄλλος οὐκ ἠδύνατο πλησιάσαι διὰ τὴν δυσωδίαν, αὐτὸς ταῖς ἰδίαις χερσὶν ἀπονίπτων τοὺς ἰχῶρας ἐπεμελεῖτο." Cf. pp. 56, 57; for the method of treatment see pp. 36–37.
42. Sirach 17:22.
43. Callinicos, *Vita S Hypatii*, p. 96.
44. *Ibid.*, p. 103.
45. *Ibid.*, pp. 25–26 *et passim.*
46. M. Leo Clugnet, "Vie et récits de l'Abbé Daniel de Scété," p. 255.
47. *Ibid.*, p. 256.
48. "Vita S Symeone Stylita," AASS, May, V (Paris and Rome, 1866), 311A.
49. "Vita S Martha," AASS, p. 400E.
50. *Ibid.*, pp. 401, 403 *et passim.*

the "unmeasurable philanthropia of God" and counseled her son to follow her example. In particular she advised him to be "a father to the orphans and a 'husband' to their mothers." [51]

Compassion toward the poor was an element of education among Byzantine families of later centuries as well. St. Eudocimos, for example, who lived during the reign of Theophilos (829–42) and came from a rich Cappadocian family, was nurtured to respect God, to love man, and to be generous to the poor. [52] His family background and education helped him to be generous to the poor who came to him. He also went out seeking poor families, orphans, and widows to whom he offered his humanitarian services. [53]

Nicon (+998) had received similar advice from his father, who admonished him to be a friend to the poor and to strangers. [54] Later this advice became Nicon's social gospel. He counseled his followers to look after the orphans, the widows, the poor, and the persecuted, and to extend hospitality to strangers and wayfarers. [55] We learn that also among the beneficiaries of Byzantine philanthropies were students. Nicetas the Paphlagonian, [56] the biographer of Patriarch Ignatios (847–58, 867–77), was an intelligent and well-educated man who became an anchorite in Pontos, and distributed his possessions to students and to the poor. [57]

The surname *eleemon* or *eleemosynary* was not restricted to John, the famous Patriarch of Alexandria whose humanitarian and philanthropic work has been mentioned before. St. Philaretos (+792) was given the same title for his extensive philanthropic works. We learn that Philaretos, a native of Pontos, was very rich; [58] his wealth consisted of many hundreds of cows, bulls,

51. *Ibid.*, pp. 407AC; cf. pp. 405, 406F, 407B, 425 *et passim*.
52. "Vita S Eudocimos," ed. Ch. M. Loparev, BIARC, XIII (1908), 201.
53. *Ibid.*, pp. 205–06, 212.
54. "Vita S. Nicon," Lampros, NE, III, no. 1 (1906), 143: "πένησι καὶ ξένοις ἀνδράσι κοινωνικὸν εἶναί σε καὶ εὐπρόσιτον."
55. *Ibid.*, p. 182: "ὦ τέκνα, τῆς φιλοξενίας μὴ ἐπιλανθάνεσθε· πτωχὸν καὶ γυμνὸν μὴ ὑπερίδητε· ἀρρώστους μὴ ὀκνεῖτε ἐπισκέπτεσθαι, πένητας κατοικτείρειν, τοῖς ἐν ἀνάγκαις βοηθεῖν ὁπόση δύναμις. Ρύεσθε ἀδικουμένους ἐκ χειρὸς ἀδίκου καὶ παρανόμου. . . . Δεῖ δὲ ὑμᾶς, ἀδελφοί, καὶ χηρῶν προΐστασθαι καὶ ὀρφανοῖς προασπίζεσθαι καὶ πτωχοῖς ἀεὶ ἐπαρκεῖν . . . πρὸς τοὺς οἰκέτας ἐπιεικῶς διακεῖσθαι καὶ φιλανθρώπως."
56. Beck, *Kirche und Theologische Literatur*, p. 548.
57. "Vita Euthymii," ed. de Boor, p. 56.
58. Fourmy-Leroy, "S Philarète," pp. 113–14; cf. A. A. Vasiliev, *Zhitie sv. Filareta Milostivago* (Odessa, 1900), p. 17.

horses, and mules, thousands of sheep, many acres of land, and other valuable possessions.[59] His biographer alleges that Philaretos was equally rich in philanthropies.[60] Even in days of poverty he carried on his humanitarian policies. When he moved to Constantinople with his family, as a result of the marriage of his granddaughter to the Emperor Constantine VI (780–97),[61] Philaretos continued his great concern for the poor. Though there seems to be much that is legendary in his *vita*, there is no need to doubt his humanitarian works.

Philaretos, while he was still a wealthy resident of Pontos, instructed his wife and daughters to prepare a great banquet, explaining that he expected "royal visitors." His family took this to mean that the emperor and his wife, together with the imperial court, were to be the guests. But Philaretos had quite different visitors in mind, since his purpose was to emulate the hospitality of Abraham and to apply the Lord's commandment.[62] He went to the agora and invited one hundred cripples, amputees, sick persons, and other destitutes to the festivity. Each visitor not only enjoyed a hearty meal but also received a gift of ten nomismata.[63] But the ladies of the household who had labored to prepare the feast were exceedingly angry.

The saint was no fool in his distribution of charities, however, and knew how to tell those in actual want from the professional beggars.[64] He had set an example for his successors to follow; on his deathbed he counseled his family to continue his humanitarian works and his love for the underprivileged.[65]

Apparently two of his sons followed their father's example. The biographer, Nicetas, who insists that he tells the truth as he had received it through his parents, the benefited poor, and by his own investigation, writes that Philaretos' son Eustathios distributed all his money to the poor, donated his estates to the monastery of St. George in Pontos and became a monk.[66] The

59. Fourmy-Leroy, "S Philarète"; cf. M. Louis Bréhier, "Les Populations rurales au IXe siècle d'après l'hagiographie byzantine," B, I (1924), pp. 177–90.
60. Fourmy-Leroy, "S Philarète," pp. 115, 119, 125.
61. *Ibid.*, p. 143; Theophanes, *Chronographia*, I, 463.
62. Cf. Matt. 25:40.
63. Fourmy-Leroy, "S Philarète," p. 147.
64. *Ibid.*, pp. 149–51.
65. *Ibid.*, pp. 153–55.
66. *Ibid.*, p. 155.

fourth son also followed Eustathios' example.[67] After the death of Philaretos, his wife went back to Pontos where she erected houses for the poor, hospitals, and homes for the aged.[68] There is no doubt that St. Philaretos' life and humanitarian work fully justify his surname, Eleemosynary.

Other philanthropist saints came from families with long histories of humanitarian works. St. Paraskeve and her brother Euthymios, who became a bishop of Madyta in southeastern Thrace, were born into such a family. When their parents died, Paraskeve and Euthymios sold all their possessions and distributed the money to the poor and the amputees.[69] Both of them became monks. Euthymios, as Bishop of Madyta, "added charities upon charities," in addition to his successful ministry in other realms. But it was not only the rich or high ecclesiastical dignitaries who practiced philanthropy; the poor offered their services of love and hospitality when the need arose. We hear that Gregory from Irenopolis, of the region of Decapolis[70] in Asia Minor, on his way to Constantinople was received by a poor family at the Isle of Princes in the Sea of Marmara and was offered their hospitality.[71] Gregory, too, exerted his influence upon individuals to distribute their possessions to the poor and to follow the solitary life.[72]

It was a tradition of the Byzantine Church to elect its bishops from among monks renowned for piety, wisdom, and love for man. Thus we often read that great bishops were great monks before their election. As a layman and a monk, Demetrianos, who later became a bishop in Cyprus, was an outstanding figure in the realm of charity. All people who needed his protection and help found in him hope and consolation, but Demetrianos extended his humanitarian work to include redemption of captives of wars and raids. In the year 911–12 the Arabs seized

67. *Ibid.*, p. 157.
68. *Ibid.*, pp. 165–66; Vasiliev, *Zhitie*, p. 37.
69. "Life of St. Paraskeve the Younger," Papadopoulos-Kerameus, «'Ανάλεκτα», I, 439.
70. Porphyrogenitos, *De Thematibus*, Bk. I, Bekker, (Bonn), p. 36; Ramsay, *Historical Geography*, p. 335.
71. F. Dvornik, *La Vie de Saint Grégoire le Decapolite et les Slaves macedoniens au IXe siècle* (Paris, 1926), p. 54: "ἐπέμενε τῇ Προκοννήσῳ, ξενιζόμενος παρά τινι πένητι. . . ." Cf. Joannou, «Μνημεῖα», p. 139.
72. Dvornik, *Saint Grégoire*, p. 65; cf. p. 59.

Cyprus and inflicted much misery. They took many captives, and burned and plundered.[73] Demetrianos, by then Bishop of Chytri, was among the captives, and was instrumental in the release of his people. His humanitarian work is highly praised by his biographer, who wrote perhaps before 965.[74]

Some Byzantines were so humanitarian that they faced deprivations themselves in order to fulfill the commandment of the Lord, or they encountered the wrath of members of their own families. The husband of St. Maria the Younger (+902) continuously complained that his wife was so liberal in her charities that they faced poverty themselves.[75] Independent of how exaggerated such information may be, there is no reason to doubt the genuine and humanitarian feelings of many Byzantines who believed in their religious commitment. (Similar sacrifices were made by religious people during the German occupation of Greece in 1941–44, of which I have personal knowledge.)

Maria's charitable work was continued by her son Marinos.[76] The religious motive is evident everywhere. Charity should not be a sort of liberality or polite kindness but rather a warm affection and a spontaneous expression of love. St. Luke the Younger (+953) exemplifies this philosophy once more, as a genuine disciple of a philanthropic God.[77] His charities were extended to destitute sailors who suffered shipwreck, and his help was both moral and material. He is praised as generous toward the poor; his life was one of service to them,[78] and he was impartial and humanitarian to all in need.[79]

73. "Life of St. Demetrianos," Grégoire, BZ, XVI (1907), 233: "Πῶς γὰρ ἦν ἀδακρὺ τὴν τοιαύτην παρελθεῖν τραγῳδίαν, ὁρῶντας ὑπὸ ἀνηλεῶν βαρβάρων ἄνδρας μὲν ὡς ἐν μακέλλῳ τοῖς ξίφεσι κατατμηθέντας, γυναῖκας ἁρπαγείσας, νήπια φειδοῦς μὴ τυχόντα, παρθένων αἰδῶ καθυβρισθεῖσαν, νεανίσκους δοριαλώτους γεγενημένους, πάντων τῶν ὑπαρχόντων ἅπαντας γυμνωθέντας, καὶ μηδὲν τῶν αἰχμαλωτισθέντων φιλανθρωπότερον ἔχοντας." Cf. George Hill, *A History of Cyprus*, I (Cambridge, 1940), 294; see also n. 4.

74. Grégoire, BZ, XVI, pp. 227, 231; Hill, *Cyprus*, n. 4.

75. "Life of St. Maria the Younger," Gedeon, «Ἑορτολόγιον», p. 297.

76. *Ibid.*, p. 301.

77. "Life of St. Luke the Younger," ed. E. Martini, AB, XIII (1894), 119: "ὃς οὐδὲ μέχρι καὶ νῦν παύεται ἢ παύσεται τὰ τῶν θαυμάτων ἐνεργῶν φιλανθρώπως, ἅτε φιλανθρώπου Θεοῦ μαθητής τε καὶ θεραπευτὴς γενόμενος. . . ."

78. *Ibid.*, pp. 104–05; cf. pp. 116–17.

79. *Ibid.*, p. 92: "μηδὲν ἀκριβολογούμενος εἰς τὴν εὐποιΐαν, ἀλλὰ . . .

Perhaps we will never know the true role that monastic establishments or individual monks played when famines and pestilences plagued the Empire. Nevertheless, many sources indicate that the headquarters of the local bishop or the local monastic community contributed greatly to the preservation of the poor. Every monastery served at one time or another as a department of welfare. Petros, Bishop of Argos (+920), endeared himself to his people through his extensive philanthropic work.[80] He saved many of the underprivileged in his diocese during a famine (sometime between 875 and 925). Some of his people were taken prisoner by Arab pirates, and others left their homes to seek asylum in the city of Argos. The bishop redeemed many hostages and provided shelter for the homeless.[81] His hymnographer did not overemphasize when he described him as "provider for the starving . . . voluntary redeemer of captives and the poor . . . common hospital to all the sick." [82]

The words of Christ, that it is difficult for a rich man to gain the heavenly kingdom of God,[83] were not forgotten by the Byzantines. A rich man, however, can enter God's kingdom through proper use of his wealth. For the Byzantines the ideal social status was the middle. On the one hand, as people not excessively rich, they were not on the verge of losing paradise; on the other, their modest possessions enabled them to contribute to charities, which would open to them the gates of Heaven. This mentality was expressed by the biographer of the brothers David, Symeon, and George. He relates that the brother-saints were born to a middle-class family. Their parents, Adrianos and Constanto, were sufficiently rich to help the poor but not excessively rich, a situation that would have endangered their salvation.[84]

The monastery of Lesbos, where the three brothers passed their lives (10th century), had become a ministry of welfare

κοινὸν πᾶσι προτιθεὶς τὸ φιλάνθρωπον." Cf. Doukakis, «Συναξαριστής», February, p. 124 *et passim.*
80. "Life of St. Petros," ed. Christos Papaoeconomou, «Ὁ Πολιοῦχος τοῦ Ἄργους Ἅγιος Πέτρος» (Athens, 1908), pp. 65–66.
81. *Ibid.,* pp. 66–68.
82. *Ibid.,* p. 175: "λιμοκτονούντων τροφεὺς ἑτοιμότατος . . . ῥύστα αὐτεπάγγελτε αἰχμαλώτων καὶ πτωχῶν . . . τῶν ἀσθενῶν κοινὸν καταφύγιον. . . ."
83. Matt. 19:23; cf. Mark 10:23–24; Luke 18:24.
84. "Acta Graeca SS. Davidis, Symeonis et Georgii Mitylenae in insula Lesbo," AB, XVIII (1899), 213.

activity, especially in times of famine. The three brothers followed the humanitarian tradition of their parents and personified the hope of the poor on their island.[85]

The philanthropic work of monasteries and individual monks was not limited to distribution of foodstuffs. Some monks were instrumental in the erection of hospitals and other welfare institutions.[86] Even isolated monasteries included hospitals and hospices for visiting or transient laymen. St. Athanasios the Athonite (+1004) constructed a hospital, a hostel, and a bathing house for the needs of the visitors and travelers who fell sick while on Mount Athos.[87]

In addition to these three institutions near the monastery, Athanasios had founded other houses of hospitality in the port city of Mount Athos which are described as *katagogia*,[88] the ancient term for xenones.

Athanasios extended his humane and civilizing activities to a previously unapproachable area and made the passage of pilgrims safe. He even built a port in a neighboring area which had lacked one. Shipwrecked sailors found a serene shelter in the monastic community of Athanasios.[89]

We may safely assume that all monasteries had special houses for hospitality. In the following chapter we shall have more to say about the xenones. In passing we may note that such institutions were attached to monasteries which existed even within the city of Constantinople. They were available to monks and laymen alike. When Symeon the New Theologian (+1022) [90] visited the Monastery of Stoudios in Constantinople, he was

85. *Ibid.*, pp. 224–25, 240–41.

86. "Life of St. Euthymios the Younger," Doukakis, «Συναξαριστής», May, p. 219.

87. "Life of St. Athanasios the Athonite," Petit, AB, XXV (1906), 35, 82; for Athanasius' life see also Paul Lemerle, "La Vie ancienne de saint Athanase l'Athonite composée au début du XIe siècle par Athanase de Lavra," *Le Millénaire du Mont Athos*, I (Editions de Chevetogne [1963]), 59–100.

88. "Life of St. Athanasios," Petit, AB, XXV, p. 36: "τῶν τε ἐν τῷ λιμένι καταγωγίων καὶ τῶν λοιπῶν αὐτουργημάτων αὐτοῦ, οὐκ ἔστι δυνατὸν διηγεῖσθαι· ἱστορίας γὰρ ἔργον τοῦτο καὶ οὐχὶ βίου διήγησις."

89. *Ibid.*, p. 47; cf. pp. 52–53, 63–64, 66 *et passim.*

90. Hans-Georg Beck, "Symeon der Theologe," BZ, XLVI (1953), 57 ff., for Symeon's writings and a different view on his name see Basil Krivocheine, "The Writings of St. Symeon the New Theologian," OCP, XX, nos. 3–4 (1954), pp. 298 ff. and 315 ff.

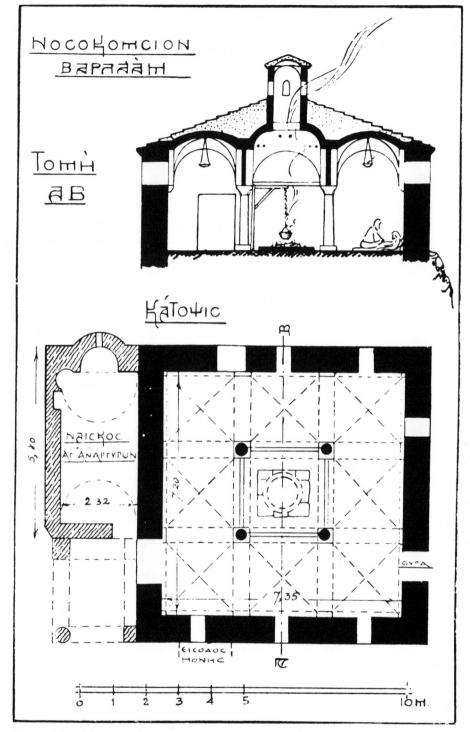

Figure 10. Hospital of Barlaam Monastery, Meteora, Greece; section and ground plan. Reproduced with permission from A. K. Orlandos, *Monastic Architecture*, p. 51.

Figure 11. Hospital of the Great Meteoron, Greece; exterior before its collapse. Photo reproduced with permission from A. K. Orlandos, *Monastic Architecture*, p. 52.

Figure 12. Hospital of the Great Meteoron, Greece; the *tetrakionion* whic. supported the central dome. Photo an reconstruction drawing reproduced wit permission from A. K. Orlandos, *Monastic Architecture*, p. 54.

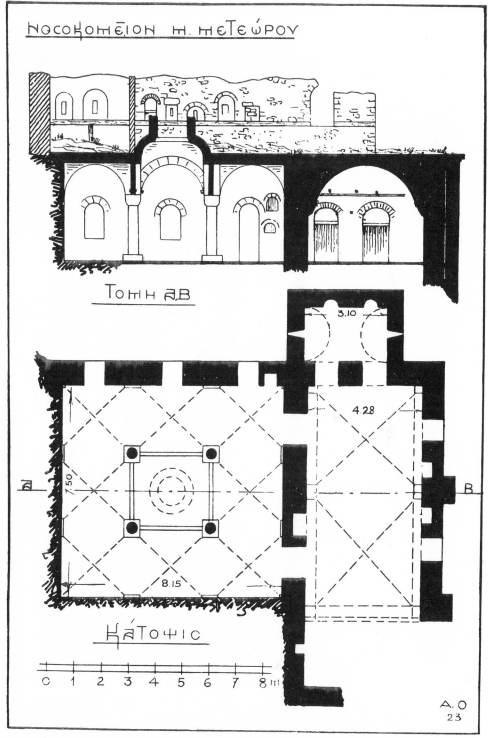

Figure 13. Hospital of a Meteora monastery; section and ground plan. Reproduced with permission from A. K. Orlandos, *Monastic Architecture*, p. 50.

assigned to the *xenia* or hospice because no cell was available.[91]

While some monastic communities were highly praised for their humanitarian work, evidence indicates that some had failed in their mission; as a consequence it took courageous men to bring them back to moral and religious order. The Monastery of St. Mamas, for example, was described as a worldly place.[92] When Symeon the New Theologian became its hegoumenos, he brought new life to it and made the monastery a center of humanitarian activity. Symeon was so generous in his charities that Stephanos, the syncellos of Patriarch Sergios II (1001–19), accused the abbot of abusing the treasury of the monastery. Stephanos asked the Patriarch to investigate Symeon's administration because of his "most abundant distribution of money to the poor." [93]

It was not unusual for a Byzantine lady to renounce the world and join a monastic community. A certain Irene who came from a socially prominent family donated her jewelry to churches and distributed her possessions to the poor,[94] after which she became the abbess of the Monastery of Chrysobalandon.[95] As the hegoumene, she continued her humanitarian work because she felt that a person who has experienced the philanthropia of God should reciprocate it to his fellow man.[96]

St. Thomais of Lesbos, whose *vita* was written between 959 and 963,[97] had no opportunity to join a convent because her parents married her against her will. Nevertheless, her anonymous biographer relates, her life was dedicated to God and her fellow man. She was so generous to the poor and needy that her husband was forced to punish her.[98] Thomais, like so many before and after her, believed that charity to the poor meant service to

91. Nicetas Stethatos, *Life of St. Symeon the New Theologian*, ed. by Irene Hausherr, "Vie de Symeon le Nouveau Théologien," *Orientalia Christiana*, XII, No. 45 (July-August, 1928), 18.

92. *Ibid.*, p. 46: "οὐχὶ μοναστῶν καταγώγιον ἢ ποίμνιον . . . ἀλλὰ κατάλυμα κοσμικῶν καὶ νεκρῶν σωμάτων πολυάνδριον."

93. *Ibid.*, p. 134: "τὴν εἰς τοὺς πένητας ἀφθονωτάτην τῶν χρημάτων διάδοσιν."

94. "Vita S Irene," AASS, July, VI (1868), 605.

95. Janin, *Géogr. Eccles.*, p. 555.

96. *Ibid.*, p. 612: a nun, "ἐλεηθεῖσα γὰρ ὑπὸ Θεοῦ, πάντας ἐλεεῖ, καὶ πᾶσι φιλανθρώπως συμπαθεῖ. . . ."

97. Beck, *Kirche und Theologische*, p. 566.

98. "Vita S Thomaidis," ed. H. Delehaye and P. Peeters, AASS, November, IV (1925), 236.

Christic.[99] Thus she not only wove clothing with her own hands in order to clothe the poor, but she defied the orders of her wealthy husband and continued her humanitarian work.[100] Her reputation as a philanthropist survived down to the thirteenth century, when Constantine Acropolites wrote a *laudation* praising the charities of Thomais.[101]

Among the outstanding figures of Byzantine monasticism who distinguished themselves in general humanitarian works, we may include also St. Michael Maleinos (+961). Michael inherited much wealth from his parents, including several servants or slaves. Riches did not spoil Michael; he freed his slaves, distributed his possessions to the poor and to institutions, and took up monastic vows.[102] Wherever he settled he continued his humanitarian concern for the underprivileged.[103]

Sometimes a monk jeopardized his reputation or even his life in order to support justice or a persecuted individual who had lost favor with the authorities. St. Paul the Younger (10th century) exerted his influence to save the life of a protospatharios named Michael.

The biographer of St. Paul narrates that Michael was entrusted with the *pronoia* of the imperial estates in the region of Mount Latros [104] or Latmos,[105] near Heracleia, during the reign of Constantine Porphyrogenitos. The Mavroi, neighbors of Michael's pronoia, were unjust and invaded Michael's estates, inflicting calamities upon the poor workers on the estates. Michael had some of the Mavroi killed and as a result was condemned to

99. "Vita S Thomaidis," *ibid.*, p. 236: "πάντα ποιοῦσαν καὶ πράττουσαν πρὸς θεραπείαν Χριστοῦ. . . ."

100. *Ibid.*, pp. 237–39.

101. Constantine Acropolites, "Laudatio S Thomaidis," ed. Delehaye and Peeters, *ibid.*, pp. 242–43: "Πένησι τὸν βίον μεριζομένη ἢ μᾶλλον ἀφειδῶς ἐξαντλοῦσα καὶ μεγαλοψύχως ἄγαν σκορπίζουσα."

102. "Vie de Saint Michel Maleinos," Louis Petit, ed., ROC, VII, no. 4 (1902), 557–58: "ἐντεῦθεν ὁ . . . Μιχαὴλ τὰ ἐκ γονικοῦ κλήρου περιελθόντα παρειληφώς, τοὺς μὲν οἰκέτας ἐλευθερίᾳ τετίμηκε λεγάτα προσεπιδούς, τὰ δὲ κινητὰ πάντα διένειμε τοῖς πτωχοῖς, καὶ ἦν ἰδεῖν πρᾶγμα θαύματος ἄξιον, ἀγέλας βοσκημάτων καὶ παντοίων εἰδῶν ἄπειρον πλῆθος ἀφειδῶς ὑπ' ἐκείνου εἰς τὰς τῶν πενήτων χεῖρας διαδιδόμενα καὶ πρὸς τὰ ἄσυλα ταμεῖα τῆς ἐκεῖθεν μακαριότητος προπεμπόμενα. . . ."

103. *Ibid.*, p. 561.

104. "Vita S Pauli Junioris in Monte Latro," Jacob Sirmond, ed., AB, XI (1892), 17.

105. Ramsay, *Historical Geography*, p. 134.

death by the court. However, the righteous testimony of the neighboring Paul saved Michael's life.[106] Nor was this the only manifestation of Paul's sense for justice. In the area of Heracleia where his monastery was founded, he was the spokesman for the poor, and his humanitarian work among them defies narration. "He was greatly philanthropos." [107] His monastery also included houses for hospitality to monks and laymen alike.[108]

In addition to the poor in general, who enjoyed the philanthropies of the monks, we hear that patients suffering from incurable diseases such as leprosy attracted not only the sympathy but the services of Byzantine monastics.[109] The monks were instructed to pursue "every good work," [110] and it was perhaps the apogee of monastic virtues for a monk to be *philanthropos, philadelphos,* and *philoxenos.*[111]

In the person of Cyril Phileotes (+1110) we find an individual who incorporates many of the good attributes of a Byzantine monk. He practiced humanitarian works, preached social justice, became the advocate of the rights of the poor, and refuted the greediness and the exploitation of the rich oligarchy. Because of his many philanthropies Cyril too was surnamed "eleemosynary" like other churchmen before him.[112] Unlike others before him, Cyril distributed not only money and foodstuffs to the poor, but added agricultural machinery to his charities. A poor farmer needed more than charity; he required equipment to cultivate his land. Thus Cyril was careful to whom he gave. He believed that philanthropies should be distributed to deserving individuals.[113] To the deserving cases Cyril was very generous, and he

106. "Vita S Pauli Junioris," ed. Sirmond, AB, XI, pp. 138–39.
107. *Ibid.,* p. 176: "φιλάνθρωπος ἄγαν καὶ εὐμενὴς ὁ ὅσιος."
108. *Ibid.,* pp. 154–55, 157–58, 165.
109. Cf. "Vita S Eudocimus," ed. Loparev, BIARC, XIII, pp. 206, 212; "Vita et Acta S Macarii Hegumeni Monasterii Pelecetes," ed. J. Van Den Gheyn, AB, XVI (1897), 148; Kataskepenos, *Cyril Phileotes,* pp. 74, 76 *et al.*
110. "Regula edita a Sancto Christodulo promonasterio Sancti Joannis Theologi, . . ." Miklosich-Muller, *Acta et Diplomata,* VI, pp. 72, 77–78.
111. "Vie de S Luc le Stylite," Albert Vogt, ed., AB, XXVIII (1909), 19; cf. pp. 20, 21, 28; C. Van de Vorst, ed., "La Vie de S Evariste Higoumene à Constantinople," AB, XLI (1923), 313 ff.; Georgios Monachos, "Vita S Lazari," AASS, November, III (1910), 510, 517, 562; Papadopoulos-Kerameus, *Varia,* p. 148.
112. Gedeon, «'Εορτολόγιον», p. 308; Kataskepenos, *Cyril Phileotes,* p. 78.
113. Kataskepenos, pp. 76–77; cf. Gedeon, pp. 310–11; Chr. Loparev, "Zhitie sv Kirilla Fileota," VV, IV (1897), 384.

even worked himself in order to contribute to their welfare. He made woolen hoods which he distributed to the poor,[114] and exerted his great influence upon others in order to make them help.[115] Even gifts given to him by Anna Dalassena, mother of Alexios Comnenos, Cyril distributed to those in want.[116]

But Cyril expressed his humanitarian concern toward the underprivileged in another way. Kataskepenos relates that Eumathios Philocales, the famous general of Alexios Comnenos and *stratopedarch* of Cyprus,[117] had grown very rich at the expense of the poor whom he had exploited. Apparently his notoriety as an unjust land magnate had reached Cyril. When Eumathios once went to pay his respects to Cyril, the courageous saint unbraided him in harsh terms. Cyril called him a devouring wolf and a tyrannical man who had no mercy for the weak and the sick.[118] He pleaded with him to change his heart and mind. Philocales promised to repent and change his ways toward the poor people who cultivated his estates, but there is no evidence that he did. Cyril had expressed his reservations about such a possibility, declaring that it is easier for an Ethiopian to change the color of his skin than for Philocales to change his ways.[119]

Despite the very bright picture that one discerns in hagiographical texts and in the charters of the monastic communities, there were men of the cloth and monasteries which failed in their vocation and social responsibilities. Eustathios, the eminent Archbishop of Thessalonica, paints a sinister picture of such monks in the twelfth century. He writes that there were monks who were gluttonous, greedy, and inconsiderate of the plight of the poor. Not only did they add wealth upon riches to their monastic communities, but actually devoured "the penny of the widow." [120] They looked for the opportunity to seize the property of the poor or weak whose land adjoined monastery property.[121]

114. Kataskepenos, p. 118.
115. *Ibid.*, p. 126.
116. *Ibid.*, p. 94.
117. Anna Comnena, *Alexiad*, IX. 2, XI. 7, Leib, II, 164; III, 34 *et passim;* cf. V. Laurent, *Les Bulles métriques dans la sigillographie byzantine* (Athens, 1932), No. 147.
118. Kataskepenos, *Cyril Phileotes*, pp. 146, 148.
119. *Ibid.*, pp. 152–53: "πρῶτον οὖν ἀλλάξεται Αἰθίοψ τὸ δέρμα αὐτοῦ . . . καὶ τότε σὺ ὁ μονόλυκος τὴν τρίχα. . . ."
120. Cf. Mark 12:40–42; Luke 20:47.
121. T. L. F. Tafel, *Eustathii Opuscula* (Francofurti ad Moenum, 1832),

While Eustathios is very critical of monastic abuses, he does not fail to praise the charitable work of other monks, and indeed proposed them as models for imitation. Such monks, worthy of their vocation, accumulated provisions and wealth not for themselves but for others. When the need arose they opened their barns to the hungry, offered their money for the redemption of prisoners of war, and contributed to other philanthropic projects.[122] Eustathios appears impartial in both his indictments of monastic abuses as well as in his commendations.[123]

Thus, Byzantine monasticism as an institution unquestionably played a very important role in the realm of social welfare and philanthropy. This aspect of Byzantine monasticism deserves perhaps further investigation. It might throw much more light on an institution badly abused in the hands of Byzantine critics. Even such an austere critic of Byzantine monasticism as the late Alexander Diomedes, of the Academy of Athens, acknowledges that a bright aspect of this important medieval institution of the Christian Greek East was the practice of philanthropia.[124] This statement is, we believe, amply confirmed by the evidence presented above.

pp. 243.87–244.1–9; cf. Ph. I. Koukoules, «Θεσσαλονίκης Εὐσταθίου τὰ Λαογραφικά», I (Athens, 1950), pp. 363–81; Charanis, "Monastic Properties," pp. 85–87.

122. *Ibid.*, p. 222.90: The good monks in Constantinople ''οὐ δαπανῶνται δὲ ἀχρείως εἰς οὐδὲν δέον, ἀλλ' ὅτε καιρὸς καλέσει δαπάνης, ἐξαντλοῦνται τὰ συνηγμένα· ὥστε ἢ ψυχὰς πεινώσας ἐμπλῆσαι ἄρτων, καὶ ἐν ἡμέραις χορτάσαι λιμοῦ, ἢ κατὰ αἰχμαλωσίας ῥυῆναι· ὡς παρασύραι μὲν κακὰ δουλώσεως, ἀποκαταστῆσαι δὲ τοὺς ἠχμαλωτισμένους εἰς τὸ ἐλευθέριον· ἢ ἀντικαταστῆναι χρόνῳ ἐγχανόντι κατὰ τῆς μονῆς, ἢ ἄλλο τι ἐνάρετον καταπράξεσθαι.''

123. Cf. *ibid.*, pp. 234.54–235.46; cf. Charanis, "Monastic Properties," pp. 86–87.

124. Diomedes, «Βυζαντιναὶ Μελέται», pp. 263, 293.

8. Philanthropy and the Byzantine State

In speaking of the Byzantine State we imply here the emperor and his administrative machinery, members of the imperial family, and court dignitaries. However, our designation is conventional and is made for practical purposes. Because it is impractical to treat the reign of every emperor in the present work, we shall limit our investigation to the philanthropies of several representative imperial houses from the fourth to the twelfth centuries.

From the very beginning many Byzantine emperors are credited with much work and legislation in alleviating public and private misery. The Byzantines expected their rulers to practice philanthropia and charity, to apply humane policies, to restrain force, and to show love to their subjects.[1] The emperor should imitate God in beneficent works, for as God governs the world so the king rules the State,[2] and the earthly king should reflect the philanthropic attributes of the heavenly King.[3]

The example of charitable works was set by the founder of

1. Cf. Baynes, *The Byzantine Empire*, p. 70.
2. Eusebios, «Εἰς Κωνσταντῖνον Τριακονταετηρικός», I, ed. Heikel, 199: "Τῆς ἀνωτάτω βασιλείας τὴν εἰκόνα φέρων ὁ τῷ Θεῷ φίλος βασιλεὺς κατὰ μίμησιν τοῦ κρείττονος τῶν ἐπὶ γῆς ἀπάντων τοὺς οἴακας διακυβερνῶν ἰθύνει."
3. *Ibid.*, p. 5: "ἦν δὴ βασιλεύς . . . πράξεσί τε βασιλικαῖς τὴν τοῦ κρείττονος ζηλῶν φιλανθρωπίαν."

111

the Christian Roman Empire, Constantine the Great. Eusebios of Caesarea writes that Constantine contributed funds to the churches to be used exclusively for their charities toward "the poor, the orphans, and destitute women." [4] Constantine also erected houses for the poor, homes for the aged, and other institutions.[5] His mother, the Empress Helen, also initiated several philanthropic projects to effect betterment in the life of the poor.[6]

Later in the fourth century the Empress Flacilla, the wife of Theodosios the Great, was especially compassionate toward lepers. Theodoretos of Cyrus relates that the empress visited patients in their houses and that she even nursed them and supplied all their needs. Her philanthropic interests were extended to the hospitals and hospices, several of which she repaired. Visiting the patients was one of her most honorable preoccupations. She offered these services as a gratitude to God who had invested her with the imperial dignity.[7]

Eudocia, the wife of the Emperor Theodosios II, also took an active part in charities. She was instrumental in the erection of several philanthropic institutions, such as hospitals, houses for strangers, gerocomeia, and the like, which she endowed lavishly.[8] She erected a number of them when she visited Jerusalem, circa 443 or 449.[9]

During the fifth century we find that measures were taken to help the poor in diverse ways. In Anastasios' reign there was a legal provision that the poor might be buried free of charge. The same emperor granted to the Church of Hagia Sophia eleven hundred workshops, whose revenue was used for charities. This grant was legalized by Justinian.[10]

The empresses, as one might have expected, occupied them-

4. Eusebios, *De Vita Constantini*, IV. 28, ed. Heikel, p. 128.

5. Ignatios of Selybria, "Βίος ἁγίου Κωνσταντίνου," Ioannou, «Μνημεῖα», p. 213.

6. Eusebios, p. 96.

7. Theodoretos of Cyrus, *Eccl. History*, V. 19, 314.

8. Nicephoros Callistos Xanthopoulos, *Ecclesiastical History*, Bk. XIV. 50, MPG, CXLVI, col. 1240B.

9. Ernst Stein-J. R. Palanque, *Histoire du Bas-Empire*, II (Paris, 1949), 214, n. 1; 215.

10. Justinian, *Novel 43*, Prooimion.

selves with charities more often than did their husbands.[11] Thus the wife of Justin I is credited with many charities. Among other works, she redeemed the debts of many poor people by paying for them herself.[12] We hear that the Emperor Justinian was frugal in his expenses for receptions and holidays in order to help the afflicted and impoverished victims of the several earthquakes which took place during his reign.[13] However, not only in times of tribulation but also on occasions of happiness Justinian was accustomed to exhibit charitable policies. When Hagia Sophia was completed, he distributed to the poor and needy up to thirty thousand *modia* of wheat.[14] Furthermore, Justinian maintained the free distribution of bread to the poor, forbidding it to be sold. The rights of the poor generally were guarded by special legislation.[15]

Members of the imperial administration were also great philanthropists. Agathias cites that during Justinian's reign prominent people visited the poor and the victims of a destructive earthquake, distributing food and clothes.[16] We know of a certain Theodore, "the most glorious copyist," nephew of John Hesychastes, Bishop of Coloneia in Asia Minor, who served the reigns of Zeno and Anastasios in several capacities, who initiated many humanitarian works. His charities and compassion for the underprivileged caused him to be admired by both the Senate and Justinian himself.[17]

The sources provide much more information about the charities and philanthropic concerns of the emperors and members of the imperial court of later centuries. Through legislation, the churches enjoyed privileges permitting them to maintain orphan-

11. See Plato Rodocanakes, «Ἡ Βασίλισσα καὶ αἱ Βυζαντιναὶ Ἀρχόντισσαι» (Athens, 1920), pp. 107–16.

12. Theophanes, *Chronographia*, I, 242.

13. George Cedrenos, *Synopsis Historion*, ed. B. G. Niebuhr, CSHB, I (Bonn, 1838), 675.

14. Pseudo-Codinos, *Patria*, Th. Preger, I, 104.

15. Cf. Justinian, *Novel 7; Chronicon Paschale*, p. 711. For the policy of the State toward the poor in the age of Justinian see my introductory article: "Philanthropia in the Age of Justinian," *GOThR*, VI, no. 2 (Winter, 1960–61), 206–26.

16. Agathias, *Epigrammata*, CSHB (Bonn, 1828), p. 288.

17. Schwartz, *Kyrillos*, p. 203.

ages, houses for the poor, and institutions for the aged and for strangers, and to continue their distributions of food and clothes to the poor. Laws were especially favorable to orphans. In addition to legislation guarding their rights,[18] the Isaurian Emperors Leo III and Constantine V emphasized that the law was also to guard the poor, and indicated that no exception would be made in favor of the powerful and the rich. The charitable institutions, churches, and dioceses were asked to extend protection to strangers and above all to orphans.[19]

Despite the adulatory character of many of our sources, there must have been much truth in their recitals of the public or private charities of the State. Even emperors who did not fare well in the accounts of contemporary chroniclers and historians are given credit when credit was due them. Genesios, for example, commended Leo V (813–20) for his sense of justice, his social consciousness, and his philanthropic activities.[20] In the ninth century the Emperor Theophilos and his wife Theodora are given much credit for their charities.[21]

Despite his iconoclastic policies, Theophilos was popular among many of his subjects for his sense of justice and his humanitarian approach to the needs of the populace. He is praised by his contemporaries as a good servant,[22] and J. B. Bury comments that Theophilos "had a passion for justice." [23] In his administration of justice Theophilos, who often presided over the imperial court of appeals, spared no persons, including individuals of his own immediate family. His sense of public duty prompted him to ride through the city once a week, visiting

18. "Ecloga, 7," Zepos-Zepos, *Jus*, II, 35–36, 44.
19. *Ibid.*, pp. 55–56: "Οἱ γὰρ αὐτοὶ εὐαγεῖς οἶκοι καὶ αἱ τοῦ θεοῦ ἐκκλησίαι, οἱ καὶ τῶν ἀλλοτρίων προϊστάμενοι καὶ τοὺς ξένους ὡς ἰδίους . . . ὑποδεχόμενοι, πολλῷ πλέον τὰ τῶν ὀρφανῶν φυλάξουσι καί . . . ἀποκατάστασιν ποιήσουσιν." Cf. p. 58.
20. Genesios, *Regum*, pp. 17–18: "Οὗτος ὁ Λέων ὁ βασιλεύς, κἂν δυσσεβής, ἀλλὰ τῶν δημοσίων πραγμάτων ἦν ἀντιληπτικώτατος, ὡς μηδὲν τῶν ὀνησιφόρων παραλιμπάνειν ἀπρόοπτον . . . πρὸς τούτοις καὶ τοῖς ἀδικοῦσι δικαίως ἐπαχθὴς ἦν. . . ." Cf. Continuatus, *Chronographia*, p. 30.
21. Regel, *Analecta*, p. 40; "Acta Graeca SS Davidis, Symeonis et Georgii Mitylenae in insula Lesbo," AB, XVIII (1899), 244.
22. George Monachos, ed. Muralt, pp. 793, 803; Genesios, 75; Theophanes Continuatus, 87–88; cf. Nicetas, *Vita Ignatii*, p. 216, who describes Theophilos as good, apart from his iconoclastic views.
23. Bury, *A History of the Eastern Roman Empire*, p. 120.

bazaars, examining the merchandise, asking the prices, and listening to the complaints and petitions of his people.²⁴

Theodora, in particular, after she was relieved of her imperial duties, dedicated herself to beneficent works.²⁵

Basil I, the founder of the Macedonian dynasty, was educated to have compassion toward the poor,²⁶ a teaching which he applied during his reign. He erected in Constantinople and in the provinces more than one hundred structures for the poor, hospitals, xenones, and other welfare institutions.²⁷

It is not irrelevant to cite here that the humanitarian concern of the imperial families in Byzantium is indicated by the fact that poor people and orphans were invited to dine with the imperial family on certain holidays of the year.²⁸

Theophano, the wife of Leo VI the Wise, was proclaimed a saint, perhaps for her immense compassion, forbearance, and prayers, but also for her innumerable charities to all the needy.²⁹ She was taught the value of eleemosyne from childhood, and considered the poor as brethren.³⁰ Though she was a queen she did not live like one. She was not only ascetic in her way of life, but was deeply concerned for those who were hungry and in want. Her biographer alleges that whatever money and objects of value came into her possession she distributed to the poor, the widows, and the orphans.³¹ Theophano established also a number of houses for the poor, hospitals, and similar institutions, which she endowed bountifully.³²

24. For some detailed accounts of Theophilos' social consciousness, see Bury, *ibid.*, pp. 120–25.
25. "Βίος καὶ συνεγκώμιον τῆς μακαρίας καὶ ἁγίας Θεοδώρας τῆς βασιλίδος," ed. Regel, *Analecta*, pp. 16–17; "Acta Graeca SS Davidis, Symeonis et Georgii, . . ." AB, XVIII, pp. 251–52.
26. Theophanes Continuatus, *Chronographia*, p. 220.
27. *Ibid.*, pp. 339–340.
28. Philotheos, *Kletorologion*, pp. 157, 158, 163.
29. Symeon Magister, *Chronographia*, p. 702.
30. "Βίος καὶ Πολιτεία τῆς ἁγίας . . . Θεοφανώ," ed. Eduard Kurtz, "Zwei griechische Texte uber die hl Theophano, die Gemahlin Kaisers Leo VI," *Memoires de l'academie imperiale des sciences de St. Petersbourg*, III, no. 2 (St. Petersburg, 1898), 4.
31. *Ibid.*, p. 14: "τὰ δὲ ἐν ταῖς χερσὶν αὐτῆς παρεμπίπτοντα χρήματα τε καὶ κτήματα, τὰ τίμια τοῖς βιωτικοῖς φαντάσματα, τοῖς πένησι διεδίδου. Τῶν δὲ πέπλων τὰ πολυτίμητα εἴδη τοῖς δεομένοις παρεῖχε, χηρῶν δὲ καὶ ὀρφανῶν τὰς αὐταρκείας ἐπεχορήγει. . . ." Cf. p. 15; Nicephoros Gregoras, "Λόγος εἰς τὴν ἁγίαν Θεοφανώ τὴν βασιλίδα," Ch. 6.
32. Gregoras, p. 41; cf. Theophanes Continuatus, *Chronographia*, p. 361.

Leo VI's concern for the philanthropic institutions of Constantinople, such as hospitals, old-age homes, orphanages, homes for travelers and others, prompted him to issue a protective novel, for their welfare and tax-free maintenance.[33] In a previous law Leo had ordered that eleven hundred workshops be given to the Great Church of Hagia Sophia, the revenue from which was to be used for welfare activities.[34] He asserts that he took this action to perpetuate a social philanthropic program which Constantine the Great had initiated and others after him had continued. The welfare charities of Hagia Sophia must have been extensive indeed.

Practically every emperor of the tenth century was engaged in charitable activity. Philanthropy was not only a policy through which an emperor endeared himself to his people, but was also a means by which his soul would receive forgiveness for sins in the life after death.[35] Consequently, imperial charity had a social and political motive as well as a religious one.

Special care was extended by the emperors for the protection of children in general. Constantine Porphyrogenitos records that every Wednesday after Easter orphans were invited to visit the palace, where they were greeted by the emperor himself. Upon their departure the orphans were kissed by the emperor and were given a purse containing money.[36] Perhaps as an indication of the humanitarian concern of the emperors, we find that orphans were brought to and participated in several official celebrations, such as Easter, the Presentation of Christ, and others.[37] Furthermore, through imperial legislation, they were well treated in orphanages and were allowed to remain in the security of the institution until they were ready for marriage.[38]

Even in personal matters the State exercised particular concern to protect the orphans. If one had become engaged by the ill advice of someone or if one regretted the engagement, the law provided that it could be dissolved without any penalty to the orphan.[39]

33. Novel 13; but cf. Gregory Kasimates, " Ἡ Κοινωνικὴ Πολιτικὴ εἰς τὰς Νεαρὰς Λέοντος τοῦ Σοφοῦ," ΕΕΒΣ, XIII (1937), p. 30.
34. Novel 12.
35. Leo VI Wise, *Tactica*, Constitution XIV, 35–36, MPG, CVII, col. 860.
36. Porphyrogenitos, *De Cerimoniis*, I, 82.
37. *Ibid.*, pp. 69, 140; cf., pp. 153, 154.
38. Porphyrogenitos, *Selectum Leges*, MPG, CXIII, col. 513.
39. *Ibid.*, col. 493.

Figure 14. Christ crowning Emperor Constantine VII Porphyrogenitos;
ivory plaque (c. 945; approximately 7$\frac{5}{16}$ × 3$\frac{11}{16}$″). Pushkin Museum of
Fine Arts, Moscow. Reproduced with permission of the Pushkin Museum.
Photo courtesy of the Victoria & Albert Museum, London.

It should be affirmed that every emperor is noted as having performed some philanthropic deed. However, among the outstanding royal figures who occupied themselves in this application are Constantine Porphyrogenitos and Romanos Lecapenos. After the great fire in the neighborhood of the Church of St. Thomas, Porphyrogenitos, "due to his exceeding goodness and his love for his citizens whom he loved as if they were of his own blood [or his own descendants], gave assistance to all and helped for the rebuilding of the houses which had suffered destruction. The people were praising and thanking the Emperor as a second God." [40]

Prisoners were not excluded from philanthropic treatment. Porphyrogenitos took special measures to improve the condition of captives, not only of those who were kept in reformatory institutions within Constantinople, but of those held in prisons of the various Themes. [41] For this principle he was proclaimed a Christ-imitator King. In receptions for foreign dignitaries, the Byzantine emperors often invited to the official dinner prisoners of war of the same nationality as the dignitaries to share in the evening's affair. On such occasions gifts and money were distributed to those prisoners who could not be invited or who could not come to the reception. [42]

Hospitals for lepers received special attention from Porphyrogenitos. He distributed gifts and money to the Zotikon hospital for lepers, which he restored and enlarged for the benefit of many more patients in need of hospitalization. [43] Theophanes Continuatus wrote that Porphyrogenitos not only visited lepers but even applied ointments upon their bodies with his own hands. [44] His philanthropy was extended to the poor and needy by the promulgation of a special novel. [45] Visiting hospitals of all kinds, in particular on every Good Friday, to distribute gifts to the patients [46] was a practice not only of Porphyrogenitos but of every emperor.

Continuatus, who gave us more information about the humanistic policies of the tenth-century emperor, adds that Por-

40. Theophanes Continuatus, *Chronographia*, p. 462.
41. *Ibid.*, p. 447.
42. Porphyrogenitos, *De Cerimoniis*.
43. Theophanes Continuatus, *Chronographia*, p. 449.
44. *Ibid.*
45. Porphyrogenitos, *Novels*, MPG, CXIII, cols. 557–69.
46. Porphyrogenitos, *De Cerimoniis*, I, 168.

phyrogenitos took special care of aged people. He transformed the stables which were built by Patriarch Theophylaktos next to the "Great Church" into an old-age home, and ordered that abundant food and clothing be given annually to the inmates.[47]

The overall philanthropic policy of Porphyrogenitos is evident in his laws directed against the rich landowners exploiting the poor and powerless farmers of the various Themes. Continuatus praises his attitude toward the poor and the legal action against the powerful. Porphyrogenitos, "wise in all," acted through legal means to stop the greediness of the powerful, who had invaded the villages and the countryside of the empire and had accumulated for themselves whole towns by exploiting the unfortunate small landholders.[48]

Romanos Lecapenos seems to have indulged in philanthropic activity much more than any other emperor.[49] Continuatus describes him as compassionate and charitable by nature.[50] His philanthropic policies can be seen in various events of his life. In the year 928 a severely cold winter destroyed the crops and caused a great famine. So many died of hunger that "the living could not bury the dead." The emperor took special measures to protect and improve the barracks of the poor against cold and snow, and ordered that money be given to them. His compassion was so keen that he invited three poor people every day to eat at his table and contributed to each of them one *nomisma*. In addition, every Wednesday and Friday he had dinner with three poor monks.[51]

Continuatus adds that during his twenty-second year as emperor Lecapenos did numerous charitable works.[52] He built special barracks and covered the arches of the embola or porticos where beggars and poor travelers used to spend their evenings.[53]

It was a tradition among the Byzantines to include provisions in their wills for poor individuals and families. They held the belief that their souls' condition would be improved after death

47. Theophanes Continuatus, *Chronographia*, p. 449.
48. *Ibid.*, pp. 447–48.
49. Cf. Steven Runciman, *The Emperor Romanus Lecapenus and His Reign* (Cambridge, 1929), pp. 75, 231.
50. Theophanes Continuatus, *Chronographia*, p. 417.
51. *Ibid.*, pp. 417–18; Symeon Magister, p. 743.
52. Theophanes Continuatus, pp. 429–30.
53. *Ibid.*, pp. 417–18; Magister, pp. 743–44.

ΡΩΜΑΝΟC
ΒΑCΙΛΕΥC
ΡΩΜΑΙΩΝ

ΕΥΔΟΚΙΑ
ΒΑCΙΛΙC
ΡΩΜΑΙΩΝ

Figure 15. Christ crowning Emperor Romanos IV Diogenes and Empress Eudocia; ivory plaque (c. 1068). Cabinet des Médailles, Bibliothèque Nationale, Paris. Photo courtesy of the Bibliothèque Nationale.

if while still living they had contributed to the poor and needy. On this basis Lecapenos ordered that after his death three myriads, or thirty thousand loaves, be distributed to the poor near his grave every day.[54]

Like other emperors before him, Lecapenos extended his philanthropy to prisons and reformatory institutions. He had ordered that every Good Friday a *nomisma* (follis) be given to each prisoner, and fifteen follis be given to each prisoner every day.[55] For the benefit of his soul after death Lecapenos built old-age homes, houses for foreigners, and hospitals for the sick.[56]

In contrast to Romanos Lecapenos, Nicephoros Phocas, though deeply religious and devout, did not build any new philanthropic institutions. He may have been humanitarian in his private life, but in his legislative activity he appears anti-philanthropic. In the year 967 he issued a novel which is an attack upon institutions of mercy.[57]

Nevertheless, this famous novel should not be viewed as anti-philanthropic. Phocas was not against charitable institutions but against the foundation of new ones. He strongly favored restoring the existing ones, which he considered sufficient. Phocas advised those who wished to erect old-age homes, hostels, and the like not to do so, but instead to use the contributions to repair the existing ones and to avoid abuses. Apparently some individuals donated large sums of money to institutions or erected new ones to satisfy their vanity. Thus he counseled that "whatever good we do, let us do it on behalf of God only and not to acquire popularity among the people." [58]

The Phocas novel was revoked by Basil II. Basil considered it not only an injustice and an insult to the philanthropic institutions but a blasphemy against God as well. Certain calamities that occurred following the death of Nicephoros were attributed to Nicephoros' policies towards monasteries and charitable institutions; thus we have the reason for its revocation by his successor.

Despite his intrigues and questionable morality, John Tzimisces

54. Theophanes Continuatus, p. 430; cf. p. 431.
55. *Ibid.;* cf. p. 423, 443.
56. *Ibid.*, pp. 417–19.
57. Rhallis-Potlis, «Σύνταγμα», V, pp. 261 ff.; cf. Charanis, "Monastic Properties," pp. 58 ff.
58. Rhallis-Potlis, pp. 263–64.

did not fall far behind in humanitarian policies. Leo Diaconos informs us that Tzimisces regularly contributed money to hospitals for lepers, and personally visited such well-known institutions as the Zotikon hospital. Together with Leo Diaconos, Continuatus confirms that Tzimisces was not ashamed or afraid to even clean with his own hands the sores of the lepers when he visited them.[59]

Just before his death Tzimisces made many donations to the poor, apparently for the benefit of his soul after death, according to Byzantine religious tradition. He did not spare the imperial treasury in order to contribute to the poor and especially to the lepers, whose bodies were eaten up by the "holy disease." He was inclined to be more philanthropic to them than to any other category of the unfortunate.[60]

As we survey the private lives of eleventh-century emperors, we find that Constantine IX Monomachos stands out because of his charities and philanthropic programs, although others may be similarly credited, such as Romanos Argyros[61] and, later in the century, Nicephoros Botaneiates.[62]

Michael Psellos relates that Constantine Monomachos was surnamed *Evergetis* or benefactor[63] because of his humanitarian personality. Although Monomachos may not have achieved much as an administrator, Psellos alleges that the emperor almost resembled the ideal ruler. In his political philosophy Monomachos was convinced that an emperor ought to exhibit compassionate feeling toward all people and especially toward his subjects. Thus, he considered himself a failure if a day passed without accomplishing some good work for the benefit of his people. He believed that an emperor must be the most philanthropic of all citizens and must set an example for his successors to follow.[64]

59. Leo Diaconos, *Historiae*, ed. C. B. Hasi, CSHB (Bonn, 1828), p. 99; cf. Theophanes Continuatus, p. 449.

60. Leo Diaconos, *Historiae*, pp. 177–78.

61. G. Schlumberger, *L'Epopée Byzantine*, III (Hachette & Cie. [Paris], 1893), pp. 96 ff.

62. Michael Attaliates, «Λόγος προσφωνητικός ... πρός ... τὸν Βοτανειάτην», ed. Immanuel Bekker, CSHB (Bonn, 1853), pp. 3–5.

63. Michael Psellos, *Chronographia*, II, 117: "Κωνσταντῖνος ὁ εὐεργέτης (οὕτω γὰρ παρὰ τοῖς πλείοσι κατωνόμασται), φημὶ δὲ τὸν Μονομάχον."

64. *Ibid.*, p. 71: "οὕτω δὴ τελευτᾷ τὸν βίον πλεῖστα μὲν εὐδοκιμηκὼς ταῖς πολιτικαῖς πράξεσιν, οὐκ ἐλάττω δὲ κἂν τοῖς ἤθεσιν ἀφεὶς παραδείγ-

Psellos adds that Constantine X was also a man of justice and compassion who tried to translate his moral convictions into actions.[65]

The charities of the imperial families and certain dignitaries during the reign of the Comnenian dynasty is an important chapter in Byzantine philanthropy. Evidence indicates that practically all of the imperial families of the late eleventh and twelfth centuries were occupied with philanthropic activity. Alexios I Comnenos is a worthy example. According to his daughter Anna, the Emperor Alexios was a humane and deeply philanthropic person. His humanitarian nature is revealed not only through his establishment of charitable institutions for the poor, the sick, and others in need, but by his personal attitude toward former enemies. It is related that the Celt rebel Ursel, who brought much destruction upon the Byzantine people in Asia,[66] was taken prisoner by Alexios. Alexios did not put him to death, nor did he punish him; on the contrary, he showed him no little "philanthropia." [67]

Alexios' attitude toward his adversary Nicephoros Bryennios, who was taken prisoner, was of the same humane nature. Nicephoros Bryennios, serving as Duke of Dyrrachium, was planning to use his position "as a jumping-off place" to overthrow Michael Ducas and become emperor himself. However, the throne was obtained by Nicephoros Botaniates, and Alexios Comnenos was appointed by the new emperor to overthrow Bryennios. Alexios was victorious and Bryennios was taken prisoner. Anna Comnena adds that "when the rebel Bryennios was turned over to Alexios by his army, Alexios sent him away as the prize of his spear to the Emperor Botaniates, without doing any injury whatsoever to his eyes. For it was not the nature of Alexios to proceed to extremes against his opponents after their capture, as he considered that capture was in itself sufficient punishment, but after their capture he treated them with philan-

ματα τοῖς ἄριστα βιοῦν ἐθέλουσιν . . . ἁπάντων ἀνθρώπων ἐγεγόνει φιλανθρωπότερος." Cf. pp. 53, 54.

65. *Ibid.*, p. 146.

66. Anna Comnena, *Alexias*, I. 1–2; cf. Kataskepenos, *Cyril Phileotes*, pp. 233–34.

67. Anna Comnena, *Alexias*, I. 4; Nicephoros Bryennios, *Historiae*, II. 19; Schlumberger, *Sigillographie*, pp. 660–66.

Figure 16. Christ enthroned between Emperor Constantine IX Mono-machos and Empress Zoë; mosaic panel, south gallery of Hagia Sophia, Istanbul (11th century). Photo courtesy of the Byzantine Institute, Washington, D.C.

Figure 17. Emperor Constantine IX Monomachos; detail from mosaic panel (see Figure 16), south gallery of Hagia Sophia, Istanbul. Photo courtesy of the Byzantine Institute, Washington, D.C.

thropia, friendliness, and liberality. He treated Bryennios with those virtues . . ." [68]

Alexios was philanthropic in his attitude, especially toward captives who were of the Christian faith. Nicephoros Bryennios, the husband of Anna Comnena, remembers that Alexios refused to kill Frankish captives "because it seemed not right to him to kill Christians." [69] The same author describes Alexios as a man "with a generous heart." [70]

Alexios expressed his humane personality by means of various philanthropic institutions and activities of which his daughter speaks with pride, as do Zonaras and others. Anna Comnena, who "swears" that she clings to the truth, says that Alexios was an excellent administrator both in peace and in war. In times of peace Alexios "judged the case of orphans, had justice attributed to widows, and looked very austerely against every case of injustice." [71] Alexios Comnenos' humane character is significantly revealed in his campaign against the Turks of Iconium. "When it was the Emperor's time for lunch he invited the men and women who were laboring under illness or old age and placed the greater part of the provisions before them." [72] This courtesy was extended to citizens of Philomelium who had been rescued by Alexios from the Turks.

When Alexios returned to Constantinople from his expedition against the Turks of Iconium, he occupied himself with the care of the captives and the strangers. "The children who had lost their parents and were afflicted with the bitter evil of orphanhood, he [Alexios Comnenos] distributed among his relations and others who, as he knew, led a well-conducted life, or sent them to the abbots of the holy monasteries with orders to bring them up, not as slaves, but as free children, and to allow them a thorough education and instruction in the Holy Writings. Some he also admitted into the orphanage, most probably to St. Paul's [73] which he had established himself and which he had converted

68. Anna Comnena, *Alexias*, I, VI. 7; English translation derived from Buckler's.
69. Bryennios, *Historiae*, II. 20.
70. *Ibid.*, IV. 15.
71. Anna Comnena, *Alexias*, XIV. 7.
72. *Ibid.*, XV. 7.
73. Anna does not mention the orphanage by name, but cf. Kataskepenos, *Cyril Phileotes*, p. 230.

Figure 18. Alexios, son of John II Comnenos, proclaimed co-Emperor in 1122; mosaic panel, south gallery of Hagia Sophia, Istanbul (first half of the 12th century). Photo courtesy of the Byzantine Institute, Washington, D.C.

more or less into a school for those anxious to learn, and told the governors of it to give these orphans a good general education. For in the quarters near the Acropolis . . . he [Alexios] built up a second city . . . and the new city was laid out in a certain number of states . . . both in length and breadth; and all round in a circle were a number of houses, dwellings for the poor, and what shows his philanthropic nature even more, there were residences for mutilated men. Here you could see them coming along singly, either blind, or lame, or with some other defect. You would have called it Solomon's porch on seeing it full of men maimed either in their limbs or in their whole bodies. This ring of houses is two-storied and semi-detached, for some of these maimed men and women live up above 'twixt earth and sky, while others creep along below on the ground floor. As for its size, anyone who wants to visit them would begin in the morning and only complete the round in the evening. Such is this city and such are its inhabitants. They have no plots of ground or vineyards or any of those things over which we imagine men spend their time, but each man and woman, just like Job, dwells in the house built for him and automatically receives everything for his food and shelter from the imperial hand." [74]

Anna further indicates the philanthropia of the emperor by stating that Alexios himself and his friends worked diligently for the relief of these unfortunate beings. He granted good and productive farms "to these brethren" in order that they might have abundant wine and bread "and all the things men eat with bread." Anna compares her father's philanthropia toward the poor of this new city with the "Savior's miracle" of the feeding of the multitudes. "The divine commandment" was the basis of Alexios' philanthropic activity. [75]

The illustrious princess describes some of the charitable work of the emperor of which she had been a witness: "I myself have seen an old woman tended by a young one and a blind man led by the hand by one who saw, and a man without feet has feet, though not his own but another's, and a man without hands

74. Anna Comnena, *Alexias*, XV. 7; cf. Theophylactos, *Oratio in Imperatorem Dominum Alexium Comnenum*, MPG, CXXVI, col. 298C; cf. col. 304.
75. When Anna refers to the "Savior's miracle" she has in mind Matt. 14:13–21 and Matt. 15:32–3. When she speaks of the "divine commandment" she probably refers to Matt. 25:31–46.

using other men's hands, and babies nursed by other mothers, and paralytics waited upon by strong men." [76] The Emperor "gave servants to every maimed man and the same care to the halt as to the healthy . . . Who could estimate the number of those who were fed daily, or the daily expense, or the care bestowed on each individual? For I attribute to him the things that lasted after him. For he assigned to them benefits from land and sea, and he provided them with as much relief from pain as possible. One of the most prominent men acts as guardian of this populous city, and its name is the Orphanage. And it is called the Orphanage because of the Emperor's kindness to orphans and to men retired from service . . . and the name which came from his care for orphans, held its ground." [77] As Alexander the Great was proud of his Alexandria in Egypt, of Bucephale in Media, and of Lysimadia in Ethiopia, likewise Alexios Comnenos was proud of the towns he had raised. In each new city Alexios would raise not only sanctuaries and monasteries but schools for orphans of every race. [78]

Anna emphasizes that she is revealing the truth, and her approach seems to be objective and analytical of her father's philanthropic policies. "I swear by the dangers the Emperor underwent for the welfare of the Roman Empire, and the struggles and disasters my father suffered on behalf of the Christians, I most certainly do not describe and write of these things in order to favor my father," for "wherever I perceive that my father made a mistake, I unhesitatingly transgress the natural law and cling to the truth, for though I hold him dear, I hold truth dearer still." [79] There is no reason to doubt the sincerity of Anna's testimony about her father's philanthropic activity.

The philanthropia of Alexios Comnenos is mentioned by another historian of the twelfth century. Joannes Zonaras, who held high positions in the imperial administration of John II Comnenos, writes in his *Epitome Historion:* "This King [Alexios Comnenos] renovated the Orphanage which had been unoccupied, and the properties of many old-age homes and new properties as well he gave to the orphanage, and placed in it numer-

76. Anna Comnena, *Alexias,* XV. 7.
77. *Ibid.,* XV. 7.
78. *Ibid.*
79. *Ibid.;* cf. also *Alexias,* XII. 3.

ous old people in need of care and goods for consumption. Furthermore he built within it residences for nuns and monks and a school for orphans or poor children. He placed teachers and educators and provisions for them as well." [80] And Michael Glycas gives similar information. He notes that a particular orphanage which was unoccupied was renovated by Alexios. Like Anna and Gregoras, Glycas agrees that the emperor granted various lands to the institutions and that the emperor added to it a school for the education of the inmates. [81]

This particular institution must have been indeed a very significant one, for it is noticed by another author who pays high honor to Alexios for this orphanage. He writes: "[Alexios Comnenos] reconstructed the benevolent orphanotrophion and kindly gave sufficient means to it, to the effect that it became a safe harbor for many suffering brethren, gathering them into thousands, providing annual rations and the rest which are needed for living. He put up residences for them and guarded them from every affliction. Who can enumerate the things which that reverent soul [person] did for this wonderful and salutary institution?" [82] The author adds a description of some of the sections of this institution, which included a school for orphans and for poor and captive children.

The Empress Irene, the wife of Alexios, was also a philanthropist. Despite her delicate nature, she would accompany Alexios on his frequent expeditions. On one of these Irene took with her gold and coined money, "and throughout the journey she gave with lavish hands to the beggars, the men clad in leather, and the naked; no one who asked of her went away empty-handed. Even when she reached the tent appointed for her, she did not immediately enter and lie down to rest, but threw it open and gave the beggars free access. For to this class she was very accessible, and allowed herself to be both seen and heard by them. And she did not only give money to the poor, but also good advice. If she noticed any of strong physique who led a lazy life, she urged them to find work and employment and earn the necessaries of life in that way, rather than grow lax through

80. Joannes Zonaras, *Epitomae Historiarum*, III, 744–45.
81. Michael Glycas, *Annales*, p. 621.
82. Anonymous, *Synopsis Chronike*, ed. Sathas, «Μεσ. Βιβλιοθήκη», VII, pp. 177–78.

sloth and go about begging from door to door. And no injunction kept the Empress away from such work." [83]

The philanthropic character of the empress is revealed by another conjecture. Michael Anemas, the ringleader of a plot to kill Alexios, was condemned to blindness by having his eyes gouged out. When Irene saw the miserable condition of Michael, who had become a spectacle to the public, she ran to the emperor "shedding bitter tears, and besought him, not once or twice, but repeatedly, to spare Michael's eyes. He [the Emperor] at once dispatched a messenger to stop the executioners . . ." [84] And when John Solomon's house was confiscated and was given to the empress because he was one of the plotters, the empress "with her usual kindness, took pity on Solomon's wife, and gave it back [to Solomon's wife] without taking the slightest thing out of it." [85]

Irene established the monastery of *Kecharitomene,* where she attached various philanthropic houses. In the Typikon Irene advised that on Christmas Day two modia and four nomismata should be given to each suppliant at the gateway of the Monastery. But charity to the poor was practiced every day. Irene insisted that it is necessary to distribute at the gateways bread, wheat, and remnants of the meals of the nuns every day. [86]

The various *mnemosyna* or memorial services which were to be held for the benefit of the soul of her husband and her son John II were to be accompanied with distribution to the poor of wheat, bread, wine, and nomismata. [87] It is important to note that Irene used language similar to that of the fathers Athanasios, Basil, and Theodore Studite, to emphasize the importance of charity. She writes that it was because of "eleemosyne" and "philanthropia" that God became man and through which man becomes God and similar to the heavenly Father. [88]

83. Anna Comnena, *Alexias,* XII. 3.
84. *Ibid.,* XII. 6.
85. *Ibid.*
86. Irene Augusta, "Typikon," Miklosich-Muller, *Acta et Diplomata,* V. 371.
87. *Ibid.,* pp. 374–77.
88. *Ibid.,* pp. 352–53: "καὶ γὰρ καὶ τὴν ὑψοποιὸν ταπείνωσιν συνεζευγμένην ἑαυτῇ δείκνυσι καὶ τὴν ἐλεημοσύνην καὶ τὴν φιλανθρωπίαν, δι' ἃ καὶ μᾶλλον ὁ θεὸς γέγονεν ἄνθρωπος καὶ ἃ καλεῖται ὁ θεὸς καὶ δι' ὧν ὁ ἄνθρωπος θεὸς ἀποδείκνυται καὶ τῷ οὐρανίῳ πατρὶ ὅμοιος.''

Irene's establishment maintained distributions of food to the poor, and also adopted orphan girls who were educated there and prepared for life.[89] Donations were accepted not for luxuries but for charities.[90] Furthermore, she left a request in her testament that upon her death and the death of her husband the monastic community make more distributions than usual.[91]

Isaac, the younger son of Alexios and Irene who occupied himself with cultural rather than military matters [92] and founded the monastery of Kosmosotera at Aenos (c. 1152), distinguished himself as a humanitarian. He writes in the typikon of his monastery that the monks should practice charities, and that distribution of meals should be made every day at the gate of the monastery to all the poor attending.[93] The distributions were more generous on certain holidays, such as the observance of the Dormition of Theotocos, when honey, wine, and money, in addition to bread, were given to the poor.[94] He charged the hegoumenos to be even more magnanimous in his charities on the day of Isaac's death.[95] Isaac's rules demonstrate that he was truly a very kind and liberal man.[96]

The Empress Irene, the prudent wife of John II Comnenos, was of the same humanitarian nature as her husband. She helped to establish the Pantocrator. John Cinnamos, her contemporary historian, points out that whatever money she had either from the emperor or from the imperial office she did not spend for luxury and cosmetics. She was intent upon doing good deeds to those who begged of her.[97] On her death the empress was exceedingly merciful and prudent, leaving much to those who had asked her for help.[98]

The information about Manuel Comnenos is scarce, and as a consequence we know very little about his notion and application of philanthropia. If we accept a poem written by Theodore

89. *Ibid.*, p. 337.
90. *Ibid.*, p. 339.
91. *Ibid.*, p. 375; cf. pp. 376–77.
92. Vasiliev, *History*, p. 490.
93. "Typicon du monastère de la Kosmosotera," Louis Petit, ed., p. 22.
94. *Ibid.*, pp. 20, 24, 25; cf. p. 50.
95. *Ibid.*, p. 25.
96. Cf. *ibid.*, pp. 49, 53, 54, 62.
97. Joannes Cinnamos, p. 10.
98. *Ibid.*, p. 202.

Prodromos on the occasion of Manuel's marriage, we may assume that Manuel too was active in charities. Theodore writes in his panygenic poem:

"There is none, and there has never been
such a great Emperor, patron of the Romans,
pious toward God and philanthropic to men

. . . .

You dedicate many and great churches to God
and numerous other philanthropic votive offerings
you always stretch out to your subjects a generous hand." [99]

The present survey indicates that philanthropia was believed in and practiced by the Byzantine State as a religious, social, and political virtue. Practically all the emperors, in one way or another, pursued the application of this noble attribute. But was the notion of philanthropia utilized by the Byzantine emperors as propaganda or was it practiced as a result of their Christian ideology? Was it an end in itself or simply political expedience to cover up inadequacies or unwelcome political measures of the crown? The numerous philanthropic institutions which were built by various emperors, and the emperors' religious attitude toward society, their Christian outlook and conviction that royal authority is divine, are indications that their social and political philosophies were imbued with Christian ethics. Of course, political motives cannot be excluded.

A few illustrations will clarify this point. We observe in the policies of such emperors a certain discordance. Their reign was marked by much humanitarian work, and yet certain cruelties perpetrated either by themselves or by their political lieutenants hardly commend them as philanthropic rulers. Justinian is credited with the erection of many charitable institutions, but his humane policies toward the aged, the sick, and the orphans must be weighed against the massacre of thousands of his people during the Nika revolt (532).[100]

We note a similar antithesis in the personality of the Empress

99. Theodore Prodromos, «Στίχοι εἰσιτήριοι τῷ Κυρῷ Μανουὴλ καὶ Σεβαστοκράτορι», ed. P. Matranga, *Anecdota Graeca* (Rome, 1850), p. 552; cf. Eustathios of Thessalonica, "Oratio XXIII. Manuelis Comneni Imp. laudatio funebris, 18," Tafel, p. 200.

100. Malalas, *Chronographia*, p. 474.

Irene (797–802). She accomplished much to relieve the needy, but her motives must have been both political and religious. We are told that she was instrumental in the establishment of several homes for the aged, houses for the poor and the stranger, and others.[101] When she became an independent ruler, she granted generous tax remissions and repealed the municipal tax paid by the citizens of Constantinople. Her social policy in general was one of generosity.[102] Nevertheless, we cannot attribute these measures to pure philanthropy or genuine religious motives. The empress needed desperately to maintain the support of the population. Political considerations motivated her humane social program.[103] The blinding of her son and her behavior before her coronation stand in sharp contrast to her charitable work.

The same inconsistency between motives and actions may be observed in the policies of the Emperor Theophilos (829–42). The illustrious emperor had a sense of justice praised by friends and enemies alike.[104] Once a week he rode about the city talking to the poor, distributing money, attending the grievances of the weak, and punishing offenders. He was always ready to defend the weak against the strong, including his own palace staff.[105] Yet this humane attitude was blackened by various acts of cruelty.[106]

The philanthropic policies of Basil I (867–86) no doubt were formulated out of political expediency. Both his personality and

101. "Vita S Nicetae Confessoris," AASS, April, I, App., XXIV. 30: " Ἐποίησεν δὲ καὶ ἄλλα πλεῖστα κατορθώματα, λέγω δὴ γηροκομία, πτωχοτροφία, ξενοδοχεῖα, καὶ φόρων κουφισμούς." Cf. Pseudo-Codinos, *Patria,* Th. Preger, III, 246.

102. Theophanes, *Chronographia,* p. 475; Theodore Studites, *Epistle No. I, 6;* MPG, XCIX, col. 929.

103. Cf. Ostrogorsky, *History,* pp. 161–62; J. B. Bury, *A History of the Eastern Roman Empire from the Fall of Irene to the Accession of Basil I* (London, 1912), pp. 2–4.

104. Nicetas, *Vita Ignatii,* p. 216; Theophanes Continuatus, *Chronographia,* p. 139; Bury, *History,* pp. 120–21, see also n. 2, p. 121.

105. Leo Grammaticos, *Chronographia,* ed. I. Bekker, CSHB (Bonn, 1842), pp. 215–16, 222–23; Bury, *History,* pp. 120, 121–123.

106. Leo Grammaticos, *Chronographia,* p. 214; Genesios, p. 51; cf. Diehl, "La Légende de l'empereur Théophile," *Seminarium Kondakovianum,* IV (Prague, 1931), 33–37; V. Grumel, "Recherches récentes sur l'iconoclasme," *Echos d'Orient,* XXIX, no. 157 (Jan.–Mar., 1930), 99.

his policies reveal the previously noted inharmony in an especially harsh light. Basil was highly commended because he erected more than one hundred public and charitable institutions and performed many philanthropies.[107] But we can hardly call Basil a humanitarian when we consider that he murdered his benefactor, the Emperor Michael III, disposed of the great Caesar Bardas, and banished the Patriarch Photios with the sole intention of fulfilling his political ambitions. He enriched himself by immoral means when he was dispatched as emissary of the Administration to examine the affairs of the wealthy widow Danielis in Patras. Nevertheless, when Basil ascended the throne, he desired to attract the people's following and impress upon them his humanitarian character, and so he distributed great sums of money among the poor masses.[108]

Basil's cruelties and unethical measures do not commend him as a philanthropist. But Basil's example suggests what has been stated earlier, that philanthropia was practiced not only for social and political but also for religious purposes, to relieve a guilty conscience, to avert the wrath of God, and to secure the salvation of the benefactor's soul.

Evidence strongly indicates, however, that philanthropia was practiced as a virtue in itself, especially by such devout emperors as Justinian, Constantine Porphyrogenitos, Romanos Lecapenos, Nicephoros Phocas (despite his anti-monastic legislation), Constantine IX, Alexios Comnenos, and John II Comnenos. Philanthropia as a virtue in its ideological conception and in its actual application was in perfect agreement with the Christian ideals with which Byzantine society was impregnated.

What Anna Comnena related in the twelfth century may well be accepted as a reflection of the spirit of the Byzantine State in toto. She describes the humane attitude of her father, the Emperor Alexios Comnenos, toward poor and needy people, and she adds that the work of philanthropia which he displayed to his people while marching against the Turks of Iconium was done as a result of the belief in the divine commandment.[109] She compares her father's philanthropic attitude toward men

107. Theophanes Continuatus, *Chronographia*, p. 256.
108. *Ibid.*, pp. 256–57; cf. Amantos, «Ἱστορία», II, 25.
109. Anna Comnena, *Alexias*, XV. 7.

and women who were suffering from illness and old age, orphans, captives, mutilated men, blind, lame, or others in need, with the "Savior's" work.[110]

Thus, while the virtue of philanthropia might have been exercised at times for political expediency by certain emperors, it is more realistic to believe that, on the whole, philanthropia was practiced under the influence of Christian ideals rather than for any other reason. The Byzantine emperor, as the first citizen, was expected to be among the first who would believe in and practice philanthropia. Only through philanthropia would he become like God.[111]

It is significant to note that while the elements of disintegration and decline were apparent in the twelfth century, altruistic thinking and humanism in practice were not lacking. The fact is that the practice of imperial philanthropia in the twelfth century highly commends the Byzantine emperors of that age.

We may observe, then, in agreement with John Cantacuzenos that the Byzantine State "was full of philanthropia"; [112] that Byzantium was a nation in which the emperor and members of the imperial court competed zealously with other dignitaries, and individuals of all classes rivaled among themselves, in the establishment of benevolent institutions and in the everyday application of the virtue of philanthropia. Philanthropia was both a lofty ideal and an everyday experience of the imperial life.

110. *Ibid.*
111. See pp. 53–57.
112. Joannes Cantacuzenos, *Historia,* p. 227.

9. Private Benefactors

Along with the charities of the Church and State dignitaries, the humble parish priest, and the unknown monk, we may include lay individuals of the middle and upper classes. Though we may never know the Byzantine "Rockefellers," there were certain magnates who deserve our attention.

During the reign of Theodosios the Great there was in Antioch a very rich man, a money dealer named Andronicos. His wife Athanasia, the daughter of another money dealer, was also very wealthy. Their religious faith influenced them strongly and made them great humanitarians. The poor and the sick found in Andronicos and Athanasia compassionate protectors. When their two children died prematurely they became even greater benefactors, freeing their slaves and distributing the major part of their wealth to the poor and to charitable institutions.[1]

Another rich man of the fourth century who became a great humanitarian to the poor of Constantinople was named Markianos (+388). He inherited immense wealth from his parents, but, rather than spending it to entertain himself, used it for the erection of charitable institutions. As one expects, the teachings of

1. "Vie et récits de l'Abbé Daniel de Scété," ed. M. Leon Clugnet, V (1900), 370: "Ἦσαν δὲ πλούσιοι σφόδρα. . . . Τὰ τοῦ ἀργυροπρατείου καὶ τῆς οὐσίας αὐτῶν εἰς τρία μέρη διεῖλον, τὸ ἓν εἰς λόγον τῶν πτωχῶν." Cf. p. 380: "ταῖς τῶν πτωχῶν καὶ νοσούντων εὐποιΐαις ἐνδελεχῶς σπουδάζοντες."

137

Christ were the determining influence in Markianos' humanitarian works.[2]

Palladios relates that during the fifth century in the city of Ancyra there were wealthy individuals who became great humanitarians to the poor. A couple named Oueros and Bosporis saved the lives of many poor when, during a great famine that befell their city, they opened their warehouse and distributed food to the hungry. It was their practice to set aside a certain amount of their annual income for the poor.[3] Magna, a rich widow of Ancyra, was thrifty in her personal expenses and distributed much of her wealth to poor individuals, to philanthropic institutions, and to the bishops for use in humanitarian endeavors.[4]

Among the philanthropists of Ancyra we may include a certain anonymous monk attached to the local bishopric for twenty years. His only purpose in life was to serve the needy. Palladios writes that this individual went out even during the night to search for the poor, perhaps beggars, and offer them his help. He visited prisoners, the sick, and others in want.[5]

The influence of the Christian Gospel upon the lives of many Byzantines perhaps can never be overestimated, particularly in the realm of philanthropy. For example, Palladios writes that there was in Alexandria an educated man name Eulogios. Because he desired the solitary life of a monk, he distributed all his possessions to the poor and to charitable concerns, and kept for himself only a few nomismata. While wandering through the agora of Alexandria and pondering whether to join a monastic community or to become a hermit, Eulogios spotted a man crippled and mutilated in his hands and feet. As if this were not enough, the man suffered from an active case of leprosy. Eulogios, in a heroic decision, took the leper under his own roof in order to serve him and express his Christian love for a "brother in Christ." Eulogios nursed the leper, washing and bathing him regularly for fifteen years.[6]

2. "Life of St. Markianos," Papadopoulos-Kerameus, «'Ανάλεκτα», IV, 260, 269; for the role of individuals in charities of the early Christian centuries see Champagny, *Char. Chrét.*, pp. 329–51.
3. Palladios, *Hist. Lausiaca*, pp. 162–63.
4. *Ibid.*, p. 163.
5. *Ibid.*, p. 164: "τοσοῦτον δέ ἐστι φιλάνθρωπος καὶ ἐλεήμων ὡς καὶ τὰς νύκτας περιιέναι καὶ ἐλεεῖν τοὺς δεομένους. Οὗτος οὐκ ἀμελεῖ οὐ φυλακῆς, οὐ νοσοκομείου, οὐ πτωχοῦ. . . ."
6. *Ibid.*, pp. 64–65.

Palladios enumerates several individuals, such as Beneria,[7] Melania,[8] Olympias,[9] Candida,[10] Melania the Younger,[11] Pammachios,[12] and others, whose daily concern it was to serve their fellow men in want. Their humanitarian work was not limited to the distribution of coins but included major undertakings in alleviating misery and want and the erection of institutions. They played major roles in helping to relieve the effects of famines and catastrophes. Ephraem of Edessa may serve as an additional illustration.

Palladios relates [13] that Edessa suffered from a great famine in which many people, particularly country people, were stricken and died.[14] Some of the rich remained apathetic to the dreadful events around them. But the deacon Ephraem (+373) crusaded to bring hope to the unfortunate.[15] He visited several wealthy people and reprimanded them for allowing countless needy people to die from hunger. They answered that there was no honest man to handle their contributions. Ephraem offered his services and was entrusted with the program, supported by the wealthy, of rehabilitation for the poor. He even provided medical services for over three hundred people.[16]

Timothy of Alexandria, considered to be the author of the history of Egyptian monasticism, writes (c. 400) [17] that there was a very wealthy businessman whose possessions amounted to twenty thousand gold pieces. He was also the owner of one hundred ships. This unnamed magnate learned of the treasures in Heaven, sold all of his belongings, and distributed the money to the poor, to philanthropic institutions, and to the churches.[18]

It was customary for Byzantines of all classes to designate the poor, orphans, or charitable institutions as beneficiaries in their

7. *Ibid.*, p. 128.
8. *Ibid.*, p. 146; cf. pp. 134 and 147.
9. *Ibid.*, p. 150; cf. "Vita S Joannes Chrysostomi," pp. 104–11.
10. Palladios, *Hist. Lausiaca*, p. 150.
11. *Ibid.*, p. 151; cf. pp. 156–57.
12. *Ibid.*, p. 157.
13. For the credibility and historical value of Palladios' *Historia Lausiaca* see Butler's introduction, p. 5.
14. Palladios, *Hist. Lausiaca*, pp. 126–27.
15. Cf. Rubens Duval, *Histoire politique, religieuse et littéraire d'Edesse* (Paris, 1892), pp. 141 ff.
16. Palladios, *Hist. Lausiaca*, pp. 126–27.
17. Altaner, *Patrology*, p. 254.
18. Timothy, *Historia Monachorum*, pp. 108–09.

wills. Eustathios Boilas,[19] a very wealthy Byzantine of the eleventh century, bequeathed land and money to former slaves, to poor people, and to orphans. He wrote in his testament: "The village of Copterion and Chouspacrati I have given to the orphan brothers Christopher and George and to their cousin, as they are poor and orphans."[20] Boilas included his freedmen in his will, allotting them four pieces of land.[21] Each piece was perhaps equal to what a pair of oxen could cultivate in a single day (zeugotopia), that is, equal to one modern acre.[22] Boilas performed his charities in memory of his dead son Romanos. He was concerned not only for the fate of his former slaves [23] but for the poor in general. "Whatever remains," he wrote, "should be distributed among my brethren and masters, that is, the poor."[24]

Symbatios and Kale Pacourianos, a very wealthy couple perhaps of the eleventh century, wrote in their will that their slaves should be set free and receive various benefits from their possessions. The husband Symbatios designated his wife as major inheritor but he also remembered his servants and the poor.[25] He asked that upon his death his wife should distribute "twelve litras" of gold nomismata to the poor and to his freedmen for the salvation of his soul.[26]

19. Speros Vryonis, Jr., "The Will of a Provincial Magnate, Eustathius Boilas (1059)," DOP, no. 11 (1957), pp. 263–77; Hr. Bartikian, *Significance of the Will of Eustathius Boilas for the study of the history of Armenia and Georgia at the time of Byzantine dominion*, XXV International Congress of Orientalists, Papers presented by the USSR Delegation (Moscow, 1960), pp. 1–17.

20. V. Beneshevich, ed., "Zavieschanie vizantiiskago boiarina XI vieka," *Zhurnal ministerstva narodnago prosvieshchenia*, IX (May, 1907), 223–24: "τὸ δὲ χωρίον τὸ Κοπτερίου καὶ τὸ Χωσπακράτη δέδωκα πρὸς Χριστοφόρον καὶ Γεώργιον τοῖς αὐταδέχφοις καὶ ὀρφανοῖς καὶ τὸν ἐξάδελφον αὐτῶν ἀπόρους καὶ ὀρφανούς." Cf. Vryonis, DOP, no. 11, p. 266, col. 1; Bartikian, *Significance*, p. 3.

21. Beneshevich, *Zavieschanie*, p. 224; cf. Bartikian, pp. 10–11.

22. But cf. Vryonis, DOP, no. 11, p. 266, col. 2.

23. Beneshevich, *Zavieschanie*, p. 228: "Τὰ δὲ οἰκογενῆ καὶ ὄντα οἰκετικά μου πρόσωπα πρὸ χρόνων ἐποιησάμην φροντίδα καὶ ἠλευθέρωσα πάντα καὶ ἐληγάτευσα . . . ἵνα εἰσὶν ἐλεύθερα παντελεύθερα καὶ πολῖται Ῥωμαίων κατὰ τοὺς κωδικίλους αὐτῶν· ἔχειν δὲ καὶ τὰ δοθέντα αὐτοὺς ζευγοτόπια ἐλεύθερα παντελεύθερα ἐπὶ διηνεκεῖς χρόνους. . . ."

24. *Ibid.*, p. 230: "τὰ δὲ περιττεύοντα εἰς τοὺς ἀδελφοὺς καὶ αὐθέντας μου τοὺς πένητας διανεμηθῶσιν."

25. Ioacheim Iberites, ed.: "Διαθήκη τοῦ Συμβατίου Κουροπαλάτου τοῦ Πακουριάνου," Ο, V, no. 60 (December, 1930), 615–16.

26. *Ibid.*, p. 616: "καὶ παράσχῃ ἡ σύμβιός μου . . . ὑπὲρ ψυχικῆς μου

Kale Pacourianos imitated the generous example of her husband and bequeathed many charities to her former servants, to slaves, to poor people, to monasteries, and, presumably, to philanthropic institutions. In her will Kale mentions twelve female servants and several monks. In addition to animals, objects, and household utilities, Kale mentioned money which should be given to her freedmen and servants, as well as to poor people in general.[27]

Gregory Pacourianos, who served as *domesticus ton scholon* under Alexios Comnenos,[28] was most probably related to Symbatios and Kale Pacourianos.[29] Gregory had become very wealthy in the service of the Empire and possessed many buildings, estates, mills, animals, and servants.[30] In addition to founding philanthropic institutions, Gregory used much of his wealth for charities. In addition, he wrote in his will that his philanthropic tradition should continue after his death. He provided that upon his death seventy-two nomismata be given to each poor man, and food and drink be given to everyone who would attend his funeral. Gregory requested that on Holy Thursday after his death an additional amount of twenty-four nomismata and food be distributed to the poor.[31]

Pacourianos made further special provisions for the protection and welfare of the old and sick among the monks. His motives were, of course, obedience to the will of God and the salvation of his soul.[32] We do not know whether he had enriched himself

σωτηρίας εἰς διανομὴν πενήτων ἐπιδώσει ἀφ' οὗπερ κέκτημαι χρυσίου τὰς δώδεκα . . . λίτρας . . . τὰς δὲ ἑτέρας ἕξ. . . ἐπιδώσει πρὸς τοὺς ἔχοντας εὑρεθῆναι ἐκδουλεύοντάς με ἐλευθέρους ἀνθρώπους μου." For an illustration of a charitable will in the later Byzantine Empire, see M. Manousakas, " Ἡ Διαθήκη τοῦ Ἀγγέλου Ἀκοτάντου (1436), ἀγνώστου Κρητικοῦ ζωγράφου," *Deltion tes Christianikes Archaeologikes Etaerias,* Series 4, II, 1960–1961 (Athens, 1962), 146–48.

27. *Iberites,* O, VI, No. 66 (June, 1931), 367–69.

28. Anna Comnena, *Alexias,* II. 4; cf. Petit, "Typikon de Pacourianos," VV, XI, Suppl. no. 1 (1904), VI–XI.

29. Constantine Amantos, "Χειρόγραφα τῆς Μονῆς τοῦ Γρηγορίου Πακουριανοῦ παρὰ τὸν Στενήμαχον," Thr, X (Athens, 1938), 250; E. Honigmann, who examines the family of Gregory Pacourianos, does not mention Symbatios and Kale at all; see his *Die Ostgrenze des Byzantinischen Reiches von 363 bis 1071* (Brussels, 1935), pp. 222–26.

30. Petit, "Typikon de Pacourianos," p. 13.

31. *Ibid.,* pp. 41–43.

32. *Ibid.*

at the expense of the poor and the peasants who cultivated his vast estates, nor how just and considerate he had been while he was their landlord. His will demonstrates, however, that he had compassion and a sense of obligation toward the underprivileged.[33]

Michael Attaleiates was another wealthy magnate of the time of Alexios Comnenos. He, too, remembered the poor in his will and provided for charitable institutions. He hoped to achieve much before his death but he requested that his will be carried out by his inheritor. His charities included the distribution of one great modion of bread every Sunday before the gate of his house in Constantinople. Six beggars were invited to dinner every day and were given upon their departure a lump of bread and four folleis. Furthermore, upon his death, two hundred and sixteen modia of wheat were to be given to widows, elderly people in need of mercy, and others in want.[34]

Attaleiates founded several institutions about which we shall have more to say later. He was indeed one of the "Rockfellers" of the Byzantine Empire. Attaleiates' wife wrote in her will that all her dowry and possessions be given to charities after her death, including an estate known as the vanitsi.[35] Michael himself, believing that man should express his philanthropia to his fellow men as God manifested His through the incarnation of Christ,[36] offered the income of his estates at Raedestos and of his properties in Constantinople for the relief of the needy and the poor. He made several provisions for the distribution of bread, wine, wheat, and money to the underprivileged.[37]

This tradition of wealthy individuals remembering charitable institutions and the needy in their wills continued in later centuries. Thus we find that the wife of Theodore Sarantinos, a wealthy citizen of Beroia in Macedonia (fourteenth century), was a habitual friend of the poor. In addition to other generosities, she distributed clothing and foodstuffs to the needy on

33. *Ibid.*, pp. 47–49 *et passim*. Cf. Theophylactos of Ochrida, *Epistles, Part 1, No. 14, Part 2, Nos. 7 and 25*, MPG, CXXVI, cols. 333 ff.
34. Sathas, «Μεσ. Βιβλιοθ.», I, 21–23.
35. *Ibid.*, p. 4.
36. *Ibid.*, p. 7.
37. *Ibid.*, pp. 7–8; cf. Nissen, *Die Diataxis des Michael Attaleiates*, pp. 22 ff.

Figure 19. Ring of Michael Attaleiates (d. 1081); gold and cloisonné enamel (Constantinople, 10th century; diameter approximately 1″ [2.3 cm.]). On the bezel, a bust of the Mother of God, with monogram; around the hoop, an engraved inscription: "Mother of God, help thy servant, Michael Attaleiates." Dumbarton Oaks Collections, Washington, D.C. Photo courtesy of the Dumbarton Oaks Collections.

Holy Thursday and Good Friday. We may safely assume that the religious significance of these two days must have induced many other wealthy Byzantines to imitate Sarantinos' example. In his will Theodore Sarantinos (c. 1326) and his wife provided that the revenue of a certain estate be distributed every year to poor monasteries for women and other poverty-stricken citizens.[38] Remembering the needy and endowing charitable institutions through their wills was very common among the Byzantines from the fourth down to the fifteenth centuries. Freedom for slaves and dowries for poor girls were prescribed in wills.[39]

It was not uncommon for a Byzantine citizen, after recovering from a serious illness, to express his thanksgiving to God by distribution of charities to orphans, widows, and others. A certain wealthy individual of Nicea, a contemporary of St. Peter of Atroa (d. 837), upon the restoration of his health from a serious infirmity, contributed to the welfare of widows, orphans, and poor people. He freed his servants and voided debts owed him.[40]

38. George I. Theocharides, «Μία Διαθήκη καὶ Μία Δίκη Βυζαντινή» (Thessalonike, 1962), p. 24.

39. Constantine Amantos, "Περὶ τῶν Βυζαντινῶν διαθηκῶν," «Πεπραγμένα τοῦ 9ου Διεθνοῦς Βυζαντινολογικοῦ Συνεδρίου», ed. S. Kyriakides, A. Xyngopoulos, and P. Zepos, II (Athens, 1956), 281–87.

40. "Vita of St. Peter of Atroa," ed. V. Laurent, La Vie merveilleuse de Saint Pierre d'Atroa, Subsidia Hagiographica, no. 29 (Bruxelles, 1956), p. 173: "ὑγιωθεὶς ὁ νοσῶν ἀνέστη . . . χήραις ἐπαρκῶν, ὀρφανοῖς εὐποιῶν, τοῖς πένησι τὰ ἑαυτοῦ μεταδιδοὺς ἐν ἁπλότητι, δούλοις καταγράφων ἐλευθερίαν, τοὺς χάρτας τῶν δανειστῶν αὐτοῦ διασχίζων."

143

We may note here that there were wealthy Byzantines who did not remember the poor or philanthropic institutions in their wills. Though Theodore Karabas belonged to the first quarter of the fourteenth century, he may serve as a typical illustration. He was a Croesus in his affluence, and owned many edifices, much real estate, and diverse possessions. In his will Karabas instructed his wife to execute his testament justly. But all his inheritance went to relatives, friends, and "spiritual children," people whom he had sponsored at baptism. Except for the monastery of Perivleptos, no hospital, xenon, gerocomeion, orphanage, or any other institution was enriched as beneficiary.[41] Nevertheless, as a rule, many wealthy Byzantines included charities in their wills to better the fate of their souls after death.[42]

Founders of monasteries instructed in their wills that the monastic establishment should maintain a policy of philanthropy toward all in want.[43]

While we encounter much evidence of the practice of charity in Byzantium, it is naive to believe that everyone was humanitarian and hospitable. In fact, we find complaints about the lack of hospitality. St. Lazaros (+1053) experienced it personally in Caesarea of Cappadocia, where he had gone to pray in St. Basil's church. After his departure from Caesarea and on his way, perhaps, to his monastery in the Galesion mountain,[44] Lazaros was forced to stay overnight in an unnamed village. None of the inhabitants offered him hospitality, for they were *aneleemones,* and he was forced to spend his evening near an oven. The following day he stayed in the same village in order to observe the Forty-Martyrs holiday, and again the people offered him nothing to eat.[45] The natives may not have been Greeks or Hellenized Byzantines.

41. "Actes de Chilandar," VV, XVII, Suppl. 5 (1911), 63.
42. Cf. Gelzer, *Leontios,* pp. 66–68; George Spyridakis, "Τὰ κατὰ τὴν τελευτὴν ἔθιμα τῶν Βυζαντινῶν . . .," EEBS, XX (1950), 85; Constantine Acropolites, " Ἑτέρα Διαθήκη," ed. M. Treu, ΔΙΕΕΕ, LV (1892), p. 50.
43. Basil Laourdas, ed., "Μητροφάνους Βίος τοῦ ὁσίου Διονυσίου τοῦ Ἀθωνίτου," *Archeion Pontou,* XXI (Athens, 1956), 68. The monks were counseled to maintain "φιλαδελφίαν, ἐλεημοσύνη, συμπάθεια . . . ξενιτείαν, ξενοδοχίαν καὶ ὅσα ὅμοια τούτοις."
44. Ramsay, *Historical Geography,* p. 110.
45. Gregorios Monachos, "Vita S Lazari," AASS, November, III (1910), 517–18: "ἔκρινε μὴ ἐξελθεῖν τῆς κώμης τῇ ἡμέρᾳ ἐκείνῃ . . . διὰ τὸ τῆς

Even some rich people who could well afford to be generous refused to offer charities or extend hospitality. Palladios writes about such a wealthy individual with no consideration for the poor, although he professed to being a Christian.[46] We may note also that bishops, who were expected to be pillars of charity, sometimes fell behind in their humanitarian obligations. Leontios of Neapolis relates that a certain Bishop Troelos in Egypt was a very greedy churchman who had accumulated an amount of money for the luxurious embellishment of his residence. However, the eleemosynary Patriarch John strongly urged him to donate the money to the Kaesarion ptochotropheion. Out of embarrassment, the greedy bishop yielded to the request, but as soon as he had donated the money he became sick.[47]

Liudprand, Bishop of Cremona and ambassador of Otto I in Constantinople,[48] had every reason to accuse the Byzantines of being hostile and lacking in philanthropia. Everywhere he went, in Constantinople, Patras, Leukas, or Corfu, the Byzantines were anything but hospitable.[49] To Liudprand the Byzantine Emperors were not *evergetae* or *philanthropoi*, as they prided themselves on being, but were instead "crafty, foxy . . . and merciless." [50] There is, however, no need to emphasize that Liudprand cannot be accepted as an objective critic.

There are other occasional inferences that the inhabitants of certain Byzantine territories, such as the Peloponnesos, lacked any sense of justice, love, and philanthropia in the first quarter of the fifteenth century. In the anonymous Byzantine satire *Mazaris*,[51] the Peloponnesos is recommended by Holobolos to Mazaris as a place of peace and humanity, happiness and prosperity. Mazaris undertakes the trip to Morea and discovers that his plight there is worse than in Hell or Tartaros. While Holobolos had assured Mazaris that his own experience there was

ἡμέρας ἐπίσημον . . . ἅμα δὲ καὶ πρὸς δοκιμὴν τῶν ἐκεῖσε ἀνελεημόνων ἀνθρώπων . . . οὐδεὶς αὐτῷ κἂν κλάσμα ἄρτου εἰς τροφὴν δέδωκεν."

46. Palladios, *Hist. Lausiaca*, p. 22.
47. Gelzer, *Leontios*, pp. 57–58.
48. Ostrogorsky, *History*, pp. 258 ff.
49. *The Works of Liudprand of Cremona*, tr. F. A. Wright (London, 1930), Ch. 63; cf. Chs. 60 and 64.
50. *Ibid., Legatio*, Ch. 40.
51. Tozer, "Byzantine Satire," pp. 235–36, 257 ff.

very satisfactory, Mazaris testifies that his reaction was very different. He found in the Peloponnesos no peace, justice, hospitality, or philanthropia.[52]

52. "Mazaris, 20," ed. Ellissen, *Analecten*, p. 232: "Μελαγχολᾷς, ἄθρω-πε, νὴ τὴν ἡμετέραν φιλίαν, ἔφην αὐτῷ [i.e. Mazaris to Holobolos]. Πλοῦτος ἐν Πελοποννήσῳ πολιτεύεται, ἢ δόσις, ἢ ἀγάπη, ἢ εἰρήνη, ἢ φιλανθρωπία, ἢ δικαιοσύνη, ἢ φιλοξενία, ἢ μετριότης, ἢ ἄλλο τι τῶν ἀγαθῶν ἁπάντων. . . ."

Part III

Philanthropic Institutions

10. Administration

Philanthropic work was institutionalized very early in the Byzantine Empire. The Church, the State, and private benefactors established numerous charitable institutions.

The Church promulgated special canons for the erection of hospitals, poorhouses, hospices, and similar establishments, and organized their administration.[1]

The Church was commissioned by her founder not only to preach a new gospel of salvation but also to feed the hungry; to quench the thirsty; to shelter the traveler; to offer hospitality to the stranger; to clothe the needy and look after the sick; to care for the orphans and the widows.[2] It is to the credit of the Byzantine Church that she realized her social mission and sought to lighten the burden of the unfortunate by founding hospitals, hostels, homes for the aged, orphanages, and other welfare institutions.[3]

The Byzantine Church emphasized the establishment of institutions which would help her missionary activities among the barbarians. Thus the episcopal headquarters and the monastic establishments became the shelter for all those in want. Preach-

1. Cf. Canons VIII and X of the Fourth Ecumenical Council.
2. Cf. Matt. 25:31–46, Gal. 2:10 *et al.*
3. Cf. Baynes-Moss, *Byzantium,* pp. XXIX–XXX; see also L'Abbé Marin, *Les Moines de Constantinople* (Paris, 1897), pp. 61–72, and P. W. Duff, "The Charitable Foundations of Byzantium," *Cambridge Legal Essays written in honour of and presented to Doctor Bond, Professor Buckland and Professor Kenny* (Cambridge, 1926), pp. 85–86.

149

ing the gospel and caring for the poor and unfortunate were excellent means for the conduct of missionary work. It was understood that supplying man's physical needs was part of the responsibility of the Church.

Monastic establishments maintained many hospitals, old-age homes, hospices, orphanages, and perhaps other charitable institutions. The monasteries had assumed the responsibilities which cities, counties, or states exercise today, in establishing and supporting philanthropic establishments. In addition to separate chambers for ill, aged, or visiting clergymen and monks, the monasteries maintained equivalent charitable institutions for laymen.[4]

The hospitals were usually built next to the "catholicon" or church of the monastery [5] for obvious reasons, while homes for the aged and xenones were usually located outside the walls of the monastery, as at the monastery of Pentele.[6]

The State, too, practiced philanthropy. From the dedication of its capital in 330 to its collapse in 1453, the Byzantine State was characterized by many manifestations of its philanthropic policies. Through special laws and the initiative of the emperors, hospitals were erected; orphanages were established where orphans were not only housed and fed but educated; special institutions for lepers were built; hospices and inns were founded in various cities and on roads of the Empire to provide food and shelter for travelers.[7]

The emperor and those in public office established numerous philanthropic institutions, in part because they were expected to be philanthropists by virtue of their offices. But one cannot draw a sharp line of demarcation between Church and State. The collection of laws known as *Epanagoge*, compiled during the reign of Basil I, defines the polity of Church and State and reveals the nature of Byzantium.[8] It was one organism—a unity composed of lay and ecclesiastical members presided over by two parallel and equal authorities, the emperor and the patriarch.[9] Both, therefore, must be given credit for the numerous philan-

4. A. K. Orlandos, «Μοναστηριακὴ ᾿Αρχιτεκτονική» (Athens, 1927), p. 49.
5. *Ibid.*, pp. 49–52.
6. Cf. *ibid.*, p. 56; see Figure 7.
7. Cf. Justinian, *Novel 120. 6;* Duff, "Charitable Foundations," pp. 90–91.
8. Zepos-Zepos, *Jus,* II, 236 ff.; cf. Leo Diaconos, *Historiae,* pp. 101–02.
9. Cf. Ostrogorsky, *History,* pp. 213–14.

thropic institutions which we encounter in the Byzantine Empire.[10]

But private initiative on the part of clergymen and laymen in establishing charitable institutions was not rare.[11] Basil the Great, John Chrysostom, Sampson, John Eleemon, Stephen the parakoemomenos of Maurice, Dexiocrates, Attaleiates, and others may be classified among many private benefactors who established and endowed philanthropic concerns.[12]

Unfortunately, our knowledge of those institutions which existed in such cities as Antioch, Alexandria, Jerusalem, Thessalonica, Chalcedon, Nicea, Corinth, and others is limited. However, we do know by name many hospitals, homes for the aged, orphanages, hospices for strangers and travelers, homes for the poor, and similar shelters for the unfortunate in Constantinople and its vicinity. Obviously, such institutions must have existed in numerous other provinces and cities of the Empire: Justinian issued a novella concerning both the establishments of the capital and those which existed in all the eparchies of his reign.[13]

10. See Etienne Chastel, *Influence de la charité*, pp. 263–302.
11. Cf. Duff, "Charitable Foundations," pp. 94–95.
12. Cf. A. H. M. Jones, *The Later Roman Empire 284–602*, II, 901. Cf. Duff, *ibid.*
13. Justinian, *Novel 120. 6:* "Καὶ ταῦτα μὲν ἐπί . . . τῶν εἰρημένων εὐαγῶν οἴκων τῶν ἐν τῇ βασιλίδι πόλει καὶ τῇ αὐτῆς περιοικίδι τυγχανόντων διετυπώσαμεν. Ἐπὶ δὲ ταῖς ἄλλαις ἁγιωτάταις ἐκκλησίαις καὶ μοναστηρίοις καὶ ξενῶσι καὶ νοσοκομείοις καὶ λοιποῖς εὐαγέσιν οἴκοις τοῖς ἐν ἁπάσαις ταῖς ἐπαρχίαις τῆς ἡμετέρας πολιτείας κειμένοις. . . ."

11. Hospitals

The hospitals which existed in the Byzantine Empire were general hospitals, leprosaria, maternity clinics, ophthalmological dispensaries, and foundling institutions. A modern historian of medicine writes that "they were in every respect perfect and nearly similar to present day institutions of this kind . . . they were the first fully equipped European hospitals."[1] This statement seems to exaggerate, and one may safely say that the organization and function of Byzantine hospitals and clinics was medieval, parallel to the scientific progress and the medical means of the Byzantine middle ages.

The care, however, which the Byzantines took in relieving human suffering and prolonging human life was admirable. Their hospitals, clinics, medicines, and methods of treatment reveal that the Byzantines knew much about medicine and that they worked extensively to promote them. "Many operations of present-day surgery, orthopedics, obstetrics-gynecology, otorhinolaryngology, as well as much of the current knowledge on hygiene, epidemiology, anthropology, and physiology, considered as scientific advances of recent years, was knowledge of medieval Greek physicians."[2] In medical knowledge and in public medical

1. G. C. Pournaropoulos, "Hospital and Social Welfare Institutions in the Medieval Greek Empire (Byzantium)," *XVIIᵉ Congrès international d'histoire de la médecine*, I (Athens, 1960), 378.
2. G. C. Pournaropoulos, "The Real Value of Medieval Greek Medicine (Byzantium)," *ibid.*, p. 357.

assistance "the Byzantines were indeed the indisputable fore-
runners of the West." ³ Professor Pournaropoulos writes that the
Byzantines made valuable contributions in many fields of medicine, such as anatomy-anthropology-physiology, hygiene-
epidemiology, therapeutics-pharmacology, pathology, general
pathology-parasitology, pediatrics, surgery-orthopedics, urology,
obstetrics-gynecology, neurology-psychiatry, otorhinolaryngology, dermatology, toxicology, physiotherapy, hydrotherapy,
stomatology, dietetics, and ophthalmology.⁴ Byzantine medicine
and organization of medical institutions were spread among the
Serbs, Roumanians, the Slavs in general, the Arabs, the Arme-
nians, and the Italians.⁵

Unfortunately, we know only a few hospitals by name, and
those mostly in Constantinople. Our knowledge of hospitals in
populous cities such as Antioch and Alexandria is not very
satisfactory. Nonetheless, hospitals and other philanthropic institutions must have existed not only in the three large centers of
the East mentioned above, but in such cities as Thessalonica,⁶
Nicea,⁷ and even in Kastoria,⁸ Hadrianople, Ephesos, Theodosiopolis, Corinth, and other provincial towns.

We must emphasize from the outset that xenones or
xenodocheia and gerocomeia also offered medical services. The
xenon of Sampson, for example, had a well-organized dispen-

3. *Ibid.*, pp. 357–58.
4. *Ibid.*, pp. 360–64; for Byzantine medicine in general, in addition to the
works cited above, see: G. C. Pournaropoulos, «Ἱστορία Βυζαντινῆς Ἰατρικῆς» (Athens, 1942); Phaedon Koukoules, BB II, VI (Athens, 1957),
9–43; Owsei Temkin, "Byzantine Medicine: Tradition and Empiricism," *Dumbarton Oaks Papers*, XVI (1962), 97–115; K. N. Alivizatos and E. P. Lekos,
"Ἡ Βυζαντινὴ Ἰατρικὴ κατὰ τὴν ἐποχὴν τῆς Ἁλώσεως τῆς Κωνσταντινουπόλεως ὑπὸ τῶν Τούρκων," XVIIᵉ *Congrès international d'histoire
de la médecine*, I (Athens, 1960), 367–377. A. Kouzis, "Contribution a l'étude
de la médecine des zenones pendant le XVᵉ siècle," B-NJ, VI (1927–1928),
76–90.
5. See the medical announcement of the Professors of Medicine, O. Temkin, R. Katic and L. Stanogevic, M. D. Grmed, N. Vatamatu, L. A. Ohanessian,
Sergio Terracina, and G. C. Pournaropoulos, XVIIᵉ *Congrès international
d'histoire de la médecine* (Athenes-Cos., 4–13 Septembre, 1960), pp. 336 ff.
6. Thessalonica is described as "πολυάνθρωπος πόλις" in the tenth century; see "Life of St. Phantinos," AASS, August VI (Paris, 1868), p. 623.
7. Theophanes Continuatus, *Chronographia*, p. 464: "πόλιν ἀρχαιόπλου-
τον καὶ πολύανδρον."
8. Kastoria is called "πολυάνθρωπος" city in the eleventh century; see
Cecaumenos, *Strategicon*, p. 32.

sary,[9] as did the xenonodocheion of Euvoulos, the establishment of Theophilos, the Myrelaion institution, and others to be mentioned later.

The erection of hospitals and clinics was the work of the Church, the emperor, or the State in general, and of pious lay benefactors. The ecclesiastical institutions were usually attached to a place of worship, which was considered a hospital in the spiritual sense. But the Church was considered not only as a hospital of the human soul but as a depository of healing power for the human body. The sick expected medical help but they never forgot to invoke a visitation by God, Jesus, and the Theotocos or a saint.[10] This tradition, invoking the divine for healing, was also common among the ancient Greeks.[11]

HOSPITALS IN THE EARLY EMPIRE

In the fourth century Basil the Great, Bishop of Caesarea in Cappadocia, established a general philanthropic institution known as the Basileias in honor of its founder. It included a hospital and is believed to be the first organized charitable system in the Christian Greek East.[12] It was established circa 372 while Basil was Caesarea's bishop. According to the historian Sozomen it was "the most celebrated hospice for the poor." [13]

But Gregory Nazianzenos, Basil's contemporary, implies that Basileias was a multi-purpose institution which, besides the hospital, also had rooms for lepers, travelers, physicians, cooks, and others. Gregory lauds it as "a new city, a storehouse of piety, the common treasury of the wealthy . . . where disease is regarded in a religious light . . . and sympathy is put to the

9. Papadopoulos-Kerameus, *Varia*, miracle 21, pp. 25–26.
10. Cf. H. J. Magoulias, "The Lives of the Saints as sources of data for the history of Byzantine medicine in the sixth and seventh centuries," BZ, LVII, No. 1 (June, 1964), 135–36.
11. Cf. Hippocrates' *Decorum* VI; W. A. Jayne, *The Healing Gods in Ancient Civilizations*, pp. 233–35, 237–38, 257–59.
12. The Roman matron Fabiola is credited as the first Christian to establish a hospital in Rome. She founded it as "a place where she might gather sufferers out of the streets, and where she might nurse the unfortunate victims of sickness and want." Jerome, "Letter 76.6," *Nicene and Post-Nicene Fathers of the Christian Church*, 2nd Series, VI (New York, 1893), 160.
13. Sozomenos, *Eccl. History*, Bk. VI, ch. 34.9, p. 291: "Προέστη δὲ καὶ Βασιλειάδος, ὃ πτωχῶν ἐστιν ἐπισημότατον καταγώγιον, ὑπὸ Βασιλείου τοῦ Καισαρείας ἐπισκόπου οἰκοδομηθέν."

test." [14] Gregory also writes that Basil's philanthropic institution, because of its purpose, was much superior to the seven gates of Thebes, the walls of Babylon, the Mausoleion of Caria, the pyramids of Egypt, the Colossos of Rhodes, majestic churches, or whatever else men admire.[15]

A third contemporary source adds that the fate of the lepers was especially miserable. Consequently, Basil included a leprosarium in the Basileias, appealing to the rich to grant him the money to establish and support it. Not only victims of leprosy but people suffering from other infirmities found shelter there. Gregory Nazianzenos, a close friend of Basil, became his co-worker there.[16] William Ramsay observes that this institution, the "New City," became the center from which "the irresistible influence of the Church permeated the whole district, as, centuries before, the cities founded by the Greek kings had been centers from which the Greek influence had slowly penetrated the country round." [17]

Basil himself counseled the monks who worked there to look after the patients as if they were brothers of Christ.[18]

Following the example of Basil, St. John Chrysostom built several hospitals in Constantinople. One of the first reforms he undertook following his election as Patriarch of Constantinople

14. Gregory Nazianzenos, "The Panegyric of St. Basil," Ch. LXIII, ed. Fernard Boulenger, *Grégoire de Nazianze Discours Funèbres* (Paris, 1908), p. 188. Cf. A. H. M. Jones, *The Later Roman Empire*, II, 901; for Basil's philanthropies see also Gregory of Nyssa, *Encomium*, Ch. 17, ed. James Aloysius Stein, *Encomium of St. Gregory on his Brother St. Basil* (Washington, 1928), pp. 36 ff.

15. Gregory of Nyssa, *Encomium*. Cf. F. H. Stead, *The Story of Social Christianity*, I (London [1924]), 105 ff.

16. Gregory the Presbyter, *Life of St. Gregory the Theologian*, MPG, XXXV, col. 273BC. Cf. P. Christou, «Ἡ Κοινωνιολογία τοῦ Μεγάλου Βασιλείου» (Athens, 1951), pp. 83–91; E. F. Morison, *St. Basil and His Rule* (London, 1912), pp. 120–30. What Morison, on p. 128, calls "other such hospitals" in Basil's diocese seem to me to be homes for the poor, properly so called.

17. W. M. Ramsay, *The Church in the Roman Empire*, 8th edition (London, 1904), p. 461.

18. St. Basil the Great, *Regulae Brevius Tractatae*, No. 155, MPG, XXXI, col. 1184B: "'Ἐπειδὴ διδασκόμεθα οἱ ὑπηρετοῦντες τοῖς ἐν τῷ ξενοδοχείῳ ἀρρώστοις μετὰ τοιαύτης διαθέσεως ὑπηρετεῖν, ὡς ἀδελφοῖς τοῦ Κυρίου ὑπηρετοῦντες." For the social ideals and work of St. Basil see the extensive study of Stanislas Giet, *Les Idées et l'Action sociales de Saint Basile* (Paris, 1941), especially pp. 400–23.

was the reorganization of church finances. When he found extraordinary extravagance in a certain bishop's expenditures, he ordered that the large sums allocated to the bishop's residence be transferred to the hospital.[19] Unfortunately, we do not know which hospital this was, nor even the founder's name. The Byzantine Empire of the fourth century also faced famines, the recurrent menace of barbaric invasions, the land-hungry power elite, and other natural catastrophes.[20] There was a pressing need for more hospitals. Chrysostom, who saw that "the need of treatment was very great, erected other hospitals, over which he appointed two devout priests, as well as physicians and cooks . . . so that strangers coming to the city, and there falling ill, could obtain medical care, as a thing which was not only good in itself, but also for the glory of the Savior."[21]

The oldest known hospital in Constantinople is the one built by Hosios Marcianos[22] near the Church of St. Irene at the Perama. This district was near the sea in the quarter of Balikpazari.[23] The founder of the hospital lived during the reign of Marcian (450–57)[24] and apparently was very rich.[25] He is credited with the establishment of other institutions and other philanthropies.[26] Nothing else is known about this hospital and no other nosocomeion of the fourth and the fifth centuries is identified by name.

19. Palladios, *Vita S. Jo. Chr.*, Ch. 5, p. 32: " ῎Ερχεται εἰς τὸ μέρος τοῦ ἀναλώματος τοῦ ἐπισκοπείου καὶ εὑρίσκει δαψίλειαν οὐ τὴν τυχοῦσαν καὶ κελεύει μετενεχθῆναι τὴν πολυτέλειαν τούτων εἰς τὸ νοσοκομεῖον."

20. A. H. M. Jones, *The Later Roman Empire*, II, 810–11, 853–55, and Ferdinand Lot, *The End of the Ancient World and the Beginnings of the Middle Ages* (New York, 1961), pp. 189 ff.

21. Palladios, *Vita S. Jo. Chr.*:   "Περιττευούσης δὲ τῆς χρείας, κτίζει πλείονα νοσοκομεῖα προσκαταστήσας δύο τῶν εὐλαβῶν πρεσβυτέρων, ἔτι μὴν καὶ ἰατροὺς καὶ μαγείρους καὶ χρηστοὺς τῶν ἀγάμων ἐργάτας τούτοις εἰς ὑπηρεσίαν, ὥστε τοὺς ἐπιχωριάζοντας ξένους καὶ ὑπὸ νόσου ληφθέντας (μάλιστα δὲ τὴν ἱερὰν καλουμένην) τυγχάνειν ἐπιμελείας, καὶ δι' αὐτὸ τὸ καλὸν καὶ διὰ τὴν τοῦ Σωτῆρος δόξαν."

22. Pseudo-Codinos, *Patria*, Th. Preger, II, p. 234.

23. Janin, *Constantinople* (Paris, 1950), p. 374.

24. If Pseudo-Codinos and Symeon Metaphrastes are correct that Marcianos lived during the reign of Marcian, then Francois Halkin erroneously places the saint's death at 388; see Halkin, *Hag. Graeca*, I, 76.

25. Pseudo-Codinos, *Patria*, Th. Preger, II, 233, and especially Symeon Metaphrastes, MPG, CXIV, col. 432B.

26. Metaphrastes, MPG, CXIV, p. 437A, 449BC ff.

Nevertheless, we know that there were xenones or hospices in the fourth century which were regular hospitals. The Empress Flacilla, wife of Theodosios the Great, restored some of them and frequently visited their patients.[27]

Like St. Basil in the previous century, Bassianos, Bishop of Ephesos during the fifth century and participant in the Council of Chalcedon,[28] established a hospital in the see of his diocese with accommodations for seventy patients.[29] According to two other authorities, who identify him as Brassianos, the hospital had rooms for eighty patients.[30]

In the same century certain important monks established hospitals not only for men of the cloth but for laymen. No one was refused admission. Among the several foundations of Sabas, the founder of the Grand Lavra near Jerusalem, was a hospital erected near the monastery.[31] Two Isaurian brothers, Theodoulos and Gelasios, were the architects of the complex, and so were called the new Beseleel and Eliab, after the architects of the Tabernacle.[32]

Theodosios the Coenobiarches (+ c. 529) not only practiced daily philanthropies, but established a number of institutions which survived for many decades. He believed that the best way to express love for one's fellow man was to visit him when he was sick and partake of his pain and affliction. Theodosios founded three houses for the sick: one was for monks and the other two for the laity—one for important personages and the other for poor and needy individuals. The third house was also to serve as a home for monks advanced in age.[33]

27. Theodoretos of Cyrus, *Eccl. History*, Bk. 5, p. 314.

28. A. Grillmeier and H. Bacht, *Das Konzil von Chalkedon*, I (Wurzburg, 1951), 276; II, 125–27; Victor Schultze, *Altchristliche Stadte und Landschaften II. Kleinasien* (Gutersloh, 1926), pp. 115–17; both identify Brassianos with Bassianos.

29. Schultze, *Altchristliche Stadte*, p. 115.

30. Filaretos Vafides, " 'Η 'Αγάπη καὶ τὰ ἔργα αὐτῆς ἐν τῇ 'Αρχαίᾳ 'Εκκλησίᾳ," *Gregorios o Palamas*, II, 363; Uhlhorn, *Christian Charity*, p. 196. But cf. Rhallis-Potlis, «Σύνταγμα», III, 428.

31. Schwartz, *Kyrillos*, Ch. 32, p. 117; see also Festugière, *Les Moines*, pp. 43 ff.

32. Schwartz, *Kyrillos*; cf. Exod. 31:2–6.

33. Symeon Metaphrastes, *Vita S Theodosii*, Ch. 33, MPG, CXIV col. 501A: "Τρεῖς οἰκοδομήσας οἴκους, τὸν μὲν τοῖς διὰ Χριστὸν ἀζύγοις ... πρὸς τὴν ἐν ἀσθενείαις τοῦ σώματος θεραπείαν ἀπένειμεν, εἶτα τοὺς δύο

In addition to building this establishment, Theodosios used the money donated by a certain rich and pious woman to erect a hospital properly so called in Jericho.[34] The hospital complex of Theodosios was thirty-five stadia west of Sabas' Grand Lavra [35] and six miles southeast of Jerusalem.[36]

THE SIXTH CENTURY

Our knowledge of hospitals and hostels in the sixth century is more satisfactory. Joshua the Stylite paints a macabre picture of the people of Edessa in the years 501–02. Famine, locusts, and pestilence had combined to bring much misery, sickness, and death to Edessa. The Church of Edessa spared neither effort nor money to relieve the victims. The state, also, played a great role in helping them, especially Demosthenes, the governor of the city. There was wailing by night and day from the pangs of hunger; bodies wasted away and became skeletons through want and disease. "The whole city was full of them, and they began to die in the porticoes and in the streets." [37] Among those who played a major role in helping the people were the oeconomoi (stewards) of the Great Church, the priests Mar Tewath-il and Mar Stratonicos; the latter eventually became a bishop of Harran.

Joshua the Stylite writes that those two priests "established an infirmary among the buildings attached to the Great Church of Edessa. Those who were very ill used to go in and lie down there; and many dead bodies were found in the infirmary, which they buried along with those at the xenodocheion.[38]

More infirmaries were established by the aristocracy of the city and by the governor. The "Greek soldiers too set up places

τοῖς ἐν κόσμῳ ζῶσι καὶ στρεφομένοις ἀνῆκε, καὶ τούτων αὐτῶν τὸν μὲν τοῖς ἐπισημοτέροις καὶ σεμνοτέροις, τὸν δὲ τοῖς εὐτελεστέροις καὶ τῆς ἑτέρων δεομένοις ἐπικουρίας. . . ." Cf. Hermann Usener, *Der Heilige Theodosios* (Leipzig, 1890), p. 40.

34. *Ibid.*, col. 501B: "Πρὸς τούτοις καὶ νοσοκομεῖον ἕτερον αὐτῷ κατεσκεύαστο, τὰ τῆς συμπαθείας ἔργα τῇ συμπαθεῖ τῷ ὄντι καὶ φιλαν-θρώπῳ ψυχῇ, ὃ καὶ δώρημα γυναικὸς ἦν κοσμίας σφόδρα καὶ τὸν τρόπον θεοφιλοῦς. . . ." Cf. Usener, *Theodosios*, p. 41.

35. Schwartz, *Kyrillos*, Ch. 29, p. 114.

36. *Ibid.*, p. 237; cf. Festugière, *Les Moines*, p. 140.

37. Joshua the Stylite, *Chronicle*, Chs. 41–42, tr. by William Wright (Cambridge, 1882), p. 31.

38. *Ibid.*, Ch. 42, p. 32.

in which the sick slept, and charged themselves with their expenses." [39]

We find a similar case in the city of Amida. John of Ephesos relates that there were many sick and destitute in that city, among them crippled, blind, and aged who had no one to look after or to console them.[40] A certain woman named Euphemia "would even go round the inns and roads and habitations . . . lest there should be any needy man or stranger laid up sick in one of them, so that she in fact found many and relieved them. And some she took into her house, and some she carried to superintendents of hospitals, and gave charge concerning them." [41]

In the large-scale program of buildings and establishments which Justinian instituted [42] were included several hospitals. He built two institutions next to the Church of the Theotocos in Jerusalem, facing each other. Both are called xenones. One of them, however, was to be utilized as a hospital for the poor [43] and was erected as a result of a petition submitted by St. Sabas to the emperor.[44] In his request Sabas emphasized the needs of foreigners and strangers who fell sick while visiting the holy city and the monastic community there.

Justinian ordered that the petition be granted. The original plan provided for a hospital of one hundred beds, but later he increased it to two hundred and endowed it with an annual revenue of one thousand eight hundred and fifty solidi.[45] Antonios Placentinos relates that Justinian's hospital included accommoda-

39. *Ibid.*, Ch. 43, p. 32.

40. John of Ephesos, "Lives of Mary and Euphemia," ed. tr. E. W. Brooks, *Patrologia Orientalis*, XVII, fasc. 1 (Paris, 1923), 180.

41. *Ibid.*, p. 180.

42. Procopios, *Buildings*, I. 1 ff., ed. Jacobus Haury, *Procopii Caesariensis Opera Omnia*, III. 2 (Leipzig, 1905), pp. 5 ff.

43. *Ibid.*, V. 6, p. 165: "Ξενῶνες δὲ τῆς ἑτέρας ἐφ᾽ ἑκάτερα δύο . . . ὁ δὲ δὴ ἕτερος ἀναπαυστήριον νοσοῦσι πτωχοῖς."

44. Schwartz, *Kyrillos*, Ch. 72, p. 175: "Πλὴν ἡμεῖς, βασιλεῦ πανευσεβέστατε, . . . ἓν δὲ νοσοκομεῖον παρακαλοῦμεν ἐν τῇ ἁγίᾳ πόλει συστήσασθαι πρὸς τὴν τῶν ἀρρωστούντων ξένων ἐπιμέλειαν. . . ."

45. A. H. M. Jones misquotes the source and accepts that "Justinian built a hospital of a hundred beds at Jerusalem." *The Later Roman Empire*, II, 901. Cyril of Scythopolis writes: "ἐκέλευσεν . . . νοσοκομεῖον κτισθῆναι ἐν τῷ μέσῳ τῆς ἁγίας πόλεως ἑκατὸν μὲν κραββατίων, πρόσοδον δὲ καθαρὰν ἀφορίσας αὐτῷ τὸ πρότερον ἐνιαυσιαίων νομισμάτων χιλίων ὀκτακοσίων πεντήκοντα, μετέπειτα δὲ διακοσίων κραββατίων ἐκέλευσεν τὸ αὐτὸ γενέσθαι νοσοκομεῖον προσθεὶς τοσαύτην . . . πρόσοδον." Schwartz, *Kyrillos*, p. 175.

tions for three thousand patients,[46] but this number seems grossly exaggerated.[47]

Recent excavations have brought to light the foundations of a building which has been identified with Justinian's hospital.[48] The proposed identification is based on two arguments. First, the dimensions of the building suggest an establishment of about the size mentioned by Cyril of Scythopolis, i.e. a hospital of two hundred beds. The second rests on the information which gives an Arabic translation of Antiochos Strategos' account of the capture of Jerusalem by the Persians in 614. According to this version one hundred and sixty-seven victims were found dead in the "royal gerocomeion." [49]

De Vaux and Milik perhaps falsely assume that a gerocomeion is the same as a nosocomeion or hostel. A nosocomeion we know was a hospital of a general nature: both Procopios and Cyril of Scythopolis wrote about "a home for the sick" and a "nosocomeion" in Jerusalem.

Charles Clermont-Ganneau, who conducted excavations in Palestine in the last quarter of the nineteenth century, observed that the meaning of gerocomeion ". . . is strictly a retreat for old people . . . it is this same word corrupted by the copyists, which we must recognise in the *gerocernio* of the Life of John the Silent by the monk Cyril . . . and also in the puzzling . . . royal *Jer(o)kumiun* of the Arabic history of the taking of Jerusalem by the Persians in 614. The qualifying adjective 'royal' applied to this latter establishment, leads one to think that it must have been one of those founded by either Eudocia or Justinian." [50]

46. Antonios Placentinos, *Itinera Hierodolymitan*, 23, ed. Paulus Geyer, *Itinera Hierosolymitana Saeculi IIII–VIII* (Prague, 1898), pp. 174–75: "De Sion ueninus in basilica sanctae Mariae, ubi est congregatio nimia monachorum, ubi sunt et xenodochia uirorum ac mulierum, susceptio peregrinorum, mensas innumerabiles, lecta aegrotorum amplius tria milia."

47. J. T. Milik, "La Topographie de Jerusalem vers la fin de l'epoque byzantine," *Mélanges de l'Université Saint Joseph*, XXXII (1960–61), 151.

48. Roland de Vaux, "Communication-Chronique archéologique," *Révue biblique*, LXXXI, no. 2 (April, 1964), p. 257; J. T. Milik, "Topographie de Jerusalem," p. 151; cf. Festugière, *Les Moines*, p. 107, and note 242.

49. Frederick C. Conybeare, "Notes and Documents—Antiochus Strategos' Account of the Sack of Jerusalem in AD 614," EHR, XXV (July, 1910), 515; J. T. Milik, *ibid.*, p. 151; de Vaux, "Communication-chronique," p. 257.

50. Charles Simon Clermont-Ganneau, *Archaeological Researches in Palestine during the Years 1873–1874*, tr. Aubrey Stewart, I (London, 1899), 247.

Figure 20. Foundations of a building in Jerusalem excavated by Roland De Vaux and identified by him as the ruins of the Hospital of Justinian. Reproduced with permission from *Revue Biblique* (April, 1964), pp. 212 ff.

The argument leads to the belief that there is no need to confuse a gerocomeion with a nosocomeion; there might have been, in addition to Eudocia's royal gerocomeion, other establishments for the aged built by Justinian or some other emperor. Furthermore, we know that the term nosocomeion was employed by contemporary authors to describe a hospital in Jerusalem built by an unknown patriarch.[51] A second point: we know that there was in Jerusalem a royal gerocomeion built about 450 by the Empress Eudocia, who established, besides several homes for the

51. R. A. Stewart Macalister, "The Rock-Cut Tombs in Wady Er-Rababi, Jerusalem," *Palestine Exploration Fund—Quarterly Statement* (London, 1900), Pl. III.

aged, houses for the poor, buildings for travelers, and the like.[52] It was Eudocia's royal gerocomeion in which John Hesychastes [53] had found shelter on his way to the holy city, and it is probably of this royal gerocomeion that the Arabic and the Georgian texts of Antiochos Strategos speak, and not of Justinian's hospital. And a third point: why should we accept the account of the Arabic translation, which mentions one hundred and sixty-seven victims, and overlook the Georgian text, of the same Greek source, now lost, which states that seven hundred and eighty people were found slaughtered in the "imperial gerocomeion"? [54]

Justinian also built and expanded hospitals in Constantinople. Some time before his reign a certain pious man, Sampson by name, had erected a xenon in the capital which was actually a home for people who were "suffering from serious illness and were destitute." [55] It was located between the churches of Hagia Sophia and St. Irene. It was destroyed during the Nika revolt,[56] for nothing was left untouched by the rioters. Justinian rebuilt it as a better and much larger building, and endowed it with a generous annual income so that more people could receive its services.[57] With the cooperation of his wife Theodora, Justinian established two more institutions of the same nature known as the House of Isidore and the House of Arcadios.[58] They were located opposite the xenon of Sampson.

52. Nic. Callistos, *Eccl. History*, Bk. XIV, Ch. 50; MPG, CXLVI, col. 1240AB.

53. Schwartz, *Kyrillos*, p. 204: " Ἐπιβὰς πλοίῳ ἦλθεν εἰς Ἱεροσόλυμα καὶ καταμένει ἐν τῷ πρὸς τῆς ἁγίας πόλεως γηροκομείῳ τῷ ὑπὸ τῆς μακαρίας κτισθέντι Εὐδοκίας, ἐν ᾧ γηροκομεῖον εὐκτήριον ἐστιν τοῦ ἁγίου μάρτυρος Γεωργίου."

54. Antiochos Strategos, *Captivitas Hierosolymae*, XXIII. 32, ed. tr. Gerard Garitte, *La Prise de Jérusalem par les Perses en 614*, CSCO (Louvain, 1960), p. 52: "Et invenimus in gerocomio regis septingentas et octoginta animas."

55. Procopios, *Buildings*, Bk. I. ii, 14–15: "ἦν δέ τις μεταξὺ ταύταις δὴ ταῖς ἐκκλησίαις ξενών, ἀνθρώποις ἀνειμένοις ἀπορουμένοις τε καὶ νοσοῦσι τὰ ἔσχατα . . . τοῦτον ἀνήρ τις θεοσεβὴς ἐν τοῖς ἄνω χρόνοις ἐδείματο, Σαμψὼν ὄνομα."

56. *Chronicon Paschale*, p. 622: "καὶ ὁ ξενὼν τοῦ Σαμψὼν ὁ μέγας ἐκαύθη, καὶ ἀπώλοντο οἱ ἐν αὐτῷ ἀνακείμενοι ἄρρωστοι."

57. Procopios, *Buildings*, Bk. I. ii. 16: " Ἰουστινιανὸς δὲ αὐτὸν ἀνῳκοδομήσατο βασιλεύς, κάλλει μὲν κατασκευῆς ἀξιώτερον, πλήθει δὲ οἰκιδίων παρὰ πολὺ μείζω· προσόδῳ τε αὐτὸν ἐπετείων δεδώρηται χρημάτων μεγάλων, ὅπως δὲ πλείοσιν ἐς ἀεὶ ταλαιπωρουμένοις ἀνθρώποις ἰῷτο τὰ πάθη."

58. *Ibid.*, Bk. I. ii. 17: "δύο ξενῶνας ἑτέρους ἀπ' ἐναντίας αὐτῷ ἔθετο ἐν ταῖς Ἰσιδώρου τε καὶ Ἀρκαδίου καλουμέναις οἰκίαις."

Figure 21. Inscriptions which indicate the existence of hospitals (*nosocomeia*) as institutions distinct from *gerocomeia* (homes for the aged). Reproduced with permission from J. T. Milik, "La Topographie de Jérusalem vers la fin de l'époque Byzantine," *Mélanges de l'Université Saint Joseph*, Vol. 37 (1961), pl. III.

In his account of the reconstruction of Antioch after its sack by the Persians in 540,[59] Procopios writes that Justinian erected buildings for the destitute sick and contributed all the means for the care and cure of their illnesses, with separate quarters for men and women.[60] Despite the fact that in his earlier days Procopios might have had a special interest in emphasizing the establishment of philanthropic institutions by Justinian,[61] there is no reason for us to doubt his information. In Bithynia, he says, at a place called Pythia, where there was a natural hot spring used as a cure by many, a hospital was already in existence. Justinian enlarged and improved it, together with its church.[62]

Again, the historian Evagrios reports that during the plague which swept through the Empire in 542 [63] Justinian built a hospital in Daphne, a suburb of Antioch: a certain monk named Thomas, who had come to the city on an errand of his monastery, became ill and died in it. Evagrios calls it a "resort for the sick." [64]

Across the Bosporos from the city of Constantinople in the suburb of Irion, there was a leprocomion, or hospital for lepers, known as Zoticon. The sources give us conflicting testimony as to the origin of this institution. Pseudo-Codinos relates that it was established by Justinian's successor Justin II and his wife Sophia (565–78): Justin built it so that the lepers might find rest there, and he endowed it with all necessary money and utensils. Zoticos, after whom the institution was named, was its first director. He had served as protovestiarios for all the city's institutions during Justin's reign.[65] According to another source,[66]

59. See Glanville Downey, *A History of Antioch in Syria from Seleucus to the Arab Conquest* (Princeton, N.J., 1961), pp. 533–46.

60. Procopios, *Buildings*, II. 10, p. 80; cf. Downey, *Antioch*, p. 553.

61. Glanville Downey, "Procopius on Antioch: A Study of Method in the 'De Aedificiis,'" B, XIV (1939), 361 ff.

62. Procopios, *Buildings*, V. iii, p. 156: "ἀλλὰ καὶ τοῦ ἀρχαγγέλου τὸ τέμενος καὶ τὸ τῶν νοσούντων ἀναπαυστήριον, μείζω τε καὶ κατὰ πολὺ ἐπιφανέστερα κατεστήσατο."

63. Downey, *Antioch*, pp. 553–57.

64. Evagrios, *Eccl. History*, Bk. IV, ch. 35, p. 185; cf. Joannes Moschos, *Pratum Spirituale*, Ch. 88, MPG, LXXXVII. 3, p. 2945AB.

65. Pseudo-Codinos, *Patria*, Th. Preger, III, 235, 267 and n. 164: "ὡσαύτως καὶ τὸν ὅσιον Ζωτικὸν τὸ Δεύτερον· καὶ ἐτύπωσεν ἀναπαύεσθαι τοὺς λωβοὺς ἐκεῖ καὶ σιτηρέσια λαμβάνειν. Παρίστατο δὲ Ζωτικὸς ὁ πρωτοβεστιάριος αὐτοῦ τοῖς κτίσμασιν." Cf. Richter, *Quellen*, p. 203; J. Pargoire, "Hieria," BIARC, IV, 41–43; Janin, *Geogr. Eccles.*, pp. 578–79; du Cange, *Constantinopolis Christiana*, Bk. IV, Ch. 9, no. 17, p. 165.

66. *Synaxarium*, pp. 359–62.

however, the leprocomion of Zoticos was founded by Emperor Constantios (337–61) in honor of St. Zoticos, whose philanthropy toward lepers cost him his life. This source relates that an epidemic of leprosy had struck Constantinople during the reign of Constantine the Great and his successors. Constantine had ordered that all the lepers should be drowned because there were no means to cure leprosy and to stop its spread. But Zoticos, who had come from Rome, had compassion on them and was able to prevent many drownings; indeed, he erected tents on the mountain or hill named Elaiones where many victims of the ailment found shelter. While Constantine was friendly to Zoticos, his son was hostile. It happened that Constantios' daughter fell sick with leprosy and the Emperor ordered that she too should be drowned. Zoticos, however, rescued her and took her to his hospital. When the Emperor was informed of this he ordered Zoticos put to death. The saint was tied between the tails of two mules and torn to death. Then the animals were driven into the sea, where his body was to be cut free and drowned. At this point, however, the animals obstinately refused to move. Constantios, learning of this, accepted it as a miracle and ordered that a "great home for lepers" [67] be built in honor of Zoticos, endowing it magnificently.

As is evident, there is much that is legendary in this narration, but its general historicity cannot be denied. Zoticos' leprosarium stood until the seventh century, when it was burned by the Slavs during a raid. Heraclios rebuilt it in wood during the fourteenth year of his reign, in 624.[68] In the tenth century it was restored once again by the Emperor John Tzimisces (969–76). In the last days of his life Tzimisces endowed it abundantly, and during personal visits to it he distributed money to the victims. He even willed half of his properties and money to it.[69] Leo

---

67. *Ibid.*, p. 362: "Ταῦτα ἀκούσας καὶ ἰδὼν ὁ βασιλεύς, . . . τὸ θεῖον ἐξιλεοῦτο μετὰ συντριμμοῦ . . . καὶ παραυτίκα προστάττει μετ' ἐπιμελείας καὶ πολλῆς τιμῆς κηδευθῆναι τὸ σῶμα τοῦ μάρτυρος καὶ σπουδῇ συντόνῳ ἀνεγεῖραι οἶκον μέγιστον τοῖς λωβοῖς, ἐκ τῶν βασιλικῶν ἀναλωμάτων τὴν ἔξοδον γενέσθαι κελεύσας καὶ προάστεια πλεῖστα . . . ἀφιερώσας."

68. George Cedrenos, *Historiarum Compendium*, I, 698–99: "ἔκτισε δὲ καὶ τὸ λωβῶν γηροκομεῖον εἰς τὰ Ἡρίου, τὸ λεγόμενον τοῦ ζωτικοῦ ἐγχόρηγον, διὰ τὸ ὑπὸ τῶν Σθλαβίνων καῆναι ξυλόστεγον ὄν. . . ."

69. Leo Diaconos, *Historiae VI. 5*, ed. C. B. Hasi (Bonn, 1878), p. 99: "τὴν δὲ τῷ καταντιπέρας Βυζαντίου τῶν λελωβημένων νοσοκομείῳ ἠφώρισε. . . ."

Diaconos adds that Tzimisces also added new houses to the existing institution.[70] Constantine Porphyrogenitos (913–59) also expanded it in order to include "all those who suffered from leprosy."[71] In the eleventh century the Zoticon was destroyed once
again by an earthquake, but was rebuilt in 1032 by the Emperor
Romanos Argyros.[72] In the thirteenth century a Russian pilgrim,
Antonios of Novgorod, writes that "in the hospital on the hill
beyond Is-Pigas, is buried the body of St. Zoticos. The Emperor
had ordered him to build a palace and instead he took the gold
and distributed it to the poor; the Emperor then ordered him to
be attached to the tails of two horses, until he should die. The
saint was buried and the people built a church there. A hospital
was founded and Christians do works of charity there."[73] It is evident that with very few variations Antonios follows the version
of the Synaxarium concerning the origin of Zoticos' leprosarium:[74] it is not necessary to relate here a third extant version
of the tale.[75]

We hear nothing more about this establishment after the report of Antonios. As for its location, there is no unanimity of
opinion. The Synaxarium speaks about the hill or "mountain beyond Byzantium called at that time Elaiones."[76] Cedrenos places
it in the region of Irion on the Asiatic coast.[77] Leo Diaconos
indicates that it stood across the Bosporos from Constantinople,[78] while Antonios mentions "the mountain or hill beyond

70. *Ibid.:* "προσεποικοδομήσας τοῖς παλαιοῖς δόμοις καὶ ἑτέρας οἰκίας."

71. Theophanes Continuatus, *Chronographia,* p. 449. 4: "χρὴ οὖν καὶ
περὶ τοῦ νοσοκομείου τοῦ ὁσίου ἐξειπεῖν. ὁ βασιλεὺς Κωνσταντῖνος . . .
κατασκευάζει, ὡς ἐπισυνάζεσθαι πάντας τοὺς τοιᾷδε νόσῳ κυριευομέ-
νους."

72. Byzantios, «Κωνσταντινούπολις», II, 238.

73. B. de Khitrowo, *Itinéraires russes en Orient* (Genève, 1889), p. 108:
"Dans l'Hôpital, fûr la montagne, au dela d'Is-Pigas, est enterré Saint Zotic;
l'empereur ordonna à ce Zotic de batir un palais, & lui, il prit l'or & le distribua
aux pauvres; l'empereur ordonna alors de l'attacher à la queue de deux
chevaux, afin qu'ils l'exterminassent; ils le trainerent par les champs & s'arrete-
rent dans un bois; le saint y fut enterré, & l'on y batit une église; on y fonda
aussi un hôpital, & les chrétiens y font l'aumone." Cf. Janin, *Geogr. Eccles.,*
p. 579.

74. *Synaxarium,* p. 360.

75. Janin, *Geogr. Eccles.*

76. *Synaxarium,* p. 360.

77. Cedrenos, *Historiarum Compendium,* I, 699.

78. Leo Diaconos, *Historiae* VI. 5, p. 99: "Τὴν δὲ τῷ καταντιπέρας Βυ-

Is-Pigas." [79] Janin accepts Antonios' account as most likely; he believes that the leprosarium faced the city and that, together with its church, it was located on the hill above Galata where Pera begins, perhaps in the region of the Tunnel.[80] However, other authorities on the topography of Constantinople (e.g. Scarlatos Byzantios) place the Zoticon on the mountain Camlica, on the evidence of the Synaxarium. J. Meliopoulos and Ph. Koukoules prefer the information of Cedrenos and Leo Diaconos and place it in the region of Irion, between Scutari and Kuzhuncuk.[81]

Another leprosarium, with a multi-purpose function, existed in the region called Argyronium, along the coast of Euxine Pontos and beyond the Church of St. Panteleemon. During the fourth century it was used as a ptochotropheion but lepers could find shelter there, too. Epiphanios of Salamis narrates that Eustathios, Bishop of Sebastia in Pontos, had entrusted its administration to a presbyter named Aerios, who turned out to be an Arian, and, because of his heresy, was obliged to resign from his post.[82] The terminology which Epiphanios used reveals that this institution was for the poor and for strangers as well as for lepers. By the time of Justinian, this leprosarium had fallen into a state of "extreme disrepair." Procopios writes that Justinian restored it completely, and that it was used to house lepers and other destitute persons.[83]

In addition to persons of the imperial court and high church dignitaries, wealthy laymen were responsible for the erection of hospitals. Andronicos and Athanasia, a couple who lived in Antioch during the age of Justinian, departed upon the death of their children for the Holy Land. Before their departure, Andro-

ζαντίου τῶν λελωβημένων νοσοκομείῳ ἠφώρισε, προσεπικοδομήσας τοῖς παλαιοῖς δόμοις τῶν τῇ ἱερᾷ νόσῳ καμνόντων καὶ ἑτέρας οἰκίας."

79. De Khitrowo, *Itinéraires russes en Orient.*
80. Janin, *Geogr. Eccles., op. cit.,* p. 579; cf., his *Constantinople Byzantine* (Paris, 1950), pp. 416–17, 419.
81. Koukoules, BBΙΙ, II, 148, and n. 7.
82. Epiphanios, *Adversus Haereses,* Bk. 3, No. 55 (75); Migne, P. G., XLII. 2, 504C: "Αὐτίκα ὕστερον καθιστᾷ τοῦτον πρεσβύτερον, τό τε ξενοδοχεῖον αὐτῷ ἐμπιστεύει, ὅπερ ἐν τῷ Πόντῳ καλεῖται πτωχοτροφεῖον. Τοιαῦτα γάρ τινα κατασκευάζουσι κατὰ φιλοξενίαν καὶ τοὺς λελωβημένους καὶ ἀδυνάτους ἐκεῖσαι ποιοῦντες καταμένειν, ἐπιχορηγοῦσι κατὰ δύναμιν οἱ τῶν ἐκκλησιῶν προστάται."
83. Procopios, *Buildings,* I. 9, p. 37.

nicos called in his brother-in-law, entrusted a great sum of money to him and advised him to build a hospital in the city and a xenodocheion for monks.[84] On the other hand, their Synaxarium relates that Andronicos charged his father-in-law to build hospitals and houses for monks.[85] A hospital of some significance was erected by Appolinarios, Patriarch of Alexandria (551–68) in the region of Alexandria named Doryzin.[86] Symeon Metaphrastes relates that Appolinarios established three institutions: a hospital proper, an institution for the aged, and a church. All three structures were close to each other and the church replaced the building which had served as a clinic for the physician-monk Cyros,[87] who lived during the age of Diocletian.

The Emperor Tiberios (578–82) is also praised for his philanthropic works: according to Manassis, he erected many homes "for the consolation of those struggling with diseases."[88] We may assume that among those institutions there were hospitals, but we have no specific information.

Andrew, Archbishop of Crete in the seventh and eighth centuries (+740), had served earlier as director of an orphanage and a home for the poor in Constantinople. Upon his election to the episcopal see of Crete, he inaugurated an extensive program of philanthropic works, building a hospital on the island for the poor and endowing it from his own finances. This hospital, known as the Xenon,[89] did not charge anything for its services.

84. M. Leon Clugnet, "Vie et récits de l'Abbé Daniel, de Scété," ROC, V (Paris, 1900), p. 372; see also his biography, p. 377.

85. *Ibid.*, p. 381: "δέδωκε τὸ πλεῖστον μέρος τῆς οὐσίας αὐτοῦ τοῖς πτωχοῖς, καὶ τοὺς ὠνητοὺς τῶν δούλων ἠλευθέρωσε· τὰ δὲ λοιπὰ τῶν ὑπαρχόντων αὐτοῦ ἀνέθετο τῷ πενθερῷ αὐτοῦ, παραγγείλας αὐτῷ ποιῆσαι νοσοκομεῖα, καὶ ξενοδοχεῖα μοναχῶν."

86. Cf. Chrysostom Papadopoulos, «Ἱστορία τῆς Ἐκκλησίας Ἀλεξανδρείας» (Alexandria, 1935), p. 453.

87. Symeon Metaphrastes, MPG, CXIV, cols. 1232–1233; Theodorus Nissen, ed., "De SS Cyri et Ioannis Vitae Formis," AB, LVII (1939), p. 70.

88. Manasses, *Synopsis Chronike*, pp. 3481–3484: "ἐπὶ παραμυθίᾳ δὲ τῶν νόσοις παλαιόντων καὶ τῶν καμνόντων τῷ λυγρῷ καὶ πολυπόνῳ γήρᾳ οἴκους ἀνήγειρε πολλοὺς καὶ πενητοτροφεῖα."

89. Nicetas, "Life of St. Andrew the Hierosolymite," Ch. 7, Papadopoulos-Kerameus, «Ἀνάλεκτα», V., p. 176: "Τοῖς σωματικοῖς ἅμα καὶ ἐξ ἐνδείας νοσοῦσιν οἶκον παραμυθίας καὶ ἰατρείας ἐκ νέας ὁ παλαιὸς οὗτος καὶ ἐν κατορθώμασι γεγηρακὼς συνεστήσατο, τὸν καλούμενον Ξενῶνα, πᾶσαν αὐτάρκειαν χρείας διὰ Χριστὸν ἐξ οἰκείας ἐπιδόσεως παρασχών."

In an unedited *laudatio*, Andrew is praised as an ever alert protector of the poor who had given a free hospital to the sick.[90]

Hospitals were founded not only by emperors and church dignitaries but by rich laymen such as Philentolos the Cypriot, a wealthy man of the seventh century. He possessed great estates (choria) and many ships; his wealth, therefore, came from both the land and the sea. Of his life we know only that his father's name was Olympios, that he himself lived in the city of Constantia when Arcadios was archbishop of the island. Philentolos' anonymous biographer describes him as a man whose charities were extended to the poor and orphans and also to the sick, for whom he built a hospital.[91] Another source also speaks of hospitals. Their exact location is unknown, but we may safely assume that they were in his home town of Constantia.

In an anonymous life of St. Philaretos the Eleemosynary (+792), the grandfather-in-law of the Emperor Constantine VI (780–97), we hear that, upon the death of Philaretos in Constantinople, his wife returned to Pontos, the region of their origin. There she occupied herself with humanitarian work and established hospitals there.[92]

As we have seen, bishops of the church were instrumental in the erection of hospitals in their dioceses. When Theophylactos was elected Bishop of Nicomedeia (d. c. 840) he initiated a program of philanthropic work which included the erection of several institutions, among them a hospital which he staffed with physicians and nurses.[93] The biographer of Theophylactos, who probably wrote sometime during the age of Photios or in any case after 843,[94] adds that it was a famous hospital and that the bishop had endowed it adequately.

Because Theophylactos had established a church named after the saint-physicians Cosmas and Damianos [95] it is probable that

90. Halkin, *Hag. Graeca*, p. 35.

91. "Περὶ τοῦ Φιλεντόλου ᾽Ολυμπίου," ed. F. Halkin, "La Vision de Kaiounos et le sort éternel de Philentolos Olympiou," AB, LXIII (1945), 62: "Πολλὰ χρήματα εἰς πτωχοὺς καὶ ὀρφανοὺς καὶ εἰς πᾶσαν ἄλλην εὐσέβειαν σκορπίσας καὶ νοσοκομεῖον (νοσοκομεῖα) ποιήσας."

92. Fourmy-Leroy, "S Philarète," p. 37; A. A. Vasiliev, *Zhitie Filareta Miloctivago* (Odessa, 1900), p. 37.

93. Anonymous, *Life of St. Theophylactos, Archbishop of Nicomedeia*, ed. A. Vogt, "S. Theophylacte de Nicomedie," AB, L (1932), 75.

94. See introduction by Vogt, *ibid.*, p. 68.

95. *Ibid.*, p. 75.

the hospital was near the church, so that the sick might have the benefit of both human and heavenly physicians in an iatreion for maladies both spiritual and physical.[96]

FOUR CENTURIES OF INCOMPLETE EVIDENCE

Among the outstanding philanthropists of the late sixth and seventh centuries, John the Eleemon, Patriarch of Alexandria, was the most famous. His biographer attributes to him the erection of several xenones and hospitals.[97] These institutions were most probably for laymen, for he built another institution for visiting clergy and ascetics.[98] When a disastrous famine befell the great city of Alexandria, many expectant mothers suffered from hunger as well as from the pains of their physical condition. The patriarch ordered that seven lying-in maternity hospitals of forty beds each be established. Here a pregnant woman could give birth and stay for seven days of recuperation.[99]

Our knowledge of hospitals from the seventh to the tenth centuries is very limited, but for the eleventh and twelfth centuries our information is more specific. What we encounter in the sources of those earlier centuries are mostly general references to philanthropic institutions. Romanos Lecapenos, for example, is credited in the tenth century with the erection of a number of such institutions, among which we find "homes for the sick."[100]

In the eleventh century Constantine IX Monomachos built a hospital next to the Church of St. George[101] in Constantinople and bestowed many favors upon it.[102] Michael Attaleiates, who

96. Cf. *ibid.*, p. 82.
97. Gelzer, *Leontios,* Ch. 7, p. 13; cf. also Ch. 9, p. 17, and Delehaye, "Une Vie," p. 22. For an English translation of John's vita see Elizabeth Dawes and Norman H. Baynes, *Three Byzantine Saints* (Oxford, 1948), pp. 195–262.
98. Gelzer, *Leontios,* Ch. 24, p. 52.
99. Delehaye, "Une Vie," p. 22: " Ἑπτὰ λοχοκομεῖα κατὰ διαφόρους τόπους τῆς πόλεως ἐδομήσατο, ἐφ᾽ ἑνὶ τούτων ἑκάστῳ ἀνὰ τεσσαράκοντα κλίνας ἀφορίσας ἐστρωμένας, ἐν αἷς ἐφ᾽ ὅλαις ἑπτὰ ἡμέραις ἑκάστην γυναῖκα τίκτουσαν διαναπαύεσθαι ἐθέσπισεν."
100. Theophanes Continuatus, *Chronographia,* p. 431: " Ὁ δὲ βασιλεὺς Ῥωμανός . . . ἀνῳκοδόμησεν . . . καὶ γερόντων τροφεῖα ξενουμένων τε καταγώγια, ἀρρωστούντων ἐνδιαιτήματα."
101. See Janin, *Geogr. Eccles.,* p. 78.
102. Michael Attaleiates, *Historia,* ed. E. Bekker, CSHB (Bonn, 1853), p. 48: "Συνῆψε δὲ τούτοις καὶ νοσοκομεῖον ἐπιμελείας ἀνάμεστον."

as high civil servant favored the feudal military aristocracy in the eleventh century, praises Nicephoros Botaneiates for his philanthropies. Attaleiates attributes to the emperor the erection or transformation of several homes for the poor and general hospitals in Constantinople and its suburbs.[103]

Alexios Comnenos, whose philanthropic policies will be discussed later, built a hospital where common illnesses were cured, and where the blind, the lame, and the lepers were treated.[104]

THE HOSPITAL OF PANTOCRATOR AND OTHER COMNENI ESTABLISHMENTS

The name of John II Comnenos, who succeeded Alexios in the year 1118, is associated with one of the most important institutions in the long history of the Byzantine Empire. In 1136 the Emperor John and his wife Irene established a great monastery known as Pantocrator, which included a hospital and related institutions. The significance of Pantocrator lies in the fact that it was a medical center in the modern sense of the term.[105] It belongs to the proleptic as well as the therapeutic kind of philanthropia. The terms of its establishment and the scope of its humanitarian functions, as evidenced by its *Typikon* or constitution, are indeed amazing and a credit to twelfth-century Byzantium.

Constantinople, as the capital of the empire and as a city of pilgrimage, had to provide for visitors and foreigners. It was not only an element of Christian tradition, which can be traced to

103. *Ibid.*, p. 278: " Ἐπὶ πλέον δὲ τῶν λοιπῶν δεσποτείαν ἐκέκτηντο τά τε πτωχοτροφεῖα καὶ νοσοκομεῖα . . . οὐ μόνον δ᾽ ἐν τῇ βασιλευούσῃ ἀλλὰ καὶ ἔν τισι τῶν ἐπινείων αὐτῆς."

104. Anna Comnena, *Alexias*, Bk. XV. 7, p. 215: " Ἔστι γὰρ ἰδεῖν τούτους κατ᾽ ἄνδρα ἕκαστον ἐπερχόμενον, ὅπου μὲν τυφλούς, ὅπου δὲ καὶ χωλούς, ὅπου δέ τι καὶ ἄλλο κακὸν ἔχοντας."

105. Pan S. Codellas, "The Pantocrator, the Imperial Byzantine Medical Center of the XIIth Century A.D. in Constantinople," *Bulletin of the History of Medicine*, XII (1942), 410; A. Orlandos, " Ἀναπαράστασις," p. 198; Oeconomos, *La Vie religieuse*, pp. 193–221. Cf. Janin, *Geogr. Eccles.*, pp. 576–78; Ferdinand Chalandon, *Jean II Comnène et Manuel I Comnène* (Paris, 1912), pp. 31–34. For the complex of the Pantocrator, see Arthur H. S. Megaw, "Notes on Recent Work of the Byzantine Institute in Istanbul," DOP, no. 17 (1963), pp. 333, 335–64; C. Lagier, *L'Orient chrétien*, II (Paris [1950]), 457–59; Constantinos, Bishop of Eirenopolis, " Ἡ διαρρύθμισις τῶν Νοσοκομείων κατὰ τὴν Βυζαντινὴν Ἐποχήν," O, XXXII (1957), 432–33.

the very early history of the empire, but a matter of statesman-
ship for the emperor to establish hostels, old-age homes, hospices
for strangers, and other philanthropic institutions. The Typikon
of the Pantocrator throws much light on the social needs of the
empire,[106] on the history of medicine, diet, and sickness, and on
the activity of the physicians and their responsibility to their
patients. Information is given also on drugs, physical therapy,
feeding of the patients, and related subjects.[107]

The monastery of Pantocrator was in every way superior to
all neighboring monasteries, including the famous one of Stoudios, which otherwise had a remarkable reputation.[108] The Typikon given the Pantocrator by John II Comnenos gives impressive
information about the organization and the function of the
Xenon, a type of general hospital. There was also a section for
the aged, a psychiatric clinic, and an out-patient service. Joannes
Cinnamos states that it was customary for the hospitals to be
called Xenones.[109] And a xenodocheion received guests, strangers,
and pilgrims. Although theoretically it was separated from the
hospital, a xenodocheion frequently became a hospital when
many of its guests became ill.[110]

There were five main clinics in the hospital of the Pantocrator.
The first clinic included ten beds for illnesses which required
surgery. The eight beds of the second clinic were assigned to
patients suffering from illnesses of the eyes and the intestines.
Twelve beds in the third were set aside for ill women. Whether
this clinic was a gynecological ward for maternity purposes is not
clear. The rest, twenty beds in two clinics, were used for general
illnesses. In addition, each clinic included an extra bed for emergency cases, and six more for extreme illness or for bedridden
patients.[111]

106. G. Schreiber, "Byzantinisches und Abendlandisches Hospital," BZ,
XLII (1943–49), 122; J. M. Hussey, *Church and Learning in the Byzantine
Empire*, pp. 185–86; and Peter Charanis, "Some Aspects of Daily Life in
Byzantium," GO Th. R., VIII, 68.
107. Dmitrievsky, *Typika*, pp. 682–702. Cf. Schreiber, "Hospital," BZ,
XLII, 123.
108. Schreiber, "Hospital," p. 122.
109. Joannes Cinnamos, *Epitome Historion*, ed. A. Meineke, CSHB (Bonn,
1836), p. 190: " Ἐκ τῶν κοινῶν ἀναλέγεσθαι νοσοκομείων, ἃ ξενῶνας
καλεῖσθαι ἔθος ἐστίν."
110. Schreiber, "Hospital," p. 140.
111. Dmitrievsky, *Typika*, p. 682.

Figure 23. Empress Irene, wife of John II Comnenos; mosaic panel, south gallery of Hagia Sophia, Istanbul (first half of the 12th century). Photo courtesy of the Byzantine Institute, Washington, D.C.

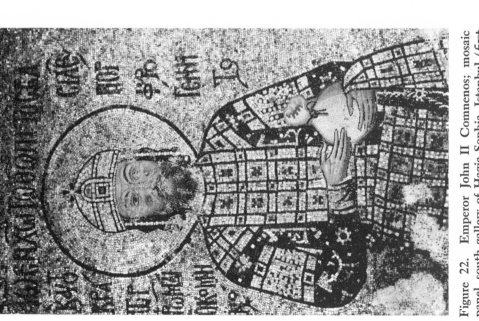

Figure 22. Emperor John II Comnenos; mosaic panel, south gallery of Hagia Sophia, Istanbul (first half of the 12th century). Photo courtesy of the Byzantine Institute, Washington, D.C.

It is of great interest to note that there were two chief physicians in charge of the pathological-general clinic of twenty beds, with three aides and two resident physicians or supernumeraries: seven physicians in all, plus a student and two nurses or attendants. The other clinics were similarly staffed.[112] In short, in a hospital of sixty-one beds there were thirty-five doctors. The Typikon adds that during each night five doctors, four male and one female, should remain in the hospital. It is revealing that in Byzantium there were women engaged in the study of medicine, and that a well-disciplined system among the doctors prevailed.[113]

Each bed had a cover resting on a bench in the oriental fashion, a blanket, a pillow, and a cover of horsehair; in the winter, two quilts.[114] The director took care of the linen. The clothes the patients brought were cleaned and ironed. The bedding was renewed each year. Discarded clothes were given to the poor.

In the women's section were two doctors, a midwife, four aides, two supernumeraries, and two attendants. In each room there was a night guard and a doctor's aide, and, for the women, a certified attendant. Doctors and personnel were organized in two teams that changed each month.[115]

The two protomenitae decided on the admission of the sick. The primikerioi took care of feeding the patients and visited them often, directed the other personnel, and gave the first medical examination to the hospitalized. A professor of medicine was attached to the hospital in order to train young doctors.[116]

112. *Ibid.*, p. 683.
113. *Ibid.*
114. *Ibid.*, p. 682.
115. *Ibid.*, p. 683: "Οὗτοι γοῦν ἅπαντες οἱ ἰατροὶ μερισθήσονται εἰς δύο, καὶ οἱ μὲν ἡμίσεις τὸν ἕνα μῆνα δουλεύσουσιν, οἱ δὲ ἕτεροι ἡμίσεις τὸν ἕτερον." *Ibid.*, p. 693.
116. V. Grumel, "La Profession medicale à Byzance à l'époque des Comnènes," REB, VII (1949), pp. 42–46. Aristotle Kouzis, "Περὶ Βυζαντινῶν νοσοκομείων καὶ ἰατρικῆς τῶν κληρικῶν . . ." *Archives of Medicine and Biology*, XV, nos. 3–4 (Athens, 1920), pp. 40–51; George Pournaropoulos, «Ἱστορία Βυζαντινῆς Ἰατρικῆς» (Athens, 1942), pp. 106–60; Pournaropoulos, "Στοιχεῖα ἐκ τῆς Ἑλληνικῆς Ἰατρικῆς κατὰ τὸν Μέσον Αἰῶνα" *Academic Medicine* (Athens, 1946), pp. 65–70; Koukoules, ΒΒΙΙ, VI, pp. 9–43; Pournaropoulos, "Hospital and Social Welfare Institutions in the Medieval Greek Empire (Byzantium)," *Histoire de la Médecine*, I (1960), pp. 379–80; Constantinos, Bishop of Eirenopolis, "Οἱ Ἰατροὶ ἐπὶ Βυζαντινῶν," O, XXXI. 1 (1956), 404–05.

Each morning the dispensary was run by four supernumerary doctors, two of whom treated the diseased while the other two took care of the wounded. They were assisted by four surgeons' aides and four doctors' aides. The director was ordered to spare no cost in the care of the sick.

The subordinate personnel included a pharmacist, three pharmacist's aides, two supernumeraries, a porter, cooks and their helpers, a miller, a baker, and a stableboy for the doctors' horses.

The diet was mostly vegetarian.[117] For drink, wine was offered in small quantities, replaced by hydromel on holidays. The sick could have two baths a week, or more if prescribed by a doctor.[118] At different times of the year the sick were given small presents of money or food. At Easter they were given three bars of soap for their bath.

The doctors, well paid for their work, were forbidden to practice medicine outside the hospital.[119]

The hospital included a chapel where religious services were conducted by two priests and two preachers. One priest was in charge of hearing confessions of the sick and of preparing them for death, while the other priest was charged with burials. The chapel was divided into two sections, one for men and one for women. Religious services were held on Wednesday, Friday, Saturday, and Sunday of each week.

The hospital buried its dead in a cemetery belonging to the monastery of Medicarios, a department of the Pantocrator located across from the city on the other side of the Golden Horn. The land was surrounded by a wall, and four men were charged with the burial services, together with one priest.

The Typikon speaks also of the structure and the work of the out-patient service, attended by four physicians. Apparently this department served many patients, who received as much attention as the regular inmates.[120] John II Comnenos charged both the physicians and the nurses, as well as the assistants, to execute their duty faithfully and to attend the patients as if they were serving the Almighty while serving the sick.[121] The Emperor demanded the full cooperation of the cooks, the maids, the priests, and the rest of the hospital personnel.

117. Dmitrievsky, *Typika*, pp. 685–86; cf. p. 688.
118. *Ibid.*, p. 686.
119. *Ibid.*, p. 693.
120. *Ibid.*, pp. 683–84.
121. *Ibid.*, p. 684.

Figure 24. Church of the Pantocrator, south flank and apse; Istanbul. From a 19th century engraving in A. G. Paspates, *Byzantinai Meletai— Topographikai kai Historikai* (1877).

Figure 25. Church of the Pantocrator, southeast view of the entire complex; Istanbul. Photo by Walter B. Denny.

Figure 26. Church of the Pantocrator, west façade; Istanbul. Photo by Walter B. Denny.

Figure 27. Church of the Pantocrator, exterior of the apse; Istanbul. Photo courtesy of Dr. Hans Buchwald.

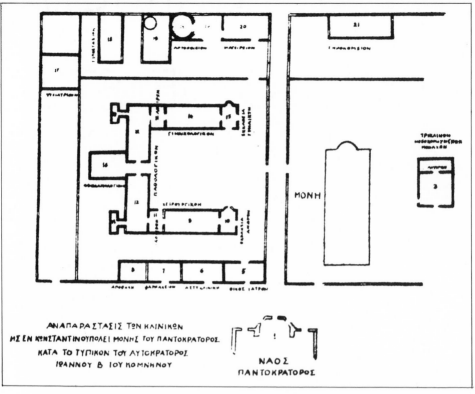

Figure 28. Hospital of Pantocrator in Constantinople; ground plans as reconstructed by A. K. Orlandos. Reproduced with permission from *Epeteris Etaerias Byzantinon Spoudon*, Vol. 17 (1941), pp. 199–201.

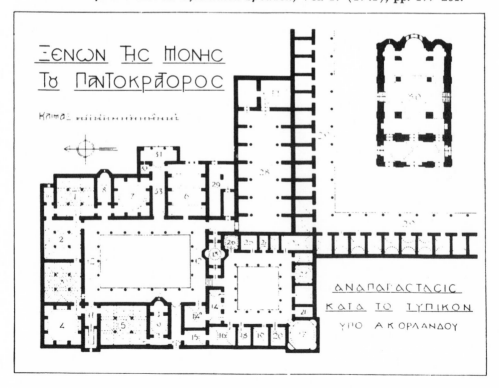

The Typikon instructs that provision is to be made in the old-age home for twenty-four totally incapacitated men, with six nurses assigned to serve them. If an old man becomes sick from an illness other than old age, he is to be transferred to the hospital (xenon).[122]

Epileptics suffering from the *hiera nosos* were not forgotten. However, due to the nature of their illness their institution was not attached to Pantocrator but was built close to an old-age home established by the Emperor Romanos.[123]

Among the institutions of the Pantocrator, there was a medical school[124] and a mausoleion for the burial of the emperors.[125] To carry on its multi-purpose functions, its founder endowed it very lavishly.[126]

The significance of the Pantocrator is indicated by the fact that coins of the twelfth century carried on one side the icon of the Pantocrator and on the reverse side a Biblical verse, such as "he who gives to the poor lends to God" or "joyfully give mercy that you may receive mercy."[127]

John II Comnenos lived up to his reputation as Calojohn, that is, good, merciful, moral John. His contemporary Nicetas Choniates writes about him: "He was a man who governed the Empire excellently, and who lived a godly life. In morals he was not lax and licentious. He was great in his donations and contributions, as his distributions to the residents of the city indicate, as well as the beautiful and great temples which he established."[128] Of all his philanthropies, however, the Pantocrator complex has attracted the most attention. It has been compared to what existed in the West of the same epoch.[129] The Greek archaeologist Orlandos has prepared a plan of the complex[130] on the basis of the data in the Typikon (Figure 28).

122. *Ibid.*, p. 694.
123. *Ibid.*, p. 695. John refers here to Romanos III Argyros, whose philanthropic activity is praised by George Cedrenos, *Historiarum Compendium*, II, 504. For the *hiera nosos* see A. Philipsborn, " Ἱερὰ νόσος und die spezial-Anstalt des Pantokrator-Krankenhauses," B, XXXIII (1963), pp. 223–30.
124. Dmitrievsky, *Typika*, p. 693.
125. *Ibid.*, pp. 664, 680 *et passim*.
126. *Ibid.*, pp. 697–99.
127. Diehl, *Societé byzantine*, p. 51.
128. Nicetas Choniates, *Joannes Comnenos*, ed. B. G. Niebuhr, CSHB (Bonn, 1835), p. 62. Cf. Vasiliev, *History*, pp. 375–77.
129. Schreiber, "Hospital," BZ, XLII (1943–49).
130. Orlandos, " Ἀναπαράστασις."

Isaac II Angelos, the last emperor of the twelfth century, did not fall behind his predecessors in philanthropia. So liberal was his policy that it affected the economy of the country. This at least is the testimony of one of his contemporaries, the historian Nicetas Choniates,[131] who writes: "The house across the port of Sophia which belonged to Isaac the Emperor he transformed into a house for poor travelers and guests. He placed into it one hundred beds and provision for one hundred men and he erected stables for an equal number of horses. . . . He converted the royal houses, which the Emperor Andronicos had erected close to the Church of the Forty Martyrs, into a hospital. He bought from the proprietor the house known as 'the house of the great droungarios' and he made it into a hospital. He donated money to the people who had suffered losses in houses or materials from a fire. . . . During Holy Week the Emperor granted amnesty to criminals condemned to death. Isaac extended charities to widows and used to give dowries to young poor girls together with all the things necessary for the wedding." [132]

The emperor did not limit his donations to individuals, families, or his relatives, but extended them to various cities by revoking taxes.[133]

The same information with a few modifications is given by Theodore Scutariotes. He avers that Isaac "built churches and temples and philanthropic institutions as very few before him had done. He restored those institutions which time had destroyed and beautified them with mosaics and beautiful colors. . . . And he transformed into a pandocheion the house of the Emperor which was by the port of Sofiana. He placed beds and food provisions in it for one hundred men and stables for an equal number of horses. The guests used to eat there every day without charge. Isaac changed into a hospital the royal houses which the tyrant Andronicos had erected close to the Church of the Forty Martyrs. Likewise the house of the Great Droungarios, which he bought from the owner, the Emperor put aside for the sick, sparing nothing for their recovery. When many of the citizens lost their houses in a fire, the Emperor consoled them

131. Nicetas Choniates, *Reign of Isaacios Angelos,* pp. 586–87.
132. *Ibid.,* pp. 584–86.
133. *Ibid.*

and gave five kentinaria to each victim of the fire. He helped many widows and he used to give to young women all the necessary things for their marriage. He used to give not only to individuals, to families, and to relatives, but he used to help whole cities by revoking their tax obligations. Even when he was angry he did not cease to be full of sympathy. Together with his wrath there was compassion." [134]

In addition to the hospital mentioned by Choniates and Scutariotes, Isaac established another hospital outside of the walls of the monastery of Kosmosotera in the region of Aenos in Western Thrace. Its Typikon makes it one of the best known of Byzantine hospitals. It had accommodations for thirty-six patients and it was fully equipped for the needs of the ill. That this hospital was not for monks only can be deduced from the emperor's Typikon: the patients upon recovery of their health could go wherever they desired. [135] The hospital, however, was under the supervision of the monks. The patients were to have baths, a good diet, and religious services. [136]

ADDITIONAL TESTIMONY

Besides the evidence for specific institutions and benefactors, the sources frequently mention a more general concern for the sick and the poor. People of all social classes and ranks did much to relieve the ill and suffering.

The condition of the lepers was especially deplorable. They were considered as "dead before the arrival of death." [137] The Byzantines under the influence of the Church nursed them because of the teaching that man is the image and the likeness of God. Thus Basil the Great taught that lepers should not be

134. Sathas, «Μεσ. Βιβλιοθ.», VII, 410–11.
135. "Typicon of the Monastery of Cosmosoteira," BIARC, XIII, 53–54: "῞Οσοι δὲ τῶν νοσούντων ἀδελφῶν ὑγιείας σὺν Θεῷ τυγχάνουσι μετὰ τὴν τοῦ προεστῶτος ἐπιμέλειαν, ἀπερχέσθωσαν ἔνθα καὶ βούλωνται, καὶ ἀντ᾽ αὐτῶν εἰσαγέσθωσαν ἕτεροι τὸν αὐτὸν ἀριθμὸν τῶν ἀδελφῶν ἀκέραιον ἀπαρτίζοντες πρὸ τῆς τῶν ὑποχωρησάντων ὑποχωρήσεως. . . ."
136. Cf. Oeconomos, *La Vie religieuse*, pp. 211–14.
137. Gregory Nazianzenos, *Oratio 43—In Laudem Basilii Magni*, MPG, XLVI, col. 480A: "Οὐκ ἔτι πρόκειται τοῖς ὀφθαλμοῖς ἡμῶν θέαμα δεινὸν καὶ ἐλεεινόν, ἄνθρωποι νεκροὶ πρὸ θανάτου, καὶ τετελευτηκότες τοῖς πλείστοις τοῦ σώματος μέλεσιν, ἀπελαυνόμενοι πόλεων, οἰκιῶν, ἀγορῶν, ὑδάτων, αὐτῶν τῶν φιλτάτων, ὀνόμασι μᾶλλον, ἢ σώμασι γνωριζόμενοι."

cast out unattended,[138] and set an example by nursing them and applying ointments upon them with his own hands.[139] John Chrysostom appealed to the rich to come to the assistance of lepers,[140] as did Gregory of Nyssa in his dramatic sermon on behalf of the poor.[141] As a result of such admonitions there were people who were not ashamed or afraid to attend lepers, the blind, and the poor.[142] A contemporary of Chrysostom, Asterios, Bishop of Amaseia, who had been a lawyer before his ordination,[143] made a similar appeal.[144]

Among laymen who showed sympathy toward the sick, the fourth-century physician Zenobios may serve as an example. The author of his *martyrium* writes that Zenobios not only served poor patients free of charge, but also gave them financial assistance when necessary.[145] Gregory Nazianzenos, before he became a clergyman, visited hospitals and worked to relieve the sick through manual labor.[146]

Sampson, the founder of the celebrated hospital of the same name, was a physician. According to his biographer, he transformed his home into a free public clinic. Not only did he treat poor patients free of charge, but also offered them food and lodging.[147]

138. *Ibid.*, col. 580B: '' 'Ἀλλ' ἐκεῖνός γε μάλιστα πάντων ἔπεισεν, ἀνθρώπους ὄντας ἀνθρώπων μὴ καταφρονεῖν, μηδ' ἀτιμάζειν Χριστὸν τὴν πάντων κεφαλὴν διὰ τῆς εἰς ἐκείνους ἀπανθρωπίας.''
139. *Ibid.*
140. Joannes Chrysostomos, *In Psalmum 48*, MPG, LV, col. 515.
141. Gregory of Nyssa, *De Pauperibus Amandis*, MPG, XLVI.
142. Joannes Chrysostomos, *Homily 58*, MPG, LVIII, col. 671: "Εἰσὶ μὲν γὰρ καὶ μικροὶ καὶ μεγάλοι κατὰ τὸν τῆς ἀρετῆς λόγον . . . καὶ ὁ μὲν θεραπεύει τραύματα τῶν λώβην ἐχόντων, ὁ δὲ χειραγωγεῖ τὸν τυφλόν, ὁ δὲ βαστάζει τὸν τὸ σκέλος πεπηρωμένον.''
143. Quasten, *Patrology*, p. 300.
144. Asterios of Amaseia, *Homilia No. 4*, MPG, XL, col. 224AB.
145. *Martyrium Sancti Martyris Zenobii*, MPG, CXV, col. 1312A; cf. col. 1309B: "Οὐκ ἀμίσθους μόνον τὰς θεραπείας ποιῶν ἀλλὰ καὶ μισθοὺς μᾶλλον σὺν αὐτοῖς παρεχόμενος.''
146. Gregory the Presbyter, *Life of St. Gregory the Theologian*, MPG, XXXV, col. 269B: "Διακονία τε καὶ λόγοις πατρικοῖς τὸ δυσαλθὲς τῆς νόσου καταπραΰνων καὶ φιλοσοφίας τὸν καιρὸν ἐγγυμναστήριον τίθεται.''
147. Symeon Metaphrastes, *Vita S Sampsoni*, MPG, CXV, col. 281D: '' 'Ἐν σμικρᾷ μέν τινι φαύλῃ διῆγεν οἰκίᾳ, ἐν δὲ τῷ πλησίον κήδεσθαι πολὺς ἦν· τὴν γὰρ οἰκίαν ταύτην φιλανθρωπίας ὑπόθεσιν καὶ ἰατρεῖον ἄμισθον ποιησάμενος, τοὺς νόσῳ πιεζομένους ξενίζων ἦν καὶ φιλαδέλφως ὑποδεχόμενος, καὶ μὴ μόνον ἐπιμελείας ἀξιῶν πάσης, . . . ἀλλὰ καὶ τροφῆς κοινωνῶν καὶ στρωμνῆς.''

General statements about emperors or their wives, bishops, and other dignitaries who established hospitals are frequent. Nicephoros Gregoras, for example, writes that the Empress Theophano established several hospitals and endowed them lavishly.[148] Romanos Lecapenos is praised because he restored various hospitals [149] in addition to the Zoticon mentioned above. Cyril of Scythopolis writes about the special interest that St. Abraamios showed toward the sick.[150] And monks were counseled to visit sick people often.[151]

In the eleventh century Michael Psellos praises the brother of Actouarios for helping the sick in various ways.[152] During the thirteenth century the celebrated philosopher, astronomer, and statesman Theodore Metochites commended the people of Nicea for their philanthropies and care of the sick. He implies that in Nicea there were hospitals and homes for the poor. It was, he said, not so much the external appearance of the buildings that was commendable as the profound compassion toward the less fortunate of the people of the city.[153]

Unfortunately we do not know any other hospital by name, either in Constantinople or in the provinces. That to nurse or visit a sick person was considered a sacred duty is beyond doubt. The spirit that lies behind this philosophy is of course Christian.

For the Byzantines, nursing the sick was a sacred duty. Canons

148. Nicephoros Gregoras, "Λόγος εἰς τὴν ἁγίαν Θεοφανὼ τὴν βασιλίδα," ed. Eduard Kurtz, "Zwei griechische texte uber die hl. Theophano, Die Gemanlin Kaisers Leo VI," *Mémoires de l'académie imperiale des sciences de St.-Petersbourg* (St. Petersburg, 1898), p. 41.

149. Theophanes Continuatus, *Chronographia*, p. 431: "ἐκαινούργησεν . . . ἀρρωστούντων ἐνδιαιτήματα."

150. Schwartz, *Kyrillos*, p. 247.

151. Life of St. Nicon, ed. S. P. Lampros, NE, III. 1, 182; cf. Life of St. Martha the Younger, AASS, May, V, 400F; Life of St. Demetrianos, ed. H. Grégoire, "Saint Demetrianos, évêque de Chytri," BZ, XVI, 231.

152. Michael Psellos, *Funeral Orations*, No. 4, Sathas, «Μεσ. Βιβλιοθ.», V. 102: " Ἔθελγες γὰρ καὶ ὑγιαίνοντας, καὶ ἐρρώνυες τοὺς κάμνοντας. Ποῖοι τῶν ἐπιφανῶν οἴκων οὐ τῆς σῆς τέχνης ἐπιμνησθήσονται; ποῖοι δὲ πένητες οὐχ ὁμοῦ τε νοσήσονται καὶ τὸν ἄμισθον εὐεργέτην ἐνθυμηθήσονται;"

153. Theodore Metochites, "Νικαεύς," Sathas, «Μεσ. Βιβλιοθ.», I, 145: "Ταῦτα δὴ ταῦτα λέγω τὰ τῶν καμνόντων ἐν νόσοις μετὰ τῆς πενίας κοινὰ καταγώγια, ὧν οὐ μᾶλλον τὸ κάλλος τῶν οἰκοδομημάτων ἔστι θαυμάζειν ἢ τὴν ὁμολογίαν τῆς φυσικῆς ἀσθενείας αἰδεῖσθαι καὶ τὴν συναίσθησιν, καὶ τὴν κατ' ἄμφω τοῦ γένους φιλανθρωπίαν, τήν τε ἐπὶ τῇ νόσῳ παρὰ τῆς τέχνης ἐπικουρίαν καὶ τὴν τῆς πενίας παραμυθίαν. . . ."

of the church or monastic establishments provided punishments for the nurses who failed in their responsibilities. Theodore Studite penalized those who neglected to feed or to care for the patients.[154] On the other hand, he emphasized how divine the work of the nurses was and encouraged them to perform their duties cheerfully that they might receive their reward from God.[155]

154. Studites, *Epistles, Poenae Monasteriales*, Nos. 67–70, MPG, XCIX, col. 1741B.

155. *Ibid., Iambus No. 17*, col. 1785D:

> "Τὸ χρῆμα θεῖον, ἀσθενῶν βάρη φέρειν.
> Τούτου λαχὼν πύκνευσον, ὦ μοι τεκνίον,
> θερμῶς προθύμως ἐκτελεῖν σου τὸν δρόμον,
> ἔωθεν εὐθὺς τοὺς κλινήρεις βλέποις,
> ἄλλον πρὸ παντὸς φαμμαλεύων τοῖς λόγοις,
> εἶτ' αὖ πρεπόντως προσφέροις σίτων δόσεις,
> ὡς χρή δ' ἑκάστῳ, συνδιακρίσει λόγον.
> Μέλος γάρ ἐστι, μὴ παρέσχου τὸν πέλας.
> Οὕτως ὑπηρετοῦντι μισθός σοι μέγας,
> φῶς ἀπρόσιτον, οὐρανῶν εὐκληρία."

12. Xenones (Hospices)

The xenon, or home for strangers, foreigners, and travelers, was a very important institution in the Byzantine world. Its primary function was to provide food and shelter for country people, visitors, and pilgrims coming to the capital or going to some other city, whether on private business or for religious purposes. It was therefore an institution found in the big city as well as in the provincial town, on the highway as well as at monastic establishments, churches, and shrines.

Traveling was not an easy undertaking in the middle ages, especially for poor people. Special attention was devoted to the problem of feeding and housing travelers from the very beginning of the Empire. The anonymous chronicler of the fourteenth century, who has been identified as Theodore Scutariotes,[1] relates that the twelve great Romans who were brought to Constantinople when it became the capital of the Christian Empire were instrumental in the establishment of several xenones.[2] Justinian and Theodora built or reconstructed several of them in Constantinople for poor strangers and travelers who had no place to stay upon their arrival at the capital, as well as for those who were traveling through the city but were "unable to pay the hire of any stay" in Constantinople. They "built a very large

1. A. Heisenberg, *Analecta Mitteilungun aus italienischen Handschriften byzantinischer Chronographen* (Munchen, 1901), pp. 5–16. Cf. Krumbacher, *Geschichte*, p. 390; Peter Charanis, "Byzantium, the West and the Origin of the First Crusade," B, XIX, 30.
2. Sathas, «Μεσ. Βιβλιοθ.», VII, 53.

xenon, destined to serve as a temporary lodging for those who should find themselves thus embarrassed." [3]

It is evident that we are concerned in this investigation about rent-free, charitable hospices and not commercial hotels properly so called.

There must have been many such establishments in other centuries as well. Speaking in generalities, Theophanes and Manassis affirm that the Emperor Tiberios II (578–82) repaired a great number of such institutions.[4] Cedrenos avers that in the eleventh century Romanos III Argyros (1028–34) restored those which were damaged by an earthquake.[5] Emperors, bishops, and other dignitaries are credited with the foundation or reconstruction of several others.[6]

Because xenon and nosocomeion are interchangeable terms, it is difficult to determine what a Byzantine writer meant when he used these words.[7] To be sure, a xenon was a house for the poor and for travelers, but it was a hospital as well. Perhaps each of them included a hospital or a clinic.[8] Of the numerous xenones of the Byzantine State we can identify by name only a few. They were erected either by Church officials, state dignitaries, members of the imperial house, or private benefactors.

XENONES DURING THE FIRST THREE CENTURIES

In the fourth century John Chrysostom had made a strong appeal on behalf of the strangers, the hungry, and the lonely. He urged his people to set aside rooms in their own houses and receive there their fellow men who needed shelter.[9] To offer hospitality to a stranger was to offer it to Christ: a hospitable

3. Procopios, *Buildings*, I. xi. Cf. Justinian, *Novel 120*, chs. 5 and 6 *et passim; Novel 59*, ch. 3.
4. Theophanes, *Chronographia*, I, 251; Manasses, *Synopsis*, pp. 3483–84.
5. George Cedrenos, *Historiarum Compendium*, II, 504.
6. Sathas, «Μεσ. Βιβλιοθ.», VII, 161 *et passim*.
7. Cf. Joannes Cinnamos, *Epitome*, p. 190.
8. Cf. Basil the Great, *Regulae Brevius Tractate*, No. 155, MPG, XXXI, 1184B; Procopios, *Buildings*, V. vi; "Typicon of the Livos Monastery," Delehaye, *Deux Typica*, p. 134; Koukoules, BBΠ, II, 148.
9. Joannes Chrysostomos, *Sermon 45—In Acta Apostolorum*, MPG, LX, 319. "Εἴ τις νομίζει χρηματισμὸν εἶναι τὰ λεγόμενα, ποιήσει ἑαυτῷ ξενοδοχεῖον ἐπὶ τῆς οἰκίας· στῆσον ἐκεῖ κλίνην, στῆσον ἐκεῖ τράπεζαν καὶ λυχνίαν."

house is a xenon of Christ.[10] He did not expect great sacrifices but simple, genuine philanthropy.[11]

This advice apparently was taken literally by some people. The parents of Cyril of Scythopolis, for example, had transformed their house in Scythopolis into a place of rest for wayfarers comparable to the xenodocheion of a monastery.[12] When Sophia, the mother of St. Sabas, left a large sum of money to her son, he used part of it to renovate the xenodocheion in Jericho and to build a second one at his Lavra outside Jerusalem.[13] On land bought from the patriarch he built a third xenodocheion in Jerusalem itself. We may assume that these institutions were used not only by visiting monks but by laymen who visited the holy city.

North of his Lavra, St. Sabas built still another xenon, and two more besides not far from the castle of David. In Jericho, in addition to the one he renovated, he established a second.[14]

In Jerusalem the monasteries of St. Euthymios and St. Theoctistos, which were administratively one during the lifetime of Euthymios, were divided twelve years after his death. Paulos became the hegoumenos of Theoctistos' monastery. In order to establish a reputation for philanthropy he spent two hundred nomismata on a xenodocheion; he meant, we hear, to have the only xenon in the holy city open to all comers.[15] A dissatisfied group in Euthymios' monastery then bought their own xenodocheion for two hundred nomismata near the castle of David.[16] As a result of this friction, the abbot Kyriacos left both parties and went off to the desert, where he founded the Lavra of Souka, which of course included a xenodocheion and a hospital.[17]

A certain illustrious Byzantine official named Acacios once visited St. Theodosios in his cave in the desert of Palestine. Out of deep respect for the hermit, Acacios secretly left one hundred

---

10. *Ibid.*, p. 320: " "Εστω τὸ τοῦ Χριστοῦ πανδοχεῖον ἡμῶν ἡ οἰκία."
11. *Ibid.*, "Οὐ κελεύω καταθῦσαι μόσχον· ἄρτον δὸς πεινῶντι, ἱμάτιον γυμνῷ, σκέπην τῷ ξένῳ."
12. Schwartz, *Kyrillos*, p. 217.
13. *Ibid.*, p. 109; cf. A. J. Festugière, *Les Moines*, pp. 42–43, n. 57.
14. *Ibid.*, p. 116.
15. *Ibid.*, p. 226: " 'Ο Παῦλος . . . δίδωσι διακόσια νομίσματα ὑπὲρ ἀγορασίας ξενοδοχείου πρὸς τὸ αὐτὸν μόνον διακατέχειν τὸ ἐν τῇ ἁγίᾳ πόλει κοινὸν ξενοδοχεῖον."
16. *Ibid.*
17. *Ibid.*

nomismata in the cave and later continued to send annual contributions to the ascetic. Upon discovering the money, Theodosios built onto the cave a xenodocheion in which he offered hospitality to anyone coming to him.[18] He especially loved the poor and strangers.[19]

It is beyond dispute that even the desert fathers and monasticism in general played an extremely important role in relieving misery and helping those in want. We are told that another monk, a priest named Isaacios, a disciple of the priest Chronios, himself a disciple of Anthony the Great, was exceedingly philanthropic and hospitable. He established a hostel in the desert of Nitria in Egypt, not only for the recuperation of sick ascetics, but for the maintenance of strangers and foreigners who visited the district to see the fathers and receive their blessings.[20] Furthermore, it was customary for monastic establishments to have xenones attached: in the monastery of Isidoros in Thebais it stood outside the walls by the gate and was administered by a presbyter.[21]

Churches, too, had houses of hospitality. Palladios relates that close to the church at Nitria was a xenon in which visitors might receive hospitality for as long as two and three years. However, they were allowed to remain idle for a single week only, after which they were put to work either in the gardens, the kitchen, or the bakery. If the guest was literate he was assigned work appropriate to his learning.[22]

The first xenon which we know by name to have existed in Constantinople was founded by St. Marcianos. When Marcianos, who built a hospital already mentioned, established the Church of St. Irene during the years 450–57 he promptly converted a

18. *Ibid.*, p. 238: " Ὁ δὲ μέγας Θεοδόσιος μετὰ τὴν τοῦ ἰλλουστρίου ἀναχώρησιν τῇ ἑξῆς ἐν τῷ σπηλαίῳ κεκρυμμένον εὑρὼν τὸ ῥηθὲν χρυσίον κτίζει ἐν πρώτοις ὑπεράνω τοῦ σπηλαίου ξενοδοχεῖον καὶ ἐδεξιοῦτο πάντα ἐρχόμενον πρὸς αὐτόν."
19. *Ibid.:* "Τρία ἐξαίρετα ἐκέκτητο κατορθώματα . . . τὴν πρὸς τοὺς ξένους καὶ πτωχοὺς δαψιλῆ καὶ ἀπροσωπόληπτον φιλοφροσύνην."
20. Palladios, *Vita S Joannis Chrysostomi*, p. 106: " Ἕτερος Ἰσαὰκ πρεσβύτερος . . . φιλόξενος εἰ καί τις ἄλλος, ὡς δι' ὑπερβολὴν φιλανθρωπίας ξενοδοχεῖον κατασκευάσαι ἐν τῇ πανερήμῳ εἰς ἀνάψυξιν καὶ τῶν ἀρρωστούντων μοναχῶν καὶ τῶν ἐπιχωριαζόντων ξένων θέας ἕνεκεν τῶν μακαρίων πατέρων. . . ."
21. Timothy, *Historia Monachorum*, p. 113.
22. Palladios, *Hist. Lausiaca*, pp. 25–26.

nearby pagan temple into a xenon.[23] We know only that its administrator carried the tenth labaron in the procession of Palm Sunday.[24]

As might be expected, the Emperor Justinian is credited with the foundation of more xenones than any other person—perhaps because Justinian found in Procopios a diligent chronicler of his architectural achievements.

In the reconstruction of Antioch after the Persian invasion of 540,[25] Justinian made provisions for housing strangers and foreigners in the city.[26] The xenon he built must have been a large one,[27] for he granted it an income of four thousand nomismata annually.[28] In Jerusalem, too, the ambitious emperor founded a xenon, one of three which he established in the holy city.[29] He also erected a xenon in Jericho.[30]

In Constantinople itself, Justinian must have founded more xenones than in any other city. However, we know only one by name, the xenon of Arcadios built by Justinian and Theodora[31] between Hagia Sophia and the Church of St. Irene. Nothing else is known about it.

The author of the *patria* relates that a patrician of Constantinople named Euboulos built a xenon during the reign of Justin I (518–27), using it at first as his residence.[32] This xenon, however, may well have been in existence before 518, for according to Theophanes[33] and Cedrenos[34] its director Paul was elected Patriarch of Antioch in that year. One wonders whether Paul could have been its director for less than a year when he was called to occupy the throne of the great *Theoupolis*.

During the Nika revolt of 532 this xenon was burned down,[35]

23. Pseudo-Codinos, *Patria*, Th. Preger, III, 234; cf. also the alternate reading in footnote.
24. Porphyrogenitos, *De Cerimoniis*, Bk. 1, Ch. 41 (32), I, 161–62.
25. See Downey, "Philanthropia," pp. 533–46.
26. Procopios, *Buildings*, II. 10, 80.
27. Malalas, *Chronographia*, p. 423.
28. *Ibid.*, p. 452.
29. Procopios, *Buildings*, V. 6.
30. *Ibid.*, V. 9.
31. *Ibid.*, I. 2; cf. Du Cange, *Constantinopolis Christiana*, IV. IX, 10; Richter, *Quellen*, p. 195.
32. Pseudo-Codinos, *Patria*, Th. Preger, III, p. 254.
33. Theophanes, *Chronographia*, I, 165.
34. Cedrenos, *Historiarum Compendium*, II, 637.
35. Chronicon Paschale, I, 622; Cedrenos, *Historiarum*, p. 647.

but it must have been reconstructed shortly thereafter.[36] It was one of those institutions which served both as a home for wayfarers and as a hospital.[37]

Procopios writes that Justinian also established a xenon called the House of Isidore in Constantinople and that the Empress Theodora labored with him in this work.[38]

The fourteenth-century Pseudo-Codinos ascribes it, however, to the brother of Euboulos, whose xenon we have just examined, named Isidoros.[39] If so, we may assume that it was erected perhaps during the reign of Justin I. According to this latter testimony Isidore transformed his house into a xenon and joined to it a church. A variant reading speaks of a gerocomeion, not a xenon.[40] We may resolve the conflict of testimony by supposing that this establishment was founded during Justin's reign by Isidore and reconstructed by Justinian after it was destroyed by the great fire of 532.[41] This establishment should not be confused with the institution built by another Isidore, a contemporary of Constantine the Great, and restored as the xenon of Theophilos in the ninth century.

Procopios adds that Isidore's xenon was situated between Hagia Sophia and the Church of St. Irene, facing the great xenon of Sampson.[42]

A xenon named after its founder, Narses, came into being during the reign of Justin II (565–78) [43] and must have existed for many more centuries after its erection. Constantine Porphyrogenitos wrote that its administrator carried the ninth labaron during the procession of Palm Sunday.[44] The xenon stood on the cliff which descends from Bazar toward the Golden Horn.[45]

Procopios writes that Justinian built—or perhaps renovated—a xenon in the place called Stadium.[46] Since Constantinople was

36. Porphyrogenitos, *De Cerimoniis*, I, 161.
37. Albert Vogt, ed., "Vie de S. Luc le stylite," AB, XXVIII, 36; cf. Richter, *Quellen*, pp. 187–88.
38. Procopios, *Buildings*, I. ii; Richter, *Quellen*, p. 195.
39. Pseudo-Codinos, *Patria*, Th. Preger, III, 254, n. 120–22.
40. *Ibid.*, p. 255.
41. Janin, *Geogr. Eccles.*, p. 572.
42. Procopios, *Buildings*, I.
43. Pseudo-Codinos, *Patria*, Th. Preger, III, 249; cf. Richter, p. 201.
44. Porphyrogenitos, *De Cerimoniis*, I, 161.
45. Janin, *Constantinople*, pp. 365–67.
46. Procopios, *Buildings*, I. xi.; cf. Du Cange, *Constantinopolis Christiana*, IV. ix, 11; Richter, *Quellen*, p. 192.

the capital of the empire, throngs of people of all conditions visited the city. Some went there on business, others seeking to make their fortune, still others to ask for some favor from the emperor or the imperial court.[47] However, because these people were unable to pay any rent, Justinian and Theodora built "a very large xenon, in order to serve as a temporary lodging" [48] for them. It was called the Stadium xenon because the location had been used previously for games and athletics. The site— "very close to the sea" as Procopios says—was near the port of Eugenios.[49]

THE HOSPICE OF SAMPSON

Among the institutions of the Byzantine Empire, the xenon of Sampson occupied a prominent position. It was both a home for poor and strangers and a hospital. Its founder was "a certain pious man named Sampson." [50] Procopios implies that Sampson had lived before the sixth century and that the institution existed before his own times. "It was," he says, "devoted to those who were at once destitute and suffering from serious illness, those who were, namely, suffering in loss of both property and health." [51]

When the xenon of Sampson was burned and destroyed in 532 Justinian rebuilt and expanded it, endowing it with a generous annual income.[52]

A second testimony about the person of Sampson differs from Procopios' account. According to tradition of the Menologium, Sampson was a descendant of the family of Constantine the Great. Sampson grew up in the "New Rome," and because of his piety and humanitarian character was ordained priest of the Great Church by the Patriarch Menas (536–52). Sampson, how-

47. Procopios, *Buildings*, I. xi.
48. *Ibid.*
49. Otto Seeck, ed., *Notitia Dignitatum Accedunt Notitia Urbis Constantinopolitanae et Laterculi Provinciarum* (Berlin, 1877), p. 232; Janin, *Geogr. Eccles.*, p. 575.
50. Procopios, *Buildings*, I. ii, 14: "ᾟν δέ τις ξενών, ἀνθρώποις ἀνειμένος ἀπορουμένοις τε καὶ νοσοῦσι τὰ ἔσχατα, εἰ πρὸς τῇ οὐσίᾳ καὶ τὸ σῶμα νοσοῖεν. Τοῦτον ἀνήρ τις θεοσεβὴς ἐν τοῖς ἄνω χρόνοις ἐδείματο, Σαμψὼν ὄνομα."
51. *Ibid.*
52. *Ibid.*

ever, was also a practicing physician, and as the story goes, had cured Justinian of a dangerous disease. In appreciation the emperor had a xenon built and named it after his benefactor.[53]

In the tenth century, Symeon Metaphrastes incorporated this tradition in his biography of Sampson. He repeats that Sampson was a philanthropic physician [54] who, because of his virtues, was ordained a priest by the Patriarch Menas. Symeon relates that at the time the emperor was suffering from an incurable disease of the genitals and the urinary system. Several physicians had failed to cure him. Sampson of course succeeded; and so the emperor named a xenon after him and placed Sampson in charge of it.[55] This tradition is followed also by the fourteenth-century author of the patria.[56]

Of these accounts Procopios' seems to be most reliable. The xenon must have been in existence before the year 532 because it was destroyed during the Nika uprising.[57] Even if it had come into existence between 527 and 532 one would question it as improbable that Justinian would have allowed his benefactor to serve as administrator of the xenon for only five to nine years. Menas was its director in 536 when he was elected Patriarch of Constantinople.[58] In the following year of 537 we find that a certain Eugenios was its administrator.[59] Besides, Procopios was contemporary to Justinian and, therefore, nearer the events which he described.

The establishment of Sampson was destroyed by another fire in December of 563,[60] and was rebuilt once again. We find it still in existence in the last quarter of the ninth century, when the Synopsis of the Basilica ordains that all privileges granted to the great Church of Hagia Sophia, to the Orphanage of the

53. Menologium, MPG, CXVII, col. 513AB: "Θεραπεύσας δὲ καὶ τὸν βασιλέα Ἰουστινιανὸν ἀπὸ πάθους δυσιάτου ἐφιλοφρονήθη παρ' ἐκείνου τὰ μέγιστα καὶ κτίσας Ξενῶνα εἰς ἀνάπαυσιν τῶν πτωχῶν καὶ ἀσθενῶν." Cf. other readings, MPG, CXV, cols. 275–77.
54. Symeon Metaphrastes, *Vita S Sampsoni*, MPG, CXV, col. 281A: "Μηδὲ ἰατρικῆς, τῆς φιλανθρώπου τέχνης, ὁ φιλανθρωπότατος ἀμελήσας."
55. *Ibid.*, col. 288–89.
56. Pseudo-Codinos, *Patria*, Th. Preger, III, 254.
57. Chronicon Paschale, I, 622; Theophanes, *Chronographia*, I, 181.
58. Malalas, *Chronographia*, p. 479; Theophanes, *Chronographia*, I, 217.
59. Justinian, *Novel* 59.3.
60. Theophanes, *Chronographia*, I, 240; Cedrenos, *Historiarum Compendium*, I, 679.

Capital, and to the "xenon which bears the name of blessed memory Sampson, as well as the buildings, establishments, church and hospices or other charitable houses which fall under its administration are to be preserved." [61]

Constantine VII Porphyrogenitos writes that the administrator of this institution carried the sixth labaron in the procession of Palm Sunday.[62] This indicates that the xenon of Sampson was held in high esteem. The xenon was still functioning in the twelfth or early thirteenth century, when the Russian Anthony of Novgorod writes: "In the xenon of St. Sampson is found his baton or staff, his epitrachilion or stole, and his clerical robes; also there is the stove upon which St. Orestes was martyred." [63] In 1204, when Constantinople fell to the Crusaders of the West, the xenon of Sampson was taken over by the Templars.[64] The fame and the reputation of the xenon of Sampson was very great and survived down to the thirteenth century, when Manuel Philes (1275–1345) expressed the wish that the nephew of Michael VIII Palaeologos might become another Sampson in his generosity to the poor.[65]

There are contradicting views as to the end of the xenon of Sampson. A. Paspates writes that it was demolished by Michael VIII Palaealogos together with other structures when the emperor repaired the imperial walls.[66] This view is accepted by K. N. Alivizatos and E. P. Lekos in their discussion of Byzantine medicine in fifteenth-century Constantinople.[67] On the other hand, R. Janin believes that the xenon survived the beginning of the fifteenth century, and identifies it with the monastery of Saint Sampson.[68] The evidence is very deficient, but considering that every Byzantine philanthropic institution was staffed by monks and under ecclesiastical directions, we may assume that the establishment of Sampson, both as a xenon and as a monastery, still existed in the fifteenth century.

61. Zepos-Zepos, *Jus*, V, 447; cf. Dmitrievsky, *Typika*, p. 83.
62. Porphyrogenitos, *De Cerimoniis*, I, 161.
63. B. de Khitrowo, *Itinéraires russes en Orient*, 1. 107.
64. Janin, *Geogr. Eccles.*, p. 574.
65. Manuel Philes, *Poem No. 213*, E. Miller, *Manuelis Philae Carmina*, I (Paris, 1855), 111.
66. Paspates, «'Ανάκτορα», p. 67.
67. Alivizatos and Lekos, " 'Η Βυζαντινὴ 'Ιατρική," *XVIIᵉ Congrès International*, I, 369.
68. Miklosich-Muller, *Acta et Diplomata*, II, 408; Janin, *Geogr. Eccles.*, p. 574; cf. *ibid.*, p. 466.

A. Obverse: A simple cross surrounded with four stars.

Reverse:

+
TOVOC
IOVCA
Mῶ

Τοῦ ὁσίου Σάμψω.

Eighth Century

B. Obverse: The Mother of God wearing the medallion of Christ, standing full face, with a cross at the edge.

Reverse:

+ TOY
OCIOY
CAMΨ
ω

Τοῦ ὁσίου Σάμψω.

Eighth Century

C. Obverse: Three saints standing full face.

Reverse:

+
CAM
Ψω
N

Σαμψῶν.

Ninth Century

Figure 29. Three Seals of the Xenon of Sampson in Constantinople, derived from *Sigillographie de l'empire byzantin*, ed. Gustave Schlumberger, p. 154.

The institution was apparently well organized, and included a group of structures. Among these was an ophthalmological clinic, for the Life of St. Artemios speaks of the surgeons and the ophthalmologists there. In the reign of Heraclios a deacon named Stephanos underwent an operation there.[69] The importance of the xenon is suggested by the survival of three of its seals of the eighth and ninth centuries.[70] (See Figure 29.)

Pseudo-Codinos writes that the "xenon of Sampson was built across from Hagia Sophia."[71] Modern scholars agree, and place it to the north of the great church.[72]

During the sixth century or the early part of the seventh, a xenon was built known as the Christodotes. The only information we possess relates that it was located next to the Church of Saint Anastasios by the portico of the Lord.[73] A deacon of Hagia Sophia named Stephanos was admitted to this institution for treatment of a chest disease. The director of the xenon entrusted Stephanos to the hands of the "chief physicians and their assistants"[74] there. The xenon was situated on the slope of the agora toward the Golden Horn.[75]

THE MACEDONIAN ERA AND ITS HOSTELS

Theophanes Continuatus narrates that Basil I (867–86), in his program of beautification and restoration of various buildings in Constantinople, included the xenon near the monastery of the Steiron[76] or St. Michael. It was established especially for the poor, and the emperor endowed it generously.[77] Its site was near the Acropolis.

69. Papadopoulos-Kerameus, *Varia*, XXI, 25–26.
70. Schlumberger, *Sigillographie*, 154.
71. Pseudo-Codinos, *Patria*, Th. Preger, III, 254, n. 119.
72. Janin, *Geogr. Eccles.*, p. 574.
73. Papadopoulos-Kerameus, *Varia*, XX, 28.
74. *Ibid.*
75. Janin, *Geogr. Eccles.*, p. 575.
76. See *ibid.*, p. 487.
77. Theophanes Continuatus, p. 339: "Τὸν δὲ τοῦ πρώτου τῶν ἀγγέλων ἐν τοῖς Τζήρου λεγομένοις θεῖον ναὸν καὶ τὴν περὶ αὐτὸν φιλάνθρωπον εἰς τοὺς πένητας ὑπουργίαν καὶ χορηγίαν ἐκεῖνος ἐστιν [ὁ Βασίλειος] ὁ περιποιησάμενος . . . καὶ τὴν διακονίαν εἰς τὸ ἀνενδεὲς τῇ τῶν προσόδων ἐπαυξήσει καταστήσας, καὶ ἐπιδαψιλευσάμενος τὸν εἰς τοὺς πένητας ἔλεον."

A much more important xenon of the ninth century was that named after Theophilos the Emperor (829–42), who restored the institution. The author of the *patria* writes that it was established on the hill of Zeugma, toward the southern part of the Golden Horn, by Constantine the Great, originally as a house of prostitution.[78] Then Isidoros, one of the twelve Latin dignitaries brought by Constantine to Constantinople in the fourth century, transformed it into his residence. After the death of Isidoros it became a monastery for women.[79] However, Symeon Magister says it was changed not into a monastery but into a reformatory institution for fallen women of the aristocratic class.[80] In the eighth century Leo III (717–41) transformed the house into a xenon or xenodocheion.[81] Later Constantine VI (780–97), the son of Irene, made it his residence after he was blinded by his mother. Upon his death his wife made it a monastery for women and joined it herself. She named it the monastery of Metanoia or Repentance.[82] It was still a monastery when the Emperor Theophilos changed in into a xenon in the year 841. Symeon Magister writes that in that year the building was about to collapse because the central beam of the triclinium was giving way. As the emperor was passing by, the sisters there begged him to restore their establishment. The emperor liked the structure so much that he transferred the inmates to another monastery and made their former convent into a xenon, decorating it lavishly and endowing it with both money and estates. The emperor also changed its name to his own.[83]

That this xenon was one of the important institutions of the capital is indicated by the fact that its administrator carried the fourth labaron in the procession of Palm Sunday.[84] It was located on the hill of Zeugma,[85] the region of present-day Unkapani. The xenon itself was probably situated in the vicinity of the Süleymaniye mosque.[86]

78. Pseudo-Codinos, *Patria,* Th. Preger, II, 185.
79. *Ibid.*
80. Symeon Magister, *Chronographia,* p. 645.
81. *Ibid.*
82. *Ibid.,* p. 646.
83. *Ibid.*
84. Porphyrogenitos, *De Cerimoniis,* I, 161.
85. Pseudo-Codinos, *Patria,* Th. Preger, II, 185.
86. Janin, *Geogr. Eccles.,* p. 572.

Another xenon of the ninth century was named for Irene. Pseudo-Codinos attributes to Empress Irene (797–802) the erection of several institutions concerned with the "death, life, and health" of man. For death she built a cemetery for the burial of foreigners, strangers, and the poor; for life she built a refectory (triclinion), and for health she built a xenon, which apparently served as a hospital also.[87]

Janin has identified this xenon with another institution known as the Paschentiou.[88] If his claim is correct, then the xenon of Irene was located near the palace, in the region of Deuteron.[89] In the procession of Palm Sunday its director carried the eighth labaron.[90]

A xenodocheion or xenon existed in the eighth or ninth century known as tou Loupadiou. A seal of the xenon from this period reveals that a certain Epiphanios, an imperial cubicularius, was its director. It shows on one side the monogram of the cross and the words "Theotocos help," on the reverse the epigraph, "Epiphanios, imperial cubicularius and xenodochos of Loupadiou."[91] We know nothing more. (See Figure 30c.)

A xenon known as tou Mavrianou was built by the Emperor Romanos Lecapenos (919–45) whose philanthropic policy was directed to many institutions and charitable works. Symeon Magister describes several of Lecapenos' philanthropic and humanitarian activities, adding that these are only a few of many.[92] Theophanes Continuatus notes that, among other things, Romanos established "a xenodocheion located at the quarters of Mavrianou"[93] and took special measures to ensure that visitors would always have plenty of clothing and food. This xenon was maintained specifically for business and court visitors to the city who had to extend their stay overnight or for several days. Next to the xenon Romanos built stables for the visitors' horses.[94] The

87. Pseudo-Codinos, *Patria*, Th. Preger, III, 246.
88. Janin, *Geogr. Eccles.*, p. 570.
89. Papadopoulos-Kerameus, *Varia*, p. 11.
90. Porphyrogenitos, *De Cerimoniis*, I, 161.
91. Schlumberger, *Sigillographie*, p. 381.
92. Symeon Magister, *Chronographia*, p. 744: "Ταῦτα ὡς ἐκ πολλῶν ὀλίγα τῶν ἀπείρων αὐτοῦ κατορθωμάτων καὶ ἐλεημοσυνῶν διεξήλθομεν."
93. Theophanes Continuatus, p. 430.
94. *Ibid.*

quarters of Mavrianou were known also as the Maurice, because the Emperor Maurice had once lived there.[95]

Romanos Lecapenos also was the founder of a group of buildings in the quarter of Myrelaion: a monastery,[96] a church, a cistern, a bath,[97] a house for the aged, and a xenon.[98] So important an establishment was this complex that Romanos' wife, his daughter, and other members of his family were buried there,[99] as well as Romanos himself.[100] There is no doubt that the xenon was of imperial origin, for it is mentioned as such in a judicial decision of Eustathios Romaios in the eleventh century. This decision reveals that imperial establishments enjoyed certain additional privileges which those founded by private benefactors did not share,[101] in this case in matters of emphyteusis or leasing.

The xenon of Myrelaion must have been in existence at least until the fourteenth century, for a physician named Romanos who lived in that century was a member of its staff.[102] This institution may have stood near the monastery in present-day Bodrumcami.[103]

During the tenth century the patrician Constantine Lips, who served as drungarius of the imperial navy under Leo VI, Romanos Lecapenos, and Constantine VII Porphyrogenitos, founded a xenon in the capital. Since the same individual had built or restored a monastery,[104] the xenon must have been nearby. Both were known by the name of their founder,[105] i.e. tou Livos or tou

95. Pseudo-Codinos, *Patria*, Th. Preger, III, 233; Byzantios, «Κωνσταντινούπολις», I, 406; but cf. Janin, *Constantinople*, pp. 358–59.

96. Monachos, *Chronicon*, ed. Muralt, p. 820; Theophanes Continuatus, *Chronographia*, pp. 402, 404, 420, 473; Symeon Magister, *Chronographia*, p. 733; Pseudo-Codinos, *Patria*, Th. Preger, III, p. 258.

97. D. Talbot Rice, "Excavations at Bodrum Camii 1930," B, VIII, 151–74.

98. Zepos-Zepos, *Jus*, IV, 53.

99. Theophanes Continuatus, *Chronographia*.

100. George Cedrenos, *Historiarum Compendium*, II, 325.

101. Zepos-Zepos, *Jus*, IV, 53.

102. Daniel de Nessel, *Catalogi Bibliothecae Caesareae Manuscriptorum*, part III, Codices Manuscriptos Medicos Graecos (Vienna, 1690), p. 53; Ioannes Mercati and Pius F. de Cavalieri, editors, *Codices Vaticani Graeci*, Bibliothecae Apostolicae Vaticanae, I (Rome, 1923), 381.

103. Janin, *Constantinople*, p. 365.

104. See Theodore Macridy with contributions by Arthur H. S. Megaw, Cyril Mango, and Ernest J. W. Hawkins, "The Monastery of Lips (fenari isa Camii) at Istanbul," DOP, No. 18 (Washington, D.C., 1964), pp. 251–315. For the question of its origin see pp. 255–56, but cf. pp. 299–301.

105. Pseudo-Codinos, *Patria*, Th. Preger, IV, p. 289. But cf. Mango and Hawkins, DOP, No. 18, p. 300.

Droungariou. This xenon might have become private property later, for we hear that Isaac II Angelos (1185–95) bought it and transformed it into a hospital, properly so called.[106] The location of the Livos was on the plateau of Lycos, near the Church of the Holy Apostles [107] in the region of Mardosaggares.[108]

Despite the criticism which the historian George Cedrenos leveled against the internal policies of the Emperor Constantine IX Monomachos, he praised that emperor's philanthropic works. Cedrenos writes that the Emperor built a monastery in the quarter of Maggana, and attached to it both homes for the aged and poor and xenones.[109] All of these are known by the name of the place where they stood. The xenon must have existed at least until the fourteenth century, when we learn the name of the chief physician, called Stephanos.[110]

This whole group of establishments was on the southwest side of the Acropolis.[111] The site took its name from an arsenal there known as Maggana.[112]

According to Pseudo-Codinos, Lausos, one of the patricians and prepositos of Constantinople during the reign of Arcadios (395–408), erected a number of buildings,[113] among them certain xenodocheia.[114] Lausos is the same dignitary to whom Palladios, Bishop of Eleonopolis, directed his famous history of Eastern monasticism. This institution was burned down during the Nika uprising,[115] but we find it in existence again during the

106. Nicetas Choniates, p. 585: "Τὸν τοῦ μεγάλου δρουγγαρίου ὀνομαζόμενον οἶκον ἐκ τοῦ δεσπόζοντος ὠνησάμενος, ὁμοίως καὶ τοῦτον εἰς ἀνάπαυμα τῶν καχεκτούντων ἀπέταξεν." Cf. Byzantios, «Κωνσταντινούπολις», I, 376–77.

107. Theophanes Continuatus, *Chronographia*, p. 371.

108. Monachos, *Chronicon*, ed. Muralt, p. 788; Byzantios, «Κωνσταντινούπολις», I, p. 376; but cf. Janin, *Constantinople*, pp. 354, 361; Macridy, *et al.*, DOP, No. 18, p. 256.

109. Cedrenos, *Historiarum Compendium*, II, 609: "Τό τε γὰρ ῥηθὲν μοναστήριον [κατὰ τὰ λεγόμενα Μάγγανα] καὶ τὰ ἐν αὐτῷ γηροτροφεῖα καὶ οἱ ξενῶνες καὶ τὰ πτωχοτροφεῖα ἐπαίνων οὐκ ἀμοιροῦσι."

110. Mercati and de Cavalieri, eds., *Codices Vaticani Graeci*, I, p. 429: " "Αλλο [εἰς ἔμφραξιν στομάχου] δοθὲν παρὰ Θεοδώρου τῶν Μαγγάνων, πρόσταξις στοματικὴ τοῦ ξενῶνος τῶν Μαγγάνων, ἐπιστολὴ ἀπὸ Θεσσαλονίκης παρὰ Στεφάνου ἀρχιατροῦ τῶν Μαγγάνων . . . περὶ στομαχικῶν σπληνικῶν καὶ ἡπατικῶν. . . ."

111. Pseudo-Codinos, *Patria*, Th. Preger, I, 141, 148.

112. *Ibid.*, III, p. 216; Byzantios, «Κωνσταντινούπολις», I, 177.

113. Pseudo-Codinos, *Patria*, Th. Preger, II, 170.

114. Cedrenos, *Historiarum Compendium*, I, 564.

115. Theophanes, *Chronographia*, I, 184.

reign of Michael III (842–867);[116] it still stood in the tenth century.[117] Pseudo-Codinos in the fourteenth century implies that remnants of it stood, such as columns.[118] The xenon and the rest of Lausos' buildings were near the hippodrome.[119]

In the tenth or eleventh century there was a xenon in the city of Nicaea. Its seal has survived, and reveals that a certain Manuel, an imperial protospatharios, was its director. On one side the seal bears the monogram of the cross and the prayer, "Lord help your servant." On the reverse it carries the inscription, "Manuel, imperial protospatharios, inspector [or director] of the xenodocheion of Nicaea."[120] We possess no other evidence. (See Figure 30A.)

An eleventh- or twelfth-century seal of an unknown xenon reveals the name of its director but contains no hint of where the xenon might have been. On one side the seal depicts the Virgin with Jesus, and the prayer, "Theotocos help," while on the opposite side it carries the words: "Sabas the humble xenodochos."[121] (See Figure 30B.)

An important xenodocheion was founded in Bithynia by the monk Michael Maleinos (+961) near his monastery. His biographer also relates that when Michael inherited a number of servants from his parents he set them free, and then distributed the rest of his inheritance to the poor and to charitable institutions.[122]

When Michael organized his monastic community in Bithynia he erected there a "great xenodocheion," which became the shelter and refuge of everyone passing by. All needy people found lodging and meals, and could receive fresh provisions for their journey.[123]

116. Monachos, *Chronicon*, ed. Muralt, p. 745.
117. Porphyrogenitos, *De Cerimoniis*, I, 154.
118. Pseudo-Codinos, *Patria*, Th. Preger, II, 170.
119. Theophanes, *Chronographia*, I, 182–84; Byzantios, «Κωνσταντινού-πολις», I, 439–40; Janin, *Geogr. Eccles.*, p. 572.
120. Schlumberger, *Sigillographie*, p. 381.
121. *Ibid.*, pp. 380–81.
122. Louis Petit, ed., "Vie de Saint Michel Maleinos," ROC, VII, No. 4 (1902), pp. 557–58.
123. *Ibid.*, p. 561. Michael erected "κοινὸν ταμεῖον καὶ σωτήριον καταγώγιον, τὸ μέγιστον λέγω ξενοδοχεῖον, ἐν ᾧ πᾶς τις ὁ κατὰ πάροδον καταλύων, ἀναπαύσεώς τε μεγίστης ἠξιωμένος καὶ ταῖς τῶν ἐπιδόσεων χορηγίαις τὸν ἐκ τῆς ὁδοιπορίας κόπον ἀποθέμενος, οὕτω τὸ ἑξῆς τῆς ὁδοῦ νεαρὸς ἀνύει καὶ πρόθυμος. . . ."

A. Seal of Manuel, Director of the Xenodocheion of Nicaea.

Obverse: An ornamented cross with the prayer, "Lord help your servant," around the edge.

+ K͞E͞ BOHΘEI TⲰ CⲰ ΔOϒΛˊ(ω)

Reverse: Inscription, "Manuel, imperial protospatharios, inspector [or director] of the xenodocheion of Nicaea."

+ MANOϒHΛ Bˊ(ασιλικω) Aˊ CΠAΘˊ(αριω),

ΕΠI TON OIKIAKON S ΞENOΔOX[Ⲱ] NIKEAC

Tenth–Eleventh Century; Collection Sorlin–Dorigny

B. Seal of Sabas, the Humble Xenodochos (Xenon Unknown).

Obverse: Bust of the Mother of God wearing the medallion of Christ, with the prayer, "Theotocos help," around the edge.

Θ͞K͞E͞ BOHΘˊ(ει) TⲰ CⲰ [ΔOϒΛⲰ]

Reverse: Inscription, "Sabas the humble xenodochos."

CABA ΕΛAXICTꙊ ΞENOΔOXHOϒ (sic)

Tenth–Eleventh Century; Collection Schlumberger

Figure 30. Three Seals of Xenon Directors, derived from *Sigillographie de l'empire byzantin*, ed. Gustave Schlumberger, pp. 380–81.

C. Seal of Epiphanios, Director of the Xenon of Loupadiou in Constantinople.

Obverse: Monogram of the cross, with the prayer, "Theotocos help," interspersed.

ΘΕΟΤΟΚΕ ΒΟΗΘΕΙ

ΤѠ CѠ ΔȣΛѠ

Reverse: Inscription, "Epiphanios, imperial cubicularius and xenodochos of Loupadiou."

ΕΠΙΦΑΝѠ Β'(ασιλικω) ΚȣΒΙΚ'(ουλαριω) [S]

ΞΕΝΟΔ'(οχω) Τȣ ΛȣΠΑΔΙ[ȣ]

Eighth–Ninth Century; Collection Sorlin–Dorigny

Figure 30.   Three Seals of Xenon Directors, derived from *Sigillographie de l'empire byzantin*, ed. Gustave Schlumberger, pp. 380–81 (*cont.*).

The monastic establishments were not isolated institutions unresponsive to the needs of the world outside, as has been demonstrated in a previous chapter. All monasteries usually had special houses for travelers, rich and poor alike, foreign guests, and pilgrims. When one considers the circumstances under which journeys were undertaken during the middle ages, monasteries must indeed have seemed oases in the desert.

A significant xenodocheion of the eleventh century was that attached to the monastery of Mount Galesion on the western coast of Asia Minor. St. Lazaros (+1053) passed his life there.[124] The mountain Galesion was just north of Ephesos,[125] and a

124. Gregorios Monachos, "Epitome Vitae S Lazari," AASS, III, cols. 535, 538; Nicephoros Gregoras, IV, 107.
125. "Epitome Vitae S Lazari," AASS, III, col. 2; Ramsay, *Historical Geography*, p. 110.

village of the same name was nearby.[126] The area was under the ecclesiastical jurisdiction of the Bishop of Ephesos who in the eleventh century, held the title of Metropolitan.[127] The monastery itself was in existence during the reign of Michael VIII Palaeologos (1259–82), and its hegoumenos Joseph is mentioned by Pachymeres.[128] The area of Ephesos was centrally located, and a highway led pilgrims from the capital and other coastal towns to the holy city. Hence a monastery in this area must have been a popular place. Our sources indicate that it attracted many travelers, strangers, and pilgrims, who found shelter in the xenodocheion of the monastery. Gregorios Monachos writes that the guests were allowed to remain there as many days as they wished and hospitality was as generous at the end as at the beginning. However, some of the visitors abused the monks' hospitality, and complaints were raised by the brothers.[129] Finally a new rule allowed the visitors to remain only three days. Upon this, the director of the xenodocheion (xenodochos) was accused of mistreating the visitors, and the hegoumenos was obliged to instruct him and the rest of the monks to be more generous, and to abolish the rule of the three-day stay. The hegoumenos emphasized that the sick should be treated especially well.[130]

XENONES DURING THE COMNENI DYNASTY

In the last quarter of the eleventh century Gregory Pacourianos, *domesticos ton scholon* under Alexios Comnenos,[131] established three xenodocheia for travelers, the poor, and pil-

126. Gregorios Monachos, "S Lazari," AASS, III, p. 556.

127. *Ibid.*, p. 526.

128. George Pachymeres, *De Michaele et Andronico Palaeologis,* ed. Immanuel Bekker, CSHB, I (Bonn, 1835), 291.

129. George Monachos, "S Lazari," AASS, III, 552–53.

130. *Ibid.*, p. 553: "Εἰπέ, ἔφη, τῷ ξενοδόχῳ, ἵνα καλῶς τοῖς ξένοις ὑπηρετῇ καὶ μὴ διώκῃ αὐτούς. Καὶ σύ, ἐξ ὧν ἂν ἔχοις εἰς τὸ κελλάριον, εἰ ἔστι τις ἄρρωστος καὶ ξένος, πάρεχε αὐτῷ πᾶν τὸ πρὸς χρείαν ἀδεῶς."

131. Anna Comnena, *Alexias,* II, 4. Cf. Petit, "Typikon de ... Pacourianos," pp. 48–49. For the history of the typikon, corrections, and related information see: Constantine Amantos, "Χειρόγραφα τῆς Μονῆς Πακουριανοῦ παρὰ τὸν Στενήμαχον," *Thr,* X (1938), 234 ff. There is a new edition of Pacourianos' Typikon with introduction and commentary in Georgian, with a Latin translation: S. Kauchtschisvli, *Typicon Gregorii Pacuriani* (Thbilisiis, 1963), pp. 205 ff.

grims. One of them was near the village of Stenimachos in Thrace, and included rooms and accommodations for many people. The second, known as the Marmarion, was situated at a bridge near the village of Pravikion in Thrace. The last was close to the monastery of St. Nicholas by the sea in eastern Thrace. Pacourianos wrote that the income of the third institution should be derived from the produce of the village of Prilogo.[132]

Pacourianos, of whom we shall say more in another chapter, endowed all three xenones very generously. They offered their free services in particular to needy people. He ordered the monks of the monastery of Petritziotissa, of which he was the founder, to respect the rights of the hostels; and he himself put those rights in writing. He ruled that distributions be made to travelers and the poor from the products of his estates: wheat, wine, meat, and whatever else was available. Near the xenon of Stenimachos he built a mill to grind the wheat.[133] Pacourianos was of Iberian origin[134] and intended the monastic community for people of his own land, but the xenones were opened to all.

The location of these institutions has not been established. However, the xenon near the village of Stenimachos must have been in the region of Philippoupolis.[135]

We have already discussed the famous institution of Pantocrator. Besides its religious centers, its hospital, and related buildings, there was also a section which served as hospice, properly so called.[136]

The size of an institution is very seldom mentioned in the sources. In the twelfth century, however, Nicetas Choniates mentions a xenon in Constantinople with accommodations for one hundred men. Originally it had been the house of Sebastocrator Isaac I Comnenos (1057–59),[137] but Isaac II Angelos (1185–95) transformed it into a xenon. Visitors were provided with lodging and with meals, and there were stables for their horses. Each

132. Petit, "Typikon de . . . Pacourianos," p. 49.
133. *Ibid.*, p. 48; cf. Amantos, *Thr.*; Beck, *Kirche und Theologische Literatur*, pp. 646, 647.
134. See E. Honigmann, *Die Ostgrenzen des byzantinischen Reiches von 363 bis 1071 nach griechischen, arabischen, Syrischen und armenischen Quellen*, pp. 222–26.
135. Petit, "Typikon de . . . Pacourianos," pp. xviii ff., 56.
136. Dmitrievsky, *Typika*, pp. 682 ff.
137. Nicetas Choniates, p. 585.

man had his own bed, and all could stay at the xenon several days without any payment.[138]

The site of Sophiana [139] which both sources mention as the location of the xenon, was near the port of the same name. We do not know much about the history of the xenon, but it is possible that it was destroyed by the Crusaders during their occupation of Constantinople after 1204.[140]

The Byzantine poet Manuel Philes (1275–1345),[141] dedicated a poem to Protostrator Michael Glabas Dukas Tarchaneiotes,[142] who established a xenon in his own name in Constantinople.[143] Glabas was motivated by his concern for poor travelers.[144] His wife helped him in this task, we learn, because she was also a friend of the poor.[145] This xenon was a "prytaneion," a true palace for the poor, the sick, and the deformed.[146]

We do not know the exact location of his xenon, but we do know that a certain Michael Tarchaneiotes Glabas was the founder of the monastery called Theotocos the Pammacaristos. If this individual was the same person who built the xenon, as Janin suggests,[147] we may assume that the xenon was located near the church.

138. Sathas, «Μεσ. Βιβλιοθ.», VII, 410–11: "Καὶ τὴν ἐν τῷ λιμένι τῶν Σοφιανῶν οἰκίαν τοῦ Σεβαστοκράτορος εἰς πανδοχεῖον μετασκευάσας ἀνδρῶν ἑκατόν, τράπεζαν καὶ κλίνας ἀνέθετο, καὶ ὑποζυγίων τοσούτων ἱππῶνας, καὶ εἰστιῶντο καθ' ἑκάστην οἱ παραβάλλοντες ἀδοτί."

139. Byzantios, «Κωνσταντινούπολις», I, 268–70.

140. Janin, *Geogr. Eccles.*, p. 575.

141. G. Moravcsik, *Byzantinoturcica*, I, 2nd ed. (Berlin, 1958), 416–17.

142. Beck, *Kirche und Theologische Literatur*, p. 711.

143. Manuel Philes, "Εἰς τὸν ξενῶνα πρωτοστράτορος τοῦ Γλαβᾶ," *Manuelis Philae Carmina*, I, 280; cf. p. 37.

144. *Ibid.*, ll. 1–4:

"Τὴν καταγωγὴν τῶν ἐπινόσων, ξένε,
ἣν ὡς ἀνεξίκακον ἐνθάδε βλέπεις,
πάλαι μὲν ὑπέθηκεν ὁ πρωτοστράτωρ
εὐσπλαγχνίας πένησιν ἐδράσας βάσεις."

145. *Ibid.*, ll. 13–14:

" Ἡ συμπαθὴς μάλιστα καὶ πτωχοτρόφος,
τοῦ συννόμου στέργουσα καὶ τὰς ἐμφάσεις."

146. *Ibid.*, p. 281, ll. 27, 28, 43 ff.

147. Janin, *Geogr. Eccles.*, p. 570, but cf. G. I. Theocharides, "Μιχαὴλ Δούκας Γλαβᾶς Ταρχανειώτης," *Epistemonike Epeteris Philosophikes Scholes Panepistemiou Thessalonikes*, VI (Thessalonike, 1957), pp. 183–206. Theocharides believes that there were two men with the same name: Protovestiarios Michael Tarchaneiotes (d. 1284) and Protostrator Michael Glabas (d. 1310–15).

Still another xenon in Constantinople was named the Krales.
It was in existence in the year 1406 [6914], when a certain monk
Nathanael, a nosocomos of the institution, urged another monk
named John to make a copy of a manuscript of Dioscurides, then
in a very bad state. Nathanael financed its transcription.[148] There
seems to be no evidence that Nathanael was director of the
xenon, as Janin writes.[149] It was founded by the Serbian Kral
Stephen Uros II Milutin (1282–1320), perhaps during the years
of his alliance with Andronicos II Palaeologos, and was attached
to the monastery of Prodromos in the quarter of Petra. In the
1440s John Argyropoulos held classes there of his school known
as *Katholicon Mouseion*.[150]

There were other xenones in Constantinople, of course, but
we do not know anything about their founders or the century in
which they were established. A xenon named tou Romanou is
mentioned by Pseudo-Codinos in his description of the Tauros
Forum. He writes that the xenon stood at the location of Alonitzion.[151]

Since it was customary for some benefactors to give their
names to institutions which they had established, we may assume
that the xenon known as Paschentiou's[152] was founded by someone of the same name. In the narration of the miracles of St.
Artemios, we read that this xenon was located near the palace
in the quarters of Deuteron.[153] There was a chapel in it where
the memory of St. Timothy, bishop of Prousa, was observed on
June 10.[154]

It is difficult to locate the site of the xenon because the quarter
of Deuteron was very extensive.[155] Because St. Timothy died

148. Bernard de Montfaucon, *Palaeographia Graeca* (Paris, 1708), p. 40;
Du Cange, *Constantinopolis Christiana*, IV. IX, 4; Amantos, *Athena*, xxxv,
p. 168.

149. Janin, *Geogr. Eccles.*, p. 572.

150. S. P. Lampros, «'Αργυροπούλεια» (Athens, 1910), pp. κά ff.; cf.
Friedrich Fuchs, *Die hoheren schulen von Konstantinopel im Mittelalter*
(Leipzig-Berlin, 1926), pp. 71–72; Giuseppe Cammelli, *Giovanni Argiro-
poulo* (Florence, 1941), pp. 33–34.

151. Pseudo-Codinos, *Patria*, Th. Preger, pp. 175–76.

152. Du Cange, *Constantinopolis Christiana*, IV. IX. 1.

153. Papadopoulos-Kerameus, *Varia*, Miracle 11, p. 11; *Synaxarium*, p.
743, col. 1.2.

154. *Ibid.*, Byzantios, «Κωνσταντινούπολις», I, 343.

155. *Ibid.*, pp. 341–43; Janin, *Constantinople*, pp. 314–17.

during the reign of Julian (361–63) and the quarters of Deuteron were in existence as early as Justinian's reign,[156] we may suggest that the Paschentiou xenon might have been an old institution.

Some donors preferred to remain anonymous. Such an anonymous Christian contributed greatly to the erection of a complex of charitable institutions near the monastery of Theotocos Evergetis. It included a xenon. The Typikon states that it was built by "a certain philochristos" for travelers and the sick. The monks were instructed by the rules of the monastery to provide needy travelers and strangers not only with lodging, but with regular meals and even used clothes and shoes. The complex included a separate burial place, called xenotaphion, for those of the "brethren" who could not journey any longer.[157]

We do not know the location of the xenon but it must have been near the monastery, that is, near Constantinople on the west side of the city.[158]

Xenones could be found even in the areas of small cities. We know, for example, that forty miles outside the town of Beroia in northern Thessaly there were houses for travelers. The narrator of the martyrdom of Alexander relates that by the river Arzos "there were many pandocheia." [159] Another manuscript, however, speaks of only one,[160] which is more probable.

THE UNKNOWN INSTITUTIONS

The xenones which we have examined in the foregoing pages must have been only a few of the many which existed. From the beginnings of the Byzantine Empire the church fathers had written about hospitality and urged the establishment of hospitable institutions. Anthemios, Bishop of Salamis in Cyprus, who built the Church of St. Barnabas, the patron saint of the island,

---

156. Procopios, *Buildings*, I. iii, p. 21; Sathas, «Μεσ. Βιβλιοθ.», VII, 117.

157. Dmitrievsky, *Typika*, p. 649.

158. Janin, *Geogr. Eccles.*, pp. 186–91.

159. "Μαρτύριον τοῦ ἁγίου . . . ᾿Αλεξάνδρου," ed. Dimitre P. Dimitrov, BIAB, VIII, 155.27: "Καὶ ἐλθὼν ὁ Τιβερειανὸς ἐν τῷ προλεχθέντι ποταμῷ ῎Αρζῳ, ὡς ἀπὸ μιλίων μ' Βεροίας, ἐν ᾧ τόπῳ ἦσαν πανδοχεῖα πολλά, ἔμεινε τὸν μάρτυρα ἐκεῖσε. . . ."

160. *Ibid.*, p. 156, note 7.

established nearby several houses for wayfarers and visitors.[161] St. Basil the Great was founder not only of that celebrated institution, the Basileias, but of several xenones in his diocese for strangers. In an epistle to Elias, Governor of Cappadocia, he wrote in 372: "Whom do we wrong when we build hospices for strangers, for those who visit us while on a journey . . . ?"[162]

In addition to monasteries, individual churches had houses near them for pilgrims, travelers, and poor people. Symeon Metaphrastes writes that when a prominent citizen of Constantinople fell in disgrace and was exiled to Thessalonike, his wife found a protector in the Patriarch John Chrysostom, who assigned her to the xenon of the church.[163] Under the influence of the same father, a certain patrician named Theodorichos donated his wealth to the pandocheion or xenon of the church.[164] Apparently Chrysostom had cultivated a strong sense of hospitality toward the stranger, the pilgrim, the poor provincial, and the visitor to Constantinople. In any case his biographer Palladios wrote that in the capital all men were xenodochoi.[165] Hospitality was considered a virtue which engendered piety,[166] and was practiced in faithful adherence to what the apostle had advised.[167] But abuses could destroy the meaning of hospitality and so Chrysostom had cautioned against it, warning that discrimination must be used with regard to the man to whom hospitality was offered.[168] The priest should not preoccupy himself with it at the expense of preaching the Gospel.[169]

During the same century, the Emperor Julian, "in imitation of the philanthropy of the Christians,"[170] had urged the establishment of xenones in every city to serve the needs not only of their own people but of foreigners as well, and had addressed a letter

161. "De S Barnaba Apostolo," Ch. 4, Sect. 45, AASS, June, II, 446E: "Πολλὰς δὲ καὶ ἑτέρας ξενίας ᾠκοδόμησε τῷ τόπῳ εἰς ἀνάπαυσιν τῶν ἐπιδημούντων ξένων."
162. Basil, *Epistles*, No. 94, II, 151.
163. Symeon Metaphrastes, MPG, CXIV, col. 1153D.
164. *Ibid.*, col. 1129B.
165. Palladios, *Vita S Jo. Chr.*, p. 72: "Εἰ δέ τις πόλιν οἰκῶν εὐνομωτά- την, οἵα ἡ Κωνσταντίνου, ἐν ᾗ πάντες εἰσὶ ξενοδόχοι."
166. *Ibid.*, p. 71.
167. Hebr. 13:2.
168. Palladios, *Vita S Jo. Chr.*, p. 71.
169. *Ibid.*, p. 72.
170. Cedrenos, *Historiarum Compendium*, p. 534.

to Arsacios, the chief pagan priest in Galatia, to that effect.[171] His policy was praised by Gregory the Theologian.[172]

During the fourth century, when the religious and cultural foundations of Byzantium were being laid, Ephraem the Syrian (c. 306–73) exerted a profound influence upon the wealthy citizens of Edessa. The city was visited by a severe famine. When the rich seemed to be indifferent to the fate of the poor, Ephraem managed to raise a great sum of money, which he used to set up three hundred beds in the public porticos. There he tended travelers as well as the local people.[173] During the reign of Constantine the Great, Leontios, Bishop of Antioch in Syria, cared for the xenones of the city himself and placed their administration in the hands of zealous men.[174] Unfortunately we do not know any of the xenones by name.

The sources often tell of individuals of various ranks who fed strangers and visitors. Bishop Paulos of an unknown century and an unidentified see [175] frequently visited strangers and foreigners in the hospital of Edessa and nursed them,[176] even before his election as bishop. Porphyrios, Bishop of Gaza (c. 347–420), after the completion of the cathedral in his diocese, distributed to each stranger who happened to be in the city the expenses for one day, and to each poor stranger or citizen he gave six obols; no poor man was left without some gift from him.[177]

The practice of remembering the poor during a celebration was customary among the Byzantines. Following the dedication

171. Julian, *Epistles*, Letter to Arsacius, High-Priest of Galatia (No. 84), I, p. 2, 145: "Ξενοδοχεῖα καθ᾽ ἑκάστην πόλιν κατάστησον πυκνά, ἵν᾽ ἀπολαύσωσιν οἱ ξένοι τῆς παρ᾽ ἡμῶν φιλανθρωπίας οὐ τῶν ἡμετέρων μόνον, ἀλλὰ καὶ τῶν ἄλλων ὅστις ἄν. . . ." Cf. Sozomenos, *Eccl. History*, pp. 217–18.

172. Gregory Nazianzenos, *Oration No. 4*, MPG, XXXV, col. 648C.

173. Sozomenos, *Eccl. History*, p. 130: " . . . καὶ λαβὼν ἀργύριον παρ᾽ αὐτῶν [τῶν πλουσίων] ἀμφὶ τὰς τριακοσίας κλίνας ἐν τοῖς δημοσίοις ἐμβόλοις εἶχε, καὶ τῶν ἀπὸ τοῦ λιμοῦ νοσούντων ἐπεμελεῖτο καὶ ξένους καὶ τοὺς κατὰ σπάνιν ἀναγκαίων ἐκ τῶν ἀγρῶν παραγενομένους ἐδεξιοῦτο."

174. Chronicon Paschale, p. 535.

175. Halkin, *Hag. Graeca*, I, 187.

176. Papadopoulos-Kerameus, «᾽Ανάλεκτα», "Life of St. Paulos the Bishop and John the Presbyter," V, 370.

177. Marcos the Deacon, "Life of St. Porphyrius Bishop of Gaza," ch. 94, ed. Henri Grégoire and M. A. Kugener, *Marc la Diacre. Vie de Porphyre evêque de Gaza* (Paris, 1930), p. 72.

of a great church in Constantinople, a few days after the election of the patriarch Eudoxios (360–69), the Emperor Constantios (337–61) made many gifts to the poor orphans, the widows, and the xenodocheia of the capital.[178]

The monastic establishments of the times were more than houses for monks or churches for endless religious services. We are told that the monastery was frequently the only hope for the poor traveler, the sick, and the homeless. Monasteries distributed food and clothes to the needy, and had special rooms in which the poor could find shelter and a hot meal. Theodosios the Coenobiarches of Jerusalem, who had established three hospitals, took additional measures to relieve the lot of strangers and poor travelers, founding xenones for them.[179] He built another and similar house for guests and foreign monks.

Theodore, Bishop of Petra, relates that the monastery of Theodosios in Palestine saved the lives of many hungry and sick people during a severe famine in the fifth or early sixth centuries.[180] We find this tradition of monastic hospitality very early in the empire. Basil the Great admonished the members of his monastic politeia to receive all strangers and provide them with all necessities.[181] The same philosophy was expressed by Sabas, the founder of the Grand Lavra in Palestine.[182]

Some time during the fifth century Eutropios and Theodora, the parents of John Calybites (c. 460), built a xenon and a large church in Constantinople. They gave all their money to the two institutions, with specific instructions that they serve the needs of strangers.[183] We do not know their location but may assume they were located in Constantinople where John Calybites was associated with the monastery of the Akoimetoi.[184] According to

178. Chronicon Paschale, p. 545: " Ὡς πολλὰς δωρεὰς ἐχαρίσατο φιλοτίμως τότε . . . καὶ τοῖς ξενοδοχείοις."
179. Theodore of Petra, *Life of St. Theodosios*, p. 34: " Ἀλλὰ καὶ τὸ τῶν καταγωγίων διάφορον ἑκάστῳ τῶν ἐπιδημούντων ἀναλόγως τὴν χρείαν χορηγοῦν, ἄλλων μὲν ἄλλως ξενοδοχουμένων, πάντων δὲ ὁμοίως θεραπευομένων."
180. *Ibid.*, pp. 36–39.
181. Basil the Great, *Regulae Fusius Tractatae*, Question No. 20, MPG, XXXI, cols. 969–73.
182. "Τύπος καὶ παράδοσις καὶ νόμος τῆς σεβασμίας λαύρας τοῦ [ἁγίου] Σάβα," ed. E. Kurtz, BZ, III, 170.
183. Symeon Metaphrastes, MPG, CXIV, 581D.
184. Byzantios, «Κωνσταντινούπολις», II, 218–19; Janin, *Geogr. Eccles.*, pp. 20–21.

Figure 31. Church of St. John Studion, interior looking toward the apse; Istanbul. Photo courtesy of the Byzantine Institute, Washington, D.C.

the chronicler Theophanes of the ninth century, the Empress Pulcheria, wife of Marcian (450–57), had built several philanthropic institutions which included homes for strangers and travelers.[185]

In addition to such great structures as Hagia Sophia, Justinian founded several hospices in various cities of the Empire in the sixth century. Procopios writes that the emperor built a hostel in Jerusalem[186] and established another guest-house in Jericho.[187] He also built xenones in Mocesos in Cappadocia,[188] which together with its many new "churches and . . . public baths and all the other structures, which are the mark of a prosperous city,"[189] raised Mocesos to the rank of Metropolis. Furthermore, he founded another great xenon in the city of Antioch[190] in Syria. Malalas recorded that Justinian endowed this xenon with an annual income of four thousand gold pieces.[191] Justinian's legislation indicates that there were many xenones for the poor and for travelers in various cities, towns, and eparchies of the empire.[192]

Another emperor of the sixth century, Tiberios I Constantine (578–82), was credited with the restoration of several xenones, which seem also to have served as hospitals.[193]

In the same century, John Moschos (b. c. 550), writes that there was a xenon in Alexandria near the pharos or lighthouse, between the Churches of St. Sophia and St. Faustos.[194] He records also that a xenon existed in the seaport of Ascalon[195] in Palestine, called the xenodocheion of the Fathers.[196]

In a similar fashion and writing in general terms, an anonymous author reports that John Eleemon, patriarch of Alexandria

185. Theophanes, *Chronographia*, I, 106.
186. Procopios, *Buildings*, V. vi, 165.
187. *Ibid.*, V. viii, 169.
188. *Ibid.*, V. iv, 158.
189. *Ibid.*, V. iv, 158.
190. Malalas, *Chronographia*, p. 423.
191. *Ibid.*, p. 452.
192. Justinian, *Novel No. 120*.
193. Cedrenos, *Historiarum Compendium*, I, 690.
194. Joannes Moschos, *Pratum Spirituale*, Ch. 106, MPG, LXXXVII. 3, p. 2965A.
195. See A. H. M. Jones, *The Cities of the Eastern Roman Provinces* (Oxford, 1937), pp. 259–60, 280–81 ff.
196. Joannes Moschos, *Pratum Spirituale*, Ch. 189, col. 3068A.

in the seventh century, founded in that city various houses for travelers and strangers.[197]

The example of the church fathers and individual benefactors was followed by members of the imperial family. In the eighth century the Empress Irene (797–802) is credited with the erection of a number of xenodocheia for poor travelers and visitors.[198]

Among the xenones of which we know very little we must include those which existed in such cities as Nicomedeia, Sag-(g)ara of Lydia—which might have been the city of Satala[199]—and Pylai.[200] The directors of their xenones are mentioned by Constantine Porphyrogenitos,[201] who classified them under the administrative jurisdiction of the Great Curator.

In a chrysobull of Isaac II Angelos issued in 1192 mention is made of a xenon located in the concession of the Pisans, near the Church of the Forty Martyrs. It had been renovated during Isaac's reign.[202] John Zonaras, again of the twelfth century, relates that there was a xenon in the neighborhood of the Church of the Saints Probos, Tarachos, and Andronicos.[203] It had been built by General Narses (who revolted against the Emperor Phocas),[204] together with the church just mentioned and the Church of St. Panteleimon.[205] Apparently there were people in the empire who founded philanthropic concerns for the benefit of their soul even to the very end of the empire. Thus we read that toward the end of the fourteenth century or the outset of the fifteenth, a xenon was built by Theodosia Cantacuzena when Matthaios (1397–1410) was Patriarch of Constantinople in the reign of Manuel II Palaeologos (1391–1425). To this xenon she offered her money and her estates. The poor and strangers were maintained there.[206]

Since traveling was a laborious and dangerous undertaking,

197. Delehaye, "Une Vie," p. 22.

198. Pseudo-Codinos, *Patria*, Th. Preger, III, 246: "Vita S Nicetae Confessoris," AASS, April, I, App., p. XXIV. 30.

199. *Historical Geography*, p. 134.

200. *Ibid.*, p. 187.

201. Porphyrogenitos, *De Cerimoniis*, p. 720. Cf. Philotheos, *Kletorologion*, p. 142.

202. Miklosich-Muller, *Acta et Diplomata*, III, 16.

203. Joannes Zonaras, *Epitomae Historiarum*, Bk. XIV, Ch. 14, ed. Theodorus Buttner-Wobst, III (Bonn, 1897), 199.

204. Theophanes, *Chronographia*, I, 292–93.

205. Zonaras, *Epitomae Historiarum*, p. 199.

206. Miklosich-Muller, *Acta et Diplomata*, II, 394–95.

214 *Philanthropic Institutions*

a xenos—that is, a foreigner, a stranger, or a traveler—was regarded with compassion, as someone who deserved the consideration and the hospitality of all. The misery which attended a stranger is movingly expressed in the poem *Logos Paregoreticos peri Dystychias Kai Eutychias.* The stranger says: "I am but a time-trodden and miserable stranger, stricken ten thousand times with misfortunes." [207]

The concern for strangers and other underprivileged, evident in a great segment of Byzantine society and especially in the monastic establishments, is beautifully expressed in another poem known as "Imberios and Margarona." Despite its romantic nature, this text manifests much of the quality of Byzantine mentality, blending the romantic element, the profoundly humanistic, the chivalrous, and the religious spirit to give us a sample of the social views of later Byzantium. Contemporary scholars [208] have demonstrated that this narration of the thirteenth century is not an unscrupulous imitation of the French romance *Pierre de Provence et la belle Maguelonne,*[209] but an independent creation related rather to the Chronicon of Morea.[210] This romance projects the admiration of the Byzantines for the hero, the athlete, the handsome and chivalrous, the rich and prestigious. More than any of these, however, it was the rich man who was the ideal, especially when he crowned his riches with good works.

207. "Λόγος Παρηγορητικὸς περὶ Δυστυχίας καὶ Εὐτυχίας," 75–76, ed. Spyridon P. Lambros, *Collection de romans grecs en langue vulgaire et en vers* (Paris, 1880), p. 292.

208. Nikos A. Bees, *Der franzosisch-mittelgriechische Ritter-roman "Imberios und Margarona" und die Grundungssage des Daphniklosters bei Athen* (Berlin-Wilmersdorf, 1924), pp. 17 ff.; Hugo Schreiner, "Neue Quellen zur Komposition und entstehungsgeschichte des Mittelgriechischen Romans Imberios und Margarona," BZ, XXX (1929–30), 121–30; *ibid.*, "Der Geschichtliche Hintergrund zu Imberios [Pierre de Provence und Margarona] La Belle Maguelonne," BZ, XLIV (1951), pp. 524–33.

209. Wilhelm Wagner, *Histoire de Imberios & Margarona—Imitation grecque du roman français Pierre de Provence et la Belle Maguelonne* (Paris, 1874), pp. 5–9; F. N. Marshall and John Mavrogordato, "Byzantine Literature," Baynes-Moss, *Byzantium*, p. 245.

210. Schreiner, "Neue Quellen . . . ," BZ, XXX, 128 ff. Cf. Emmanuel Kriaras, «Βυζαντινὰ Ἱπποτικὰ Μυθιστορήματα» (Athens, 1955), pp. 206–09. Cf. Borje Knos, *L'Histoire de la littérature néo-grecque* (Uppsala, 1962), pp. 121–24; Marcel Pichard, "Sur les fondements historiques des romans 'D'Imberios et de Margarona' et 'De Pierre de Provence et de la Belle Maguelonne,'" REB, X (1952), 84–92; Hugo Schreiner, "Der Alteste Imberiostext," *Akten des XI. Internationalen Byzantinistenkongresses Munchen, 1958* (Munich, 1960), pp. 556–62.

It was the evergetis (benefactor) who was immortalized. The father of Imberios was such a man,[211] and Margarona, one of the two protagonists of the romance, devoted the wealth of her supposedly dead husband to the erection of a xenon of one hundred beds for the "sick, the poor, and the strangers." What is more, although the romance is largely legendary, its author insists that Margarona did actually and in cold fact establish such an institution. It stood next to the monastery of which she was the abbess, and the nuns served as nurses and attendants.[212] The monastery has since been identified as the famous complex of Daphni[213] in Attica, which included several large structures: a xenon properly so called, a hospital, and perhaps a school.[214] Whatever the truth of the matter, "Imberios and Margarona" reveals how much the Byzantines revered those who cared for the stranger and the destitute. The alien was accepted as the likeness of Christ who had himself become a stranger upon the earth. The same notion is expressed in another late Byzantine source which was transcribed in the sixteenth century by Acacios, Bishop of Naupactos and Arta.[215]

211. " Ἡμπέριος καὶ Μαργαρώνα," ed. Lambros, *Collection de Romans Grecs en Langue Vulgaire et en vers*, ll. 20–24, p. 240; Emile Legrand, *Bibliothèque grecque vulgaire*, I (Paris, 1880), ll. 20–25, p. 284. G. Meyer, *Programm des K. K. Deutschen Ober–Gymnasiums der Kleinseite* (Prague, 1876), ll. 19–23, p. 1; cf. Wagner, *Histoire* . . . , ll. 17–19, p. 11.

212. "Imperios and Margarona," Lambros, *Collection*, ll. 670–77, p. 278:
" Ὁρίζει ἡ πανέμμορφος, ὡραία Μαργαρῶνα
νὰ κτίσουν ἑκατὸ κελλιὰ καὶ ἑκατὸν κρεββάτια,
νὰ ἀναπαύσῃ ἀσθενεῖς, πτωχόν τε δὲ καὶ ξένον.
Ξενῶναν ἐγκατέστησεν ἡ ὡραία Μαργαρῶνα.
Ξένοι καὶ ἄρρωστοι πτωχοὶ εἰς τὸν ξενῶνα ὑπᾶσιν
καὶ ἡ καλογρηαὶς νὰ βλέπουσιν τοὺς ἀστενεῖς, τοὺς ξένους,
νὰ στέκουν εἰς παράστασιν τί θέλουν οἱ ἀρρῶστοι."

213. Bees, *Ritter-roman*, pp. 51 ff.; Schreiner, "Der Geschichtliche Hintergrund . . . ," BZ, XLIV, pp. 530 ff.

214. Gabriel Millet, *Le Monastère de Daphni–Histoire, Architecture, Mosaiques* (Paris, 1899), p. 8; see also pl. II; cf. George Lambakis, «Χριστιανικὴ Ἀρχαιολογία τῆς Μονῆς Δαφνίου» (Athens, 1889), p. 88.

215. "Περὶ Ξενιτείας," Wagner, *Carmina*, p. 206:
"Εἴ τις γὰρ ἔχει τοῦ Θεοῦ τὸν φόβον 'ς τὴν ψυχήν του,
ἂς βλέπει κι' ἂς προσεύχεται, ξένον μὴν ὀνειδίσῃ,
ἐπεὶ 'ς τὸν κόσμον ὁ Θεὸς ἔπλασεν καὶ τοὺς ξένους.
νὰ πῶ κατὰ ἀλήθειαν τὸ ἀψευδὲς ἐτοῦτο·
ἀτός του ὁ παντοκράτορας ὁ ποιητὴς τῶν πάντων,
ἀτός του ξένος ἔγινεν καὶ φάνηκε 'ς τὸν κόσμον,
κ' αὐτός του πρῶτος ἔδειξεν τῶν ξένων ταῖς πικρίαις,
ταῖς θλίψεις καὶ τὰ βάσανα καὶ ταῖς ἀναισχυντίαις."

The conclusion is clear. Fragmentary as our sources may be, they nevertheless suggest that there were very many xenones, xenodocheia, and pandocheia in the Byzantine Empire.[216] In the preceding pages we have examined those institutions intended for philanthropic purposes. It is beyond the scope of the present work to include the philanthropy of those establishments in which private business was conducted.

The function and the importance of a charitable xenon was beautifully expressed by Theodore the Studite, who wrote in the last quarter of the eighth or the beginning of the ninth century:

> "Come forward to the hospitable house
> Oh, tired travellers,
> partake of our hospitality [eat]
> desirable bread which delights a heart, [drink]
> delicious wine which is plenty,
> be covered by blankets which protect from cold
> which have been given to me, oh friends,
> by the omniscient God. . . .
>
> . . . .
>
> in order that in this hospitable manner
> may I gain the bosom of Abraham." [217]

ADMINISTRATION

A xenon or xenodocheion was administered by a xenodochos. The xenodochos was appointed in some cases by the founder of

216. Cf. Justinian, *Novel 43*, Preface, p. 270; Justinian legislated concerning "πολλούς . . . εὐαγεῖς ξενῶνας."

217. Studites, *Epistles*, No. 29, MPG, XCIX, col. 1792A:

"Προβᾶτε, δεῦτε, τῇ ξενιζούσῃ στέγῃ
ἄνδρες πορευταί, τοῖς πόνοις κεκμηκότες,
μετεκλάβοιτε τῶν ἐμῶν ξενισμάτων,
ἄρτου ποθητοῦ, τοῦ τρέφοντος καρδίαν,
ποτοῦ γλυκείου, τοῦ ῥέοντος ἀφθόνως,
σκεπασμάτων τε τῶν ψύχους ἀλλοτρίων.
"Ἅ μοι παρέσχε τῷ Θεογνώστῳ, φίλοι,
ἐκ τῶν πανόλκων δωρεῶν αὐτοῦ χάριν,
Ὁ Δεσπότης μου Χριστός, ὁ πλουτοβρύτης.
Ἐπευλογοῦντες αὐτόν, ὡς κοσμοτρόφον,
κἀμοὶ προσευχὴν ἀντιποιοῦντες μόνον,
ὅπως ἐκεῖθεν τῷ φιλοξένῳ τρόπῳ
τοὺς Ἀβραὰμ τύχοιμι κόλπους εἰσδύναι."

Figure 32.   St. Theodore Studites, mosaic panel, Monastery of Nea Mone, Chios, Greece. Photo courtesy of Pericles Papahadjidakis.

the institution, in others by the imperial court, but most frequently by the local bishop. However, even when the local
bishop did not appoint the directors of the xenones, both the
canons of the Church and the laws of the State held him responsible for their general administration, as indeed also for all charitable enterprises in his diocese. The Church canons and State
laws held the bishop responsible for all church properties, for the
distribution of charities, and for the administration of social welfare in his diocese. Usually the bishop assigned various trustworthy individuals to direct the institutions of which he was the
supreme overseer. Thus the forty-first canon of the Apostles commanded the bishops to be in charge of all ecclesiastical functions
and to relegate and carry out the philanthropic functions through
the presbyters and the deacons.[218] The same spirit is expressed
in later canons [219] as well as in imperial legislation which, after
the bishop, held the governor of the eparchy responsible for the
philanthropic institutions of his charge, usually called *evage
oikoi* or *evage systemata*.[220]

Previous legislation was reaffirmed and clarified by the Emperors Basil I (867–86), Leo VI (886–912), and Alexander (912–
13) in their epanagoge, which commanded: "The *oeconomoi*
and *xenodochoi*, the *nosocomoi* and *ptochotrophoi*, and the administrators of all other philanthropic houses and besides, all
clergymen whatsoever shall be responsible to their bishop to
whose jurisdiction they belong and to whom their administration
is entrusted. . . ." [221] The bishop was forbidden to appropriate

218. "Forty-first Apostolic Canon," Rhallis-Potlis, «Σύνταγμα», II, 57:
"Προστάσσομεν, τὸν ἐπίσκοπον ἐξουσίαν ἔχειν τῶν τῆς Ἐκκλησίας πραγμάτων . . . καὶ τοῖς δεομένοις . . . ἐπιχορηγεῖσθαι." Cf. Auguste Rivet,
Le Régime des biens de l'eglise avant Justinien (Lyon, 1891), pp. 52–93.
219. Cf. "the thirty-eighth Apostolic Canon," Rhallis-Potlis, «Σύνταγμα»,
II, 52; "the twenty-fifth canon of the Council of Antioch," *ibid.*, III, 168;
"the twelfth canon of the seventh Ecumenical Council," 592–93 *et passim*.
220. Cf. Justinian, *Novel No. 7*, Prooimion, Ch. 12, epilogue, pp. 48–51,
62–63; *Novel No. 12*, Ch. 5, p. 581; *Novel No. 131*, Chs. 7, 10, 11, pp. 657,
659; Heraclios, "Νόμος Βεβαιῶν τοῖς Ὁσιωτάτοις," Rhallis-Potlis,
«Σύνταγμα», V, 225–29; "Synopsis Basilicorum," Zepos-Zepos, *Jus*, V, 264–
65, 294–95 *et passim*.
221. *Epanagoge*, Title Nine, paragraph 19, Zepos-Zepos, *Jus*, II, 256:
"Τοὺς οἰκονόμους καὶ ξενοδόχους καὶ νοσοκόμους καὶ πτωχοτρόφους
καὶ τοὺς τῶν ἄλλων εὐαγῶν οἴκων διοικητὰς καὶ τοὺς ἄλλους ἅπαντας
κληρικοὺς κελεύομεν ὑπὲρ τῶν ἐμπιστευθεισῶν αὐτοῖς διοικήσεων παρὰ
τῷ ἰδίῳ ἐπισκόπῳ ᾧ ὑπόκεινται, ἀποκρίνεσθαι, καὶ τοὺς λογισμοὺς τῆς

for himself or his relatives anything belonging to a philanthropic establishment.[222]

According to John Zonaras, the twelfth-century canonist, the eighth canon of the Council of Chalcedon placed the directors of all philanthropic institutions under the bishop.[223] His contemporary Theodore Balsamon,[224] another canonist, agrees with him.[225] Furthermore, the eighth canon of the Council of Chalcedon provided penalties for clergymen or laymen who refused to accept the order of the bishop.[226]

The office of xenodochos, understood as administrator of a charitable establishment, existed as early as in the third century after Christ. We know that one Isidore served as director of the xenones of the Alexandrian church and received ordination from St. Athanasios.[227] In the fifth century John Hesychastes, then Bishop of Coloneia in Asia Minor, joined the Grand Lavra of St. Sabas in Jerusalem without revealing his ecclesiastical rank and was assigned to serve as director of the house for strangers and guests. Cyril Scythopolites writes that as xenodochos John had to cook and labor for the benefit of the guests.[228] Cyril also tells us that the xenodochos under the general supervision of the oeconomos, was in charge of the meals and general welfare not only of visitors and foreigners but of all the monks of the establishment as well.[229]

If consideration for others and concern for the public welfare is the mark of a broad-minded and a tolerant individual—as modern psychology maintains—then the Byzantines were more broad-

ἰδίας διοικήσεως πληροῦσθαι καὶ εἰσπράττεσθαι." Cf. Justinian, *Novel 59*, chs. 3 and 4, pp. 319–20; see also August Knecht, *System des Justinianischen Kirchenvermogensrechtes* (Stuttgart, 1905), pp. 43–55.

222. In addition to church and state legislation cited above cf. also Photios, «Νομοκάνων», Rhallis-Potlis, «Σύνταγμα», I, 239–41 *et passim*.

223. *Ibid.*, II, 234–35: "Πάντας τοὺς ἐν ταῖς ἐκκλησίαις καὶ πόλεσι κληρικούς . . . οἱ θεῖοι κανόνες τοῖς ἐπισκόποις ὑπείκειν κελεύουσι· διὸ καὶ ὁ παρὼν κανὼν τοὺς τῶν πτωχείων κληρικοὺς τῷ ἐπισκόπῳ ὑπέταξε. Πτωχεῖα δὲ εἰσὶ τὰ εἰς πτωχῶν ἀφωρισμένα πρόνοιαν καὶ διοίκησιν, τὰ γηροκομεῖα δηλονότι, καὶ ὀρφανοτροφεῖα, καὶ τὰ τοιαῦτα."

224. Beck, *Kirche und Theologische Literatur*, p. 657.

225. Rhallis-Potlis, «Σύνταγμα», II, 234–35: "Πτωχεῖα δὲ λέγονται, πάντα τὰ εἰς πτωχῶν πρόνοιαν ἀφορισθέντα."

226. *Ibid.*, p. 234.

227. Palladios, *Vita S Jo. Chr.*, p. 35.

228. Schwartz, *Kyrillos*, p. 206.

229. *Ibid.*, pp. 130–31, 136–37.

220   Philanthropic Institutions

minded and tolerant than they have usually been thought to be.
They were sensitive people with an admirable passion for social
service. Hagiographical texts regularly tell of men who became
monks in order to offer their services to God and their fellow
men.

Along with the several persons cited above we may include a
soldier named Egersios who abandoned his military career and
joined the monastery of St. Hypatios (+445) in Bithynia. Here
he was made xenodochos and proved very successful in his
services to people, extending hospitality not only to traveling
monks but to many poor people.[230]

A xenodochos was often an important personage, and many
of them became bishops. The Patriarch of Antioch, Paul II (519–
21), was in charge of the xenon of Euboulos in Constantinople
before he was elected to the patriarchal throne.[231] Usually the
administration of a xenon was assigned to a presbyter with an
established reputation for virtue and knowledge.[232] This was
only wise, for Justinian's legislation entrusted the xenodochos
with the authority to sell or mortgage the estates of the institution in case of emergency.[233] It was forbidden to acquire the
office by simony.[234] Penalties were set for bad administration:
Theodore Studites issued a canon penalizing with ninety pros-
trations the xenodochos who failed to receive well any strangers,
visitors, and pilgrims.[235]

The office of xenodochos became so important in the following
centuries that many xenodochoi came to occupy important positions in state and religious ceremonies. The xenodochoi of six
xenones identified by name participated in the annual procession
of Palm Sunday in Constantinople.[236] They were assigned to the
jurisdiction of the chartularius of Sakellion,[237] had the rank of

230. Callinicos, *Life of St. Hypatios*, ed. in series Seminarii Philologorum
Bonnensis Sodales, *Callinici de Vita S. Hypatii Liber* (Leipzig, 1895), p. 82:
"Καὶ γενόμενος ξενοδόχος ἐφ' ἑκάστης ἡμέρας ἐξενοδόχει καὶ μονά-
ζοντας καὶ πτωχοὺς ἱκανούς. . . ."
231. Malalas, *Chronographia*, p. 411; Theophanes, *Chronographia*, I, 165.
232. Palladios, *Hist. Lausiaca*, p. 15.
233. Justinian, *Novel 120*; cf. *Novel 7*.
234. "Epanagoge VIII. 13," Zepos-Zepos, *Jus*, II, 252.
235. Studites, *Epistles*, "Poenae Monasteriales," No. 82, MPG, XCIX, col.
1744C.
236. Porphyrogenitos, *De Cerimoniis*, Bk. 1, Ch. 41(32), I, 161–62.
237. Philotheos, *Kletorologion*, pp. 141–42; cf. *ibid.*, pp. 152, 162.

spatharius,[238] and were to give regular reports to their bishop.[239]

So important was this office that the patriarch himself took interest in it. Photios, for example, addressed letters of reproach to two unworthy administrators: to a deacon George, and to a certain Damianos. George, it seems, had sold his soul and perhaps the property of his charge for wine. Photios recommends temperance,[240] points out the spiritual dangers of excess,[241] and urges him to replace his greediness with eleemosyne.[242] To Damianos, the celebrated patriarch emphasizes that the director of a xenon is expected to be a man both just and considerate of the poor.[243] Photios was especially sensitive to their fate.[244]

Unworthy administrators were not the only problems of the xenones. Many guests and visitors were of questionable morality and intentions. Because the xenones offered hospitality to all kinds of people a xenon sometimes threatened to become a house of ill fame. Thefts, murders, prostitution, and heavy drinking were common evils.[245] Such xenones enjoyed a bad reputation as in antiquity.[246] However, special laws for the protection of travelers and guests in hospices held the director responsible for any irregularities and abuses that occurred with his cooperation or knowledge. He was not, of course, held responsible if the crime was committed by one of the guests.[247]

238. *Ibid.*, p. 152.
239. Porphyrogenitos, *Selectus legum*, Title 9, Par. 18, MPG, CXIII, col. 488.
240. Photios, *Epistles*, No. 110, ed. Valetas, p. 432: "Πανταχοῦ τὸ μηδὲν ἄγαν ὑπολαμβάνειν κράτιστον."
241. *Ibid.*, No. 183, p. 511.
242. *Ibid.*, No. 185, p. 512.
243. *Ibid.*, Nos. 187, 188, 189, pp. 512–14.
244. *Ibid.;* note especially Letter No. 187: "Λῦσον, ἄνθρωπε, τῷ πένητι τὴν συμφοράν, ἀποδιδοὺς τὸ ἀδίκημα, καὶ τὰ τραύματα θεραπεύων εὐεργεσίας ἐλαίῳ. Εἰ δὲ τοῦ πένητος ὑπερορᾷς, ἀλλ᾽ οὖν τὴν ἐμὴν λῦσον συμφοράν· μᾶλλον δὲ τὴν σήν. ἡ σὴ γὰρ μείζων καὶ τῆς τοῦ πένητος καὶ ἡμῶν, κἂν οὔπω ταύτης, οἶμαι, συναίσθησιν ἔχῃς."
245. Cf. Joannes Chrysostomos, *Homilia de Capto Eutropio*, MPG, LII, col. 401; J. B. Aufhauser, ed., *Miracula S Georgii*, VIII (Leipzig, 1913), 94, 97; Anonymous, "De Officiis Regiis Libellus," ed. Wassiliewsky and Jernstedt, p. 99; Koukoules, ΒΒΠ, II, Pt. 1, 139–40. Cf. "Life of St. Theodore Sykeon," Ioannou, «Μνημεῖα», pp. 363–64.
246. Cf. Eustathios Makrembolites—the Philosopher, "Τὸ καθ᾽ Ὑσμίνην καὶ Ὑσμινίαν Δρᾶμα," Ch. 8, Par. 5, ed. Rudolph Hercher, *Erotici Scriptores Graeci*, II (Leipzig, 1859), 240.
247. Zepos-Zepos, *Jus*, VII, 279.

13. Gerocomeia (Homes for the Aged)

The Byzantines, as the Christian heirs of classical Greek culture,[1] paid special honor to old age. Their church prayed that the last days of man's earthly life might be peaceful, painless, and dignified,[2] and beseeched that God might not forsake a man in the time of life when his strength and health fails him.[3] Besides, the Church joined with the Byzantine State and private persons to establish many homes for the aged. We can identify more than thirty of these gerocomeia by name.[4] Most were named after their founders.

Of course, there were many gerocomeia besides those we know by name. Our sources speak of many gerocomeia in terms too general to allow us to identify them. Theophanes and Cedrenos, for example, record that the Emperor Tiberios I Constantine rebuilt not only churches but "many xenones and gerocomeia."[5] Manassis notes that Tiberios "erected many houses for the consolation of those suffering from mournful old age."[6] The Empress Irene (797–802) founded many more homes for the aged.[7]

1. Richardson, *Old Age Among the Ancient Greeks,* pp. 48–58.
2. Cf. Goar, *Euchologion,* pp. 32, 60 *et passim.*
3. Cf. Ps. 71:9.
4. Justinian, *Novel* 7, Chs. I–III *et passim;* Porphyrogenitos, *De Cerimoniis,* Bk. 1, Ch. 41(32), I, 107.
5. Theophanes, *Chronographia,* I, 251; Cedrenos, *Synopsis,* I, 690.
6. Manasses, *Synopsis,* vv. 3478–3483.
7. Pseudo-Codinos, *Patria,* Th. Preger, III, 246; Theophanes, *Chronographia,* I, 486.

Though some of these general statements refer to institutions in the capital, we may safely assume that gerocomeia existed in other major or provincial cities too, such as Antioch, Alexandria, Jerusalem, Thessalonica, Heracleia, Nicaea, Ephesos, Nicomedia, and Corinth.

GEROCOMEIA IN THE EARLY BYZANTINE EMPIRE

Perhaps the oldest known gerocomeion in Constantinople was in the quarter of Psamathia and was called by that name in the fourteenth century. Pseudo-Codinos relates that Helen, the mother of Constantine the Great, had built it, together with a palace and a church.[8] There is no other evidence. The toponym, however, has survived to the present day as Psamathia (Samatya in Turkish). The region is at the extreme west of Constantinople near the sea.[9]

A house for the aged attributed by tradition to the fourth century was known by the name of Euphrata. The thirteenth-century chronicler Theodore Scutariotes of Cyzicos relates that the house had belonged to one Euphratas who came to Constantinople from Rome with other patricians during the reign of Constantine the Great.[10] We learn that it was a very large structure and located in the quarter of Dimakellion.[11] When Scutariotes wrote, the gerocomeion was still in existence. He specifically states that "it is still called the Euphratas, even today." [12] The quarter of Dimakellion was in the region of present-day Humkapi, where old and used clothes are sold.[13]

One of the oldest gerocomeia known to have existed in Constantinople was built by Anthemios, the Byzantine magistrate who was sent to Rome in 467 as Emperor of the West. Our source

8. Pseudo-Codinos, *Patria,* Th. Preger, III, 216; cf. Richter, *Quellen,* p. 134. Cf. Ignatios of Selybria, Ioannou, «Μνημεῖα», p. 213.

9. Byzantios, «Κωνσταντινούπολις», I, 304; Janin, "Monastères byzantins. Les Couvents secondaires de Psamathia (Constantinople)," EO, XXXII (July-September, 1933), 325–31; cf. *Vita S Euthymii,* ed. de Boor, pp. 14–17.

10. Sathas, «Μεσ. Βιβλιοθ.», VII, 53.

11. Byzantios, «Κωνσταντινούπολις», I, 430; Janin, *Constantinople,* p. 327.

12. Sathas, «Μεσ. Βιβλιοθ.», VII, 53: "Οὕτω τοῦ Εὐφραθᾶ καλουμένου ἕως τοῦ νῦν."

13. Byzantios, «Κωνσταντινούπολις», pp. 438–39; Janin, *Constantinople,* pp. 321, 327, 352–53.

Pseudo-Codinos implies that before he left for his new assignment Anthemios transformed his house into a gerocomeion.[14] Whether this house belonged to the grandfather of Anthemios, whose name was also Anthemios,[15] is not clear. This institution was located in the western section of the city near the cistern of Mocios.[16]

During the reign of Arcadios (395–408), the patrician Florentios transformed his residence into a retreat for the aged.[17] The institution inherited its benefactor's name, and was located in the quarter of the old gardens of Serail.[18]

A patrician named Dexiocrates of the reign of Theodosios II (408–50) also changed his house into a gerocomeion and established a chapel there. Here again Pseudo-Codinos is our source.[19] This institution may have been of some significance because we know that one of its administrators was elected to the throne of Constantinople as Patriarch John the Fifth (669–75).[20] It was located on the Golden Horn, perhaps as far up as the present-day Ayakapi.[21]

The Emperor Marcian (450–57) and his virgin wife Pulcheria had established an institution for the aged in the neighborhood known as Prasina. Pseudo-Codinos writes that the place was so named because the stables of the Greens once stood there.[22] The author of the *Patria* relates that in the eighth century Ardabasdos, the strategos of the Armeniakon theme [23] who had helped Leo III the Isaurian (717–41) to seize the imperial throne,[24] had confiscated the house as his residence.[25] Perhaps it was after

14. Pseudo-Codinos, *Patria*, Th. Preger, III, 251; Richter, *op. cit.*, p. 163; Du Cange, *Constantinopolis Christiana*, IV. IX. 32, p. 166.

15. See Janin, *Geogr. Eccles.*, p. 565.

16. Janin, *Constantinople*, pp. 290–91.

17. Pseudo-Codinos, *Patria*, Th. Preger, III, p. 251; Richter, *Quellen*, p. 150.

18. Janin, *Constantinople*, pp. 378–79.

19. Pseudo-Codinos, *Patria*, Th. Preger, III, 241.

20. Ephraemios, *Patriarcharum*, ll. 9842–47.

21. Janin, *Constantinople*, pp. 317–18.

22. Pseudo-Codinos, *Patria*, Th. Preger, III, 239; Richter, *Quellen*, p. 171.

23. Not the Armenian Emperor Ardabasdus as Janin, *Geogr. Eccles.*, p. 569, suggests.

24. Manasses, *Synopsis*, ll. 4169–74; Ostrogorsky, *History*, p. 137; see a more detailed account in Amantos, «'Ιστορία», I, p. 329.

25. Pseudo-Codinos, *Patria*, Th. Preger.

he was blinded [26] in 743 [27] by his brother-in-law Constantine V (741–75) that he re-established it as a gerocomeion and endowed it generously.[28]

The location has not been identified. Janin writes that it might have been in the neighborhood of Zeugma [29] but furnishes no evidence to support his hypothesis.

In the fifth century, a number of gerocomeia also existed in Palestine. As a city of pilgrimages, Jerusalem was always in need of buildings to accommodate the throngs of visitors and curious adventurers: hospitals, hospices, and inns. In addition, establishments for the aged were needed.

In Jerusalem St. Theodosios, whose hospitals have been noted in a previous chapter, founded a home for aged monastics.[30] It must have been located near his monastery, with the rest of his philanthropic institutions—that is, seven kilometers west of the Grand Lavra of Sabas and nine kilometers from Jerusalem.[31]

About 408–50 the Empress Eudocia-Athenais also established a gerocomeion in Jerusalem, which included a chapel in honor of St. George.[32] While Euphemios was the Patriarch of Constantinople (489–95), John Hesychastes was the guest of the gerocomeion. Cyril of Scythopolis notes that it stood around a courtyard.[33]

In 1873 an inscription was discovered in Jerusalem on the north side of the great square tower, near the gate Bab es Sahera in the north quarters. It says that a Byzantine couple, Joannes and Berine, had built here a home for aged "poor" or "humble" women.[34] That this implies "poor in spirit" as Charles Clermont-Ganneau suggests,[35] can be only a conjecture. This gerocomeion

26. Theophanes, *Chronographia*, II, 420.
27. Ostrogorsky, "Die Chronologie des Theophanes im 7. und 8. Jahrhundert," BNJ, VII, 18.
28. Pseudo-Codinos, *Patria*, Th. Preger.
29. Janin, *Geogr. Eccles.*, p. 569.
30. Theodore of Petra, *Life of St. Theodosios*, ed. Usener, p. 41.
31. Schwartz, *Kyrillos*, pp. 114, 237; cf. Festugière, *Les Moines*, p. 140.
32. Schwartz, *Kyrillos*, p. 204.
33. *Ibid.*
34. Charles Simon Clermont-Ganneau, *Archaeological Researches in Palestine during the Years 1873–1874*, p. 247: "Γεροκομεῖον γυναικῶν ταπεινῶν συσταθὲν διὰ τῆς ἁγίας Θεοτόκου, ὑπὸ Ἰωάννου καὶ Βερίνης Βυζαντίων." (Greek text restored.) Cf. R. P. Germer-Durand, "Épigraphie chrétienne de Jérusalem," *Revue biblique*, I (1892), 583.
35. *Ibid.*, p. 248.

was in existence during the fifth century. Finally there was the gerocomeion of the Patriarch, built, we may suppose, by an unknown patriarch of Jerusalem. The Georgian version of Antiochos Strategos' account of the capture of Jerusalem by the Persians in 614 records that three hundred and eighteen dead were found near it,[36] so that we may suppose it was in existence at least as early as the sixth century.

Indeed, the sixth century appears to have been rich in philanthropic establishments for the aged. We know by name at least six such institutions of this period.

A house for the elderly, named Narses, indicates that it inherited the name of its benefactor. According to Pseudo-Codinos, Narses the patrician and protospatharius who lived during the reign of Justin and Sophia (565–78) built a complex consisting of a church, a hospice, and a house for senior citizens.[37] According to Theophanes, Narses built them in the year 570 [6063].[38]

Several scholars have discussed the location of the Narses, but Janin, who has studied the problem in detail, believes that it was in the present-day Zindankapi or Odunkapi.[39]

Another establishment for the advanced in age was known as the Isidorou. Pseudo-Codinos relates that the place had been the residence of a certain Isidore, the brother of the patrician Euboulos in the reign of Justin I (518–27). Later he transformed it into an institution for the aged and added a chapel.[40] There is no further information about it. Janin suggests that this establishment might have included a chamber for strangers, a xenon, which was known under the same name.[41] However, his hypothesis is not supported by any evidence, nor is the evidence sufficient to identify this house with one of the xenones by the same name which we have already discussed.

During the reign of Justinian (527–65) we hear of an institu-

36. Antiochos Strategos, *Captivitas Hierosolymae*, ed., tr. Gerard Garitte, p. 52: "Et invenimus in gerocomio patriarchae trecentas et duodeveginti animas." Milik, "La Topographie de Jérusalem," p. 133, agrees with this figure.
37. Pseudo-Codinos, *Patria*, Th. Preger, III, 249.
38. Theophanes, *Chronographia*, I, 243–44.
39. Janin, "Etudes de topographie byzantine," EO, XXXVI, 288–308; see especially pp. 290–92, 299; cf. also Janin, *Constantinople*, pp. 365–67.
40. Pseudo-Codinos, *Patria*, Th. Preger, III, 254–55.
41. Janin, *Geogr. Eccles.*, p. 567.

tion for the aged named ta Petrou. Named after its founder Peter the Patrician,[42] at the beginning it had served as his residence. Later he transformed it into a gerocomeion with a chapel. Peter the Patrician was probably the "prudent and meek" envoy from Thessalonica who was delegated by Justinian to Italy and served the imperial administration well in various capacities.[43] The identification of the site remains difficult, and it is not certain, as has been suggested, that it was located in the region of Petrion, though to be sure there stood there another home for the aged, a number of churches, monasteries, and a palace.[44]

From the last quarter of the sixth century we learn of three gerocomeia. One was known by the name Karianou. Pseudo-Codinos asserts that it was founded by Emperor Maurice (582–602) who also built a church there and some porticos.[45] The toponym derives its origin from the patrician Karianos[46] who had once built his house on the site. Later the area came to have a palace[47] and (perhaps) other buildings. Janin has proposed that the name may derive from the marble called Carie of which it was built.[48] The site of the Karianou was at the Blachernae.[49]

An important foundation for the aged was erected in Constantinople by Stephanos the parakoemomenos of the Emperor Maurice (582–602). It was located at the quarter of Armatiou, where Stephen had constructed also a cistern and baths.[50] The

42. Pseudo-Codinos, *Patria,* Th. Preger, III, 249. Cf. Richter, *Quellen,* p. 191.

43. Procopios, *History of the Wars,* V. iii, 30.

44. Chronicon Paschale, p. 494; Theophanes, *Chronographia,* I, 368; Theophanes Continuatus, *Chronographia,* p. 275–325, 397; Pseudo-Codinos, *Patria,* Th. Preger, III, 239, 240, 264; Byzantios, «Κωνσταντινούπολις», I, 563–67; Janin, *Constantinople,* pp. 375–76 ff.

45. Pseudo-Codinos, *Patria,* Th. Preger, III, 241; cf. Du Cange, *Constantinopolis Christiana,* II. vi, 12, Richter, *Quellen,* pp. 341–42; Symeon Magister, *Chronographia,* p. 653.

46. Pseudo-Codinos, *Patria.*

47. Theophanes Continuatus, *Chronographia,* pp. 95, 174; Symeon Magister, *Chronographia,* p. 653 ff.

48. Janin, *Constantinople,* pp. 341–42.

49. Byzantios, «Κωνσταντινούπολις», I, 594; J. B. Papadopoulos, *Les Palais et les églises des Blachernes* (Athens, 1928), pp. 161–62 *et passim.*

50. Pseudo-Codinos, *Patria,* Th. Preger, III, 238–39; E. Kurtz, "Zwei griechische Texte uber diehl. Theophano," BZ, III, 18; Du Cange, *Constantinopolis Christiana,* IV. IX. 21; *Synaxarium,* p. 492; Gedeon, «Ἑορτολόγιον», p. 78.

Figure 33. The *Gerocomeion* in the Quarter of Armatiou in Constantinople, derived from a miniature in a Byzantine manuscript. Reproduced with permission from *Epeteris Etaerias Byzantinon Spoudon*, Vol. 17 (1941), p. 206.

establishment had also a clinic for strangers and provincial citizens who fell sick while visiting the capital. A copy of its typikon made in 1446 at the orders of its administrator Dositheos testifies to its later existence: [51] it is the only philanthropic institution which we know to have existed from the beginnings until the collapse of the empire. The region of Armatiou where the

51. Bartholomeos of Koutloumousion, «Ὑπόμνημα περὶ τῆς ἐν Χαλκῇ Μονῆς τῆς Θεοτόκου» (Constantinople, 1845), cited by Gedeon, p. 78, n. 111; Janin, *Geogr. Eccles.*, p. 566, n. 2; Marie Vogel and Victor Gardthausen, *Die griechischen Schreiber des Mittelalters und der Renaissance* (Leipzig, 1909), p. 92: " Ἐξόδου τοῦ τιμιωτάτου ἐν ἱερομονάχοις κυρίου Δοσιθέου καὶ καθηγουμένου τοῦ εὐαγοῦς Ξενῶνος τοῦ Ἀρματίου.’ " It is apparent that Janin is wrong in referring to Dositheos as Dorothea or Dorothy and as the "hieromoine et cathigoumene," in *Geogr. Eccles.*, p. 566.

228

house stood was on the Golden Horn in the neighborhood known today as Unkapani.[52]

Stephen built a second gerocomeion known as the house of Sagma.[53] Whether the name is that of its location is not known. There is no further information about it.

Stephen was, not unreasonably, canonized, and his memory is observed on February 26.

In the life of the physician-monk Cyros we learn that as soon as Patriarch Appolinarios was elected to the see of Alexandria in the year 551, he inaugurated a program of philanthropic work. Among other foundations, Appolinarios erected a specific house for the aged near the Church of the Three Children in the region of Doryzin.[54] There must have been many bishops in the Byzantine Empire who imitated Appolinarios' example.

THE GAP IN EVIDENCE

In the seventh century, a foundation for the aged stood in the Scala region and was known by the same name. We do not know anything about its founder or its site. The only information we have about it we owe to the fourteenth-century ecclesiastical historian Nicephoros Callistos Xanthopoulos,[55] who writes that when Patriarch Thomas II was elected to the Ecumenical throne in the year 667 [56] he was in charge of the gerocomeion of Scala.[57] Thomas' election from that office to the throne of Constantinople suggests that this establishment might have been of some importance. The quarter of Scala has not been identified, but the word may have been a corruption of

52. A. D. Mordtmann, *Esquisse topographique de Constantinople* (Lille, 1892), p. 10, par. 16; Gedeon, «Ἑορτολόγιον», pp. 78–79; Byzantios, «Κωνσταντινούπολις», I, 348–49; R. Janin, "*Topographie de Constantinople byzantine quelques quartiers mal connus*," *Memorial Louis Petit-Mélanges d'histoire et d'archéologie byzantines* (Bucarest, 1948), pp. 218–22.

53. *Synaxarium*, p. 492.

54. Theodorus Nissen, ed., "De SS Cyri et Iohannis Vitae Formis," AB, LVII (1939), 70; Symeon Metaphrastes, MPG, CXIV, cols. 1232–33.

55. Beck, *Kirche und Theologische Literatur*, pp. 705 ff.

56. *Ibid.*, pp. 108, 803; cf. Ephraemios, *Patriarcharum*, ll. 9839–41; Grumel, *Chronologie*, I, 435.

57. Nicephoros Callistos Xanthopoulos, *Patriarcharum Constantinopolitanorum Catalogum*, MPG, CXLVII, 457B; «Ἐκκλησιαστικὴ Ἀλήθεια», V (1885), 273, cited by Janin, *Geogr. Eccles.*, p. 569, n. 5.

Scallae, which in turn may have been a perversion of Chelas [58] or Chalas [59] or Challaes.[60] In such a case, the institution was located in present-day Bebek on the Bosporos.[61]

The patrician Severos, the adopted brother of the Emperor Constans II (641–68) founded a retreat for the elderly and gave it his name.[62] It had served as Severos' residence in the beginning. His wife added a church nearby, perhaps as a token of gratitude to God for her husband's survival of the emperor's catastrophe in Sicily.[63] Pseudo-Codinos adds that it was Severos who led the Byzantine fleet back to the east [64] after the emperor's defeat. The gerocomeion was built near the Forum Tauros.[65] The neighborhood must have been a distinguished one,[66] for there stood nearby a palace, the Church of St. Mark, the Church of St. John the Baptist, a Church of St. Theodoros, a bath, and perhaps other public structures.[67] The Tauros is the region of present-day Boyazit.[68]

Petros was elected to the patriarchal throne of Constantinople in 654,[69] during the reign of Constans II (641–68). He was at that time the administrator of a gerocomeion [70] called St. Clem-

58. Pierre Gilles, *De Bosporo Thracio* (Lyon, 1561), pp. 156–159.

59. Chronicon Paschale, pp. 722, 723.

60. *Synaxarium*, p. 846; Byzantios, «Κωνσταντινούπολις», I, 121.

61. Janin, *Constantinople*, p. 436; cf. p. 428; cf. Gedeon, «Ἑορτολόγιον», p. 139. Gedeon suggests that the region of Scallae was on the east side of Bosporos.

62. Pseudo-Codinos, *Patria*, Th. Preger, III, 251–52; cf. Du Cange, *Constantinopolis Christiana*, IV. IX. 31; Richter, *Quellen*, p. 211.

63. Theophanes, *Chronographia*, I, 351–52.

64. Pseudo-Codinos, *Patria*, Th. Preger. This testimony contradicts Theophanes' account, which relates that the son of Constans, Constantine IV (668–685) made a successful expedition to Italy to avenge his father's death and eventually brought the Byzantines back to the East. E. W. Brooks, in "The Sicilian expedition of Constantine IV," BZ, XVII (1908), 455–59, has demonstrated that such an expedition did not occur. But cf. H. Grégoire, "Notules Epigraphiques," B, XIII, 170, n. 1.

65. Pseudo-Codinos, *Patria*, Th. Preger.

66. *Ibid.*, II, pp. 175–77; *Synaxarium*, p. 630; Dmitrievsky, *Typika*, I, 43; Gedeon, «Ἑορτολόγιον», p. 52.

67. Pseudo-Codinos, *Patria*, Th. Preger; Janin, *Constantinople*, pp. 69–72; Byzantios, «Κωνσταντινούπολις», I, 411–15.

68. Janin, *Constantinople*.

69. Beck, *Kirche und Theologische Literatur*, pp. 432–33; cf. Grumel, *Chronologie*, p. 435.

70. Nicephoros Callistos Xanthopoulos, *Patriarcharum*, MPG, CXLVII, col. 457A.

ent's, and had served in that capacity twelve years and four months.[71] St. Clement's may have stood near the Church of St. Clement. The church was located on the far side of the Anaplous, in the region of Eudoxiou [72] where the modern village Bebek lies.[73]

In the last quarter of the seventh and the first half of the eighth centuries, Andrew, Archbishop of Crete,[74] undertook many philanthropic works in his diocese. In addition to the hospital already discussed, Andrew erected a home for the aged.[75] Nothing else is known about it.

In the eighth century in the quarter of Petrion [76] stood a gerocomeion named the Geragathes.[77] Pseudo-Codinos recites an amusing anecdote about it: the Geragathes was built by Agathe, the daughter of a patrician perhaps named Peter, during the reign of Constantine V Copronymos (741–75). Agathe, alas, remained an old maid, and even in advanced age preserved her beauty and her virginity. Thereafter the institution was called the *Geragathes*, i.e. the Old-Agathe's. Pseudo-Codinos adds that Agathe collected icons in the old-age home, but that the emperor had them all burned. He also, according to Pseudo-Codinos, took her virginity [78]—perhaps by marriage. The Geragathe was in the quarter of Petrion or Petra. Whether this toponym is derived from the name of Agathe's father, or another patrician of the same name who was contemporary with Justinian,[79] is not clear. A region known as Petrion did indeed exist in the first half of the sixth century,[80] but it may have been called Petrion or Petri and Petra because the location was stony.[81]

71. *Synaxarium*, p. 418.
72. Janin, *Geogr. Eccles.*, pp. 291, 567.
73. Gedeon, «Ἑορτολόγιον», p. 63, par. 23; Janin, *Constantinople*, p. 429.
74. See Krumbacher, *Geschichte*, pp. 165–66, 673–74; Beck, *Kirche und Theologische Literatur*, pp. 500 ff.
75. Ch. Loparev, "Περὶ τινων βίων ἁγίων Ἑλληνιστὶ γεγραμμένων," VV, IV, 346.
76. For the topography see: Byzantios, «Κωνσταντινούπολις», I, 563–67; Mordtmann, *Esquisse topographique de Constantinople*, No. 68, p. 41; R. Janin, "Le Petrion de Constantinople," EO, XXXVI, 31–51.
77. Pseudo-Codinos, *Patria*, Th. Preger, III, 240.
78. *Ibid.*; cf. Du Cange, *Constantinopolis Christiana*, IV. IX. 25; Richter, *Quellen*, pp. 375–76.
79. Procopios, *Anecdota*, pp. 134, 135, 137, 138 ff.
80. *Acta Conciliorum Oecumenicorum*, ed. Edward Schwartz, III (Berlin, 1940), 35, 36, 173 ff.
81. Byzantios, «Κωνσταντινούπολις», I, 563.

We do not know of any other foundations of the eighth and the ninth centuries. Perhaps due to their more satisfactory historical literature, the following three centuries offer a few more foundations for the aged.

GEROCOMEIA UNDER THE MACEDONIANS
AND THE COMNENI

The Patriarch Theophylaktos (933–56),[82] we hear, had erected stables near the Church of Hagia Sophia. The continuator of Theophanes alleges that Constantine Porphyrogenitos (913–59) transformed them into a gerocomeion, ordering that the inmates were to be given food and clothing annually in abundance.[83]

At about the same time Porphyrogenitos' wife, the Empress Helen, founded and gave her name to a complex of buildings including a gerocomeion.[84] It was located in the district of the old Petri,[85] probably in the area of present-day Petrikapi.[86] Continuatus observes further that the empress was so devoted to it that when she became seriously sick, the emperor issued a chrysobull granting the institution special privileges and rights and assigning to it special estates and other properties. The founder was very much pleased.[87]

Legislation of the period also mentions a gerocomeion near the monastery of the Myrelaion.[88] We know that the monastery owed its origin to the Emperor Romanos Lecapenos[89] and so may suppose that he built the gerocomeion, too. The Myrelaion, as we have said, was probably in the precinct in which the mosque Bodrumcami today stands. The mosque was erected on the site of a Byzantine church.[90]

---

82. Grumel, *Chronologie*, p. 436.
83. Theophanes Continuatus, *Chronographia*, p. 449; cf. Du Cange, *Constantinopolis Christiana*, IV. IX. 28; Richter, *Quellen*, p. 233.
84. Continuatus, *Chronographia*, pp. 458–59.
85. *Ibid.*
86. Byzantios, «Κωνσταντινούπολις», I, 567; Mordtmann, *Esquisse topographique*, p. 129; Janin, *Constantinople*, pp. 375–76.
87. Theophanes Continuatus, *Chronographia*, pp. 458–59.
88. Zepos-Zepos, *Jus*, IV, 53; cf. *Jus*, I, xxxii.
89. Theophanes Continuatus, *Chronographia*, pp. 404, 473.
90. Byzantios, «Κωνσταντινούπολις», I, 280–81; Janin, *Constantinople*, p. 365; Rice, "Excavations at Bodrum Cami," B, VIII, 151–74.

Porphyrogenitos' father, Emperor Leo VI Wise (886–912), also took measures for the benefit of the aged. He expelled the inmates of a house of prostitution in the vicinity of Kyphe and transformed it into a gerocomeion.[91] His son Constantine VII remarks that the emperor used to visit this institution on Good Friday on his return from church services at the Blachernae, and distributed gratuities to the senior citizens there. He implies that the institution included more than one structure and that there was a section for lepers.[92] Where it stood we do not know, but Janin speculates that it may have been situated along the Golden Horn.[93]

The last institution of the tenth century known by name is the Eugeniou. But the only information we possess is found in a reference in the Book of Ceremonies of Constantine VII Porphyrogenitos: the administrator of this foundation for the elderly addressed a eulogy to the emperor when he came to take his bath at the Blachernae.[94] A seal of the ninth century has survived.[95] The location of this establishment was frequently mentioned by the Byzantines [96]—on the Golden Horn, perhaps where the station Sirkessi stands today.[97] (See Figure 34.)

Constantine IX Monomachos (1042–54) founded a number of structures, including a gerocomeion, in the quarters known as Maggana. George Cedrenos says that they were near the monastery of St. George.[98]

The region of Maggana, frequently mentioned by the Byzan-

---

91. Theophanes Continuatus, *Chronographia*, p. 370; Monachos, *Chronicon*, p. 865; cf. Du Cange, *Constantinopolis Christiana*, IV. IX. 33; Richter, *Quellen*, p. 228.

92. Porphyrogenitos, *De Cerimoniis*, I, 168.

93. Janin, *Geogr. Eccles.*, p. 568.

94. Porphyrogenitos, *De Cerimoniis*, Bk. 2, ch. 12, Bonn ed., p. 556.

95. Schlumberger, *Sigillographie*, p. 154. It reads: "Κυριτζίῳ ὑπάτῳ καὶ γηροκόμῳ τῶν Εὐγενίου."

96. Pseudo-Codinos, *Patria*, Th. Preger, I, 141, 142, 148; III, 220; John Cantacuzenos, *Historia*, III, 76, 213, 214, 232; George Pachymeres, ed. Emmanuel Bekker, CSHB, III (Bonn, 1835), 96, 134; Nicephoros Gregoras, *Byzantina Historia*, ed. Ludovicus Schopenus, CSHB, I (Bonn, 1829), 167, 275.

97. Byzantios, «Κωνσταντινούπολις», I, 149; Janin, *Geogr. Eccles.*, pp. 566–67.

98. George Cedrenos, *Historiarum Compendium*, 608–09; Sathas, «Μεσ. Βιβλιοθ.», VII, 409; Monachos, *Chronicon*, II, 759.

Obverse: Monogram of the cross, with the prayer, "Theotocos help," interspersed.

ΘΕΟΤΟΚΕ ΒΟΗΘΕΙ

Τῼ Ϲῼ ΔΥΛῼ.

Reverse: Inscription, "Kyritsios, chief gerocomos of Eugeniou."

+ ΚΥΡΙ
ΤΖΙῼΥΠΑ
ΤῼϹΓΗΡΟΚ,Τ,
ΕΥΓΕΝΙΥ

Κυριτζίω ὑπάτω καὶ γηροκώμω τῶν Εὐγενίου.

Figure 34. Seal of Kyritsios, Gerocomos of Eugeniou, a *Gerocomeion* in Constantinople, derived from *Sigillographie de l'empire byzantin*, ed. Gustave Schlumberger, p. 154.

tines,[99] was near the Acropolis [100] and received its name because war materials and machines for building walls were kept there.[101]

In a document issued by Patriarch Callistos, who occupied the throne of Constantinople from 1350 to 1353 and from 1355 to 1363,[102] we learn that the monastery of Maggana was in existence in 1351.[103] We may infer that the homes for the aged were still in existence, too. Modern historians disagree as to the exact site of Maggana, but incline to place it in the region southeast of the Acropolis.[104]

One of the three emperors named Romanos—either Romanos I

99. Theophanes Continuatus, *Chronographia*, p. 337; Pseudo-Codinos, *Patria*, Th. Preger, III, 292; *Life of St. Ignatios*, MPG, CV, 540; Theophanes, *Chronographia*, I, 435.

100. Pseudo-Codinos, *Patria*, Th. Preger, I, 141, 148.

101. *Ibid.*, III, 216.

102. Beck, *Kirche und Theologische Literatur*, p. 774 ff.

103. Miklosich-Muller, *Acta et Diplomata*, I, 317.

104. Byzantios, «Κωνσταντινούπολις», I, 177–79; Janin, *Constantinople*, pp. 355–56 ff.; Richter, *Quellen*, pp. 401–03; R. Demangel and E. Mamboury, *Le Quartier des Manganes et la I^ne région de Constantinople* (Paris, 1939), pp. 19–47; see also Plates III, VI, VII.

Lecapenos (920–44), Romanos II (959–63) or Romanos III Argyros (1028–34)—gave his name to a gerocomeion mentioned in the first half of the twelfth century. Our information about it has come to us in six words of the Typikon of the celebrated Pantocrator. It relates that the Emperor John II Comnenos (1118–43) decided to build a house for elderly people suffering from leprosy, and chose to erect it near the home for the aged of the Emperor Romanos.[105] Whether this gerocomeion was built by Romanos Argyros or is identified with the Myrelaion, as Janin suggests,[106] is not clear.

As for the gerocomeion of the Pantocrator complex, we are told that it was founded by John II Comnenos, who ordered the erection there of an establishment for the aged where twenty-four "crippled, lame, and incapable" men could find shelter and protection. Six nurses were assigned to it. The director of the Pantocrator was expressly instructed not to admit any person in good health or able to earn his own living.[107] The inmates of the gerocomeion were given bread, wine, dry beans, oil, cheese,[108] money, clothes, and wood for fire and heat; special gifts were given them on various holidays. A priest was assigned to serve the religious needs of the inmates. The emperor prescribed that if any inmate became sick, a physician of the hospital should be summoned to look after him; if his illness was very serious, he was transferred to the hospital and stayed there until he had recuperated. Each of the inmates was given a bath twice each month in the hospital baths. A gerocomos under the supervision of the hegoumenos of the monastery was appointed to supervise the gerocomeion. A special bath was prescribed on Holy Thursday for all the residents and patients of the Pantocrator, and they were given gifts.[109]

We have already noted that Isaac II Angelos (1185–95) had founded a hospital. He also established an institution for senior

105. Dmitrievsky, *Typika*, 695.
106. Janin, *Geogr. Eccles.*, p. 569.
107. Dmitrievsky, *Typika*, 694.
108. See E. Jeanselme, *Calcul de la ration alimentaire des malades de l'hôpital et de l'asile des vieillards annexes au monastère du Pantocrator à Byzance (1136),* Extrait du 2ᵉ congrès d'histoire de la médecine (Evreux, 1922), pp. 6 ff.
109. Dmitrievsky, *Typika*, 694–95.

citizens, perhaps on the place where the monastery of Cosmoso-teira and its infirmary stood. He endowed it with all necessary provisions.[110]

Three more gerocomeia of this period are known by name, but their founders and the year in which they were erected are un-known. The Melobiou is known only through a mention in the synaxare, which states that on April fifteenth of each year the liturgy in memory of the saints Theodore and Pausilypos was conducted in a chapel, probably that of the Melobiou.[111] We possess no other knowledge of the saints nor of the location of the house.[112]

Just as obscure is the mention of a gerocomeion named after St. Elias. A legal pronouncement of the time notes that the gerocomeion of St. Elias had been allocated space for a church.[113] Though there were several churches and a monastery named for the prophet Elias in the capital and its vicinity,[114] to which the gerocomeion in question might have been attached, Janin's sug-gestion that it was at St. Elias of the Petrion [115] is only a con-jecture.[116] It seems improbable that this gerocomeion can be identified with a similar establishment known as the Petria. A legal notice indicates that the Petria was erected by an emperor or a member of the imperial family.[117] Janin argued that two seals of the twelfth and thirteenth centuries must have belonged to this establishment.[118] However, the evidence does not support Janin's allegation: the seals belong to the monastery of Petrion and not to the gerocomeion properly so called.[119] The monastery was a royal institution where dethroned empresses regularly took

110. *Typicon of the Monastery of Cosmosoteira,* ed. L. Petit, BIARC, VI, 65–66; cf. p. 67.
111. *Synaxarium,* pp. 603–04, Synaxaria Selecta, H.
112. Cf. Janin, *Geogr. Eccles.,* p. 568.
113. Zepos-Zepos, *Jus,* IV, 53: " Ὁ ἅγιος ἡλίας τὸ γηροκομεῖον τόπους ἐκδέδωκε πρὸς ἐκκλησίαν."
114. See Janin, *Geogr. Eccles.,* pp. 143–46.
115. This important region has been discussed earlier. Cf. Richter, *Quellen,* p. 183; Du Cange, *Constantinopolis Christiana,* IV. V. 1; Byzantios, «Κωνσταντινούπολις», pp. 563–67.
116. Janin, *Geogr. Eccles.,* p. 567.
117. Zepos-Zepos, *Jus,* IV, 53.
118. Janin, *Geogr. Eccles.,* p. 568.
119. Schlumberger, *Sigillographie,* p. 156.

monastic vows.[120] To be sure, the second seal may include the gerocomeion among "the royal estates of Petrion," [121] of which it says that one Nicholas was supervisor. The vicinity of Petrion, where the gerocomeion was located, was along the Golden Horn, to the southeast of present-day Phanar.

A seal of the eleventh century bears the name of the administrator of still another institution for the aged. His name was Vasilios,[122] a patrician, judge of Velos and gerotrophos of Tirithoni; I have not been able to identify the city where his gerocomeion was located. (See Figure 35A.) Another seal of the eleventh century bears only the name of a gerocomos named Vasilios Leucatenos.[123] If his patronym indicates also his place of residence,[124] we may assume that his gerocomeion was on the island of Leucas or Leucadia in the theme of Cephalenia. (See Figure 35B.)

That an institution for the aged was held in esteem was manifested by the behavior of the emperor himself. Constantine Porphyrogenitos writes that the imperial head visited every home for the elderly on each Holy Thursday.[125] During his visit the emperor distributed gifts to the senior citizens and performed his other customary duties. The emperor visited the Kyphe establishments for the aged on Good Friday, where he also distributed benefactions.[126]

There may well have been many homes for the aged in the tenth century, for Nicephoros Phocas (963–69) issued a novella against the erection of additional homes.[127] This was repealed subsequently by the Emperor Basil II (976–1025).[128]

120. Byzantios, «Κωνσταντινούπολις», I, 563.
121. Schlumberger, *Sigillographie:* ῎Νικολάῳ ἐπισκεπτῆτι τῶν βασιλικῶν κτημάτων τοῦ Πετρίου.''
122. C. M. Constantopoulos, «Βυζαντινὰ Μολυβδόβουλα» (Athens, 1930), p. 16.
123. V. Laurent, *Le Corpus des sceaux de l'empire byzantin,* V (Paris, 1963), No. 134, pp. 107–08.
124. Cf. Miklosich-Muller, *Acta et Diplomata,* IV, 203, where the patronym indicates the land of origin.
125. Porphyrogenitos, *De Cerimoniis,* I, 165.
126. *Ibid.,* p. 168.
127. Rhallis-Potlis, «Σύνταγμα», V, 261 ff.
128. *Ibid.,* p. 270.

A. Seal of Vasilios, Patrician, Judge of Velos, and Gerotrophos of Tirithoni (Location Unknown), derived from *Byzantina Molybdoboula,* ed. C. M. Constantopoulos, p. 16.

Obverse: The Mother of God wearing the medallion of Christ, hands raised in an *orans* gesture, standing full face, with monograms.

$\overline{\text{MHP}} - \overline{\text{OV}}$

Reverse:

+O͞K͞E RO	Θ(εοτό)κε β(οή)ϑ(ε
RACIΛEIω	Βασιλείῳ
ΠΡΙΑΝΘΥΠΑ	π(ατ)ρι(κίῳ), ἀνϑυ.
Τ΄ΚΡΙΤΗΤ8RH	-τ(ῳ), κριτῇ τοῦ Β
ΛΣΓΗΡΟΤΡΟ	·λ(ου) καὶ γηροτρό
φωΤωΤΙΡΙ	φῳ τῷ Τιρί-
ΘωΝΙ	ϑωνι.

Eleventh Century

B. Seal of Vasilios Leucatenos, Gerocomos (Gerocomeion Unknown), derived from *Le Corpus des sceaux de l'empire byzantin,* ed. V. Laurent, Vol. V, No. 134, pp. 107–08.

Obverse:

+KER, Θ,	+
RACIΛEIω	K(ύρι)ε β(οή)θ(ει)
ΧΑΡΤ8ΛΑ	Βασιλείῳ
ΡΙωΓΗΡω	χαρτουλα-
ΚΟΜω	ρίῳ γηρω-
	κόμῳ

Reverse:

SEΠΙΤ,	(καὶ) ἐπὶ τ(οῦ)
Π͞ΡΙΑΡΧΙΚ	π(ατ)ριαρχικ(οῦ)
CEKPET, Tω	σεκρέτ(ου) τῷ
ΛEVKAT,	Λευκατ(η)-
N,	ν(ῷ)

Eleventh Century; Dumbarton Oaks (Collection Shaw, No. 1108)

Figure 35. Seals of Directors of Two *Gerocomeia.*

THE DIRECTOR

The director of an institution for the aged was known as gerocomos, gerotrophos, gerocomicos, or gerodocomos.[129]

As early as the fourth century we find that the director of an institution for the aged was a highly respected person, not unlikely to become a patrician or to be elevated to an episcopal throne. A fourth-century bishop of Trimithous in Cyprus, named John, had been a gerocomos, a patrician, and a physician before he was elected a bishop.[130] The office also ranked high in the administrative machinery of the empire in other centuries. Constantine Porphyrogenitos writes that during the vesper services and liturgy for the commemoration of prophet Elias, the directors of the gerocomeia of the city offered golden crosses to the emperor. These services were held at the Church of the All-Holy Theotocos [131] in the Pharos.[132]

In the reign of the Emperor Constantine X Dukas (1059–67), the gerotrophos was counted among the dignitaries of the administrative bureaucracy who were bound to respect a chrysobull which the Emperor issued concerning the rights and privileges of the monastery called the Great Lavra.[133]

The gerocomos' work was generally supervised by his bishop, who was the legal overseer of the evage systemata or charitable institutions in his diocese.[134] A gerocomos had the rank of a spatharios [135] and ranked sixth, after the chartularios of

129. See Theodore of Paphos, *Life of St. Spyridon*, ed. Paul Van Den Ven, pp. 91–92, P. 15–16; Justinian, *Novel No. 7*, ch. 12, epilogue; Constantine Porphyrogenitos, *De Cerimoniis*, ed. A. Vogt, I, p. 107; Louis Bréhier, "La Vie chrétienne en Orient," *Histoire de l'église*, ed. Augustin Fliche and Victor Martin, IV, 554; Ph. Koukoules, Β Β Π, II. 1, 170–171; August Knecht, *System des Justinianischen Kirchenvermogensrechtes*, pp. 54–55.

130. Theodore of Paphos, *Life of St. Spyridon*, ed. Paul Van Den Ven, pp. 91–92, P. 15–16.

131. Porphyrogenitos, *De Cerimoniis*, I, 107; cf. Byzantios, «Κωνσταντινούπολις», I, 215.

132. Theophanes, I, 502; Symeon Magister, pp. 681, 727; *Synaxarium*, p. 725; Janin, *Geogr. Eccles.*, pp. 241–45; Byzantios «Κωνσταντινούπολις», I, 214–15, 522–23.

133. *Actes de Lavra*, p. 74; cf. other Chrysobulls, pp. 77, 81, 84, 97, 100, 103, 112.

134. Cf. Zepos-Zepos, *Jus*, II, 256; see earlier discussions above of administration of the *xenones*.

135. Philotheos, *Kletorologion*, ed. Bury, p. 512.

sakellion.[136] In the eleventh century, however, the administration of the institutions for the aged was removed from the jurisdiction of the chartularios of sakellion.[137]

136. *Ibid.*, p. 141; see Bury, *ibid.*, pp. 84–86, 93–95.
137. Franz Dolger, *Beitrage zur Geschichte der byzantinischen Finanz-verwaltung, besonders des 10 und 11 Jahrhunderts* (Munchen, 1927), p. 15; cf. Ph. Koukoules, B B Π, II, 1, 170.

14. Orphanages

Orphans have always received special care and sympathy in human societies from early antiquity, and in the religious society of Byzantium they must have fared relatively well. However, we can identify only a few orphanages in Byzantine times. Still, the silence of our sources may indicate that orphanages were departments of other philanthropic complexes, for, as we have seen in the previous chapter, the Church, the State, and Byzantine society in general had taken the necessary measures for the nurture and welfare of orphans.

That there were more orphanages than those which we know by name is clear from Justinian's Novella 131. Justinian orders that "the orphanotrophoi or administrators of orphanages discharge the duties and honors of trustees and curators, that they may sue and be sued in cases concerning the property belonging to their institutions or to the inmates as individuals" and that they "shall receive property belonging to the orphans or the orphanages of which they are the directors. . . . "[1] Justinian's law assumes that there were orphanages both in the capital and in the provinces.[2] He made, however, a special provision for one

1. Justinian, *Novel No. 131*, Ch. 15, 664: "Οἱ δέ ὀρφανοτρόφοι ἐπιτρόπων καὶ κουρατώρων τάξιν ἐχέτωσαν, οὕτω μέντοι ἵνα καὶ χωρὶς ἱκανοδοσίας καὶ ἐνάγωσι καὶ ἐνάγωνται περὶ τῶν πραγμάτων τῶν τοῖς ὀρφανοῖς κυρίως καὶ αὐτοῖς τοῖς ὀρφανοτροφείοις ἀνηκόντων." See also "Synopsis Basilicorum," Zepos-Zepos, *Jus*, V, 455.
2. Justinian, *Novel No. 131*, Ch. 15, 664: " 'Εν δὲ ταῖς ἐπαρχίαις παρὰ τοῖς ἄρχουσιν αὐτῶν ἢ τοῖς ἐκδίκοις τῶν τόπων λαμβάνειν τοὺς ὀρφανοτρόφους καὶ φυλάττειν. . . ."

particular orphanage which existed in the capital, ordering that this orphanage should enjoy the same privileges reserved for the Church of Holy Wisdom and the Sampson complex.[3]

THE ORPHANAGE OF ST. ZOTICOS

The orphanage mentioned in Justinian's law has been since identified as that of St. Zoticos. We have already pointed out that there existed a leper hospital with the same name.[4] Probably both were named after their founder. The "Zoticos orphanotropheion" is mentioned also in a novella of the Emperor Heraclios addressed to the Patriarch Sergios I (610–38), under whose care he had placed the orphanage.[5] It must have been an important institution, for in the fifth century we find that its director was elected to the patriarchal throne of Constantinople as Acacios (472–88).[6]

In the reign of Justinian, Cyril of Scythopolis refers to an orphanage of importance in the capital. In the controversy between the Orthodox and Origenist monks of Palestine, the Origenists resorted to threats and violence. Gelasios, the Orthodox hegoumenos of the Grand Lavra of Sabas, decided to travel to Constantinople to press charges against the Origenists. At that time Justinian's court was under the influence of Theodore Ascidas, Bishop of Cappadocia and a member of the Origenist party. When Theodore was informed of Gelasios' coming he ordered that neither the patriarchate nor the palace nor the orphanage should offer hospitality to him.[7] Cyril's report thus reveals that an orphanage might provide shelter for visiting religious dignitaries.

3. *Ibid.*
4. Cf. Pseudo-Codinos, *Patria*, Th. Preger, p. 267; see also alternate reading of paragraph 164.
5. Heraclios, *Novel No. 4*, ed. Rhallis-Potlis, IV, 240.
6. Evagrios, *Eccl. History*, Bk. II. 11, ed. Bidez-Parmentier, p. 63; cf. Beck, *Kirche und Theologische Literatur*, p. 104, n. 6. Beck's reference to V. Benesevich, "Die Byzantinische Ranglisten," *Byzantinisch-Neugriechische Jahrbucher*, IV (1927), 149, is misleading. I failed to find any relationship between Acacios' election and the context of page 149 of Benesevich's study.
7. Schwartz, *Kyrillos*, pp. 194–95: "Αὐτοῦ δὲ κατὰ τὸ Βυζάντιον γεγονότος μηνύεται τῷ 'Ασκιδᾷ ἡ αὐτοῦ παρουσία καὶ παραγγέλονται οἵ τε τοῦ ὀρφανοτροφείου καὶ τοῦ Πατριαρχείου καὶ τοῦ παλατίου μοναχὸν ἀπὸ 'Ιεροσολύμων μὴ δέξασθαι."

Because this orphanage is not mentioned by name it is difficult to identify it either with the orphanage of St. Zoticos or with St. Paul's, but it might well have been the latter.

THE ORPHANAGE OF ST. PAUL

The only other orphanage of this period known by name was that of St. Paul in Constantinople. Pseudo-Codinos credits the Emperor Justin II (565–78) and his wife Sophia with having built this institution,[8] and notes that they had also built other structures.[9] Theophanes adds that Justin II built the Church of the Holy Apostles in the area where the orphanage stood,[10] but implies that the orphanage had been founded by someone else. We know that a Church of St. Paul was destroyed by fire during the reign of Zeno (474–75, 476–91) and was rebuilt by Justin. If we assume that the orphanage of St. Paul was attached to the Church of St. Paul, then the orphanage may also have been in existence before the sixth century, and may have been rebuilt by Justin II. In that event, it may be the anonymous orphanage mentioned by Cyril of Scythopolis, but this is only a conjecture.

The St. Paul orphanage continued to offer its services for many centuries. Theophanes writes that it was taxed in the early part of the ninth century,[11] when the Emperor Nicephoros I (802–11) was in need of money for his war against the Slavs and the Bulgars. Nicephoros levied a hearth tax on all monasteries and churches, as well as upon "the numerous charitable institutions in Byzantium."[12] He also taxed the tenants of the monasteries, churches, orphanages, the xenones, and the gerocomeia.[13]

The St. Paul orphanage was also the place where a Theodotos

8. Pseudo-Codinos, *Patria*, Th. Preger, III, 235: "Τὸν δὲ ἅγιον Παῦλον τὸ ὀρφανοτροφεῖον ἀνήγειρεν 'Ιουστῖνος καὶ Σοφία." Cf. Du Cange, *Constantinopolis Christiana*, IV. IX. 19; Richter, *Quellen*, p. 138.
9. *Ibid.*, III, p. 267.
10. Theophanes, *Chronographia*, I, 244.
11. *Ibid.*, p. 486.
12. Ostrogorsky, *History*, p. 167; cf. Peter Charanis, "Nicephorus I, The Savior of Greece from the Slavs," *Byzantina Metabyzantina*, I, pt. I (1946), 76–77; cf. Continuatus, *Chronographia*, p. 8.
13. Theophanes, *Chronographia*, pp. 486–87: ". . . τοὺς τῶν εὐαγῶν οἴκων παροίκους τούς τε ὀρφανοτροφείου καὶ τῶν ξενώνων καὶ γηροκομείων τε καὶ ἐκκλησιῶν καὶ μοναστηρίων βασιλικῶν τὰ καπνικὰ ἀπαιτεῖσθαι. . . ."

Philanthropic Institutions

Melissenos Kassiteras, who later ascended the patriarchal throne (815–21), met the future Leo V just before he deposed Michael I Rangabe (811–13).[14]

In the year 1032 a great earthquake damaged many buildings both on the Asiatic coast and in Constantinople.[15] St. Paul's also was ruined, but it was promptly repaired by the Emperor Romanos III Argyros (1028–34).[16]

St. Paul's must have had rooms other than those used for the orphans. The author of the Strategicon,[17] relates that the orphanage served also as a refuge for bankrupt individuals.[18]

During the eleventh century St. Paul's must have suffered further damage, for its doors were closed.[19] Later, it was completely reconstructed and transformed by the Emperor Alexios Comnenos (1081–1118), as part of the extensive program of rehabilitation and philanthropic works he undertook upon his return from his expedition against the Turks of Iconium. He also built a number of establishments for indigents, for the blind, for the crippled, for the aged and disabled, and for veterans, making a "new city," like the Basileias of the fourth century or a "second city inside the Queen of cities," in the words of Anna Comnena.[20]

Among these, St. Paul's orphanage must have been especially impressive, for it was praised by others[21] less favorably inclined

14. Theophanes Continuatus, *Chronographia*, p. 23; Symeon Magister, *Chronographia*, p. 605.

15. George Cedrenos, II, 503–04.

16. *Ibid.*, p. 504.

17. The question of authorship is still unsettled. See Paul Lemerle, *Prolegomenes à une édition critique et commentée des "Conseils et Récits" de Kekaumenos* (Brussels, 1960); Ostrogorsky, *History*, p. 281; see also note no. 2 where bibliography on authorship is cited.

18. Cecaumenos, *Strategicon*, ed. Wassiliewsky-Jernstedt, p. 39.

19. John Zonaras, *Epitome Historion*, III, pp. 744–45: cf. Michael Glycas, *Annales*, ed. by Immanuel Bekker, CSHB (Bonn, 1836), p. 621: "Τὸ δὲ ὀρφανοτροφεῖον ἤδη ἐσχολακὸς ἀνακαινίζει ὁ διαληφθεὶς βασιλεύς" [i.e. Alexios Comnenos]; cf. Sathas, «Μεσ. Βιβλιοθ.», VII, 177.

20. Anna Comnena, *Alexias*, Bk. XV, ch. 7, p. 215: " 'Ενταῦθα πόλιν ἑτέραν ἐν τῇ βασιλίδι πόλει ἐδείματο." For an English translation see E. A. S. Dawes, *The Alexiad of the Princess Anna Comnena* (London, 1928), p. 409. See also Juan Arcadio Lascaris Comneno, "Los Orfanotrofios Griegos y su Perduracion en Bizancio" (A proposito de Alexiada, XV. VII. 3–9), *Actas del primer Congrese espanol de Estudios Clasicos*, Madrid 15–19 de Abril 1956 (Madrid, 1958), pp. 508–513.

21. Kataskepenos, *Cyril Phileotes*, p. 230; cf. Lysimaque Oeconomos, *La vie religieuse*, pp. 214–15.

to Alexios than his illustrious daughter. The Emperor also built a school for those orphans anxious to improve themselves, and assigned to it teachers and governors whom he instructed to give the orphans "a good general education." [22]

The complex around St. Paul's Church must have been very extensive: to visit the whole of it required an entire day, according to Anna,[23] and both she and Theodore Scutariotes allege that thousands lived there.[24] To assure their subsistence, Alexios granted to his "new city" many estates and made it financially "a safe harbor for many. . . ." [25] Furthermore, Anna avers that thirty years after her father's death, at the time she wrote her memoirs, the orphanage was administered by one of the most important personages of the empire.[26] Unfortunately she gives no name, but her mention of St. Paul's indicates how important this complex must have been.

We do not know the fate of St. Paul's during the pillage of Constantinople in 1204. In the thirteenth century, however, George Pachymeres (1242–c. 1310) writes that after the Empire was restored by the Greeks in 1261, the Emperor Michael VIII Palaeologos (1259–82), at the petition of the Patriarch Germanos III (1265–67), established a school near the "old orphanage" near the Church of St. Paul.[27] He appointed a director and supported the headmaster and the students. During his visits there on holidays, the emperor tested the students and gave them gifts.[28] It is not clear, however, whether this new school was only for the inmates of the orphanage or also for the general public.

22. Anna Comnena, *Alexias;* John Zonaras, *Epitome Historion,* III, 744–45; Michael Glycas, *Chronicon,* pp. 621–22. For education in the age of the Comneni see Georgia Buckler, *Anna Comnena* (London, 1929), pp. 178–87; for education in the orphanage, pp. 176–77, 185–86 *et passim.*

23. Anna Comnena, *Alexias:* "Εἴ τις ἐθέλει τούτους ἰδεῖν, ἀρξάμενος πρωΐθεν εἰς ἑσπέραν ἂν τὸν κύκλον συνετέλεσε."

24. *Ibid.;* anonymous, *Synopsis Chronike,* ed. Sathas, «Μεσ. Βιβλιοθ.», VII, 177. Anna calls it a "μυρίανδρος πόλις" and Scutariotes relates that the number amounted in "χιλιάδας."

25. Sathas, «Μεσ. Βιβλιοθ.», VII, 177; Anna Comnena, *Alexias,* XV. 7.

26. Anna Comnena, *Alexias:* "Προκάθηται γὰρ ἀνὴρ τις τῶν ἐνδοξοτάτων φροντιστὴς τῆς μυριάνδρου ταυτησὶ πόλεως."

27. George Pachymeres, I, 284: ". . . συστήσασθαι δὲ καὶ κατὰ τὸν τοῦ μεγάλου Παύλου νεὼν ἐν τοῖς ἀρχαίοις ὀρφανοτροφείοις γραμματικευομένων σχολήν. . . ."

28. *Ibid.*

Nor is it clear that the phrase "at the old orphanage" does not simply mean that the school was located on the site where the orphanage once stood, for we know that when George Codinos or Pseudo-Codinos wrote his manual on secular and ecclesiastical offices, during the reign of the Emperor John VI Cantacuzenos (1347–54) or soon after, the orphanage did not exist and the office of orphanotrophos was everywhere extinct.[29]

Anna Comnena writes that the orphanage was near the Church of St. Paul "in the quarter of the Acropolis, where the mouth of the sea widens;" [30] so that the institution must have been located southeast of the Acropolis where the Straits of Bosporos widen and unite with the Sea of Marmara. Nevertheless, Scarlatos Byzantios placed the orphanage in the region called the Eugeniou, present-day Yahkosk.[31] Manuel Gedeon locates it on the extreme northwest of the Acropolis at the point of Serail.[32] Louis Bréhier places it north of the Acropolis,[33] while R. Janin locates it next to the quarter called the Spoudaeou,[34] of which the site is unknown.

These authors, although they have observed that Anna Comnena placed St. Paul's "on the highest spot in the city" where it "stood out like a citadel," [35] have overlooked perhaps Anna's earlier note that the location was "in the quarter near the Acropolis, where the mouth of the *pontos* widens." [36]

A highly educated woman, Anna could hardly have used the term *pontos* to describe the "gulf of the *keras*" [37] if the institution were at the mouth of the promontory of Constantinople, for in

29. Codinos, *De officialibus*, p. 41: " 'Ο 'Ορφανοτρόφος ἦν μὲν φροντίζων καὶ ἐπιμελούμενος πάλαι τῶν ὀρφανῶν, νῦν δὲ οὐδαμῶς κέκτηταί τινα ὑπηρεσίαν." Cf. Louis Bréhier, *Vie et mort*, p. 596; *ibid.*, *Les Institutions*, pp. 525–26; R. Guilland, "Les Chapitres relatifs aux fonctions des dignitaires," BS, XIII. 2 (1952–1953), 139; *ibid.*, "Observations sur la liste des dignitaires du Pseudo-Codinos," REB, XII (1954), 59–60.
30. Anna Comnena, *Alexias*, XV. 7: " 'Εν γὰρ τοῖς πρὸς τὴν ἀκρόπολιν μέρεσιν, ἔνθα καὶ τὸ στόμα τοῦ πόντου ἀνοίγεται. . . . "
31. Byzantios, «Κωνσταντινούπολις», I, 149.
32. Gedeon, «'Εορτολόγιον», p. 118, col. 2.
33. Bréhier, *Les Institutions*, p. 526.
34. Janin, *Geogr. Eccles.*, p. 581.
35. Byzantios, «Κωνσταντινούπολις», I, 150; quoted from Anna Comnena, *Alexias*, p. 215. 3–4.
36. Anna Comnena, *Alexias*, p. 214, 30–31.
37. Cf. Leo Sternbach, *Analecta Avarica* (Cracoviae, 1900), p. 12: 8–12; p. 15: 5–15 *et passim*.

the Middle Ages pontos meant open sea. The "mouth of pontos," then, must mean the opening of the Bosporos into the Sea of Marmara. Besides, in the area south of the Acropolis stood also the Church of St. Paul to which the orphanage was probably attached.[38] This church, we know, was near the monastery and its Church of the Saints Sergios and Bacchos.[39] All these clues, plus the testimony of Anna Comnena that the orphanage was located where the pontos widens, lead us to the conclusion that the famous orphanage stood in the region south or southwest of the Acropolis.

A second problem is whether St. Paul's orphanage is identical with the Zoticon. Certain scholars believe that the St. Paul's which Pseudo-Codinos says was built by the Emperor Justin was not a new edifice but only a reconstruction of the Zoticon.[40] Nevertheless, topographical evidence suggests that the Zoticon and St. Paul's were two different orphanages.[41] The Zoticon is usually placed at the site of Irion on the Asiatic coast [42] or present-day Scutari,[43] while St. Paul's must have been on the side of the Acropolis. J. B. Bury suggests that both orphanages may have been under the same administrator.[44]

OTHER HOMES FOR CHILDREN

Orphans were cared for elsewhere, too. Monasteries, churches, and headquarters of the dioceses must have made provisions for orphans. The monastery of Gregory Pacourianos will serve as an example. Gregory, who served as great *domesticos* under Alexios I Comnenos—as we have seen in a previous chapter—records in the typikon of the monastery of Petritziotissa that he took extra measures "in the interests of very young children." It is not clear

38. Pseudo-Codinos, *Patria*, Th. Preger, III, 235.
39. Alexander Van Millingen, *Byzantine Churches in Constantinople* (London, 1912), p. 63.
40. Byzantios, «Κωνσταντινούπολις», I, 149–50; Amantos, " Ἡ Ἑλληνικὴ Φιλανθρωπία," p. 153; Bréhier, *Les Institutions*, p. 526.
41. Cf. Bury, *The Imperial Administrative System in the Ninth Century*, pp. 103–04.
42. *Synaxarium*, p. 860, col. 1; Cedrenos, I, 699; Pargoire, "Hieria," pp. 48–50.
43. Byzantios, «Κωνσταντινούπολις», II, 226.
44. Bury, *The Imperial Administrative System in the Ninth Century*, pp. 103–04.

from this phrase whether he had built a special house for orphans
next to the monastery or whether he simply took orphans into
the monastery itself. In any case he ruled that "little children"
should be given all necessary provisions, and assigned a priest
to supervise their education. Six of the children were to be
trained for the priesthood.[45] We possess no further information.

An institution closely related to the orphanage properly so
called was the *Brephotropheion* or foundling home, most probably meant for infants born out of wedlock.[46] The Christian
Church had manifested special concern for deserted infants from
its beginnings,[47] but we find specific reference to foundling homes
only in the sixth century, when Justinian's seventh novella to the
patriarch Epiphanios (520–35) lists brephotropheia among the
establishments to be governed by his legislation.[48]

At one time, it seems, foundling homes were tax-exempt, but
such establishments were both numerous and wealthy. Justinian
prescribed that only the eleven hundred shops which belonged
to Hagia Sophia were to be free from taxation.[49] In the ninth
century we find that a donation of five hundred nomismata to a
home for infants was not taxable.[50]

These laws imply that institutions for deserted infants were
not rare, although we know but very few by name. In Constantinople a brephotropheion stood near the monastery of St.
Philip the Apostle.[51] For in the *Libellus monachorum ad
Agapetum* we find the signature of Anastasios, a presbyter and
the second in charge of the monastery of St. Philip the Apostle,
which is said to be near the brephotropheion.[52] The location of

45. "Typikon of Gregory Pacourianos," ed. Petit, p. 50.
46. Cf. Anna Comnena, *Alexias*, XV. 7; Koukoules, ΒΒ II, II. 1, 154–56.
47. Basil the Great, *Homilia VIII in Hexaemeron*, 6, MPG, XXIX, cols.
177–80; cf. Gregory of Nyssa, *De Vita S Macrinae*, MPG, XLVI, col. 988AB;
see especially Symeon Metaphrastes, *Vita S Clementis Ancyrani*, ch. 2, MPG,
CXIV, col. 824AB.
48. Justinian, *Novel No. 7*, preface and ch. 2.
49. *Ibid., Novel No. 43*, ch. 1.
50. Photios, *Nomocanon*, Bk. 2. 1, canon 19, ed. Rhallis-Potlis, «Σύνταγμα», I, pp. 100 ff.
51. For the monastery and its location see Janin, *Geogr. Eccles.*, pp.
509–10; but cf. Gedeon, «Ἑορτολόγιον», p. 192.
52. *Acta Conciliorum Oecumenicorum*, ed. Schwartz, III, p. 145, No. 57:
"'Αναστάσιος ἐλέει θεοῦ πρεσβύτερος καὶ δευτεράριος μονῆς τοῦ ἁγίου
καὶ ἐνδόξου ἀποστόλου Φιλίππου τοῦ ἐν τῷ βρεφοτροφείῳ ἀξιώσας ὑπέ-
γραψα. . . ."

the monastery and foundling home has not been identified with absolute certainty. There were two monasteries and churches of St. Philip in Constantinople, one next to the cistern of Mocios,[53] and the other across the Bosporos at the town of Neapolis.[54] However, it was most probably to the latter that the brephotropheion was attached, together with other philanthropic establishments.[55] Mention of the monastery of St. Philip in the biography of St. Cyril Phileotes (+1110) hints that the brephotropheion was in existence in the twelfth century.

THE OFFICE OF ORPHANOTROPHOS

The officer or orphanotrophos who administered the orphanage held an important post, and frequently became bishop or even patriarch. In the eleventh century an orphanotrophos even ran the affairs of the empire. However, we have most information about the orphanotrophos of St. Paul's orphanage in Constantinople.

The first orphanotrophos known by name is perhaps St. Zoticos who, as we have noted, may have been the original founder of the Zoticon. He lived during the reign of Constantios (337–61).[56] The Patriarch Acacios (472–88), who lent his name to the Acacian schism [57] had been before his election to the throne of Constantinople the director of this orphanage.[58] A few years after Acacios, Euphemios, administrator of the orphanage at Neapolis (Zoticon), was elected Patriarch of the capital.[59]

Even outside Constantinople the office of orphanotrophos was highly respected. When a bishop of Nicaea was forced to abdicate from his hierarchical throne, he became the director of an

53. Gedeon, «Ἑορτολόγιον», p. 192; Janin, *Geogr. Eccles.*, pp. 508–09.
54. Kataskepenos, *Cyril Phileotes*, p. 99; cf. ibid., p. 86; R. Janin, "L'Eglise byzantine sur les rives du Bosphore (Côte Asiatique)," REB, XII (1954), 85–86.
55. Cf. Ephraemios, vv. 9746–49, 9835–38.
56. *Synaxarium*, p. 359, col. 1.
57. See Edward Schwartz, *Publizistische Sammlungen zum Acacianischen Schisma* (Munchen, 1934), pp. 161 ff.; L. Duchesne, *Histoire ancienne de l'église*, III (Paris, 1928), 486 ff.
58. Evagrios, *Eccl. History*, ed. Bidez-Parmentier, p. 63; Ephraemios, vv. 9735–39.
59. Ephraemios, vv. 9747–49.

orphanage.[60] Nicetas, the biographer of Archbishop Andreas of Crete, writes that before his election to the see of Crete, Andreas was the director of a large orphanage in Constantinople,[61] perhaps St. Paul's.

The director of the St. Paul's gradually became a very important administrative officer. In the religious procession in the Hippodrome on Palm Sunday the Orphanotrophos was assigned, when the Emperor was ready at the Chrysotriclinos, to carry the "symbol of faith," that is, the cross, to the Emperor so that he might kiss it.[62]

As in the beginning of the ninth century the same orphanage served as the meeting place of conspirators plotting to seize the throne, so also in the tenth century its director seems to have been engaged in a plot against the government. In any case, in the interpolation of the chronicle of George Monachos we are told that one Paul, the director of an orphanage perhaps to be identified as St. Paul's, was sent into exile by the Emperor Romanos Lecapenos (920–44).[63]

The administrator of St. Paul's orphanage best known for his role in the affairs of the state was a certain John, called Orphanotrophos.[64] John, the brother of the future Michael IV (1034–41), was deeply involved in the intrigues of the imperial court, and so managed to arrange the marriage of the Empress Zoe to his younger brother, who thereupon ascended the Byzantine throne. When Michael fell ill, it was John who ran the government [65] with great success. His administrative experience as the director of St. Paul's seems to have served him well.[66] Before his brother's illness, John served as a sort of minister for internal

60. "Vita S Ignatii," MPG, CV, col. 537.

61. Nicetas, *Life of St. Andrew the Hierosolymite*, ed. Papadopoulos-Kerameus, «'Ανάλεκτα», V, 174.

62. Porphyrogenitos, *De Cerimoniis*, I, 160–61.

63. George Monachos, *Chronicon*, ed. Muralt, p. 817; Symeon Magister, p. 732.

64. R. Janin, "Un Ministre byzantin—Jean l'Orphanotrophe (XIᵉ siècle)," EO, XXXIV (1931), 431 ff.

65. Michael Psellos, *Michael V*, ch. 2, ed. Renauld, I, 86: " 'Ο ... ὀρφανοτρόφος 'Ιωάννης, ὃς δὴ καὶ τὸ ξύμπαν κράτος τηνικαῦτα διώκει...." Cf. Cecaumenos, *de Of. Reg.*, ed. Wassiliewsky-Jernstedt, p. 99; Bury, *The Imperial Administrative System*, p. 104; Janin, "Un Ministre byzantin," EO, XXXIV, pp. 431 ff.; Amantos, «'Ιστορία», II, 183 ff.

66. Psellos, *Michael IV*, ch. 2, ed. Renauld, I, 54: "... ἀνὴρ δεινότατος περὶ τὰς ἐνθυμήσεις καὶ περὶ τὰς πράξεις δραστήριος."

security. When Alousianos, the son of King Aaron of Bulgaria, was caught in a plot against the emperor, Michael placed him under the vigilant eyes of John. To escape his surveillance was considered no mean triumph.[67] His influence, however, was his downfall. When Michael V (1041–42) succeeded Michael IV, his first decision was to exile the Orphanotrophos, thus "tearing down . . . the pillar of the family" of Michael IV.[68]

Usually the director of an orphanage was a monk, a clergyman, or a public official. Photios, the scholar and Patriarch of Constantinople, addressed a letter to an orphanotrophos named George who was a deacon.[69] Nicephoros Ouranos, the general of Basil II (976–1025), wrote a letter to an orphanotrophos named John, who was also judge in the theme of Armeniacon.[70] That public officials were appointed to administer an orphanage is established by the Tacticon composed during the reign of Michael III and Theodora (845–56) from which we hear of an orphanotrophos of the patrician rank.[71] In the same century Theodore the Studite addressed a letter to an orphanotrophos Leo, also a patrician, and calls Leo's wife a patricia.[72]

As early as the age of Justinian, the orphanotrophos was the legal trustee and guardian of the properties of the orphanage and of the orphans themselves. They could sue for and could dispose of the property entrusted to them.[73] Justinian's laws on this point were reaffirmed by the Macedonian emperors.[74]

A few seals have survived which belonged either to orphanages

67. *Ibid.*, *Michael IV*, ch. 47, ed. Renauld, I, 80: "Διέδρα οὖν καὶ τὴν πολυόμματον τοῦ ὀρφανοτρόφου δύναμιν, καὶ οὐδὲ τούτῳ γέγονεν ἁλωτός."

68. *Ibid.*, *Michael V*, ch. 42, ed. Renauld, I, 111: ". . .τὸν ὀρφανοτρόφον ὁ βασιλεύων [Μιχαὴλ Ε΄], ἀπήλασεν, ὥσπερ δὴ τὸν τοῦ γένους στύλον κατενεγκών. . . ." Cf. Michael Attaleiates, *Historia*, pp. 11–12.

69. Photios, *Epistle No. 186*, ed. Valetas, p. 512. Photios does not identify the orphanage.

70. Gustav Karlsson, *Idéologie et cérémonial dans l'épistolographie byzantine* (Uppsala, 1959), p. 19.

71. "Τακτικὸν ἐν ἐπιτόμῳ γενόμενον ἐπὶ Μιχαὴλ . . . καὶ Θεοδώρας τῆς . . . αὐτοῦ μητρός," ed. Th. Uspenski, BARC, III (Sophia, 1898), 117; cf. also Bury, *The Imperial Administrative System*, p. 104.

72. Theodore Studites, *Epistle No. 29*, MPG, XCIX, col. 1004C; cf. Bury, *The Imperial Administrative System*, p. 104.

73. Justinian, *Novel 131*, ch. 15; cf. Knecht, *System des Justinianischen*, pp. 51–52.

74. "Synopsis Basilicorum," Zepos-Zepos, *Jus*, V, 455.

or to their directors.[75] A seal bearing busts of saints Peter and Paul and on the reverse the word orphanotrophi[on] is assigned by Gustave Schlumberger to the reign of Justinian and the Zoticon.[76] However, Bury is surely right in attributing it to the reign of Justin II and Sophia (565–78) and so to St. Paul's.[77] (See Figure 36A.)

Three more seals have been accepted as belonging to St. Paul's. The first has the inscription: "Michael [called] Tetrapolites, cleric, and supervisor of the nurses of the orphanage."[78] The writing covers both sides and indicates that Michael was a native of the region of Tetrapolis in Asia Minor.[79] (See Figure 36B.)

The second seal belongs to the tenth or eleventh century and depicts the bust of St. Porphyrios and either St. Julian or St. Bacchos the Younger. On the reverse side appears: "first seal of the students of the orphanage."[80] It might have belonged to St. Paul's. (See Figure 36c.)

The third seal bears the name of John the Orphanotrophos, whom we have mentioned above. It belongs, of course, to the eleventh century.[81] (See Figure 36D.)

That the office of orphanotrophos was of significance even in the last centuries of the empire is further verified by a seal of the thirteenth century. On the one side it has a bust of the Theotocos Blachernitissa and on the reverse the inscription: "Theotocos help thy servant Nicetas, Bishop of Ionopolis and Chartularios of the Great Orphanage."[82] (See Figure 35E.)

Documents of the later period of the Byzantine Empire indicate that the orphanotrophos continued to serve as a close associate of the imperial court. In January of 1316 Andronicos II Palaeologos (1282–1328) assigned an orphanotrophos named Tryphon Kedrenos to arbitrate certain disputes concerning monastic, ecclesiastical, and personal properties in the Theme of

75. Schlumberger, *Sigillographie*, p. 379.
76. *Ibid.*, p. 380; *ibid.*, *Mélanges d'archéologie byzantine* (Paris, 1895), pp. 299–300.
77. Bury, *The Imperial Administrative System*, p. 103.
78. Schlumberger, *Sigillographie*, p. 379; *ibid.*, *Mélanges*, pp. 297–98.
79. Ramsay, *Historical Geography*, p. 425.
80. Schlumberger, *Sigillographie*, p. 379; *ibid.*, *Mélanges*, p. 298.
81. Schlumberger, *Sigillographie; ibid.*, *Mélanges*, p. 299; *ibid.*, "Monuments numismatiques," pp. 207–208.
82. Schlumberger, *Sigillographie*, p. 155.

A. Seal of St. Paul's (or Zoticon's) Orphanage in Constantinople.

Obverse: Profile busts of SS. Peter and Paul, face to face, with a small cross above them.

Reverse: Large monogram encircled with the word, "orphanotrophi[on]."

 + ΟΡΦΑΝΟΤΡΟΦΙ'

Sixth Century; Collection Schlumberger

B. Seal of Michael Tetrapolites, Deacon, Cleric, and Supervisor of Nurses at St. Paul's Orphanage in Constantinople.

Obverse:

 + ΜΙΧΑΗΛ ΔΙΑΚΟΝ'(ος) ΚΛΗΡΙΚΟC.

Reverse:

 [S] Α'ΝΟC' (for ΠΡѠΤΟΝΟCΟΚΟΜΟC)

Τȣ ΟΡΦΑΝ'Τ' (for ΟΡΦΑΝΟΤΡΟΦΙΟΥ)

Ο ΤΕΤΡΑΠΟΛΙ'(της)

Eleventh Century; Collection Schlumberger

Figure 36. Five Seals Relating to Orphanages and their Officers, derived from *Sigillographie de l'empire byzantin*, ed. Gustave Schlumberger, pp. 155, 379–80.

C. "First Seal of the Students of the Orphanage," possibly St. Paul's Orphanage in Constantinople.

Obverse: Busts of two saints (St. Porphyrios, as inscribed, and either St. Julian or St. Bacchos the Younger), full face.

Ō A͞(γιος) ΠΟΡΦΥΡΙΟC

Reverse:

ΠΡѠΤΗ ΜΑΘΗΤѠΝ CΦΡΑΓΙC

ΟΡΦΑΝΟΤΡΟΦΟΥ (for ΟΡΦΑΝΟΤΡΟΦΙΟΥ)

Tenth–Eleventh Century; Cabinet des Médailles, Paris

D. Seal of John Orphanotrophos, Director of St. Paul's Orphanage in Constantinople.

Obverse: Bust of St. Nicholas, inscribed (partially effaced).

Ο ΑΓΙΟC ΝΙΚΟΛΑΟC

Reverse: Inscription, "Lord, protect your servant John, monk and orphanotropos."

+ K͞E B'Θ' TѠ CѠ ΔΥ(λω) Ι͞Ѡ(αννη)

ΜΟΝΑΧ(ω) S ΟΡΦΑΝΟΤΡΟΦ(ω)

Eleventh Century; Collection Schlumberger

Figure 36. Five Seals Relating to Orphanages and their Officers, derived from *Sigillographie de l'empire byzantin*, ed. Gustave Schlumberger, pp. 155, 379–80 (*cont.*).

E. Seal of Nicetas, Bishop of Ionopolis and Chartularios of the Great Orphanage in Constantinople.

Obverse: Bust of the Mother of God wearing the medallion of Christ, with monograms.

Reverse:

ΘΚΕΒ,Θ,
ΤѠϹѠΔꙜΛ,
ΝΙΚΗΤ,ΕΠΙ
ϹΚΟΠ,ΙѠΝΟ·
ΠΟΛ,Ϛ ΧΤΛ
ΤꙜΜΟΡΦΑ
Ν,ΤΡΟΦ,

Θεοτόκε βοήθει τῷ σῷ δούλῳ

Νικήτᾳ ἐπισκόπῳ Ἰωνοπόλεως καὶ

χαρτουλαρίῳ τοῦ Μεγάλου Ὀρφανοτροφίου.

Thirteenth Century

Figure 36. Five Seals Relating to Orphanages and their Officers, derived from *Sigillographie de l'empire byzantin*, ed. Gustave Schlumberger, pp. 155, 379–80 (*cont.*).

Boleros, Mosynopolis, Serrae, and Strymon in Macedonia,[83] a task likely to be given only to an important administrative personage.

During the first half of the same century we hear of orphanotrophoi named Edessenos,[84] Antonios Sigalas,[85] Constantinos,[86] and others.[87] However, the office of orphanotrophos was extinct or insignificant by the middle of the fourteenth century or shortly after.[88]

While the aim of Byzantine Christians was to reach perfection in the practice of the Christian religion, it was only to be ex-

83. Franz Dolger, *Aus den Schatzkammern des heiligen Berges* (Munich, 1948), pp. 207–08.

84. Christopher Ktenas, "Τὰ Κειμηλιαρχεῖα τῆς ἐν Ἁγίῳ Ὄρει Ἱερᾶς . . . Μονῆς τοῦ Δοχειαρίου," EEBS, VII (1930), 110.

85. Stilpon Kyriakides, «Βυζαντιναὶ Μελέται», II–V (Thessalonike, 1937), p. 74.

86. Miklosich-Muller, *Acta et Diplomata*, V, 110.

87. Dolger, *Aus den Schatzkammern des heiligen Berges*, p. 206.

88. Codinos, *De Officialibus*, p. 41.

pected that many of them proved all too mortal. Orphanotrophoi were no exception. Some of them used their office for private gains or public influence: e.g. John Orphanotrophos was criticized not only for his involvement in politics but for irregularities in the administration of St. Paul's. John seems to have used his office to support poor relatives in Paphlagonia, as a result of which the people turned against both him and his relatives.[89]

What has already been said about the officers of other philanthropic institutions may be repeated here. An orphanotrophos, usually a monk or a clergyman, was responsible to his bishop as overseer of the charitable establishments of the diocese,[90] so that, in theory at least, any clergyman who tried to buy for the office of orphanotrophos was punished and removed.[91]

89. Michael Attaliates, *Historia,* pp. 11–12; cf. Michael Psellos, *Michael IV,* ch. 11, ed. Renauld, I, 58.
90. Cf. Zonaras commentary on the eighth canon of the Council of Chalcedon, Rhallis-Potlis, «Σύνταγμα», II, 234–35.
91. Rhallis-Potlis, «Σύνταγμα», VI, 514. For the office of orphanotrophos see also R. Guilland, "Etudes sur l'histoire administrative de l'empire byzantin —L'Orphanotrophe," REB, XXIII (1965), 205–21.

15. Ptocheia (Houses for the Poor)

The Byzantines maintained a special institution for the poor named *ptocheion* or *ptochotropheion*. A man was designated as "poor" if his revenues and possessions were worth less than fifty nomismata.[1] This legal distinction of the sixth century was incorporated and maintained by Byzantine legislation of later centuries as well.[2] Among other disadvantages the poor were forbidden to stand as witnesses.

We have no statistical evidence as to the proportion of the poor people in the Byzantine Empire to the rest of the population. John Chrysostom, in one of his sermons delivered in Antioch between 386 and 388 [3] when the imperial government had imposed an increase in taxation,[4] estimated that the poor of Antioch amounted to one tenth of the inhabitants. He remarked that one tenth more were very rich, the remaining eight tenths making up

1. Justinian, *Pandect*, Bk. 48, title 2, par. 10: "nonnulli propter paupertatem, ut sunt qui nimus quam quiquaginta aureos habent," ed. Theodore Mommsen, *Digesta Justiniani Augusti*, II, second print (Berlin, 1963), p. 798; for an English translation see S. P. Scott, *The Civil Law*, XI (Cincinnati, 1932), 18.
2. Prochiron, Title 27, par. 22: "Οἱ πένητες οὐ μαρτυροῦσιν. Πένης δὲ ἐστὶν ὁ μὴ ἔχων πεντήκοντα νομισμάτων περιουσίαν." Zepos-Zepos, *Jus*, II, 181; cf. *Epanagoge legis*, Title 12, par. 8, *ibid.*, II, 262; Mattheos Blastaris, *Syntagma*, ed. Rhallis-Potlis, «Σύνταγμα», VI, 230; A. Christophilopoulos, «Τὸ Ἐπαρχιακὸν Βιβλίον Λέοντος τοῦ Σοφοῦ καὶ αἱ Συντεχνίαι ἐν Βυζαντίῳ» (Athens, 1935), p. 85, note 5.
3. C. Marriott, "Preface," *Nicene and Post-Nicene Fathers of the Christian Church*, ed. Philip Schaff, X, p. ix; but cf. Quasten, *Patrology*, III, 437.
4. Altaner, *Patrology*, p. 374.

the middle class.⁵ He appealed to the middle class as follows:
"The very rich indeed are but few, but those that come next to
them are many; again the poor are much fewer than these. Nevertheless, although therefore there are so many that are able to
feed the hungry, many go to sleep in their hunger." ⁶ The same
church father estimates that the poor of Constantinople were less
than fifty thousand. He pronounced this number in one of the
sermons which he delivered in Constantinople after his election
to the patriarchal throne, sometime between his consecration on
February 26, 398 and before June 9, 404, when he was banished
to exile. He had made an appeal to the Christian population of
approximately one hundred thousand to support the poor. He
writes that the rest of the population were pagans and Jews.⁷
If the fifty thousand poor made the one tenth of the total population of Constantinople, as Chrysostom had estimated the poor
of Antioch, then the inhabitants of the capital might have been
close to four hundred thousand, not an extravagant number for
the beginnings of the fifth century.⁸ Nonetheless, it is very diffi-

5. Joannes Chrysostomos, *In Matthaeum Homilia LXVI*, 3, MPG, LVIII,
630: " Ἔστι τὸ δέκατον μέρος πλουσίων, καὶ τὸ δέκατον πενήτων τῶν
οὐδὲν ὅλως ἐχόντων· οἱ δὲ λοιποὶ τῶν μέσων εἰσί." For poverty and social
justice in the later Byzantine Empire and especially during the fourteenth
century, see Alexios Makrembolites, "Διάλογος πλουσίων καὶ πενήτων,"
ed. Jhor Ševčenko, "Alexios Makrembolites and his 'Dialogue between the
Rich and the Poor,'" pp. 203–15; cf. Ševčenko's comments, pp. 196–97, 199;
Demetrios Cydones, «Ῥωμαίοις συμβουλευτικός», MPG, CLIV, 961–1008;
ibid., Correspondence, ed. R. J. Loenertz, *Demetrius Cydones. Correspondence*, I, No. 114 (Vatican, 1956), 152; Apostolos E. Bakalopoulos,
«Ἱστορία τοῦ Νέου Ἑλληνισμοῦ», I (Thessalonike, 1961), 118–23 *et passim*.
6. Joannes Chrysostomos, MPG, LVIII, 630; English translation is from
Nicene and Post-Nicene Fathers, X, 407, col. 1.
7. Joannes Chrysostomos, *In Acta Apostolorum Homilia XI. 3*, MPG, LX,
col. 97: "Εἰπὲ γάρ μοι, ἡ πόλις ἡμῖν εἰς πόσον μιγάδων ἀριθμὸν νῦν
τελεῖ; πόσους βούλεσθε εἶναι Χριστιανούς; βούλεσθε δέκα μυριάδας, τὸ
δὲ ἄλλο Ἑλλήνων καὶ Ἰουδαίων; ... πόσος δὲ ἀριθμός ἐστι πενήτων; Οὐκ
οἶμαι πλέον μυριάδων πέντε." But cf. J. B. Bury, *History of the Later
Roman Empire*, I, 88, see also note 3.
8. Cf. Bury, *History of the Later Roman Empire*, I, p. 88, and J. C. Russell,
Late Ancient and Medieval Population, Transactions of the American Philosophical Society (Philadelphia, 1958), p. 77. Russell's estimate of 80,000–
150,000 is too small. Cf. Russell's revised estimate "Recent Advances in Mediaeval Demography," *Speculum*, XL. 1 (January, 1965), 91. See also
A. Kriesis, "Uber die Wohnhaustyp der fruheren Konstantinopel," BZ, 53. 1
(1960), 322–27; D. Jacoby, "La population de Constantinople à l'époque
byzantine: un problème de démographie urbaine," B, XXXI. 1 (1961),

cult for us to determine the accuracy of Chrysostom's estimate of the poor either of Antioch or of Constantinople. We know, however, that the Church was the true force behind the various charities that were organized in every Byzantine city. Much of the wealth of the Church and monastic establishments of later centuries [9] was used for the poor, who had multiplied,[10] and for the maintenance of philanthropic institutions.

It was for this class of people that the Byzantine Church and State took special measures. Special houses known as *ptocheia* or *ptochotropheia* were built to shelter poor people [11] unable to work and in dire need of support. Chrysostom avers that his church in Antioch, when he delivered his famous sermons on the occasion of the imperial statues, had been supporting many widows, prisoners, maimed, orphans, and others in want, three thousand in all.[12] This charitable work was carried on despite the fact that the revenue of his church was one of the lowest in the city.[13]

The same charitable policy of the Church was exercised by John Eleemon in Alexandria in the seventh century. He had compiled a list of more than seven thousand poor who were supported by his philanthropic program.[14] We may safely assume that Chrysostom's example and John Eleemon's concern for the poor were not unique. Other religious leaders, members of the imperial court, and ordinary citizens did a great deal to relieve the poor, as we have seen in a previous chapter. Here we are concerned with the establishments properly called ptocheia or ptochotropheia.

Those institutions were for the benefit of poor people who could not work because of some previous illness, or because they were incapacitated by old age or by other reasons beyond their control. The poor who could support themselves had no place

81–110. For Byzantine cities in the early Byzantine centuries see George Ostrogorsky, "Byzantine Cities in the Early Middle Ages," DOP, XIII, pp. 47–66; Ostrogorsky, *History*, p. 42, see also note one.

9. Cf. Peter Charanis, "Monastic Properties," DOP, IV, pp. 53–118.

10. Cf. Charanis, "Social Structure," pp. 40 ff.

11. Cf. Sozomenos, *Eccl. History* 9. 1, ed. Bidez, p. 391; Michael Attaleiates, *Diataxis*, ed. Sathas, «Μεσ. Βιβλιοθ.», I ,pp. 8–9.

12. Joannes Chrysostomos, MPG, LVIII, 630: "Εἰς τὸν τῶν τρισχιλίων ἀριθμὸν ὁ κατάλογος αὐτῶν ἔφθασε."

13. Joannes Chrysostomos, *ibid.*

14. Gelzer, *Leontios*, pp. 8–9.

in an institution. Provincial citizens, for example, coming to the capital for no sound reason while in good health and able to work could not receive any help and were sent back to their towns.[15] This policy also accounted for the beggars. It was the concern of the Quaestor of the city to find them employment. If the healthy beggars refused to work they were expelled from the capital.[16] A ptocheion included also a clinic and many times served as a home for the aged.[17]

Of the numerous ptocheia which must have existed in many cities and towns of the Byzantine Empire we can identify several by name. The evidence comes to us in general terms; we lack knowledge in many specifics, such as exact location, size of an institution, and number of its inmates, the diet, and general conditions in a ptocheion. We know, for example, that St. Basil included a house for the poor in his celebrated philanthropic complex of Basileias,[18] but we possess no further information about it.

It is understandable why Byzantine authors do not provide us with more details; no modern historian either would have thought to present a detailed account of charitable institutions in a general history of a state, a country, or even a city unless he had a reason to deal exclusively with them. With the exception of Procopios and perhaps Anna Comnena, no Byzantine author wrote specifically about the institutions, their administration, or the buildings themselves. Any reference to them seems to have been casual. From general statements, therefore, we must deduce certain specifics and to infer that there must have been many more institutions than those which we can identify.

Thus in the diocese of Caesarea several ptocheia must have existed in addition to the great complex of Basileias. Basil the Great, writing to the prefect's accountant, introduces a *chorepiscopos* who was in charge of such an institution. He writes: "You [i.e. the accountant] will have the kindness to inspect the home for the poor in the district under his [i.e. the chorepis-

15. Justinian, *Novel No. 80*, ch. 4.
16. *Ibid.*, *Novel No. 80*, ch. 5.
17. Sozomenos, *Eccl. History*, IX. 1; Attaleiates, *Diataxis*, ed. Sathas, «Μεσ. Βιбλιοθ.», I, 8–9; Rhallis-Potlis, «Σύνταγμα», II, 234–35.
18. Sozomenos, *Eccl. History*, VI. 34, p. 291; Gregory Nazianzenos, "The Panegyric of St. Basil," ed. Boulenger, p. 188. Cf. Ignatios of Selybria, ed. Ioannou, «Μνημεῖα», p. 213.

copos'] care and to exempt it entirely from taxation. For it has already pleased your colleague to make the small property of the poor immune from assessment." [19]

Basil indicates also that there were several establishments for the poor in the city of Amasea, in the eparchy of Pontos on the river Iris. He writes that, according to information he possessed, an accountant of the prefect had been supporting one. Basil had appealed to this second imperial officer and had requested his support for another church-owned ptochotropheion whose director was a chorepiscopos.[20]

The fact that bishops were also administrators of institutions for the poor reveals the importance attached to their function.

Basil's close friend Gregory the Theologian bequeathed his property to the church of his former see, the city of Nazianzos, to be used solely for the relief of the poor. He assigned three individuals, two deacons and one monk, to serve as directors of his funds.[21] They are described as ptochotrophoi, a term which implies the existence of institutions for the poor. Nevertheless they might not have been directors of ptochotropheia, properly speaking. The term ptochotropoi probably meant that they were entrusted with the funds to be used for the poor.

Gregory is explicit, however, when he writes of an institution for the poor. He wrote that in Cappadocia there was a big establishment for the poor whose director was a presbyter named Sakerdos.[22] It possessed various estates donated to it by a certain Kastor.

Contemporary to the Cappadocian fathers, while Macedonios I was Patriarch of Constantinople (341–48, 350–56), a certain deacon named Eleusios was also an important trustee or perhaps in charge of several poor-houses.[23] During the same golden age of the Christian Church a ptochotropheion existed on the coast of the Euxine Pontos north of the city of Sebasteia. It was prob-

19. Basil the Great, *Epistle No. 142*, ed. Deferrari, II, 345.

20. *Epistle No. 143, ibid.*, p. 347.

21. Gregory Nazianzenos, *Exemplum Testamenti*, MPG, XXXVII, col. 389AB.

22. *Ibid., Epistle No. 211*, MPG, XXXVII, col. 348C: " Ὁ τιμιώτατος καὶ θεοφιλέστατος υἱὸς ἡμῶν Σακερδῶς, ὁ συμπρεσβύτερος, πτωχείου προέστηκε τῶν ἐπισήμων πολυανθρώπου."

23. Sozomenos, *Eccl. History*, IV. 20: ". . . σπουδαῖος ἐπίτροπος πτωχείων."

ably a department of the Argyronium philanthropic complex which we have already discussed. It had been established some time in the fourth century and was known in the beginning as the Ptochotropheion.[24] Administratively it came under the jurisdiction of the bishop of Sebasteia and generally served many social purposes.

Among church leaders who pursued both prophylactic and analeptic works of philanthropy for the needy, John the Alms-Giver or Eleemon was undoubtedly an outstanding example. He had established several refuges for the poor in Egypt.[25] One of them, known as Kaesarion, had long vaulted chambers and wooden platforms. Its floors were covered with square rush-mats for the protection of the inmates and to prevent drafts. The celebrated patriarch visited this establishment often, and gave the poor money and gifts according to the importance of the holiday observed on the day of his visit.[26]

Byzantine emperors did not linger behind the bishops in works of philanthropy toward the poor. The bishops followed the admonition of their Lord who had commanded them to attend His brethren the poor. The emperors, too, as images of their prototype the heavenly King, were expected to look after the poor. Thus, at the very outset of the Byzantine State we find Constantine the Great (324–37) taking protective measures for the poor. The trustworthy historian Eusebios (who might have had a special reason to emphasize the Christian metamorphosis of Constantine) writes that the first Emperor contributed immensely to the churches in order that they might continue their philanthropic work toward "the poor, the orphans, and destitute women."[27] His mother Helen had also initiated many philanthropies for relief of the poor.[28] Though we have no specific reference to the establishment of any definite ptocheia by them, it seems safe to make such an assumption because they had constructed various institutions in the past.

24. Epiphanios, *Adversus Haereses,* III, No. 55(75), MPG, XLII. 2, col. 504C.

25. Delehaye, "Une Vie," pp. 22, 55 *et passim.*

26. Gelzer, *Leontios,* pp. 57–58.

27. Eusebios, *De Vita Constantini,* Bk. IV, 28, ed. Heikel, I, 128: ''Ταῖς δ' ἐκκλησίαις τοῦ Θεοῦ καθ' ὑπεροχὴν ἐξαίρετον πλεῖσθ' ὅσα παρεῖχεν, . . . ἐπὶ χορηγίᾳ πενήτων. . . .''

28. *Ibid.,* p. 96: ''Πλεῖστά θ' ὅσα πένησι γυμνοῖς καὶ ἀπεριστάτοις ἐδίδου. . . .

Their nephew, the romantic Julian (361–63), who abhorred Christianity in all its forms, nevertheless endeavored to imitate Christian philanthropic philosophy. A Christian historian did not hesitate to give him credit for his concern for the poor.[29] The apostate emperor also encouraged the pagan priests to follow the example of their Christian colleagues in works of philanthropy.[30]

Women of the imperial court were often more compassionate than the men. Thus Eudocia, wife of Emperor Theodosios II (408–50), built several homes for the poor. Cyril of Scythopolis wrote that she built numerous institutions, churches, monasteries, poor-houses, and homes for the aged.[31] Despite the pleonastic language of Cyril, there must have been a sense of truth in what he wrote. Among the many poor-houses Eudocia had built was a special ptocheion for epileptics with accommodations for four hundred persons. It was located at Phordisiis in Palestine, perhaps within the walls of Jerusalem.[32] Eudocia's sister-in-law, who succeeded Theodosios in 450 with her husband Marcianos (450–57), was described by Byzantine authors as very philanthropic and was given credit for the erection of many poor-houses.[33] She endowed them with all her wealth, which was to be shared with other philanthropic and social establishments.

Among the poor-houses one could find special institutions for

---

29. Sozomenos, *Eccl. History*, V. 16.

30. Sozomenos, *Eccl. History*, V. 16; Julian, *Epistle to Theodore the Chief-Priest*, No. 89, ed. Bidez, I, part 2, 156: " Ἀσκητέα τοίνυν πρὸ. πάντων ἡ φιλανθρωπία· ταύτῃ γὰρ ἕπεται πολλὰ μὲν καὶ ἄλλα τῶν ἀγαθῶν, ἐξαίρετον δὲ δὴ καὶ μέγιστον ἡ παρὰ τῶν θεῶν εὐμένεια." Cf. J. Kabiersch, *Untersuchungen zum Begriff der Philanthropia bei dem Kaiser Julian* (Weisbaden, 1960); Glanville Downey, "Philanthropia," *Historia*, IV (1955), 201.

31. Ch. 35, Schwartz, *Kyrillos*, p. 53: "Μοναστήρια δὲ καὶ πτωχεῖα καὶ γηροκομεῖα τοσαῦτα ἅπερ τῆς ἐμῆς οὐκ ἔστι δυνάμεως ἀριθμεῖν. . . ." Symeon Metaphrastes, *Vita S. Euthymii*, MPG, CXIV, col. 677CD; cf. Raymond Genier, *Vie de Saint Euthyme le Grand (377–473) Les Moines et l'église en Palestine au Ve siècle* (Paris, 1909), pp. 206 ff.; Festugière, *Les Moines*, pp. 101–103; Nicephoros Callistos Xanthopoulos, *Ecclesiastical History*, Bk. 14, ch. 50, MPG, CXLVI, col. 1240B.

32. Nicephoros Callistos Xanthopoulos, *Ecclesiastical History*, MPG, CXLVI, col. 1240B: " Ἐν δὲ Φορδισίοις πτωχεῖον ἀνίστη, ἐν ᾧ τετρακόσιοι τῇ ἱερᾷ νόσῳ προσειλημμένοι ἐνδιαίτημα εἶχον." Cf. J. I. Milik, "La Topographie de Jérusalem vers la fin de l'époque byzantine," p. 150, note 2.

33. Theophanes, *Chronographia*, I, 106; George Cedrenos, I, p. 587; George Monachos, II, 610.

poor people suffering from leprosy. Palladios, the historian of early monasticism, mentions one such establishment in Alexandria. At the time of his journey to the Egyptian monastic communities in circa 388,[34] the Alexandria ptocheion was administered by a presbyter named Makarios, who must have been a clever man. It was through unethical persuasion that he received five hundred nomismata for his establishment from a very rich but greedy woman.[35] His reputation, however, as a "lover of the poor" survived longer than his foxy methods.

This ptocheion had two floors: the upper floor was occupied by women and the lower by men. All residents were crippled from leprosy.[36]

Among the emperors of the sixth century Justinian undoubtedly was the chief in erecting or renovating buildings for the poor. This, at least, is the impression we get from the historical literature of his times. In addition to the splendid establishments which he erected in several cities and towns of the empire, Justinian founded or renovated several ptocheia. He rehabilitated the ptocheion named after St. Romanos in Apameia.[37] He raised a new one in Bostra,[38] and reconstructed the poor-houses of Kouricos[39] and Saint Conon.[40] He built also a ptochotropheion in the Emporium of the harbor city of Perga in Pamphylia, which he dedicated to Saint Michael.[41]

During the second half of the seventh century we find that an institution for the poor existed in the region of Eugeniou in Constantinople. Andrew, the celebrated hymnographer and Archbishop of Crete, had been appointed by the Emperor Justinian II (685–95, 705–11) to serve as its administrator after his ordination to the order of deacon around 685.[42] It was from this position that he was chosen as head of the Cretan Church.

34. Altaner, *Patrology*, p. 254.
35. Palladios, *Hist. Lausiaca,* ed. Butler, VI, 23.
36. *Ibid.,* VI, 24.
37. Procopios, *Buildings,* V. 9, 27.
38. *Ibid.,* V. 9, 22.
39. *Ibid.,* V. 9, 34.
40. *Ibid.,* V. 9, 35.
41. *Ibid.,* V. 9, 38.
42. Nicetas, *Life of St. Andrew the Hierosolymite,* ed. Papadopoulos-Kerameus, «'Ανάλεκτα», V, 174; cf. S. Eustratiades, " 'Ανδρέας Κρήτης ὁ 'Ιεροσολυμίτης," *Nea Sion,* vol. 29. 12 (Jerusalem, 1934), p. 675.

It is only logical that one should expect many ptocheia to have existed in the capital city. Justinian ruled that the ptocheia were subject to the same law which was to govern the ecclesiastical properties, thus implying that there were many ptocheia [43] which were not exempted from taxes.[44] Many institutions for the poor must have been maintained in later centuries as well. We are told that Basil I (867–86) was very generous to them.[45]

Despite this generally favorable picture, only three more ptocheia are known by name. The first was located in the town of Neapolis on the Bosporos. We know that in the year 489 its administrator, named Euphemios, was elected by the Synod to succeed Flavitas on the throne of the Constantinopolitan Patriarchate. The election of a ptochotrophos to the Ecumenical See indicates that the office was held in high esteem and that it was entrusted to capable individuals (and usually ones of dependable orthodoxy). This hypothesis is further supported by another patriarchal election. We know that the patriarch Nicephoros I (806–15) had been forced by the iconoclastic party to administer the "very great ptocheion" [46] before he was elected patriarch. There is no reason to identify this ptocheion with the Great Orphanage as a modern author suggests.[47] They were two distinct institutions, and the offices of ptochotrophos and orphanotrophos were well-established several centuries before in Justinian's legislation, as we have already seen. Furthermore, we know that in Constantinople there existed a second ptocheion which was designated as "the ptocheion," that is, the greatest and most important of all poor-houses.[48] It was near the Church of Saints

---

43. Justinian, *Novel 7*, Praefatio, p. 49; cf. *Novel 43*, ch. I, p. 271; *Novel 120*, ch. 6, pp. 582–83.

44. *Ibid.*, *Novel 43*, pp. 269–73.

45. Genesios, *Regum,* IV, ed. I. Bekker, CSHB (Bonn, 1834), 128. Cf. Theophanes Continuatus, p. 462; Leo VI the Wise, «Λόγος Ἐπιτάφιος . . .», ed. A. Vogt and I. Hausherr, "Oraison funèbre de Basile I par son fils Leon VI le Sage," OCP, XXVI. 1, No. 77 (1932), 58, 60 *et passim.*

46. Ignatios, *Vita S. Nicephori,* ed. de Boor, p. 152: " "Οθεν καὶ τοῦ μεγίστου πτωχείου τῶν κατὰ τὴν βασιλίδα ἐπιτροπεύειν προτροπῇ βιαίᾳ τῶν κρατούντων ἡ χάρις ἠξίωσε . . . καί . . . ἐγχειρίζουσα τῇ μερικῇ διεξαγωγῇ τὴν τῆς καθολικῆς ἐκκλησίας κυβέρνησιν." See also Ignatios, MPG, C, col. 60D.

47. Paul J. Alexander, *The Patriarch Nicephorus of Constantinople* (Oxford, 1958), pp. 63–64.

48. Dmitrievsky, *Typika,* I, p. 88; *Synaxarium,* col. 801, and Synaxaria Selecta, 31.

Archippos and Philemon. We are informed that this church was located in the region of Elaia [49] (Elaia was probably above modern Galata [50]). Nicephorus might have been the ptochotrophos of this particular ptocheion.

The third institution for the poor which we can identify was founded by Michael IV the Paphlogonian (1034–41). He was motivated by his desire to receive forgiveness for his sins and to please God.[51] Psellos, the source of this information, does not write in which quarter it was founded nor tell us anything about its size. He adds, however, that the emperor endowed it lavishly.[52]

In the Greek peninsula proper ptocheia must have existed in such cities as Thessalonica, Corinth, Kastoria, and other towns. In the excavations of Athens in 1877 an inscription was discovered with the biblical quotation: "Thou openest thy hand, thou satisfiest the desire of every living thing." [53] With it other inscriptions were unearthed and were accepted as belonging to the tenth or the eleventh centuries. We may assume that the first inscription belonged to one of those two centuries. Panaretos Constantinides, who studied them, suggests that it was an epigraph attached to a ptochotropheion.[54] The institution might have been in the region of Asclepieon where the excavations were conducted.

In Constantinople in the twelfth century, Alexios Comnenos added a number of houses for the poor to his great philanthropic complex,[55] the "new city" which we have already mentioned. Many of the residents of those establishments were not only poor but handicapped, either blind, lame, or with some other defect. The houses were two-storied and close to each other.[56]

The land magnate and imperial officer Michael Attaleiates, one

49. *Synaxarium*, col. 804.
50. Janin, *Constantinople*, pp. 416–17.
51. Michael Psellos, *Michael IV*, ch. 36, ed. Renauld, I, 74: "Πρυτανεῖον νέον ἐπῳκοδόμησε πτωχοτροφεῖον τοῦτο ἐπονομάσας, καὶ χρυσοῦ ρεῦμα ἐντεῦθεν πολὺ τοῖς ἀσκεῖν προαιρουμένοις ἀφῆκεν."
52. *Ibid.*
53. Ps. 145:16.
54. P. Constantinides, " ᾿Αθηνῶν ᾿Ανέκδοτοι Χριστιανικαὶ ἐπιγραφαί," *Parnassos*, VI (Athens, 1882), 80–85.
55. Anna Comnena, *Alexias XV*. 7, III, 215: "Κύκλῳ δὶ ταύτης ἑστᾶσιν οἰκήματα πυκνά, κατοικίαι πενήτων."
56. *Ibid.*

of the most important personages of the twelfth century, used his wealth for the relief of the poor. On his estates in Rhaedestos on the Sea of Marmara, with a considerable investment of time and labor, he transformed an ancient building ruined by decay and earthquake into a house for the poor.[57] He also purchased an adjoining building from Psorarios and Narses and attached it to the other, making one large establishment to serve as a ptocheion for the local population and as a resting place for needy travelers.[58]

Attaleiates possessed additional houses in Constantinople. He writes that he changed the house he had acquired from his sister-in-law Anastaso (his wife's sister), and dedicated it as a house for the poor. A *katogeon* or one-story structure was attached to it known as the *Triclinos*. This was connected with the Church of *Prodromos*, and had an exit and entrance to another house which he had bought from the aunt of his wife Euphrosyne. These two, the ground-floor building and the regular house, were united and made into another institution for the poor.[59]

These establishments were placed under one administrator "in honor of Jesus Christ the All-Merciful." All were to be known as the "Ptochotropheion of Paniktermon." [60] He did all this to comply with the "philanthropic" commandment of Christ. He endowed them richly and secured them legally in order that no one would violate their autonomy and sacred function. He invoked an anathema upon any violator of his rules.

He also built a church and ruled that the institutions be served by monks, among whom he mentioned the oeconomos or steward, the *ecclesiarches* who would be responsible for the church services and the prayer life of the institution.[61] They would be responsible to his inheritor, either his son or grandson, in either case to one of his descendants. If there were no *ptochotrophos* descendant of his family, the *oeconomos* assumed responsibility for the total institution.

Because the number of monks serving the ptochotropheion was considerable, Attaleiates instituted also a monastery for

57. Michael Attaleiates, *Diataxis*, ed. Sathas, «Μεσ. Βιβλιοθ.», I, 8.
58. *Ibid.*, p. 9.
59. *Ibid.*, p. 10.
60. *Ibid.*
61. *Ibid.*, p. 16.

them.[62] He made provisions for the poor inmates and the monks alike. The surpluses should be distributed to the beggars and other poor whom he calls "brethren in Christ."[63]

The *diataxis* of Attaleiates states that no one should violate the recorded rules of the establishment unless one is *"misanthropos* and behaves contrary to the philanthropos and merciful God."[64] Furthermore, Attaleiates endowed his establishment with several estates and money.[65] He ruled that if his family should disappear from the face of the earth, all his properties, monies, possessions, and valuable objects should be turned over to his philanthropic institutions.[66]

An institution for the poor must have been a common establishment from the early centuries of the Byzantine Empire not only in Constantinople but in other cities as well. The deaconess Olympias,[67] the faithful disciple of John Chrysostom, distributed all her vast wealth to the poor, for the release of captives of war and to institutions. Among them we find the ptochotropheia.[68]

Another rich woman of Alexandria who lived during the reign of Theodosios II (408–50)[69] was advised that she could free herself from material possessions by distributing them to philanthropic establishments, including ptocheia.[70]

Such general references to establishments for the poor are found to the very end of the Byzantine world. Suffice it to mention here one particular example of the thirteenth century. During the reign of John III Doucas Vatatzes (1222–54) of the Empire of Nicaea, after the Latin occupation of Constantinople,

62. *Ibid.*, p. 17.
63. *Ibid.:* "...τὰ δὲ λοιπὰ διανέμωνται τοῖς ἐν Χριστῷ ἀδελφοῖς μου τοῖς δεομένοις."
64. *Ibid.*, pp. 18–19.
65. *Ibid.*, p. 19.
66. *Ibid.*, pp. 20–21.
67. See A. M. Malingrey, *Jean Chrysostom Lettres à Olympias*, Sources Chrétiennes (Paris, 1947), pp. 6–15.
68. Palladios, *Hist. Lausiaca*, ch. 144, MPG, XXIV, col. 1249: "Γεγονυῖα ... κοινωνὸς δὲ καὶ διάκονος πάντων τῶν δεομένων. Αὕτη πάντα τὸν ἄπειρον ἐκεῖνον καὶ ἀμέτρητον πλοῦτον διασκορπίσασα, πᾶσιν ἁπλῶς καὶ ἀδιακρίτως ἐπήρκεσεν ... ἀλλ' ἐπήρκεσεν ... καὶ πτωχοτροφείοις. ..." Cf. Butler's ed. of Palladios, pp. 149–150, and Chrysostom's *Letters to Olympias*, No. 8.10a, ed. Malingrey, pp. 133–134.
69. Symeon Metaphrastes, *Vita et Conversatio Sanctae Euphrosynes Alexandrinae*, MPG, CXIV, col. 305A.
70. "Vita Sanctae Euphrosynae," ed. A. Boucherie, AB, II, 199.

his wife the Empress Irene built churches and monasteries in such cities as Magnesia, Nicaea, and Prousa, and also adequately endowed the extant ptocheia.[71]

While a ptocheion served the masses of the poor, the Byzantines practiced charity to beggars, captives, orphans, and other poverty-stricken individuals not confined in organized institutions.

The ptochotrophos or director of a poor-house was an ecclesiastically important office. As we have already seen, two patriarchs of Constantinople, Euphemios (489–95) and Nicephoros I (806–15), were directors of ptochotropheia when they were elected to the throne. Andreas, Archbishop of Crete, was also the administrator of the ptocheion of Eugeniou in Constantinople before he was elected a bishop.[72]

The eighth canon of the Council of Chalcedon also indicates that the ptochotrophos was an ecclesiastical office. The canon places the director of a poor-house under the jurisdiction of the local bishop.[73] St. Basil the Great, on the other hand, ruled that any cleric who had acquired this office with bribes and improper means should be removed from his position.[74]

---

71. Nicephoros Gregoras, I, 45; cf. George Acropolites, *Annales,* pp. 56, 67.
72. Nicetas, *Life of St. Andrew the Hierosolymite,* ed. Papadopoulos-Kerameus, «'Ανάλεκτα», V, 174.
73. Rhallis-Potlis, «Σύνταγμα», II, 234; cf. Knecht, *System des Justinianischen Kirchenvermogensrechtes,* pp. 50–51.
74. Rhallis-Potlis, «Σύνταγμα», VI, 514.

16. Other Institutions

In addition to the major institutions which we have investigated in the preceding pages we find in Byzantine society other establishments for social services, either proleptic or therapeutic in nature.

REFORMATORY HOUSES

Prostitution was one of the less flattering aspects of a Christian civilization such as the Byzantine. Poverty, social conditions, economic considerations, and above all human nature contributed to the existence of moral and legal outcasts in Byzantine society.[1] Their fate was the same as it had been in previous societies. William Lecky, the nineteenth-century historian of morals and ideas, ably expressed the sentiments of all societies when he wrote that the prostitute is a figure "certainly the most mournful, and in some respects the most awful . . . who counterfeits with a cold heart the transports of affection, and submits herself as the passive instrument of lust; who is scorned and insulted as the vilest of her sex. . . . She remains, while creeds and civilizations rise and fall, the eternal priestess of humanity, blasted for the sins of the people."[2]

1. For prostitution in Byzantine society see Phaedon Koukoules, B B II, II, 2 (Athens, 1948), 117–62; Peter Charanis, "Some Aspects of Daily Life in Byzantium," pp. 60–62. "Vita S. Andrea Salo," AASS, May, VI, Corollarium, pp. 13–14. See also the sources cited in the following notes of this section.
2. Lecky, *Eur. Morals*, II, 282–83.

In Byzantine society, while some viewed the fallen woman as a means of entertainment, others accepted her as a creature made after the "image and the likeness of God"; a human being who deserves the compassion and love of society. Therefore unlike other social and religious systems, Byzantine society adopted a rather charitable attitude toward the persons of prostitutes, though the legislation of the State and the Church was severe against prostitution as such.[3] Robert Byron rightly observes that "the story of the prostitute indicates the whole tenor of Byzantine society. That society was one in which practice of the true Christian ideal was possible; not of a tithe to the poor or the turning of the other cheek; but of the sympathy for others, of the understanding of fellow-beings born of the Greek instinct to scatter the pretensions of one man above another." [4]

In the Byzantine world much effort was exerted so that civil disabilities and stigmas were removed from this class of women who had never met with sympathy before. A brilliant example was set by the Empress Theodora. The illustrious wife of Justinian I was one of the most beneficent empresses of the Byzantine Empire. Not only was she alert in exerting her influence for the cause of justice where justice was at stake,[5] but she initiated several measures to assist miserable individuals of her own sex who had fallen prey to procurers and whoremongers. We are told that she redeemed prostitutes from their masters by paying from her own purse. Once she offered five nomismata to a whoremonger for each woman under his patronage. She not only gave orders against procurers but when setting free certain such women, she gave one nomisma to each one of them.[6] Justinian followed her example.[7]

Individuals of the monastic ranks considered it their duty to work for the moral restoration of fallen women. We are told that St. Vitalios worked to secure many prostitutes' repentance and to return them to a life of morals and dignity. He not only

---

3. Cf. Justinian, *Novel 51*, pp. 295–96; *Novel 17. 7*, pp. 121–22; Zepos-Zepos, *Jus*, V, 471–72. For church and patristic Canons see Rhallis-Potlis, «Σύνταγμα», I, 301–02; vol. IV, 216, 308, 309, 400, 437 *et passim*.

4. Robert Byron, *The Byzantine Achievement*, p. 237.

5. John Lydos, *De Magistratibus*, III. 69, 263: "κρείττων τῶν ὄντων ὁτεδήποτε ἐπὶ συνέσει, καὶ συμπαθείᾳ τῶν ἀδικουμένων ἀγρυπνοῦσα [ἡ Θεοδώρα]."

6. Malalas, p. 440.

7. Agathias, p. 307.

visited houses of ill fame in order to persuade prostitutes to abandon their ignoble profession, but he also prayed for their repentance. The result of his moral crusade was that some abandoned their sinful work altogether, others married and commenced a new life, and a third group, leaving the worldly life, found refuge in monasteries.[8]

We have two other instances of organized philanthropy toward fallen women, one in the sixth and the other in the eleventh century. Procopios, who often exaggerates, writes that "there was a throng of women in Byzantium who had carried on in brothels a business of lechery, not of their own free will, but under force of lust."[9] To clean up the city, Justinian and Theodora banished brothel-keepers and erected a special institution to provide the needs of the former prostitutes.

It was through the efforts of Theodora that Justinian issued a special novel[10] against procuring and the exploitation of poor and minor girls. The novel, as well as the chronicler John Malalas, indicate that unscrupulous procurers visited villages and country towns where they approached poor families. Poverty pressed upon the unfortunate parents to sell their girls to procurers, who promised the girls shoes, clothes, and other necessities. However, when the girls were brought to Constantinople, they were confined in dens and miserable houses for the practice of prostitution. The money, of course, was collected by the masters.[11]

The celebrated queen expressed her concern for fallen women in more concrete terms. There was a neglected palace on the Euxine sea across from Constantinople. They converted it into a convent named *Metanoia* or "Repentance" to serve as a refuge for fallen women who had repented of their ignoble past.[12] Procopios adds that more than five hundred of them were placed in that institution,[13] and that the illustrious sovereigns endowed it with a plentiful income.[14]

8. Gelzer, *Leontios*, p. 73; cf. "Life of St. Gregory the Decapolites," ed. F. Dvornik, *La Vie de Saint Grégoire le Decapolite*, pp. 56–57.

9. Procopios, *Buildings*, I. 9, 35–36. English translation is from H. B. Dewing and Glanville Downey, p. 75; cf. Koukoules, BB II, II, 144.

10. Justinian, *Novel 14.*

11. *Ibid., Novel 14,* "Prooimion"; Malalas, pp. 440–41.

12. Procopios, *Buildings*, I. 9; cf. *ibid., Anecdota*, XVII. 5; Malalas, pp. 440–41.

13. Procopios, *Anecdota*, XVII. 5–6.

14. Procopios, *Buildings*, I. 9.

The second such establishment was the work of the Emperor Michael IV (1034–41). Psellos writes that after the days of pleasure had passed for Michael and Zoe, the emperor displayed much piety and desired the salvation of his soul. The celebrated philosopher maintains that he is not eulogizing Michael but that he is simply narrating events.[15]

In his catalogue of Michael's good deeds, Psellos includes "an edifice of enormous size and very great beauty" which the Emperor Michael IV founded to house harlots who were ready to reform.[16] The Emperor had issued a proclamation which, in the words of Michael Psellos, "all women who trafficked in their beauty, provided they were willing to renounce their trade and live in luxury, were to find sanctuary in this building: they were to change their own clothes for the habit of nuns, and all fear of poverty would be banished from their lives for ever. . . . Thereupon a great swarm of prostitutes descended upon his refuge, relying on the Emperor's proclamation, and changed both their garments and their manner of life, a youthful band enrolled in the service of God, as soldiers of virtue." [17]

It is not irrelevant to emphasize that because of the humane attitude and the religious philosophy of the Byzantines toward repentant prostitutes, we find a number of saints among them who previously had been great sinners.[18] For the foundation of this policy the Byzantines referred to the Scriptures. While the New Testament speaks caustically against fornication, adultery, and sins of the flesh,[19] the repentant sinner is always accepted by the Church. The example was set by Christ himself. When the Scribes and the Pharisees brought before Him for condemnation a woman taken in adultery, Christ uttered the now-famous words: "He that is without sin among you, let him first cast a stone at her." [20] Elsewhere Jesus indicated that repentant harlots go into the Kingdom of God before the priests and pretentious religious individuals.[21] One can easily discern how much this

15. Michael Psellos, *Michael IV*, ch. 34, ed. Renauld, I, 73–74.
16. *Ibid.*, ch. 36, Renauld, I, 74–75.
17. Michael Psellos, *Michael IV*, ch. 36; English translation, E. R. A. Sewter, *The Chronographia of Michael Psellus* (London, 1952), pp. 73–74.
18. Sophronios of Jerusalem, *Vita Mariae Aegyptiae*, MPG, LXXX. 3, col. 3697 ff.
19. Acts 25:20; Rom. 1:29; 1 Cor. 6:18; 1 Thes. 4:3, *et al.*
20. John 8:3–3.
21. Matt. 21:31.

Christian philosophy influenced the Byzantines toward the fallen woman.

XENOTAPHEIA

Among the diverse philanthropic institutions in Byzantium we may classify also the xenotapheion or the cemetery especially put aside for the burial of poor strangers or poor local people. We do not know much about this tradition, but there is evidence that in Byzantium either the Church, the State, or individual philanthropists undertook the expenses for the burial of the poor and had special sections for them. In Constantinople such a cemetery was near the cistern of Mocios.[22]

On the part of the State we are told that the Empress Pulcheria, the wife of Marcianos (450–57) was instrumental in the establishment of *xenotapheia*. Because the noun is in the plural one wonders how many she had built. Both Theophanes and George Monachos imply that Pulcheria had established more than one.[23] Later in the eighth and early ninth century the Empress Irene (797–802) is given credit for her measures toward the poor. Pseudo-Codinos must have had in mind certain specific cemeteries for the poor and the strangers when he wrote that Irene established *ta xenotapheia*.[24]

Justinian's legislation implies that the poor were afforded a free funeral and burial in a special cemetery.[25] Later in the tenth century Leo VI (886–912) issued a law concerning the shops of Hagia Sophia. Much of this income was used for philanthropic purposes, including the funeral expenses of the poor and perhaps of strangers who had died while visiting the capital.[26]

Xenotapheia existed in other cities as well. There was one in the small city of Daphne outside of Antioch.[27] John Moschos, the source of this information, implies that the strangers were buried

22. Phaedon Koukoules, "Βυζαντινῶν Νεκρικὰ Ἔθιμα," EEBS, XVI, 42, note 1.

23. Theophanes, *Chronographia*, I, 106; George Monachos, II, 610.

24. Pseudo-Codinos, *Patria*, Th. Preger, III, 246.

25. Justinian, *Novel 59*, ch. 7 *et passim*.

26. Leo VI Wise, *Novel 12*, Zepos-Zepos, *Jus*, I, 70.

27. Joannes Moschos, *Pratum Spirituale*, ch. 88, MPG, LXXX. 3, col. 2945B; cf. "Vita S. Marthae Matris S. Symeonis Junioris," AASS, May V, 407C. M. I. Gedeon, "Διαθήκη Ἰωάννου Πρμοκυρίου," *Ekklesiastike Aletheia*, IX (1888–1889), p. 295, col. 1.

in a somewhat different manner than the local citizenry. Perhaps the religious ceremony was briefer than the ordinary one,[28] the corpse was not washed, and the brief service was without candles and incense. In a similar manner Saint Symeon the Salos (sixth century) was buried in a xenotapheion.[29]

The underlying philosophy for charity toward dead strangers and the poor is expressed by Theodore the Studite. In a letter to the consul Thomas, Theodore emphasized that because of love for God and man, God's image and likeness, the monks of the cloister of the Studion and himself had dedicated their services to those who either because of poverty or because they were foreigners and had no relatives in the capital were left unattended even at death.[30]

HOMES FOR THE BLIND

We have seen that Byzantine hospitals included ophthalmological clinics,[31] and among the physicians there was an ophthalmologist or *ophthalmicos iatros*.[32] Additional but insufficient evidence indicates that the Byzantines had special institutions for the blind. In the narrations of the "miracles" of St. Anastasios (+628) we read that a *typhlocomion* or home for the blind was in Jerusalem.[33] Considering the sympathy with which the Byzan-

28. Moschos, MPG, LXXX. 3, col. 2945B: ". . . ὡς ξένον ἔθαψαν αὐτὸν ἐν τῷ ξενοταφίῳ." For funerals and their tradition see Phaedon Koukoules, "Βυζαντινῶν Νεκρικὰ Ἔθιμα," EEBS, XVI, 3–80; George Spyridakis, "Τὰ κατὰ τὴν τελευτὴν ἔθιμα τῶν Βυζαντινῶν ἐκ τῶν Ἁγιολογικῶν Πηγῶν," EEBS, xx, 75–171.

29. Leontios of Neapolis, "Vita S. Symeone Salo Confessore," AASS, July, I, 150A; *ibid.*, MPG, XCIII, col. 1744D.

30. Theodore Studites, *Epistles*, Bk. I, No. 13, MPG, XCIX, col. 953A: "Εὐλαβῶς εἰς τὸ θεῖον ἀπιδόντες καὶ πρὸς τὸ ὁμόφυλον τὴν ἀγαπητικὴν διάθεσιν ἀναλαβόντες, καθήκαμεν ἑαυτοὺς εἰς τόδε τὸ ἀσεβές [εὐσεβές;] σύστημα, καθὼς ὑποτέτακται, πρόνοιαν ποιούμενοι τῶν ἀπρονοήτων σκηνωμάτων, εἴτ᾽ οὖν νενεκρωμένων, καὶ ἐκ πενίας ἤ ἐκ ξενιτείας μὴ ἐχόντων πῶς ἐκκομίζεσθαι καὶ ἐνθάπτεσθαι ἐν ταύτῃ τῇ βασιλευούσῃ τῶν πόλεων... ὁ καθεὶς ὡς ἔχει δυνάμεως, καταβολὴν ποιούμενοι πρός τε ἀγορασίαν ἐνταφίων, καὶ τὰ τῶν εἰς ταφὴν ἄλλων συντελοῦντα, διορίζομεν ἐν Κυρίῳ τάδε. . . ."

31. Dmitrievsky, *Typika*, I, 682.

32. Julius Polydeukes, " Ἑρμηνεύματα [καὶ] Καθημερινὴ Ὁμιλία," ed. Anatole Boucherie, *Notices et extraits des manuscrits de la Bibliothèque Nationale*, XXIII, part 2 (Paris, 1872), 351.

33. "Miracula S Anastasii Persae," No. XII, AASS, January, III, 52: "His vero miraculis alteram gratiam decet adjungere, Sancti scilicet com-

tine Church and society looked upon the blind and the deformed, we may assume that the typhlocomeion in Jerusalem
was not the exception. The Church maintained the fifty-seventh
apostolic canon by which anyone ridiculing a blind, a deaf, or
a lame man could suffer the penalty of excommunication. According to the canonists Zonaras, Balsamon, and Aristenos, the canon
implied that the blind and the crippled in general deserved
understanding and the philanthropic help of the community.[34]

There must have been other philanthropic institutions of which
we know very little or nothing, such as *parthenones* and *cherotropheia*. *Parthenones* might have been orphanages or homes for
deserted girls. We find them in the fourth century [35] as well as
in the tenth [36] and the fifteenth,[37] in Constantinople and in
smaller cities. The *cherotropheion*, an institution perhaps for
poor widows found in the early Byzantine Empire,[38] may not
have survived after the fifth century, although protection was
extended to widows in Byzantium in later centuries as well.[39]

miserationem. Mulier quaedam, Photi nomine, ministra effecta sacri typh-
locomii, sive caecorum domicilii. . . ." Cf. J. I. Milik, "La Topographie de
Jérusalem . . . ," p. 150, note 2.

34. "Fifty-Seventh Apostolic Canon," ed. Rhallis-Potlis, «Σύνταγμα»,
II, pp. 74–75, where the commentaries of the canonists are cited.

35. "Life of St. Hypatios Archbishop of Gangra," ed. Theophilos Ioannou,
«Μνημεῖα», p. 256.

36. "Life of St. Paraskeve the Younger," ed. Papadopoulos-Kerameus,
«'Ανάλεκτα», I, 443.

37. Andronicos Kallistos, *Monodia de Constantinopoli Capta*, MPG, CLXI,
col. 1134A.

38. Sozomenos, *Eccl. History*, V. 15. Sozomenos relates that Eleusios
bishop of Cyzicos erected *cherotropheia*. Cf. Chrysostomos, MPG, LVIII, col.
630; Symeon Metaphrastes, MPG, CXIV, col. 1097c.

39. See Nicetas Choniates, 585. 20. For the protection of widows in the
fourth and fifth centuries see Koukoules, ΒΒΠ., II, 162–64.

Part IV

Conclusion

17. Conclusion

The preceding pages have been an endeavor, as it were, to construct a Byzantine mosaic in the sphere of Byzantine social history. Tesserae have been selected from every century of the Byzantine era, and we have tried to paint a well-balanced picture. Our reconstruction may be weak, perhaps less beautiful than a Byzantine mosaic is supposed to be.[1] Nevertheless, we have before us a view of an aspect of Byzantine civilization and culture. Emperors and patriarchs, state officials and church dignitaries, wealthy magnates and poor citizens, learned theologians and illiterate monks, serious historians and popular chroniclers expounded their views on the concept of philanthropia, delineating the work of the charitable institutions of what was, despite the views of some modern scholars, a really glorious empire.

At the outset of this work we adopted as our hypothesis the claims of the Byzantine authors Theophylactos Simocattes, Photios, Nicholas Mysticos, Alexios Makrembolites, and John Cantacuzenos[2] that philanthropia flourished among the Byzantines. The evidence by which to judge that hypothesis has now been furnished. The reader will draw his own conclusions. Nonetheless, the author feels obligated to record his own judgment.

It is hardly necessary to remark that the theoretical concept

1. Cf. O. M. Dalton, *Byzantine Art and Archaeology* (New York, reprint, 1961), pp. 323–25; D. V. Ainalov, *The Hellenistic Origins of Byzantine Art,* tr. E. Sobolevitch and S. Sobolevitch (New Brunswick, N.J., 1961), pp. 272–74.

2. See my Preface, p. x.

of philanthropia had become fixed and stereotyped in the Byzantine Empire as early as the fourth century. In the usage of the term, there is marked continuity from Greek classical antiquity to the Byzantine world although, in Byzantium, the concept of philanthropia assumed a more religious significance. This continuity is evident both in theory and in practice. The ancient Greeks practiced philanthropy extensively: hospitality, compassion, and consideration for their fellow men. We do not share the view that the ancient world was "a world without love." [3] On the contrary, there was much concern for those in want.[4] The difference between ancient Greek and medieval Byzantine philanthropia may be viewed as one of scope and catholicity, perhaps also one of depth. Ancient Greek philanthropia was individualistic, limited, and aimed at a rather subjective satisfaction, while medieval Greek-Christian philanthropia was a collective, well-organized ideal pursued by the entire society. Furthermore, philanthropia as a concept in antiquity remained a philosophic yearning and quest rather than an applied virtue. Its application, as we saw, was incidental and limited, while the Christian ideology of Byzantium had broadened and deepened the spirit of love and concern for man. It had heightened their regard and view for the dignity, worth, and destiny of every human being. The humane values of the Byzantines contributed greatly to social advances and improved the quality of human life among the underprivileged members of their society. Wealthy patrons made great contributions to charitable institutions and distributed charities to needy individuals either in return for the prayers of the Church and the beneficiaries or in order to give up worldly concerns and follow the monastic life. The definite purpose that guided many Byzantine philanthropists was to please God, to receive forgiveness of sins, and to manifest love of their fellow men. To these reasons we must add that much philanthropy was practiced in order to relieve immediate social conditions and to achieve certain social objectives, such as to help victims of pestilences and to redeem prisoners of war.

Further, philanthropia sought, as it were, to satisfy not only the philanthropist himself but the very source of philanthropia,

3. Cf. Uhlhorn, p. 5.
4. Cf. Bolkestein, pp. 67 ff.; A. H. M. Jones, *The Later Roman Empire*, II, 970–71.

God. As a consequence Christian philanthropia embraced all men, for man is God's supreme creature. Under the impact of Christianity, Greek philanthropia blossomed into a passion of agape.

A further difference between the ancient Graeco-Roman world and Graeco-Christian Byzantium was that in the former man was viewed primarily as a social and political being. In the Byzantine thought-world, however, man was accepted as the "image and the likeness of God," who, as a rebellious son of God, was called back to the house of his father by means of the philanthropia of his brother Jesus Christ. Thus while philanthropy in the ancient world was limited in principle, motive, and practice, in the Byzantine Empire philanthropia flourished as a genuine, selfless, and idealistic principle, and was all-embracing in practice.

No Byzantine text comes closer to a definition of philanthropia as selfless love, altruism, and Christian agape, which is manifested to friends and enemies alike, than the Pseudo-Clementine homilies, probably of the fourth century.[5] In a compact form the unidentified author expressed what we have discussed throughout the first chapter of this work. Philanthropia as a concept is much more than mere affection, pity, friendship, and compassion. It is Christian love which manifests itself in words and deeds to needy friends and adversaries alike; it is love which benefits every man because he is a man.[6] He is the genuine philanthropic man who serves even his enemies. The philanthropist is an imitator of God, doing good to the just and the unjust, as God himself supplies all men everywhere with His sun and His heavenly rains.[7]

Therefore, there is little doubt that philanthropia as an element of the culture of the Byzantine Empire was rooted in moral

5. Altaner, *Patrology*, p. 105.
6. Pseudo-Clementines, *Homily*, XII. 25: "τί ποτ' ἐστὶ φιλανθρωπίας μέγεθος, ἥτις ἐστὶν ἡ ἄνευ τοῦ φυσικῶς πείθοντος, ἡ πρὸς οἷον δήποτε στοργή, καθὸ ἄνθρωπός ἐστιν . . . ἡ δὲ φιλανθρωπία ἄνευ τοῦ φυσικῶς πείθοντος πάντα ἄνθρωπον, καθὸ ἄνθρωπός ἐστι, φιλοῦσα εὐεργετεῖ." Cf. *Epitome of Clementines*, 93.
7. Pseudo-Clementines, *Homily*, XII. 26: "Φιλάνθρωπος ἐστὶν ὁ καὶ ἐχθροὺς εὐεργετῶν . . . Χρὴ οὖν τὸν φιλανθρωπίαν ἀσκοῦντα μιμητὴν εἶναι τοῦ Θεοῦ, εὐεργετοῦντα δικαίους καὶ ἀδίκους, ὡς αὐτὸς ὁ Θεὸς πᾶσιν ἐν τῷ νῦν κόσμῳ τόν τε ἥλιον καὶ τοὺς ὑετοὺς αὐτοῦ παρέχων." Cf. *Epitome of Clementines*, 94.

and religious thought. Because the Byzantines believed in a
Philanthropos Theos, they, too, were moved to be humanitarian
and express philanthropia toward their fellow men. They gave
help to the poor, the orphans, the widows, the strangers, and
others in want, and they formed institutions to prevent and
alleviate misery and distress. The State administration and the
Church, monastic establishments and private citizens, took measures to prevent poverty, sickness, and misery; and when they
could not prevent them, they organized institutions to relieve
their victims.

The Byzantine Church was conscious of her social responsibilities toward the community as well as toward the individual
in want. The social consciousness of the Church pursued a policy
for both a spiritual and an earthly transformation of man. She
prayed and worked for a total metamorphosis of the cosmos and
for the rehabilitation of the social order. This concept is profoundly expressed in a prayer by St. Basil the Great, whose social
work we have examined. St. Basil writes: "[O God] . . . rear
the infants . . . support the aged . . . accompany those who
voyage; journey with those who journey; defend the widows;
protect the orphans; free the captives; heal the sick. Remember,
O God, those who are under trial, and in the mines, and in
prison, and in bitter labors, and in all affliction, distress, and
tribulation." [8]

Monastic communities, on the other hand, expressed their
social philosophy in numerous deeds and acts of philanthropy
and concern for man. Social consciousness was not alien to Byzantine monasticism. We have cited many texts which reveal
that social action was a vital preoccupation of the Church and
her monasteries. The monks were indeed the "nerves and the
foundations of the Church," in the words of Theodore Studites.
They made up the social army which had undertaken to secure
the spiritual renewal of the Church and the social rehabilitation

8. Goar, *Euchologion,* p. 146: "...τὰ νήπια ἔκθρεψον...τὸ γῆρας
περικράτησον... τοῖς πλέουσι σύμπλευσον· τοῖς ὁδοιποροῦσι συνόδευσον...
χηρῶν πρόστηθι· ὀρφανῶν ὑπεράσπισον· αἰχμαλώτους ῥῦσαι· νοσοῦντας
ἴασαι. Τῶν ἐν βήμασι καὶ μετάλλοις καὶ ἐξορίαις καὶ πικραῖς δουλείαις
καὶ πάσῃ θλίψει καὶ ἀνάγκῃ καὶ περιστάσει ὄντων μνημόνευσον ὁ
Θεός. . . ." For a critical edition of the Liturgy see Panagiotis N.
Trembelas, «Αἱ Τρεῖς Λειτουργίαι» (Athens, 1935), pp. 186–87.

of the needy and the destitute.[9] Thus, disparaging views that the Church of Byzantium has never been concerned with the fate of man on earth are unfounded.[10] She has bequeathed a rich tradition in social philosophy and in social projects.

Philanthropy in Byzantium was not practiced as a result of coercion on the part of the State machinery or the Emperor as is sometimes the case in socialist societies today. It was a voluntary manifestation of love and human consideration. The Byzantine Empire was not a socialist state. Its welfare program did not destroy self-reliance, self-respect, or initiative. Byzantine philanthropy did not make the poor servile and dependent, weak in character, resigned, and parasitic. We have shown that the Byzantines believed that "if any one will not work, let him not eat." [11] Of course, we will never know how many actually practiced philanthropy and how many of the beneficiaries really deserved it.

Nevertheless, we know that ambitious and industrious citizens, though poor and humble in origin, could improve their lot and even become high officials, even emperors or patriarchs.[12] In many respects, after the seventh century Byzantium was not a closed society in the middle ages. To a great measure the Byzantine Empire was the land of opportunity.

Nonetheless, one discerns in Byzantine society a certain inconsistency. There was a passion for philanthropia in the sense of altruistic love, but there was much hatred as well. We see abundant philanthropy and charity, but also much poverty and misery. We find many "men of God" walking side by side with "men of the flesh." Piety and godliness contrast with excessive religiosity and superstition. There was abundant wealth, but many times it was in the hands of the few, and there were many poor and underprivileged. Many factors contributed to the disparities between wealth and poverty: the Christian concept that God bears with conditions and the social structure; government regulations concerning trade and industry, economic life and

9. Cf. Carnegie S. Calian, "Social Consciousness in Eastern Orthodoxy," *The Christian Century*, LXXXII, No. 42 (October 20, 1965), 1284–86.
10. Cf. Adolf Harnack, *What is Christianity?*, trans. by Thomas B. Saunders, Second Edition, Revised (New York, 1906), pp. 256–62.
11. Cf. 2 Thes. 3:10.
12. Cf. Charanis, "Social Structure," pp. 40 ff. Cf. George Every, *The Byzantine Patriarchate, 451–1204*, pp. 8 ff.

guilds; the strong centralization of the Byzantine State. Thus many poor were not able to rise up against their superiors, but neither were the wealthy free to devour the poor.[13] Their moral and religious philosophy viewed the differences in social status and economic conditions as forces not to separate and alienate one class of people from another but to make them depend more upon each other and to unite them closer in the bond of the philanthropia of God. Thus the performance of philanthropic work was considered as an obligation owed to God and man alike. This view, however, had its merits as well as its shortcomings. While the Byzantines are commendable for the numerous charities and their great concern for philanthropic institutions, they seem to have done little to prevent poverty in a systematic manner or to help the poor to become independent. We find many provisions for the poor but not much concern that constant almsgiving may perpetuate poverty and maintain the status quo in the social structure. Instead of finding means to drive the poor out of poverty, their moral philosophy and religious feelings made poverty easy to endure and to continue. The monastery, for example, or the local congregation and diocese, instead of serving as centers of charitable distributions to the poor, could have given lands to the poor and properties to cultivate; that is, they could have created the presuppositions for self-help instead of carrying on a purely religious and sentimental attitude toward charity. The state and city authorities should have provided conditions in which the poor would have been in a position to take care of themselves. On many occasions it was probable that the benefactors, by relieving their own moral duties and religious sentiments, did more harm than good to the poor. In their generosity many Byzantines apparently did not think of the adverse consequences.

However, the existence of extremes of wealth and poverty or the measure of immobility does not indicate that there was no middle class in the Byzantine Empire. As we have seen, the middle class may have been the major segment of Byzantine society for several centuries. If estimates of Chrysostom and John Eleemon of the poor in Antioch, Alexandria, and Constantinople between the last quarter of the fourth century and the

13. Cf. "The Book of the Eparch," *Prooimion*, ed. Zepos-Zepos, *Jus*, II, 371; cf. "Epanagoge," *ibid.*, p. 37.

first quarter of the seventh are approximately correct, the poor must have composed some ten per cent of the total population, or a little more.

The disaccord of which we speak above, however, has never been absent from any society [14] including our own. It is to the credit of the Byzantines that they tried to improve the lot of the poor through active philanthropy and charity. In many respects the Church was the bulwark of social justice and the monastery was a haven for the hungry, the destitute, and the wayfarers. It is easy for any writer to emphasize the negative: the cruelties, the poverty, the mutilations—the *apanthropia* or *misanthropia* in Byzantine civilization. Yet he ought not to overlook the positive aspect, its *philanthropia*. The Byzantines bequeathed to modern man certain values of lasting worth. For example, there were periods in the Byzantine Empire when the death penalty was seldom employed.[15] In particular during the reign of John II Comnenos (1118–43), whose numerous philanthropies we have described elsewhere, the death penalty was practically abolished; it was never once employed; mutilation, as well, was never carried out in John's reign.[16]

Public philanthropy and private charity were among the best aspects of Byzantine civilization. The Church and the monastic institutions were concerned not only with the salvation of man's soul and with metaphysical questions, but manifested also a humanitarian spirit, a warm interest in man's temporal welfare, a dedicated and active concern that man's hunger, pain, and disease be alleviated. The humble contribution of the monk or the peasant, the organized philanthropy of the Church and the support given to humanitarian endeavors by the State, the manual services of men and women of all classes and ranks, the generous contributions of emperors, bishops, or magnates contributed greatly to assuaging the miseries of Byzantine society whether caused by the constant barbaric invasions, by natural catastrophes, or by human injustices.

14. Cf. Downey, "Who is my Neighbor?", pp. 8 ff.
15. Steven Runciman, *Byzantine Civilization* (New York, 1956), pp. 85–86.
16. Nicetas Choniates, *Historia*, 63: "μηδένα διὰ ξυμπάσης αὐτῷ τῆς ἀρχῆς ἢ ψυχῆς στερήσας ἢ ἐς τὸ σῶμα ὁσονοῦν λυμηνάμενος. . . ." Cf. Runciman, *Byzantine Civilization*, p. 86. J. B. Bury, too, did not doubt Choniates's testimony that under John II Comnenos no one was put to death. See *The Cambridge Medieval History*, I, ed. J. M. Hussey (Cambridge, 1966), Preface, p. xix.

The Byzantines laid much weight upon social justice. It was praised when it was evident and regretted when it was absent. John III Dukas Vatatzes (1222–54) is praised because during his reign as ruler of the Nicean Empire he had succeeded in establishing justice and order.[17] On the other hand, among other catastrophes that fell upon the waning Empire of the fourteenth century was a failure of social justice, for rich and powerful magnates were now exploiting the poor and weak. Thus Pletho Gemistos insisted that restoration of social justice was a prerequisite for the revival of the Empire.[18] This concept of social justice had been expressed in the Book of the Prefect (tenth century), in the following words: "God, who created the world and put everything in order, engraved the law with his own hand on the tables, and set it forth for all to see so that it might prevent by a happy discipline the members of the human family from throwing themselves one upon the other and the stronger from crushing the weaker. He desired that all should be weighed among them with a just balance. It is for this reason that it has appeared good to our serenity also to formulate the dispositions which result from the law, so that mankind is governed as is fitting and so that one person does not oppress another." [19]

The concept and sense of equality, social justice, and philanthropia in general which was expressed by Serapion of Thmuis (d. after 362) impregnated the thought-world of Byzantium. Serapion writes: "We pray thee, O God of mercy, for the free and the slaves, for men and women, for the aged and the chil-

17. Nicephoros Gregoras, I, 44: ''ἦσάν γε μὴν ἄμφω τὴν βασιλείαν ἰθύνοντες πάνυ σεμνῶς καὶ κοσμίως καὶ πλείστην ποιούμενοι πρόνοιαν τοῦ δικαιοσύνην τε καὶ εὐνομίαν ἀνθεῖν ἐν ταῖς πόλεσι, πλεονεξίαν τε ἀπεῖναι καὶ ἁρπαγήν.''

18. George Gemistos, ''Εἰς Μανουὴλ Παλαιολόγον περὶ τῶν ἐν Πελοποννήσῳ Πραγμάτων,'' ed. Sp. Lampros, «Παλαιολόγεια καὶ Πελοποννησιακά», III (Athens, 1926), 247, 261–62. Cf. Bakalopoulos, «Ἱστορία τοῦ Νέου Ἑλληνισμοῦ», I, 174 ff.

19. ''Book of the Eparch,'' Zepos-Zepos, *Jus*, II, 371: ''Τὴν τῶν ὄντων ὁ Θεὸς σύστασιν δημιουργήσας ἐν κόσμῳ καὶ εὐταξίᾳ τὸ πᾶν συναρμόσας, δακτύλῳ ἰδίῳ νόμῳ ἐγχαράξας ταῖς πλαξίν, ἐνεδήλωσεν ἀριδηλότατα, ὡς ἂν δι' αὐτοῦ τὸ τῶν ἀνθρώπων φῦλον εὖ διατιθέμενον μὴ ἀναισχύντως ἐπιπηδᾷ τῷ ἑτέρῳ θάτερος μήτε μὴν ὁ κρείττων τὸν ἐλάττονα καταβλάπτῃ, ἀλλὰ πάντα δικαίῳ διαταλαντεύηται. Διὰ τοῦτο καὶ τὴν ἡμετέραν γαληνότητα τὰ ῥηθησόμενα νόμων ἐχόμενα διαθεῖναι εὐδόκησεν . . . καὶ μὴ θάτερος καταδυναστεύῃ θάτερον.'' E. N. Freshfield, *Roman Law in the Later Roman Empire* (Cambridge, 1938), p. 1; cf. ''Epanagoge,'' Zepos-Zepos, *Jus*, II, 317.

dren, and manifest Your philanthropia to all. . . . We beseech Thee for the travellers . . . for the bereaved, the captives and the poor. Relieve every one, free the captives, redeem the poor, console all. . . . We beseech Thee for the sick; grant them health . . . for Thou art the Saviour and Benefactor." [20] Here we may agree with the anonymous biographer of Joannes Acatios or Acatzes [21] that Constantinople and the Byzantine Empire in general was a country in which hospitality was offered to the stranger, charitable institutions were maintained, and the poor were received and entertained. [22] When it fell to the Turks one of its last writers lamented that even its numerous hospitals, xenones, ptochotropheia, gerocomeia, and other philanthropic institutions were destroyed and could not offer their services to the throngs of miserable captives. [23]

The whole State and Constantinople in particular enjoyed the reputation of a hospitable city to citizens and non-citizens alike. Even when the capital had been impoverished in the last two centuries, it maintained its charities and care for the poor and the strangers. Another eyewitness of its collapse lamented that when it fell under the Turks, the famous city could no longer maintain its many philanthropic institutions. [24] Despite, however,

20. Serapion of Thmuis, "Εὐχὴ ὑπὲρ Λαοῦ," ed. Georg Wobbermin, *Altchristliche liturgische Stucke aus der Kirche Aegyptens nebst einem dogmatischen brief des bischofs Serapion von Thmuis* (Leipzig, 1899), p. 19: "Δεόμεθα θεὲ τῶν οἰκτιρμῶν ὑπὲρ ἐλευθέρων καὶ δούλων, ἀρρένων καὶ γυναικῶν, γερόντων καὶ παιδίων, πενήτων καὶ πλουσίων· πᾶσιν τὸ ἴδιόν σου δεῖξον χρηστόν· καὶ τὴν ἰδίαν σου πᾶσιν πρότεινον φιλανθρωπίαν . . . παρακαλοῦμεν ὑπὲρ ἀποδημούντων . . . ὑπὲρ τεθλιμμένων καὶ δεδεμένων καὶ πενήτων . . . σὺ γὰρ εἶ ὁ σωτὴρ καὶ εὐεργέτης." Cf. Murray, *A Study of the Life of Andreas*, p. 115.

21. Halkin, *Hag. Graeca*, I, 226.

22. Theodore Dousas and Leo Allatius, "In Georgium Acropolitam Notae," ed. by Immanuel Bekker, *Georgii Acropolitae Annales*, CSHB (Bonn, 1836), p. 206.

23. Andronicos Kallistos, *Monodia de Constantinopoli Capta*, MPG, CLXI, col. 1135A: "ποῦ δὲ σεμνεῖα καὶ παρθενῶνες . . . ποῦ δὲ νοσοκομεῖα καὶ πτωχοτροφεῖα ὧν ἡ πόλις πολλὴν ἐποίει σπουδήν;" cf. col. 1140D. With the fall of Constantinople all beneficiaries lost: "οἱ γέροντες τὴν γηροκομῶσαν . . . οἱ γεωργοὶ τὴν δικαιοσύνην . . . οἱ ὁδοιπόροι τὴν ἀνάπαυλαν . . . οἱ πένητες τὴν πορίζουσαν, οἱ πτωχοὶ τὴν τρέφουσαν, οἱ αἰχμάλωτοι τὴν ῥύουσαν, οἱ ὀρφανοὶ τὴν μητέρα, αἱ χῆραι τὴν προστάτιν."

24. George Scholarios, "Θρῆνος . . . ἐν τῷ ὄρει τοῦ Μενοικέως ἐν τῇ Μονῇ τοῦ Τιμίου Προδρόμου," by Louis Petit, X. A. Siderides and Martin Jugie, *Oeuvres complètes de Georges Scholarios*, I (Paris, 1928), 287; cf. p. 294, 4–8.

the social injustices, the poverty, and the social paralysis of the
last decades of the Byzantine state, philanthropia was still one
of the finest elements of its civilization and culture.

Thus, Andronikos Kallistos, who was aware of the philanthropic virtues of his compatriots and his State, could not com-
prehend how the *Philanthropos Theos* of the Byzantines, who
had manifested His philanthropia to them in so many and diverse
ways for a period of more than ten centuries, had abandoned
them now to massacres, humiliation, and slavery.[25]

Perhaps it was the *dikaeosyne* and not the philanthropia of
God that was disclosed on Tuesday, May 29, 1453. Perhaps many
Byzantines had forgotten. It is at least certain that the wealthy
of the fourteenth century, for example, refused to support the
needy. Social injustice was great. The aristocracy even refused
to place their wealth at the disposal of their Emperor when their
country was on the brink of destruction.[26] That is among other
reasons the calamities that fell upon Constantinople and the
Byzantine Empire in general were attributed to lack of philanthropy and goodness; to the absence of social justice, to greediness, selfishness, and other immoral and materialistic concerns.[27]

Nevertheless, we have seen that much evidence corroborates
the claims of Theophylactos Simocattes, Photios, Nicholas
Mysticos, John Cantacuzenos, Alexios Makrembolites, and other
Byzantine authors that, in general, the Byzantine Empire was a
most philanthropic state. The Byzantines were profoundly concerned with the human person and the reality of God; thus they
adhered to ultimate values, and their social behavior was often
guided by principles of eternal worth.

25. Andronikos Kallistos, MPG, CLXI, col. 1136: "ὦ θειότατε βασιλεῦ,
πῶς οὕτω φιλάνθρωπος ὢν κατὰ πάντα τρόπον φιλανθρωπίαν ὑπὲρ τοῦ
γένους [τῶν Ἑλλήνων] οὐκ ἀμελήσας ποιεῖν, νῦν ἠνέσχου καταλιπεῖν
ἡμᾶς εἰς δυστυχίαν καὶ δουλείαν τοσαύτην . . . "
26. Cf. Georgios Scholarios, "Πρὸς τὸν βασιλέα [Κωνσταντῖνον τὸν
Παλαιολόγον] Ἀπολογητικός," ed. Sp. Lampros, «Παλαιολόγεια καὶ
Πελοποννησιακά», II (Athens, 1924), 95–96: Leonardus Chiensis, *Historia
Constantinopolitanae Urbis a Mahumett II Captae*, MPG, CLIX, col. 934AB.
27. See George Zoras, «Περὶ τὴν Ἅλωσιν τῆς Κωνσταντινουπόλεως»
(Athens, 1959), pp. 166–69. Cf. *ibid.*, p. 168:
      "οἱ πάντες ἦσαν πονηροί, χωρὶς ἀγαθωσύνην,
      καὶ μόνον τρεῖς ἢ τέσσαρες εἶχαν δικαιοσύνην."

Envoi

" Ἡδὺς ὁ λιμὴν τοῖς πλέουσι τυγχάνει
καὶ τοῖς γραφεῦσι τέρμα τῆς βίβλου πάλιν·
ἄμφω γὰρ ἀνάπαυλαν εἰσφέρει πόνων." [1]

[1] Timothy Monachos, " Ἔκθεσις καὶ Ὑποτύπωσις," ed. A. Dmitrievsky, *Typika*, p. 655.

Bibliography

Only works immediately relevant to Byzantine philanthropia and institutions are included. Works of classical Greek authors and Church writers cited in Chapter 1, "The Hellenic and Christian Background," are omitted. Not included here are auxiliary articles and books cited in the footnotes.

General Works

Altaner, Berthold. *Patrology.* Tr. Hild C. Graef. Edinburgh-London: 1958.

Beck, Hans Georg. *Kirche und Theologische Literatur im Byzantinischen Reich.* Munich: 1959.

Bible, The. Revised Standard Version. New York: 1957.

Demetrakos, D. «Μέγα Λεξικὸν τῆς Ἑλληνικῆς Γλώσσης», 9 vols. Athens: 1949–1950.

Dolger, Franz. *Regesten der Kaiserurkunden des Ostromischen Reiches.* Corpus der Griechischen Urkunden des Mittelalters und der Neueren Zeit, 2 vols. Munich and Berlin: 1924–1925.

Ehrhard, A. *Uberlieferung und Bestand der hagiographischen und homiletischen Literatur der griechischen Kirche von den anfangen bis zum ende des 16. jahrhunderts,* 3 vols. Leipzig: 1937–1952.

Grumel, V. *La Chronologie.* Traité d'études byzantines. Paris: 1958.

Grumel, V. *Les Régestes des actes du patriarcat de Constantinople.* Bucarest: 1947.

290

Halkin, François. *Bibliotheca Hagiographica Graeca.* 3 vols. Third edition. Brussels: 1957.

Krumbacher, Karl. *Geschichte der Byzantinischen Litteratur.* Munich: 1897.

Liddell, H. G. and Scott, Robert. *A Greek-English Lexicon.* New edition by H. S. Jones. Oxford: 1958.

Moravcsik, Gyula. *Byzantinoturcica.* Vol. I. Berlin: 1958.

Quasten, Johannes. *Patrology.* Vol. III. Westminster, Md.: 1960.

Ramsay, William M. *The Historical Geography of Asia Minor.* Reprint. Amsterdam: 1962.

Sophocles, E. A. *Greek Lexicon of the Roman and Byzantine Periods.* New York: 1900.

Sources

Acropolites, Constantine. *Laudatio S Thomaidis,* ed. H. Delehaye and P. Peeters. *Acta Sanctorum.* November, Vol. IV. Brussels: 1925.

———. " Ἑτέρα Διαθήκη," ed. M. Treu. *Deltion tes historikes kai ethnologikes etaerias tes Ellados.* Vol. IV. Athens: 1892.

Acropolites, George. *Annales, ed.* Immanuel Bekker. Bonn: 1836.

"Acta Graeca SS Davidis, Symeonis et Georgii, Mitylenae in insula Lesbo," *Analecta Bollandiana.* Vol. XVIII. Brussels: 1899.

"Actes de Chilandar," ed. Louis Petit and B. Korablev. *Vizantiiskii Vremennik.* Vol. XVII, Supplement No. 5, St. Petersburg: 1911.

Actes de Lavra, ed. G. Rouillard and Paul Collomp. Vol. I. Paris: 1937.

Agapetos, Deacon. *Exposito Capitum Admonitoriorum,* ed. Migne. *Patrologia Graeca.* Vol. LXXXVI. 1.

Agathias. *Historiarum,* ed. B. G. Niebuhr. Bonn: 1828.

"Miracula S. Anastasii Persae," No. XII, *Acta Sanctorum* January. Vol. III. Paris: 1863.

Anastasios Sinaites. *Quaestiones,* ed. Migne. *Patrologia Graeca.* Vol. LXXXIX.

Antiochos Strategos. *Captivitas Hierosolyme,* ed. tr. Gerard Garitte. *La Prise de Jérusalem par les Perses en 614,* Corpus Scriptorum Christianorum Orientalium. Louvain: 1960.

Antonios Placentinos. *Itinera Hierosolymitan,* ed. Paul Geyer. *Itinera Hierosolumitana Saeculi III–VIII.* Prague: 1898.

Ashburner, Walter. "The Farmer's Law," *Journal of Hellenic Studies*. Vol. XXX. 1910.

Asterios of Amaseia. *Homilia No. 4*, ed. Migne. *Patrologia Graeca*. Vol. CXV.

Athanasios of Alexandria. *De Incarnatione*, ed. Frank L. Cross. *Athanasius De Incarnatione*. London: 1939.

———. *Epistles*, tr. Archibald Robertson. *Nicene and Post-Nicene Fathers*. Vol. IV. Grand Rapids, Mich: 1953.

———. *Oratio II Contra Arianos; Vita S Antoni; Epistola Episcoporum Aegypti et Libyae*, ed. Migne. *Patrologia Graeca*. Vol. XXVI.

———. *Historia Arianorum*, ed. Migne. *Patrologia Graeca*. Vol. XXV.

Attaleiates, Michael. *Diataxis*, ed. Constantine N. Sathas. «Μεσαιωνικὴ Βιβλιοθήκη». Vol. I. Venice: 1872.

———. *Historia, ed.* Immanuel Bekker. Bonn: 1853.

Aufhauser, J. B. *Miracula S. Georgii*. Leipzig: 1913.

"De S. Barnaba Apostolo," *Acta Sanctorum*, Vol. II. June. Paris and Rome: 1867.

Basil I. *Paraenesis to Leo*, and *Second Paraenesis*, ed. Migne. *Patrologia Graeca*. Vol. CVII.

Basil the Great. *Epistles*, ed. tr. R. J. Deferrari. *Saint Basil—the Letters*. Loeb Classical Library. Vol. II. London: 1928.

———. *Homilia VIII in Hexaemeron*, ed. Migne. *Patrologia Graeca*. Vol. XXIX.

———. *In Illud Dictum Evangelii*, ed. Migne. *Patrologia Graeca*. Vol. XXXI.

———. *Homilia in Divites*, ed. Migne. *Patrologia Graeca*. Vol. XXXI.

———. *Regulae Brevius Tractatae* and *Regulae Fusius Tractatae*, ed. Migne. *Patrologia Graeca*. Vol. XXXI.

———. *Sermo Asceticus*, ed. Migne. *Patrologia Graeca*. Vol. XXXI.

———. *De Spiritu Sancto*, ed. Benoit-Bruche, *Basil de Césarée Traité du Saint-Esprit*. Paris: 1946.

Beneshevich, V. "Zavieschanie vizantiiskago boiarina XI vieka," *Zhurnal ministerstva narodnago prosvieshchenia*. Vol. IX. May, 1907.

de Boor, Charles. *Vita S Euthymii*. Berlin: 1888.

Boucherie, A. "Vita Sanctae Euphrosynae," *Analecta Bollandiana*. Vol. II. Paris-Brussels: 1883.

Callinicos. *De Vita S Hypatii Liber.* Seminarii Philologorum Bonnensis Sodales. Leipzig: 1895.

Cecaumenos. *Strategicon,* ed. B. Wassiliewsky and V. Jernstedt. *Cecaumeni Strategicon et . . . de Officiis Regiis Libellus.* St. Petersburg: 1896.

Cedrenos, George. *Historiarum Compendium,* ed. Immanuel Bekker. Vols. I and II. Bonn: 1838.

Choniates, Nicetas. *Historia,* ed. Immanuel Bekker. Bonn: 1835.

Chronicon Paschale, ed. L. Dindorf. Bonn: 1832.

Clugnet, M. Leon. "Vie et récits de l'abbé Daniel de Scété," *Revue de l'orient chrétien.* Vol. V. Paris: 1900.

Codinos, George. *De Officialibus Palatii Constantinopolitani,* ed. Immanuel Bekker. Bonn: 1839.

Codinos, George [Pseudo]. *Scriptores Originum Constantinopolitanarum,* ed. Theodore Preger. Leipzig: 1901–1907.

Comnena, Anna. *Alexias,* ed. Bernard Leib. *Anne Comnène Alexiade.* 3 vols. Paris: 1937–1945.

Constantine Porphyrogenitos. *De Cerimoniis,* ed. Albert Vogt. *Constantine VII Porphyrogenète. Le Livre de Cérémonies.* Vols. I and II. Paris: 1935–1939.

———. *Selectus Legum,* ed. Migne. *Patrologia Graeca.* Vol. CXIII.

Cydones, Demetrios. *Epistolae,* ed. Raymond L. Loenertz. *Demetrius Cydones Correspondence.* Vol. I. Vatican City: 1956.

Cyrillos of Alexandria. *Homilae Paschales,* ed. Migne. *Patrologia Graeca.* Vol. LXXVII.

Darrouzès Jean. *Epistoliers byzantins de Xe siècle.* Paris: 1960.

Dawes, Elizabeth, and Norman H. Baynes. *Three Byzantine Saints.* Oxford: 1948.

Decrees and Canons of the Seven Ecumenical Councils. The Nicene and Post-Nicene Fathers. Vol. XIV. Grand Rapids, Mich.: 1956.

Delehaye, Hippolyte. *Deux Typica byzantins de l'époque des Paleologues.* Brussels: 1921.

———. "Monumenta Latrensia Hagiographica," *Milet.* Vol. III. 1. Berlin: 1913.

———. *Synaxarium Ecclesiae Constantinopolitanae.* Propylaeum ad Acta Sanctorum Novembris. Brussels: 1902.

———. "Une Vie inédite de Saint Jean l'aumonier," *Analecta Bollandiana.* Vol. XLV. Brussels: 1927.

Dimitrov, Dimitre P. "Μαρτύριον τοῦ ἁγίου . . . Ἀλεξάνδρου."

Bulletin de l'institut archéologique bulgare. Vol. VIII. 1934.

Dindorf, Wilhelm. *Themistii Orationes.* Hildesheim: 1961.

Dmitrievsky, A. *Euchologion.* Kiev: 1894.

——. *Opisanie Liturgicheskikh Rukopisei.* Vol. I. Typika. Kiev: 1895.

Dolger, Frank. *Aus den Schatzkammern des heiligen Berges.* Munich: 1948.

Doukakis, Constantine. "Life of Saint Gregory, Bishop of Assos." «Μέγας Συναξαριστής». March. Athens: 1891.

Dvornik, F. *La Vie de Saint Grégoire le décapolite et les Slaves macédoniens au IXe Siècle.* Paris: 1926.

"Εἰς Βασιλέα," ed. Bruno Keil. *Aelii Aristidis.* Vol. II. Berlin: 1898.

Efstratiades, S. "Τυπικὸν . . . Μάμαντος," *Hellenica.* Vol. I, no. 2. Athens: 1928.

Ellissen, Adolf, ed. *Analekten der mittel-und-neugriechischen Literatur.* Vol. IV. Leipzig: 1860.

Ephraemios, *Imperatorum et Patriarcharum,* ed. Immanuel Bekker. *Corpus Scriptorum Historiae Byzantinae.* Bonn: 1840.

Epiphanios. *Adversus Haereses,* ed. Migne. *Patrologia Graeca.* Vol. XLII, part 2.

Eusebios of Caesarea. *De Vita Constantini,* ed. Ivar A. Heikel. *Eusebius Werke.* Vol. I. Leipzig: 1902.

——. *Ecclesiastical History,* ed. Edward Schwartz. *Eusebius Werke.* Vol. II, part 2. Leipzig: 1908.

——. *Fragments to Marcellus,* ed. Erich Klostermann. *Eusebius Werke.* Leipzig: 1906.

Eustathios of Thessalonica. *Laudatio S Philothei Opsiciani.* Migne, *Patrologia Graeca.* Vol. CXXXVI.

——. "Oratio ad Manuelem Imperatorem," ed. W. Regel. *Fontes Rerum Byzantinarum.* Vol. 1, part I. St. Petersburg: 1892.

——. *Oratio in Psalmum XLVIII,* ed. Migne. *Patrologia Graeca.* Vol. CXXXVI.

Evagrios. *Ecclesiastical History,* ed. J. Bidez and I. Parmentier. *The Ecclesiastical History of Evagrius with the Scholia.* London, 1898.

Fourmy, Marie-Henriette, and Maurice Leroy. "La Vie de S. Phila-rète," *Byzantion.* Vol. IX, Fasc. 1. 1934.

Gedeon, Manuel. «Βυζαντινὸν Ἑορτολόγιον». Constantinople: 1899.

Genesios, *Regum,* ed. Immanuel Bekker. Bonn: 1834.

George Monachos. *Chronicon,* ed. Charles de Boor. Vols. I and II. Leipzig: 1904.

Georgios Monachos. *Chronicon,* ed. E. Muralt. St. Petersburg: 1859.

Gheyn, J. Van Den. "Vita et Acta S Macarii Hegumeni Monasterii Pelecetes," *Analecta Bollandiana.* Vol. XVI. 1897.

Glycas, Michael. *Annales,* ed. Immanuel Bekker. Bonn: 1856.

Goar, Jacobus. *Euchologion Sive Rituale Graecorum.* Venice: 1730.

Grégoire, H. and M. A. Kugener. *Marc la Diacre. Vie de Porphyre, évêque de Gaza.* Paris: 1930.

——. "Saint Demetrianos, évêque de Chytri," *Byzantinische Zeitschrift.* Vol. XVI. 1907.

Gregoras, Nicephoros. *Byzantinae Historiae,* ed. L. Schopenus. *Corpus Scriptorum Historiae Byzantininae.* Vol. I. Bonn: 1829.

Gregorios Monachos. "Vita S Lazari," *Acta Sanctorum.* November. Vol. III. Brussels: 1910.

Gregory Nazianzenos. *Exemplum Testamenti,* ed. Migne. *Patrologia Graeca.* Vol. XXXVII.

——. *Epistolae,* ed. Migne. *Patrologia Graeca.* Vol. XXXVII.

——. *Oratio IV,* ed. Migne. *Patrologia Graeca.* Vol. XXXV.

——. *Oratio XLIII—In Laudem Basilii Magni,* ed. Migne. *Patrologia Graeca.* Vol. XLVI.

——. *Oratio XIV—De Pauperum Amore,* ed. Migne, *Patrologia Graeca.* Vol. XXXV.

——. "The Panegyric of St. Basil," ed. Fernard Boulenger. *Grégoire de Nazianze. Discours funèbres.* Paris: 1908.

Gregory of Nyssa. *De Pauperibus Amandis,* ed. Migne. *Patrologia Graeca.* Vol. XLVI.

——. *De Vita S. Macrinae,* ed. Migne. *Patrologia Graeca.* Vol. XLVI.

——. "Encomium," ed. James A. Stein. *Encomium of St. Gregory on his Brother St. Basil.* Washington: 1928.

Gregory the Presbyter. *Life of St. Gregory the Theologian,* ed. Migne. *Patrologia Graeca.* Vol. XXXV.

Halkin, F. "La Vision de Kaiounos et le sort éternel de Philentolos Olympion," *Analecta Bollandiana.* Vol. LXIII. Brussels: 1945.

——. "Περὶ τοῦ Φιλεντόλου ᾿Ολυμπίου," *Analecta Bollandiana.* Vol. LXIII. Brussels: 1945.

Heisenberg, A. *Nicephori Blemmydae Curriculum vitae et Carmina.* Leipzig: 1896.

Ignatios. *Vita S. Nicephori*, ed. Charles de Boor. *Nicephori Archiepiscopi Constantinopolitani Opuscula Historica*. Leipzig: 1880.

Ignatios the Deacon. *Vita Tarasii Archiepiscopi Constantinopolitani*, ed. I. A. Heikel. *Acta Societatis Scientiarum Fennicae*. Vol. XVII. Helsingfors: 1891.

Ioacheim Iberites. "Διαθήκη τοῦ Συμβατίου Κουροπαλάτου τοῦ Πακουριάνου," *Orthodoxia*. Vol. V, No. 60. December, 1930.

Ioannou, Theophilos. «Μνημεῖα Ἁγιολογικά». Venice: 1884.

Joannes Cantacuzenos. *Historia*, ed. L. Schopenus. Vol. III. Bonn: 1832.

Joannes Chrysostomos. *Ecloga*, ed. Migne. *Patrologia Graeca*. Vol. LXIII.

————. *De Eleemosynis*, ed. Migne. *Patrologia Graeca*. Vol. LX.

————. *Homilia de Capto Eutropio*, ed. Migne. *Patrologia Graeca*. Vol. LII.

————. "Homilies XXVI and XXVIII," *Commentarius in Sanctum Joannem Apostolum et Evangelistam*, ed. Migne. *Patrologia Graeca*. Vol. LIX.

————. *In Matthaeum Homilia LXVI*, ed. Migne. *Patrologia Graeca*. Vol. LVIII.

————. *In Psalmum 48*, ed. Migne. *Patrologia Graeca*. Vol. LV.

————. *Oratio LVIII*, ed. Migne. *Patrologia Graeca*. Vol. LVIII.

Joannes Cinnamos. *Epitome*, ed. A. Meinek. *Corpus Scriptorum Historiae Byzantinae*. Bonn: 1836.

Joannes Climacos. *Scala Paradisi*, ed. Migne. *Patrologia Graeca*. Vol. LXXXVIII.

Joannes Moschos. *Pratum Spirituale*, ed. Migne. *Patrologia Graeca*. Vol. LXXXVII. part 3.

John of Ephesos. "Lives of Mary and Euphemia," ed. tr. E. W. Brooks. *Patrologia Orientalis*. Vol. XVII, Fasc. 1. Paris: 1923.

Joshua the Stylite. *Chronicle*, tr. William Wright. Cambridge: 1882.

Julian. *Epistles*, ed. J. Bidez. *L'Empereur Julien, oeuvres complètes*. Vol. I, part 2. Paris: 1924.

Justinian. *Novels*, ed. R. Schoell and G. Kroll. *Corpus Juris Civilis*. Vol. III. Berlin: 1928.

Kabasilas, Nicholas. *Life in Christ*, ed. W. Gass and M. Heinze. *Die Mystik des Nikolaus Cabasilas*. Leipzig: 1899.

de Khitrowo, B. *Itinéraires russes en orient*. Geneva: 1889.

Kurtz, Eduard. "Τύπος καὶ Παράδοσις τῆς Λαύρας τοῦ [ἀγίου] Σάββα." *Byzantinische Zeitschrift.* Vol. III. 1894.

―――. "Zwei griechische texte uber die hl. Theophano, Die Gemanlin Kaisers Leo VI," *Mémoires de l'Académie Imperiale des Sciences de St.-Petersbourg.* St. Petersburg: 1898.

Lampros, Spyridon. "Διαθήκη Παύλου τοῦ Λατρηνοῦ." NE Vol. 12. Athens, 1915.

―――. "Λόγος Παρηγορητικὸς περὶ Δυστυχίας καὶ Εὐτυχίας," and "Ἡμπέριος καὶ Μαργαρώνα," *Collection de romans grecs en langue vulgaire et en vers.* Paris: 1880.

―――. "Life of St. Nicon," *Neos Hellenomnemon.* Vol. III, part 1. Athens: 1906.

―――. "Ὁ Μαρκιανὸς Κῶδιξ 524." *Neos Hellenomnemon.* Vol. VIII. Athens: 1911.

Laourdas, Basil. "Μητροφάνους Βίος τοῦ ὁσίου Διονυσίου τοῦ Ἀθωνίτου," *Archeion Pontou.* Vol. XXI. Athens: 1956.

Latysev, Basil. *Menologii Anonymi Byzantini.* Fasciculus I and 2. St. Petersburg: 1911 and 1912.

Leo Diaconos. *Historiae,* ed. C. B. Hasi. Bonn: 1878.

Leontios of Neapolis. *Life of St. John the Eleemosynary,* ed. H. Gelzer. *Leontios' von Neapolis, Lebendes heiligen Iohannes des barinherzigen erzbischofs von Alexandrien.* Leipzig: 1893.

―――. "Vita S. Symeone Sale Confessore," *Acta Sanctorum,* July. Vol. I. Paris and Rome: 1867.

Loparev, Ch. M. "Life of St. Eudocimos," *Bulletin de l'institut russe à Constantinople.* Vol. XIII. 1908.

―――. "Zhitie sv Kirilla Fileota." *Vizantiiskii Vremennik.* Vol. IV. 1897.

―――. "Περί τινων βίων ἀγίων Ἑλληνιστὶ γεγραμμένων." *Vizantiiskii Vremennik.* Vol. IV. 1897.

Liudprand of Cremona. *Works,* tr. F. A. Wright. London: 1930.

Makarios. *Homilies,* ed. H. Dorries. *Die 50 Geistlichen Homilien des Makarios.* Berlin: 1964.

Makrembolites, Eustathios. "Τὸ καθ' Ὑσμίνην καὶ Ὑσμινίαν Δρᾶμα," ed. Rudolph Hercher. *Erotici Scriptores Graeci.* Vol. II. Leipzig: 1859.

Malalas, Joannes. *Chronographia,* ed. Ludwig Dindorf. Bonn: 1831.

Malingrey, A. M. *Jean Chrysostom. Lettres à Olympias.* Sources chrétiennes. Paris: 1947.

Manasses, Constantine. *Synopsis Chronike*, ed. B. G. Niebuhr. *Corpus Scriptorum Historiae Byzantinae*. Bonn: 1837.

Mansi, Joannes D. *Sacrorum Conciliorum Nova et Amplissima Collectio*. Vol. XVI. Venice: 1902.

"Life of St. Martha the Younger," *Acta Sanctorum*, May. Vol. V. Paris and Rome: 1866.

Martini, E. "Life of St. Luke the Younger," *Analecta Bollandiana*. Vol. XIII. 1894.

Martyrium Sancti Martyris Zenobii, ed. Migne. *Patrologia Graeca*. Vol. CXV.

Matranga, P. *Anecdota Graeca*. Rome: 1850.

Maximos the Confessor. *Capita Theologica*, ed Migne. *Patrologia Graeca*. Vol. XCI.

———. *De Caritate*, ed. Migne. *Patrologia Graeca*. Vol. XC.

Menologium, ed. Migne. *Patrologia Graeca*. Vol. CXVII.

Mercati, Ioannis and Pius F. de Cavalieri. *Codices Vaticani Graeci, Bibliothecae Apostolicae Vaticanae*. Vol. I. Rome: 1923.

———. "Gli aneddoti d'un Codice Bolognese," *Byzantische Zeitschrift*. Vol. VI. 1897.

Metaphrastes, Symeon. *Vita S. Joannis Calybitae*, ed. Migne. *Patrologia Graeca*. Vol. CXIV.

———. *Vita S. Joannis Chrysostomi*, ed. Migne. *Patrologia Graeca*. Vol. CXIV.

———. *Vita S. Clementis Ancyrani*, ed. Migne. *Patrologia Graeca*. Vol. CXIV.

———. *Vita et Conversatio Sanctae Euphrosynes Alexandrinae*, ed. Migne. *Patrologia Graeca*. Vol. CXIV.

———. *Vita S. Euthymii*, ed. Migne. *Patrologia Graeca*. Vol. CXIV.

———. *Vita S. Marciani Presbyteri*, ed. Migne. *Patrologia Graeca*. Vol. CXIV.

———. *Precationes*, ed. Migne. *Patrologia Graeca*. Vol. CXIV.

———. *Vita S. Sampsonii*, ed. Migne. *Patrologia Graeca*. Vol. CXIV.

———. *Vita S. Theodosii*, ed. Migne. *Patrologia Graeca*. Vol. CXIV.

———. *Vita SS Cyri et Joannis*, ed. Migne. *Patrologia Graeca*, Vol. CXIV.

Metochites, Theodoros. "Νιχαεύς," ed. Constantine Sathas. «Μεσαιωνικὴ Βιβλιοθήκη». Vol. I. Venice: 1872.

Meyer, Ph. *Die Haupturkenden fur die Geschichte der Athosklos- ter.* Leipzig: 1894.

Miklosich, Fr. and J. Muller. *Acta et Diplomata Graeca Medii Aevi Sacra et Profana.* 6 vols. Venice: 1860–1890.

Mommsen, Theodore. *Digesta Justiniani Augusti.* Vol. II, second printing. Berlin: 1963.

Morrison, E. F. *St. Basil and His Rule.* London: 1912.

Murray, Sara. *A Study of the Life of Andreas, The Fool for the Sake of Christ.* Borna-Leipzig: 1910.

Neilos of Ancyra. *Peristeria,* ed. Migne. *Patrologia Graeca.* Vol. LXXIX.

Neophytos. "Τυπικὴ Διαθήκη," ed. Frederick E. Warren. *Archae- ologia.* Vol. XLVII. London: 1882.

de Nessel, Daniel. *Catalogia Bibliothecae Caesareae Manuscripto- rum.* Vienna: 1690.

Nicene and Post-Nicene Fathers of the Christian Church, ed. Philip Schaff. Vol. X. New York, 1888.

Nicephoros Blemmydes. *Oratio de Regis Officiis,* ed. Migne, *Patro- logia Graeca.* Vol. CXLII.

Nicephoros Callistos Xanthopoulos, *Ecclesiastical History,* ed. Migne, *Patrologia Graeca.* Vol. CXLVI.

———. *Patriarcharum Constantinopolitanorum,* ed. Migne. *Patro- logia Graeca.* Vol. CXLVII.

Nicetas. *Life of St. Andrew the Hierosolymite,* ed. Papadopoulos- Kerameus. «'Ανάλεκτα 'Ιεροσολυμιτικῆς Σταχυολογίας». Vol. V. St. Petersburg: 1898.

Nicholas Kataskepenos. *Life of St. Cyril Phileotes,* ed. Etienne Sar- gologos. *La Vie de Saint Cyrille le philéote, moine byzantin.* Brussels: 1964.

Nicholas Mysticos. *Epistles,* ed. Migne. *Patrologia Graeca.* Vol. CXI.

———. " 'Ομιλία εἰς τὴν ἅλωσιν τῆς Θεσσαλονίκης," ed. John Tsaras. *Makedonica.* Vol. I. 1940.

Nicholas, Patriarch of Constantinople. "De Vita Monastica," ed. Angelo Maii. *Scriptorum Veterum Nova Collectio.* Vol. IX. Rome: 1837.

Nissen, Th., ed., "De SS Cyri et Johannis Vitae Formis," *Analecta Bollandiana.* Vol. LVII. 1939.

Pachymeres, George. *De Michaele et Andronico Palaeologis,* ed.

Immanuel Bekker. *Corpus Scriptorum Historiae Byzantinae.* Vol. I. Bonn: 1835.

Palladios. *History Lausiaca,* ed. Cuthbert Butler. *The Lausiac History of Palladius.* Cambridge: 1898.

———. *Vita S Joannis Chrysostomi,* ed. P. R. Coleman-Norton. *Paladii Dialogus de Vita S Joannis Chrysostomi.* Cambridge: 1928.

Papadopoulos, N. P. «Εὐχολόγιον τὸ Μέγα». Athens, n. d.

Papadopoulos-Kerameus, A. "Life of St. Paraskeve the Younger," «'Ανάλεκτα 'Ιεροσολυμιτικῆς Σταχυολογίας». Vol. I. St. Petersburg: 1891.

———. "Life of Saint Paulus the Bishop and John the Presbyter." «'Ανάλεκτα 'Ιεροσολυμιτικῆς Σταχυολογίας». Vol. V. St. Petersburg: 1898.

———. *Varia Graeca Sacra.* St. Petersburg: 1909.

Papaoeconomou, Christos. «'Ο Πολιοῦχος τοῦ "Αργους "Αγιος Πέτρος». Athens: 1908.

Papoulia, Basilike. "Die Vita des Heiligen Philotheos vom Athos," *Sudost-Forschungen.* Vol. XXII. 1963.

Pertusi, Agostino. *Giorgio di Pisidia Poemi.* Buchkunstverlag Ettal: 1960.

Petit, Louis. "Life of St. Athanasios the Athonite." *Analecta Bollandiana.* Vol. XXV. 1906.

———. "Διάταξις . . . Μανουὴλ Μοναχοῦ." *Bulletin de l'institut russe à Constantinople.* Vol. VI. 1900.

———. "Le Monastère de Notre-Dame de Pitié," *Bulletin de l'institut russe à Constantinople.* Vol. VI. 1900.

———. "Typikon de Grégoire Pacourianos pour le monastère de Petritzos (Backovo)," *Vizantiiskii Vremennik.* Vol. XI, Supplement No. 1. St. Petersburg: 1904.

———. "Typicon of the Monastery of Cosmosoteira." *Bulletin de l'institut russe à Constantinople.* Vol. XIII. 1908.

———. "Vie de Saint Michel Maleinos." *Revue de l'orient chrétien.* Vol. VII, no. 4. 1902.

Petrides, S. "Le Typikon de Nil Damilas pour le monastère de femmes de Daeonia en Créte," *Bulletin de l'Institut russe à Constantinople.* Vol. XV. Sofia: 1911.

Philotheos. *Kletorologion,* edited by J. B. Bury. *The Administrative System in the Ninth Century with a Revised Text of the Kletorologion of Philotheos.* London: 1911.

Philes, Manuel. *Poems,* ed. E. Miller. *Manuelis Philae Carmina.* Vol. I. Paris: 1855.

Photios. *Epistles,* ed. Joannis N. Valetas. London: 1864.

Photopoulos, Philemon. «'Ανέκδοτα». *Nea Sion.* Vol. XII. Jerusalem: 1912.

Polydeukes, Julios. " Έρμηνεύματα [καί] Καθημερινὴ 'Ομιλία," ed. Anatole Boucherie. *Notices et extraits des manuscrits de la Bibliothèque Nationale.* Vol. XXIII, a.

Procopios of Caesarea. *Opera Omnia,* ed. Jacobus Haury. *Procopii Caesariensis Opera Omnia.* Leipzig: 1905.

Psellos, Michael. *Chronographia,* ed. Emile Renauld. *Michel Psellos Chronographie.* 2 vols. Paris: 1926–1928.

———. "Funeral Orations, No. 4," ed. Constantine Sathas. «Μεσαιωνικὴ Βιβλιοθήκη». Vol. V. Paris: 1878.

Regel, W. "De Theophili imperatoris absolutione," *Analecta Byzantino-Russica.* St. Petersburg: 1891.

———. *Fontes Rerum Byzantinorum.* Vol. I, part 1. St. Petersburg: 1892.

Rhallis, G. A. and M. Potlis. «Σύνταγμα τῶν θείων καὶ ἱερῶν Κανόνων». 6 vols. Athens: 1852–1859.

Riedel, W. and W. E. Crum. *The Canons of Athanasius of Alexandria.* Oxford: 1904.

Synopsis Chronike, ed. Constantine N. Sathas. «Μεσαιωνικὴ Βιβλιοθήκη». Vol. VII. Paris: 1894.

Schwartz, Edward. *Acta Conciliorum Oecumenicorum.* Vol. III. Berlin: 1940.

———. *Kyrillos von Skythopolis.* Leipzig: 1939.

De Scientia Politica, ed. Angelo Mai. *Scriptorum Veterum Nova Collectio.* Vol. II. Rome: 1827.

Scott, S. P. *The Civil Law.* Vol. XVI. Cincinnati: 1932.

Seeck, Otto. *Notitia Dignitatum Accedunt Notitia Urbis Constantinopolitanae et Laterculi Prouinciarum.* Berlin: 1877.

Ševečenko, Ihor. "Alexios Makrembolites and his Dialogue between the Rich and the Poor," *Zbornik Radoba.* Vol. LXV. Belgrade: 1960.

Sewter, E. R. A. *The Chronographia of Michael Psellus.* London: 1952.

Sirmond, Jacob. "Vita S Pauli Junioris in Monte Latro," *Analecta Bollandiana.* Vol. XI. Brussels: 1892.

Sophronios of Jerusalem. *Vita Mariae Aegyptiae* .Migne, *Patrologia Graeca.* Vol. LXXXVII, part 3.

Sozomenos. *Ecclesiastical History,* ed. Joseph Bidez. *Sozomenus Kirchengeschichte.* Berlin: 1960.

Sternbach, Leo. *Analecta Avarica.* Cracow: 1900.

Stethatos, Nicetas. *Life of St. Symeon the New Theologian,* ed. Irene Hausherr, *Orientalia Christiana.* Vol. XII. July–August, 1928.

Symeon Magister, *Chronographia,* ed. Immanuel Bekker. *Corpus Scriptorum Historiae Byzantinae.* Bonn: 1838.

Symeon of Thessalonica. *De Eleemosynis,* ed. Migne. *Patrologia Graeca.* Vol. CXX.

———. *De Fine et Exitu nostro e vita,* ed. Migne. *Patrologia Graeca.* Vol. CLV.

Synesios. *De Regno,* ed. Migne. *Patrologia Graeca.* Vol. LXVI.

Tafel, T. L. F. *Eustathii Opuscula.* Frankfurt: 1832.

Theodore of Paphos. *Life of St. Spyridon,* ed. Paul Van Den Ven. *La Légende de S. Spyridon, évêque de Trimithonte.* Louvain: 1953.

Theodore Studites. *Epistles,* ed. Migne. *Patrologia Graeca.* Vol. XCIX.

———. *Poenae Monasteriales,* ed. Migne. *Patrologia Graeca.* Vol. XCIX. *Iambi de Variis Argumentisana.*

———. *Small Catechism,* ed. Immanuel Auvray. *Sancti Patris nostri et Confessoris Theodori Studitis Praepositi Parva Catechesis.* Paris: 1891.

Theodoretos of Cyrus. *Ecclesiastical History,* ed. Leon Parmentier. *Theodoret Kirchengeschichte,* 2nd edition by F. Scheidweiler, Berlin: 1954.

Theodulos Monachos. *Oratio de Regis Officiis,* ed. Migne. *Patrologia Graeca.* Vol. CXLV.

Theophanes Confessor. *Chronographia,* ed. Carl de Boor. 2 vols. Leipzig: 1883.

Theophanes Continuatus.*Chronographia,* ed. Immanuel Bekker. Bonn: 1938.

Theophylactos of Ochrida. *Epistles,* ed. Migne. *Patrologia Graeca.* Vol. CXXVI.

———. *Institutio Regia,* ed. Migne. *Patrologia Graeca.* Vol. CXXVI.

————. *Oratio im Imperatorem Dominum Alexium Comnenum,* ed. Migne. *Patrologia Graeca.* Vol. CXXVI.

Theophylactos of Simocatta. *Historia,* ed. Charles de Boor. Leipzig: 1887.

Timothy of Alexandria. *Historia Monachorum in Aegypto,* edited by A. J. Festugière. Subsidia Hagiographica No. 34. Brussels: 1961.

Tsiknopoulos, J. P. «Νεοφύτου Πρεσβυτέρου Μοναχοῦ καὶ Ἐγκλείστου Τυπικὴ σὺν Θεῷ Διαθήκη». Larnaca: 1952.

Tunitskij, N. L. *Monumenta ad SS. Cyrilli et Methodii successorum vitas resque gestas pertinentia.* Sergiev Posad: 1918.

Vasiliev, A. A. *Zhitie Filareta Miloctivago.* Odessa: 1900.

Vasilievskii, V. G. "Life of St. George, Archbishop of Amastris," *Trudy.* Vol. III. Petrograd: 1915.

————. "Synaxare of Stephanus Confessor, Archbishop of Sougdaia." *Trudy.* Vol. III. Petrograd: 1915.

"Vita S Andrea Salo," *Acta Sanctorum.* May, Vol. VI. Paris and Rome: 1866.

"Vita S Irene." *Acta Sanctorum.* July, Vol. VI. Paris: 1868.

"Vita S Lazari. " *Acta Sanctorum.* November, Vol. III. Brussels: 1910.

"Vita S Martha." *Acta Sanctorum.* May, Vol. V. Paris and Rome: 1866.

"Vita S Phantinus." *Acta Sanctorum.* August, Vol. VI. Paris: 1868.

"Vita S Symeone Stylite." *Acta Sanctorum.* May, Vol. V. Paris and Rome: 1866.

"Vita S Thomaidis." *Acta Sanctorum.* November, Vol. IV. Brussels: 1925.

Vogt., A. "S Théophylacte de Nicomédie." *Analecta Bollandiana.* Vol. L. 1932.

Vogt, Albert. "Vie de S. Luc le Stylite," *Analecta Bollandiana.* Vol. XXVIII. 1909.

Vogt, A., and I. Hausherr. "Oraison Funèbre de Basile I par son fils Leon VI le Sage," *Orientalia Christiana.* Vol. XXVI. 1, No. 77. 1932.

Vorst, C. Van de. "La Vie de S. Evariste, higoumène à Constantinople," *Analecta Bollandiana.* Vol. XLI.

Vryonis, Speros, Jr. "The Will of a Provincial Magnate, Eustathius Boilas (1059)," *Dumbarton Oaks Papers,* No. 11. Washington: 1957.

Usener, Hermann. *Der Heilige Theodosios.* Leipzig: 1890.

Uspenski, Th. "Τακτικόν . . . Μιχαήλ. . . καὶ Θεοδώρας. . . ." *Bulletin de l'institut russe à Constantinople.* Vol. III. Sophia: 1898.

Wagner, Wilhelm. *Carmina Graeci Medii Aevi.* Leipzig: 1874.

Zepos, J., and P. Zepos. *Jus Graeco-Romanum.* Vol. I. Athens, 1931.

Zonaras, Joannes. *Epitomae Historiarum,* ed. Theodorus Buttner-Wobst. Vol. III. Bonn: 1897.

Modern Works

Agourides, Savas. «Ἡ Κοινοκτημοσύνη ἐν τῇ πρώτῃ Ἐκκλησίᾳ». Thessalonike: 1963.

———. "The Social Character of Orthodoxy," *The Greek Orthodox Theological Review,* Vol. VIII, Nos. 1 and 2 (Summer 1962–Winter 1962–1963), pp. 7–20.

Alexander, Paul J. *The Patriarch Nicephorus of Constantinople.* Oxford: 1958.

Alivizatos, C. N., and E. P. Lekos. "Ἡ Βυζαντινὴ Ἰατρικὴ κατὰ τὴν ἐποχὴν τῆς Ἁλώσεως τῆς Κωνσταντινουπόλεως ὑπὸ τῶν Τούρκων." *XVIIᵉ Congrès international d'histoire de la médecine.* Vol. I. Athens: 1960.

Alivizatos, Hamilcar S. "Ἡ Βιβλικὴ καὶ Ἱστορικοδογματικὴ βάσις τῆς Κοινωνικῆς καὶ Ἠθικῆς Ἀποστολῆς τῆς Ἐκκλησίας." Athens: 1933.

Amantos, Constantine. "Ἡ Ἑλληνικὴ Φιλανθρωπία κατὰ τοὺς Μεσαιωνικοὺς χρόνους." *Athena.* Vol. XXXV. Athens: 1923.

———. Ἕνας Κυπριώτης Πατριάρχης, *Kypriaka Grammata.* Vol. I, No. 21–24, 15 July–1 Sept. 1935.

———. «Ἱστορία τοῦ Βυζαντινοῦ Κράτους». Vol. I, second edition. Athens: 1953. Vol. II. Athens: 1957.

———. "Χειρόγραφα τῆς Μονῆς τοῦ Γρηγορίου Πακουριανοῦ παρὰ τὸν Στενήμαχον." *Thrakika.* Vol. X. Athens: 1938.

———. "Περὶ τῶν Βυζαντινῶν διαθηκῶν," Πεπραγμένα τοῦ 9ου Διεθνοῦς Βυζαντινολογικοῦ Συνεδρίου, ed. S. Kyriakides, A. Xynogopoulos and P. Zepos, Vol. II. Athens: 1956.

———. "Zu den wohltätigen Stiftungen von Byzanz," *Orientalia Christiana Periodica.* Vol. XXII. 1955.

Andreades. A. M. «Ἱστορία τῆς Ἑλληνικῆς Δημοσίας Οἰκονομίας». Vol. I, part 1. Athens: 1918.

Anonymous," "Σελίδες ἀπὸ τὸν Βυζαντινὸν Χριστιανισμόν," *Zoe*, Vol. XLII. Athens, 1952.

Bakalopoulos, Apostolos E. «Ἰστορία τοῦ Νέου Ἑλληνισμοῦ». Vol. I. Thessalonike: 1961.

Bartikian, H. *Significance of the Will of Eustathius Boilas for the study of the history of Armenia and Georgia at the time of Byzantine dominion,* XXV International Congress of Orientalists. Papers presented by the USSR Delegation. Moscow: 1960.

Baynes, Norman H. *Byzantine Studies and Other Essays.* London: 1960.

————. *The Byzantine Empire.* London: 1946.

Baynes, Norman H., and H. St. L. B. Moss. *Byzantium.* Oxford: 1961.

Baur, Chrysostomus. *Der heilige Johannes Chrysostomus und seine zeit.* Vol. I. Munich: 1929.

Bell, H. I. "Philanthropia in the Papyri of the Roman Period," *Hommages à Joseph Bidez et à Franz Cumont.* Vol. II. Brussels: 1949.

Benesevich, V. "Die Byzantinische Ranglisten," *Byzantinisch-Neugriechische Jahrbucher.* Vol. V. 1927.

Bonis, Constantine. " Ἡ Κοινωνικὴ Δικαιοσύνη κατὰ τοὺς Πατέρας τῆς Ἐκκλησίας," *Orthodoxos Skepsis.* Vol. I.18. Athens: October, 1958.

————. "Τὰ Ἰδεώδη τοῦ μοναχικοῦ βίου ἐν Βυζαντίῳ κατὰ τὴν ια′ ἑκατονταετηρίδα," *Theologia.* Vol. XVI, No. 64. Athens: 1938.

Bréhier, Louis. *La Civilisation byzantine.* Paris: 1950.

————. "La Vie chrétienne en Orient," *Histoire de l'Eglise,* ed. Augustin Fliche and Victor Martin. Vol. IV. Blond and Gay, 1948.

————. *Vie et mort de Byzance.* Paris: 1947.

————. *Les Institutions de l'empire byzantin.* Paris: 1949.

————. "Les Populations rurales au IXe siècle d'après l'hagiographie byzantine," *Byzantion.* Vol. I. 1924.

Buckler, Georgia. *Anna Comnena.* London: 1929.

Bury, J. B. *History of the Later Roman Empire.* 2 vols. New York: 1958.

————. *A History of the Eastern Roman Empire* (A.D. 802–867) reprint. New York: 1965.

Byron, Robert. *The Byzantine Achievement.* London: 1929.

Byzantios, Scarlatos D. «Ἡ Κωνσταντινούπολις». 3 vols. Athens: 1862.

Cambridge Medieval History, The, ed. H. M. Gwatkin and J. P. Whitney. Vol. I. Cambridge: 1957.

Chalandon, Ferdinand. Jean II Comnène et Manuel I Comnène. Paris: 1912.

de Champagny, Franz. La Charité chrétienne dans les premiers siècles de l'église. Paris: 1854.

Charanis, Peter. "Coronation and its Constitutional Significance in the Later Roman Empire," Byzantion. Vol. XV. 1940–1941.

———. "The Monastic Properties and the State in the Byzantine Empire." Dumbarton Oaks Papers. Vol. IV. Cambridge, Mass.: 1948.

———. "On the Social Structure of the Later Roman Empire," Byzantion. Vol. XVII. 1945.

———. "Some Aspects of Daily Life in Byzantium," The Greek Orthodox Theological Review. Vol. VIII, Nos. 1–2. Summer 1962—Winter 1962–1963.

Chastel, Etienne. Etudes historiques sur l'influence de la charité. Paris: 1953.

Christophilopoulos, A. «Τὸ Ἐπαρχιακὸν Βιβλίον Λέοντος τοῦ Σοφοῦ καὶ αἱ Συντεχνίαι ἐν Βυζαντίῳ». Athens: 1935.

Christou, P. «Ἡ Κοινωνιολογία τοῦ Μεγάλου Βασιλείου». Athens: 1951.

Codellas, P. S. "The Pantocrator, the Imperial Byzantine Medical Center of the XIIth Century AD in Constantinople," Bulletin of the History of Medicine. Vol. XII. 1942.

Comneno, D. Juan Arcadio Lascaris. "Los Orfanotrófios Griegos y su perduración en Bizancio" (A Propósito de Alexiada, XV, VII, 3–9), Actas del primer Congreso español de Estudios Clásicos, Madrid, 15–19 de Abril 1956. Madrid: 1958.

Constantelos, Demetrios J. "Philanthropy in the Age of Justinian," The Greek Orthodox Theological Review. Vol. VI. 2. Winter, 1960–1961.

———. "Philanthropia as an Imperial Virtue in the Byzantine Empire of the Tenth Century," Anglican Theological Review XLIV. 4. October, 1962.

Constantinides, P. "Ἀθηνῶν Ἀνέκδοτοι Χριστιανικαὶ Ἐπιγραφαί," Parnassos. Vol. VI. Athens: 1882.

Constantinos, Bishop of Eirenopolis. "Οἱ Ἰατροὶ ἐπὶ Βυζαντινῶν," *Orthodoxia*. Vol. XXXI.1. 1956.

———. " Ἡ διαρρύθμησις τῶν Νοσοκομείων κατὰ τὴν Βυζαντινὴν ἐποχήν," *Orthodoxia*. Vol. XXXII. 1957.

Constantopoulos, C. M. «Βυζαντινὰ Μολυβδόβουλα». Athens: 1930.

Conybeare, Frederick C. "Notes and Documents—Antiochus Strategos' Account of the Sack of Jerusalem in AD 614," *English Historical Review*. Vol. XXV. July, 1910.

Deaut, Roger Le. "Φιλανθρωπία dans la littérature grecque jusqu'au nouveau testament," *Mélanges Eugène Tisserant*. Vol. I. Rome: 1964.

Demangel, R., and E. Mamboury. *Le Quartier des Manganes et la I*^{re} *région de Constantinople*. Paris: 1939.

Demetropoulos, P. «Ἡ Πίστις τῆς Ἀρχαίας Ἐκκλησίας ὡς κανὼν ζωῆς καὶ ὁ Κόσμος». Athens: 1959.

Diehl, Charles. *Byzantium: Greatness and Decline*, tr. Naomi Walford. New Brunswick, N.J.: 1957.

———. *Justinien et la civilisation byzantine au VI*^{e} *siècle*. Paris: 1901.

———. *La Société byzantine à l'époque des Comnènes*. Paris: 1929.

Diomedes, Alexander N. «Βυζαντιναὶ Μελέται». Vol. I. Athens: 1951.

Dittenberger, W. *Sylloge Inscriptionum Graecorum*. Vol. II. Leipzig: 1917.

Dolger, Franz. *Beitrage zur Geschichte der byzantinischen Finanzverwaltung, besonders des 10 and 11 Jarhunderts*. Munich: 1927.

Downey, Glanville. *A History of Antioch in Syria from Seleucus to the Arab Conquest*. Princeton, N.J.: 1961.

———. "The Perspective of the Early Church Historians," *Greek-Roman and Byzantine Studies*, Vol. VI. 1. Spring, 1965.

———. "Philanthropia in Religion and Statecraft in the Fourth Century after Christ," *Historia*. Vol. IV. 1955.

———. "Themistius and the Defense of Hellenism in the Fourth Century," *The Harvard Theological Review*. Vol. L. 4. October, 1957.

———. "Who is My Neighbor? The Greek and Roman Answer," *Anglican Theological Review*. January, 1965.

Du Cange, Charles de Fresne. *Historia Byzantin—Constantinopolis Christiana*. Paris: 1682.

Duchesne, L. *Histoire ancienne de l'église.* Vol. III. Paris: 1928.

Duff, P. W. "The Charitable Foundations of Byzantium," *Cambridge Legal Essays Written in Honour of and Presented to Dr. Bond, Professor Buckland, and Professor Kenny.* Cambridge: 1926.

Durand, R. P. Germer-. "Epigraphie chrétienne de Jérusalem," *Revue biblique.* Vol. I. 1892.

Eustratiades, S. "'Ανδρέας ὁ Κρήτης ὁ 'Ιεροσολυμίτης," *Nea Sion.* Vol. XXIX, No. 12. Jerusalem: 1934.

Every, George. *The Byzantine Patriarchate 451–1204.* Second Revised Edition. London: 1962.

Ferguson, John. *Moral Values in the Ancient World.* London: 1958.

Festugière, A. J. *Les Moines d'orient III/2 Les Moines de Palestine.* Paris: 1962.

Florovsky, Georges. "The Social Problem in the Eastern Orthodox Church," *The Journal of Religious Thought,* Vol. VIII, No. 1. Autumn–Winter 1950–51.

———. "St. John Chrysostom: The Prophet of Charity," *St. Vladimir's Seminary Quarterly,* Vol. IV, Nos. 3–4. 1955.

Freshfield, E. N. *Roman Law in the Later Roman Empire,* Vol. IV. Cambridge: 1938.

Fytrakis, A. J. «Οἱ Μοναχοὶ ὡς Κοινωνικοὶ Διδάσκαλοι καὶ Ἐργάται ἐν τῇ Ἀρχαίᾳ Ἀνατολικῇ Ἐκκλησίᾳ». Athens: 1950.

Ganneau, Charles Simon Clermont-. *Archaeological Researches in Palestine during the Years 1873–1874,* tr. Aubrey Stewart. Vol. I. London: 1899.

Gedeon, M. I. "Διαθήκη Ἰωάννου Πριμοκυρίου," *Ekklesiastike Aletheia,* Vol. IX. 1888–1889.

———. "Διαθήκη Μαξίμου μοναχοῦ κτίτορος τῆς ἐν Λυδίᾳ Μονῆς Κοτινῆς," *Mikrasiatika Chronika,* Vol. II. Athens: 1936.

———. «Ὁ Ἄθως». Constantinople: 1885.

Genier, Raymond. *Vie de Saint Euthyme le Grand (377–473). Les Moines et l'eglise en Palestine au Ve siècle.* Paris: 1909.

Gibbon, Edward. *The History of the Decline and Fall of the Roman Empire.* Vol. III. London: 1887.

Gigante, Marcello, "Sulla Concezione Bizantina dell Imperatore nel VII Secolo," *Synteleia,* Vincenzo Arangio-Ruiz. Naples: 1964.

Gilles, Pierre. *De Bosporo Thracio.* Lyon: 1561.

Grillmeier, A., and H. Bacht. *Das Konzil von Chalcedon.* Vol. I. Wurzburg: 1951.

Grumel, V. "La Profession médicale à Byzance à l'époque des Comnènes," *Revue des études byzantine.* Vol. VII. 1949.

Guilland, R., "Etudes sur l'histoire administrative de l'empire byzantin—L'Orphanotrophe," *Revue des études byzantines,* Vol. XXIII. 1965.

———. "Les Chapitres relatifs aux fonctions des dignitaires." *Byzantinoslavica.* Vol. XIII. 2. 1952–1953.

———. "Observations sur la liste des dignitaires de Pseudo-Codinus," *Revue des études byzantines.* Vol. XII. 1954.

Harnack, A. *Die Mission und Ausbreitung des Christentums.* Vol. IV. Leipzig: 1924.

Hesseling, D. C. *Essai sur la civilisation byzantine.* Paris: 1907.

Honigman, E. *Die Ostgrenze des Byzantinischen Reiches von 363 bis 1071.* Brussels: 1935.

Hunger, Herbert. Φιλανθρωπία —*Eine griechische Wortpragung auf ihrem Wege von Aischylos bis Theodoros Metochites.* Graz—Vienna: 1963.

———. *Prooimion-Elemente der Byzantinischen Kaiseridee in den Arengen der urkunden.* Vienna: 1964.

Hussey, J. M. "Byzantine Monasticism." *Historia.* Vol. XXIV, No. 93. June, 1939.

———. *The Byzantine World.* London: 1957.

———. *Church and Learning in the Byzantine Empire,* Second Issue. New York: 1963.

Imbert, Jean. *Les Hôpitaux en droit canonique.* Paris: 1947.

Janin, R. *Constantinople byzantine.* Paris: 1950.

———. *La Géographie écclésiastique de l'empire byzantin.* Paris: 1953.

———. "Monastères byzantins. Les couvents secondaires de Psamathia (Constantinople)," *Echos d'orient.* Vol. XXXII. July–September, 1933.

———. "L'Eglise byzantine sur les rives du Bosphore (côte asiatique)," *Revue des études byzantines.* Vol. XII. 1954.

———. "Etudes de topographie byzantine," *Echos d'orient.* Vol. XXXVI. July–September, 1937.

———. "Le Monachisme byzantin au moyen âge, commende et typica (X^e–XIVe siècle)," *Revue des études byzantines.* Vol. XXII. Paris: 1964.

———. "Les Monastères du Christ Philanthrope à Constantinople." *Revue des études byzantines.* Vol. IV. Paris: 1946.

Janin, R. "Le Pétrion de Constantinople." *Echos D'orient*. Vol. XXVI. 1937.

———. "Topographie de Constantinople byzantine quelques quartiers mal connus," *Mémorial Louis Petit—Mélanges d'histoire et d'archéologie byzantines*. Bucarest: 1948.

———. "Un Ministre byzantin—Jean l'Orphanotrophe (XIᵉ siècle)." *Echos d'Orient*. Vol. XXXIV. 1931.

Jeanselme, E. *Calcul de la ration alimentaire des malades de l'hôpital et de l'asile des vieillards annexes au monastère du Pantocrator à Byzance (1136)*. Extrait de 2ᵉ congrès d'histoire de la médecine. Evreux: 1922.

Jeanselme, E., and L. Oeconomos. "Les Oeuvres d'assistance et les hôpitaux byzantins au siècle des Comnènes." *Communication faite au Iᵉʳ congrès de l'histoire de l'art de guerir, Anvers 1920*. Anvers: 1921.

Jones, A. H. M. *The Cities of the Eastern Roman Provinces*. Oxford: 1937.

———. "The Greeks under the Roman Empire," *Dumbarton Oaks Papers*. Vol. XVII. Washington: 1963.

———. *The Later Roman Empire 284–602*. 2 vols. Norman, Okla.: 1964.

Kabiersch, J. *Untersuchungen zum Begriff der Philanthropia bei dem Kaiser Julian*. Wiesbaden: 1960.

Karayiannopoulos, John E. "Βυζαντινὸν Κράτος καὶ Βυζαντινὴ Κοινωνία," *Megale Hellenike Encyclopaideia*, Supplement, Vol. II. Athens, n. d.

Karlsson, Gustav. *Idéologie et cérémonial dans l'épistolographie byzantine*. Uppsala: 1959.

Kasimates, Gregory. " Ἡ Κοινωνικὴ Πολιτικὴ εἰς τὰς Νεαρὰς Λέοντος τοῦ Σοφοῦ," *Epeteris Etaerias Byzantinon Spoudon*, Vol. XIII. 1937.

Knecht, August. *System des Justinianischen Kirchenvermogensrechtes*. Stuttgart: 1905.

Kotsones, Jerome. "Τό «Φιλάνθρωπον» εἰς τοὺς Κανόνας τοῦ Μ. Βασιλείου." *Aktines*, Vol. XVIII, No. 156. Athens: 1955.

———. "Τὸ Χριστιανικὸν «φιλάνθρωπον» καὶ οἱ ἱεροὶ Κανόνες τῆς Ἐκκλησίας." *Aktines*, Vol. XVIII, No. 162. Athens: 1955.

Koukoules, Phaedon. «Βυζαντινῶν Βίος καὶ Πολιτισμός». Vol. II, part 1. Athens: 1948. Vol. VI. Athens: 1957.

―――. «Βυζαντινῶν Νεκρικὰ ῎Εθιμα», *Epeteris Etaerias Byzantinon Spoudon*. Vol. XVI. Athens: 1940.

―――. "L'Assistance aux indigents dans l'empire byzantin," *Mémorial Louis Petit—Mélanges d'histoire et d'archéologie byzantines*. Bucarest: 1948.

Kousis, Aristotle. "Contribution à l'étude de la médecine des zenones pendant le XVᵉ siècle," *Byzantinisch-Neugriechische Jahrbucher*. Vol. VI. 1927–1928.

―――. "Περὶ Βυζαντινῶν Νοσοκομείων καὶ ἰατρικῆς τῶν κληρικῶν. . . . " *Archives of Medicine and Biology*. Vol. XV, Nos. 3–4. Athens: 1920.

Kriaras, Emmanuel. «Βυζαντινὰ Ἱπποτικὰ Μυθιστορήματα». Athens: 1955.

Krivocheine, Basil. "Mt. Athos in the Spiritual Life of the Orthodox Church," *The Christian East*, New Series. Vol. II, no. 2. Autumn, 1952.

―――. "The Brother-Loving Poor Man," *The Christian East*, New Series. Vol. II, nos. 7 and 8. Winter 1953–1954.

Ktenas, Christopher. "Τὰ Κειμηλιαρχεῖα τῆς ἐν ἁγίῳ ῎Ορει Ἱερᾶς . . . Μονῆς τοῦ Δοχειαρίου." *Epeteris Etaerias Byzantinon Spoudon*. Vol. VII. Athens: 1930.

Kyriakides, Stilpon. «Βυζαντιναὶ Μελέται». Vols. II–V. Thessalonike: 1937.

Lallemand, Leon. *Histoire de la charité*. 2 vols. Paris: 1902–1903.

Lambakis, George. «Χριστιανικὴ Ἀρχαιολογία τῆς Μονῆς Δαφνίου». Athens: 1889.

Laurent, V. *Les Bulles métriques dans la sigillographie byzantine*. Athens: 1932.

―――. *Le Corpus de sceaux de l'empire byzantin*. Vol. V. Paris: 1963.

―――. "Une Princesse byzantine au cloître." *Echos d'orient*. Vol. XXIX. 1930.

Lecky, William. *History of European Morals from Augustus to Charlemagne*. Vol. II. New York: 1955.

Leclercq, H. "Charité," *Dictionnaire d'archéologie chrétienne et de liturgie*. Vol. II. Paris: 1903.

Lenger, Marie-Therese. "La Notion de 'bienfait' (philanthropon) royal et les ordonnances des rois Lagides," *Studi in onore di Vincenzo Arangio-Ruiz*. Vol. I. 1953.

Lorenz, S. *De Progressu Notionis* «Φιλανθρωπία». Leipzig: 1914.

Louillet, G. Da Costa. "Saints de Constantinople aux VIIIe, IXe et Xe siècles," *Byzantion*. Vol. XXIV. 1954.

Macalister, R. A. Stewart. "The Rock-cut Tombs in Wady Er-Rababi, Jerusalem," *Palestine Exploration Fund—Quarterly Statement*. London: 1900.

Magoulias, H. J. "The Lives of the Saints as Sources of Data for the History of Byzantine Medicine in the Sixth and Seventh Centuries," *Byzantinische Zeitschrift*. Vol. LVII, No. 1. June, 1964.

Marin, Abbé. *Les Moines de Constantinople*. Paris: 1897.

Megaw, Arthur H. S. "Notes on Recent Work of the Byzantine Institute in Istanbul," *Dumbarton Oaks Papers*, No. 17. Washington: 1963.

Meletes, George B. «Ὁ Ἅγιος τῆς Ἀγάπης Ἰωάννης ὁ Ἐλεήμων.» Athens, 1964.

Milik, J. T. "La Topographie de Jérusalem vers la fin de l'époque byzantine," *Mélanges de l'Université Saint Joseph*. Vol. XXXII. 1960–1961.

Millet, Gabriel. *La Monastère de Daphni—Histoire, Architecture, Mosaiques*. Paris: 1899.

Millingen, Alexander Van. *Byzantine Churches in Constantinople*. London: 1912.

Monnier, Alexandre. *Histoire de l'assistance publique dans les temps anciens et modernes*. Paris: 1866.

de Montfaucon, Bernard. *Palaegraphia Graeca*. Paris: 1708.

Mordtmann, A. D. *Esquisse topographique de Constantinople*. Lille: 1892.

Mpratsiotes, Panayiotes. «Τὸ Νόημα τῆς Χριστιανικῆς Ἀγάπης.» Athens, 1956.

Niederev, Frances J. "Early Medieval Charity," *Church History*. Vol. XXI. 1952.

Nissiotis, N. A. "Church and Society in Greek Orthodox Theology," *Christian Social Ethics in a Changing World*, ed. John C. Bennett. New York: 1966.

Nygren, Anders. *Agape and Eros*, tr. Philip S. Watson. Philadelphia: 1953.

Oeconomos, L. *La Vie religieuse dans l'empire byzantin au temps des Comnènes et des Anges*. Paris: 1918.

Orlandos, Anastasios. "Ἡ Ἀναπαράστασις τοῦ Ξενῶνος τῆς ἐν Κωνσταντινουπόλει Μονῆς τοῦ Παντοκράτορος," *Epeteris Etaerias Byzantinon Spoudon*. Vol. XVII. 1941.

Ostrogorsky, George. *History of the Byzantine State,* tr. Joan Hussey. New Brunswick, N.J.: 1957.

Papadopoulos, Chrysostomos, «Ὁ ῞Οσιος Λουκᾶς ὁ "Νέος" (896–953)». Athens: 1935.

Papadopoulos, Jean B. *Les Palais et les églises des Blachernes.* Athens: 1928.

————. "Τὰ Ἱερὰ Χρήματα εἰς τὴν Ἀρχαίαν Ἑλληνικὴν καὶ Βυζαντινὴν Περίοδον," *Epeteris Etaerias Byzantinon Spoudon.* Vol. XIX. 1949.

Pargoire, J. "Hieria," *Bulletin de l'institut archéologique russe de Constantinople.* Vol. IV. 2. Sophia: 1899.

Paspates, A. G. «Τὰ Βυζαντινὰ Ἀνάκτορα». Athens: 1885.

————. «Βυζαντιναὶ Μελέται—Τοπογραφικαὶ καὶ Ἱστορικαί». Constantinople: 1877.

Philipsborn, A. "Ἱερὰ νόσος un die spezial-Anstalt des Pantokrator-Krankenhauses," *Byzantion.* Vol. XXXIII. 1963.

Plassman, Otto. *Das Almosen bei Joannes Chrysostomus.* Münster: 1961.

Pournaropoulos, G. C. "Hospital and Social Welfare Institutions in the Medieval Greek Empire (Byzantium)," *XVIIᵉ Congrès international d'histoire de la médecine.* Vol. I. Athens: 1960.

————. «Ἱστορία Βυζαντινῆς Ἰατρικῆς». Athens: 1942.

————. "The Real Value of Medieval Greek Medicine (Byzantium)." *XVIIᵉ Congrès international d'histoire de la médecine.* Vol. I. Athens: 1960

————. "Στοιχεῖα ἐκ τῆς Ἑλληνικῆς Ἰατρικῆς κατὰ τὸν Μέσον Αἰῶνα," *Academaike Iatrike.* Athens: 1946.

Ramsay, William M. *The Church in the Roman Empire,* eighth edition. London: 1904.

Rice, R. Talbot. "Excavations at Bodrum Camii, 1930," *Byzantion.* Vol. VIII. 1937.

Richardson, B. E. *Old Age Among the Ancient Greeks.* Baltimore: 1933.

Richter, J. P. *Quellen der Byzantinischen Kunstgeschichte.* Vienna: 1897.

Rivet, Auguste, *Le Régime des biens de l'église avant Justinien.* Lyons: 1891.

Rodocanakes, Plato. «Ἡ Βασίλισσα καὶ αἱ Βυζαντιναὶ Ἀρχόντισσαι.» Athens: 1920.

de Ruiter, S. Tromp. "De vocis quae est φιλανθρωπία significatione atque usu," *Mnemosyne*. Vol. LIX. 1932.

Runciman, Steven. *Byzantine Civilization*. New York: 1956.

Savramis, Demosthenes. *Zur Soziologie des Byzantinischen Monchtums*. Leyden/Cologne: 1962.

Schlumberger, Gustave. *Mélanges d'archéologie byzantine*. Paris: 1895.

————. *Sigillographie de l'empire byzantin*. Paris: 1914.

————. "Monuments numismatiques et sphragistiques du moyen age byzantin," *Revue archéologique*, New Series. Vol. XL. July–December, 1880.

Schreiber, G. "Byzantinisches und Abendlandisches Hospital," *Byzantinische Zeitschrift*. Vol. XLII. 1943–1949.

Schultze, Victor. *Altchristliche Stadte und Landschaften II Kleinasien*. Gutersloh: 1926.

Siotes, Markos. «Ἡ Φροντὶς τῆς πρώτης Ἐκκλησίας ὑπὲρ τῶν Ὀρφανῶν Κορασίδων». Athens: 1964.

Soteriou, George A. «Αἱ Μοναὶ τῆς Ἑλλάδος καὶ ἡ Ἐθνική των δρᾶσις κατὰ τοὺς Βυζαντινοὺς Χρόνους». Athens: 1936.

————. «Χριστιανικὴ καὶ Βυζαντινὴ Ἀρχαιολογία». Vol. I. Athens: 1962.

Spicq, Ceslaus. *Agape in the New Testament*, tr. Marie A. McNamara and Mary H. Richter, Vols. I, II, and III, St. Louis: B. Herder, 1963, 1965, and 1966.

Spyridakis, George. "Τὰ κατὰ τὴν τελευτὴν ἔθιμα τῶν Βυζαντινῶν ἐκ τῶν Ἁγιολογικῶν Πηγῶν," *Epeteris Etaerias Byzantinon Spoudon*. Vol. 20. Athens: 1950.

Stein, Ernest-Palanque, J. R. *Histoire du Bas-Empire*. Vol. II. Paris: 1949.

Stephana, Febe. "Ἡ Διακόνισσα στό Βυζάντιο," *Aktines*. Vol. IX. No. 59. 1946.

Stephanides, B. «Ἐκκλησιαστικὴ Ἱστορία». Athens: 1948.

Temkin, Owsei. "Byzantine Medicine: Tradition and Empiricism," *Dumbarton Oaks Papers*. Vol. XVI. Washington: 1962.

Theocharides, George I. «Μία Διαθήκη καὶ Μία Δίκη Βυζαντινή». Thessalonike: 1962.

————. "Μιχαὴλ Δούκας Γλαβᾶς Ταρχανειώτης," *Epistemonike Epeteris Philosophikes Scholes Panepistemiou Thessalonikes*. Vol. VII. Thessalonike: 1957.

Theodorou, A. "Das Monchtum der Orthodoxen Ostkirche." *Die Orthodoxe Kirche in Griechischer sicht,* ed. P. Bratsiotis. Vol. I, Part I. Stuttgart: 1960.

Theodorou, Evangelos. «Ἡ "Χειροτονία" ἤ "χειροθεσία" τῶν διακονισσῶν». Athens: 1954.

————. «Ἡρωΐδες τῆς Χριστιανικῆς ἀγάπης—αἱ διακόνισσαι διὰ τῶν αἰώνων». Athens: 1949.

Theoharis, Maria S. " Ὁ Τάφος τοῦ Μεγάλου Δομεστίχου Πακουριανοῦ," *Kathemerine.* Athens: July 11, 1965.

Troeltsch, Ernst, *The Social Teaching of the Christian Churches,* tr. Olive Wyon, Vol. I. New York: 1960.

Uhlhorn, G. *Christian Charity in the Ancient Church,* tr. from German. New York: 1883.

Vafides, Filaretos. " Ἡ Ἀγάπη καὶ τὰ ἔργα αὐτῆς ἐν τῇ Ἀρχαίᾳ Ἐκκλησίᾳ," *Gregorios o Palamas.* Vol. II. 1927.

Vance, J. Milton. *Beitrage zur Byzantinischen Kulturgeschichte.* Jena: 1907.

Vasiliev, A. A. *History of the Byzantine Empire 323–1453.* Madison, Wisc.: 1952.

de Vaux, Roland. "Communication-Chronique Archéologique," *Revue biblique.* Vol. LXXI, No. 2. April, 1964.

————. "Les Hôpitaux de Justinien à Jerusalem, d'après les dernières fouilles," *Académie des inscriptions et belles lettres.* Vol. III. Paris: 1965.

Vogel, Marie and Gardthausen, Victor. *Die griechischen Schreiber des Mittelalters und der Renaissance.* Leipzig: 1909.

Winslow, Donald F., "Gregory of Nazianzus and Love for the Poor," *Anglican Theological Review.* Vol. XLVII. 1965.

Xanalatos, Diogenes A. "Θεοφύλακτος ὁ Βουλγαρίας καὶ ἡ δρᾶσις του ἐν Ἀχρίδι," *Theologia.* Vol. XVI, No. 63. 1938.

————. *Beitrage zur wirtschaftsund Sozialgeschichte Makedoniens im Mittelalter, hauptsachich auf Grund der Briefe des Erzbischots Theophylaktos von Achrida.* Munich: 1937.

Zakythinos, Dionysios A. «Ἱστορία τοῦ Βυζαντινοῦ Κράτους». Vol. I. Athens: 1953.

————. «Βυζάντιον—Κράτος καὶ Κοινωνία Ἱστορικὴ Ἐπισκόπησις». Athens: 1951.

Index

Aaron, king of Bulgaria, 251
Abraamios, bishop of Krateia, 74, 183
Abraham, 92, 98, 216
Acacian schism, 249
Acacios (official), 187–88
Acacios, bishop of Naupactos and Arta, 215
Acacios, Patriarch (478–88), 242, 249
Academy of Athens, 110
Acatios, Joannes, 287
Acatzes, 287
Acropolis, Constantinople, 128, 195, 199, 234; orphanage near, 246, 247
Acropolites, Constantine, cited, 84n, 107, 144n
Acropolites, George, cited, 269n, 287n
Acta Apostolorum, In (Chrysostomos), 186nn, 187nn, 258n
Acta Conciliorum Oecumenicorum (Schwartz), 231n, 248n
Acta et Diplomata Graeca Medii Aevi Sacra et Profana (Miklosich and Muller), 24n, 25n, 26n, 35n, 41n, 60nn, 69n, 91n, 108n, 131nn, 132nn, 193n, 213nn, 234n, 237n, 255n
"Acta Graeca SS Davidis, Symeonis et Georgii, Mitylenae in insula Lesbo" (*Analecta Bollandiana*), 38n, 101n, 102n, 114n, 115n
Acta Sanctorum, cited, 25n, 35n, 41n, 93n, 96nn, 97n, 106n, 107nn, 108n, 134n, 144n, 153n, 183n, 202n, 203nn, 208n, 213n, 270n, 274n, 275nn

316

"Actes de Chilandar" 37n, 144n
Actes de Lavra (Rouillard and Collomp, eds.), 26n, 239n
Actouarios, brother of, 183
Acts, cited, 10n, 13nn, 29n, 273n
"Adhortatio Patriarchae ad Basilium, regem Moscovii" (Antonios), 60nn, 61n
Adrianople, 79
Adrianos and Constanto (parents of the brother saints), 101
Adversus Haereses (Epiphanios), 167n, 262
Aelii Aristidis (Keil, ed.), 50n
Aerios the Arian, 167
Aeschylos, quoted, 4
Aetherios (bishop), 71
Against Celsos (Origen), 30nn
agape, 3, 12, 31, 66, 280; monastery charities and, 25–26; New Testament on, 13–14, 29, 30; as the supreme attribute, 22, 33, 36–37, 38
Agape and Eros (Nygren), 12n, 31n
Agape in the New Testament (Spicq), 12n
Agapetos, deacon, on kingship, 43, 46, 49
Agathe, 231
Agathias, cited, 113n, 271n
Agathoupolis, 69
aged, the, 22, 66, 136; bishops and, 14; Greek, 5, 6, 8, 10, 19, 222; homes for, 222–40 (*see also* gerocomeia); monastery aid to, 94, 172; monks, 141, 157; in poorhouses, 260; private aid to, 142; slaves, 15; women, 57

Agesilaos, king of Sparta (398–360 B.C.), 8, 11

Agesilaos (Xenophon), 8*nn*

Agourides, Savas, 13*n*

agriculture, 108, 119, 142, 284; farms for the crippled, 128; land bequests, 140

Ainalov, D. V., cited, 279*n*

Akoimetoi, monastery of the, 210

Alexander, martyr, 207

Alexander (teacher), 80

Alexander the Great, 129

Alexander (912–13), 218

Alexander, Paul J., cited, 60*n*, 265*n*

Alexandria, Egypt, 30, 94, 129, 151; gerocomeia in, 223, 229; hospitals in, 153, 168, 264; poor of, 74, 259, 264, 284; private philanthropy in, 138, 268; xenones in, 212, 213

Alexiad, The (Dawes), 27*n*, 244*n*

Alexias, Anne Comnène Alexiade (Anna Comnena), 27*n*, 86*nn*, 109*n*, 123*nn*, 126*nn*, 128*nn*, 129*nn*, 131*nn*, 135*n*, 136*n*, 141*n*, 171*n*, 203*n*, 244*n*, 245*nn*, 246*nn*, 266*nn*

Alexios Comnenos (1081–1118), 84, 109, 132, 142; city for the maimed, 128–29, 244, 266; deaconess order and, 86; Gregory Pacourianos and, 141, 203; hospital of, 171; motives of, 26–27, 135–36; orphans and, 126, 128, 129–30, 244–45, 247; prisoners and, 123, 126; St. Cyril Phileotes and, 55

Alexios Comnenos (son of John II Comnenos), 55–56

"Alexios Makrembolites and his Dialogue between the Rich and the Poor" (Ševčenko), 39*n*

Alivizatos, K. N., cited, 153*n*, 193

Allatius, Leo, cited, 287*n*

Almosen bei Joannes Chrysostomus, Das (Plassman), 24*n*, 71*nn*

Al-Muktadir, calif of Baghdad, 53

Alonitzion quarter, Constantinople, 206

Alousianos, of Bulgaria, 251

Altaner, Berthold, cited, 139*n*, 257*n*, 264*n*, 281*n*

Altchristliche liturgische Stucke aus der Kirche Aegyptens nebst einem dogmatischen brief des bischofs Serapion von Thmuis (Wobbermin), 287*n*

Altchristliche Stadte und Landschaften II Kleinasien (Schultze), 157*n*

"Alteste Imberiostext, Der" (Schreiner), 214*n*

Amantos, Constantine, cited, xi*n*, 135*n*, 141*n*, 143*n*, 203*n*, 204*n*, 224*n*, 247*n*, 250*n*

Amasea, 261

Amastris, 78, 79

Amida, 159

"Amour de l'Hellénisme au Christianisme, L'" (Spanneut), 10*n*

Analecta Avarica (Sternbach), 246*n*

Analecta Bollandiana (periodical), cited, 35*n*, 38*n*, 78*n*, 100*nn*, 101*n*, 102*nn*, 107*n*, 108*nn*, 114*n*, 115*n*, 168*n*, 169*n*, 170*nn*, 190*n*, 213*n*, 229*n*, 262*n*, 268*n*

Analecta Byzantino-Russica (Regel), 38*n*, 114*n*, 115*n*

Analecta Mitteilungun aus italienischen Handschriften byzantinischer Chronographen (Heisenberg), 185*n*

Analecta Patristica (Diekamp), 33*n*, 36*nn*

Analekten der mittel-und-neugriechischen Literatur (Ellissen, ed.), 60*n*, 146*n*

Anaplous, 231

Anastastios (presbyter), 248

Anastasios (+628), saint, 275

Anastasios I (491–518), emperor, 112, 113

Anastasios Sinaites, 68*n*

Anastaso, 267

Ancyra, 78, 138

Andreades, A. M., cited, 55*n*

Andreas, archbishop of Crete (d.740), 34, 231, 250; poorhouses and, 75, 168–69, 264, 269

Andronicos (money-lender), 137, 167–68

Andronicos I Comnenos (1110–1185), emperor, 180

Andronicos II Palaeologos (1282–1328), emperor, 206, 252

"Anecdota" (Photopoulos), 84*n*

Anecdota (Procopios), 231*n*, 272*n*

Anecdota Graeca (Matranga, ed.), 133*n*

"Aneddoti d'un Codice Bolognese, Gli" (Mercati and de Cavalieri), 57*nn*

Anemas, Michael, 131

angels, 36, 41

Anglican Theological Review (periodical), 11*n*, 285*n*

Anna Comnena, cited, 27*n*, 109*n*, 131*n*, 135–36, 141*n*, 171*n*, 203*n*, 248*n*, 260, 266*nn*; on Alexios' "Orphanage," 128–29, 244–45, 246, 247; deaconess order and, 86; on justice, 126; on prisoners of war, 123; son of, 56

Anna Comnena (Buckler), 86*n*, 245*n*

Anna Dalassena, 109

Annales (Acropolites), 269*n*

Annales (Glycas), 130*n*, 244*n*

Ante-Nicene Fathers, The (Roberts and Donaldson, eds.), 15*n*

Anthemios, bishop of Salamis, 207–208

Anthemios, emperor of the West, 223–24

Anthony, saint, 93, 188

Anthony of Novgorod, 166, 167, 193

Antigone (Sophocles), 8*n*

Antioch, 151, 153, 223; the poor in, 68, 71, 137, 257, 258, 259, 274, 284; xenones in, 189, 209, 212, 220

Antiochos Strategos, 160, 162, 226

Antonios IV, patriarch (1391–97), on kingship, 60–61

Antonios of Novgorod, 166, 167, 193

Antonios Placentinos, 159–60

Apameia, 264

Apollo, 7

Apollonia, 69

Apologeticus (Tertullian), 13*n*, 14*n*, 15*n*

Apologia (Aristides), 14*nn*, 15*n*

Apostolic Church, 13–14, 24, 29, 207

Apostolic Constitutions, 13*n*, 14*n*, 15*n*, 24, 67, 86

Apostolic Diaconate of the Church of Greece, 13*n*

Appolinarios, Patriarch of Alexandria (551–68), 168, 229

Arabs, 78, 99–100, 101, 153

Arangio-Ruiz, Vincenzo, cited, 49*n*

Arcadios, emperor (395–407), 45, 199, 224

Arcadios, archbishop of Constantia, 23, 169

Arcadios, xenon of, 189

Archaeologia (periodical), 91*nn*

Archaeological Researches in Palestine during the years 1873–1874 (Clermont-Ganneau), 160*n*, 225*nn*

"Archaeology in Greece, 1899–1900" (Rosanquet), 7*n*

Archeion Pontou (periodical), 144*n*

Archives of Medicine and Biology (periodical), 174*n*

Ardabasdos, strategos, 224–25

Argos, Greece, 7, 101

Argyronium, 167, 262

Argyropoulos, John, 206

Aristides, Aelius, 14*nn*, 15

Aristinos, 68*n*, 276

Aristogiton (Demosthenes), 6*n*

Aristotelis De Republica Libri (Bekker, ed.), 6*n*

Aristotle, cited, 6, 7*n*, 8*n*, 10, 43

Armatiou quarter, Constantinople, 227, 228

Armenia, 80, 153

Arnakis, G. G., cited, 28*n*

Arsacios, priest, 16, 209

Arsenoita, Egypt, 94

Artemios, saint, 195, 206

Arzos River, 207

Ascalon, Palestine, 212

Ascidas, Theodore, bishop of Cappadocia, 242

Asclepieion, Greece, 266

Asclepios, 41; Epidauros temple, 7

Ashburner, Walter, cited, 49*n*

Asiana, 71

Asterios, bishop of Amaseia, 182

Athanasia, 137, 167–68

Athanasios the Athonite (+1004), 92, 102

Athanasios, bishop of Adramyttion, 84

Athanasios the Great, saint, 31–32, 33, 38, 68n, 70, 131, 219

Athanasius De Incarnatione (Cross), 32n

Athena (periodical), xin, 247n

Athenagoras, metropolitan of Paramythia and Parga, 87n

Athenian Constitution (Aristotle), 7n

Atheniensium Respublica (Aristotle), 8n

Athens, Greece, 6, 8, 9, 10, 110; excavations, 266

Athos, port, 92, 102

Attaliates, *see* Michael Attaliates

Attica, 215

Aufhauser, J. B., cited 221n

Aus den Schatzkammern des heiligen Berges (Dolger), 255n

Aus der Werkstatt des Vollendeten (von Harnack), 90n

"Authorship of the Strategikon of Cecaumenos" (Buckler), 54n

Auvray, Emmanuel, 35n

Ayakapi, 224

Bab es Sahera gate, Jerusalem, 225

Bacchos the Younger, saint, 252

Bacht, H., cited, 157n

Bakalopoulos, Apostolos E., cited, 258n

Balsamon, Theodore, 68n, 86, 276

baptism, 24, 85, 144

Bardas, Caesar, 135

Barker, Ernest, cited, 49n, 50nn, 54n

Barnabas, saint, 207; cited, 14nn

Bartholomeos of Koutloumousion, quoted, 228n

Bartikian, H., cited, 140nn

Basil the Great, saint, 32, 85n, 150, 151, 248n, 269; Basileias of, 154–55, 157, 208, 260; charities of, 68–69, 71, 74, 93, 131; on God's philanthropy, 33–34, 38, 282; lepers and, 181–82; on mercy, 19n, 21, 35n; monasticism and, 89, 90n; on taxation, 260–61; on wealth, 22–23; xenones and, 186n, 208, 210

Basil I, emperor (867–86), quoted, 51; institutions established by, 52, 115, 134–35, 195, 218, 265

Basil II, emperor (976–1025), 52, 121, 237, 251

Basil, prince of Moscow, 60

Basil de Cesaree Traite du Saint-Esprit (Benoit Bruche), 33n

Basileias, 154–55, 157, 208, 244, 260

Basilicorum Libri, 86n

Bassianos, bishop of Ephesos, 157

Bate, H. N., cited, 84n

bathing, 102, 198, 212, 227; Blachernae, 233; Pantocrator, 235

Baur, Chrysostomus, 68n

Baynes, Norman H., cited, 3n, 43n, 49n, 55n, 65nn, 89n, 111n, 149n, 214n

Bebek on the Bosporos, 230, 231

Beck, Frederick A. G., 5n

Beck, Hans Georg, cited, 54n, 84n, 97n, 102n, 106n, 204n, 205n, 219n, 229nn, 230n, 231n, 234n, 242n

Bees, Nikos A., cited, 214n, 215n

beggars, 5, 19, 26, 27, 269; employment of, 260; Empress Irene and, 130; Michael Attaleiates and, 142, 268; shelter for, 119

Beitrage zur Byzantinischen Kulturgeschichte (Vance), 68n

Beitrage zur Geschichte der byzantinischen Finanzverwaltung, besonders des 10 und 11 Jahrhunderts (Dolger), 240n

Beitrage zur wirtschaftsund Sozialgeschichte Makedoniens im Mittelalter, hauptsachich auf Grund der Briefe des Erzbischots Theophylaktos von Achrida (Xanalatos), 84n

Bell, H. I., cited, 3n, 10n

Beneria, 139

Benesevich, V., cited, 140nn, 242n

Beroia, Macedonia, 142, 207

Beseleel, 157

Bias (c. 570 B.C.), 9

Bias (Diogenes Laertios), 9n

Bibliotheca Hagiographica Graeca (Halkin), 78n, 156n, 169n, 209n, 287n

Bibliothèque Grecque Vulgaire (Legrand), 215*n*
Bidez, J., cited, 16*n*, 45*n*, 209*n*, 263*n. See also Sozomenus Kirchengeschichte*
bishops, 203; Chrysostom's discipline of, 156; duties of, 14–15, 67, 68–69, 70–71, 74, 75, 78–79, 80, 84, 86, 101, 138, 145, 149, 169, 209, 218–19, 239–40, 256, 261, 262, 269; election of, 99; private gifts to, 138; royal authority and, 81, 84. *See also individual names*
Bithynia, 74, 96, 164; xenones, 200, 220
Blachernae district, Constantinople, 227, 233
Blastaris, Mattheos, cited, 257*n*
blind, homes for, 275–76
Bodrumcami mosque, 232
Boilas, Eustathios, 140
Boilas, Romanos, 140
Boleros, Macedonia, 255
Bolkestein, Hendrik, cited, 9*n*, 280*n*
Bonis, Constantine G., cited, 89*n*
Bonwetsch, D. G. N., 31*n*
Book of Ceremonies (Constantine VII Porphyrogenitos), *see Cerimoniis, De*
"Book of the Eparch, The" (Zepos, ed.), 284*n*, 286*n*
Book of the Prefect, 286
Boor, Charles de, cited, 81*nn*, 97*n*, 223*n*
Boris, king of Bulgaria, 50
Bosporis, 138
Bosporos, The, 164, 166, 230, 249, 265; Golden Horn of, 195, 196, 224, 229, 233, 237; Sea of Marmara and, 246, 247
Bosporo Thracio, De (Gilles), 230*n*
Bostra, 264
Boucherie, Anatole, cited, 268*n*, 275*n*
Boulenger, Fernard, 68*n*, 155*n*, 260*n*
Boyazit, 230
Bréhier, Louis, cited, 98*n*, 239*n*, 246, 247*n*
Brephotropheion (foundling home), 248

Brockhaus, Heinrich, 41*n*
Brooks, E. W., cited, 159*n*, 230*n*
Bruche, Benoit, 33*n*
Bruck, E. F., 16*n*
Bryennios the Younger, Nicephoros, 56, 126
Bucephale, Media, 129
Buckler, Georgina, cited, 54*nn*, 55*n*, 86*n*, 245*n*
Buildings (Procopios), 159*nn*, 162*nn*, 167*n*, 186*nn*, 189*nn*, 190*nn*, 191*nn*, 207*n*, 212*nn*, 264*nn*, 272*nn*
Bulgaria, 50, 52–53, 79, 243, 251
Bulles métriques dans la sigillographie byzantine, Les (Laurent), 109*n*
Bulletin of the History of Medicine (periodical), 171*n*
Bulletin de l'institut archéologique bulgare (periodical), 45*nn*
Bulletin de l'institut archéologique russe à Constantinople (periodical), 26*n*, 27*n*, 39*n*, 91*n*, 93*nn*, 97*n*, 108*n*, 132*nn*, 164*n*, 181*n*, 236*n*, 247*n*, 251*n*
burial, 15, 112, 197, 198; Pantocrator, 175, 179; of travelers, 207, 274–75
Burnet, Joannes, 4*n*
Bury, J. B.: on the death penalty, 285*n*; on John Chrysostom, 68, 258*nn*; on orphanages, 247, 250*n*, 251*n*, 252; on Theophilos, 114, 115*n*
Bury, R. G., 6*n*
Byron, Robert, quoted, 66, 271
Byzantina Metabyzantina (periodical), 243*n*
Byzantinae Historiae (Gregoras), 115*nn*, 233*n*, 269*n*
Byzantine Achievement, The (Byron), 66*n*, 271*n*
Byzantine Art and Archaeology (Dalton), 279*n*
Byzantine Churches in Constantinople (Millingen), 247*n*
"Byzantine Cities in the Early Middle Ages" (Ostrogorsky), 258*n*
Byzantine Empire, The (Baynes), 3*n*, 65*n*, 111*n*

"Byzantine Literature" (Marshall and Mavrogordato), 214n
"Byzantine Medicine: Tradition and Empiricism" (Temkin), 153n
"Byzantine Monasticism" (Hussey), 89n, 90n
Byzantine Patriarchate 451–1204 (Every), 283n
"Byzantine Satire" (Tozer), 145n
Byzantine Studies and Other Essays (Baynes), 43nn, 65n, 89n
Byzantinisch-Neugriechische Jahrbucher, 153n, 174n, 225n, 242n
"Byzantinisches und Abenlandisches Hospital" (Schreiber), 172nn, 179nn
"Byzantinische Ranglisten, Die" (Benesevich), 242n
Byzantinische Zeitschrift (periodical), 54n, 57nn, 92n, 100n, 154n, 172nn, 179nn, 183nn, 210n, 214n, 215n, 230n
Byzantinoslavica (periodical), 246n
Byzantinoturcica (Moravcsik), 205n
Byzantion (periodical), 54n, 58n, 59nn, 60n, 97n, 98n, 99nn, 169n, 179n, 185n, 198n, 232n, 258n, 259n, 283n
Byzantios, Scarlatos: on gerocomeia, 223nn, 227nn, 229n, 230nn, 231nn, 232nn, 233n, 234n, 236n, 237n, 239nn; on orphanages, 246, 247nn; on xenones, 198n, 199nn, 200n, 210n; on the Zoticon, 166n, 167
Byzantium: Church-State unity in, 65–66, 150, 222, 279, 283; economic structure of, 283–85; fall of, 287–88; Greek restoration (1261), 245; imperial duties in, 43–61, 111, 135–36, 150; lay charities in, 137–46, 151; monastic influence in, 95, 150, 285; philanthropic thought in, 18–28, 279–88; theology in, 29–41, 149–50. *See also specific placenames*
Byzantium (Baynes and Moss), 49n, 55n, 149n, 214n
"Byzantium, the West and the Origin of the First Crusade" (Charanis), 185n

Caesarea of Cappadocia, 144, 260
Calcul de la ration alimentaire des malades de l'hôpital et de l'asile des vieillards annexes au monastère du Pantocrator a Byzance (Jeanselme), 235n
Calian, Carnegie S., cited, 283n
Callinicos, cited, 92n, 93nn, 96nn, 220n
Callistos, patriarch (1350–53, 1355–63), 234
Calybites, Eutropios and Theodora, 210
Calybites, John (c. 460), 210
Cambridge Legal Essays Written in Honour of and Presented to Dr. Bond, Professor Buckland, and Professor Kenny, 149n, 150n, 151n
Cambridge Medieval History, The (Gwatkin and Whitney, eds.), 285n
Cameniates, Joannes, cited, 38n
Cammelli, Giuseppe, cited, 206n
Candida, 139
Canons of Athanasius of Alexandria (Riedel and Crum), 70n
Cantacuzenos, *see* John VI Cantacuzenos
Capita Theologica (Maximos the Confessor), 35nn, 49n
Cappadocia, 208, 212, 261
Cappadocian Fathers, 32
Captivitas Hierosolyme (Antiochos Strategos), 162n, 226n
Caritate, De (Maximos the Confessor), 22nn, 25n
Carmina Graeca Medii Aevi (Wagner), 26nn, 27n, 56nn
Catalogia Bibliothecae Caesareae Manuscriptorum (de Nessel), 198n
Catholic and Apostolic (Bate), 84n
Cavalieri, Pius F. de, 198n, 199n
Cecaumenos, 56n, 153n, 244; on kingship, 54–55
Cecaumeni Strategicon et . . . de officiis Regiis Libellus (Wassiliewsky and Jernstadt, eds.), 54–55, 56n, 153n, 244n, 250n
Cedrenos, George, 179n, 263n; on earthquake, 113n, 244nn; on

gerocomeia, 223; on xenones, 186, 189, 198n, 199, 208n, 212n, 222; on the Zoticon, 165n, 166n, 167, 247n

Celsos, 30

Celts, 123

cemeteries, 175, 197, 198, 207; xenotapheia, 274–75. *See also* strangers, burial of

Cephalenia, 237

Cerimoniis, De (Constantine Porphyrogenitos), 233; cited, 50n, 52nn, 116nn, 118nn, 189n, 190nn, 193n, 196n, 197n, 200n, 213n, 220n, 222n, 237nn, 239nn, 250n

Chadwick, Henry, 30n

Chalandon, Ferdinand, cited, 171n

Chalcedon, 151

Champagny, Franz de, cited, 16n, 69n, 87n, 138n

"Chapitres Relatifs aux fonctions des Dignitaires, Les" (Guilland), 246n

Charanis, Peter, xin, 18n, 172n, 185n, 243n, 270n, 283n; on kingship, 54n, 58n, 59n, 60n; on monasticism, 110nn, 121n, 259nn

"Charitable Foundations of Byzantium, The" (Duff), 149n, 150n, 151n

"Charité" (Leclercq), 16n

Charité chrétienne dans les premiers siècles de l'eglise, La (de Champagny), 16n, 69n, 87n, 138n

Charity and Social Life (Loch), 7n

Chastel, Etienne, 16n, 87n, 151n

cherotropheion, 276

Chiensis, Leonardus, cited, 288n

children, 14, 116; illegitimate, 248; infant baptism, 85; law and, 48. *See also* orphans

Chimmerious, Armenia, 80

choirs, 86

Choniates, Nicetas, *see* Nicetas Choniates

Chouspacrati, 140

Christian Century (periodical), 283n

Christian Charity in the Ancient Church (Uhlhorn), 16n, 157n, 280n

Christianity: Byzantine development of, 66, 136, 149–51, 271, 273–74, 275–76, 281; Greek influences in, 3–16, 43, 46, 222; kingship and, 43–61, 133, 136; pagan reception of, 15–16, 31, 208–209, 263; theocentricity of, 11–12, 13; war and, 126, 129

Christmas, 88, 131

Christodotes, xenon, 195

Christophilopoulos, A., cited, 257n

Christou, P., cited, 155n

Chronicle (Joshua the Stylite), 158nn, 159n

Chronicon (Glycas), 245n

Chronicon (Gregorios Monachos), 114n, 198n, 199n, 200n, 233n, 250n, 263n

Chronicon of Morea, 214

Chronicon Paschale (Dindorf, ed.), 35n, 113n, 162n, 189n, 192n, 209n, 210n, 227n, 230n

Chronios, 188

Chronographia (Leo Grammaticos), 134n

Chronographia (Malalas), 133n, 189nn, 192n, 212nn, 220n, 271n, 272nn

Chronographia (Psellos), 53nn, 122nn, 123n, 273n

Chronographia of Michael Psellus, The (Sewter), 273n

Chronographia (Symeon Magister), 35n, 115n, 119nn, 196nn, 197n, 198n, 227nn, 239n

Chronographia (Theophanes), 98n, 113n, 134n, 186n, 189n, 192nn, 199n, 200n, 212n, 213n, 220n, 222n, 225n, 226n, 227n, 230n, 239n, 243nn, 263n, 274n

Chronographia (Theophanes Continuatus), 26n, 52n, 114nn, 115nn, 118nn, 119nn, 121nn, 122nn, 134n, 135nn, 153n, 166n, 170n, 183n, 195n, 197nn, 198n, 199n, 200n, 227n, 230n, 232nn, 233n, 234n, 243nn, 244n, 265n

Chronologie, La (Grumel), 229n, 230n, 232n

"Chronologie des Theophanes im 7. und 8. Jahrhundert, Die" (Ostrogorsky), 225n

Chrysobalandon, monastery of, 106

"Chrysobull of the Emperor Andronicus II, A" (Alexander), 60n

Chrysostom, John, saint, 22n, 221n, 276n; charities of, 68, 69, 71, 74, 93, 145, 151, 268; on forgiveness of sins, 24; on God's justice, 34; on hospitality, 186–87, 208; hospitals of, 155–56; lepers and, 182; on the poor, 257–59, 284

Chrysotriclinos, 250

Church and Learning in the Byzantine Empire (Hussey), 27n, 172n

church buildings, 24, 52, 75, 79, 93, 168; deaconesses and, 85–86; dedication of, 133, 209–10, 227, 267; xenones in, 188, 190, 198, 208. *See also specific churches*

Church History (periodical), 16n

church philanthropy, 11, 13, 28, 67–87, 149, 279; aged and, 222; deserted children and, 248; hospitality and, 218; imperial support of, 65–66, 113–14, 150–51; medicine and, 154, 158, 168, 169–70; the poor and, 259, 285. *See also specific churchmen and institutions*

Church Quarterly Review (periodical), 84n

Church in the Roman Empire, The (Ramsay), 155n

Cicero, 3n

Ciganto, Marcello, 49n

Cimon, 9, 11

Cimon (Plutarch), 9n

Cinnamos, John, 186n; on Irene, 132; on Pantocrator, 172

Cities and Bishoprics of Phrygia (Ramsay), 7n

Cities of the Eastern Roman Provinces, The (Jones), 74n, 212n

Civil Law, The (Scott), 257n

Classical World, The (periodical), 45n

Clement of Alexandria (d. c. 215), 30–31, 43

Clement, bishop of Ochrida (+916), 81

Clermont-Ganneau, Charles, 160, 225

clinics, 152, 154, 186, 275; in gerocomeia, 228; Greek, 7, 8; in the Pantocrator, 172, 174, 175; in poor-houses, 260

Clugnet, M. Leon, 35n, 92n, 96nn, 137n, 168nn

Codellas, Pan S., cited, 171n

Codex Theodosianus XVI, 85n

Codices Vaticani Graeci (Mercati and Cavalieri), 198n, 199n

Codinos, George, *see* Pseudo-Codinos, George

Coelesti Hierarchia, De (Dionysios the Areopagite), 36nn

coinage, 179

Collection de romans grecs en langue vulgaire et en vers, 214n, 215nn

Collomp, Paul, 26n, 239n

Commentarius in Sanctum Joannem Apostolum et Evangelistam (Chrysostomos), 34n

Commentarius in S. Matthaeum Evangelistam (Chrysostomos), 24n

"Communication-Chronique Archéologique" (de Vaux), 160nn

Comneno, Juan Arcadio Lascaris, 244n

Comparative Studies in Society and History (periodical), 18n

"Concept of Philanthropia in Plutarch's Lives, The" (Martin, Jr.), 4n, 11n

"Confession of Faith, The" (royal), 60

Congrès d'histoire de la médecine (2e, 1922), 235n; (XVIIe, 1960), 152n, 153n, 174n, 193n

Congrès international des études byzantines (IVe), *Actes*, 52n

Congreso español de Estudios Clásicos, Madrid, 15–19 de Abril 1956, *Actas* del primer, 244n

Constans II, emperor (641–68), 230

Constantelos, Demetrios J., cited, 113n

Constantia (city), 169

Constantine the Great, 223; charities of, 112, 116; laws of, 48, 165,

262; prostitutes and, 196; Sampson and, 191; xenones and, 209

Constantine V Copronymos, emperor (741–75), 114, 225, 231

Constantine VI, emperor (780–97), 98, 169; blinding of, 134, 196

Constantine VII Porphyrogenitos, emperor, 50n, 51n, 52nn, 99n, 107, 116, 135, 233, 250n; gerocomeia and, 118–19, 222n, 232, 237, 239; on xenones, 189n, 190, 193n, 196n, 197n, 200n, 213, 220n, 221n; the Zoticon and, 166

Constantine IX Monomachos, emperor (1042–55), 53, 56, 122, 135, 170, 198, 233

Constantine X Dukas, emperor (1059–67), 123, 239

Constantine, crown prince (son of Michael VII), 58

Constantinides, P., cited, 266n

Constantinople, 71, 76, 98, 115, 151; brothels of, 272; gerocomeia in, 116, 223–25, 227, 229–37; hospitals in, 116, 153, 155–56, 162, 164–67, 170–79, 195, 244–45; Latin occupation of, 268; Liudprand in, 145; Michael Attaleiates house in, 142, 267; municipal taxation, 134; orphanages, 86, 116, 126, 128, 129–30, 168, 241–52, 276; poor in, 258–59; 260, 265–66, 267–68, 284; Russian attack (860), 79; sack of 1204, 245; St. Philaretes in, 169; xenones of, 102, 106, 116, 162, 185–86, 188–200, 204–208, 210, 213, 220

Constantinople, University of, 80

Constantinople byzantine (Janin), 156n, 167n, 190n, 198nn, 199n, 206n, 223nn, 224nn, 226n, 227n, 230nn, 231n, 232nn, 234n, 266n

Constantinopolis Christiana, see *Historia Byzantin—Constantinopolis Christiana* (Du Cange)

Constantinos, bishop of Eirenopolis, cited, 171n, 174n

Constantinos (orphanotrophos), 255

Constantios II, emperor (337–61), 45, 165, 210, 249

Constantopoulos, C. M., cited, 237n

"Contribution à l'étude de la médecine des zenones pendant le XVe siècle" (Kousis), 153n, 174n

Conybeare, Frederick C., cited, 160n

Copterion, 140

Corfu, 145

Corinth, 151, 153, 223, 266

Corinthiaca (Pausanias), 7n

I *Corinthians,* 12n, 13nn, 29n, 273n

II *Corinthians,* 12n, 13nn

Cornelius (c. 250), bishop, 15

"Coronation and its Constitutional Significance in the Later Roman Empire" (Charanis), 54n, 58n, 59nn, 60n

Corpus Juris Civilis (Schoell and Kroll, eds.), 48nn, 85nn, 112n, 113n, 150n, 151n, 186n, 192n, 212n, 216n, 218nn, 220n, 222n, 239n, 241n, 242n, 248n, 251n, 257n, 260n, 265nn, 271n, 274n

Corpus de sceaux de l'empire byzantin, Le (Laurent), 75n, 237n

Corpus Scriptorum Historiae Byzantinae, xin, 56nn, 113n, 115n, 122nn, 132nn, 150n, 165n, 166n, 168n, 172n, 179n, 186n, 199n, 203n, 204n, 222n, 224n, 229n, 233n, 245n, 249n, 269n, 276n, 285n, 286n, 287n

Corpus Scriptorum Christianorum Orientalium, cited, 162n, 226n

Cosmas, saint, 169

Cosmosoteira, monastery of, 27, 132, 181, 236

Council of Chalcedon (451), 69, 85, 157, 269; on episcopal duties, 219

Council of Nicaea (325), 69

Council in Trullo (692), 70, 85

Crateia, 74

Cremona, Italy, 145

Crete, 7, 75, 168, 250, 264

cripples, 10, 66, 76, 98, 99, 136, 259, 276; Alexios' city for, 128–29, 244; Eulogios and, 138; in gerocomeia, 235

Cross, Frank L., 32n

Crucifixion, The, 36

Crum, W. E., 70n

Crusades, The, 193, 205

Cydones, Demetrios, 60n, 258n

Cyprian (d. 258), saint, 15
Cyprus, 69, 91, 109, 207; Arab seizure (911–12), 99–100
Cyrillos of Alexandria, 68n
Cyril Phileotes (Kataskepenos), 21n, 22n, 25nn, 35nn, 55n, 60n, 108n, 109nn, 126n, 244n, 249n
Cyril of Scythopolis, 35, 71, 183, 263; on John Hesychastes, 219, 225; on Justinian's hospital, 160; on orphanages, 242, 243; parents of, 187
Cyros (physician), 168, 229

Dalton, O. M., cited, 279n
Damianos, xenodochos, 221
Damianos, saint, 169
Daniel of Scete, abbot, 35n, 92n, 137n, 168nn; in Egypt, 96
Daphne, 164, 274
Daphni, monastery of, 215
Darrouzès, Jean, 35n, 80nn
David, Symeon and George, brother-saints, 101–102
David, Castle of, 187
Dawes, E. A. S., 27n, 244n
deacons, 70, 75, 84–87
Deaut, Roger Le, 3n, 10nn
Decapolis, 99
Decarreaux, Jean, cited, 89n
Decorum (Hippocrates), 154n
Decrees and Canons of the Seven Ecumenical Councils, 69n
Definitiones (Plato), 4n
Delehaye, Hippolyte, cited, 19nn, 25n, 35n, 39n, 80n, 81nn, 90n, 91nn, 92n, 106n, 107nn, 186n, 213n, 262n
Demangel, R., cited, 234n
Demetrianos, Bishop of Chytri, 99–100
Demetrius Cydones Correspondence (Loenertz, ed.), 60n
Demetropoulos, P., cited, 16n
Demosthenes, 6, 9
Demosthenes, governor of Edessa, 158
Den Ven, Paul Van, 69n
Denys L'Areopagite Sources Chrétiennes (Heil), 36n
Deuteron quarter, Constantinople, 197, 206–207

Deux Typica byzantins de l'époque des Paleologues (Delehaye), 19nn, 25n, 35n, 90n, 91nn, 170nn, 186n
Dewing, H. B., 272n
Dexiocrates, 151, 224
diaconia, 70, 75, 84–87
Dialogue with Trypho (Justin), 15n, 29n
Diataxis (Michael Attaleiates), 259n, 260n, 267nn, 268nn
Diataxis des Michael Attaleiates, Die (Nissen), 142n
Dictionnaire d'archéologie chrétienne et de liturgie (Leclercq), 16n
Didache of the Twelve Apostles, 13n, 14n
Diehl, Charles, 55n, 134n, 179n
Diekamp, Franz, 33n, 36nn
Dienst der Frau in den ersten Jahrhunderten der christlichen Kirche, Der (Zscharnack), 84n
Digesta Justiniani Augusti (Mommsen), 257n
Dikaeosyne, see justice
Dimakellion quarter, Constantinople, 223
Dimitrov, Dimitre P., cited, 207nn
Dindorf, Wilhelm, 45nn
Dio Chrysostomos, 49
Diocletian, 168
Diogenes Laertios, cited, 9n
Diomedes, Alexander N., cited, 28n, 110
Dionysios of Alexandria (d. 264–65), quoted, 20
Dionysios the Areopagite, saint, 36n, 37n
Dioscurides, 206
Dittenberger, W., 10n
Divine Liturgy, The (Basil the Great), 33n
Divinis Nominibus, De (Dionysios the Areopagite), 37n
Dmitrievsky, A., cited, 25n, 26n, 28n, 34n, 91n, 92n, 93n, 172nn, 174nn, 175nn, 179nn, 193n, 204n, 207n, 230n, 235nn, 265n, 275n
Dodds, E. R., cited, 41n
Dolger, Franz, cited, 240n, 255nn
Donaldson, James, 15n
Dormition of Theotocos, 88, 91, 132

Dorries, H., 20*nn*

Doryzin quarter, Alexandria, 168, 229

Dositheos, 228

Doukakis, Constantine Chr., 79*n*, 84*n*, 101*n*, 102*n*

Dousas, Theodore, cited, 287*n*

Downey, Glanville, cited, 11*n*, 45*nn*, 46*n*, 164*nn*, 189*n*, 263*n*, 272*n*, 285*n*

"Droit divin à Byzance, Le" (Guilland), 54*n*

Droungariou, tou, 198–99

Du Cange, Charles de Fresne, cited, 164*n*, 189*n*, 190*n*, 206*nn*, 224*n*, 227*nn*, 230*n*, 231*n*, 233*n*, 236*n*, 243*n*

Ducas, Michael, *see* Michael VII Ducas, emperor

Duchesne, L., cited, 249*n*

Duff, P. W., cited, 149*n*, 150*n*, 151*n*

Dumbarton Oaks Papers, cited, 43*nn*, 53*n*, 110*n*, 121*n*, 140*nn*, 153*n*, 171*n*, 198*n*, 199*n*, 258*n*, 259*n*

Duval, Rubens, cited, 139*n*

Dvornik, F., 99*nn*, 272*n*

Dyrrachium, 79

Dyrrachium, Duke of, 123

"Early Medieval Charity" (Niederev), 16*n*

earthquakes, 113, 166, 186, 244, 267

Easter, 88, 116

Ecclesiastica Hierarchia (Dionysios the Areopagite), 37*n*

Ecclesiastical History (Eusebios of Caesarea), 15*n*

Ecclesiastical History (Evagrios), 164*n*, 242*n*, 249*n*

Ecclesiastical History (Nicephoras Callistos Xanthopoulos), 162*n*, 263*nn*

Ecclesiastical History (Sozomenos), 16*n*, 31*nn*, 46*n*, 70*n*, 71*n*, 85*n*, 154*n*, 209*n*, 259*n*, 260*nn*, 261*n*, 263*nn*, 276*n*

Ecclesiastical History (Theodoretos of Cyrus), 31*n*, 39*n*, 85*n*, 112*n*, 157*n*

Echos d'orient (periodical), 41*n*, 134*n*, 223*n*, 226*n*, 231*n*, 250*n*

Ecloga (Chrysostomos), 22*n*

Ecloga (Leo III), 49–50

Ecumenical Councils, 69, 70, 85, 149*n*, 157, 219, 269

Edessa, Syria, 96, 139, 158; famine in, 209

Edessenos, orphanotrophos, 255

education, 50, 51, 58, 206; compassion and, 97, 115; medical, 174, 179; of orphans, 126, 128, 129, 130, 132, 150, 245, 248

Efstratiades, S., cited, 39*n*, 93*n*

Egersios, soldier, 220

"Eglise byzantine sur les rives du Bosphore, L'" (Janin), 249*n*

Egypt, 94, 96, 129, 139, 145; poorhouses in, 262, 264; xenones in, 188. *See also specific cities*

Ekklesiastike Aletheia (periodical), 274*n*

Elaeon, monastery of, 94

Elaia quarter, Constantinople, 266

Eleemosyna Sermo, De (Chrysostomos), 68*n*

Eleemosynis, De (Chrysostomos), 24*n*

Eleemosynis, De (Symeon of Thessalonica), 25*n*

Eleusios, deacon, 261

Eliab, 157

Elias, prophet, 236

Elias, Governor of Cappadocia, 208

Ellissen, Adolf, cited, 60*n*, 146*n*

Emendanda vita monachica, De (Eustathios of Thessalonica), 23*n*

Empereur Julien, oeuvres complètes, L' (Bidez, ed.), 16*n*, 45*n*, 209*n*, 263*n*

"Emperor and the Imperial Administration, The" (Ensslin), 49*n*

Emperor Romanus Lecapenus and his Reign, The (Runciman), 119*n*, 285*nn*

emperors, 111–36, 150; bishops and, 81, 262; God and, 26–27, 28, 31, 43, 61, 111, 135–36, 262. *See also individual names*

"Empire and Desert: Antinomies of Christian History" (Florovsky), 90*n*

"Encomium" (Gregory of Nyssa), 155nn

Encomium of St. Gregory on His Brother St. Basil (Stein), 155n

End of the Ancient World and the Beginnings of the Middle Ages, The (Lot), 156n

English Historical Review (periodical), 160n

Ensslin, Wilhelm, 49n

Epaminondas, 9, 11

Epaminondas (Nepos), 9n

Epanagoge, 150, 218–19

Epeteris Etaerias Byzantinon Spoudon (periodical), 7n, 87n, 116n, 144n, 171n, 179n, 205n, 255n, 274n, 275n

Ephesians, 12n

Ephesos, 153, 157, 202–203, 223

Ephraemios, cited, 224n, 229n, 249nn

Ephraem the Syrian, 139, 209

Epidauros, 7

epidemiology, 152–53

Epigrammata (Agathias), 113n

"Epigraphie chrétienne de Jérusalem" (Germer-Durand), 225n

epilepsy, 179

Epiphanios, cubicularius, 197

Epiphanios (d. 403), bishop of Constantia, 70, 167, 262n

Epiphanios, patriarch (520–35), 248

Epiphany, 88

Epistle of Barnabas, 14nn

Epistle to the Philippians (Polycarp), 13n

Epistle to the Smyrneans, 13n, 14n

Epistles (Athanasios the Great), 68n

Epistles (Cyprian), 15n

Epistles (Julian), 16n, 45n, 209n, 263n

Epistles (Nicholas Mysticos), xn, 37n, 52n, 53nn, 79n

Epistles (Photios), xn, 35n, 37n, 50nn, 221nn, 251n

Epistles (Theodore Studites), 79n, 134n, 184n, 216n, 220n, 251n, 275n

Epistles (Theophylactos of Ochrida), 37n, 55n, 81n, 84n, 142n

Epistle to Theodore the Chief-Priest (Julian), 263n

Epistola Episcoporum Aegypti et Libyae Nonaginta (Athanasios), 32n

Epistolae (Cydones), 60n

Epistoliers byzantins du Xe *siècle* (Darrouzès), 35n, 80nn

Epitomae Historiarum (Zonaras), 68n, 130n, 213nn, 244n, 245n

Epitome (Pseudo-Clementine), 29n, 281nn

Epitome Historion (Joannes Cinnamos), 132nn, 172n, 186n

Erotici Scriptores Graeci (Hercher), 221n

Esquisse topographique de Constantinople (Mordtmann), 229n, 231n, 232n

Essai sur la civilization byzantine (Hesseling), 61n

Essays and Hymns of Synesius of Cyrene (Fitzgerald, tr.), 46n

"Etudes sur l'histoire administrative de l'empire byzantin—L'Orphanotrophe" (Guilland), 256n

Etudes historiques sur l'influence de la charité (Chastel), 16n, 87n, 151n

"Etudes de topographie byzantine" (Janin), 226n

Euboulos, 154, 226; xenon of, 189, 190, 220

Euchaita, Armenia, 80

Euchologion (Dmitrievsky), 34n

Euchologion Sive Rituale Graecorum (Goar), 34n, 41n, 222n, 282n

Eudocia (Athenais), empress of Theodosios II, 112, 160–62, 225, 263

Eudoxios, patriarch (360–69), 210

Eudoxiou, Constantinople, 231

Eugenios, port of, 191

Eugeniou gerocomeion, 233

Eugeniou region, Constantinople, 264, 269

Eulogios, 96, 138

Euphemia, 159

Euphemios, patriarch (489–95), 225, 249, 265, 269

Euphrata gerocomeion, Constantinople, 223

Euphratas, 223

Euphrosyne, 267

eusebia (piety), 45, 46, 50, 60
Eusebios of Caesarea, 15n, 31; on
　　Constantine the Great, 112, 262;
　　kingship and, 43, 45, 111nn
"Eusebius and the Christian Em-
　　pire" (Baynes), 43n
Eusebius Werke (Klostermann, ed.),
　　31n
Eustathii Opuscula (Tafel), 109n
Eustathios, bishop of Sebastia in
　　Pontos, 167
Eustathios, son of Philaretos, 98–99
Eustathios of Thessalonica (b. c.
　　1125), 23n, 24, 79–80, 133n; on
　　kingship, 56–57; on monastic
　　philanthropy, 109–10
Eustratiades, S., cited, 264n
Euthymios, bishop of Madyta, 99
Euthymios, patriarch (907–12), 81
Euthymios, saint, 187
Euxine Pontos, 261, 272
Evagrios, 164, 242n, 249n
Every, George, cited, 283n
"Excavations at Bodrum Camii,
　　1930" (Rice), 198n, 232n
Excidio Thessalonicensi, De (Jo-
　　annes Cameniates), 38n
Exemplum Testamenti (Gregory
　　Nazianzenos), 261nn
Expeditio Persica (George of
　　Pisidia), 49n
Exposito Capitum Admonitoriorum
　　(Agapetos), 46n

famine, 68, 79, 80, 101; hospitals
　　and, 156, 158, 170, 209; Palestine,
　　210; private aid in, 138, 139;
　　Romanos Lecapenos and, 119.
　　See also food
Farag, Farag Fofail, cited, 89n
"Farmer's Law, The" (Ashburner),
　　49n
Fathers, xenodocheion of the,
　　Ascalon, 212
Felicetti-Liebenfels, Walter, 41n
Ferguson, John, cited, 3n, 11n, 31n
Festugière, A. J., 158n, 160n, 187n,
　　225n, 263n
"Fifty-Seventh Apostolic Canon"
　　(Rhallis-Potlis, ed.), 276n
Fine et Exitu nostro e vita, De
　　(Symeon of Thessalonica), 25n

fires, 180–81, 189, 190, 192, 243
First Apologia (Justin), 13n, 15n,
　　29n
Fitzgerald, Augustine, 46n
*Five Theological Orations of
　　Gregory of Nazianzenos* (Mason),
　　32n
Flacilla, empress, 112, 157
Flavitas, patriarch, 265
Fliche, Augustin, 239n
Florentios, gerocomeion of, 224
Florovsky, Georges, cited, 90n
Fontes Rerum Byzantinorum
　　(Regel), 56n, 57nn
food, 10; banquet of Philaretos, 98;
　　Church distribution of, 14, 15,
　　114; famine relief, 68, 79, 80;
　　hospital, 172, 174, 175; imperial
　　gifts of, 113, 118, 119, 121, 126,
　　128, 132, 232; monastery distribu-
　　tion of, 88, 90, 91, 94, 102, 131,
　　132, 200, 204, 207, 210, 235;
　　private gifts of, 138, 139, 141,
　　142–43, 204; refectories, 196, 197
Forty Martyrs, Church of the, 180,
　　213
Forty-Martyrs holiday, 144
Fourmy, Marie-Henriette, cited, 97n,
　　98nn, 99nn, 169n
Fragments to Marcellus (Eusebios of
　　Caesarea), 31n
Franks, 126
*Franzosisch-mittelgriechische Ritter-
　　roman "Imberios und Margarona"
　　und die Grundungssage des
　　Daphniklosters bei Athen* (Bees),
　　214n, 215n
Freshfield, E. N., cited, 286n
Fuchs, Friedrich, cited, 206n
funds: Church, 13, 70, 71, 78, 79,
　　81, 112, 116, 156, 259, 261;
　　funeral, 274; Greek "sacred
　　treasuries," 7–8, 11; hospital, 159,
　　169, 175; imperial, 27–28, 57,
　　112, 122, 179, 263, 287; monastic,
　　91, 109–10; private, 15, 68–69,
　　70, 78, 81, 93, 94, 97–98, 101,
　　106, 107, 137–38, 139–46, 168,
　　169, 214, 267, 280; for recon-
　　struction of institutions, 121, 180,
　　195, 196; for xenones, 187–88,
　　189, 195, 204, 212, 220

"Funeral Orations, No. 4" (Psellos), 183n

Fytrakis, A. J., 89n

Galata, 266

Galatia, 16, 94, 209

Galatians, Epistles of Saint Paul to the, 13n

Gardthausen, Victor, cited, 228n

Garitte, Gerard, cited, 162n, 226n

Gass, W., 38n

Gay, J., cited, 53n

Gedeon, Manuel, cited, 90n, 92n, 100nn, 108n, 246n, 248n, 249n, 274n; on gerocomeia, 227n, 228n, 230n, 231n

Gelasios, 157, 242

Gelzer, H., 74nn, 75nn, 144n, 145n, 170nn, 259n, 262n, 272n

Gemistos, Pletho, 286

General History of the Christian Religion and Church (Neander), 16n, 67n

Genesios, cited, 114, 134n, 265n

Genier, Raymond, cited, 263n

Gennadios II (George Scholarios), 287n, 288n

Géographie ecclésiastique de l'empire byzantin, La (Janin), cited, xin, 92n, 106nn, 164n, 166nn, 167n, 170n, 171n, 190n, 191n, 193nn, 195nn, 196n, 197n, 200n, 205nn, 206n, 224nn, 225n, 226n, 228n, 229n, 231n, 233nn, 235n, 236nn, 239n, 246n, 248n

George, archbishop of Amastris (d. c. 807), 78–79

George, deacon, 221, 251

George of Pisidia, 49

George, saint, 225

Georgii Acropolitae Annales, 287n

Georgios Monachos, *see* Gregorios Monachos

"Georgium Acropolitam Notae, In" (Dousas and Allatius), 287n

Geragathes, gerocomeion, 231

Germanos III, patriarch (1265–67), 245

Germany, 100

Germer-Durand, R. P., cited, 225n

gerocomeia, 99, 222–40; Church, 69, 71, 80, 86, 168, 190; imperial establishment of, 52, 55, 112, 116, 119, 121, 129–30, 134, 160–61, 198, 199, 232–33, 236, 237, 244; medical services, 153–54, 179, 233, 235; monastic, 150, 157, 235–37; wartime destruction of, 287

gerocomos, office of, 239–40

Geschichte der Byzantinischen Ikonenmalerei (Felicetti-Liebenfels), 41n

Geschichte der Byzantinischen Litteratur (Krumbacher), 231n

Geschichte des Griechish-Romaischen Rechts (Lingenthal), 50n

"Geschichtliche Hintergrund zu Imberios (Pierre de Provence und Margarona) La Belle Maguelonne, Der," 214n, 215n

Gheyn, J. Van Den, 35n, 108n

Gibbon, Edward, cited, xin, 16n

Giet, Stanislas, cited, 155n

Gilles, Pierre, cited, 230n

Giorgio di Pisidia Poemi (Pertusi), 49n

Giovanni Argiropoulo (Cammelli), 206n

Glabas, Michael Tarchaneiotes, xenon, 205

Glycas, Michael, cited, 130, 244n, 245n

Goar, Jacobus, cited, 34n, 41n, 222n, 282n

God: fall of Byzantium and, 288; gratitude toward, 27, 28, 33, 112, 143–44; healing and, 143–44, 154, 183–84; kingship and, 43–61, 111, 135–36; man's relation to, 4, 8, 10, 11, 12, 13, 19, 21, 26, 27, 29, 30–37, 38–39, 41, 46, 67, 80, 81, 84, 92, 93, 94, 97, 131, 275, 280–81; mercy of, 19, 20, 29, 34, 35, 39, 51, 58, 286–87; sin and, 23, 32, 33, 39, 135. *See also* Jesus Christ

Golden Horn, 195, 196; gerocomeia on, 224, 229, 233, 237

Good Friday, 88, 118, 121, 143, 237

Gortyn, Crete, 7

Grand Lavra, Jerusalem, 157, 158, 187, 210, 225; Constantine X and, 239; John Hesychastes and, 219; Origenist monks and, 242

Greece, 3–16, 18–19, 25, 29, 31, 41, 280, 281; aged in, 6, 8–10, 19, 222; Byzantine restoration (1261), 245; German occupation (1941–44), 100; kingship concept in, 43, 46; medicine in, 154, 158–59; poor-houses in, 266. See also specific placenames

Greek Apologists, 29

Greek Education (Beck), 5n

Greek Orthodox Theological Review, xin, 90n, 113n, 172n, 270n

Greek-Roman and Byzantine Studies (periodical), 45n, 46n

"Greeks under the Roman Empire, The" (Jones), 43nn

Greeks and the Irrational, The (Dodds), 41n

Grégoire, H., cited, 100nn, 183n, 209n, 230n

Grégoire de Nazianze Discours Funèbres (Boulenger), 68n, 155n, 260n

Gregoras, Nicephoros, cited, 115nn, 183, 233n, 269n, 286n

Gregorios Monachos, saint, 108n, 114n, 233n, 250, 263n, 274; on xenones, 198n, 199n, 200n, 202nn, 203

Gregorios, bishop of Assos, 84

Gregorios o Palamas, 16n, 157n

Gregory, from Irenopolis, 99

Gregory Nazianzenos, saint, 71, 182, 209; on the imitation of God, 20, 21n, 32; on St. Basil, 68n, 69n, 154–55; will of, 261

Gregory of Nyssa, saint, 32, 182; cited, 19n, 68n, 155nn, 248n

Gregory the Presbyter, cited, 155n, 182n

Gregory the Theologian, see Gregory Nazianzenos, saint

Griechischen Schreiber des Mittelalters und der Renaissance, Die (Vogel and Gardthausen), 228n

Griffith, G. T., 10nn

Grillmeier, A., cited, 157n

Grmed, M. D., 153n

Grumel, V., cited, 53n, 134n, 174n, 229n, 230n, 232n

Guilland, Rodolphe, cited, 54n, 246n, 256n

Gulick, C. B., cited, 6n, 7n

Gwatkin, H. M., 285n

Hadrianople, 153

Hagia Sophia, Constantinople, 76, 85, 162, 212, 242; completion of, 113; gerocomeion at, 119, 232; workshops, 112, 116, 248, 274; xenones near, 189, 190, 191–95

Halkin, François, cited, 24n, 41n, 78n, 156n, 169n, 209n, 287n

Halmyrissos, Thrace, 95

Harnack, Adolf von, cited, 16n, 90n, 283n

Harun-al-Raschid, 78

Harvard Essays on Classical Subjects (Smyth, ed.), 6n

Harvard Theological Review, 45n

Hatch, Edwin, 16n

Haupturkenden fur die Geschichte der Athoskloster, Die (Meyer), 92n

Hausherr, Irenée, 106n, 265n

Hawkins, Ernest J. W., cited, 198n

Healing Gods of Ancient Civilizations, The (Jayne), 7n, 154n

Hebrews, 21n, 208n

Heikel, I. A., 45n

Heil, Gunter, 36n

Heilige Johannes Chrysostomus und seine zeit, Der (Baur), 68n

Heilige Theodosios, Der (Usener), 93n, 158nn

Heinze, M., 38n

Heisenberg, A., cited, 185n

Helen, empress of Constantine Porphyrogenitos, 112, 232

Helen, saint, 223, 262

Hell, 23

Hellenica (periodical), 39n, 93n

Hellenistic Civilization (Tarn and Griffith), 10nn

Hellenistic Origins of Byzantine Art, The (Ainalov), 279n

Hera, sanctuary of, 7

Heracleia, 107–108, 223

Heracles, 8, 9

Heraclios, emperor (610–41), 195, 218n; deaconess order and, 85;

kingship theory and, 49; the Zoticon and, 165, 242

Hercher, Rudolph, cited, 221*n*

hermits, 20, 88, 138, 187–88

Hesiod, 5

Hesseling, D. C., 61*n*

Hesychastes, John, *see* John Hesychastes

Hierapolis, 7

"Hieria" (Pargoire), 164*n*, 247*n*

Hill, George, cited, 100*nn*

Hippocrates, 8, 95, 154*n*

Hippodamos, 6

Hippodrome, 250

Histoire ancienne de l'église (Duchesne), 249*n*

Histoire de l'assistance publique dans les temps anciens et modernes (Monnier), 5*n*, 10*n*

Histoire du Bas-Empire (Stein), 112*n*

Histoire de la charité (Lallemand), 5*n*, 16*n*

Histoire de l'education dans l'antiquité (Marrou), 5*n*

Histoire de l'église (Fliche and Martin, eds.), 239*n*

Histoire de Imberios & Margarona —Imitation Grecque du Roman Français Pierre de Provence et la Belle Maguelonne (Wagner), 214*n*, 215*n*

Histoire de la littérature néogrecque, L' (Knos), 214*n*

Histoire politique, religieuse et littéraire d'Edesse (Duval), 139*n*

Historia (Joannes Cantacuzenos), xin, 136*n*, 233*n*

Historia (Nicetas Choniates), 56*nn*, 199*n*, 204*n*, 276*n*, 285*n*

Historia (periodical), 45*nn*, 89*n*, 90*n*, 189*n*, 263*n*

Historia (Simocattes), ix*n*, x*nn*

Historia Arianorum (Athanasios of Alexandria), 33*n*

Historia Byzantin—Constantinople Christiana (Du Cange), 164*n*, 189*n*, 190*n*, 206*nn*, 224*n*, 227*nn*, 230*n*, 231*n*, 233*n*, 236*n*, 243*n*

Historia Constantinopolitanae Urbis a Mahummet II Captae (Leonardus Chiensis), 288*n*

Historiae (Bryennios), 126*nn*

Historiae (Leo Diaconos), 122*nn*, 150*n*, 165*n*, 166*nn*

Historia Monachorum (Timothy), 35*n*, 91*n*, 94*nn*, 139*n*, 188*n*

Historiarum (Agathias), 271*n*

Historiarum Compendium (Cedrenos), 165*n*, 166*n*, 179*n*, 186*n*, 189*nn*, 198*n*, 199*nn*, 208*n*, 212*n*, 233*n*, 244*nn*, 247*n*, 263*n*

Historical Geography of Asia Minor, The (Ramsay), 74*n*, 78*nn*, 80*n*, 99*n*, 107*n*, 144*n*, 202*n*, 213*nn*, 252*n*

History of Antioch in Syria from Seleucus to the Arab Conquest, A (Downey), 164*nn*

History of the Byzantine Empire 323–1453, A (Vasiliev), 56*n*, 132*n*, 179*n*

History of the Byzantine State (Ostrogorsky), 18*n*, 55*n*, 71*n*, 74*n*, 78*n*, 91*n*, 134*n*, 145*n*, 150*n*, 224*n*, 243*n*, 244*n*, 258*n*

History of Cyprus, A (Hill), 100*nn*

History of the Decline and Fall of the Roman Empire, The (Gibbon), xin, 16*n*

History of the Eastern Roman Empire, A (Bury), 114*n*, 115*n*, 134*nn*

History of European Morals from Augustus to Charlemagne (Lecky), 11*n*, 12*n*, 16*n*, 67*nn*, 270*n*

History of the Later Roman Empire (Bury), 68*n*, 258*nn*

History Lausiaca (Palladios), 21*n*, 22*n*, 94*nn*, 95*n*, 138*nn*, 139*nn*, 145*n*, 188*n*, 220*n*, 264*nn*, 268*n*

History of the Peloponnesian War (Thucydides), 6*n*

History of the Wars (Procopios), 227*n*

Hoheren schulen von Konstantinopel im Mittelalter, Die (Fuchs), 206*n*

Holy Apostles, Church of the, Constantinople, 199, 243

Holy Thursday, 88, 141, 143, 235, 237

Holy Week, 180

Holy Wisdom, Church of the, Constantinople, *see* Hagia Sophia
Homer, 5, 6
Homer's Epigrams (Hesiod), 5n
Homilia de Capto Eutropio (Chrysostomos), 221n
Homilia dicta tempore famis et siccitatis (Basil the Great), 68n
Homilia in Divites (Basil the Great), 19n, 21n, 68n
Homilia VIII in Hexaemeron (Basil the Great), 248n
Homilia No. 4 (Asterios of Amaseia), 182n
Homiliae Paschales (Cyrillos of Alexandria), 68n
Homilien (Makarios), 20nn
Homily XI (Chrysostomos), 258n
Homily XXVIII (Chrysostomos), 34nn
Homily 58 (Chrysostomos), 182n
Homily (Pseudo-Clementine), 29n, 281nn
Hommages à Joseph Bidez et à Franz Cumont, 3n, 10n
Honigmann, E., cited, 141n, 204n
Hornus, Jean-Michel, 36n, 37n
Hosea, 19n
hospices, *see* xenones
"Hospital and Social Welfare Institutions in the Medieval Greek Empire (Byzantium)" (Pournaropoulos), 152n, 174n
hospitality, 14, 26, 76, 144–45, 215, 282, 287; Apostolic Church, 12, 13, 207; Chrysostom on, 186–87, 208; of the desert fathers, 188; monastic, 89, 91, 92, 94, 96, 98, 108, 210; patriarchal, 21, 98; Studities on, 216. *See also* xenones
hospitals, 152–84, 252, 275; canon law on, 69; of Chrysostom, 71; deaconesses in, 86; Greek, 7; imperial concern for, 52, 54, 112, 115, 116, 118, 121, 122, 150, 157, 159–60, 161–62, 164, 170–71, 172, 183, 198; monastery, 24, 102, 150, 157–58, 159, 171–79, 181, 187, 204, 225, 235; Syrian, 153, 162, 209; of Theophylactos, 78; wife of Philaretos and, 99;

xenones and, 186, 195. *See also* leprosaria
House of Arcadios, 162
House of the Great Droungarios, 180
House of Isidore, 162, 190
humanism, 66, 67, 136, 214
Humkapi quarter, Constantinople, 223
Hunger, Herbert, cited, 3n, 48n
Hussey, J. M., cited, 27n, 89n, 90n, 172n
hygiene, 152–53
Hypatios, archbishop of Gangra, 93
Hypatios of Ephesos (d. between 537–38 and 552), 33n, 36
Hypatios, saint, 95–96, 220

Iamboi (Theodore Studites), 24n
Iberites, Ioacheim, cited, 140nn, 141n
Iconium, 126, 135, 244
Idées et l'action sociales de Saint Basile, Les (Giet), 155n
Idéologie et cérémonial dans l'epistolographi byzantine (Karlsson), 251n
Ignatios, bishop of Antioch, 14, 69
Ignatios, metropolitan of Nicomedeia, 80
Ignatios, patriarch (847–58, 867–77), 97
Ignatios the Deacon, 76, 265nn
Ignatios, saint, 13n, 14n
Ignatios of Selybria, 112n, 223n, 260n
Iliad (Homer), 5, 6n
Illud Dictum Evangelii, In (Basil the Great), 23nn
"Imberios and Margarona," 214–15
Imperatorum et Patriarcharum (Ephraemios), 224n, 229n, 249nn
Imperial Administrative System in the Ninth Century, The (Bury), 247nn, 250n, 251n, 252n
Imperial Court, 81, 114; philanthropy and, 26, 27, 111, 112–13, 123, 259. *See also* emperors; state philanthropy
Incarnation doctrine, 30, 32, 36, 37, 38, 92; Irene Augusta and, 131;

kingship and, 56; Michael Attaleiates and, 142

Incarnatione, De (Athanasios of Alexandria), 32*nn*

Inédits byzantins d'Ochrida, Candie et Moscou (Halkin), 24*n*, 41*n*

Influence of Greek Ideals on Christianity, The (Hatch), 16*n*

Innocent, pope, 95

Institutio Regia (Theophylactos of Ochrida), 58*nn*

institutions, 12–13, 14, 18, 24, 65–66, 260; administration of, 149–51, 220–21, 239–40, 241–42, 249–56, 261, 262, 267; Church establishment of, 69, 71, 74, 76, 78, 79, 80, 86, 93, 149–50, 170; Greek, 6, 7, 9–10, 11, 19; imperial philanthropy and, 52, 54, 55, 112, 115, 119, 121, 123, 128–30, 133, 134, 135, 150–51, 195, 200, 262–67; leasing of, 198; private concern for, 99, 102, 137, 138, 139, 141, 142, 143, 144, 151, 169; Turkish destruction of, 287. *See also specific kinds of institution,* i.e., churches; gerocomeia; hospitals; leprosaria; monasteries; orphanages; ptochotropheia; xenones, xenotapheia

Institutions de l'empire byzantin, Les (Bréhier), 246*nn*, 247*n*

International Congress of Orientalists (XXV), 140*nn*

Internationalen Byzantinistenkongresses Munchen, 1958, XI, *Akten,* 214*n*

Ioannou, Theophilos, cited, 19*n*, 94*n*, 99*n*, 112*n*, 221*n*, 223*n*, 260*n*, 276*n*

Irene, saint, 106

Irene Augusta, empress of Alexios Comnenos, 130–32, 196; death of Alexios and, 27; gerocomeia of, 222; motives of, 134; xenones and, 197, 213; xenotapheia of, 274

Irene, empress of John II Comnenos, 132, 171

Irene, empress of John III Doucas Vatatzes, 268–69

Irion, Zoticon and, 164–67, 247

Iris River, 261

Isaac I Comnenos (1057–59), 27, 84, 132, 204

Isaac II Angelos (1185–95), 180–81, 199, 204, 213, 235–36

Isaacios, priest, 188

Isauria, 71

Isaurian dynasty, 114, 157

Isidore, xenon of, 190

Isidore of Alexandria, 219

Isidoros, 196

Isidoros, monastery, 188

Isidoros, xenon, 190

Isidorou gerocomeion, 226

Isle of Princes, 99

Isocrates, 9, 43

Is-Pigas, 166, 167

Italy, 153, 227

Itinera Hierosolymitan (Antonios Placentinos), 160*n*

Itinera Hierosolymitana Saeculi III–VIII (Geyer, ed.), 160*n*

Itinéraires russes en orient (de Khitrowo), 166*n*, 167*n*, 193*n*

Jacoby, D., cited, 258*n*

James, 12*n*

Janin, R., cited, xin, 41*n*, 89*n*, 92*n*, 106*n*, 156*n*, 170*n*, 171*n*, 266*n*; on gerocomeia, 223*n*, 224*nn*, 225, 226, 227, 228*n*, 229*nn*, 230*nn*, 231*n*, 232*nn*, 233*nn*, 234*n*, 235, 236, 239*n*; on orphanages, 246, 248*n*, 249*n*, 250*nn*; on xenones, 190*nn*, 191*n*, 193, 195*nn*, 196*n*, 197, 198*nn*, 199*n*, 200*n*, 205, 206, 207*n*; on the Zoticon, 164*n*, 166*nn*, 167*n*

Jayne, Walter A., cited, 7*n*, 154*n*

Jean Chrysostom, Lettres à Olympias (Malingrey), 268*n*

Jean II Comnène et Manuel I Comnène (Chalandon), 171*n*

Jeanselme, E., cited, 235*n*

Jejunio Homilia I, De (Basil the Great), 68*n*

Jenkins, Romilly, cited, 50*n*, 53*n*

Jericho, 158, 187, 189, 212

Jernstedt, V., 54–55, 56*n*, 153*n*, 244, 250*n*

Jerome, saint, 39, 154*n*

Jerusalem, 71, 95, 112; gerocomeia in, 160–62, 223, 225, 226, 239; hospitals in, 151, 157, 158, 159–60; institutions for the blind in, 275–76; poor-houses in, 263; xenones in, 187, 189, 210, 212, 219

Jesus Christ: hospitality and, 186–87, 215; incarnation of, 30, 32, 36, 37, 38, 56, 92, 131, 142; monasticism and, 88–89, 90, 95, 101, 107; philanthropy and, 10, 11, 12, 13, 14, 15, 22, 23–24, 30, 37, 41, 59, 67, 74, 95, 138, 149–50, 281; the poor and, 262, 267, 268; sins of the flesh and, 273

Joannes and Berine gerocomeia, 225

Joannes of Climacos, 21, 35n

Joannes Comnenos (Nicetas Choniates), 179n

John, 12nn, 29n, 30n, 273n

John (copyist), 206

John I Tzimisces, emperor (969–76), 121–22, 165–66

John II Comnenos, emperor (1118–43), 55, 57, 129, 131; gerocomeia and, 235; motives of, 135; Pantocrator monastery of, 27, 132, 171–79; prisoners and, 285

John III Doucas Vatatzes, emperor (1222–54), 59, 268, 286

John VI Cantacuzenos, emperor (1347–54), xin, 136, 233n, 246, 279, 288

John, brother of Alexios Comnenos, 84

John of Damascos (Joannes Damascenos), 20, 32, 34; cited, 21n, 24n, 35n, 68n

John the Eleemosynary, patriarch (d. 620), 74, 97, 151, 170

John of Ephesos, quoted, 159

John the Evangelist, saint, 39

John the Fifth, patriarch (669–75), 224

John Hesychastes, bishop of Coloneia, 113, 162, 219, 225

John Moschos (b.c. 550), 85n, 88n, 164n, 212, 274–75

John, bishop of Trimithous, 239

John the Orphanotrophos, 250–51, 252, 256

Jones, A. H. M., cited, 11n, 43nn, 74n, 151n, 155n, 156n, 159n, 212n, 280n

Joseph, hegoumenos, 203

Joshua the Stylite, 159n; quoted, 158

Journal of Hellenic Studies, 7n, 49n

Journal of Religious Thought, 90n

Journal of Theological Studies, 50n

Judaism, 12

Julian, emperor (361–63), 207; quoted on Christian charities, 16, 208, 209n, 263; kingship theory and, 45, 49

Julian, saint, 252

Julian of Adramyttion, 36

Jus Graeco-Romanum (Zepos and Zepos), 50n, 51nn, 52nn, 85n, 114nn, 150n, 193n, 198nn, 218nn, 220n, 221n, 232n, 236nn, 239n, 257n, 274n, 284n, 286nn

justice, 12, 15, 19, 20; Byzantine failures in, 145–46, 285, 286, 288; Church concern for, 71, 74, 75, 76, 78, 80, 81, 84, 285; of God, 31, 34, 37–38, 39; imperial, 48, 49–50, 51–52, 53–55, 56, 57, 81, 114, 119, 121, 126, 134, 271, 286; monastic efforts for, 107–108, 109

Justin I, emperor (518–27), 96, 113, 189, 190, 226

Justin II, emperor (565–78), 164, 190, 226, 243, 247, 252

Justin the Philosopher (d.c. 165), 13n, 15, 29, 43

Justinian, emperor (527–65), 207, 222n, 226, 227, 239n, 271; diaconate and, 85; hospitals and, 159–60, 161, 162, 164, 167, 252; laws of, 112, 113, 150n, 151, 212, 218nn, 220, 241, 242, 248, 251, 257n, 265, 272, 274; philanthropy of, 46, 48, 113, 133, 135; poor-houses and, 257n, 260n, 264–65, 274; xenones of, 185, 186n, 189, 190–91, 192, 212, 216n, 220

Kabasilas, Nicholas (d. c. 1370), 38

Kabbadias, P., cited, 41n

Kabiersch, J., cited, 45n, 263n

Kaegi, Walter E., Jr., 45n

Kaesarion ptochotropheion, 145, 262

Kallistos, Andronicos, cited, 276n, 287n, 288

Karabas, Theodore, 144

Karianos, 227

Karianou, gerocomeion, 227

Karlsson, Gustav, cited, 251n

Karvelas, G. I., cited, 41n

Kasimates, Gregory, cited, 116n

Kastor, 261

Kastoria, 153, 265

katagogia, 7, 102. *See also* xenones

Kataskepenos, Nicholas, cited, 21n, 22n, 25nn, 35nn, 55n, 60n, 108nn, 109, 126n, 244n, 249n

Katholicon Mouseion, 206

Katic, R., 153n

Kauchtschiscvli, S., cited, 203n

Kecharitomene, monastery of, 131

Kedrenos, Tryphon, 252

Kerameus, P., *see* Papadopoulos, A., and P. Kerameus

Khitrowo, B. de., 166n, 167n, 193n

Kirchenvater und Sozialen Erbrecht (Bruck), 16n

Kirche und Theologische Literatur in Byzantinischen Reich (Beck), 84n, 97n, 106n, 204n, 205n, 219n, 229nn, 230n, 231n, 234n, 242n

Kletorologion (Philotheos), 115n, 213n, 220n, 221n, 240nn

Klostermann, Erich, 31n

Knecht, August, cited, 218n, 239n, 251n, 269n

Knights Templar, 193

Knos, Borje, cited, 214n

Konzil von Chalcedon, Das (Grillmeier and Bacht), 157n

Kosmosotera, *see* Cosmosoteira, monastery

Koukoules, Phaedon, cited, xin, 61n, 110n, 153n, 167, 186n, 221n, 239n, 240n, 248n, 270n, 272n, 274n, 275n, 276n

Kouricos, poor-house, 264

Kousis, Aristotle, cited, 153n, 174n

Krales xenon, 206

Kral Stephen Uros II Milutin (1282–1320), 206

Kriaras, Emmanuel, cited, 214n

Kriesis, A., cited, 258n

Krivocheine, Basil, cited, 102n

Kroll, G., *see* Corpus Juris Civilis (Schoell and Kroll, eds.)

"Kronung Symeons von Bulgarien durch den Patriarchen Nikolaos Mystikos, Die" (Ostrogorsky), 52n

Krumbacher, Karl, 231n

Ktenas, Christopher, cited, 255n

Kugener, M. A., cited, 209n

Kunst in den Athos-Klostern, Die (Brockhaus), 41n

Kurtz, Eduard, cited, 92n, 115nn, 183n, 210n, 227n

Kuzhuncuk, 167

Kyphe, 233, 237

Kyriacos, abbot, 187

Kyriakides, Stilpon, cited, 255n

Kyrillos von Skythopolis (Schwartz), 35n, 71n, 74n, 94n, 95n, 113n, 157nn, 158nn, 159n, 162n, 183n, 187nn, 188nn, 219nn, 225nn, 242n, 263n

Lagier, C., cited, 171n

Lallemand, Leon, 5n, 16n

Lampros, Spyridon, cited, 37n, 56n, 97nn, 183n, 206n, 214n, 215nn, 286n, 288n

Laourdas, Basil, cited, 144n

Late Ancient and Medieval Population (Russell), 258n

Later Roman Empire 284–602, The (Jones), 11n, 151n, 155n, 156n, 159n, 280n

"Laudatio S. Paul Junionis" (Delehaye, ed.), 92n

Laudatio S. Philothei Opsiciani (Eustathios of Thessalonica), 80n

Laudatio S. Thomaidis (Acropolites), 107n

Laudibus Constantini, De (Eusebios), 45n

Laurent, V., cited, 41n, 75, 109n, 143n, 237n

Lausiac History of Palladios, The, 21n, 22n, 94nn, 95n, 138nn, 139nn, 145n, 188n, 220n, 264nn, 268n

Lausos, xenon of, 199–200

Lavra of Souka, 187

laws: Canon, 67–68, 69, 70, 85, 149, 183–84, 218, 220, 269, 276; Greek, 6; imperial, 46, 48, 49, 51, 52, 61, 85, 112, 113–14, 116, 118, 119 121, 150, 151, 212, 218, 220, 232, 239, 241–42, 248, 251; on leprosy, 165; on orphans, 114, 116, 126, 241–42, 248, 251; on poverty, 257, 262, 265; on prostitution, 271, 272; restrictive, 121, 135, 237

Lazaros, saint, 144, 202

Lecky, William, cited, 11n, 12n, 16n, 67, 270

Leclercq, H., 16n

Legatio (Liudprand of Cremona), 145n

"Légende de l'Empereur Theophile, La" (Diehl), 134n

Légende de S. Spiridon évêque de Trimithonte, La (Van Den Ven), 69n

Leges (Plato), 4n, 6n, 7n

Legrand, Emile, cited, 215n

Lekos, E. P., 153n, 193

Lemerle, Paul, cited, 54n, 102n, 244n

Lenger, Marie-Therese, 3n

Leo III, emperor (717–41), 114, 224; kingship theory and, 49–50, 51; xenon of, 196

Leo V, emperor (813–20), 114, 244

Leo VI the Wise, emperor (886–912), 26n, 34, 81, 115, 198, 265n; diaconate and, 86; gerocomeia and, 233; laws of, 51, 116, 218, 274

Leo Diaconos, 122, 150n; on the Zoticon, 165–66, 167

Leo Grammaticos, 134nn

Leontios, bishop of Antioch, 209

Leontios of Neapolis, 74–75, 145, 275n

Leontios' von Neapolis, Lebendes heiligen Iohannes des barinherzigen erzbischofs von Alexandrien (Gelzer), 74nn, 75nn, 144n, 145n, 170nn, 259n, 262n, 272n

Leo, orphanotrophos, 251

lepers, 55, 76, 78; Church attitudes toward, 181–82; epidemics of leprosy, 165; imperial concern for, 112, 118, 122, 150, 164–67, 171; monastic aid to, 94, 95, 108; private help for, 138, 182

leprosaria, 86, 118, 122, 150, 152; the Basileias, 154, 155; gerocomeia and, 233, 235; poor-houses and, 264; the Zoticon, 164–67, 242

Leroy, Maurice, 97n, 98nn, 99nn, 169n

Lesbos, monastery of, 101–102

Letter to James (Pseudo-Clementine), 29n

Leucas, 145, 237

Leucatenos, Vasilios, 237

Libanios, 43, 45

Libellus monachorum ad Agapetum, 248

Life in Christ (Kabasilas), 38n

"Life of Hypatios, Archbishop of Gangra" (Ioannou), 94n, 276n

Life of St. Andrew the Hierosolymite (Nicetas), 168n, 250n, 264n, 269n

"Life of St. Artemios," 195, 206

"Life of St. Athanasios, the Athonite" (Petit), 102nn

"Life of St. Demetrianos" (Grégoire), 100nn, 183n

"Life of St. Eudocimos" (Loparev), 93n, 108n

"Life of St. Euthymios the Younger" (Doukakis), 102n

"Life of St. George, Archbishop of Amastris" (Vasilievskii), 78nn, 79n

"Life of Saint Gregory, Bishop of Assos" (Doukakis), 84n

Life of St. Gregory, the Theologian (Gregory the Presbyter), 155n, 182n

Life of St. Ignatios, 234

"Life of St. Luke the Younger" (Martini, ed.), 100nn

"Life of St. Maria the Younger" (Gedeon), 100nn

"Life of St. Markianos" (Papadopoulos-Kerameus), 138n

"Life of St. Martha the Younger" (*Acta Sanctorum*), 183n

"Life of St. Nicon" (Lampros), 183n

"Life of St. Petros" (Papaoeconomou), 101n

"Life of St. Phantinos" (*Acta Sanctorum*), 153n

"Life of St. Paraskeve the Younger" (Papadopoulos-Kerameus), 99n, 276n

"Life of Saint Paulos the Bishop and John the Presbyter" (Papadopoulos-Kerameus), 209n

"Life of St. Porphyrios, Bishop of Gaza" (Marcos the Deacon), 209n

Life of St. Sabas (Cyril of Scythopolis), 35n

Life of St. Spyridon (Theodore of Paphos), 69n, 239nn

Life of St. Symeon the New Theologian (Stethatos), 106nn

"Life of St. Theodore Sykeon" (Ioannou), 19n, 221n

Life of St. Theodosios (Theodore of Petra), 93n, 210nn, 225n

Life of St. Theophylactos, Archbishop of Nicomedeia (anonymous), 78nn, 169nn, 170n

Lingenthal, Zacharia von, 50n

Lips, Constantine, 198

Lips, monastery of, 91

Liturgy of John Chrysostom, 34

Liturgy of the Presanctified Gifts, 34

Liturgy of St. Basil, 33–34

Liudprand, bishop of Cremona, 145

"Lives of Mary and Euphemia" (John of Ephesos), 159nn

"Lives of the Saints as Sources of Data for the History of Byzantine Medicine in the Sixth and Seventh Centuries" (Magoulias), 154n

Livos, tou, 198–99

loans, 6–7

Loch, C.S., cited, 7n

Loeb Classical Library, 6n, 9nn, 13n, 16n

Loenertz, Raymond J., 60n

Logos, *see* Jesus Christ

Logos Paregoreticos peri Dystychias Kai Eutychias, 214n, 215nn

Loparev, Ch. M., cited, 93n, 97n, 108n, 231n

Lorenz, S., cited, 3n

Lot, Ferdinand, cited, 156n

Loupadiou, tou, 197

Luke, 10, 13n, 19n, 24n, 101n

Luke the Younger, saint, 100

Lycos, 199

Lydos, John, cited, 271n

Lysimadia, Ethiopia, 129

Macalister, R. A. Stewart, cited, 161n

Macarios, 20nn

Macedonia, 79, 115, 251, 255

Macedonios, patriarch (341–48, 350–56), 261

McNamara, Maria A., 12n

Macridy, Theodore, cited, 198n, 199n

Macurdy, Grace H., cited, 4n

Madyta, 99

Maggana quarter, Constantinople, 199, 233–34

Maggana xenon, 199

Magister, Symeon, *see* Symeon Magister

Magistratibus, De (Lydos), 271n

Magna, 138

Magnesia, 269

Magoulias, H. J., cited, 154n

Mai, Angelo, cited, 39n, 49n

Makarios, presbyter, 264

Makedonica (periodical), 38n

Makedonica (Tsaras), 38n

Makrembolites, Eustathios, cited, 221n

Malalas, Joannes, 133n, 189nn, 192n, 220n, 271n; on Justinian, 212, 272

Malingrey, A. M., cited, 268n

Malta, Italy, 10

Mamboury, E., cited, 234n

man, 61, 66; Christian love of God and, 11, 12, 13, 67, 93, 94, 97, 131, 275, 281; God's love for, 3–4, 10, 19, 30–37, 38–39, 80, 81, 92, 282; God's mercy toward, 19, 20, 29, 34, 35, 39, 46; passions of, 80, 93

Manasses, Constantine, 168, 186, 222, 224n

Mandate (Shepherd of Hermas), 14n

Mango, Cyril, 198n

Mansi, Joannes D., 69n

Manuel, protospatharios, 200
Manuel Comnenos, 56, 57, 132–33
Manuel II Palaeologos, emperor (1391–1425), 212
Manuelis Philae Carmina (Miller), 193n, 205nn
Marc la Diacre, Vie de Porphyre, évêque de Gaza (Grégoire), 209n
Marcellus, 31
Marcian (450–57), 156, 188–89, 212, 224; poor and, 263, 274
Marcianos, Hosios, 156
Marcos the Deacon, cited, 209n
Mardosaggares region, Constantinople, 199
Maria the Younger, saint, 100
Marin, abbé, 88n, 149n
Marinos, son of St. Maria, 100
Mark, 11n, 13n, 101n, 109n
Markianos (+388), 137–38
Marmara, Sea of, 99, 246, 247, 267
Marmarion xenon, 204
Marriott, C., cited, 257n
Marrou, H. J., cited, 5n
Marshall, F. N., cited, 214n
Mar Stratonicos, 158
Mar Tewath-il, 158
Martha, saint, 96
Martin, Hubert, Jr., cited, 4n, 11n
Martin, Victor, 239n
Martini, E., 100nn
Martyrium Sancti Martyris Zenobii, 182n
Mason, A. J., 32n
maternity clinics, 152, 170, 172
Matranga, P., 133n
Matthaeum Homilia LXVI, In (Chrysostomos), 258n
Matthaios, patriarch (1397–1410), 213
Matthew, 11n, 12n, 13nn, 19n, 20n, 95n, 98n, 101n, 128n, 149n, 273n
Maurice, emperor (582–602), 198, 227
Mavrianou, tou, 197, 198
Mavrogordato, John, cited, 214n
Mavroi, 107
Maximos the Confessor, cited, 22, 25n, 32, 35, 37n, 38, 49n
Mazaris (anonymous), 145
"Mazaris, 20" (Ellissen, ed.), 146n
Medicarios, monastery of, 175

medicine, 152–53; at the Pancrator, 171–79. *See also* hospitals
Megale Hellenike Encyclopaideia, 41n
Megaw, Arthur H. S., cited, 171n, 198n
Mélanges d'archéologie byzantine (Schlumberger), 252n
Mélanges Charles Diehl, 53n
Mélanges Eugène Tisserant, 3n, 10n
Mélanges de Sciences Religieuse, 10n
Mélanges de l'Université Saint Joseph, 160nn, 226n, 263n, 275n
Melania, 139
Melania the Younger, 139
Meliopoulos, J., on the Zoticon, 167
Melobiou, gerocomeia, 236
Memorabilia (Xenophon), 4n, 8n
Mémorial Louis Petit—Mélanges d'histoire et d'archéologie byzantines, 229n
Menaeon, 41n
Menas, patriarch (536–52), 191, 192
Menologium, 192n
Mercati, Ioannis, 198n; quoted, 57nn, 19n
Messenia, 9
Metanoia, monastery of, 196, 272
Metaphrastes, Symeon, *see* Symeon Metaphrastes, saint
metempsychosis, 30
Methodios, cited, 31n
Methodius (Bonwetsch), 31n
Metochites, Theodore, 183
Meyer, G., cited, 215n
Meyer, Ph., 92n
Michael Maleinos, saint, 107–108, 200
Michael I Rangabe, emperor (811–13), 244
Michael III, emperor (845–56), 135, 200, 251
Michael IV, emperor (1034–41), 250, 251, 266, 272
Michael IV (Michael Psellos), 250n, 251n, 256n, 266nn, 273nn
Michael V, emperor (1041–42), 251
Michael V (Michael Psellos), 250n, 251n
Michael VII Ducas, emperor (1071–78), 55, 58, 123

Michael VIII Palaeologos, emperor (1259–82), 193, 203, 245
Michael, bishop of Synnadon, 79
Michael, protospatharios, 107–108
Michael the Rhetorician, 57
Michael Attaliates, 37, 151; on Nicephoros Botaneiates, 122n, 170–71; the poor and, 27, 28, 256n, 259n, 260n, 266–68; will of, 142
Michaele et Andronico Palaeologis, De (Pachymeres), 203n, 233n, 245n
Michael Tetrapolites, 252
Michel Psellos Chronographie (Renauld, ed.), 53nn, 122nn, 123n
Migne, J. P., *see Patrologia Graeca* (Migne, ed.)
Miklosich, Fr., *see Acta et Diplomata Graeca Medii Aevi Sacra et Profana* (Miklosich and Muller, eds.)
Mikrasiatika Chronika (periodical), 90n
Milet, 39n, 80n, 81n
Miletos, 80
Milik, J. T., cited, 160, 226n, 263n, 275n
Millénaire du Mont Athos, Le, 102n
Miller, E., cited, 193n, 205nn
Millet, Gabriel, 215n
Millingen, Alexander van, cited, 247n
Miltiades, 9
"Ministre byzantin—Jean l'Orphanotrophe (XIe siècle)" (Janin), 250nn
"Ministries of Women in the Primitive Church" (Turner), 84n, 85n
Ministry of Deaconesses, The (Robinson), 84n, 85n
"Miracula S. Anastasii Persae" (*Acta Sanctorum*), 275n
Miracula S. Georgii (Aufhauser), 221n
Mission und Ausbreitung des Christentums, Die (Harnack), 16n
missionaries, 149, 150
mnemosyna, 131
Mnemosyne (periodical), 3n
Mocesos, Cappadocia, 212
Mocios, cistern of, 249, 274
Moines de Constantinople, Les (Marin), 88n, 149n

Moines d'orient, Les (Festugière), 158n, 160n, 187n, 225n, 263n
Mommsen, Theodore, cited, 257n
"Monachisme byzantin au moyen age, commende et typica (Xe–XIVe siècle), Le" (Janin), 89n
Monachus et Eremita (Joannes Moschos), 88n, 212nn
monarchy, *see* emperors
Monastère de Daphni—Histoire, Architecture, Mosaiques (Millet), 215n
"Monastère de Notre-Dame de Pitié" (Petit), 39n
"Monastères byzantins. Les Couvents secondaires de Psamathia (Constantinople)" (Janin), 223n
"Monastères du Christ Philanthrope a Constantinople, Les" (Janin), 41n
monasteries, 19, 20, 24, 25–26, 41, 280; Church relationship, 65–66, 75, 88; establishment of, 27–28, 52, 79, 94, 130, 131, 198, 200, 202–204, 267–68; imperial attitudes toward, 121, 132; Origenist, 242; philanthropic activity of, 88–110, 132, 144, 149, 150, 171–79, 181, 183, 187, 188, 210, 220, 247–48, 259, 271–72, 275, 279, 282–83, 284, 285; private aid to, 139, 141, 143, 144, 267–68; war orphans in, 126, 129. *See also specific monasteries*
"Monastic Properties and the State in the Byzantine Empire, The" (Charanis), 110nn, 121n, 259n
"Monastery of Lips (fenari isa Camii) at Istanbul, The" (Macridy, *et al*), 198n, 199n
"Monchtum der Orthodoxen Ostkirche, Das" (Theodorou), 89n
Monks and Civilization (Decarreaux), 89n
Monnier, Alexandre, 5n, 10n, 11n
Monodia de Constantinopoli Capta (Kallistos), 276n, 287n, 288n
Montfaucon, Bernard de, cited, 206n
"Monumenta Latrensia Hagiographica" (Delehaye), 39n, 80n, 81nn

"Monuments numismatiques et sphragistiques du moyen age byzantin" (Schlumberger), 20n

Monumenta ad SS. Cyrilli et Methodii successorum vitas resque gestas vertinentia (Tunitskij), 81n

Moral Values in the Ancient World (Ferguson), 3n, 11n, 31n

Moravcsik, Gyula, 205n

Mordtmann, A. D., cited, 229n, 231n, 232n

Morea, 145, 214

Morison, E. F., 155n

Moss, H. St. L. B., 49n, 55n, 149n, 214n

Mosynopolis, Macedonia, 255

Mount Athos, monastery of, 92, 102

Mount Camlica, 167

Mount Elaiones, 165, 166

Mount Galesion, 144, 202–203

Mount Latros (Latmos), 107

Muller, J., *see Acta et Diplomata Graeca Medii Aevi, Sacra et Profana* (Miklosich and Muller, eds.)

Murray, Sara, cited, 19nn

Muslims, 78, 232

Myrelaion, monastery of, 154, 198, 232, 235

Mystik des Nikolaus Cabasilas, Die (Kabasilas), 38n

Narses, general, 213, 226, 267

Narses gerocomeion, 226

Narses xenon, 190, 213, 226

Nathanael, nosocomos, 206

Nazianzenos, Gregory, *see* Gregory of Nazianzos, saint

Nazianzos, 261

Neander, Augustus, 16n, 67n

Neapolis, 249, 265

Nea Sion (periodical), 84n, 264n

Neilos of Ancyra, 68n

Neilos Damilas, Typikon of, 26

Neophytos, 91

Neos Hellenomnemon (periodical), 37n, 56n, 97n, 183n

Nepos, Cornelius, cited, 9n

"Neue Quellen zur Komposition und entstehungsgeschichte des Mittelgriechischen Romans Imberios und Margarona" (Schreiner), 214nn

New Testament, 26, 29, 30, 138, 273. *See also specific Books*

Nessel, Daniel de, cited, 198n

Nicaea, 143, 151, 153, 268, 269, 286; gerocomeia, 223; hospitals, 183; orphanages, 249–50; xenones, 200

Nicene and Post-Nicene Fathers of the Christian Church (Schaff, ed.), 68n, 69n, 154n, 258n; Preface, 257n

Nicephoros I, emperor (802–11), 243

"Nicephoros I, the Savior of Greece from the Slavs" (Charanis), 243n

Nicephoros II Phocas, emperor (963–69), 52, 81, 121, 135, 213, 237

Nicephoros III Botaneiates, emperor (1078–81), 122, 171

Nicephoros I, patriarch (806–15), 265, 266, 269

Nicephoros Blemmydes, 59

Nicephoros Callistos Xanthopoulos, cited, 162n, 229, 230n, 263nn

Nicephoros, bishop of Miletos, 80–81

Nicetas, bishop of Ionopolis, 97, 98, 252

Nicetas Choniates, cited, 114n, 134n, 168n, 264n, 269n; on Isaac II Angelos, 180, 181, 199n, 204; on John II Comnenos, 179, 285n; on kingship, 56; on orphanages, 250; on widows, 276n

Nicholas Mysticos, patriarch of Constantinople, xn, 32, 37n, 39n, 279, 288; Bulgarian war relief and, 79; kingship theory and, 52–53

Nicomedeia, 213, 223

Nicon (+998), 97

Niederer, Frances J., cited, 16n

Niehbuhr, B. G., 113n, 179n, 222n

Nika revolt (532), 133, 162, 189, 192, 199

"Nikoulitza et les historiens byzantins contemporains" (Valdenberg), 54nn

Nissen, Th., cited, 142n, 168n, 229n

Nitria, Egypt, 188

Nomocanon (Photios), 85*n*, 219*n*, 248*n*

"Note on the 'Letter to the Emir' of Nicholas Mysticos" (Jenkins), 53*n*

"Notes and Documents—Antiochus Strategos' Account of the Sack of Jerusalem in AD 614" (Conybeare), 160*n*

"Notes on Recent Work of the Byzantine Institute in Istanbul" (Megaw), 171*n*

Notices et Extraits des Manuscripts de la Bibliothèque Nationale (Boucherie), 275*n*

"Notion de 'bienfait' (philanthropon) royal et les ordonnances des rois Lagides, La" (Lenger), 3*n*

"Notions of Humanity Among the Greeks" (Gulick), 6*n*, 7*n*

Notitia Dignitatum Accedunt Notitia Urbis Constantinopolitanae et Laterculi Provinciarum (Seeck), 191*n*

"Notules Epigraphiques" (Grégoire), 230*n*

Novel No. 4 (Heraclios), 242*n*

Novel 12 (Leo VI, the Wise), 274*n*

Novel XXII (Heraclios), 85*n*, 218*n*

novels, *see* laws

Novels (Justinian), 48*nn*, 85*nn*, 112*n*, 113*n*, 150*n*, 151*n*, 186*n*, 192*n*, 212*n*, 216*n*, 218*nn*, 220*n*, 222*n*, 239*n*, 260*n*, 265*nn*, 271*n*, 274*n*; on orphans, 241*n*, 242*n*, 248*n*, 251*n*

Novels (Porphyrogenitos), 118*n*

Numa (Plutarch), 4*n*

nuns, 86

Nygren, Anders, 12*n*, 31*n*

Nyssa, Gregory, *see* Gregory of Nyssa, saint

"Observations sur la liste des dignitaires de Pseudo-Codinus" (Guilland), 246*n*

obstetrics–gynecology, 152–53

Ochrida, diocese of, 81

Odyssey (Homer), 5*n*

Oeconomicos (Xenophon), 8*n*

Oeconomos, Lysimaque, 86*n*, 171*n*, 181*n*, 244*n*

Oeuvres complètes de George Scholarios, 287*n*, 288*n*

Officialibus Palatii Constantinopolitani, De (Pseudo-Codinos), 60*n*, 246*n*, 255*n*

"Officiis Regiis Libellus, De" (anonymous), 221*n*

Ohanessian, L. A., 153*n*

Old Age Among the Ancient Greeks (Richardson), 6*nn*, 222*n*

"Old Royal House" in Constantinople, 76

Old Testament, 21

Olympias, 139

Olympias, deaconess, 268

On the Chersonese (Demosthenes), 9*n*

"On the Early History and Modern Revival of Deaconesses" (*Church Quarterly Review*), 84*n*

On the Resurrection (Methodios), 31*n*

ophthalmology, 152, 172, 195, 275

"Oraison funèbre de Basile I par son fils Leon VI le Sage" (Vogt and Hausherr), 265*n*

Oratio IV (Gregory Nazianzenos), 209*n*

Oratio No. 15 (Gregory Nazianzenos), 20*n*, 21*n*

Oratio II Contra Arianos (Athanasios of Alexandria), 32*nn*

Oratio Contra Gentes (Athanasios of Alexandria), 32*n*

Oratio im Imperatorem Dominum Alexium Comnenum (Theophylactos of Ochrida), 28*n*

"Oratio XXIII. Manuelis Comneni Imp. laudatio funebris, 18" (Eustathios of Thessalonica), 133*n*

Oration (Themistios), 45*nn*

Oratio XLIII—In Laudem Basilii Magni (Gregory Nazianzenos), 68*n*, 69*n*, 181*n*, 182*nn*

Oratio XIV—De Pauperum Amore (Gregory Nazianzenos), 68*n*

Oratio in Psalmum XLVIII (Eustathios of Thessalonica), 24*n*

Oratio de Regis Officiis (Nicephoros Blemmydes), 59*nn*

Oratio de Regis Officiis (Theodulos Monachos), 60*n*
ordination, 85, 86
Orestes, saint, 193
"Orfanotrofios Griegos y su Perduracion en Bizancio, Los" (Comneno), 244*n*
Orientalia Christiana Analecta, 33*n*, 36*n*
Orientalia Christiana Periodica, 33*n*, 102*n*, 106*n*, 265*n*
Orient chrétien, L' (Lagier), 171*n*
Origen, 30–31, 39
Origenist monks, 242
Orlandos, Anastasios, cited, 150*nn*, 171*n*, 179
Orphanage of the Capital, 192–93, 244–47, 265
orphanages, 80, 86, 149, 150, 168, 241–56; Alexios I and, 126, 128, 129–30; for girls, 94, 132, 276; legislation on, 69, 113–14, 116; Phrygian, 79
orphanotrophoi, office of, 241, 246, 249–50, 265
orphans: Christian charity toward, 12, 13, 14, 15, 25, 32, 33, 55, 66, 149, 269, 282; Church concern for, 66, 69, 70, 71, 74, 75, 76, 78, 81, 85, 88, 92, 97, 149, 241, 248, 259; foster homes for, 126; Greek concern for, 5–6, 8, 10, 19; imperial philanthropy and, 51, 54, 112, 115, 116, 126, 132, 136, 150, 210, 241–47; legal rights of, 114, 116, 126, 241–42, 251; orphanages, 241–56 (*see also* orphanages); private bequests to, 139–40
Orthodoxe Kirche in Griechischer sicht, Die (Bratsiotis, ed.), 89*n*
Orthodoxia (periodical), 140*nn*, 141*n*, 171*n*, 174*n*
orthopedics, 152–53
orthros, 35
Ostgrenze des Byzantinischen Reiches von 363 bis 1071, Die (Honigman), 141*n*, 204*n*
Ostrogorsky, George, cited, 18*n*, 52*n*, 55*n*, 71*n*, 74*n*, 78*n*, 91*n*, 134*n*, 145*n*, 150*n*, 224*n*, 225*n*, 243*n*, 244*n*, 258*n*

otorhinolaryngology, 152–53
Oueros, 138
Ouranos, Nicephoros, 251
Oxyrhynchos, Egypt, 94

Pachymeres, George (1242–c.1310), cited, 37*n*, 203, 233*n*, 245
Pacourianos, Gregory, 141–42, 203–204, 247–48
Pacourianos, Symbatios and Kale, 140–41
Paedagogos (Clement of Alexandria), 30*nn*
paganism: Christian charities and, 14–16, 22, 31, 208–209, 263; kingship and, 53
Palaegraphia Graeca (Montfaucon), 206*n*
Palais et les églises des Blachernes, Les (Papadopoulos), 227*n*
Palamas, Gregorios, 39*n*, 157*n*
Palanque, J. R., cited, 112*n*
Palestine, 35, 167, 187, 210; excavations, 160; gerocomeia, 225; Origenist party of, 242; poor-houses in, 263. *See also specific placenames*
Palestine Exploration Fund—Quarterly Statement, 161*n*
Palladii Dialogus de Vita S. Joannes Chrysostomi, 21*n*, 71*nn*, 139*n*, 156*nn*, 188*n*, 208*nn*, 219*n*
Palladios of Eleonopolis (d.c. 431), 21, 22*n*, 71*nn*, 95*n*, 156*nn*; Lausos and, 199; on poor-houses, 264, 268*n*; on private charity, 138–39, 145; on wealth, 94; on xenones, 188, 208, 219*n*, 220*n*
Palm Sunday, procession, 189, 190, 193, 196, 197, 220, 250
Pammachios, 139
Pamphylia, 264
Panaretos, Constantinides, 266
Pandect (Justinian), 257*n*
"Panegyric of St. Basil, The" (Gregory Nazianzenos), 155*n*, 260*n*
Pantocrator, monastery of, 235; establishment, 27–28, 132; gerocomeion of, 235; hospital of, 171–79, 204; *Typikon,* 171, 172, 174, 175, 179, 235

"Pantocrator, the Imperial Byzantine Medical Center of the XIIth Century AD in Constantinople, The" (Codellas), 171*n*

Papadopoulos-Kerameus, A., cited, 35*n*, 37*n*, 41*n*, 75*nn*, 84*n*, 99*n*, 108*n*, 138*n*, 154*n*, 250*n*, 264*n*, 269*n*, 276*n*; on xenones, 195*nn*, 197*n*, 206*nn*, 209*n*

Papadopoulos, Chrysostomos, cited, 168*n*

Papadopoulos, Jean B., cited, 7*n*, 227*n*

Papadopoulos, N. P., 33*n*, 34*n*

Papaoeconomou, Christos, cited, 101*nn*

Paphlagonia, 74, 256

Paphos, 91

Papoulia, Basilike, 35*n*

Parable (Shepherd of Hermas), 14*n*

Paradise, 23, 26, 28

Paraenesis to Leo (Basil I), 51*nn*

Paraphrasis (Pachymeres), 37*n*

Paraskeve, saint, 99

Pargoire, J., 164*n*, 247*n*

Parnassos (periodical), 266*n*

parthenones, 276

Paschentiou, 197, 206–207

Paspates, A., 193

Patras, 145

Patria (Pseudo-Codinos), 26*nn*, 113*n*, 134*n*, 156*nn*, 164*n*, 242*n*, 243*nn*, 247*n*, 274*n*; on gerocomeia, 222*n*, 223*n*, 224*nn*, 225*n*, 226*nn*, 227*nn*, 230*nn*, 231*nn*, 233*n*, 234*nn*; on xenones, 189*nn*, 190*nn*, 192*n*, 195*n*, 196*nn*, 197*n*, 198*nn*, 199*nn*, 200*n*, 206*n*, 213*n*

Patriarch, gerocomeion of the, 226

"Patriarche Nicolas et son rôle politique, Le" (Gay), 53*n*

Patriarch Nicephorus of Constantinople, The (Alexander), 265*n*

Patriarcharum Constantinopolitanorum (Nicephoros Callistos Xanthopoulos), 229*n*, 230*n*

patriarchs (Biblical), 21. *See also individual Biblical figures*

Patrologia Graeca (Migne, ed.), x*n*, 68*nn*, 69*n*, 70*n*, 71*nn*, 79*n*, 80*n*, 81*n*, 84*n*, 118*n*, 134*n*, 142*n*, 155*n*, 157*n*, 158*n*, 162*n*, 167*n*, 181*n*, 182*nn*, 184*n*, 186*nn*, 187*nn*, 192*nn*, 209*n*, 216*n*, 220*n*, 221*n*, 230*n*, 234*n*, 248*nn*, 249*n*, 251*n*, 273*n*, 275*n*, 276*n*; texts on charity, 19*n*, 20*n*, 21*n*, 22*n*, 23*n*, 24*n*, 25*n*; on God's love for man, 32*n*, 33*n*, 34*n*, 35*nn*, 37*n*; on kingship, 45*n*, 46*n*, 49*n*, 51*nn*, 55*n*, 58*n*, 59*n*, 60*n*; on poor-houses, 258*n*, 261*nn*, 262*n*, 263*n*, 268*n*; on Turkish conquest, 287*n*, 288*nn*

Patrologia Orientalis (Brooks, ed.), 159*n*

Patrology (Altaner), 139*n*, 257*n*, 264*n*, 281*n*

Patrology (Quasten), 29*n*, 182*n*

Paul, saint, 10, 252

Paul the Younger, saint, 107, 108

Paul II, patriarch (519–21), 189, 220

Pauperibus Amandis, De (Gregory of Nyssa), 19*n*, 68*n*, 182*n*

Pausanias, cited, 7*n*

Pausilypos, saint, 236

Peeters, P., cited, 106*n*, 107*nn*

Peisistratos, 7

Peloponnesos, 145–46

Pentecost, 88

Pentele, monastery, 150

Perga, Pamphylia, 264

Pericles, 11; on orphans, 6

Peristeria (Neilos of Ancyra), 68*n*

Perivleptos, monastery, 144

Perrin, B., cited, 9*n*

Persia, 74, 75; Jerusalem attack (614), 160, 162, 226; sack of Antioch (540), 164, 189

"Perspective of the Early Church Historians, The" (Downey), 46*n*

Pertusi, Agostino, 49*n*

Peter, saint, 252

Peter, 12*nn*

Peter of Atroa, saint, 143

Peter the Patrician, 227

Petit, Louis, cited, 27*n*, 39*n*, 91*n*, 92*n*, 102*nn*, 107*nn*, 132*nn*, 141*nn*, 142*nn*, 200*nn*, 203*n*, 204*nn*, 236*n*, 248*n*, 287*n*

Petra quarter, Constantinople, 206

Petria gerocomeion, 236

Petrides, S., cited, 26*n*

Petrikapi, 232

Petrion monastery, 236–37

Petrion quarter, Constantinople, 227, 231, 236, 237

"Pétrion de Constantinople, Le" (Janin), 231*n*

Petritziotissa monastery, 204, 247–48

Petros, bishop of Argos (+920), 101

Petrou, ta, gerocomeion, 227

Phanar, 237

"Philanthropia dans la littérature grecque jusqu'au nouveau testament" (le Deaut), 3*n*, 10*nn*

Philanthropia—Eine griechische Wortpragung auf ihrem Wege von Aischylos bis Theodoros Metochites (Hunger), 3*n*

"Philanthropia in the Papyri of the Roman Period" (Bell), 3*n*, 10*n*

"Philanthropia in Religion and Statecraft in the Fourth Century after Christ" (Downey), 45*nn*, 189*n*, 263*n*

Philanthropos Soter monastery, 41

philanthropy: Christian theology and, 29–41, 67, 116, 133, 149–50, 275; Greek sources of, 3–16, 18–19, 25, 41, 280, 281; motivation of, 18–28, 94–95, 106–107, 109, 114, 116, 119, 121, 133–35, 141–42, 143–44, 171–72, 214–15, 216, 219–20, 255–56, 266, 275, 280–81, 284. *See also* Church philanthropy; private philanthropy; State philanthropy

"Philanthropy in the Age of Justinian" (Constantelos), 113*n*

Philaretos, metropolitan of Euchaita, 80

Philaretos, saint, 97–98, 99, 169

Philentolos the Cypriot, 23, 169

Phileotes, Cyril (+110): charities of, 108–109, 249; on philanthropy, 25, 55

Philes, Manuel (1275–1345), 193, 205

Philip of Macedonia, 9

Philippoupolis, Thrace, 204

Philipsborn, A., cited, 179*n*

Philocales, Eumathios, 109

Philomelium, 126

Philoromos, 94

philosophy, philanthropic, 18–28, 55, 61, 67, 280. *See also individual philosophers*

Philotheos, *Kletorologion* of, 115*n*, 213*n*, 220*n*, 221*n*, 240*n*

Philotheos, priest, 80

Phocas, *see* Nicephoros II Phocas

Phordisiis, Palestine, 263

Photios, patriarch, x*n*, 35*n*, 37*n*, 50, 85*n*, 169, 279, 288; banishment of, 135; orphanages and, 248*n*, 251; xenones and, 219*n*, 221

Photopoulos, Philemon, 84*n*

Phrygia, 79

physicians, 95, 154; free care and, 8, 10, 182; God and, 33; Maggana, 199; monks as, 168, 229; ophthalmological, 275; Pantocrator, 172, 174, 175, 179; sainted, 169; Sampson xenon, 192, 195

physiology, 152–53

Pichard, Marcel, cited, 214*n*

Pierre de Provence et la belle Maguelonne, 214

plague, 164

Plassman, Otto, cited, 24*n*, 71*n*

Plato, 4, 6, 7*n*, 43

Platonis (Burnet, ed.), 4*n*

Platonism, metempsychosis theory of, 30

Plutarch, 4*n*; quoted, 9

Plutarchi Vitae Parallelae (Sintenis, ed.), 4*n*

Poems (Manuel Philes), 193*n*, 205*nn*

Poenae Monasteriales (Theodore Studites), 184*n*

Politica (Aristotle), 6*nn*, 10*n*

politics, philanthropic, 18, 28, 43–61, 95, 111–36, 150–51, 250, 283–84. *See also* emperors; state philanthropy

Polycarp, 13*n*

Polydeukes, Julios, cited, 275*n*

Pontos, 97, 98, 99, 169; leprosarium in, 167; poor of, 261

"Population de Constantinople à l'époque byzantine: un problème de démographie urbaine" (Jacoby), 258*n*

"Populations rurales au IXe siècle

d'après l'hagiographie byzantine, Les" (Bréhier), 98n

Porphyrios, bishop of Gaza (c.347–420), 209

Porphyrios, saint, 252

Porphyrogenitos, *see* Constantine VII Porphyrogenitos

Potlis, M., *see* Rhallis, G. A., and M. Potlis

Pournaropoulos, G. C., cited, 152nn, 153nn, 174n; quoted, 152, 153

poverty, 12, 21, 22, 26, 32, 66, 282, 287; Apostolic Church and, 13–14; bequests and, 119, 121, 139–40, 141–44; burial and, 274–75; Byzantine economic structure and, 283–85; Church concern for, 68, 69, 70, 71, 74–75, 76, 78, 79, 81, 84, 85, 86, 88, 113–14, 149; "deserving" concept, 25, 108–109, 208, 283; educational attitudes toward, 97, 115; Greek, 5, 6–7, 8, 10–11; imperial concern for, 54–55, 57, 114, 130–31, 132, 134, 200, 262–66; monastery aid for, 89–90, 91, 92, 93, 94–96, 98, 99, 101, 102, 106, 107, 108, 150, 210, 284, 285; monastic, 20, 24, 150; poor-houses for, 257–69 (*see also* ptochotropheia); private concern for, 137, 138, 140, 141–42, 143–46, 266–68; prostitution and, 270, 271, 272; Roman, 16; sacrifices and, 14, 15, 19; travel and, 185–221

Prasina quarter, Constantine, 224

Pratum Spirituale (Joannes Moschos), 85n, 88n, 164n, 274n

Pravikion, Thrace, 204

prayer, 20, 27, 35; charity and, 21; for the dead, 38; healing and, 154; monasticism and, 93

Prayer of Serapion of Thmuis, 34n, 287n

Precationes (Symeon Metaphrastes), 37n

Precepts (Hippocrates), 8nn

priests, 67, 68, 70, 79, 80, 175; education of, 248; pagan, 263

Prilogo, Thrace, 204

"Princesse byzantine au cloître, Une" (Laurent), 41n

Prise de Jérusalem par les Perses en 614 (Antiochos Strategos), 162n, 226n

prisoners, 15, 66; Alexios and, 123, 126, 130, 131, 136; amnesty for, 180; bishops and, 14, 70, 71; death penalty, 285; fall of Byzantium and, 287; gifts to, 118, 121, 269; God and, 33; Greek concern for, 5, 8, 9, 10; political, 131, 133; ransom of, 9, 25, 27, 71, 99–100, 110, 268, 280; in reformatories, 196, 270–74; sanctuary for, 76

private philanthropy, 11, 15, 24, 65, 137–46, 279; medicine and, 154, 167–68, 169, 182; poor-houses and, 259, 267–68, 285; xenones and, 206, 207. *See also individual names*

Procopios of Caesarea, cited, 227n, 231n, 260n, 264nn, 272; on hospitals, 159nn, 160, 162nn, 164, 167; on xenones, 186nn, 189, 190–91, 192, 207n, 212

Procopii Caesariensis Opera Omnia (Procopios of Caesarea), 159nn, 162nn, 164nn, 167n, 186nn, 189nn, 190nn, 191nn, 207n, 212nn, 264nn, 272nn

"Procopius on Antioch: A Study of Method in the 'De Aedificiis'" (Downey), 164n

Prodromos, Theodore, 132–33

Prodromos, Church of, Constantinople, 267

Prodromos, monastery, 206

"Profession médicale à Byzance à l'époque des Comnènes, La" (Grumel), 174n

Program des K. K. Deutschen Ober-Gymnasiums der Kleinseite (Meyer), 215n

Progressu Notionis Philanthropia (Lorenz), 3n

Prolegomenes à une édition critique et commentée des "Conseils et Récits" de Kekaumenos (Lemerle), 54n, 244n

Prooimion–Elementeder Byzantinischen Kaiseridee in den Aregnen der urkunden (Hunger), 48n

Prometheus, 4
Prometheus Bound (Aeschylos), 4nn
prostitution, 196, 221, 233, 270–74
Prousa, 269
Proverbs, 19nn
"prytaneion," 205
Psalms, 19nn, 222n, 266n
Psalmum 48, In (Chrysostomos), 182n
Psamathia quarter, Constantinople, 223
Psellos, Michael, 53, 122–23, 250nn, 251nn, 256n; on Michael IV, 273; on poor-houses, 266; on the sick, 183
Pseudo-athanasianische "IVte Rede gegen die Arianer," Die (Stegmann), 32n
Pseudo-Clementine, 29n, 281
Pseudo-Codinos, George, 26nn, 60n, 113n, 134n, 156n; on gerocomeia, 222n, 223n, 224, 225n, 226, 227, 230nn, 231, 233n, 234nn; on orphanages, 242n, 243, 246, 247, 255n; on Sicilian defeat, 230; on xenones, 189nn, 190, 192n, 195, 196nn, 197, 198nn, 199, 200, 206, 213n; on xenotapheia, 274; on the Zoticon, 164, 247
Pseudo-Dionysios the Areopagite, 36–37
Psorarios, 267
Ptocheion, The, Constantinople, 265–66
Ptochomeion of Michael Attaliates, 27, 28
ptochotropheia (poor-houses), 55, 145, 257–69, 287; of Alexios, 128–29, 244, 266; of Andreas of Crete, 168; of Basil I, 52, 115; canon law on, 69, 149; of Constantine the Great, 112; of Constantine Monomachos, 199; of Glabas, 205; of Irene (797–802), 134; of Lecapenos, 119; lepers in, 167; of Michael Attaliates, 27, 28; of Philaretos' wife, 99
Ptochotropheion of Paniktermon, Constantinople, 267
Ptochotropheion of Sebasteia, 261–62
ptochotrophos, office of, 265, 269

"Public Finances" (Andreades), 55n
Publizistische Sammlungen zum Acacianischen Schisma (Schwartz), 249n
Pulcheria, empress of Marcian (450–57), 212, 224, 274
Pylai, 213
Pythia, Bithynia, 164

Quasten, Johannes, cited, 29n, 182n
Quaestiones (Anastasios Sinaites), 68n
Quality of Mercy—The Gentler Virtues in Greek Literature (Macurdy), 4n
Quartier des Manganes et la I^{ne} Région de Constantinople, Le (Demangel and Mamboury), 234n
Quellen der Byzantinischen Kunstgeschichte (Richter), 164n, 189n, 190nn, 223n, 224nn, 227nn, 230n, 231n, 232n, 233n, 234n, 236n, 243n

Raedestos, 142
Raedestos ptochotropheion, 28, 267
Ramsay, William M., cited, 7, 74n, 78nn, 80n, 99n, 107n, 144n, 155, 202n, 213nn, 252n
"Real Value of Medieval Greek Medicine (Byzantium), The" (Pournaropoulos), 152n, 153nn
"Recent Advances in Mediaeval Demography" (Russell), 258n
"Recherches récentes sur l'iconoclasme" (Grumel), 134n
"Recherches récentes sur le pseudo-Denys l'Areopagite, Les" (Hornus), 36n
Regel, W., cited, 38n, 56n, 57nn, 114n, 115n
Régestes des actes du patriarcat de Constantinople, Les (Grumel), 53n
Régime des biens de l'eglise avant Justinien, Le (Rivet), 218n
Regno, De (Synesios), 45n, 46nn
Regulae Brevius Tractatae (Basil the Great), 35n, 155n, 186n
Regulae Fusius Tractatae (Basil the Great), 89nn, 90n, 210n

Regum (Genesios), 114*nn*, 134*n*, 265*n*

Reign of Isaacios Angelos (Nicetas Choniates), 180*nn*

Renauld, Emile, 53*nn*, 122*nn*, 123*n*

"Research on Julian the Apostate: 1945–1964" (Kaegi, Jr.), 45*n*

Revue archéologique, 20*n*

Revue biblique, 160*nn*

Revue des études byzantine, 41*n*, 54*n*, 89*n*, 174*n*, 214*n*, 246*n*, 249*n*, 256*n*

Revue d'Histoire et de Philosophie Religieuses, 36*n*

Revue de l'orient chrétien, 35*n*, 92*n*, 96*nn*, 107*nn*, 137*n*, 168*nn*

Rhallis, G. A., and Potlis, M., cited, 67*n*, 68*n*, 69*n*, 70*nn*, 85*n*, 86*nn*, 121*nn*, 157*n*, 218*nn*, 219*nn*, 237*nn*, 248*n*, 256*nn*, 257*n*, 269*nn*, 271*n*, 276*n*

Rhodes, Greece, 10

Rice, R. Talbot, cited, 198*n*, 232*n*

Richard the Lionhearted, 91

Richardson, B. E., cited, 6*nn*, 222*n*

Richter, J. P., cited, 164*n*, 189*n*, 190*nn*, 243*n*; on gerocomeia, 223*n*, 244*nn*, 227*nn*, 230*n*, 231*n*, 232*n*, 233*n*, 234*n*, 236*n*

Richter, Mary H., 12*n*

Riedel, W., 70*n*

Rivet, Auguste, cited, 218*n*

Roberts, Alexander, 15*n*

Robertson, Archibald, 68*n*

Robinson, Cecilia, cited, 84*n*, 85*n*

"Rock-cut Tombs in Wady Er-Rababi, Jerusalem, The" (Macalister), 161*n*

Rodocanakes, Plato, 113*n*

Romaios, Eustathios, 198

Roman Law in the Later Roman Empire (Freshfield), 286*n*

Romanos I Lecapenos, emperor (920–44), 26, 118, 119, 121, 135; gerocomeia and, 232, 234–35; hospitals and, 170, 179, 183; orphanages and, 250; xenones and, 197, 198

Romanos II, emperor (959–63), 235

Romanos III Argyros, emperor (1028–34), 122, 166, 235; earthquake and, 244; xenones, 186

Romanos Melodos, saint, 34

Romanos, physician, 198

Romanou, tou, 206

Romans, 12*nn*, 13*nn*, 29*n*, 273*n*

Rome, 10, 12, 31, 165; Anthemios in, 223; kingship theory and, 46; laws of, 48

Rome, Church of, 15, 16

Rosanquet, R. C., 7*n*

Rouillard, G., 26*n*, 239*n*

Roumania, 153

Ruiter, S. Tromp. de, 3*n*

Runciman, Steven, cited, 119*n*, 285*nn*

Russell, J. C., cited, 258*n*

Russia, 60, 79, 166, 193

Russian Attack on Constantinople, The (Vasiliev), 79*n*

Sabas, saint (d. 532), 92, 157, 159, 225; xenones and, 187, 210, 219

Sacra Parallela (Joannes Damascenos), 20*nn*, 21*n*, 24*n*, 35*n*, 68*n*

sacrifice, 14, 16, 68, 100, 106–107; after illness, 143–44; mercy and, 19; monastic, 20, 24; in the name of the dead, 25, 38, 121, 122, 131, 132, 140, 141

Sacrorum Conciliorum nova et amplissima collectio (Mansi), 69*n*

Saggara of Lydia, 213

Sagma, gerocomeion of, 229

Saint Anastasios, Church of, Constantinople, 195

Saint Andronicos, Church of, Constantinople, 213

"S. Barnaba Apostolo, De" (*Acta Sanctorum*), 208*n*

St. Barnabas, Church of, Cyprus, 207

St. Basil and His Rule (Morison), 155*n*

Saint Basil—The Letters (Deferrari, ed.), 85*n*, 208*n*, 261*n*

St. Clement, Church of, Constantinople, 231

St. Clement's gerocomeion, 230–31

Saint Conon poor-house, 264

St. Elias gerocomeion, 236

St. Elias monastery, 236

"S. Epiphani Vita" (*Patrologia Graeca*), 70*n*

St. Euthymios monasteries, 187

St. Faustos, Church of, Alexandria, 212

St. George, Church of, Constantinople, 170

St. George's monastery, Constantinople, 233

St. George's monastery, Pontos, 98

Saint Hypatios, monastery of, 220

St. Irene, Church of, Constantinople, 156, 162; xenones near, 188–89, 190

St. John the Baptist, Church of, Constantinople, 230

St. John the Forerunner's Day, 91

St. Mamas, monastery of, 106

St. Mark, Church of, Constantinople, 230

St. Mark, See of, 74

St. Michael, Church of, Constantinople, 75

St. Michael, monastery of, 195

Saint Michael ptochotropheion, Perga, 264

St. Nicholas, monastery of, 204

St. Panteleimon, Church of, Constantinople, 167, 213

St. Paul, Church of, Constantinople, 86, 126; orphanage of, 243, 245, 246, 247, 249, 250, 252, 256

St. Philip the Apostle, monastery of, 248–49

Saint Probos, Church of, Constantinople, 213

St. Romanos, ptocheion of, 264

St. Sabas, monastery of, 92, 157, 219

Saint Sampson, monastery of, 193

St. Sophia, Church of, Alexandria, 212

St. Sophia, Church of, Constantinople, *see* Hagia Sophia, Constantinople

St. Tarachos, Church of, Constantinople, 213

St. Theoctistos, monastery of, 187

St. Theodoros, Church of, Constantinople, 230

"S. Théophylacte de Nicomédie" (Vogt), 78*nn*

St. Thomas, Church of, 118

St. Zoticos, orphanage of, 242, 243, 252. *See also* Zoticon, The.

Saints Archippos and Philemon, Church of, 265–66

"SS Cyri et Johannis Vitae Formis, De" (Nissen, ed.), 168*n*, 229*n*

"SS Hierone et Sociis Martyribus, De" (*Acta Sanctorum*), 41*n*

Saints Sergios and Bacchos, Church of, 247

Sakellion, chartularius of, 220, 240

Sakerdos, 261

Salamis, Cyprus, 207

Salmydessos, 69

salvation, 20, 21, 23–25, 26, 27, 28; by Grace, 35; by works, 135, 141

Sampson, saint, 151, 182; orphanage, 242; xenon of, 153, 162, 190, 191–95

Sancti Patris nostri et Confessoris Theodori Studitis Praepositi Parva Catechesis (Auvray), 35*n*

Saracens, 38, 53

Sarantinos, Theodore, 142, 143

Satala, 213

Sathas, Constantine N., cited, 130*n*, 131*nn*, 183*n*, 185*n*, 186*n*, 205*n*, 207*n*, 223*n*, 233*n*, 244*n*, 245*nn*; on Michael Attaliates, 27*nn*, 28*n*, 37*nn*, 142*nn*, 260*n*, 267*n*

Savramis, Demosthenes, 89*n*

Scala gerocomeion, Constantinople, 229–30

Scala Paradisi (Joannes Climacos), 21*nn*, 35*n*

Scete, Constantinople, 96

Schaff, Philip, cited, 68*n*, 69*n*, 154*n*, 257*n*, 258*n*

Scheltema, H. J., 86*n*

Schlumberger, Gustave, cited, 20*n*, 122*n*; on seals, 195*n*, 197*n*, 200*nn*, 233*n*, 236*n*, 237*n*, 252

Schoell, R., *see Corpus Juris Civilis* (Schoell and Kroll, eds.)

Scholarios, George (Gennadios II), cited, 287*n*, 288*n*

Scholia in Librum de Divinis Nominibus (Maximos the Confessor), 37*n*

Schopenus, L., cited, xi*n*

Schreiber, G., cited, 172*nn*, 179*nn*

Schreiner, Hugo, cited, 214*nn*, 215*n*

Schultze, Victor, cited, 157*n*

Schwartz, Edward, cited, 35*n*, 71*n*, 74*n*, 94*n*, 95*n*, 113*n*, 157*nn*, 158*nn*, 159*nn*, 162*n*, 183*n*, 187*nn*, 188*nn*, 219*nn*, 225*nn*, 231*n*, 242*n*, 248*n*, 249*n*, 263*n*

Scientia Politica, De (Anonymous), 49*n*

Scott, S. P., cited, 257*n*

Scriptorum Veterum Nova Collectio (Mai, ed.), 39*n*, 49*n*

Scriptures, 51, 126, 179. *See also specific Books*

Scutari, 167, 247

Scutariotes, Theodore: quoted, 180–81; on gerocomeia, 223; on orphanages, 245; on xenones, 185

Scythopolis, 187

Sea of Marmara, 99, 246, 247, 267

Sebasteia, 261, 262

Second Paraenesis (Basil I), 51*n*

Seeck, Otto, cited, 197*n*

Selectus Legum (Constantine Porphyrogenitos), 51*nn*, 116*nn*, 221*n*

Seminarium Kondakovianum, 134*n*

Senate, 27, 113

Serapion of Thmuis (d. after 362), 75; quoted, 286–87

Serapion, priest, 94

Serail gardens, Constantinople, 224, 246

Serbia, 153, 206

Sergios I, patriarch (610–38), 242

Sergios II, patriarch (1001–19), 106

Sermo Asceticus (Basil the Great), 89*n*

Sermon 45 (Joannes Chrysostomos), 186*nn*, 187*nn*, 258*n*

Serrae, Macedonia, 255

Ševčenko, Ihor, cited, 39*n*, 258*n*

Severos gerocomeion, 230

Sewter, E. R. A., cited, 273*n*

Shepherd of Hermas, 14*n*

shipwreck victims, 15, 70, 75, 92, 100, 102

"Sicilian expedition of Constantine IV, The" (Brooks), 230*n*

Sicily, 230

sickness, 22, 66, 282, 287; Apostolic Church on, 13; bishops and, 14, 71, 74, 76, 78, 156; deaconess order and, 85, 86; God and, 33, 154, 183–84; in Greece, 5, 6, 7, 8,

10; imperial concern for, 26, 27, 112, 115, 118, 121, 122, 126, 128–29, 136, 179–81, 183; medical knowledge and, 152–53, 171–79; monastery aid for, 88, 89, 93, 94, 95, 96, 98, 99, 101, 102, 108, 138, 150, 159, 168, 171–79, 183, 203, 207, 210; of monks, 141, 150, 157, 170, 181; old age and, 179, 235; private concern for, 136, 138, 139, 159, 169, 182, 183; sacrifice after, 143–44. *See also* hospitals; leprosaria

Sigalas, Antonios, 255

Sigillographie de l'empire byzantin (Schlumberger), 195*n*, 197*n*, 200*nn*, 233*n*, 236*n*, 237*n*, 252*nn*

Significance of the Will of Eustathius Boilas for the study of the history of Armenia and Georgia at the time of Byzantine dominion (Bartikian), 140*nn*

Süleymaniye mosque, 196

Simocattes, Theophylactos, ix, *xnn*, 279, 288

sin: forgiveness of, 19, 20, 23–25, 28, 34, 35, 38–39, 116, 266, 280; original, 29, 32, 33, 39; prostitution and, 270–74; punishment for, 36–37, 39, 135

Sintenis, Carolus, 4*n*

Siotes, Markos, 13*n*

Sirach, 96*n*

Sirkessi, 233

Sirmond, Jacob, cited, 107*n*, 108*nn*

slaves, 10, 12; aged, 15; bequests to, 140, 141, 143; freeing of, 107, 137, 140, 143, 200; war orphans, 126

Slavs, 165, 243

Small Catechism (Theodore Studites), 35*n*, 37*n*, 38*n*

Smyrna, 14

Smyth, Herbert W., 6*n*

Sobolevitch, E. and S., cited, 279*n*

"Social Consciousness in Eastern Orthodoxy" (Calian), 283*n*

Socialism, 283

Social and Political Thought in Byzantium (Barker), 49*n*, 50*nn*, 54*n*

"Social Problem in the Eastern Orthodox Church, The" (Florovsky), 90n

"Social Structure of the Later Roman Empire, On the" (Charanis), 259n, 283n

"Société byzantine à l'époque des Comnènes, La" (Diehl), 55n, 179n

society: Church involvement in, 65–66, 67–87; kingship and, 51–52, 55, 57, 61, 133; medical history and, 172; monasticism and, 88–90, 95, 282–83, 285; orphans and, 241; philanthropic function in, 4-5, 8, 9, 12, 18, 20, 23, 55, 61, 66, 135–36, 276, 279–88; prostitution and, 270–71

Sociological and Moral Studies in the Field of Coptic Monasticism (Farag), 89n

Socrates, 8

Sodom, 21

Solomon, John, 131

"Some Aspects of Daily Life in Byzantium" (Charanis), xin, 172n, 270n

Sophia, empress of Byzantium (565–78), 164, 226, 243, 252

Sophia, mother of St. Sabas, 187

Sophia, port of, 180

Sophiana xenon, 205

Sophocles, 8n

Sophronios of Jerusalem, cited, 273n

Soteriou, George A., cited, 89n

Sozomenos, *Kirchengeschichte* of, 16n, 31, 46n, 70, 71n, 85n, 154n, 209n, 259n, 260nn, 261n, 263nn, 276n

"Spaneas" (Alexios Comnenos), 26–27

Spanneut, M., cited, 10n

Spanodromos, 94

Sparta, Greece, 8

Speculum (periodical), 258n

Spicq, Ceslaus, cited, 12n

Spiritu Sancto, De (Basil the Great), 33n

Spoudaeou, 246

Spyridakis, George, 144n, 275n

Spyridon of Trimithous, 69

Stadium xenon, Constantinople, 190–91

Stanogevic, L., 153n

state philanthropy, 11, 26–28, 65–66, 111–36, 279; age and, 333; burial costs and, 274; coercion and, 283; hospitality and, 218; kingship and, 43–61, 111, 150–51; medicine and, 154, 158; orphans and, 241; prisoners and, 285. *See also* emperors; laws; *and see specific institutions*

Stead, F. H., cited, 155n

Stegmann, Anton, 32n

Stein, James Aloysius, 155n

Steiron, 195

Stenimachos xenon, 204

Stephana, F., 84n

Stephanos, deacon, 195

Stephanos, physician, 199

Stephanos, saint, 227–28, 229

Stephanos, saint, parakoemomenos of Maurice, 151, 227–28, 229

Stephanos, syncellos, 106

Sternbach, Leo, cited, 246n

Stethatos, Nicetas, 106nn

Stoics, 11

Story of Social Christianity, The (Stead), 155n

Stein, Ernest, cited, 112n

Stoudios, monastery of, Constantinople, 102, 106, 172, 275

strangers: burial of in xenotapheia, 274–75; poverty and, 185–21; theological metaphor of Jesus, 215. *See also* cemeteries; hospitality; xenones; xenotapheia

Strategicon of Cecaumenos: on imperial justice, 54–55, 56n; on Kastoria, 153n; on orphanages, 244, 250n

Stroumnitza, Thrace, 39

Strymon, Macedonia, 255

Studia Patristica et Byzantina, 49n

Studi in onore di Vincenzo Arangio-Ruiz, 3n

Studites, *see* Theodore Studites

Study of the Life of Andreas, The Fool for the Sake of Christ (Murray), 19nn

Sudost-Forschungen (periodical), 35n

"Sulla Concezione Byzantina dell'

Imperatore nel VII Secolo" (Cigante), 49n
surgery, 152–53, 172, 175, 195
"Sur les fondements historiques des Romans 'D'Imberios et de Margarona' et 'De Pierre de Provence et de la Belle Maguelonne'" (Pichard), 214n
Sylloge Inscriptionum Graecorum (Dittenberger), 10n
Symeon, king of Bulgaria, 52–53, 79
Symeon Magister, 35n, 115n, 196, 227nn, 239n; on Romanos Lecapenos, 119nn, 197, 198n
Symeon Metaphrastes, saint, cited, 71nn, 93n, 210n, 229n, 248n, 263n, 268n, 276n; on Chrysostom, 208; on hospitals, 156nn, 157n, 158n, 168, 182n; on the Incarnation, 37; on Sampson, 192
Symeon the New Theologian (+1022), 102, 106
Symeon the Salos, saint, 275
Symeon of Studios, 38
Symeon Stylites, the Younger, saint, 96
"Symeon der Theologie" (Beck), 102n
Symeon of Thessalonica (d. 1429), quoted, 25
"Synaxare of Stephanus Confessor, Archbishop of Sougdaia" (Vasilievskii), 78nn
Synaxarium Ecclesiae Constantinopolitanae, cited, 164n, 165n, 206n, 227n, 229n, 230nn, 231n, 239n, 247n, 249n, 265n, 266n; on Andronicos, 168; on the Melobiou, 236; on the Zoticon, 166–67
Syncellos, office of the, 87
Synesios of Cyrene (b. 370–75, d. 413–14), kingship theory and, 43, 45, 46n, 49
Synod of Gangra (343?), 67–68
Synopsis of the Basilica, 192–93
"Synopsis Basilicorum" (Zepos and Zepos), 241n, 251n
Synopsis Chronike (Manasses), 168n, 186n, 222n, 224n
Synopsis Chronike (Sathas, ed.), 130n, 245n

Synopsis Historion (Cedrenos), 113n, 222n
Syntagma (Blastaris), 257n
Synteleia (Arangio-Ruiz), 49n
Syria, 74, 96; taxation, 257; xenones of, 189, 209, 212
System des Justinianischen Kirchenvermogensrechtes (Knecht), 218n, 239n, 251n, 269n

Tabernacle, 157
Tactica (Leo VI, the Wise), 26n, 116n
Tacticon, 251
Tafel, T. L. F., cited, 109n
Tarasios, patriarch (784–806), 76, 78
Tarchaneiotes, Michael Glabas Dukas, 205
Tarentum, 10
Tarn, William, 10nn
Tauros Forum, Constantinople, 206, 230
taxation, 91, 116, 257, 265; military, 243; municipal, 134; revocation of, 180, 181, 248, 261
Temkin, Owsei, cited, 153nn
Terracina, Sergio, 153n
Tertullian (d.c. 220), 13n, 14n; quoted, 15
Tetrapolis, 252
Thebais, Egypt, 96, 188
Thebes, 9
Thematibus, De (Constantine Porphyrogenitos), 99n
Themistii Orationes (Dindorf), 45nn
Themistios, kingship and, 43, 45, 49
"Themistius and the Defense of Hellenism in the Fourth Century" (Downey), 45n
Theocharides, George I., cited, 143n, 205n
Theoctistos, monastery of, 187
Theodora, empress, 38, 114, 115, 162; orphanages and, 251; prostitutes and, 271, 272; xenones and, 185, 189, 190, 191
Theodore, saint, 236
Theodore, "the most glorious copyist," 113
Theodore Doukas Lascares, emperor, 34

Theodore of Paphos, 69n, 239nn
Theodore of Petra, cited, 93n, 210, 225n
Theodore Studites, 32, 35n, 37n, 38, 79n, 134n; on monasticism, 88; on nursing, 184; on orphanages, 251; on salvation, 24, 282; on xenones, 216, 220; on xenotapheia, 275
Theodoret Kirchengeschichte, 31n, 39n, 85n, 112n, 157n
Theodoretos of Cyrus, 39n, 85n, 157n; on Flacilla, 112; on God's justice, 31
Theodorichos, 208
Theodorou, A., 89n
Theodorou, Evangelos, 84n
Theodosia Cantacuzena, 213
Theodosiopolis, 153
Theodosios, saint, 187–88, 225
Theodosios the Great, emperor (379–95), 112, 137, 157
Theodosios II, emperor (408–50), 31, 112, 224, 263, 268
Theodosios the Coenobiarches (+c. 529), 157–58, 210
Theodosios, monastery of, 210, 225
Theodotos Melissenos Kassiteras (815–21), 243–44
Theodulos Monachos, 60n
Theologia (periodical), 81n, 84n, 89n
Theological Oration (Gregory Nazianzenos), 32n
theology, 18; medicine and, 154, 183–84; monasticism and, 88–89; philanthropy and, 29?41, 55, 61, 67, 80, 116, 149–50, 281–82
Theodoulos, 157
Theophanes, cited, 98n, 113n, 134n, 192nn, 199n, 200n, 213n, 220n, 225n, 227n, 230n, 239n, 263n; on gerocomeia, 226; on orphanages, 243; on xenones, 186, 189, 212, 222; on xenotapheia, 274
Theophanes Continuatus, cited, 26n, 52n, 114nn, 115nn, 121nn, 122n, 134n, 135nn, 153n, 166n, 170n, 183n, 227n, 230n, 232nn, 233n, 234n, 243nn, 244n, 265n; on Constantine Porphyrogenitos, 118–19, 232; on John I Tzimisces, 122; on

xenones, 195, 197, 198n, 199n, 200n
Theophanes (Palamas), 39n
Theophano, empress of Leo VI, 115, 183
Theophilos, emperor (829–42), 38, 97, 114–15, 134, 154; xenones of, 190, 196
Theophilos of Antioch, quoted, 29
Theophilos, patriarch of Alexandria, 70
Theophilos xenon, 196
Theophylactos of Ochrida (1091–1108), 32, 84, 128n, 142n; on Clement, 81; on kingship, 55, 58
Theophylactos, patriarch (933–56), 119, 232
Theophylactos (d.c. 840), archbishop of Nicomedeia, 78, 169–70
Theotocos, Church of the, Blachernae, 85, 252
Theotocos, Church of the, Jerusalem, 159
Theotocos Eleousa, monastery of, 39
Theotocos Evergetis, monastery of, 207
Theotocos the Pammacaristos, monastery, 205
Thessalonians, 273n, 283n
Thessalonica, 38, 151, 153, 208, 222, 227, 266
Thessaly, 207
Thomas II, patriarch, 229
Thomas, consul, 275
Thomais, saint, 106–107
Thrakika (periodical), 141n, 203n
Thrace, 39, 79, 95, 99, 204
Three Children, Church of the, Alexandria, 229
Thucydides, cited, 6n, 7n
Tiberios I Constantine, emperor (578–82), 212, 222
Tiberios II, emperor (698–705), 168, 186, 212
Timarion (anonymous), 60
Timothy Monachos, quoted, 289
Timothy of Alexandria, cited, 35n, 92n, 94nn, 139, 188n
Timothy, bishop of Prousa, 206–207
Tirithoni, 237
Titus, 10, 29n
To Autolycos (Theophilos), 29n

To Philip (Isocrates), 9nn

"Topographie de Constantinople byzantine, quelques quartiers mal connus" (Janin), 229n

"Topographie de Jerusalem vers la fin de l'Epoque Byzantine" (Milik), 160nn, 226n, 263n, 275n

"Transfer of Populations as a Policy in the Byzantine Empire, The" (Charanis), 18n

Treatise (Cyprian), 15n

Trembelas, Panagiotis N., cited, 282n

Trimithous, Cyprus, 239

Troelos, bishop, 145

Trudy (Vasilievskii), 78n, 79n

Tsaras, John, 38n

Tsiknopoulos, J. P., 91n

Tunitskij, N. L., 81n

Turkey, 28, 69, 126, 135, 244, 287

Turner, C. H., cited, 84n, 85n

typhlocomeia, 275–76

Typicon Gregorii Pacuriani (Kauchtschischvili, tr.), 203n

"Typicon of the Monastery Evergetis" (Dmitrievsky), 93n

"Typicon of the Monastery of Cosmosoteira" (Petit), 132nn, 236n

"Typicon of the Monastery of St. Mamas" (Efstratiades), 93n

"Typicon of the Monastery of Theotocos of Elegmon," 91n, 92n

"Typicon Neilou" (Miklosich-Muller), 91nn

"Typicon of Theotocos Eleousa" (Petit), 91n

typika, 90, 91, 92, 93, 131, 132, 207. *See also specific monasteries*

Typika (Dmitrievsky), cited, 25n, 26n, 28n, 34n, 91n, 92n, 93n, 172nn, 174nn, 175nn, 179nn, 193n, 204n, 207n, 230n, 235nn, 265n, 275n

"Typikon" (Irene Augusta), 131nn, 132nn

"Typikon de Grégoire Pacourianos pour le monastère de Petritzos (Backovo)" (Petit), 141nn, 142n, 203n, 204nn, 248n

"Typikon of the Livos Monastery" (Delehaye), 186n

"Typikon du monastère de la Kosmosoteira" (Petit), 27n

"Typikon de Nil Damilas pour le monastère de femmes de Daeonia en Créte, Le" (Petrides), 26n

Tzimisces, John, *see* John I Tzimisces

"Uber die Wohnhaustyp de fruheren Konstantinopel" (Kriesis), 258n

Uhlhorn, G., 16n, 157n, 280n

Unkapani district, Constantinople, 196, 229

Untersuchungen zum Begriff der Philanthropia bei dem Kaiser Julian (Kabiersch), 45n, 263n

Ursel, 123

Usener, Hermann, 93n, 158nn

Vademecum der Byzantinischen Aristokrate. Das Sogenannte Strategikon des Kekaumenos (Beck), 54n

Vafides, Filaretos, cited, 16n, 157n

Valdenberg, Vladimir, 54nn

Valetas, Joannes N., xn

Vance, J. Milton, 68n

Van den Ven, Paul, 69n, 239n

Van der Wal, N., 86n

Varia Graeca Sacra (Papadopoulos-Kerameus), 35n, 37n, 84n, 108n, 154n, 195nn, 197n, 206nn

Vasiliev, A. A., cited, 56n, 79n, 97n, 99n, 132n, 169n, 179n

Vasilievskii, V. G., cited, 78nn, 79n

Vasilios, 237

Vatamatu, N., 153n

Vaux, Roland de, cited, 160nn

Velos, 237

vespers, 35

Vevaias Elpidos, monastery of, 90

"Vie ancienne de saint Athanase l'Athonite composée au début du XIe siècle par Athanase de Lavra, La" (Lemerle), 102n

"Vie chrétienne en orient, La" (Bréhier), 239n

"Vie inédite de Saint Jean l'aumonier, Une" (Delehaye), 170nn, 213n, 262n

Vie Merveilleuse de Saint Pierre D'Atroa, La (Laurent), 143n

Vie et mort de Byzance (Bréhier), 246n

"Vie et récits de l'abbé Daniel de Scété" (Clugnet), 35n, 92n, 96nn, 137n, 168nn

Vie religieuse dans l'empire byzantin au temps des Comnènes et des anges, La (Oeconomos), 86n, 171n, 181n, 244n

Vie de Saint Euthyme le Grand (377–473) (Genier), 263n

"Vie de S. Evariste, higoumène à Constantinople, La" (Vorst), 108n

Vie de Saint Grégoire le décapolite et les Slaves macédoniens au XIᵉ siecle, La (Dvornik), 99nn, 272n

"Vie de S. Luc le Stylite" (Vogt), 198n, 190n

"Vie de Saint Michel Maleinos" (Petit), 107nn, 200nn

"Vie de S. Philarète, La" (Fourmy), 97n, 98nn, 99nn, 169n

"Vie de Symeon le Nouveau Théologien" (*Orientalia Christiana*), 106nn

Virgin, Church of the, Constantinople, 75

"Vision de Kaiounos et le sort éternel de Philentolos Olympion, La" (Halkin), 169n

"Vita et Acta S. Macarii Hegumeni Monasterii Pelecetes" (Gheyn), 35n, 108n

Vita Constantini, De (Eusebios of Caesarea), 111nn, 112nn, 262nn

Vita et Conversatio Sanctae Euphrosynes Alexandrinae (Symeon Metaphrastes), 268n

"Vita Euthymii" (De Boor), 81nn, 97n, 223n

"Vita des Heiligen Philotheos vom Athos, Die" (Papoulia), 35n

Vita Ignatii (Nicetas), 114n, 134n

Vita Mariae Aegyptiae (Sophronios of Jerusalem), 273n

"Vita Monastica, De" (Nicholas, Patriarch of Constantinople), 39n

"Vita S. Andrea Salo" (*Acta Sanctorum*), 270n

Vita S. Antoni (Athanasios), 32n

Vita S. Clementis Ancyrani (Symeon Metaphrastes), 248n

"Vita S. Eudocimos" (Loparev, ed.), 97n

"Vita Sanctae Euphrosynae" (Boucherie), 268n

Vita S. Euthymii (Symeon Metaphrastes), 263n

Vita S. Hypatii Liber, De (Callinicos), 92n, 95nn, 96nn, 220n

"Vita S Ignatii" (*Patrologia Graeca*), 249n

"Vita S. Irene" (*Acta Sanctorum*), 106n

Vita S Joannis Chrysostomi (Palladios), 71nn, 139n, 156nn, 188n, 208nn, 219n

"Vita S. Joanni Hesychasti" (Cyril of Scythopolis), 35n

"Vita S Lazari" (Gregorios Monachos), 35n, 108n, 144n, 202nn, 203nn

Vita S. Macrinae, De (Gregory of Nyssa), 248n

"Vita S Martha" (*Acta Sanctorum*), 93n, 96nn, 97n

"Vita S. Marthae Matris S. Symeonis Juniori" (*Acta Sanctorum*), 274n

Vita S. Nicephori (Ignatios the Deacon), 265n

"Vita S. Nicephori" (Delehaye, ed.), 80n, 81nn

"Vita S Nicetae Confessoris" (*Acta Sanctorum*), 134n, 213n

"Vita S Nicon" (Lampros), 97nn

"Vita S Pauli Junioris in Monte Latro" (Sirmond), 107n, 108nn

"Vita of St. Peter of Atroa" (Laurent, ed.), 143n

Vita S. Sampsonii (Symeon Metaphrastes), 182n, 192nn

"Vita S. Symeone Sale Confessore" (Leontios of Neapolis), 275n

"Vita S. Symeone Stylite" (*Acta Sanctorum*), 96n

Vita S. Theodosii (Symeon Metaphrastes), 157n, 158n

"Vita S Thomaidis" (Delehaye and Peeters), 106n, 107nn

Vita Tarasii Archiepiscopi Constantinopolitani (Ignatios the Deacon), 76nn

Vitalios, saint, 271–72

Vizantiiskii Vremennik (periodical), 37n, 108n, 141nn, 142n, 144n, 204nn, 231n, 248n
Vogel, Marie, cited, 228n
Vogt, Albert, cited, 78nn, 108n, 169nn, 170n, 190n, 265n
Vorst, C. Van de, cited, 108n
Vryonis, Speros, Jr., cited, 140nn

Wagner, Wilhelm, cited, 26nn, 27n, 56nn, 214n, 215n
warfare, 41, 50, 78, 79; Christian attitudes in, 123, 126, 135; destruction of institutions in, 287; hospitals and, 156, 158–59, 160; taxation for, 243
Warren, Frederick E., cited, 91nn
Wassiliewsky, B., cited, 54–55, 56n, 153n, 244, 250n
wealth, 22–23, 283–84, 288. *See also* funds; poverty
Webster's New International Dictionary of the English Language (Neilson, ed.), 18n
What is Christianity? (Harnack), 283n
Whitney, J. P., 285n
"Who is My Neighbor? The Greek and Roman Answer" (Downey), 11n, 285n
widows, *see* women, widowed
"Will of a Provincial Magnate, Eustathius Boilas (1059), The" (Vryonis), 140nn
Wobbermin, Georg, 287n
Wohltatigkeit und Armenpflege im Vorchristlichen Altertum (Bolkestein), 9n, 280n
women, 22, 23, 57, 112; deacons, 84–87, 268; doctors, 174; dowry gifts, 9, 143, 180, 181; empresses, 112–13, 263 (*see also individual names*); leprosaria and, 264; maternity care for, 152, 170, 172; monasteries and, 90, 91, 143, 196, 271–72, 273; orphaned girls, 94; parthenones for, 276; private philanthropies of, 98, 99, 106–107, 138, 141, 142–43, 158, 159; reformatories for, 196, 270–74; widowed, 13, 14, 15, 25, 32, 33,

51, 54, 66, 69, 70, 71, 75, 76, 78, 79, 81, 92, 97, 126, 142, 149, 180, 210, 259, 276, 282
work: ethic of, 13, 25, 130–31, 259–60, 283; monastic, 89–90, 92, 94, 109; in xenones, 188
Works of Liudprand of Cremona, The (Wright, tr.), 145n
Works and Days (Hesiod), 5n
Wright, F. A., 145n
Wright, W. C., cited, 16n
Wright, William, 158nn, 159n
"Writings Familiar to Cecaumenos" (Buckler), 54n, 55n
"Writings of St. Symeon the New Theologian, The" (Krivocheine), 102n

Xanalatos, Diogenes A., 81n, 84n
xenodochos, office of, 216, 218, 219, 220–21
Xenon, The (of Andrew of Crete), 168–69
xenones, 7, 52, 55, 170, 185–221, 226; Church, 69, 74, 76, 79, 80, 149; imperial philanthropy and, 112, 115, 116, 121, 134, 150, 185–86, 195–96, 197, 198–99, 212, 213, 222; lepers in, 167; medical services in, 153–54, 156, 157, 159–60, 162, 172, 180, 186, 187, 188, 190, 195, 197, 209; monastery, 91, 102, 106, 108, 150, 168, 188, 196, 198, 200, 202–203, 204, 206, 207, 214, 220; wartime destruction of, 287
Xenophon, 4n, 8
xenotapheia, 274–75; *see also* cemeteries; strangers, burial of

Yahkosk, 246

Zakythinos, Dionysios A., 52nn, 61n
Zaoutsis, Stylianos, 81
"Zavieschanie vizantiiskago boiarina XI vieka" (Beneshevich), 140nn
Zbornik Radova (periodical), 39n, 258n
Zeno (474–75, 476–91), 243
Zeno, bishop of Maiuma, 71, 113

Zenobios, physician, 182

Zepos, J., and P. Zepos, *see Jus Graeco-Romanum* (Zepos and Zepos)

Zeugma, hill of, 196, 225

Zhitie Filareta Miloctivago (Vasiliev), 97n, 99n, 169n

"Zhitie sv Kirilla Fileota" (Loparev), 108n

Zhurnal ministerstva narodnago prosvieshchenia (periodical), 140nn

Zoe, empress of Michael IV, 250, 273

Zonaras, Joannes, cited, 68n, 126, 129–30, 244n, 245n, 256n; on episcopal duties, 219; on the 57th canon, 276; on Narses xenon, 213

Zoras, George, cited, 288n

Zoticon, The, 118, 164–67, 183, 242, 247, 249; seals and, 252

Zoticos, saint, 165, 166, 242, 249

Zscharnack, Leopold, 84n

Zur Soziologie des Byzantinischen Monchtums (Savramis), 89n

"Zwei griechische texte uber die hl. Theophano, Die" (Kurtz), 115nn, 183n, 227n

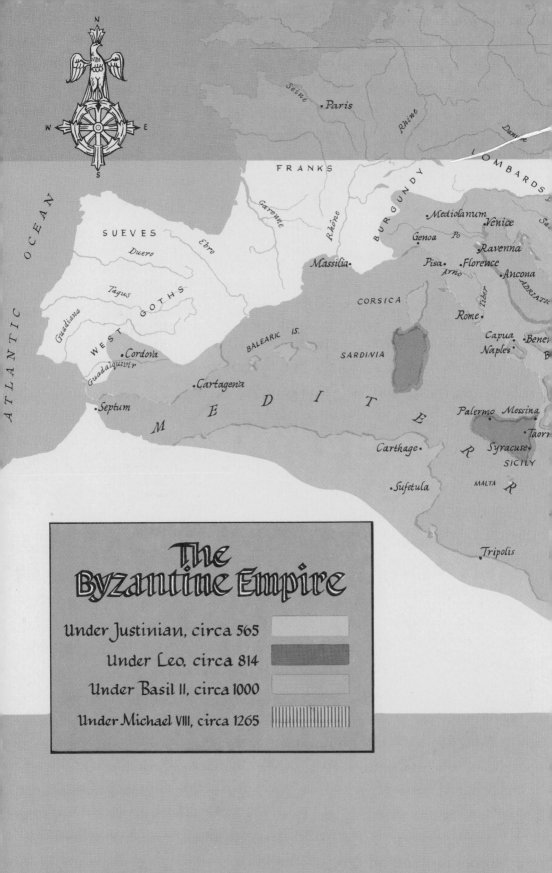

N

W E

S

ATLANTIC OCEAN

Paris

Seine

Rhine

Danube

FRANKS

LOMBARDS

BURGUNDY

Garonne

Rhône

Mediolanum
Genoa
Po
Venice

SUEVES

Duero

Ebro

Massilia

Pisa
Ravenna
Florence
Arno
Ancona

ADRIATIC

Tagus

GOTHS

CORSICA

Tiber

Rome

Guadiana

WEST

Cordova

Capua
Naples
Bene
B

Guadalquivir

BALEARIC IS.

SARDINIA

Cartagena

MEDITER

E

Septum

M

R

Palermo
Messina
Taorm

Carthage

Syracuse
SICILY

R

Sufetula

MALTA

Tripolis

The Byzantine Empire

Under Justinian, circa 565

Under Leo, circa 814

Under Basil II, circa 1000

Under Michael VIII, circa 1265